ENGLISH AND EUROPEAN PERSPECTIVES ON CONTRACT AND COMMERCIAL LAW

The purpose of this book is to honour the influential and wide-ranging work of Professor Hugh Beale, who retires from full-time teaching at Warwick University this year. It contains essays by twenty-five very distinguished authors, each of whom has worked with Professor Beale as a co-author, as a teaching colleague, during his time as Law Commissioner of England and Wales, or as part of the study groups working in Europe on contract and commercial law. The essays reflect different aspects of Professor Beale's interests. Some concentrate on English contract law, either from a historical or a current perspective, while others are focused on aspects of European contract law. There are four essays looking at current issues relating to security and financing, and, as befits a former Law Commissioner, three essays on law reform. The essays in the final section discuss trends in transnational and European commercial law. This book brings together the reflections of eminent writers from all over Europe on important issues facing contract and commercial law, and will be of interest to all scholars and practitioners working in these areas.

English and European Perspectives on Contract and Commercial Law

Essays in Honour of Hugh Beale

Edited by

Louise Gullifer
and
Stefan Vogenauer

·HART·
PUBLISHING
OXFORD AND PORTLAND, OREGON
2017

Hart Publishing
An imprint of Bloomsbury Publishing Plc

Hart Publishing Ltd
Kemp House
Chawley Park
Cumnor Hill
Oxford OX2 9PH
UK

Bloomsbury Publishing Plc
50 Bedford Square
London
WC1B 3DP
UK

www.hartpub.co.uk
www.bloomsbury.com

Published in North America (US and Canada) by
Hart Publishing
c/o International Specialized Book Services
920 NE 58th Avenue, Suite 300
Portland, OR 97213-3786
USA

www.isbs.com

HART PUBLISHING, the Hart/Stag logo, BLOOMSBURY and the Diana logo are trademarks of Bloomsbury Publishing Plc

First published in hardback, 2014
Paperback edition, 2017

British Library Cataloguing-in-Publication Data
A catalogue record for this book is available from the British Library.

ISBN: PB: 978-1-50991-297-1
HB: 978-1-84946-549-6

Typeset by Compuscript Ltd, Shannon
Printed and bound in Great Britain by
Lightning Source UK Ltd

Preface

Hugh Beale is one of the most influential English private lawyers of his generation. His scholarly writings impress both by their learning and the broad range of topics addressed. The main focus of Hugh's scholarship has been contract law: he has written extensively in this area, is the co-author of a leading student textbook and is the general editor of the authoritative *Chitty on Contracts*. However, he has also made significant contributions to the law of security and financing. Moreover, Hugh is one of the few English scholars who have seriously engaged with the ongoing attempts to harmonise contract law across Europe, arguably the most important contemporary development in private law. Indeed, he is the only English lawyer who has been right at the heart of this initiative and shaped it more than anyone else. It is not only at the European level that Hugh has combined his academic work with his active interest in law reform. As a Law Commissioner of England and Wales from 2000 to 2007 he initiated many projects for the reform of English law.

Those who know Hugh and his ongoing involvement in the debates on English and European private law will probably be as surprised as we were to learn that he has now reached the statutory age of retirement and is about to scale down his teaching. We both felt that this would be an appropriate moment to honour his massive contribution to the law. This volume is an attempt to do so. It contains a selection of essays that aim to reflect Hugh's various interests, ranging from the English law of contract and its history to European contract law, the law of security and financing, trends in transnational and European commercial law and law reform in general. Each of these areas is understood broadly. The range of contributors reflects both the English and the European dimension of Hugh's work. It is perhaps testimony to his popularity amongst his colleagues that our invitations to contribute to this volume were received with great enthusiasm and accepted almost without exception.

We are tremendously grateful to the contributors for letting us have such a fascinating array of essays. Thanks are also due to Richard Hart and Sinead Moloney of Hart Publishing for their support of this book project. Mel Hamill and Tom Adams expertly steered the volume through the production process. Emma Gullifer provided invaluable support in checking footnotes. Perhaps most importantly, Jane Beale was instrumental in concealing the enterprise from Hugh until it had reached a stage where it would be impossible for him to stop it.

Our biggest thanks go, of course, to Hugh himself. We have both worked in various functions with him over the years, as co-authors and/or co-teachers. He has been a tremendous source of support for the Faculty of Law at the University of Oxford, as a Visiting Professor, a Research Fellow of the Institute of European and Comparative Law and one of the Senior Research Fellows at the new Harris Manchester College Commercial Law Centre. We have benefited from Hugh's insights, kindness, patience and generosity all along. In many respects he is a role model in the way he goes about his job. We very much hope that his impending retirement from full-time teaching will rather strengthen than diminish his involvement in analysing and shaping the law in the years to come.

Louise Gullifer
Stefan Vogenauer
Oxford, 7 November 2014

Foreword: Hugh Beale and the Law Commission

LORD CARNWATH, LORD TOULSON
AND TAMARA GORIELY

Lord Carnwath (Chairman of the Law Commission 1998–2002) writes:
At the end of 1998 I became Chairman of the Law Commission. One of my first tasks was to assist in the recruitment of two new Commissioners, one to replace the common law Commissioner, Andrew Burrows. Lord Irvine, then Lord Chancellor, who was a strong supporter of the Commission's work, encouraged me to take my time to find out who were the leading academics in the field, and to see if they could be encouraged to apply. As soon as I began making inquiries, I became aware for the first time of Hugh Beale, whose name came at the top of everyone's list. I invited him to visit me at the Commission, where he made a strong impression of authority, calmness and charm. I was delighted that he decided to apply, and came through a strong field to secure the post.

From the start he proved to be an ideal choice. He quickly attuned himself to the combination of academic rigour and practical realism which the Commission's work requires. Apart from the major projects which he initiated and led to completion, he played a full part in all the work of the Commission. In the early days, he worked on the completion of a number of projects, including damages under the Human Rights Act 1998, to which he brought valuable new insights. Among the joys of the Commission is the interaction of practitioners and academics, and the high level of debate and discussion which accompanies the preparation of the reports. Although each Commissioner will have projects in his or her specialist field, all are expected to contribute to the debate on every report. Hugh's contribution to the debates was always incisive and illuminating. He could be highly critical but always with courtesy and good humour. I have a particularly strong memory of a debate on our report on criminal fraud, which recommended the creation of a new offence. Although crime was not Hugh's subject, his interventions brought a wholly new perspective and discipline to our discussion, and help to set the form of what became the Fraud Act 2006.

His major projects for the Commission were brought to fruition after I had left the Commission. Tamara Goriely, who worked with Hugh for five years as a team lawyer between 2002 and 2007, has provided below a more detailed appreciation of his work.

Lord Toulson (Chairman of the Law Commission 2002–2006) writes:
I had the privilege of succeeding Robert Carnwath and being welcomed to the Law Commission by Hugh Beale, who was then the most senior Commissioner. I was

extremely fortunate. Hugh became my role model as a Commissioner. His attention to detail and intellectual powers of analysis were colossal. He would always look beyond and beneath the intricacies to what he considered were or should be the real underlying principles. He was a tireless campaigner for reform in areas where he considered that the law was over complex, unfair or simply out of date, and he combined a willingness to be radical with an acute sense of what was practical.

Hugh was also particularly good in his dealings with fellow Commissioners, staff, consultees and government. I echo Robert Carnwath's comments about his contribution to projects which were not his own. Where there were disagreements he would always seek to understand, rather than merely argue against, views which differed from his own, in an attempt to see if they could be reconciled in a way which was principled and not simply a fudge. Personally, I learned much from our debates and the manner in which he approached them. The same qualities were apparent in his patient approach to consultees and critics, even when they were unreasonable, and in his dealings with government. He won not only respect, but affection, from those who worked for him, as well the admiration and affection of his colleagues.

Tamara Goriely (team lawyer Law Commission) writes:
Hugh Beale was a Commissioner at the Law Commission from 2000 to 2007, leading the Commercial and Common Law Team. During this time he was responsible for a very wide range of projects. Three subjects were particularly close to his heart.

First, Hugh believed passionately in a new functional approach to security law. His review was extremely ambitious, with a consultation paper in 2002, a consultative report in 2004 and a final report in 2005. The second was unfair terms. Hugh believed that contract law should reflect the legitimate expectation of the parties. He wrote the consultation paper himself and was fully involved in the final report and draft Bill published in 2005. Finally, when I first met Hugh, he shared with me his desire to reform insurance law, particularly the insured's duty of disclosure. He was not deterred by the failure of the Law Commission's 1980 report and worked tirelessly to persuade the Treasury that we should return to the subject. We published the first consultation paper on the day he left the Commission in July 2007.

In addition, Hugh produced many other reports. He completed Professor Burrows' work on limitation of actions (2001) and damages under the Human Rights Act 1998 (October 2000). He published reports on pre-judgment interest on debts and damages (2004) and the forfeiture rule and the law of succession (2005). He furthered the project started by Professor Burrows on illegality in contract and trusts, writing a consultation paper on the illegality defence in tort (2001). He then developed the policy, which was eventually published in a final report in 2010. Last, but not least, he worked at an international level to harmonise the law by which investors 'own' intermediated securities. He analysed successive drafts of the UNIDROIT Convention on Substantive Rules regarding Intermediated Securities and, in 2008, recommended that the United Kingdom should ratify the Convention, subject to specific amendments.

Hugh was a Commissioner during the Blair Government (1997 to 2007). In retrospect, these years were not favourable to implementing Law Commission reports (or indeed to any reforms not developed within the heart of government). None of Hugh's recommendations were implemented while he was a Commissioner.

Since 2007, however, his work has been recognised and slowly implemented. In particular, the Consumer Insurance (Disclosure and Representations) Act 2012 came into force on 6 April 2013. It largely follows the consumer proposals in the 2007 consultation paper. The report on forfeiture and the law of succession was taken up by Greg Knight, MP and implemented through a Private Member's Bill. Thus the Estates of Deceased Persons (Forfeiture Rule and Law of Succession) Act 2011 came into force on 1 February 2012. In 2013, the Law Commission updated the unfair terms recommendations affecting consumers (see *Unfair Terms in Consumer Contracts: Advice to the Department of Business Innovation and Skills* (March 2013)). These recommendations are now reflected in Part 2 of the Consumer Rights Bill, introduced into Parliament in January 2014.

On security interests, a power to amend the scheme for registration of charges was included in section 894 of the Companies Act 2006. In April 2013, the Companies Act 2006 (Amendment of Part 25) Regulations 2013, SI 2013/600 came into force, giving effect to many of the Law Commission proposals concerning registration of charges. The broader proposals (regarding priority, the Land Registry and the sale of receivables) will need to await another day.

Finally, a personal note: I joined the team in 2002 and worked closely with Hugh for five years. During that time, his work output was prodigious. It was not unusual for him to come up with an idea on Friday, and hand the surprised team lawyer several chapters of a report the following Monday. Everyone remarked on what a pleasure he was to work with. He was unfailingly courteous at all times—though I would sometimes shudder when he leaned over and said 'With respect, Tammy'. I knew a devastating intellectual critique of my suggestion was on it way. Fellow Commissioners report a similar experience, preceded by the words 'Forgive me, Chairman'.

Hugh believed passionately in the Law Commission and its statutory purpose. Section 3 of the Law Commission Act 1965 states that the Law Commission should 'review all the law' of England and Wales with 'a view to its systematic development and reform'. Lesser mortals have suggested that this is impossible: one cannot review all of insurance law, or all of security law. But Hugh never shirked a challenge, and worked tirelessly to produce intellectually coherent, systematic bodies of law in which each element reflected underlying principle. It was often painful to him when others put political expediency above principle, or truncated his broad sweeping vision into measures to be implemented. But the advantage of principle is that it stands the test of time. People will return to read Hugh's reports for many years—and, slowly, his ideas are reaching the statute book.

Contents

Contributors

Christian von Bar, FBA, Professor of Law and Director of European Legal Studies Institute, University of Osnabrück

Paul Brand, Professor of English Legal History, University of Oxford and Senior Research Fellow, All Souls' College, Oxford

Michael Bridge, FBA, Cassel Professor of Commercial Law, London School of Economics, and Professor of Law, National University of Singapore

Andrew Burrows QC (Hon), FBA, Professor of the Law of England, University of Oxford, and Senior Research Fellow, All Souls' College, Oxford

Lord Carnwath, Justice of the Supreme Court of the United Kingdom

Mindy Chen-Wishart, Reader in Contract Law, University of Oxford and Fellow and Tutor in Law, Merton College, Oxford

Eric Clive, Visiting Professor, University of Edinburgh

Bénédicte Fauvarque-Cosson, Professor of Law, Université Panthéon-Assas, Paris II

Michael Furmston, Professor of Law, Singapore Management University

Roy Goode, Emeritus Professor of Law in the University of Oxford and Emeritus Fellow of St John's College, Oxford

Tamara Goriely, Commercial and Common Law Team Manager, Law Commission of England and Wales

Louise Gullifer, Professor of Commercial Law, University of Oxford and Fellow and Tutor in Law, Harris Manchester College, Oxford

Arthur S Hartkamp, Professor of European Private Law, Radboud University, Nijmegen

Martijn W Hesselink, Professor of European Private Law, University of Amsterdam

Thomas Krebs, Fellow and Tutor in Law, Brasenose College and University Lecturer in Commercial Law, University of Oxford

Ole Lando, Professor Emeritus, Copenhagen Business School

Eva Lomnicka, Professor of Law, Dickson Poon School of Law, King's College London and Barrister, 4 New Square Chambers

Catharine MacMillan, Professor of Law and Legal History, University of Reading

Ewan McKendrick, Registrar and Professor of English Private Law, University of Oxford, Fellow of Lady Margaret Hall

Wolf-Georg Ringe, Professor of International Commercial Law at Copenhagen Business School and the Faculty of Law, University of Oxford

Jacobien W Rutgers, Reader in Private and Private International Law, Vrije Universiteit Amsterdam

Lord Toulson, Justice of the Supreme Court of the United Kingdom

Christian Twigg-Flesner, Professor of Commercial Law, University of Hull

Anna Veneziano, Professor of Comparative Law, University of Teramo (Italy); Professor of European Property Law, University of Amsterdam (The Netherlands); Deputy Secretary-General of the Institute for the Unification of Private Law (UNIDROIT).

Stefan Vogenauer, Linklaters Professor of Comparative Law, University of Oxford, Director of the Oxford Institute of European and Comparative Law, and Fellow of Brasenose College, Oxford

Simon Whittaker, Professor of European Comparative Law, University of Oxford and Fellow and Tutor in Law, St John's College, Oxford

Sarah Worthington, Downing Professor of the Laws of England, University of Cambridge, and Fellow, Trinity College, Cambridge

Reinhard Zimmermann, Director, Max Planck Institute for Comparative and International Private Law, Hamburg

Table of Cases

European Union

Australia

Germany

The Netherlands

United Kingdom

United States of America

Tables of Legislation

Domestic Legislation

Austria

France

Germany

Greece

Italy

The Netherlands

Norway

Portugal

Spain

Switzerland

United Kingdom

Statutes

Statutory Instruments

United States of America

European Union Legislation

Treaties and Conventions

Regulations

Directives

International Instruments

Legal History

1

Merchants and the Legislative Process in Thirteenth Century England

The Making of the Statutes of Acton Burnel (1283) and Merchants (1285)

PAUL BRAND

THIS CHAPTER IS about how the legislative process worked in later thirteenth-century England. Its main focus is on the making of two related pieces of legislation: the Statute of Acton Burnel of 1283 and the Statute of Merchants of 1285. The Statute of Acton Burnel introduced a new system allowing, but not requiring, the official registration of debts plus a set of administrative procedures to compel the repayment of unpaid debts registered in this way. These included the forced sale of the debtor's movable goods (including any burgage properties he held), and the imprisonment of the debtor until the debt was paid. Little is generally known about the drafting process that preceded the enactment of thirteenth-century legislation.[1] In the case of the Statute of Acton Burnel, however, there survives one highly revealing official draft. This seems to have been prepared in advance of the discussion of the legislation at the Parliament held at Shrewsbury and Acton Burnel in late September and early October 1283. It has plenty of space between the lines to incorporate drafting changes and it apparently records the changes which were made during the course of the discussion in Parliament. As will be seen, these were not simply minor drafting alterations but introduced significant changes in the procedures envisaged for levying unpaid debts. These in turn suggest major opposition in principle to the scheme as originally envisaged. But the modified system put in place by the 1283 Statute seems not to have been found satisfactory either, for less than two years later Parliament returned in the Statute of Merchants of 1285 to make further major changes in the system for enforcing the payment of debts and less major changes in the system for recording them. Members of

[1] The main exception to this are the various drafts associated with the enactment of the Provisions of Westminster of 1259: see Paul Brand, 'The Making of English Thirteenth-century Legislation: Some New Evidence' in Andrew Lewis, Paul Brand and Paul Mitchell (eds), *Law in the City: Proceedings of the Seventeenth British Legal History Conference, London, 2005* (Dublin, 2007) 42–53 (and earlier works cited there). But these drafts are the product of a particular political context and reveal little of the normal drafting process.

England's Jewish community were the only group specifically excluded from using the system established by these Statutes. The irony is that Jewish creditors had long been required to use their own generically similar system of official registration of debts and they had also been able to use a system of quasi-administrative procedures for levying unpaid registered debts, which in some important respects prefigures the system established for Christian creditors in 1283 and amended in 1285. In the final part of the essay a brief account of this system will be given and comparisons made between it and the system established in 1283 and modified in 1285.

It was in June 1283 that summonses went out for a Parliament which was to meet at Shrewsbury at the end of September.[2] This was not somewhere Parliament normally met. Many of the main judicial and administrative organs of royal government had been at Shrewsbury since the autumn of 1282 while the king was conducting a military campaign in Wales but they were on the way back to Westminster by the time Parliament was held. The reason for Parliament meeting at Shrewsbury was not administrative convenience but symbolic. The king wanted Parliament to meet as close as possible to Wales because the main stated purpose of the Parliament was to witness the trial and condemnation of the recently captured Daffydd of Wales. Parliament may have started a little later than scheduled and it seems then to have remained in session until the end of October. It did much more than witness a significant political trial. It also dealt, like other Parliaments of this period, with a variety of other business. This included answering and taking action on petitions and the discussion and approval of legislation. Although Parliament had been summoned to Shrewsbury it seems to have moved part of the way through its session to Acton Burnel, perhaps after the trial of Daffydd had been concluded, and after the representatives of the counties had gone home. It was probably only after the move to Acton Burnel that the debt registration legislation was approved. The Statute of Merchants of 1285 refers to the earlier Statute as having been made at a Parliament held at Acton Burnel,[3] and the earlier legislation is referred to as the 'Statute of Acton Burnel' in a document of 1284,[4] and the contemporary Close Roll enrolment of the text also ties it to Acton Burnel.[5] Acton Burnel was just seven miles south east of Shrewsbury and it was the birthplace of Robert Burnel, bishop of Bath and Wells and the king's chancellor. Burnel erected a substantial fortified manor house there that is still standing. Other almost contemporary texts of the legislation refer to it as the 'Statutes made at Shrewsbury',[6] but this was probably because the legislation had been approved in a Parliament which had initially been summoned to Shrewsbury. The debt registration legislation was probably approved and possibly (but not certainly) published in the second week of October, well before Parliament

[2] Paul Brand (ed), *The Parliament Rolls of Medieval England, 1275–1504*, vol I, *Edward I, 1275–1294* (Woodbridge, 2005) 41.

[3] *Statutes of the Realm*, I, 98.

[4] TNA: PRO C 241/1, no 144: an acknowledgement of a debt under the provisions of the statute with an acknowledgment that *alioquin quod currerent super eum pena et districcio in statuto domini regis apud Acton Burnel proviso* (27 November 1284).

[5] *Statutes of the Realm*, I, 54, note.

[6] TNA: PRO, C 74/1, m 46 (Great Roll of Statutes): *Ceu sunt les estatuz fez a Salopesbury* or E 164/9, f 40: *ceo sunt les estatuz fez a Salopesbury al parlement prochein apres la feste seint Michel lan del regne le rey Eadward fiz le rey Henry unzine.*

itself dissolved. The Close Roll enrolment of the statute, which must be virtually contemporary, dates it to 12 October 1283.[7]

The legislation envisaged the creation of local debt registries in just three of the largest English urban centres: London, York and Bristol.[8] The process of registering a debt was to begin with the personal appearance of the debtor and the creditor[9] before the mayor of one of these towns and a clerk who had been specially appointed by the king for recording debt acknowledgments in the town concerned. The debtor was to acknowledge the amount of the debt and the date (or dates) for its payment. By November 1284, and perhaps from the very beginning, the debtor would also need to specifically acknowledge that he was submitting himself to the enforcement measures contained in the legislation.[10] The acknowledgment was to be enrolled on an official roll of acknowledgments written in the hand of the king's clerk. It was also to be recorded in a separate individual bond written by the same clerk and sealed not just by the debtor (as a private bond would have been) but also by a special royal seal provided for this purpose. This seal was to be in the joint custody of the mayor and the king's clerk in each town. The king was to receive a fee of one penny in the pound on each such acknowledgement, a relatively modest fee. This was supposedly for the costs of the clerk, and no further fees for the subsequent collection of the debt are mentioned. If the creditor required the additional assurance of pledges or mainpernors for the payment, in case the debtor was unable to pay, the creditor was able to ensure that they too made acknowledgments in the same way and to have them also recorded both on the roll and in individual bonds.

The legislation makes no provision about what was to happen if the debt was paid on or before time. It does not require the debt to be paid in the presence of those before whom it had been acknowledged. Nor does it provide that the enrolled record of the debt should then be cancelled as having been paid. It presumably assumes that the debtor will simply ensure that the bond is defaced and surrendered and that this will by itself constitute sufficient proof of payment. Its main provisions are about what is to be done if the debt remains unpaid. The creditor has to start the ball rolling by appearing before the mayor and the king's clerk with his bond and having them check that bond against the enrolment, to ensure that the debt has indeed been acknowledged and that the date for payment is past. All this can, however, be done without any need to inform the debtor or to ensure his presence at the debt registry. The mayor is then to act at once to have the debt levied from the chattels (comprising both movable possessions and devisable burgages[11]) belonging to the debtor within the city or town, by selling such chattels and handing the proceeds over to the creditor. If no purchaser can be found, the mayor is to hand the chattels over to the creditor at the valuation set by appraisers. They were to be

[7] *Statutes of the Realm,* I, 54, note.

[8] The legislation is most readily accessible in *Statutes of the Realm*, I, 53–54.

[9] Only once at the beginning of this section is he described specifically as a 'merchant' (*marchaunt*); elsewhere he is simply a creditor (*creaunzour*).

[10] See n 1 above.

[11] The legislation is careful to only make 'devisable' burgages subject to execution, those that under town custom were at the free post-mortem disposal of the debtor. If there were restrictions on his powers of disposal intended to ensure the burgage passed to his heirs they were excluded. In Bristol, only acquired and not inherited burgages were devisable in this way.

working under the discipline set by the creditor's ability to oblige them to take the chattels at their own valuation if they had valued them too highly (out of favour for the debtor).[12] The legislation also makes provision for the possibility that the debtor will have no assets within the jurisdiction of the town where the debt had been acknowledged but may have elsewhere, perhaps envisaging that the registration system will be used for debts owed by those who had no direct connection with the towns where the registries were located and intending to facilitate this use. In that case, the creditor may get the mayor to notify the king's chancellor of the acknowledgment of the debt and then himself get the chancellor to send a writ to the sheriff of the county where the debtor does have movables to authorise him to levy the debt from them in much the same way as the mayor would have done if they had been found in the town, either by sale or through delivery at the appraised valuation to the creditor. If neither of these procedures was feasible or fully effective imprisonment of the debtor was available, but evidently only as a last resort. The legislation envisaged that this might then lead to the debtor himself reaching agreement with, or otherwise satisfying, the creditor, or that his friends (*amis*), which could mean either unrelated friends or more likely his relatives, would do so on his behalf.[13] In general, the creditor was only to be entitled to the unpaid debt he was owed, but the legislation also made special provision for the foreign merchant (*merchaunt estraunge*)[14] who needed to stay on in England until his debt was levied. Such a creditor was to remain in England at the cost of the debtor until he had recovered his debt. If there had been mainpernors or pledges for the debt, execution was only to take place against their movables if the debtor was unable to pay in full. There is no suggestion that the mainpernors or pledges will themselves be liable to imprisonment.

Although there is some damage to the surviving text of the draft version of this legislation (a single sheet of parchment now in The National Archives in Kew) most of it can still be read and certainly enough to reveal what had been in the original draft before it came to Parliament and what was inserted or deleted in the course of discussion there.[15] This indicates that the system for the registration of debts was in pretty much its final form from the very beginning and also that these registries were from the beginning envisaged as being in the same three major towns. Only the provision for the payment of a fee of penny in the pound to the king on acknowledgments is shown by this text to be an addition made in the course of discussion in Parliament, or just possibly even later.[16] The draft section on the process to be followed if the debt is not paid is the one which shows the greatest alteration.

[12] The legislation provided, in effect, that the debtor had only himself to blame if the valuation was too low since he could have sold them for more beforehand if he had wished.

[13] The legislation also made provision for the debtor who could not even pay for his own food and drink in gaol. The creditor was to provide him with bread and water but the debtor was not to be released until this expense had also been repaid.

[14] The expression is ambiguous. It could simply mean a merchant from a different town. But it seems more likely in the wider context of the legislation that it refers to a foreign merchant.

[15] Paul Brand, 'A Working Draft of the Statute of Acton Burnell (1283)' in Paul Brand and Sean Cunningham (eds), *Foundations of Medieval Scholarship: Records Edited in Honour of David Crook* (York, 2008) 25–33.

[16] This in turn helps to explain why even in the final text it is to be found not in the section to which it seems to belong, that on the registration system, but almost at the end of the Statute.

As initially drafted, only the movables of the debtor were to be subject to immediate execution, either by sale or by delivery to the creditor. If execution on the movables did not pay the debt, however, what was originally envisaged was a proclamation by the mayor of the compulsory sale (at a future date) of the debtor's non-movable property. This was not, as later, to be restricted to devisable burgages but to cover any non-movable property (in towns these would generally be burgages), whether it had come to the debtor by inheritance or by acquisition.[17] The debtor then had 40 days to make his own private sale in order to satisfy the creditor. After 40 days the debtor lost this power, with the mayor being given a further eight days to complete the forced sale. It was only as a result of discussion at Parliament that execution came to be confined to devisable burgages and that the 40 day grace period during which the debtor himself might validly sell his non-movable property disappeared. The draft also suggests that an even more drastic change took place as a result of parliamentary discussion in the provisions for levying debts on assets outside the registration towns. As originally drafted, the legislation would have authorised sheriffs, once they were in receipt of chancery authorisation, to levy debts through the forced sale not just of movables but also of non-movable property. There is nothing in the text to suggest this was to be limited to what a later generation would call 'chattels real' (such as leases and wardships) and clear that it was intended to cover any kind of real property. After discussion the legislation was amended to restrict the sheriff's powers of execution to movable property. In effect, this left the debtor's real property (although normally his largest capital asset) outside the direct reach of his creditor, though the creditor might still use his power to procure the debtor's imprisonment for an unlimited period of time to gain indirect access to such assets or their cash value.

The draft legislation and the final text both provide in their preamble an explanation of why the legislation was being enacted. This was in order to meet the needs of merchants, and especially of foreign merchants.[18] Such merchants had, it is said, fallen into poverty (*chez en poverte*) because when they had 'lent' (*preste*) their goods to people (meaning, perhaps, had sold their merchandise on credit for future payment) there was no speedy mechanism for the recovery of the money owed if it was not paid on the day fixed for payment. As a result of this, it was said, many merchants had ceased coming to 'this land' (England) with their merchandise. In a passage added to the draft during discussion this in turn was said to be to the damage of 'merchants' (*marchaunz*), evidently native merchants wishing to trade with their foreign counterparts, and of the whole kingdom. The whole scheme is, then, to be seen as an attempt to ensure the swift recovery of debts, primarily those owed to foreign merchants, and in support of the wider economic interests of the country. The best method of doing this was seen to be that of allowing the registration of debts in official registries and with a purely administrative mechanism for levying the debt which did not use the courts and allowed for the forced sale of chattels and, as originally envisaged, the forced sale of lands as well, with the imprisonment of

[17] This seems to be a wider category than is covered by the devisable burgages of the final legislation.

[18] The marginal heading to the text of the statute on the Close Roll calls it *Statutum editum pro mercatoribus ad debita sua celeriter recuperanda*: *Statutes of the Realm*, I, 53, note.

the debtor as the ultimate weapon of persuasion to ensure the debtor or his friends or kin paid up. There is nothing to suggest that the legislation had been directly suggested by the foreign merchants that it was intended to benefit, let alone drafted by them, but that their supposed interests may have been central to the whole scheme is suggested by two further pieces of evidence. One is the specific provision made in the legislation for the payment of the costs of foreign merchants staying until their debt had been levied.[19] The second is the fact that only two days after the making of the Statute of Acton Burnel a different piece of legislation (perhaps better described as an ordinance rather than as a statute) was ordered to be proclaimed in London by the mayor and sheriffs, evidently as a result of discussion and approval at the same Parliament.[20] Its purpose seems to have been to stop banking or exchange transactions being made outside England (but relating to commercial transactions in England) because they were seen as impeding the flow of foreign silver into England and as leading to a decline in the international trade that was promoted by the influx of such silver. This, then, too was apparently prompted by a similar perceived diminution in the activities of foreign merchants in England. If the foreign merchants themselves were not the authors or direct inspiration for the legislation, who was? One possibility seems to be Robert Burnel himself. It may be no coincidence that the legislation was made at his birth place. It may also be no coincidence that the legislation made chancery (and more specifically the chancellor, Burnel) an essential link in the procedure for the extra-urban mechanism for the enforcement for debts. More fancifully perhaps, the statute merchant clerks, with their own versions of the royal seal, could perhaps be seen as detached parts of the chancery, though nothing in the legislation suggests this directly. If the legislation was inspired and even drafted by Burnel he may have been acting not so much on the prompting of the foreign merchants as on that of their English counterparts. Burnel certainly had a close personal tie with at least one such English merchant. He is Richard of Bedford, who belonged to a mercantile family connected with the town of Wilton. In May 1279 this same Richard of Bedford was given a protection with *volumus* when going overseas with the chancellor,[21] and after his death in 1289 Burnel can be found acting as one of his executors.[22] From litigation brought in the 1279 Kent eyre we know that Richard was already borrowing money from his relatives for mercantile ventures in 1256, much of which he subsequently lost owing to various misfortunes,[23] and as late as 1288 we hear of him (still described as a merchant) suing a German abbot and various merchants for the sums they owed him at Boston fair.[24] But even if the legislation was primarily intended to facilitate the commercial activities of foreign merchants, there was from the beginning no attempt to restrict its use to them, or even to merchants, as creditors. Indeed both the draft version (as far as can be seen) and the final version make it absolutely clear that it was to apply to any parties who wished to use the debt registration system. Only Jews were

[19] See p 6 above.
[20] *CCR 1279–88*, 244. The full text is printed in Ryley, *Placita Parliamentaria*, 444.
[21] *CPR 1272–81*, 314.
[22] *CPR 1281–92*, 403; TNA: PRO, CP 40/89, m 48d.
[23] TNA: PRO, JUST 1/370, m 19d.
[24] *CPR 1281–92*, 306.

excluded from taking advantage of it. If this legislation was inspired or drafted by Robert Burnel he may also have had somewhere in his mind broader considerations: the possibility of creating a more efficient and more reliable way of recording debts and enforcing debt payments which would capture this business for the king and royal government, perhaps at the expense of the towns and cities themselves. The changes made in the course of discussion, however, suggest that Burnel or whoever drafted the legislation may have underestimated the degree of opposition that the compulsory sale of land (apart from the very limited category of devisable burgages) would meet and that this opposition would be sufficient to ensure major changes in the legislation at a comparatively late stage. Presumably this opposition came from the 'landed interest' in the later thirteenth-century English Parliament, in particular from those lords who did not want to be made to accept new mercantile tenants for the lands within their fee.

Less than two years after the original legislation on debt registries and the new administrative processes for the collection of registered debts was enacted, Parliament returned to the same subject to pass a second piece of legislation that made more major changes in the scheme. One contemporary or almost contemporary text calls this the 'Statutes for Merchants and Bad Debtors' (*statuta pro mercatoribus et malis debitoribus*) but private copyists of statutes seem generally to have called it simply the 'Statute of Merchants' (*statutum mercatorum*).[25] The Statute was enacted at the Easter Parliament of 1285 held at Westminster which opened at the end of April and lasted until late June.[26] Various other items of business are known to have been transacted there, including the enactment of one other major piece of legislation, the Statute of Westminster II. Westminster II is said by one annalist to have been published in Westminster Hall on 29 June; one text of the Statute of Merchants suggests that it may have been approved and/or published on the previous day, 28 June.[27] The Statute of Merchants begins by rehearsing the preamble to the Statute of Acton Burnel and claiming that the enactment and enforcement of that Statute had meant that merchants since its enactment had recovered their debts with much less trouble. So far, so good. But, it seems, not everything had been working as planned. The merchants whom the legislation had been intended to help had made a complaint to the king (presumably by a petition submitted to this Parliament) that sheriffs (nothing is said about mayors) had been misinterpreting the Statute and sometimes even maliciously delaying its execution. This had led to the king having the Statute of Acton Burnel recited (*fist reciter*), presumably read out, at the Westminster Parliament and then making further legislation to 'clarify' some of the articles of the Statute (*pur declarer aquns articles de sun statut*). In practice, however, the Statute of Merchants did much more than that would seem to imply. The Statute was a reissue of the original legislation but with very significant amendments: in effect it very largely superseded it.

The amended scheme envisaged the establishment of debt registries not just in the three towns originally named in the Statute of Acton Burnel but also in whichever

[25] *Statutes of the Realm*, I, 98, note.
[26] *Parliamentary Rolls of Medieval England I*, 43.
[27] *Annales Monastici*, iv 304; *Statutes of the Realm*, I, 100, note.

towns the king should determine, and a later clause extended the operation of the debt registration scheme to the English lordship of Ireland as well. Extension outside the original three English towns had, in fact, already been taking place before 1285. Surviving notifications of unpaid debts show that even prior to this specific statutory authorisation registries had also been established in Lincoln, Winchester, and perhaps Shrewsbury.[28] What looks from its position in the text to have been a relatively late addition to the Statute also extended the debt registration system to fairs, which played an important role in national and international trade. The oral process of acknowledging a debt no longer had to be made before the mayor of a town but could now be made before his equivalent (*ou autre chief gardeyn de vile*) in towns without a mayor,[29] or before a temporary sworn substitute for either of these (*autre prodhome a ceo esleu e jure*) if they were temporarily unable to act.[30] At fairs the keeper of the fair and the community of merchants present were to choose two London merchants before whom (jointly or individually) acknowledgments could be made. In towns the second person before whom the debt was to be acknowledged was now to be at least one of what were now intended to be two clerks for each registry, or both if possible; at fairs there was only to be a single clerk despatched from chancery to the fair (with the seal). The form of the debt acknowledgment was unchanged, but the statute now also mentioned a requirement (probably already being observed in practice) that the debtor have the 'penalty of the statute' read to him so that he could not say later that it was not the penalty which he had agreed. The original scheme mentioned only a single roll of acknowledgments kept by the clerk,[31] but an additional safeguard was now offered by requiring a second roll of these to be kept by the mayor. A further safeguard was introduced in respect of the written obligation, which could be written by either of the two clerks. The king's seal attached to such acknowledgments was to be in two pieces. The larger part was to be in the custody of the mayor, the smaller in the custody of the senior clerk (an improvement perhaps on the original scheme of joint custody of an undivided seal). The king's fee remained the same except at fairs where it was fixed at 50 per cent higher.

The most important of the changes, though, were those made in the procedures authorised to ensure the repayment of overdue debts. The first of these was to establish imprisonment of the debtor as the first, not the last, step in compelling payment, provided the debtor was a layman. The legislation also makes it explicit that the custodian of the gaol is to be under an obligation to accept such a prisoner and adds that this custodian will be liable for the debt himself if he refuses to accept the prisoner or fails to keep him in secure custody. If the mayor or mayoral equivalent is unable to find the debtor and arrest him he was to send the record of the debt acknowledgement to the chancellor and he (presumably acting

[28] TNA: PROC 241/1, nos 144 (Lincoln, 1284), 134 (Winchester, 1284), 35 (?Shrewsbury).

[29] This is again prefigured before 1285 by acknowledgments in Bristol made before the constable of the castle: C 241/1, no 135 (1284). In early July 1285 (just after the publication of the statute) London too temporarily lost its mayor: *CPR 1281–92*, 182.

[30] This too may have been prefigured in earlier practice. In 1284 Adam of Northampton, citizen of Winchester, acted in Winchester debt acknowledgements: C 241/1, nos 134–33.

[31] Now that there were two clerks it had to be determined that the roll should be kept by the first appointed of the two clerks.

on information provided by the creditor as to his location) was to send a writ to the appropriate sheriff to make the arrest. This legislation also makes the sureties who have acknowledged they are 'principal debtors' (as sureties for debt normally did) liable to immediate arrest, just like the debtor. As has been seen, the Statute of Acton Burnel did not apparently envisage this even when imprisonment was a last, not a first, option. After arrest the debtor was to have a grace period of a quarter of a year (significantly longer than the grace period prior to the compulsory sale of lands envisaged in the draft legislation of 1283) during which he could sell his chattels and also his lands to pay off the debt. The careful draftsman made it plain that such a sale would be valid even though normally any sale of land made by one in prison was *ipso facto* invalid and could be voided. If he failed to do this after that three-month period, all the debtor's chattels were to be handed over to the creditor (evidently at a valuation set by appraisers).[32] He was also to gain possession of all of the debtor's lands[33] at a reasonable valuation (again apparently set by the appraisers) to hold until he had recovered his debt. This was in effect a lease of the land, but one protected by the actions of novel disseisin (or redisseisin) as if it was a freehold. It was also like a lease in the sense that the legislation specifically preserved the continuing right of the debtor to sell his land, provided that the creditor did not lose out on any improvements he had made to the land while holding it. This final part of the process, but only this part, was to be overseen by the courts, a significant break from the previous enforcement mechanism in which the courts had played no part at all. The chancery writ authorising the sheriff to act was to require him to report back on what he had done to the justices of either the Common Bench or the King's Bench, who could then order further action as needed (including writs to any sheriff to ensure the debtor's arrest, if he was not yet in custody). The provisions of Acton Burnel as to the recovery of additional expenses as well as the original debt were also expanded and extended. The creditor was to have damages and necessary and reasonable costs for travel, suits, delays and expenses. It is only the 'merchant' (*marchaunt*) who was to enjoy such expenses, but since the creditor is described as the 'merchant' throughout this statute,[34] it may have been intended to apply to all creditors. There is nothing in the language this time (in contrast to the Statute of 1283) to suggest that it was meant to apply only to foreign merchants. One other new provision in the Statute dealt with the situation where the debtor or a surety had died before the debt had been paid. The obligation to pay the debt, now that it was in effect secured on the debtor's lands, was to be transmissible to the heir to those lands, not the debtor's executors, and they were not to be liable to imprisonment, only to measures against their lands.

In the light of the speed with which this legislation superseded the Statute of Acton Burnel it looks at least possible that the debt registration system established

[32] For evidence of the use of appraisers see CP 40/123, m 45d (1298) but note that the court's order here preceded a successful arrest and ran in parallel with a further attempt to ensure one.

[33] The lands liable to execution included all the lands the debtor held on the day he made the acknowledgment. This was probably to ensure against collusive grants to defraud the creditor made before the debt was due and during the period between arrest and execution.

[34] Although the Statute of Merchants takes over from the Statute of Acton Burnel the clause that says the legislation applies to anyone who wishes to use it other than Jews.

by the Statute of Acton Burnel in 1283 and the associated enforcement procedures created by that Statute, may have been intended from the first as no more than a pilot scheme to see how well such a system would work and what changes might be needed to make it more effective. That is certainly how it worked in practice. As has been seen, initially there were just three local debt registries but their number had already increased before the enactment of the Statute of Merchants of 1285 and that Statute gave a general authority for establishing them in future both in England and in Ireland wherever the king thought fit, and also authorised a debt registry of the same general kind to operate in fairs. It was probably experience in running the registries that suggested the need for two clerks in each registry, and to make possible the operation of registries in towns without mayors and where temporary substitutes were needed for mayors or other chief officials and also at fairs. Practical experience and the need to guard against possible dishonesty may also have dictated the decision to have a duplicate roll and to divide the official seal into two separate pieces. Imprisonment of the debtor for an unlimited term as way of constraining him to pay his debt was something new in 1283. In the initial scheme it was to be used very much as a last resort, perhaps for that very reason, in order to render it acceptable. Once it had become acceptable to use imprisonment for private debt the drafters of the 1285 Statute of Merchants revealed their view of just how useful imprisonment was in compelling payment when they moved it from a final resort to the first resort. The drafters of the 1285 Statute of Merchants were also able to revisit what the history of the drafting of the 1283 Statute of Acton Burnel reveals to have been the fraught question of giving the creditor recourse to the real property assets of the debtor, especially the extra-urban real property assets. Instead of entrusting local sheriffs (or mayors) with a power of compulsory sale of such assets (as originally proposed), the 1285 Statute came up with the ingenious idea of giving the creditor a fully protected leasehold interest in such assets to run until the debt was paid off. In effect this gave the creditor a temporary lien on the whole of the debtor's property and that this was what it was is also indicated by the way that liability for the debt was transmitted under the terms of the Statute to the debtor's heir, and also by the fact that the lien was specifically stated in the Statute to obtain over lands which the debtor alienated between the time of acknowledging the debt and the time for its payment. One other notable change was the introduction of oversight of part of the enforcement process by the two main central royal courts (King's Bench and the Common Bench), partially judicialising what had previously looked like a purely administrative process. It is possible that all these changes were suggested by the merchants whose complaints about shrieval misconduct were the apparent pretext for this legislation, but it seems more likely that these changes were the result of a wider consideration in the king's council, and perhaps in Parliament as a whole, in the summer of 1285.

As has already been noted, the only group excluded from the use of the new debt registration procedure were members of the Jewish community and this exclusion was spelled out not just in the initial Statute of Acton Burnel of 1283 but also in the Statute of Merchants of 1285.[35] Ironically, there had been a system for the official

[35] *Statutes of the Realm*, I, 54, 100.

registration system of all debts owed to Jewish creditors by Christian debtors (but in practice only for all debts secured on the lands of Christian debtors) for almost a century by 1283, ever since its establishment in the reign of King Richard I in 1194. It too worked through a series of local registries, known as chirograph chests. Initially there were only six or seven of these, but by 1220 there were 17, and later even more. The original intention seems to have been to make the use of these registries compulsory, but in practice there continued to be some use of non-registered debt obligations. These too worked through personal appearances of the debtor and creditor at the chirograph chest and acknowledgment of the debt there. In this case, however, the appearance was not before the mayor but before a group of two Jewish and two Christian officials of each chest (known as chirographers), and one or (but only in the biggest towns) two clerks. These wrote bonds, but instead of a single copy sealed by the debtor and by the king's seal (as under the later scheme) Jewish debt bonds took the form of duplicate and later triplicate chirographs, of which only one was sealed and that only by the debtor's seal. One copy of the chirograph was kept in the sealed chirograph chest and from 1239 onwards this was the sealed copy. As under the later scheme, there was also a roll recording the debts written by the clerk. As originally planned there was also intended to be a roll recording payments made on debts but there seems to be no evidence of this in later practice.[36] The main difference between the two schemes lay in their purpose. The main purpose of the 1283 and 1285 systems was to provide a debt registration system and swifter debt recovery system for the benefit of creditors, and initially particularly foreign merchants, with the king's interest in all this very much secondary. The 1194 system was primarily intended from the first to serve the king's interests: giving him a record of the sums owed to all the Jews of England on which the king and his commissioners could base Jewish taxation and through seizure of Jewish debts ensure that it was paid; giving him a way of knowing what was owed to Jewish creditors when they died from which he was able to levy his share.[37] Any benefit to Jewish creditors seems to have been secondary.

There are also interesting comparisons to be made between the two systems in respect of the levying of unpaid debts. Only the system for the use of Christian creditors used imprisonment of the debtor as a weapon, whether at the end (as in 1283) or the beginning (as in 1285) of the enforcement process. No such process seems ever to have been available for Jewish creditors and was perhaps unthinkable in twelfth- and thirteenth-century England. In both systems the first recourse for the debtor in levying his debt from the debtor's property was on his chattels. For the Jewish creditor this was originally something authorised by a writ issued by the Exchequer of the Jews to the local sheriff on production of the creditor's part of the chirograph but without any prior judicial process; for the Christian creditor it might simply be authorised by the mayor or (if the debtor had only extra-urban property) required notification to chancery and then a writ to the sheriff. But the Statute of Jewry of 1275 complicated matters, allowing the Jewish creditor no more

[36] Paul Brand (ed), *Plea Rolls of the Exchequer of the Jews* (Jewish Historical Society of England, 2005) vol IV, 6.

[37] ibid 7–9.

than half of the debtor's chattels and requiring a valuation before they were put into possession of them.[38] As has been seen, the Christian creditor was originally to have been entitled to have his debtor's real property sold to levy his debt under the original draft scheme, but then lost that right and ended up under the Statute of Merchants with a right to a fully protected leasehold interest in the lands. The Jewish creditor also originally seems to have got a similar limited interest in all his debtor's lands, but again after 1275 was allowed possession of only half of them, not including the debtor's house, until the debt was levied.[39] This may suggest that the Jewish creditor model was one not just known to the drafters of this part of the 1285 Statute but also utilised by them. If it was the model, there was certainly no direct acknowledgment of that fact and that is hardly surprising since the Jewish community in England was increasingly marginalised by the mid-1280s and was to be expelled from England in 1290. One other major difference prior to 1275 was in the provision in Jewish bonds for a continuing payment of interest on the loan after the debt became due, which became part of the debt levied through the official procedures. This was prohibited by the Statute of Jewry of 1275. This was never something allowed to Christian creditors under the debt registration scheme.

In the draft version of the Statute of Acton Burnel, the Statute of Acton Burnel of 1283 and the Statute of Merchants of 1285, there survives a remarkable sequence of legislation and legislative drafts in which we can see the draftsmen and the English Parliament developing and refining a scheme for local debt registries and for streamlined and effective enforcement of the payment of the debts recorded under the scheme, at least in part in response to practical experience of the working of what seems to have amounted to a pilot scheme, some of them channelled through complaints received from some of the users. As has been seen, the legislation was developed in response to the perceived needs of merchants and amended in part in response to their complaints, but the amendment of the original draft legislation and the compromise scheme of leasehold tenancies for the creditor eventually adopted in the 1285 Statute of Merchants gives some real sense of the compromises required to meet the objection of rural landlords. Merchants and mercantile transactions made important contributions to the later thirteenth-century English economy but their political influence was much less than that of the country gentry and the nobility.

[38] ibid 12.
[39] ibid 12.

2

Contract Terms Between Unequal Parties in Victorian England

CATHARINE MACMILLAN*

PROFESSOR BEALE WAS a Law Commissioner when the Law Commission issued a joint *Report on Unfair Terms in Contracts*.[1] The Report considered the concept of an unfair term imposed by one party into a contract and made certain recommendations as to how English law should regulate such terms. That such terms could be incorporated into contracts arose from nineteenth-century cases.[2] While the Victorians were not unduly concerned with unfair terms there were concerns expressed about contracts between unequal parties. This situation arises, in the words of Lord Denning MR, where 'the parties have not met on equal terms—when the one is so strong in bargaining power and the other so weak—that as a matter of common fairness, it is not right that the strong should be allowed to push the weak to the wall'.[3] We are concerned here not with undue influence, where the parties contract in the context of an existing relationship of trust and confidence, but where the parties deal as strangers. Nineteenth-century courts of equity would intervene in instances where the parties were not equals and one party exploited the weakness of the other. English law has resisted the full development of a doctrine of unconscionability despite the existence of a body of cases upon which such a development could have occurred. This chapter examines when equity intervened in cases of inequality in the nineteenth century and explores the reasons why they did not form the basis of a larger legal doctrine.

FRAUD AND CONTRACTUAL FAIRNESS IN THE NINETEENTH CENTURY

Legal historians have been concerned to explain how the changes in contract law during the nineteenth century related to the broader economic and political changes of the period. The view was advanced that an earlier approach of paternalistic

* I am grateful to Charlotte Smith for her comments on an earlier draft; all errors and omissions are my own.

[1] Law Com No 292, 2005; Scot Law Com No 199.

[2] See, eg, *Parker v South Eastern Railway Company; Gabell v South Eastern Railway Company* (1877) 2 CPD 416 (CA).

[3] *Lloyds Bank v Bundy* [1974] 1 QB 326 (CA), 336–37. The attempt to establish a general principle of inequality of bargaining power was disapproved of by the House of Lords: *National Westminster Bank plc v Morgan* [1985] AC 686.

values in enforcing conceptions of contractual fairness gave way to an approach that sought to protect individual rights acquired by contract. These legal changes were explained in the context of changing political and economic theories that advanced a system of laissez-faire capitalism. The adoption of a will theory suited the needs of a modern industrialist society.[4] Later scholars have distanced political and economic change from legal change and refuted this earlier approach.[5] The law had its own internal discourse and judges did not decide the cases before them on the basis of political theory. Contractual fairness is central to this larger discussion and examinations have already been undertaken as to the extent to which courts protected parties from hard bargains.[6] In comparing the equitable and legal treatments of such bargains it has been observed that the difference between these two systems lay more in their different structures: 'law and equity in effect dealt with distinct problems, and used different procedures'.[7] The inquisitorial procedure of equity allowed it to consider questions that the common law could not. To this can be added that the greater remedial flexibility of courts of equity encouraged different conceptions of substantive law, although these conceptions were not necessarily antithetical to the common law.

Courts of common law had little scope to consider issues of contractual unfairness beyond positive fraud,[8] despite attempts to seek a fair solution to particular problems by use of warranties, trade customs or particular representations.[9] Equity, as a court of conscience, had the jurisdiction and the means to scrutinise the fairness or reasonability of a contract in relation to fraud. Lord Hardwicke, in *Earl of Chesterfield v Janssen*,[10] explained that the court had the jurisdiction to relieve against every species of fraud. The five categories he set out formed the basis of equitable relief into the nineteenth century. The nature of this equitable jurisdiction over fraud was a fluid one. Writing to Kames, addressing the general question of whether or not a court of equity should be governed by general rules, Hardwicke used fraud as a specific instance in which such rules should be avoided:

> But as to relief against frauds, no invariable rules can be established. Fraud is infinite, and were a court of Equity once to lay down rules, how far they would go, and no further, in extending their relief against it, or to define strictly the species or evidence to it, the jurisdiction would be cramped, and perpetually eluded by new schemes, which the fertility of man's invention would contrive.[11]

[4] PS Atiyah, *The Rise and Fall of Freedom of Contract* (Oxford University Press, 1979).

[5] Michael Lobban, 'Part II: Contract' in William Cornish et al, *The Oxford History of the Laws of England*, vol XII, *1820–1914: Private Law* (Oxford University Press, 2010) 296–300. For the American counterparts to this discussion, see Morton J Horwitz, *The Transformation of American Law, 1780–1860* (Oxford University Press, 1977) and the challenges made to it by AWB Simpson, 'The Horwitz Thesis and the History of Contracts' (1979) 46 *University of Chicago LR* 533 and Peter Karsten, *Head versus Heart: Judge-made Law in Nineteenth Century America* (Chapel Hill, NC, University of North Carolina Press, 1997).

[6] Michael Lobban, 'Contractual Fraud in Law and Equity, c1750–c1850' (1997) 17 *Oxford J Legal Stud* 441 and JL Barton, 'The Enforcement of Hard Bargains' (1987) 103 *LQR* 118.

[7] Lobban, 'Contractual Fraud in Law and Equity, c1750–c1850', n 6 above, 443–44.

[8] ibid 457–66.

[9] ibid 466–71.

[10] *Chesterfield v Janssen* (1751) 2 Ves Sen 125, 156–57; 28 ER 82, 100.

[11] Letter from Lord Hardwicke to Lord Kames, 30 June 1750, in Joseph Parkes, *A History of the Court of Chancery* (Longman, Rees, Orme, Brown and Green, 1828) 508.

It was from concern as to this 'fertility of invention', rather than a lack of conception as to the nature of the protection to be granted, that equity sought to retain a flexible jurisdiction in dealing with fraud. Equitable relief was twofold. The first was to set aside the contract, to find that the fraud rendered the contract voidable; the second was to refuse specific performance and leave the plaintiff to his remedy in an action for damages at common law.[12]

Two of Lord Hardwicke's categories, actual fraud and fraud upon those not party to the contract (or against public policy) do not concern us. His remaining categories, fraud apparent from the nature of the bargain, fraud presumed from the circumstances and the condition of the parties, and the fraud involved in 'catching bargains' with expectant heirs, all involved instances where relief was provided where parties met on unequal terms outside an existing relationship.

UNEQUITABLE AND UNCONSCIENTIOUS BARGAINS

Lord Hardwicke's second species of fraud arose from the bargain: 'it may be apparent from the intrinsic nature and subject of the bargain itself; such as no man in his sense and not under delusion would make on the one hand, and as no honest and fair man would, accept on the other; which are unequitable and unconscientious bargains'.[13] The fraud existed not only because of the weakness of one party but because the other took advantage of this weakness. While this category was broadly phrased it was little used and primarily considered when an asset was sold at undervalue. In principle a transaction could be impugned for an inadequate consideration but in practice few cases were so resolved. As Lord Eldon stated, 'unless inadequacy of price is such as shocks the conscience, and amounts in itself to conclusive and decisive evidence of fraud in the transaction, it is not itself a sufficient ground for refusing specific performance'.[14] Thurlow LC disapproved of inequality as a basis for setting aside a transaction and was of the view that 'to set aside a conveyance, there must be an inequality so strong, gross, and manifest, that it must be impossible to state it to a man of common sense, without producing an exclamation at the inequality of it'.[15]

There is a hint, but no more, that equity was reluctant to set aside contracts solely on the basis that too much had been paid.[16] Examples existed of contracts set aside

[12] Lobban, 'Contractual Fraud in Law and Equity, c1750–c1850', n 6 above, 448–50.

[13] *Chesterfield v Janssen*, n 10 above, 155, 100.

[14] *Coles v Trecothick* (1804) 9 Ves Jun 234, 246; 32 ER 592, 597. Where the parties were in a 'confidential relation' adequacy would be more 'jealously scrutinised': *Coles v Trecothick* (1804) 2 Ves Jun Supp 164; 34 ER 1040. Courts refrained from establishing a precise amount. In *Butler v Miller* (1867) IR 1 Eq 195, Walsh MR stated, obiter, that conscience was shocked where half the price or less was received: 211–12.

[15] *Gwynne v Heaton* (1778) 1 Bro C C 1, 9; 28 ER 949, 953.

[16] *Abbott v Sworder* (1852) 4 De G & Sm 448; 64 ER 907. A solicitor had overpaid for the value of a farm but not so much as to shock the conscience and specific performance would not be refused.

for inadequacy of consideration alone[17] or a refusal to grant specific performance[18] but the nineteenth-century tendency was against such actions.[19] Courts of Chancery expressed reservations about setting aside contracts solely on the ground of inadequacy of consideration because the value of a thing 'admits of no precise standard' and to intervene on such basis would 'shake the commercial intercourse of the nation'.[20] While successive courts kept open the possibility that a contract could be set aside on the ground of an inadequate consideration they generally declined to do so solely on that basis.[21] During the course of the nineteenth century one finds fewer courts concerned about undervalue as such, as the investigation for potential fraud became focused on other aspects.

Because inequality of terms, taken to mean an inadequate consideration, only hinted at an inequality between the parties it was the case that where some other factor was present besides an inadequate consideration, courts would intervene. Undervalue could indicate abuse of a confidential relationship,[22] or that a weak man had been pressed,[23] or that advantage had been taken of a distressed party[24] or one of feeble intellect,[25] or that oppression had occurred.[26]

PRESUMED FROM THE CIRCUMSTANCES AND CONDITIONS OF THE CONTRACTING PARTIES

The presence of these other features indicates that what equity was concerned about was the advantage taken of a party not on an equal footing. Undervalue was not an independent ground for equitable intervention but an indication that intervention was required on other grounds. Lord Hardwicke's second species of fraud thus informed his third, that which arises from the nature and the circumstances of the contracting parties. Equity would prevent a party from 'taking surreptitious advantage of the weakness or necessity of another: which knowingly to do so is equally against the conscience as to take advantage of his ignorance'.[27]

Weakness resulting in inequality arose in two general ways: those intrinsic to the individual and those extrinsic to the individual. In the first group were those cases of physical or mental impairment. In the second group were factors related to the

17 *Heathcote v Paignon* (1787) 2 Bro Ch C 167; 29 ER 96 was a rare exception where inadequacy of consideration was the ground for setting aside the sale of an annuity.

18 *Young v Clerk* (1720) Pr Ch 538; 24 ER 241. In *Falcke v Gray* (1859) 4 Drew 651; 62 ER 250. Kindersley MR would have refused specific performance of contract of sale of chattels on undervalue alone.

19 *Moth v Atwood* (1801) 5 Ves Jun 845; 31 ER 889. Arden MR was of the view that although the undervalue was substantial the vendor was determined to sell.

20 *Griffith v Spratley* (1787) 1 Cox CC 383, 388; 29 ER 1213, 1215 per Eyre LCB.

21 *Clark v Malpas* (1862) 4 De G F & J 401; 45 ER 1238; *Summers v Griffiths* (1866) 35 Beav 27; 55 ER 804; *Tennent v Tennents* (1867) LR 2 ScDiv 6 (HL), 9 per Lord Westbury.

22 *Crowe v Ballard* (1790) 1 Ves Jun 215; 30 ER 308; *Huguenin v Baseley* (1807) 14 Ves Jun 273; 33 ER 526.

23 *Gartside v Isherwood* (1783) 1 Bro C C 558; 28 ER 1297.

24 *Wood v Abrey* (1818) 3 Madd 417; 56 ER 558; *James v Kerr* (1889) 40 Ch D 449 (Ch D).

25 *Longmate v Ledger* (1860) 2 Giff 157; 66 ER 67.

26 *Cockell v Taylor* (1852) 15 Beav 103; 51 ER 475.

27 *Chesterfield v Janssen*, n 10 above, 156; 100.

individual's condition in life. Most cases in which relief was given exhibited one or more elements common to one or both of these groups: 'taking the whole history together, it may present so many features of unconscientiousness, extortion, and unfair dealing on the one side and weakness on the other, as to compel the Court to exercise its equitable jurisdiction'.[28] The basis for equitable intervention lay in preventing the unacceptable consequences of a stronger party knowingly taking advantage of another's weakness.

A number of intrinsic individual weaknesses worked to place a party on an unequal footing. Mental disability was troublesome for both Victorian medics and lawyers.[29] Could a binding contract be entered into with one who was insane or of unsound mind? A distinction was made between lunatics, persons who lost their use of reason, and idiots, persons who had been born without understanding and where it was presumed none would ever be acquired.[30] Where a person had been found to be a lunatic his situation was governed by statute. Difficulties arose when such a determination had not been made. By the mid-eighteenth century it was established that while a man could not plead his own disability to set aside his deed,[31] another could use the disability to set it aside[32] and it could also be set aside where only the insane party was prejudiced.[33] There are indications by Lord Hardwicke that these restrictions could be overcome where insanity was an aspect of fraud.[34] The lunatic was capable of contracting where his state of mind was unknown to the other party who took no advantage of the lunatic.[35] An executed contract would not be set aside in such circumstances out of necessity for 'a contrary doctrine would render all ordinary dealings between man and man unsafe'[36] and extensive and inconvenient consequences would follow.[37] While contrary views to this were expressed which denied that a person of unsound mind was capable of contracting at all,[38] equity generally declined to give relief in a sale and purchase where the party dealt with a person of unsound mind but without knowledge of this disability.[39] Where there was knowledge that the person was of unsound mind the conscience of the other party was affected and it was the effect upon the conscience that triggered equitable

[28] *Nevill v Snelling* (1889) 15 Ch D 679 (Ch), 703 per Denman J.

[29] See John Charles Bucknill and Daniel Hack Tuke, *A Manual of Psychological Medicine* (John Churchill, 1862) and I Ray, *A Treatise on the Medical Jurisprudence of Insanity*, 5th edn (Little, Brown and Company, 1871).

[30] The various forms of mental disability and its legal treatment are to be found in Leonard Shelford, *A Practical Treatise on the Law concerning Lunatics, Idiots and Persons of Unsound Mind* (S Sweet, 1833) ch I.

[31] *Re Beverley's Case* (1603) 4 Co Rep 123b; 76 ER 1118.

[32] *Thompson v Leach* (1690) 3 Mod Rep 301; 87 ER 199.

[33] *Ridler v Ridler* (1729) 1 Eq Cas Abr 279; 21 ER 1045.

[34] *Bennet v Vade* (1742) 2 Atk 324; 26 ER 597. See *Sergeson v Sealey* (1742) 2 Atk 412; 26 ER 648, where the purchase of real property by a lunatic was supervised by the lunatic's only son who thought the bargain a fair one; relief was declined. See also, *Price v Berrington* (1851) 3 Mac & G 486; 42 ER 348.

[35] *Molton v Cambroux* (1848) 2 Exch 487; 154 ER 584; *Imperial Loan Co v Stone* [1892] 1 QB 599 (CA).

[36] *Elliot v Ince* (1857) 7 De G M & G 475, 487; 44 ER 186, 190 per Cranworth LC.

[37] *Niell v Morley* (1804) 9 Ves Jun 478; 32 ER 687. Grant MR expressed concern about restoring the parties to their original positions, particularly if reliance had been placed upon an apparent valid contract. The party was left to his remedy at law.

[38] *Harrod v Harrod* (1854) 1 K & J 4, 7; 69 ER 344, 346.

[39] *Elliot v Ince*, n 36 above. The situation was otherwise where, as here, the provisions of a settlement were altered.

intervention. Equity would not provide relief from a contract entered into with a lunatic during a lucid interval where no other factors pointed to an undue advantage being obtained from him.[40]

A weak-minded person with the appearance of sufficient understanding to govern himself and a memory capable of acquiring knowledge was not considered to have a mental disability.[41] Where this weakness of mind left the individual unable to protect himself when contracting, equity would intervene. The mental incapacity could be less than what might have been necessary for a commission of lunacy to act.[42] Page Wood V-C was of the view that it was a fraud to lead a party into a contract which they did not understand,[43] although this was only correct where they suffered from some unsoundness of mind.[44] 'Good faith should be observed in all transactions, between man and man'[45] stated Lord Wynford and for this reason, a deed would be set aside where it had been entered into by an ill man of weakened intellect of whom advantage had been taken. Story concluded that where a person was of weak understanding and thus liable to imposition, contracts would be held void if the nature of the contract justified the conclusion that the person had 'been imposed upon, circumvented, overcome by cunning, or artifice, or undue influence'.[46]

Intoxication was largely governed by the same rules, for here the party was *non compos mentis* by his own act. Where drunkenness created an inequality between the parties equity might relieve a party from their contract or decline to assist one who had obtained a contract from a drunkard. The drunkenness had to result in an extreme state of intoxication and an unfair advantage taken by the other party of the drunkard's state, or contrivance had been made to draw him into drink.[47] Equity would also set aside a contract where the drunkenness was so extreme as to invalidate the contract at law. Intoxication is a matter of degree and where the drunkard had only impaired rather than destroyed his capacity equity would not intercede to avoid his act.[48]

Equity also recognised that physical disabilities operated to create inequality between the parties. Old age, infirmity and illness coupled with some form of inadequacy in exchange and a lack of advice were all reasons given to relieve contracts.[49] Illness and infirmity often appeared in contexts in which the law would now presume undue

[40] *Hall v Warren* (1804) 9 Ves Jun 605; 32 ER 738: an important factor was that the price of the sale was independently set.

[41] Shelford, *A Practical Treatise on the Law*, n 30 above, 3.

[42] *Blachford v Christian* (1829) 1 Knapp 73; 12 ER 248.

[43] *Harrod v Harrod*, n 38 above, 7; 246.

[44] *Anderson v Elsworth* (1861) 3 Giff 154; 66 ER 363 (a case of a voluntary deed); *Gartside v Isherwood* (1783) 1 Bro C C 558; 28 ER 1297. Contrary observations were made in *Osmond v Fitzroy* (1731) 3 P Will 129, 130; 24 ER 997, but the weaknesses complained of may not have been of mind as such.

[45] *Blachford v Christian*, n 42 above, 77; 250.

[46] Joseph Story, *Commentaries on Equity Jurisprudence, as Administered in England and America*, 13th edn (by Melville Bigelow, Boston, NJ, Little, Brown and Company, 1886) vol 1 paras 238, 249–50.

[47] *Cooke v Clayworth* (1811) 18 Ves Jun 13; 34 ER 222. *Say v Barwick* (1812) 1 V & B 195; 35 ER 76. At law, complete intoxication would support a plea of *non est factum* to a deed, of *non concessit* to a grant and of *non assumpsit* to a promise for the drunkard 'had not an agreeing mind': *Pitt v Smith* (1811) 3 Camp 33, 34; 170 ER 1296, per Lord Ellenborough.

[48] *Shaw v Thackray* (1853) 1 Sm & G 537; 65 ER 235.

[49] *Clark v Malpas* (1862) 31 Beav 80; 54 ER 1067; aff'd 4 De G, F & J 401; 45 ER 1238.

influence: a surgeon and his patient;[50] a dentist and his patient;[51] an apothecary and his patient;[52] or between family members.[53] Equity did provide relief absent such a relationship when one of the parties was elderly and, almost invariably, infirm in body or mind. Age alone was not a ground upon which to base relief for it was not indicative on its own that a party had been imposed upon or advantage taken. As Buller J observed 'we have seen the greatest abilities at an age greater than 75'.[54] While old age was frequently pled, the importance of it depended upon the context in which the transaction took place. In *Harrison v Guest*,[55] a very ill and bedridden man of 71, acting without advice or assistance, conveyed his property to Guest in exchange for accommodation, food and an attendant in Guest's home for the remainder of his life. The exchange was grossly inadequate for the vendor only lived for six weeks as Guest's guest. Cranworth LC held that where parties dealt at arm's length and in absence of a fiduciary relation, the burden of proof was upon the party seeking to set aside the transaction to show that he had been imposed upon. In this case Hunt had sought out Guest to offer the conveyance. Nothing indicated imposition nor that Guest snapped at Hunt's offer. Hunt understood what he was doing, acted in his own interests and benefitted from the exchange: 'he was in a more cleanly and happy state, with more comforts about him'.[56]

In contrast, in *Longmate v Ledger*,[57] Stuart V-C set aside a contract between a creditor and a debtor who was 'a man advanced in years [72] and of a weak and eccentric disposition',[58] acting without advice. While the vendor had offered the property to the purchaser, he had done so under the influence of a quarrel with his daughter and while his debt to the purchaser made a great impression upon him. While the purchaser did nothing to induce the vendor into the contract it was one where the price was wholly inadequate. In such circumstances the contract could not stand 'on the ground of inequality between the contracting parties'.[59]

Equity regarded certain factors extrinsic to the individual as tending to create an inequality of circumstances between the parties. Three, often combined, were of particular concern: illiteracy, financial distress and social class. Illiteracy, more common before compulsory education from 1880, was presented as a factor contributing to inequality but not accepted as a ground on its own.[60] It was significant when combined with a lack of independent advice because it served to emphasise the dependence upon the other for an understanding of the transaction.

[50] *Popham v Brooke* (1828) 5 Russ 8; 38 ER 930.
[51] *Allen v Davis* (1850) 4 De G & S; 64 ER 767.
[52] *Priestly v Wilkinson* (1790) 1 Ves Jun 214; 30 ER 307.
[53] *Willan v Willan* (1814) 2 Dow 274; 3 ER 863.
[54] *Lewis v Pead* (1789) 1 Ves Jun 19; 30 ER 210. In *Rosher v Williams* (1875) LR 20 Eq 210, the court declined assistance on the grounds of advanced age (92) alone.
[55] *Harrison v Guest* (1855) 6 De G M & G 424; 43 ER 1298.
[56] ibid 437, 1303.
[57] *Longmate v Ledger* (1860) 2 Giff 157; 66 ER 67.
[58] ibid 163, 69.
[59] ibid 165, 70.
[60] *Clark v Malpas*, n 49 above; *Summers v Griffiths* (1866) 35 Beav 27; 55 ER 804.

Financial distress was relevant to the inquiry of 'whether the parties really did meet on equal terms'.[61] Inequality was established where a vendor was in distressed circumstances and a purchaser took advantage of that distress. Other factors reinforced the inequality. In *Wood v Abrey*,[62] an impecunious father and son, ignorant of the value of their estates, sold them at a gross undervalue upon the purchaser's proposal and in absence of independent advice. In *Ford v Olden*,[63] Stuart V-C found that a small grocer struggling under debts he could not meet had been taken advantage of by his mortgagee and the influence of the mortgagee's position, coupled with an undervalue, was sufficient to set aside the transaction. Disadvantage would not be found where the impecunious had received independent advice, but where this advice was influenced by the competing desires of the adviser, the effect of the advice would be disallowed.[64] Towards the end of the nineteenth century, judges began to compare the position of the financially distressed as analogous to that of the expectant heir.

The third factor that tended towards inequality between the parties arose when, to use a Victorian aphorism, one party came from a different 'station in life' than the other. The factor had two aspects. One from a lower social class was more in need of protection and, conversely, one from a higher social class owed a form of implied duty to his social inferior not to take exploit the situation. A bargain between a humble man in mean circumstances and an affluent man, in which the former was taken by surprise by the latter to a contract advantageous only to the affluent, was one the court would avoid. Kenyon MR observed that, while it was difficult to lay down principles in such circumstances, 'if the party is in a situation, in which he is not a free agent, and is not equal to protecting himself, this Court will protect him'.[65] A large number of successful claimants for equitable relief were women of inferior social status dealing with their male 'social superior'.[66] In *Baker v Monk*,[67] an elderly widow of humble status, impoverished, illiterate, infirm and charged with the care of her bed-ridden father-in-law, contracted (without advice) to sell her property at an undervalue to the Mayor of Favesham upon his proposal. The decision of Romilly MR to set aside the transaction was upheld on appeal. The differences between the parties 'rendered it incumbent on the Appellant to throw further protection around this lady before he made the bargain with her'.[68] Knight Bruce LJ gave an indication that the reasons for disallowing the transaction were ones not only of conscience but also of public policy: 'this is a case in which society is as much interested as are individuals'.[69]

[61] *Wood v Abrey* (1818) 3 Madd 417, 423; 56 ER 558, 560, per Leach V-C.

[62] ibid.

[63] *Ford v Olden* (1867) LR 3 Eq 461 (Ch).

[64] *James v Kerr* (1887) 40 Ch D 449 (Ch); *Fry v Lane* (1888) 40 Ch D 321 (Ch).

[65] *Evans v Llewellin* (1787) 1 Cox C C 333, 340; 29 ER 1193, 1194.

[66] *Summer v Griffiths* (1866) 35 Beav 27; 55 ER 804; *Rees v De Bernardy* [1896] 2 Ch 437 (Ch). In *Haygarth v Wearing* (1871) LR 12 EQ 320, Wickens V-C set aside a contract between a schoolmistress and a mill-owner, noting that 'he was more or less of a man of business; she was as far as possible removed form a woman of business': 327.

[67] *Baker v Monk* (1864) 33 Beav 419; 55 ER 430; aff'd 4 De G J & S 388; 46 ER 968.

[68] ibid 393; 970.

[69] ibid 389; 969.

The importance of advice to the disadvantaged party appears in *Curson v Belworthy*.[70] An uneducated and illiterate labourer in greatly distressed circumstances conveyed his interest in land to a landowner at severe undervalue. Equity would not interfere with the transaction, though, because the labourer had the advice of his three younger brothers (who had urged him not to sell) and his wife, a 'shrewd and vigilant woman'.[71] The case is unusual because the general tendency of the courts was to require, in cases where the weaknesses of a party made them incapable of making a bargain, that they obtain professional advice.[72] It was incumbent upon the stronger party to suggest the weaker take independent advice.[73] While it was often said that this should be legal advice the intercession of a solicitor, as such, was not insisted on, although if a solicitor had provided advice it acted as evidence that he had explained the nature and character of the transaction to the weaker party.[74]

CATCHING BARGAINS WITH HEIRS, REVERSIONERS OR EXPECTANTS

In some instances equity extended relief to dealings between strangers where one of the parties had a particular status the nature of which entitled the party to protection. One such instance was sailors dealing with their prize money.[75] A second instance of this status-based intervention was that of the expectant heir.[76] Throughout the nineteenth century relief was sought under this head far more than either of the heads of fraud considered above, only to fall away rapidly in the early twentieth century. Lord Hardwicke's final species of fraud upon which equity would give relief was of catching bargains with heirs, reversioners or expectants in the life of the father. This head of fraud contained elements of all the other heads of fraud, sometimes actual fraud and sometimes fraud presumed or inferred from the circumstances or conditions of the contracting parties: 'weakness on one side, usury on the other, or extortion or advantage taken of that weakness ... an appearance of fraud from the ... intrinsic unconscionableness of the bargain'.[77] Such a transaction worked a fraud not only upon the impecunious heir but also upon his family, for the transaction mislead the ancestor into believing he had left his estate to the heir when it would instead pass 'to a set of artful persons'.[78] Concern with the family's posi-

[70] *Curson v Belworthy* (1852) 3 HLC 742; 10 ER 294. See also *Longmate v Ledger*, n 25 above.

[71] *Curson v Belworthy*, n 70 above, 756; 300.

[72] *Harrison v Guest*, n 55 above; *Clark* v *Malpas*, n 49.

[73] *Baker v Monk*, n 67 above.

[74] *Denton v Donner* (1856) 23 Beav 285; 53 ER 112.

[75] *Baldwin v Rochford* (1748) 1 Wils KB 229; 95 ER 589; *Taylour v Rochfort* (1751) 2 Ves Sen 281; 28 ER 182; *How v Weldon* (1754) 2 Ves Sen 516; 28 ER 330. Lord Hardwicke declined to include them to his identified species in *Chesterfield v Janssen*, n 10 above.

[76] The term came to cover a wide category of persons: Daniel Rankin MacAlpin, *The Law relating to Money-Lenders and Borrowers* (London, Reeves and Turner, 1880) 287.

[77] *Chesterfield v Janssen*, n 10 above, 157; 101.

[78] ibid 157; 101 per Lord Hardwicke.

tion predominates in the consideration of these cases and the equitable jurisdiction was exercised to 'prevent the ruin of families'.[79]

These issues arose from a system of landholding in which the attempt was made to preserve a family's wealth indefinitely from one generation to the next by the use of a strict settlement.[80] The strict settlement functioned by giving a life estate to the owner of the land with remainders in tail to his children. Trustees placed within the arrangement preserved contingent remainders and raised money for the maintenance of family members. Within each generation the settlement was renewed when the eldest son, upon his majority, surrendered his fee tail for a life estate accompanied by an allowance. While a son could refuse to allow a resettlement, this rarely occurred. The workings of this system meant that adult children were dependent upon their father, or trustees, for an allowance. At the same time, these adult children knew the dependency would end upon the ancestor's death. Increased longevity in the nineteenth century worked, though, to lengthen the period of dependency.[81] The temptation to either borrow against their expectancy or to sell it was often enormous.

Equity extended protection to the expectant heir or reversioner[82] who received an inadequate value in exchange for their interest.[83] While the protection seems initially to have encompassed a reversioner or a remainderman it came to encompass 'every one who has the hope of succession to the property of an ancestor'.[84] The protection was a generous one because it was not prevented by the applicant's mature age;[85] nor that the applicant understood the transaction;[86] nor the applicant's lack of pecuniary distress.[87] If an heir sought out his lender or purchaser, this only served to emphasise his necessity.[88] The courts attached particular importance to the character of an heir[89] because a contract with an expectant heir was one where 'the parties do not meet upon equal terms—there is distress on one side and

[79] ibid. Where the heir entered into contractual arrangements within the family, equity would not automatically intervene (*Harwood v Tooke* (1812) 2 Sim 192; 57 ER 76; *Twedell v Twedell* (1822) TR 1, 13; 37 ER 992, 997; *Wethered v Wethered* (1828) 2 Sim 183; 57 ER 757) or where a father was aware of a son's dealings (*King v Hamlet* (1835) 3 Cl & F 218; 6 ER 1419) equitable relief was not automatic because the family interest was not necessarily compromised.

[80] The process is described by Stuart Anderson, 'Property' in Cornish et al, *The Oxford History of the Laws of England*, n 5 above, ch 3 and Eileen Spring, 'The Settlement of Land in Nineteenth-Century England' (1964) 8 *American Journal of Legal History* 209, 209–16.

[81] The greatest increase in life expectancy was experienced by higher socio-economic groups: D Friedlander et al, 'Socio-Economic Characteristics and Life Expectancies in Nineteenth-Century England: A District Analysis' (1985) 39 *Population Studies* 137.

[82] *Nott v Hill* (1682) 1 Vern 167; 23 ER 391; *Shelly v Nash* (1818) 3 Madd 232; 56 ER 494.

[83] Where the consideration was grossly inadequate in exchanges with heirs, 'the Court has never suffered it to stand': *Gwynne v Heaton* (1778) 1 Bro CC 1, 6; 28 ER 949, 951, per Thurlow LC. Inadequacy of consideration was the material consideration: *Peacock v Evans* (1809) 16 Ves Jun 512, 516; 33 ER 1079, 1080.

[84] *Beynon v Cook* (1875) LR 10 Ch App 389, 391, per Jessel MR.

[85] *Davis v Duke of Marlborough* (1819) 2 Swan 108; 36 ER 555.

[86] *Wiseman v Beake* (1690) 2 Vern 121; 23 ER 688; *Evans v Cheshire* (1806) Ves Sen Supp 300; 28 ER 532.

[87] *Bromley v Smith* (1859) 26 Beav 644; 53 ER 1047.

[88] *Gwynne v Heaton*, n 15 above.

[89] Frederick White and Owen Tudor, *A Selection of the Leading Cases in Equity with Notes*, 4th edn (London, Sweet and Maxwell, 1872) vol I, 594, relying upon Swanston's note to *Davis v Duke of Marlborough*, n 85 above.

greediness of gain on the other'.[90] The heir could not reveal his financial distress to his family for this might endanger his expectancy and the need to conceal his wants made the heir 'a slave to the person with whom he treated'.[91] The concealment deprived the heir of proper advice about the nature of the transaction. Equity's concern for the heir extended beyond the inequality of his position with his lender or purchaser to the effect upon the heir of the money he received. It could go to 'feed riot'[92] as the money lent would support the heir's extravagances, leading him to a dissolute, debauched or destructive life. The availability of such money also encouraged disobedience amongst heirs[93] and the court sought to protect a family estate by preventing 'the seducing [of] an heir apparent from a dependence on his ancestor'.[94] An heir who was no longer dependent upon his ancestor might refuse to cooperate in the process necessary to resettle the family estate, for the heir's agreement was procured by his need for money.

Where equity presumed that inequality existed in a transaction between an heir and another, the onus lay upon the other to establish that there had been no advantage taken,[95] that a fair price had been paid,[96] and that the bargain was reasonable.[97] Absent the establishment of such factors, equity would set aside a contract with an expectant heir solely on the ground that the value received was inadequate.[98] A sale by auction established a fair market price[99] as did an independent valuation.[100] Subsequent ratification by the heir once removed from the pressures of his necessities acted to prevent equitable relief.[101]

Two legislative developments had an impact upon the equitable relief of heirs. The first was the repeal of the usury Acts in 1854.[102] The repeal removed the principal challenge at law to extortionate contracts with heirs, namely, that the loan was usurious. The result was to leave equity without a complement in law and, henceforth, the principal basis for challenge lay in equity.[103] As Stuart V-C observed, the repeal of the usury laws brought into operation to a greater extent 'the principle of the Court which prevented any oppressive bargain, or any advantage exacted from a

90 ibid 596.

91 *Chesterfield v Janssen*, n 10 above, 131; 86 (per counsel for the plaintiff).

92 ibid 91; 141 (per counsel for the defendant).

93 *Baugh v Price* (1752) 1 Wil K B 320; 95 ER 640.

94 *Cole v Gibbons; Martin v Cole* (1734) 3 P W 290, 293; 24 ER 1070, 1071, per Talbot LC.

95 *Gowland v De Faria* (1810) 17 Ves Jun 20; 34 ER 8.

96 *Shelly v Nash* (1818) 3 Madd 232; 56 ER 494.

97 *Davis v Duke of Marlborough*, n 85 above, 139; 566, per Eldon LC.

98 *Jones v Ricketts* (1862) 31 Beav 130; 54 ER 1087. The court generally set aside the bargain and had the security stand as security for the amount advanced with interest at about 5 per cent per annum: Macalpin, *The Law relating to Money-Lenders and Borrowers*, n 76 above, 287–88.

99 *Earl of Aldborough v Trye* (1840) 7 Cl & F 436; 7 ER 1136.

100 *Tynte v Hodge* (1864) 2 H & M 287; 71 ER 474.

101 *Gwynn v Heaton*, n 15 above; *King v Hamlet*, n 79 above.

102 An Act to repeal the Laws relating to Usury and to the Enrolment of Annuities, 1854 (17 & 18 Vict c 90).

103 In *Chesterfield v Janssen*, n 10 above, the first issue had been whether or not the bargain was a usurious loan for this was 'to give the party a short remedy'. See also Warren Swain and Karen Fairweather, 'Usury and the Judicial Regulation of Financial Transactions in Seventeenth- and Eighteenth-century England' in Mel Kenny, James Devenney and Lorna Fox O'Mahony (eds), *Unconscionability in European Private Financial Transactions* (Cambridge University Press, 2010).

man under grievous necessity and want of money, from prevailing against him'.[104] Chancery rejected the proposition that the repeal of the usury laws altered their rules as to dealings with expectant heirs.[105] The second enactment was the Sales of Reversions Act 1867.[106] Growing unease with the equitable practice of setting aside sales of reversions on the ground of inadequate value alone, a practice which disabled an heir from parting with his reversion, led to the statute which attempted to curtail the relief. A bona fide purchase made without fraud or unfair dealing could not be set aside merely because of undervalue.[107]

This attempt to curtail the equitable relief afforded to heirs largely failed. In *Earl of Aylesford v Morris*,[108] Lord Selborne reaffirmed the equitable jurisdiction to set aside the sale of reversions on the basis that the Act prohibited setting aside sales where only the undervalue was present. The abolition of the usury laws did not remove the court's ability to scrutinise a bargain for the presence of fraud. A presumption of fraud still arose where there was an inequality between the parties.[109] Fraud did not mean deceit, 'it means an unconscientious use of the power arising out of these circumstances and conditions; and when the relative position of the parties is such as primâ facie to raise this presumption, the transaction cannot stand unless the person claiming the benefit of it is able to repel the presumption by contrary evidence, proving it to have been in point of fact fair, just, and reasonable'.[110] These grounds for relief were broad enough to extend to a range of transactions characterised by an inequality between the parties. In this instance, Lord Selborne held that the heir was still deserving of equity's protection because of the vulnerability which arose from his lack of will or power to take care of himself and with no one else to take care of him. On the other side, the money-lender was interested only in taking advantage of the heir's weakness.

Although the decision was greeted with controversy by contemporaries, partly out of concern for the sanctity of commercial transactions and the imprecision of equitable relief,[111] the House of Lords in *O'Rorke v Bolingbroke* upheld it.[112] Bolingbroke, to fund his education, sold his reversion to O'Rorke on terms negotiated by his father during his minority. The son had no independent adviser. The father, upon whose life the reversion was dependent, was in ill-health and died shortly after the transaction. After Bolingbroke received the annuity payments he sought to set aside the transaction. Lord Blackburn agreed that Lord Selborne had accurately stated the law but then found that in the case before him it did not apply. Undervalue was not of great importance since the Sales of Reversions Act 1867.

[104] *Barrett v Hartley* (1866) LR 2 Eq 789, 795. The development was an acknowledged one: Patrick Hastings, *The Law Relating to Money-Lenders* (London, Butterworth & Co, 1905) 13.

[105] *Croft v Graham* (1863) 2 De G J & S 155; 46 ER 332.

[106] 31 Vict c 4.

[107] ibid s 1.

[108] *Earl of Aylesford v Morris* (1873) LR 8 Ch App 484. The case is examined in detail in Catharine MacMillan, 'Earl of Aylesford v Morris (1873)' in Charles Mitchell and Paul Mitchell (eds), *Landmark Cases in Equity* (Oxford, Hart Publishing, 2012).

[109] *Aylesford v Morris*, n 108 above, 490. The equitable jurisdiction of the court over unconscionable bargains had been affirmed earlier by Stuart V-C in *Tyler v Yates* (1870) LR 11 Eq 265.

[110] *Aylesford v Morris*, n 108 above, 491.

[111] MacMillan, 'Earl of Aylesford v Morris (1873)', n 108 above, 342–43.

[112] *O'Rorke v Bolingbroke* (1877) 2 App Cas 814 (HL).

His concerns lay with the purchaser who offered a fair, 'even liberal' price which because of a latent defect (the father's imminent demise) turned out to be inadequate. Here the bargain was made bona fide and without fraud or unfair dealing. Lord Hatherley, the panel's sole equity judge, dissented. After explaining the equitable jurisdiction, he found that Bolingbroke was within equity's protection for he was not on equal terms with O'Rorke. He was an expectant heir, unable to understand the value of the interest or to estimate proposals for it. He was 'fettered' by the bargain obtained by his father. The absence of an independent adviser was critical, though, for any adviser would have inquired into the father's health and advised him against a sale when his 'hopeless ill-health' was ascertained.

That there was a division between equity and common law judges over the case is seen in the astounding letter sent by Lord Justice Christian to *The Times*.[113] While Christian LJ purported to accept the House of Lords' decision overturning his own decision in the Irish Chancery, he stated that he could not accept the 'grave charge' of Lord Blackburn (whom he described as 'more familiar with the Queen's Bench than the Court of Chancery') that Christian LJ had made his decision without regard for the proven facts or that he needed a 'lecture from my Lord Blackburn as to what is "of the essence of justice"'. The letter was, in reality, a criticism on the composition of the panel and that a case, 'one purely of equity', should have only one judge of equity training. The thinly veiled implication was that the other judges did not understand the nature of the equitable jurisdiction and that Blackburn's reasoning was ridiculous. The *Solicitor's Journal* wrote that readers must have viewed the letter with 'a keen sense of astonishment'.[114] The disagreement between the common law judges and the equity judge pointed to the ultimate decline of this equitable relief.

Despite Lord Selborne's broad approach in *Aylesford v Morris*, the final decades of the nineteenth century saw little expansion of the scope of this equitable protection from heirs to other situations of inequality between the parties. In *Nevill v Snelling*,[115] Denman J applied the principle to an instance where a young man borrowed money on unconscionable terms that he did not fully understand from a professional money-lender. The young man in question, though, was the third son of the Marquis of Abergavenny and it was clear that he both had general expectations of inheritance and that the money-lender lent on the basis that the father would undoubtedly pay on the notes to save his son from the disgrace of bankruptcy. In *Fry v Lane*,[116] Kay J set aside the sale of reversionary interests by two poor and ignorant men who sold at considerable undervalue, without valuation and without proper advice. Relief was granted because the parties did not deal on 'equal terms'.[117] In *James v Kerr*,[118] a transaction with an impecunious heir was set aside

[113] 3 August 1877, 6. Christian LJ's indignation was likely compounded by the presence of Lord O'Hagan, a man he publicly criticised for his lack of knowledge of Chancery matters: *Oxford Dictionary of National Biography*, entry for Jonathan Christian, available at www.oxforddnb.com.idpproxy.reading.ac.uk/view/article/50586?docPos=8.

[114] 4 August 1877, 765.

[115] *Nevill v Snelling* (1880) LR 15 Ch D 679 (Ch D).

[116] *Fry v Lane* (1888) LR 40 Ch D 312 (Ch D).

[117] ibid 323, quoting Leach V-C in *Wood v Abrey* (1818) 3 Madd 417; 56 ER 558.

[118] *James v Kerr* (1888) LR 40 Ch D 449 (Ch D).

where the lenders thought that they were doing the borrower a service, not without risk, on terms that were fair.

ABSENCE OF A BROADER DOCTRINE

Why did these cases of inequality leading to an unconscientious use of power not develop into a broader doctrine? It is suggested that while there was no deliberate resistance to the further development as such, a number of factors combined to impede such a development. The first was that legislative changes removed both the need to resort to equitable relief and the number of cases in which equitable relief was sought.

Many of the transactions involving heirs concerned professional money-lenders, a category of trader held in particular opprobrium by Victorians. These money-lenders sought out their clientele (or victims) by means of circular advertisements and schemes whereby easy advancements were soon followed by the most oppressive of interest rates. Many of their loans were made during the heir's minority and the Infants Relief Act 1874[119] provided that such a contract was void. Money-lenders preyed not only upon heirs but also upon the poor. The result was that a Select Committee was formed in 1897 to inquire into the 'alleged evils attending Money Lending transactions at high rates of interest, or under oppressive conditions as to repayment'.[120] Witnesses before the Committee testified as to the position of the county courts in bankruptcy matters. While equitable adjustments could be made, deeds could only be set aside where there was fraud or mistake[121] and not where the dealings between the parties were unconscionable. As one judge testified, 'the equity jurisdiction of the court ... I do not think is sufficient'.[122] What he needed was the ability to set aside money-lending transactions according to the equity that Chancery exercised in the cases of exorbitant bargains with expectant heirs.[123]

The Committee was keen not to interfere with 'legitimate trading' and confined its recommendations to 'money-lenders'.[124] While the Committee was against the establishment of a maximum rate of interest, because a high rate of interest was not incompatible with fair dealing and because the ingenuity of lenders would allow the circumvention of such a ceiling, the Committee did recommend that 'the courts have absolute and unfettered discretion in dealing with these transactions'.[125] The resulting Money Lenders Act 1900 provided that where the transaction was harsh and unconscionable, such that a court of equity would give relief, the court could reopen the transaction to examine the circumstances and do what it judged reasonable.[126]

[119] 37 & 38 Vict c 62, s 1.

[120] *Report from the Select Committee on Money Lending* (PP 1897, 364) ii.

[121] County Courts Act 1888 (51 & 52 Vict c 43), s 67(8).

[122] *Report from the Select Committee on Money Lending*, n 120 above, Judge Owen, 204 q4410.

[123] ibid 206–7 qq 4431–44. Judge AL Smith, of the Westminster County Court, sought the same equitable powers: 222–24, qq 4657–66. See also, Hugh HL Bellot, 'The Money-Lenders Act 1900' (1901) 26 *Law Mat and Rev Quart Rev Juris*, 5th ser 456, 467.

[124] Report from the Select Committee on Money Lending (PP 1898, 260) v.

[125] ibid vi.

[126] 63 & 64 Vict c 51, s 1(1).

From the outset, judges disagreed as to the ambit of the Act. An early decision found that while the rate of interest charged was harsh and unconscionable, equity would not grant relief only on the grounds that the charges were excessive.[127] While the House of Lords rejected this approach,[128] courts struggled to apply the equitable concepts: 'The difficulty is that the words remaining are so vague. Harsh and unconscionable are not easy words to construe when the rules of the Court of Equity have been put out of consideration'.[129] The House of Lords held that the Act gave courts the power to prevent oppression by examining a transaction on its merits to determine whether or not there had been an abuse of power.[130] In this determination, the older equitable jurisdiction was a guide.[131] The Money Lenders Act 1900 went some way to remove the need for the relief equity provided to the expectant heir.[132] It is, thus, not surprising that these cases of unconscionable bargains with expectant heirs disappeared in the twentieth century, as such cases were judicially resolved within a legislative framework.[133]

A more profound legislative change lay in the Judicature Acts of 1873 to 1875.[134] An effect of fusion was to subject various equitable concepts, including contractual unfairness, to a common law mindset which inhibited the equitable practices.[135] The different approaches of common law judges and equity judges to the same set of facts in the determination of inequality has been seen above in *O'Rorke v Bolingbroke*. The Judicature Acts had the effect of placing judges trained in the common law to decide equity cases.[136] A result of this appears to have been a disinclination to extend or even maintain certain equitable doctrines, of which this was one.

Finally, other legislative enactments acted to alter a world that contained the dependent expectant heir. The structure of family settlements was to undergo profound changes as a result of the Settled Land Act 1882[137] which allowed greater scope for dealing with the land. The logic of the Married Woman's Property Act 1882[138] was also to work against a system of complicated family settlements. The decline in value of landed estates from the 1890s onward acted to undermine the aristocracy at the pinnacle of this system.

[127] *Wilton & Co v Osborne* [1901] 2 KB 110 (KBD).

[128] *Samuel v Newbold* [1906] AC 461 (HL).

[129] *Carringtons Ltd v Smith* [1906] 1 KB 79 (KBD), 86, per Channell J.

[130] *Samuel v Newbold*, n 128.

[131] ibid 470, per Lord Macnaghten referring to *Gwynne v Heaton*, n 83 above.

[132] See Joseph Bridges Matthews, *The Law of Money-Lending* (London, Sweet and Maxwell, 1906) Part II, for a consideration of how courts approached their task under the Act. See Owen Davies Tudor and Frederick Thomas White, *A Selection of Leading Cases in Equity*, 8th edn (by William Joseph Whittaker, Edward William Sutton and Percy Vaughan, London, Sweet and Maxwell, 1910) vol I, 336–42, for their consideration of the Money Lenders Act 1900, in relation to 'catching bargains'.

[133] The 1900 Act was amended by the Money Lenders Act 1911 (1 & 2 Geo V c 38); both were replaced by the Moneylenders Act 1927 (17 & 18 Geo V c 21).

[134] 36 & 37 Vict c 36; 38 & 39 Vict c 77.

[135] Stephen Waddams, 'Equity in English Contract Law: The Impact of the Judicature Acts (1873–75)' (2012) 33 *JLH* 185, 188–92.

[136] See also, Patrick Polden, 'Mingling the Waters: Personalities, Politics and the Making of the Supreme Court of Judicature' (2002) 61 *CLJ* 575.

[137] 45 & 46 Vict c 38.

[138] 45 & 46 Vict c 75.

In addition to these legislative changes, changes occurred within the way courts of equity approached inequality in contracts. The focus came to rest on the nature of the relationship between the parties.[139] In *Hunter v Atkins*,[140] Lord Brougham sought to categorise three forms of relationships in which equity would protect a party from an advantage being taken. Although Romilly MR expressed reservations about such categorisation, fearing that the ability of the court to intercede would be limited by confining relief to categories,[141] this is what was to happen in *Allcard v Skinner*.[142] Lindley LJ formulated two situations in which relief would be granted: first where there had been unfair and improper conduct accompanied by a possible personal advantage obtained by one placed 'in some close and confidential relation to the donor'; the second where 'the position of the donor to the donee has been such that it has been the duty of the donee to advise the donor'.[143] The case exemplified Victorian concerns about religious sisterhoods and was widely reported.[144] Although it concerned a gift, it came to be regarded within a short period of time as 'the leading modern case on Undue Influence' in contract.[145] The effect of the case was explained as one where once the relationship had been established, the burden of proof lay upon the donee to establish that the donor had independent advice or subsequently ratified the transaction.[146]

The development of a relationship-based doctrine of undue influence had the effect of stultifying the development of the much smaller number of instances of inequality between strangers. Undue influence, as it came to be formulated, availed itself of neat categories of relationships. Both lawyers and lay participants more easily understood these than a fluid conception of factors leading to inequality. These categories of relationship offered a form of certainty, definiteness and predictability. They also had the effect of imposing a liability upon an often quasi-professional relationship. Equity throughout the nineteenth century adopted a more rigid regard for precedent and the movement that favoured undue influence was a part of this larger process.

A final element that acted to stultify what might have become a broader doctrine of unconscionability was the way in which the late nineteenth century treatise writers considered these earlier cases. Towards the end of the century, contract law became not only what lawyers and judges conceived it to be but, also, increasingly, what treatises stated the law to be. Throughout the century jurists wrote treatises on contract law and, in so doing, transformed it. The most significant of these transformations was the attempt to structure English contract law around the will

[139] See, eg, *Huguenin v Baseley* (1807) 14 Ves 273; 33 ER 526, which was regarded as a leading case on undue influence: Owen Davies Tudor, *Leading Cases in Equity* (London, William Maxwell, 1850) vol II, 406.

[140] (1834) 3 My & K 113; 40 ER 43.

[141] *Hobday v Peters (No 1)* (1860) 28 Beav 349, 351; 54 ER 400, 401.

[142] *Allcard v Skinner* (1887) 36 Ch D 145 (CA).

[143] ibid 181.

[144] The historical context of the case is covered by Charlotte Smith, 'Allcard v Smith (1887)' in Charles Mitchell and Paul Mitchell (eds), *Landmark Cases in the Law of Restitution* (Oxford, Hart Publishing, 2006).

[145] Frederick Pollock, 'Reviews and Notices' (1903) 19 *LQR* 107.

[146] Tudor and White, *A Selection of Leading Cases in Equity*, n 132 above, 281.

theory. One of the most prominent jurists in this process was Frederick Pollock and his approach to the categories of inequality examined here is intriguing.

Pollock was of the firm view that the Chancery jurisdiction as to unconscionable bargains was based on the principle that '"the necessitous man is not a free man" ... [he] is acting under coercion: his poverty but not his will consents: and a Court of Equity is bound to come to the rescue'.[147] While a contemporary was quick to observe that 'this is scarcely correct',[148] the approach Pollock set out prevailed. His long-lived treatise, *Principles of Contract*,[149] reconstructed certain equitable doctrines around a will theory[150] as he sought to formulate contract on a scientific basis. In a chapter entitled 'Duress and Undue Influence', Pollock wrote that if the consent of one party was obtained by the other in circumstances where the consent was not free, the contract was voidable by this party.[151] In an often-confusing treatment of the subject, Pollock considered the equitable cases largely by considering and cataloguing relationships between parties where undue influence was a concern. Pollock greatly admired Lindley LJ (to whom his treatise was dedicated) and following his decision in *Allcard v Skinner*, Pollock placed the case at the forefront of his discussion on undue influence.[152]

In a brief examination, Pollock accepted that equity would intervene in instances where there was an inequality between the contracting parties but he explained this intervention on the basis of the codification in the Indian Contract Act, namely, that such an agreement gave rise to the question as to whether or not consent had been freely given.[153] On the whole, he disapproved of such cases, equating them to the law concerned with inadequacy of consideration and contended that such factors should not be the basis for setting aside a contract.[154] The cases of catching bargains with heirs were ones that Pollock viewed as establishing exceptions to the rules of evidence requiring the lender or purchaser to establish that the other party's consent was freely obtained.[155] Although Pollock moved away from a will-based theory of contract law in his third edition,[156] he did not change his treatment of these unequal bargains as failures of consent.

Principles of Contract had three effects. By emphasising a consent basis for contract, it re-explained the equitable intervention in instances of inequality between the parties on a different basis. The intervention arose not to prevent an unfair

[147] Frederick Pollock, 'Notes' (1905) 21 *LQR* 101, 103, commenting upon *Saunders v Newbold* [1905] 1 Ch 260 and paraphrasing Lord Northington in *Vernon v Bethell* (1762) 2 Eden 110; 28 ER 838 for his explanation.

[148] Hugh HL Bellot, *The Legal Principles and Practice of Bargains with Money-Lenders* (London, Stevens and Haynes, 1906) 151.

[149] Frederick Pollock, *Principles of Contract at Law and in Equity* (London, Stevens and Sons, 1876).

[150] Another instance is in relation to contractual mistake: Catharine MacMillan, *Mistakes in Contract Law* (Oxford, Hart Publishing, 2010) ch 6.

[151] Pollock, *Principles of Contract at Law and in Equity*, n 149 above, 500.

[152] Frederick Pollock, *Principles of Contract*, 5th edn (London, Stevens and Sons, 1889) 580–81.

[153] ibid 521.

[154] ibid 539.

[155] ibid 532–33.

[156] Frederick Pollock, *Principles of Contract Law: Being a Treatise on the General Principles concerning the Validity of Agreements in the Law of England*, 3rd edn (Stevens and Sons, 1881). He approved of *O'Rorke v Bolingbroke*, n 112 above, 601–2.

advantage taken of a weaker party because it was unconscientious but as instances where the contract was voidable because of impaired consent. The cases did not really support such a theory and were minimised in comparison to those concerned with undue influence. The second effect was that an ambition to establish legal classifications in a scientific treatise resulted in an emphasis upon categories of relationships giving rise to undue influence. Finally, this exercise in establishing a scientific and predictive treatise worked towards rigidifying the equitable jurisdiction concerned with fraud away from its original fluidity.

Other treatise writers followed Pollock's lead both in categorising the equitable relief for inequality as a defect in consent and in a preference for categorising undue influence cases.[157] Anson coyly refrained from discussing this form of equitable fraud as a failure of consent but tucked his consideration of 'undue influence' at the end of a chapter entitled 'The Reality of Consent'.[158] Over time his treatment of the subject developed it as one of undue influence between parties who were not strangers rather than unconscionable bargains between unequal strangers.[159]

The treatment accorded by the contract treatise writers to this form of equitable relief was a distinct contrast to that provided by those who had earlier written about the equitable treatment of fraud. Equity provided relief to prevent 'unconscientious circumvention' of the law.[160] Relief was provided because advantage had been taken of distress.[161] Tudor and White, in their note to *Chesterfield v Janssen*, focused upon the cases involving expectant heirs and observed that the reason for the relief was that the parties did not meet upon equal terms.[162] Equitable relief was given because where an undue advantage was taken, a court would protect this weaker party. Half a century later, this approach was still adhered to as the authors described the cases where the court gave relief for the hardness or unfairness of a bargain as arising from 'an unconscientious use of the power' arising out of the circumstances of the

[157] Martin Leake eschewed treating these inequality cases as failures of consent but did place them under a heading of 'undue influence' and directed his discussion towards categories of undue influence, of parties dealing with those they knew: S Martin Leake, *A Digest of the Principles of the Law of Contracts*, 3rd edn (London, Stevens and Sons, 1892) 354–61. See also the lengthy description and categorisation of undue influence cases in Sydney Edward Williams, *Kerr on Fraud and Mistake*, 4th edn (London, Sweet and Maxwell, 1910) 145–93 and the brief account of unconscionable bargains: 193–96.

[158] Sir William R Anson, *Principles of the English Law of Contract* (Oxford, Clarendon Press, 1879) 156–62.

[159] Sir William R Anson, *Principles of the English Law of Contract*, 10th edn (Oxford, Clarendon Press, 1903) 192–98.

[160] George Jeremy, *A Treatise on the Equity Jurisdiction of the High Court of Chancery* (London, J & WT Clarke, 1828) 385. Note, though, Joseph Story's explanation that a free and full consent was needed by parties to a contract and that equity intervened where this was absent: *Commentaries on Equity Jurisprudence*, 4th edn (Little, Brown and Company, 1846) vol I, paras 222–23 at 244–45. See also, Snell's explanation that the court relieved the expectant heir because his circumstances prevented him from exercising the 'full power of deliberate consent which is essential to a valid contract': Edmund Henry Turner Snell, *The Principles of Equity* (London, Stevens and Haynes, 1868) 383.

[161] John Eykyn Hovenden, *A General Treatise on the Principles and Practice by which Courts of Equity are Guided as to the Prevention or Remedial Correction of Fraud* (London, S Sweet, 1825) 497.

[162] Frederick Thomas White and Owen Davies Tudor, *A Selection of Leading Cases in Equity* (London, William Maxwell, 1849) vol I, 396.

parties.[163] At the same time, though, the will-based theories of Pollock began to enter the equity treatises. White and Tudor's *Leading Cases in Equity* began to refer to Pollock in the seventh edition of 1897.[164] The will-based contract jurists had come to influence the approach of the equity lawyers in a post-fusion world

CONCLUSIONS

Victorian concerns about inequality between the parties to a contract could result in legal intervention. The circumstances in which this occurred in contracts between strangers were limited and diminished throughout the century. They arose in response to particular social, cultural and economic concerns and as these were modified, so too, did the apparent necessity for this intervention. The law, both judicial and legislative, changed in ways that inhibited the development of a broader doctrine. As jurists wrote about the law in a particular way they contributed to the development of a doctrine of undue influence based on the relationship of the contracting parties rather than the inequalities that might exist when strangers contracted. English contract law did not reject a doctrine of unconscionability or inequality in the nineteenth century. It simply developed a different set of legal responses to the circumstances that came before the courts.

[163] Frederick Thomas White and Owen Davies Tudor, *A Selection of the Leading Cases in Equity*, 7th edn (by Thomas Snow, London, Sweet and Maxwell, 1897) 308. Undue influence was separated and considered in a note on *Huguenin v Baseley*, n 139 above, 247. The approach was maintained at the end of the century in other works: Andrew Thomson, *A Compendium of Equity* (London, William Clowes and Sons, 1899) ch 17.

[164] White and Tudor, *A Selection of the Leading Cases in Equity*, n 163 above.

Law Reform

3

Alternatives to Legislation: Restatements and Judicial Law Reform

ANDREW BURROWS*

MY FRIENDSHIP WITH Hugh Beale dates back to the annual conference of the Society of Public Teachers of Law (now the Society of Legal Scholars) in Bristol in 1983. Ever since then, I have admired greatly his exceptional abilities as a lawyer and communicator. With shared academic interests in contract law and law reform, I have had the privilege of working directly with Hugh as part of his *Chitty* team and on projects in Hungary and Germany. With typical modesty, he helped me enormously in my work at the Law Commission that led to the Contracts (Rights of Third Parties) Act 1999 and I was delighted when he succeeded me as the Law Commissioner in charge of the commercial and common law projects.

In this chapter, I want to look at two areas that I hope will be of interest to Hugh. Each may be regarded as an alternative to legislation: first, Restatements of English law and, secondly, judicial law reform. In particular, I want to draw on my own experience of these, the first in ongoing work and the second in respect of work I did at the Law Commission in the last century.

RESTATEMENTS

Type and Purpose of Restatement

It is not intended that the Restatements I am working on should be enacted as legislation. Rather the hope is that they will enhance the accessibility and coherence of the English common law and will be non-binding but persuasive authority. If one imagines a legislative code—albeit rather alien to the English tradition—and then one thinks of the alternative of a non-binding code, then a Restatement, being very similar indeed to a non-binding code, can be viewed as an alternative to legislation.

Clearly, a Restatement is a novel concept in relation to English law. In contrast, the Restatements produced by the American Law Institute are well-known as

* Versions of this essay were presented at Portcullis House, London, on 15 November 2013, at a conference on 'Statute Law and Alternative Solutions: Codification, Restatement, Common Law' organised by the Statute Law Society, and at King's College, London on 3 March 2014.

non-legislative, but powerfully persuasive, statements of the law applying across the United States. While knowing what the law is in England and Wales does not raise the multi-jurisdictional problems encountered in the United States, there are nevertheless real benefits to be gained in setting out what the common law is in England and Wales in as clear and accessible a form as possible. Brilliant as the common law methodology is, its major disadvantage is its lack of accessibility, especially to those who are not trained as common lawyers. Allied to that is that, in certain areas, the structure and coherence of the common law may not be obvious or may be lacking. Some of the terminology used may also need modernising.

For those reasons, it had long seemed to me that the non-existence of Restatements was a lacuna in the English approach to law and I have been delighted to have had the chance to try to address this in my ongoing Restatement projects. So far this has led to the publication in December 2012 of *A Restatement of the English Law of Unjust Enrichment* (RELUE) by Oxford University Press and I am at present part-way through work on restating the English law of contract.

Before I go any further, it is important to stress that I am talking about Restatements of the common law, in the sense of judge-made law including equity. I am not talking about restating statute law. Indeed, if an area were largely statute-based, a Restatement (or at least the type of Restatement I am concerned with) would in my view be an inappropriate instrument. True it is that, occasionally, statute is so intertwined with the common law that it is important in presenting a coherent and accurate picture of the common law to refer to a statute in a Restatement. So, for example, in RELUE we included reference to the restitution of benefits conferred under a contract discharged for frustration as laid down in the Law Reform (Frustrated Contracts) Act 1943. Similarly, that Restatement includes an outline of the law on limitation of actions which is contained in the Limitation Act 1980. Quite how much statute law is included in a Restatement is a matter of judgement and depends on the nature of the area being restated. As it happens, almost all of the law of unjust enrichment is judge-made law. In contrast, in the Contract Restatement so much of the law is statutory that we will necessarily, I think, have to make clear at the outset that the Restatement is restating merely what is often referred to as the general law of contract and even that will need to include some statutory material if it is to be coherent and accurate.

So what the finished RELUE book comprises is a 36 section Restatement with numerous subsections and an 80,000 word commentary which copies across the relevant section from the Restatement (which is put in a grey-shaded box) and then contains the commentary on that section. The commentary makes extensive use of hypothetical or real examples in the belief that this is commonly the best way of understanding the law. The leading cases have been cited but, while there is some reference to the academic literature, the aim of the commentary is to explain the Restatement, not to reproduce the textbooks in this area.

The word 'Restatement' might suggest that these projects are purely concerned to state the present law. That would be marginally misleading. What is being aimed for is the best interpretation of the present law. In some limited circumstances (perhaps less limited in the law of unjust enrichment than the law of contract because the latter is more settled), one may require a decision of the Supreme Court to lay down the law as set out in the Restatement. In other words, on some matters the

Restatement takes a principled interpretation of the law that may be regarded as going further than the existing cases. The commentary makes clear where this is so.

The question arises, however, as to what difference there is between this type of principled Restatement of the law within a single jurisdiction and a *non-binding* code. They are clearly very similar. However, the essential difference is that a code, unlike a Restatement, does not need to be tied to the existing law. When one is dealing, as I am, with a Restatement within a single jurisdiction, this notion of being tied to the existing law is relatively straightforward and requires that the Restatement is within the interpretative reach of the courts. The notion of being tied to the existing law is more complex where one has a multi-jurisdictional Restatement as in the United States or if one is trying to set out the law across Europe. But the essential point distinguishing a non-binding code from a Restatement, whether a single or multi-jurisdictional Restatement, is that with a code, unlike a Restatement, one can simply start with a blank sheet of paper, decide on what is the best legal rule, and then set that out in the code. One cannot do that with a Restatement. So, for example, I do not think it is open to us in restating the English law of contract to depart from the doctrine of consideration or to decide that specific performance should be the primary remedy for breach of contract because such departures are in my view not within the interpretative reach of even the Supreme Court. Similarly, in RELUE, in my view it was not open to restate the English law by adopting an absence of basis rather than unjust factor approach. True it is that it is a matter of judgement as to what lies within the interpretative reach of the courts; and the more radical one is willing to be, the closer one comes to a code.

Linked to this is that, as their title makes clear, these Restatements are not purported *European* Restatements. There are, of course, ongoing attempts—and Hugh Beale has been much involved with some of them—to harmonise areas of private law across Europe. So, for example, particularly relevant to the unjust enrichment project were the European model rules for 'Unjustified Enrichment' in Book VII of the *Draft Common Frame of Reference* (prepared by the Study Group on a European Civil Code and the Research Group on EC Private Law (Acquis Group)); and the proposed EU Regulation on a Common European Sales Law (CESL) which has some provisions on restitution after termination of a contract for the sale of goods. I make no point about whether or not European legal harmonisation is a desirable or feasible goal. But what I do say, especially when one looks at the attempted harmonised rules on unjustified enrichment, is that it is essential that the subtleties of English law are properly understood before there is consideration of whether they should be abandoned in favour of a European approach. Some may agree with the sceptical view of the late Lord Rodger of Earlsferry (although note that he was focusing on a legislative European code) who wrote as follows in an article entitled, '"Say not the Struggle Naught Availeth": the Costs and Benefits of Mixed Legal Systems':[1]

> [I]t is boring enough to find branches of McDonalds, the Body Shop, and Benneton in every major European city without finding exactly the same law too. To find ourselves tied into

[1] Lord Rodger of Earlsferry, '"Say not the Struggle Naught Availeth": The Costs and Benefits of Mixed Legal Systems' (2003) 78 *Tulane Law Review* 419, 431.

> a monolithic codified system in which all final decisions are taken in the colourless prose of a court in Luxembourg—presumably increased to an even more enormous number of judges—is unattractive, to say the least.

He went on:

> Nor do I believe that the practical advantages would be so great as actually to justify the change, if politics are kept out of the picture. In the United Kingdom we have rubbed along very well for almost 300 years with two separate systems of private law which differ in many ways ... if the British experience shows anything, it is that having a unified form of contract law is not in fact necessary for developing a strong common market. Scots law has been able to exist quite satisfactorily over the last 200 years while trade has spread to create a single market throughout the United Kingdom. If businesses really want to work under one particular legal system rather than another, they can, and do, arrange it by inserting appropriate terms in their contracts.

Working Methods and the Use of an Advisory Group

The working methods of the American Law Institute, which was founded in 1923 and whose primary purpose is to produce the American Restatements, are well known. The Institute comprises practitioners, judges and academics and has a large membership of up to 4,000 and a Council of up to 65. For each Restatement a Reporter or Reporters are appointed who have responsibility for the drafting of the Restatement, assisted by an advisory committee and a larger consultative group. The drafts of the different parts of the Restatements are drawn up in the form of Preliminary Drafts which must be approved by the advisory committee and consultative group and the final version must be approved by a meeting of the members as a whole. The numbers of people involved and the potential input is therefore very large and, given also the approval required, the projects take many years to complete. Indeed, some have been abandoned part way through. So, for example, the most recent *Third Restatement of Restitution and Unjust Enrichment*, published in 2011, took some 13 years to complete. The *Second Restatement of Restitution* was abandoned in the 1980s.

For *A Restatement of the English Law of Unjust Enrichment* I was anxious to avoid such a long-drawn out process and therefore opted for a streamlined approach. Having said that, I thought it essential that that this would not just be the work of academics and I therefore put together a small advisory group, half of whom were academics and half of whom were judges or practitioners. In addition to the Restatement being a novelty in this jurisdiction, the idea of academics, judges and practitioners coming together to work on a legal project was also a novelty. My own view is that it worked extremely well and that we all learnt a great deal from each other. It was a rich and rewarding collaborative exercise.

The working methods we adopted for RELUE were as follows. Over a period of about 18 months, four all-day meetings of the advisory group were held. In advance of those meetings, drafts of parts of the Restatement and the commentary were prepared by me and circulated electronically. Comments were then sent back and revised versions of the Restatement and Commentary were again sent out in advance of each meeting. Those drafts were then discussed at the meetings. They were further revised in the light of the discussions. Further invaluable assistance on drafting was given by retired Parliamentary Counsel. I had first encountered Parliamentary Counsel during my time at the Law Commission in the 1990s and had come to admire greatly their skills as lawyers and 'wordsmiths'. The whole RELUE project from start to publication by Oxford University Press took about two years.

One point that has to be stressed is that I alone accepted responsibility for the Restatement. It was my head alone that was (and is) on the block. To try to reach agreement on many of the issues would have been impossible and, in my view, some sort of compromise on a difficult issue is not the best way of producing a principled outcome. One further advantage of the approach adopted was that those on the advisory group, perhaps especially the judges, felt able to express their views freely without having to commit themselves to a particular formulation. Not having to reach a consensus also allowed us to push along at a good pace. The disadvantage, of course, is that one loses some of the status of this being a group-approved Restatement: but in my view the advantages of efficiency and producing a principled outcome outweigh that disadvantage. And it is certainly not correct to think that this is nothing more than the Restatement I would have produced had there been no advisory group. My views were throughout being tested and refined and in some respects changed by the discussions of the advisory group.

Five Points on the Content of RELUE

I cannot let this opportunity pass by without saying something very briefly about the content of RELUE.

(i) It is a Restatement of the English law of unjust enrichment, it is not a Restatement of the English law of restitution. Unjust enrichment describes an event or cause of action. Restitution describes a response or remedy. It used to be thought that it did not really matter whether in this area one focused on the event or on the response, not least because restitution is almost invariably the only response to unjust enrichment. But following the work of the late Peter Birks it has now become widely accepted, especially by the academics but also by some influential judges (and this explains the change of title from *The Law of Restitution* to *The Law of Unjust Enrichment* of the latest 2011 edition of *Goff and Jones*)[2] that it really does matter which one focuses on because restitution may be the response to events or causes of action other than unjust enrichment. In particular, restitution may be the response to a wrong, ie instead of the standard monetary remedy of compensation, restitution stripping all or some of the defendant's gains may be a remedy for a tort or an equitable wrong or even, after *Attorney-General v Blake*,[3] a breach of contract. Those types of claim, where the wrong is the cause of action, raise different questions from an unjust enrichment claim. So the Restatement does not include

[2] C Mitchell, P Mitchell and S Watterson, *Goff and Jones' The Law of Unjust Enrichment* 8th edn (London, Sweet and Maxwell, 2011).

[3] *Attorney-General v Blake* [2001] 1 AC 268.

restitution for wrongs: like the new edition of *Goff and Jones*, its scope is controlled by the event or cause of unjust enrichment, not the response or remedy of restitution.

(ii) The Restatement is underpinned by the fourfold conceptual structure for unjust enrichment that has come to be recognised by the English courts.[4] According to this, every unjust enrichment claim involves asking four distinct questions:

— First, has the defendant been enriched? (The 'enrichment' question.)
— Second, was the enrichment at the claimant's expense? (The 'at the expense of' question.)
— Third, was the enrichment at the claimant's expense unjust? (The 'unjust' question.)
— Fourth, are there any defences? (The 'defences' question.)

(iii) While all four of those questions give rise to many fascinating issues, some of which remain unresolved, the most important theoretical question is the third, the unjust question. The Restatement adopts the standard English approach to that question whereby the claimant must identify an unjust factor such as, for example, mistake, failure of consideration, duress, undue influence, or the unlawful obtaining of a benefit by a public authority (the so-called *Woolwich* principle). This contrasts with the traditional civilian approach to the unjust question, which looks instead at whether there is an absence of juristic basis.

(iv) The Restatement accepts that the restitution that responds to an unjust enrichment may be personal or, in certain circumstances, proprietary. The standard restitutionary response is a personal right to a 'monetary restitutionary award' measured by the value of the enrichment received by the defendant. As a personal right this is enforceable only against the defendant or his representatives. The term 'monetary restitutionary award' is used in the Restatement as a modern simplification of the archaic terminology (such as an award of money had and received to the claimant's use or an award of money paid to the defendant's use or a quantum meruit or an account) that has traditionally bedevilled the law on restitutionary remedies. Apart from that standard personal remedy, the restitution can in certain circumstances be proprietary: and there are four main examples of proprietary restitutionary responses established in the unjust enrichment cases, namely, a lien, subrogation to a discharged security, rescission (or rectification) revesting title, and a beneficial interest under a constructive or resulting trust. The major practical importance of proprietary restitution is that, in contrast to personal restitution, it gives priority to the claimant on the defendant's insolvency.

(v) Finally, the law of unjust enrichment comprises aspects of both common law and equity. In the law of unjust enrichment, hardly anything today turns on whether a rule or principle is historically derived from the common law courts or the Court of Chancery. In particular, it is a myth to think that equity is more discretionary and less principled than the common law. So it is that the Restatement presents an integrated view of common law and equity within this area. Indeed, with one minor exception, there is no reference at all in the Restatement to the historical labelling of common law and equity, although that distinction is occasionally referred to in the commentary.

[4] See, most recently, *Benedetti v Sawiris* [2013] UKSC 50; [2013] 3 WLR 351.

Reaction

Time alone will tell whether in our common law single jurisdictional system a Restatement of English law is regarded as a worthwhile means of filling a gap between judge-made law and legislation. Meanwhile I have been sufficiently encouraged by initial reactions to move on to restating the English law of contract.

JUDICIAL LAW REFORM

Perhaps oddly for a former Law Commissioner, I have never been a great fan of legislative reform of the non-criminal common law. Indeed, my years at the Law Commission merely served to reinforce my legislative scepticism. That scepticism is built on two main concerns about legislative law reform. The first is that the vagaries of the legislative process mean that whether time is found for legislation depends almost entirely on whether one can fit one's law reform within the political imperatives of the day and has little or no relationship to the quality of, or necessity for, the reform proposed. The second is that, while legislative drafting and progressive judicial interpretation can overcome the difficulties, there is some risk that legislative reform, as opposed to judicial reform, may freeze the law in a way that makes desirable change, and the correcting of mistakes, difficult. At root my approach may rest on a belief that our judges are to be trusted on developments of the common law in a way that our politicians should not be.

This legislative scepticism means that, for example, I think judges should be very wary of leaving possible reform of the common law to the legislature.[5] As a general proposition, I regard arguments to that effect as an abdication of judicial responsibility and as masks for what are often good reasons for favouring keeping the law as it is which the judges should be prepared to defend rationally and openly. Even worse are arguments that, because the legislature has not enacted some reform, it is the intention of Parliament that there should be no reform of it. The truth is that there is a myriad of reasons why Parliament may not have legislated on a matter and it is incorrect to regard it as necessarily reflecting a considered choice. Again, where there is legislation in place, I regard the role of the judges as being to treat the legislation as 'always speaking' and hence to ensure, so far as the wording permits this, that the statute remains fit for purpose.[6] Put another way, judges in interpreting statutes should adopt, so far as the words permit, common law methodology.

[5] For this argument see my article 'The Relationship between Common Law and Statute in the Law of Obligations' (2012) 128 *Law Quarterly Review* 232, 247–48. For a disappointing recent example, see some of the Supreme Court's reasoning in *R (Prudential plc) v Special Commissioner of Income Tax* [2013] UKSC 1; [2013] 2AC 185 on the question of whether legal professional privilege should be extended to accountants giving legal advice.

[6] This is sometimes referred to as statutes having an 'ambulatory' meaning. Examples of an application or acceptance of this by the courts include *Royal College of Nursing v Dept of Health and Social Security* [1981] AC 800; *R v Ireland* [1998] AC 147; *R (on the application of Quintavalle) v Secretary of State for Health* [2003] UKHL 13; [2003] 2 AC 687; *Yemshaw v Hounslow LBC* [2011] UKSC 3; [2011] 1 WLR 433. For criticism, which I do not agree with, of that last decision, see the casenote on *Yemshaw* by Richard Ekins, 'Updating the Meaning of Violence' (2013) 129 *Law Quarterly Review* 17.

On the question of whether to develop the common law or to leave it to the legislature,[7] I always have in the forefront of my mind the brilliant speech of Lord Goff in *Woolwich Equitable Building Society v IRC*,[8] which repays careful examination by every lawyer and law student. Faced with the argument that it would be preferable to rely on legislation rather than to develop the common law so as to allow restitution of money paid pursuant to an ultra vires demand by a public authority, Lord Goff said the following:[9]

> [It is argued that] for your Lordships' House to recognise such a principle would overstep the boundary which we traditionally set for ourselves, separating the legitimate development of the law by the judges from legislation. It was strongly urged by [counsel for the Revenue] in his powerful argument ... that we would indeed be trespassing beyond that boundary if we were to accept the argument of Woolwich. I feel bound however to say that, although I am well aware of the existence of the boundary, I am never quite sure where to find it. Its position seems to vary from case to case. Indeed, if it were to be as firmly and clearly drawn as some of our mentors would wish, I cannot help feeling that a number of leading cases in your Lordships' House would never have been decided the way they were. For example, the minority view would have prevailed in *Donoghue v Stevenson*;[10] our modern law of judicial review would have never developed from its old, ineffectual, origins; and *Mareva* injunctions would never have seen the light of day.

And later he went on to point out that the opportunity for the judges to develop a particular area of the law rarely arises and should be seized where it does arise; and that in some areas, where central government has a vested interest in maintaining the present law, there is no practical prospect of legislation:

> [T]his opportunity will never come again. If we do not take it now, it will be gone forever. [Moreover,] I fear that, however compelling the principle of justice may be, it would never be sufficient to persuade a government to propose its legislative recognition by Parliament; caution, otherwise known as the Treasury, would never allow this to happen.[11]

Against that background, explaining my legislative scepticism and my preference for judicial development of the non-criminal common law, I would like to draw your attention to two Law Commission projects that I was involved in to show that judicial law reform may be the best route forward even where legislation might seem, at least at first sight, the more obvious solution. The first was the level of damages for pain, suffering and loss of amenity in personal injury cases. The second was the reform of the law on the defence of illegality.

[7] For general considerations of this question, see, eg 'The Judge as Lawmaker: An English Perspective' in Tom Bingham, *The Business of Judging: Selected Essays and Speeches* (Oxford University Press, 2000) ch 2; Sir Philip Sales, 'Judges and Lawmakers: Values into Law' (2012) *Cambridge Law Journal* 287, 291–93; Sir Philip Sales, 'Rationality, Proportionality, and the Development of the Law' (2013) 129 *Law Quarterly Review* 225, 232–34; Lord Dyson, 'Where the Common Law Fears to Tread', ALBA Lecture 2012 (2013) 34 *Statute Law Review* 1.

[8] *Woolwich Equitable Building Society v IRC* [1993] AC 70.

[9] ibid at 173.

[10] *Donoghue v Stevenson* [1932] AC 562.

[11] *Woolwich Equitable Building Society*, n 8 above, at 176.

Level of Damages for Non-Pecuniary Loss in Personal Injury Cases

What I am about to discuss is the story behind the Court of Appeal's decision on a series of conjoined appeals in *Heil v Rankin*.[12] As part of a project on damages for personal injury, the Law Commission considered whether the level of damages for pain, suffering and loss of amenity was too low.[13] The traditional approach to the level of such damages was for them to be fixed by appellate judges in particular cases in line with what was considered to be 'fair, just and reasonable'; and that in subsequent cases the awards would be updated for inflation by applying the increase in the Retail Prices Index since the previous relevant decision. Greater consistency was instigated by the publication, beginning in 1992, of the Judicial College's *Guidelines for the Assessment of General Damages in Personal Injury Cases*.[14] These Guidelines synthesised in a readily accessible form the past decisions without seeking to change the level set by them.

The Law Commission concluded on various grounds that the level of damages for pain, suffering and loss of amenity in cases of more serious injury had become too low and should be increased. The Law Commission's own consultation exercise, a survey of lay opinion conducted with the assistance of the Office for National Statistics, the increase in life expectancy, and the level of awards given in Northern Ireland, were all factors that the Law Commission considered relevant in making that recommendation.

Of particular importance to the theme of this chapter is the method by which the Law Commission recommended that the uplift should be brought about. Rather than recommending legislation, the Law Commission proposed that the level could and should be increased across the board by the Court of Appeal (or House of Lords) seeking to hear together a number of appeals dealing with injuries of different severity.[15] It was argued that fixing the appropriate level of awards for non-pecuniary loss fell within the powers of the judiciary and it was more likely that this method of 'reform' would be successful than waiting for legislative action. Support had been obtained in advance of publishing the Report from Lord Woolf MR and the Lord Chief Justice Lord Bingham. After meeting with us, Lord Woolf raised the matter on the Law Commission's behalf with the Judges' Council; and Lord Bingham CJ wrote to the Law Commission as follows:

> I would myself think it possible to arrange for the Court of Appeal to hear a number of different appeals on quantum in personal injury cases, covering a range of different injuries and factual situations, and to invite the appointment of an amicus. I think it would be important to have independent representations, since the court would have to consider the effect on insurers of a sudden increase in levels of compensation if the court were to be invited to rule in favour of such a general increase.[16]

[12] *Heil v Rankin* [2001] QB 272.
[13] Law Commission, *Damages for Personal Injury: Non-Pecuniary Loss* (Law Com No 257, 1999).
[14] The 12th edn was published in 2013.
[15] Law Com No 257, paras 3.140–3.165.
[16] ibid para 3.165, n 195.

With that support, the Law Commission was confident that a way would indeed be found to bring the cases before the Court of Appeal although, as a fall-back position, we did recommend legislation should the courts fail to make the recommended increase.

So it was that eight conjoined appeals came before a specially convened five-judge Court of Appeal in *Heil v Rankin*. An amicus instructed by the Treasury Solicitor assisted the court with oral and written submissions, and written submissions were accepted from the Association of Personal Injury Lawyers and from various insurers and groups representing insurance interests.

A significant part of the judgment of the Court of Appeal dealt with whether the Court of Appeal was the appropriate forum for considering what to do about the Law Commission's report. In particular, the defendants were arguing that this was a matter for Parliament and not for the courts. Lord Woolf, giving the judgment of the court, summarised the defendants' arguments as follows:

> [It has been] contended that it would be unsuitable and inappropriate to seek to alter the level of awards by judicial determination. It is argued that Parliament is the appropriate forum in which such a change should be made. There could then be a full and proper public debate as to the justification for the increase in general damages which the Commission have recommended. All interested parties would then be able to make representations to their Members of Parliament. Existing and prospective litigants would know the progress and likely outcome. Parliament is in the position to achieve a change in levels which would be prospective only and can cater for the effects on the insurance industry by means of clearly defined commencement dates and transitional provisions. If the courts interfere, this would create undesirable uncertainty about the prospects of further changes which would not arise if Parliament dealt with the issue.[17]

Lord Woolf rejected those arguments. While he accepted that 'the level of awards does involve questions of social policy',[18] what the courts were being asked to do fell within their traditional remit of fixing the level of damages for non-pecuniary loss, and if Parliament wished to intervene subsequently, it could of course do so. Although prospective rather than retrospective reform might have been preferable, the judges were experienced in making the social policy decisions needed in this area and for them not to do so would be to neglect their responsibility. In Lord Woolf's words:

> [I]t is appropriate for the court to consider the Commission's recommendation. What is involved is part of the traditional role of the courts. It is a role in which juries previously were involved. Now it is the established role of the judiciary. It is a role which, as a result of their accumulated experience, the judiciary is well qualified to perform. Parliament can still intervene. It has, however, shown no inclination that it intends to do so. If it should decide to do so then the fact that the courts have already considered the question will be of assistance to Parliament. Until Parliament does so, the courts cannot avoid their responsibility. While a public debate on this subject would no doubt be salutary, the contribution which it could make to the actual decision of the court is limited. The court has the report of the Commission. It also has the other material which the parties have placed before it. It

[17] [2001] QB 272, para 10.
[18] ibid para 41.

> is in as good a position as it is likely to be to make a decision in the context of the present appeals. We see no reason to accede to [counsel for the defendants' submission] that we should postpone doing so. To postpone would be to neglect our responsibility to provide certainty in this area as soon as it is practical to do so.[19]

As it was, the Court of Appeal decided that what the Law Commission had recommended (that damages of more than £3,000 should be uplifted by at least 50 per cent) went too far. Instead the decision made was that levels of damages over £10,000 should be increased on a tapered basis with the highest awards lifted by 33 per cent. So while the previous highest award for the most serious injury was £150,000 that was increased to £200,000. That level of increase changed the law and has been the basis for all subsequent decisions and of all subsequent editions of the Judicial College's Guidelines.

The upshot is that, while we at the Law Commission did not achieve fully what we had hoped in terms of the precise level of increase, the decision in *Heil v Rankin* was a triumph in terms of the methodology of law reform. It showed what could be achieved by a close working relationship between the Law Commission and the judiciary. I am convinced that, had we waited for legislation, we would still be waiting, as is borne out by other unimplemented recommendations for legislation that we made, not least in relation to reforms of the Fatal Accidents Act 1976 or the Limitation Act 1980.

Illegality as a Defence in Private Law

Although perhaps less obviously 'a success', the Law Commission's project on illegality is another example of the Law Commission being instrumental in bringing about desirable *judicial* law reform.

The defence of illegality in private law has long perplexed the courts. Technical rules, some based on Latin maxims, such as *ex turpi causa non oritur actio* ('no action arises from a disgraceful cause') and *in pari delicto potior est conditio defendentis* ('where both parties are equally in the wrong the position of the defendant is the stronger') have tended to hold sway; and there has been little scope for the courts to address the underlying policies at stake and, in particular, whether the denial of the cause of action or remedy by reason of the illegality is a proportionate reaction. When I first instigated a project on this area, it was confined to illegal transactions (illegality in the context of contracts and trusts) but ultimately the work was expanded to include the law of tort. Early on, and when I was still at the Commission, our provisional proposal had been for legislation by which the courts would be given a structured discretion to decide on what the impact of the claimant's illegality should be in relation to an otherwise valid claim based on contract, trust or unjust enrichment.[20] Many years later, after I had left the Commission, the

[19] ibid para 48.

[20] Law Commission, *Illegal Transactions: The Effect of Illegality on Contracts and Trusts* (Law Com CP No 154, 1999).

recommendation in the Law Commission's final report, *The Illegality Defence*,[21] was that, subject to one exception, to deal with the House of Lords' decision supporting the 'reliance principle' in the context of trusts in *Tinsley v Milligan*,[22] reform was essentially within the interpretative reach of the courts and that judicial law reform was the preferable way forward.

So in its final report the Law Commission approved the approach favoured in its earlier consultation paper, *The Illegality Defence: A Consultative Report*,[23] that the courts should articulate and balance the various polices in play in deciding the central question of whether the denial of the claimant's normal rights was a proportionate response to the claimant's illegality. The policies articulated were furthering the purposes of the rule which the illegal conduct has infringed, consistency, that the claimant should not profit from his or her own wrong, deterrence, and maintaining the integrity of the legal system.

Despite my intuitive preference for judicial law reform, I was very doubtful whether the judges could bring about the necessary reform in this area. On the face of it, it required too much of an upheaval of precedent. Hence my earlier preference for a statutory structured discretion. I wrote as follows about the final recommendation of the Law Commission:

> A problem for the largely non-statutory reform now favoured by the Law Commission is that it is clearly somewhat unusual for the courts, at common law, to articulate and balance policies in the way recommended; and it is unclear, for example, whether one would need to wait for the Supreme Court to signal this as the correct judicial approach. Moreover, it seems unsatisfactory to leave the 'no reliance' *Tinsley v Milligan* approach in play outside the proposed statutory reform of trusts. The wide-ranging statutory solution, previously preferred, would avoid such uncertainty and would sweep up reform of *Tinsley v Milligan* at the same time.[24]

Similar scepticism regarding a non-statutory solution was put forward by Lord Sumption in a lecture in 2012 to the Chancery Bar Association.[25]

However, I am pleased to say that Lord Sumption and I have been proved wrong. In its Report, the Commission had already seen signs of support for its favoured approach from the House of Lords in the tort case of *Gray v Thames Trains Ltd*,[26] in which Lord Hoffmann said, 'The maxim *ex turpi causa* expresses not so much a

[21] Law Commission, *The Illegality Defence* (Law Com No 320, 2010).

[22] *Tinsley v Milligan* [1995] 1 AC 340.

[23] Law Commission, *The Illegality Defence: A Consultative Report* (Law Com CP No 189, 2009) esp paras 2.35, 3.142 and 4.44.

[24] Andrew Burrows, *The Law of Restitution*, 3rd edn (Oxford University Press, 2011) 601.

[25] Lord Sumption, 'Reflections on the Law of Illegality' (Chancery Bar Association, London, 23 April 2012). This was subsequently published in [2012] *Restitution Law Review* 1. The final paragraph of that lecture was as follows: 'It is true that in some cases the courts have been able to escape the harshness of the law, but they have done it by cheating, a process which is not conducive to either clarity or coherence in the law. The government is, I believe, still considering its response to the Law Commission's final report. We may be permitted to hope that it will prefer the more imaginative proposals which the Commission had put forward in its early consultation documents to the abandonment of the cause which is evident in its final report'.

[26] *Gray v Thames Trains Ltd* [2009] UKHL 33; [2009] 1 AC 1339.

principle as a policy. Furthermore that policy is not based upon a single justification but on a group of reasons which vary in different situations'.[27]

Crucially, the Law Commission's approach has recently been explicitly approved and applied by the Court of Appeal in two cases. In *Les Laboratoires Servier v Apotex Inc*,[28] the leading judgment was given by Etherton LJ, who was Chair of the Law Commission at the time of much of its work on illegality. The claim was for damages under a cross-undertaking in damages given by Servier who had been granted an injunction against Apotex to restrain infringement of a patent. It transpired that Servier should not have been granted that injunction because it had no valid patent in this jurisdiction. The question was whether Apotex's illegality, by acting in breach of a valid Canadian patent, constituted a defence to Apotex's claim for damages under the cross-undertaking. It was held that, in the light of the policies in play and, taking into account in assessing those policies whether the illegality was trivial or inadvertent, the illegality should not be a defence so that Apotex was entitled to damages. Etherton LJ said as follows:[29]

> Following its Consultation Paper No 160 on 'The Illegality Defence in Tort', the Law Commission in its 2009 Consultation Paper No 189 and its 2010 final Report (Law Com No 320) on 'The Illegality Defence' recommended that the illegality defence should be allowed where its application can be firmly justified by one or more of the following policies underlying its existence: furthering the purpose of the rule which the illegal conduct has infringed; consistency; the claimant should not profit from his or her own wrong; deterrence; and maintaining the integrity of the legal system. As the cases plainly show, this does not mean that the illegality defence will always apply where one or more of those policy rationales is relevant. It means that, if the illegality defence applies at all, it must find its justification firmly in one or more of them ... I do not accept, therefore, [counsel for Servier's] strictly exclusive four-part categorisation of the circumstances in which, notwithstanding illegality, the claimant is not barred from recovery by the illegality principle. I readily acknowledge that his categorisation is a useful way of analysing the cases ... My objection is that it imposes an unwarranted inflexibility in a difficult area, whereas what is required in each case is an intense analysis of the particular facts and of the proper application of the various policy considerations underlying the illegality principle so as to produce a just and proportionate response to the illegality. That is not the same as an unbridled discretion.

Etherton LJ's judgment and the approach of the Law Commission were then supported by the Court of Appeal in the contract illegality case of *Parkingeye Ltd v Somerfield Stores Ltd*.[30] Here, Somerfield and Parkingeye entered into a contract whereby Parkingeye would operate a number of Somerfield car parks and would deal with the 'fines' for those who outstayed their free parking time. Somerfield repudiated the contract and, subject to the illegality defence, were held liable to Parkingeye for £350,000. The question at issue was whether Parkingeye's illegal conduct in performing the contract was a defence to that contract claim. The illegality in question was that Parkingeye had been chasing up customers who had failed to pay with third and fourth letters that were not merely aggressive but contained

[27] ibid para 30.
[28] *Les Laboratoires Servier v Apotex Inc* [2012] EWCA Civ 593, esp paras 66, 73 and 75.
[29] ibid paras 66, 75.
[30] *Parkingeye Ltd v Somerfield Stores Ltd* [2012] EWCA Civ 1338; [2013] QB 840.

false statements. At first instance that illegality was held not to be a defence and that was upheld by the Court of Appeal. Sir Robin Jacob (with whom Laws LJ agreed) and Toulson LJ both relied on the recommendation of the Law Commission and the judgment of Etherton LJ in the *Servier* case.

Sir Robin Jacob said:[31]

> In applying the 'disproportionate' test I do not think I am exercising a judicial discretion. It was settled by *Tinsley v Milligan*[32] that a defence of illegality point cannot be solved by applying a discretion based on public conscience. Proportionality as I see it is something rather different. It involves the assessment of how far refusal of the remedy furthers one or more of the specific policies underlying the defence of illegality. Those policies Etherton LJ identified in *Les Laboratoires Servier v Apotex Inc*,[33] (from the Law Commission report) as: 'furthering the purpose of the rule which the illegal conduct has infringed; consistency; the claimant should not profit from his or her own wrong; deterrence; and maintaining the integrity of the legal system'. Etherton LJ was careful to add: 'As the cases plainly show, this does not mean that the illegality defence will always apply where one or more of those policy rationales is relevant. It means that, if the illegality defence applies at all, it must find its justification firmly in one or more of them'.

Sir Robin Jacob concluded: 'I do not think the facts of this case, considered with a sense of proportionality, involve such an invasion of any of the policy rationales as to deprive Parkingeye of its remedy'.[34]

Similarly, Toulson LJ concluded as follows: 'In summary, the disallowance of Parkingeye's claim on the ground of illegality is not compelled by the authorities, and it would not be a just and proportionate response to the illegality'.[35]

The law on illegality, through the work of the Law Commission and taken up by progressive reforming judges, has therefore been put on a more flexible basis that allows the courts to cut through to the underlying policies and to reach a proportionate result. That has been done without the legislation that I, for one, thought would be needed. It is a great example of what can be achieved by judicial law reform. I suspect that, had the Law Commission gone through with the initial proposal for legislation, we would still be waiting. A Bill to reform the illegality defence is hardly likely to have set the political pulses racing in Whitehall.

CONCLUSION

The message of this chapter is that, if like me, you trust judges and have some scepticism about legislation in relation to English private law, there are alternatives. The Restatement project seeks to remedy the lack of accessibility that the common law might otherwise be thought to suffer from in contrast to legislation. And reform of the common law can be achieved by the judges, even in areas where it might at first sight seem that legislation is the only way forward.

31 ibid para 39.
32 *Tinsley*, n 22 above.
33 *Les Laboratoires Servier*, n 28 above, para 66.
34 *Parkingeye Ltd*, n 30 above, para 40.
35 ibid para 79.

4

The Impact of Rule-making by Financial Services Regulators on the Common Law

The Lessons of PPI

EVA LOMNICKA

GENERAL

SINCE THE ADVENT of detailed regulatory regimes that impose standards of behaviour on the firms they regulate, the courts have had to consider how to accommodate those standards into the common law. This has been a particular issue in the financial services sphere[1] where the regulatory regimes have been superimposed on relationships that were already primarily governed by obligations law: contractual, tortious and fiduciary. The first wave of detailed regulation under the Financial Services Act (FSA) 1986 prompted a Law Commission consideration of the interplay between fiduciary duties and regulatory rules, centred on the management of the multifarious conflicts of interest that the sector gave rise to after 'Big Bang'.[2] Its conclusion was that as the case law[3] recognised that contractual terms generally could define the extent of fiduciary duties owed, there was no need to recommend any wholesale reform.[4] The issue again forms one aspect of the Law Commission's present consultation on the fiduciary duties of investment intermediaries, with particular focus on the pensions sector.[5] When the regulatory standards are 'voluntary' in the sense of not having statutory backing, the courts are left with considerable freedom in deciding what their impact should be. Unsurprisingly they

[1] But in that context, as noted below, the Financial Ombudsman Service (FOS) is able to side-step this problem and decide cases 'by reference to what is, in the opinion of the ombudsman, fair and reasonable in all the circumstances of the case' (Financial Services and Markets Act 2000 (FSMA), s 228(2)) and hence on grounds that do not need to reflect the strict legal position.

[2] Law Commission, *Fiduciary Duties and Regulatory Rules*, Cm 3049 (Law Com No 236, 1995), preceded by Law Commission, *Fiduciary Duties and Regulatory Rules* (Law Com CP No 124, 1992).

[3] In particular *Kelly v Cooper* [1993] AC 205, decided during the consultation period.

[4] It only recommended legislation to clarify that no liability should arise if a firm operated 'Chinese Walls' complying with statutory regulatory rules.

[5] Law Commission, *Fiduciary Duties of Investment Intermediaries* (Law Com CP No 25, 2013). A final report is expected in June 2014.

have looked to professional standards articulated by professional bodies[6] or trade associations[7] to inform existing common law standards, but always reserving the right to insist that the common law might find those standards wanting.[8] So, most obviously, in the context of deciding if professionals have breached their obligation of exercising due care and skill, professional standards have generally been accepted as setting the benchmark, at least as a minimum.[9] An alternative analysis that is available where there is a contractual relationship between the protagonists is to regard the regulatory standards as giving rise to implied terms.[10]

The courts do not have as much freedom when dealing with regulatory provisions imposed under statutory powers, as how Parliament intended the regime to relate to the existing common law becomes the paramount consideration. However, that merely changes the focus of the inquiry that the courts need to undertake.

BREACH OF STATUTORY DUTY ACTION

The imposition of a statutory framework on a regulatory regime brings with it the additional possibility of the breach of statutory duty action for transgressions of duties imposed under statutory powers. Increasingly, given the history of extensive case law on whether such actionability arises at all, modern regulatory statutes usually seek to make the position clear. Accordingly, the Consumer Credit Act 1974 spells out the consequences for breaches of its regime (sometimes criminal[11] and sometimes civil)[12] but then includes a general provision stating that no further consequences follow.[13] The Financial Services and Markets Act 2000 (FSMA)

[6] On the relevance of the Guidance issued by the Consultative Committee of Accountancy Bodies as to auditors liability, see *Lloyd Cheyham & Co v Littlejohn & Co* [1987] BCLC 303, 313 (Woolf J). See also *Dawson International Plc v Coats Paton Plc* [1989] BCLC 233 (affd [1990] BCLC 560); *Revenue and Customs Commissioners v William Grant & Sons Distillers Ltd* [2007] UKHL 15, paras 2, 38; *Macquarie Internationale Investments Ltd v Glencore UK Ltd* [2010] EWCA Civ 697, para 51. See generally, John Powell and Roger Stewart (eds), *Jackson and Powell on Professional Liability*, 7th edn (London, Sweet and Maxwell, 2012) paras 2-007–2-012 and *passim*.

[7] Most recently, see *Plevin v Paragon Personal Finance Ltd* [2013] EWCA Civ 1658 (considered below) on the relevance of the Finance Industry Standards Association (FISA) and Finance and Leasing Association (FLA) voluntary codes.

[8] For cases where solicitors and financial advisers (respectively) were held negligent despite complying with current industry practice, see *Edward Wong Finance Co Ltd v Johnson, Stokes and Master* [1984] AC 296 and *Loosemore v Financial Concepts* [2001] Lloyd's Rep PN 235.

[9] See cases at n 6 above and, generally, John Powell and Roger Stewart (eds), *Jackson and Powell on Professional Liability*, n 6 above.

[10] *Larussa-Chigi v CS First Boston Ltd* [1998] CLC 277: Thomas J suggested (obiter) that the London Code of Conduct (then published by the Bank of England to govern wholesale money markets) would be impliedly incorporated. *cf Clarion Ltd v National Provident Institution* [2000] 1 WLR 188 (Rimer J held that the SIB Principles (forerunner to the FCA Principles for Business, considered below) were not implied into the contract in question) and *Bear Stearns Bank plc v Forum Global Equity Ltd* [2007] EWHC 1576 (Smith J held that the Loan Market Association rules were not implied).

[11] Many (viz. those imposed under Consumer Credit Act (CCA) 1974, ss 39, 45, 51, 51A, 160A, 167) have now been repealed since the transfer of regulation from the Office of Fair Trading (OFT) to the FCA and the regulation of licensing (now 'authorisation') and advertising (now 'financial promotion') under FSMA, which only uses the criminal sanction in limited circumstances.

[12] CCA 1974, ss 55(2), 61B(3), 65(1), 77, 77A, 78, 79, 86D, 105(7)(a), (b), 107–9, 110, 111(2), 124(1), (2).

[13] CCA 1974, s 170(1).

(as did its predecessor, the FSA 1986) also spells out the precise consequences of contravention of various aspects of its regime.

The breach of statutory duty action is a central feature of the FSMA regime.[14] Hence FSMA, section 138D (and its predecessors FSMA, section 150[15] and the FSA 1986, sections 62–62A) provides that contravention of a 'rule' made by the regulator is 'actionable at the suit of a private person who suffers loss as a result of the contravention, subject to the defences and other incidents applying to actions for breach of statutory duty'.

To confer some constitutional legitimacy on this law-making power of the regulators, rule-making under FSMA must generally be preceded by an extensive consultation process followed by a 'feedback' statement by the regulator that responds to representations made.[16] Part of that consultation process involves consulting various 'Panels'. As far as the Financial Conduct Authority (FCA) is concerned, it must establish and maintain a 'Consumer Panel'[17] and three 'Practitioner Panels'.[18] The fact that the opportunity is given (in particular to those affected by the regime) to comment on and challenge the proposals, clearly gives the resulting rules a particularly authoritative status, although as with all law-making the relative strengths of the various lobbying groups should not be ignored. It is notable that in practice the bulk of responses and lobbying comes from the well-resourced trade bodies of the various practitioners affected, as well as the individual practitioners themselves.

The (limited) scope of this actionability provision in FSMA, section 138D should be noted. In particular, only contraventions of certain provisions are actionable: breaches of certain 'rules'. Which provisions give rise to actionability is partly determined by the statute itself and partly by the regulators. The statute provides that only breach of regulatory 'rules' (and not other provisions such as Guidance)[19] is actionable. Moreover, it explicitly excludes certain rules[20] from this consequence. Otherwise it is up to the regulators to decide which of their regulatory provisions are to give rise to such civil claims. First, when drafting the rule-books the regulators determine which of their provisions are to have the status of 'rules' as opposed

[14] In the United States, such an action became a much used additional enforcement mechanism for the securities regulation regime (especially civil claims for breach of SEC rule 10b-5 made under the Securities Exchange Act 1934, see *Blue Chip Stamps v Manor Drug Stores* 421 US 723; 44 L Ed 2d 539; 95 S Ct 1917 (1975)) and when the United Kingdom first introduced its financial services regulatory regime in the Financial Services Act (FSA) 1986, the decision was made to follow suit. For discussion of FSMA, s 138D and its predecessors, see Gerald McMeel and John Virgo, *McMeel and Virgo on Financial Advice and Financial Products: Law and Liability*, 2nd edn (Oxford University Press, 2012); John Powell and Roger Stewart (eds), *Jackson and Powell on Professional Liability*, n 6 above, para 14-070 *et seq*; *Encyclopedia of Financial Services Law* (London, Sweet and Maxwell, Looseleaf) para 2A-309.

[15] FSMA, s 150 was replaced by FSMA, s 138D on 1 April 2012 (by the Financial Services Act 2012, s 24) when the Financial Conduct Authority (FCA) and Prudential Regulation Authority (PRA) replaced the Financial Services Authority (FSA).

[16] FSMA, s 138I (FCA), s 138J (PRA), but note the exemptions in s 138L and s 138M.

[17] FSMA, ss 1M and 1Q; and see s 1R: duty to consult representations made by Panels.

[18] FSMA, ss 1M and 1N (FCA Practitioner Panel), s 1O (Smaller Business Practitioner Panel) and s 1P (Markets Practitioner Panel); and see s 1R: duty to consult representations made by Panels.

[19] Made under FSMA, s 139A.

[20] See s 138D(5). The following rules are not actionable: (a) the 'Part 6' rules (listing rules etc) made by the FCA under Pt VI (s 73A); (b) rules made under s 137O (the Threshold Condition Code); (c) rules under s 192J (provision of information by parent undertakings); (d) financial resources rules. See also s 138C: so-called evidential 'rules', breach of which is not actionable.

to 'guidance' or 'evidential rules'. Secondly, the regulators are also given power to withdraw or confer the actionability sanction in relation to each of their 'rules'.[21] Hence, whilst contraventions of all regulatory provisions[22] are subject to disciplinary sanctions by the regulators,[23] the regulators can also decide, by designating provisions as 'rules' and rendering them actionable or not, whether to visit contravention of such provisions with the added sanction of a potential civil suit against the regulated firm by private persons[24] suffering loss.

The rule-books presently vary in their levels of specificity. The original rule-books under the FSA 1986 were drafted with what was regarded as an excessive degree of precision and the predecessor to FSMA, section 138D[25] was partly blamed. As the rules imposed civil liability for breach, they were deliberately drafted like statutes in order to enable businesses to regulate their affairs so as to be sure they escaped civil liability. It was feared that drafting vague and imprecise rules would be an invitation to litigation, leaving the courts (rather than the regulators) with the role of defining the liability more precisely.[26] The result therefore was lengthy and 'legalistic' rule-books that were not only difficult to understand and navigate but that also lacked the focus of the overarching principles that the regime aimed to implement.

One response was the introduction of the original 'Ten Commandments' or 'Statements of Principle'[27] that spelt out, in easily understood general propositions, the basic obligations regarding both the conduct and financial standing that regulated firms needed to live up to. For example, the first Principle now states that a firm 'must conduct its business with integrity' and the sixth requires a firm to 'pay due regard to the interests of its customers and treat them fairly'.[28] The sanctions for non-compliance with these principles were initially precisely spelt out by statute:[29] disciplinary action by the regulator but, given their 'high level' wording, not civil actionability. When the Financial Services Authority (FSA) took over regulation under FSMA, the number of principles increased to 11.[30] Hence the biblical epithet

[21] For PRA rules to be actionable, the PRA must so provide: s 138D(1). All FCA rules are actionable, unless the FCA provides otherwise: s 138D(2), (3). Most significantly, the FCA has provided that its Principles for Business in the PRIN Module of its Handbook (considered at n 77 below) are *not* actionable.

[22] In so far as they give rise to a 'relevant requirement' (defined in FSMA, s 204A) and hence grounds for the imposition of a penalty (FSMA, s 206), public censure (FSMA, s 205) and suspension of permission (FSMA, s 206A). Variation or cancellation of permission is available on wider grounds (FSMA, s 55J).

[23] And, as noted below, all such contraventions are relevant to FOS determinations.

[24] The action is only generally available to 'private persons' as defined (essentially to exclude business clients) in regulations made by the Treasury under FSMA, s 138D(6): see FSMA (Rights of Action) Regulations 2001, SI 2001/2256, regs 6, 3.

[25] FSA 1986, ss 62–62A (re-enacted as FSMA, s 150 before that was replaced by FSMA, s 138D).

[26] As was the US experience when the courts recognised a right of action for breach of the imprecisely worded SEC Rule 10b-5, see n 4 above and, generally, Eva Lomnicka, 'Private Damages Claims for Breaches of Securities Regulation Law' in Richard Plender (ed), *Legal History and Comparative Law: Essays in Honour of Albert Kiralfy* (London, Frank Cass, 1990).

[27] The model was the (then) Takeover Code's General Principles.

[28] This Principle was the basis of the extensive 'Treating Customer Fairly' (TCF) initiative launched by the FSA in July 2006 (Financial Service Authority, *Treating Customers Fairly: Towards Fair Outcomes for Consumers*) to require firms to achieve six 'TCF outcomes' when dealing with consumers.

[29] FSA 1986, s 47A.

[30] The PRA will have eight 'Fundamental Rules' (rather than 'Principles for Business'): see Bank of England, *Consultation Paper: The PRA Rulebook* (CP2/14, 2014).

has sadly been abandoned and they are now known as the 'Principles for Business' (or PRIN after the acronym of the Module of the Handbook in which they feature). Although FSMA itself no longer explicitly provides that breach of the Principles is not actionable, that position is maintained in that the Financial Conduct Authority (FCA) has used its power to provide that although the Principles are 'rules', breach is not actionable under FSMA, section 138D.

But whilst answering one question (is there a right of action for breach of the regime?) FSMA, section 138D raises the further question of how determinative of other issues such a provision is. To what extent does this exhaust or at least limit the judges' freedom to develop the underlying common law?

If an actionable rule has been breached, FSMA, section 138D provides a straightforward route to liability. And in so far as additional causes of action based on the common law duty of care and skill arise, they generally[31] add little as the courts have regarded common law liability as largely co-extensive with that imposed under FSMA, section 135D.[32] But if the actionable rules are complied with, a more difficult question arises: should the courts nevertheless recognise that other liability might arise at common law. The PPI (mis-)selling saga brought this problem to the fore.

THE PPI SAGA

Background

The widespread (mis-)selling of payment protection insurance (PPI)[33] has, in particular, required the courts to grapple with the interplay between the regulatory rules and the common law. PPI became a very profitable[34] 'financial product' that, although available on a stand-alone basis on the open market, was typically sold at the same time as a loan was provided. The sale of PPI in conjunction with loans usually had some or all of the following features. The PPI policy was usually optional[35]

[31] The courts do reserve the right to determine otherwise: see *Gorham v British Telecommunications Plc* [2001] 1 WLR 2129: although the rules only gave a right of action to the client of an adviser, the Court of Appeal applied *White v Jones* [1995] 2 AC 207 and permitted his wife to claim at common law. But *cf Green and another v RBS Plc* [2013] EWCA Civ 119: the duty in *Hedley Byrne v Heller* [1964] AC 465 was not extended to impose a duty of disclosure, although COB rules so provided.

[32] A conclusion drawn (and of course supported by the cited case law) in McMeel and Virgo, *McMeel and Virgo on Financial Advice and Financial Products*, n 14 above, para V.1.20 and John Powell and Roger Stewart (eds), *Jackson and Powell on Professional Liability*, n 6 above, para 14-072. See also P Reynolds, 'Selling Financial Products: The Interface between Regulatory and Common Law Standards' (2014) 29(5) *Journal of International Banking Law and Regulation* 269.

[33] Sometimes called credit or loan protection insurance. It insures against an inability to repay a loan in certain events (eg illness, accident or unemployment of the borrower) and sometimes includes life cover.

[34] The Competition Commission's Final Report of 29 January 2009 (Competition Commission, *Market Investigation into Payment Protection Insurance* (2009), available at www.competition-commission.org.uk/assets/competitioncommission/docs/pdf/non-inquiry/rep_pub/reports/2009/fulltext/542) estimated that the 12 largest distributors of PPI made profits (after tax) in excess of the cost of capital of £1.4 billion in 2006 representing a return on equity of 490 per cent.

[35] Hence it did not form part of the 'total charge for credit' and hence the (necessarily) cited 'APR' (annual percentage rate of charge).

but often the borrower gained the impression[36] that it was a precondition of the grant of the loan.[37] The cost of the insurance was typically considerably in excess of that available on the open market.[38] Payment was usually by single premium (rather than 'pay-as-you-go' periodic premiums) that was added to the amount of the loan. This had two consequences: early repayment of the loan usually did not result in a pro rata refund of the premium[39] and the lender made an added profit on the extra credit advanced to pay for the premium. Often the period of cover was shorter than the period of the loan.[40] The seller of the PPI, whether the lender or the borrower's broker, was typically paid a commission by the PPI insurer, which generally amounted to a large proportion[41] of the premium paid (and borrowed) by the borrower. Finally, PPI was sometimes sold to persons who did not need it, being already covered against the risks of not being able to repay their loan, and it was often poor value in that the total cost of the policy exceeded the benefits payable.[42]

The sale of such insurance is regulated in great detail by the ICOBS rule-book now issued by the FCA.[43] This activity has been regulated in this way since 2005, under the predecessor rule-book, ICOB, issued by the FCA's predecessor the FSA. The regulation was prompted by the need to implement the Insurance Mediation Directive.[44] Some of the features of the PPI sales process noted above were clearly in breach of the ICOB regulatory regime. For example, the seller of PPI is obliged to take reasonable steps to ensure that any personal recommendation to buy PPI is suitable, by undertaking a process to obtain information about[45] and then assess the customer's 'demands and needs'.[46] In addition, the amount of the premium and the

[36] The documentation had to state that PPI was optional but the sales process often suggested otherwise.

[37] In any event, a borrower could be forgiven for assuming that, although PPI was not compulsory, a borrower protected by PPI would be more attractive to a lender than one without: see Financial Services Authority, *ICOB Review Interim Report: Consumer Experiences and Outcomes in General Insurance Markets* (2007), available at www.fsa.gov.uk/pubs/other/ICOB_review.pdf, para 5.5.8: '44% of [sample of borrowers] also thought that a loan application was more likely to be approved if they agreed to take out PPI at the same time'.

[38] The Competition Commission's Final Report, n 34 above, found that many consumers were unaware that they could buy PPI from other sources.

[39] This was particularly disadvantageous to the borrower who refinanced their borrowing by terminating the old loan early (and hence terminating the PPI with the loss of unexpired cover) and taking out a new loan with a new PPI policy. See *Harrison v Black Horse Ltd* [2011] EWCA Civ 1128 and *Conlon v Black Horse Ltd* [2013] EWCA Civ 1658 (three loans in 10 months and hence three PPI premiums charged).

[40] As in *Harrison*, n 39 above (23 year loan but five year PPI) and *Plevin*, n 7 above (10 year loan but five year PPI).

[41] The Competition Commission's Final Report, n 34 above, found that commission was typically 50–80 per cent for personal loans (it was 87 per cent in *Harrison*, n 39 above, see below) and 40–65 per cent for mortgages.

[42] And the Competition Commission's Final Report, n 34, found that typically only between 11–28 per cent of the gross written premium was paid out in claims.

[43] Financial Conduct Authority, *Insurance: Conduct of Business Sourcebook* (FCA Handbook), in force on 6 January 2008, replacing Financial Services Authority, *Insurance: Conduct of Business* (ICOB) (FSA Handbook) in force 14 January 2005. The replacement of ICOB by ICOBS was part of the FSA's move towards 'Principles-based Regulation' (PBR) and hence ICOBS is drafted in more general 'principles-based' terms.

[44] Council Directive 2002/92/EC of the European Parliament and of the Council of 9 December 2002 on insurance mediation [2003] OJ L9 (Insurance Mediation Directive).

[45] ICOB, 4.3.1R; 4.3.2R.

[46] ICOB, 4.3.6R–4.3.7G. In *Harrison*, n 39 above, Tomlinson LJ noted that the 'inelegant phrase "demands and needs"' was taken from art 12.3 of the Directive. He added (at para 42): 'Perhaps it has lost something in translation'.

fact that it is optional has to be disclosed. However, if the lender sells the policy to a consumer, it is not obliged to reveal either the fact of or amount of the commission it receives from the insurer. This is in contrast to the usual position under ICOB/ICOBS which provides that a seller of 'non-investment insurance'[47] to a 'commercial customer' (that is, a customer who is not a consumer)[48] must disclose its commission on request.[49]

Although the Directive gives a specific list of what information has to be disclosed by the intermediary to the potential policy-holder,[50] that information does not include either the fact of or amount of commission payable by the insurer to the intermediary. However, under English law, if the intermediary is the *agent* of the policy-holder, fiduciary principles applicable to 'secret profits' come into play. The issue was considered by the Court of Appeal in *Wilson v Hurstanger Ltd*[51] where a (sub-prime) mortgage lender paid a commission to the borrower's broker. In that case a (vague) disclosure by the broker to the borrower that commission might be paid was held to negate secrecy and hence deprive the commission of the characteristic of being a 'secret' profit, with all the attendant draconian remedies that follow the paying of 'bribes'.[52] However, in order for the commission to be retained and have no further equitable remedial consequences (such as a vitiating affect on the consequent loan agreement) the borrower has to give his 'informed consent' to the broker receiving commission; mere disclosure is not enough.[53] Whether there is 'informed consent' is clearly an issue of fact and it was held in that case (involving 'the non-status lending market' where borrowers were 'likely to be vulnerable and unsophisticated'),[54] invoking the Office of Fair Trading (OFT)'s *Non-status Lending Guidelines*,[55] that this required informing the borrowers both that commission was to be paid and the size of the commission. The court added that it should also have been made clear that the borrower was being asked to consent to the payment of

[47] ie ordinary insurance and not that with an investment element (which is regulated, as are all 'investments', by the Financial Conduct Authority, *Conduct of Business Sourcebook* (COBS) (FCA Handbook) (not the ICOBS rules).

[48] See the definitions of 'commercial customer' and 'consumer' in the FCA 'Glossary'.

[49] ICOBS, 4.4.1R (ex-ICOB, 4.6.1R). The Guidance to the Rule notes the fiduciary principle that imposes a duty to account on *agents* of the policy-holder (see discussion on *Wilson v Hurstanger Ltd* [2007] EWCA Civ 299, below). It adds (somewhat confusingly but apparently paraphrasing ICOBS, 4.4.1R and hence dealing with *both* the fiduciary and non-fiduciary context (as did the fuller ex-ICOB, 4.6.2G)): 'but where a customer employs an insurance intermediary by way of business and does not remunerate him, and where it is usual for the firm to be remunerated by way of commission paid by the insurer out of premium payable by the customer, then there is no duty to account but if the customer asks what the firm's remuneration is, it must tell him'.

[50] Insurance Mediation Directive, art 12.

[51] *Wilson v Hurstanger Ltd* [2007] EWCA Civ 299.

[52] Including damages for fraud covering any actual loss sustained by entering into the tainted transaction.

[53] Peter Watts (ed), *Bowstead and Reynolds on Agency*, 19th edn (London, Sweet and Maxwell, 2012) para 44, regarded as an accurate statement of law in *Wilson*, n 51 above, para 36.

[54] ibid para 37.

[55] Issued in July 1997 (updated November 1997) to give *guidance* (with no statutory underpinning) on the OFT's approach to licensing. See para 6 ('brokers should disclose at the outset … any brokerage fee or commission payable by the borrower or lender') and para 15 ('any customer booklet … should warn that the broker or other intermediary may not be in a position to give unbiased advice if they are tied to the lender or are paid a fee or commission by the lender').

commission and (again as recommended by the OFT Guidelines) a warning that this might preclude the giving of unbiased advice should have been included.

During the requisite consultation process that preceded the issuing of ICOB, the FSA specifically consulted on whether to require disclosure of commission over and above that required by the ordinary fiduciary law, in particular, where the lender (rather than a broker who is the borrower's agent and so obliged to disclose in accordance with fiduciary principles) sold the PPI policy.[56] It decided *not* to extend the fiduciary principle beyond a fiduciary relationship in the consumer context. Noting that the ICOB rules would require 'product' disclosure of both the amount of the premium separately and whether the PPI was compulsory (which the FSA said would facilitate 'shopping around'), a number of reasons were given for not requiring commission disclosure to retail customers: it might confuse and be unhelpful to the customer in focusing on the amount of commission rather than on how suitable the policy was, it would result in 'information overload' and it would be difficult to operate and regulate.[57] The assertion that disclosure of the PPI premium and the fact that the PPI was optional would facilitate 'shopping around' proved unfounded.[58]

As is well known, the selling of PPI to consumers in conjunction with loans became a very widespread and profitable practice. Some PPI was undoubtedly missold in the sense that ICOB/ICOBS was breached. However, even sales that were *not* in breach of ICOB/ICOBS began attracting complaints and it became clear that normal competitive forces were not operating in this market. Regulatory action eventually culminated[59] in the prohibition by the FSA of the sale of single premium PPI[60] and by the Competition Commission of the sale of other PPI policies at the same time as the provision of credit.[61]

[56] See (i) Financial Services Authority, *Insurance Selling and Administration: The FSA's High-level Approach to Regulation* (FSA, CP160, 2002) and (ii) Financial Services Authority, *Insurance Selling and Administration and Other Miscellaneous Amendments* (FSA, CP187, 2003). The final proposals were contained in Financial Services Authority, *Insurance Selling and Administration and Other Miscellaneous Amendments: Feedback on CP187 and Made Text* (FSA, PS04/01, 2004) para 4.21.

[57] FSA CP No 160, paras 11.6–11.8. See also FSA CP No 187, para 8.3 ('nothing in the responses to CP160 caused us to change our view') and FSA PS 04/01, para 4.21 ('we continue to believe that requiring disclosure of commission to retail customers would not add to consumer protection').

[58] See the Competition Commission's Final Report, n 34 above. It is a moot point whether it would have made any difference to its conclusion had the FSA had a 'competition' objective (see now FSMA, s 1B(3)(c)) and duty (see now FSMA, s 1B(4)), both of which have since been imposed on the FCA.

[59] The main milestones were as follows (and see the FSA's interventions, noted at n 65 below): (i) in September 2005 the Citizens Advice Bureau submitted a 'super-complaint' to the OFT and the OFT carried out a 'market survey' which indicated that the market was 'not working well'; (ii) the OFT referred the matter to the Competition Commission under the Enterprise Act 2002, s 131 to determine if competition was restricted or distorted; (iii) on 5 June 2008 the Competition Commission made 'Provisional Findings' that there was limited competition in the market; (iv) on 29 January 2009 the Competition Commission issued its Final Report, n 34 above; (v) Barclays Bank Plc (essentially, unsuccessfully) challenged aspects of the Report before the Competition Appeals Tribunal; (vi) in October 2010 the Competition Commission issued its Final Remittal Report confirming it would issue the Order noted in n 61 below.

[60] In February 2009 the FSA halted the selling of single premium PPI sales on unsecured loans by writing to chief executives requesting its removal from the marketplace.

[61] See the Competition Commission, *Payment Protection Insurance Market Investigation Order* (2011), available at www.webarchive.nationalarchives.gov.uk/+/http://www.competition-commission.org.uk/inquiries/ref2010/ppi_remittal/pdf/ppi_market_investigation_order_(2011).pdf, in force 6 April 2012. PPI can only be sold seven days after the credit agreement and information has to be provided enabling borrowers to 'shop around'.

Breach of ICOB/ICOBS 'rules' is actionable and FSMA, section 138D provides a quick route to redress through the courts.[62] But what is the position of firms that *comply* with the detailed provisions of ICOB/ICOBS? Whilst clearly protecting them from section 138D claims, does such compliance protect the firm from all other adverse legal consequences? Or do the courts still have room for manoeuvre in augmenting the explicit legal obligations that regulators impose, with all the attendant uncertainties that this would bring? This issue arose in two different PPI litigation contexts, with different results.

Redress in the Event of Compliance

One of the many[63] regulatory responses to PPI (mis-)selling was a Policy Statement, *The Assessment and Redress of Payment Protection Insurance Complaints*,[64] from the FSA[65] prompted by its 'serious concerns about widespread weaknesses in previous PPI selling practices'. Amongst its 'package of measures',[66] the Policy Statement relied on the Principles for Business[67] in requiring regulated firms that sold PPI to compensate clients in cases where listed 'common fallings' (some *not* amounting to breaches of ICOB)[68] had occurred. For example, the rules[69] set out very specifically the documentary material that had to be provided to a retail customer. Yet the FSA relied on the Principles[70] in order to require firms to pay redress when they had not given *further* explanations as to any mismatch between the term of cover of the PPI policy and the length of the loan and/or *further oral* explanations that (if

[62] And from the Financial Services Compensation Scheme (see FSMA, Pt XV and Financial Conduct Authority, *Compensation* (FCA Handbook), if the firm is insolvent (as the broker was in *Plevin v Paragon Personal Finance Ltd* [2013] EWCA Civ 1658).

[63] See n 59 above and n 65 below.

[64] Financial Services Authority, *The Assessment and Redress of Payment Protection Insurance Complaints* (FSA, PS10/12, 2010), preceded by Financial Services Authority, *The Assessment and Redress of Payment Protection Insurance Complaints, updated 20 November 2009* (FSA, CP09/23, 2009) and Financial Services Authority, *The Assessment and Redress of Payment Protection Insurance Complaints, Feedback on CP09/23 and Further Consultation* (FSA, CP10/06, 2010).

[65] The FSA had been investigating the sale of PPI since 2005. See (i) Financial Services Authority, *The Sale of Payment Protection Insurance: Results of Thematic Work* (Thematic Report) (2005), available at www.fsa.gov.uk/pubs/other/ppi_thematic_report.pdf; (ii) Financial Services Authority, *The Sale of Payment Protection Insurance: Results of Follow-up Thematic Work* (Follow-up Thematic Report) (2006), available at www.fsa.gov.uk/pubs/other/ppi_thematic.pdf; (iii) Financial Services Authority, *ICOB Review Interim Report* (2007); and (iv) Financial Services Authority, *The Sale of Payment Protection Insurance: Thematic Update* (Thematic Update) (2007), available at www.fsa.gov.uk/pubs/other/ppi_thematic_update.pdf. FOS (see below) under the so-called 'wider-implications' process (whereby FOS had to notify the FSA of any issues it considered had such implications for the financial services sector) notified the FSA in July 2008 of the large volume of PPI (mis-)selling complaints it was receiving. FOS upheld 89 per cent of PPI complaints made to it in the year ended 31 March 2009.

[66] Including amendments to Financial Services Authority, *Dispute Resolution: Complaints* (FSA Handbook) concerning the Financial Ombudsman Service (FOS).

[67] See p 55 above.

[68] Non-disclosure of commission was not listed as a 'common failing', perhaps because this would have been too great a *volte farce* for the FSA which, as noted at p 58 above, had specifically decided, when drafting ICOB, not to require such disclosure.

[69] ICOB, 5.3.1R.

[70] In particular Principle 7: 'A firm must pay due regard to the information needs of its clients, and communicate information to them in a way which is clear, fair and not misleading'.

this was the case) an early termination of a single premium PPI policy would not lead to a pro rata rebate of the premium. Hence, processes and systems devised to comply with the detail of the ICOB regime did not protect firms from liability to clients. This led to judicial review proceedings by the main banking trade body, the British Bankers Association (BBA): *R (on the application of the British Bankers Association) v Financial Services Authority* ('the BBA case').[71] The objection was clear: the regulator had decided that only breaches of certain 'rules' and not Principles gave rise to actionability by clients. Hence (it was argued) the regulator could not circumvent this statutory framework (which it had itself devised) which limited the civil liability of regulated firms to clients, by requiring firms nevertheless to pay their clients redress for breaches of the Principles.

That framework appeared to have been endorsed by the limited scope of 'consumer redress schemes' (CRSs) that the FSA was (and the FCA now is) able to put in place under FSMA.[72] FSMA enabled the FSA[73] to make rules requiring regulated firms to establish and operate a CRS for providing redress to consumers where loss had been caused to them by 'widespread or regular failure'. FSMA expressly provides that the loss must be such as to be remediable by 'legal proceedings'[74] and it was accepted in the BBA case that such a CRS could not be used in respect of breaches of Principles.[75] (Hence in the Policy Statement the FSA purported to use its general powers (in particular its rule-making powers as to complaints handling by regulated firms) to deal with PPI (mis-)selling, an approach it regarded as 'swifter and more appropriate than a [CRS]'.)

Although clearly not 'actionable' nor (therefore) enforceable by a CRS, the Principles are nevertheless a very significant part of the financial services regulatory regime.[76] As the Guidance to the Principles for Business states:

> [S]ince the Principles are also designed as a general statement of regulatory requirements applicable in new or unforeseen situations, and in situations in which there is no need for guidance, the appropriate regulator's other rules and guidance should not be viewed as exhausting the implications of the Principles themselves.[77]

[71] *R (on the application of the British Bankers Association) v Financial Services Authority* [2011] EWHC 999 (Admin).

[72] The present provisions (FSMA, ss 404–404G) were substituted for the original, more limited provision for 'reviewing past business' (old FSMA, s 404), on 12 October 2010, by the Financial Services Act 2010, s 14, but apply to events occurring before that date. The FCA has exercised these powers in respect of the mis-selling of the Arch cru funds: see Financial Conduct Authority, *Consumer Redress Schemes Sourcebook* (FCA Handbook) (and previously, Financial Service Authority, *Consumer Redress Scheme in respect of Unsuitable Advice to Invest in Arch cru Funds* (FSA PS12/9, 2012), preceded by Financial Services Authority, *Redress Scheme for Arch cru Investors* (FSA CP12/9, 2012)).

[73] After consultation with the FOS.

[74] FSMA, s 404(1)(b).

[75] *British Bankers Association*, n 71 above, para 194.

[76] For example, as noted at n 28 above, Principle 6 ('A firm must pay due regard to the interests of its customers and treat them fairly') was used as the basis of the extensive 'Treating Customer Fairly' (TCF) initiative launched by the FSA.

[77] Financial Conduct Authority, *Principles for Businesses* (FCA Handbook) 1.1.9G.

There is no doubt that *disciplinary* action can be taken by the regulator for breach of a Principle without having to rely on a breach of a more specific rule.[78] Disciplinary action may take many forms and some of it can result in regulated firms being liable to pay monetary compensation to their clients. In particular, the regulators have power under FSMA, section 384 to require regulated firms to compensate those suffering loss resulting from a contravention of a 'relevant requirement' which clearly covers a breach of the Principles.[79] They may also apply to the court for an order to similar effect under FSMA, section 382. However, this is dependent on the regulator taking the initiative.

Whilst the aggrieved client cannot compel the regulators to act under FSMA, section 384 or section 382, retail clients do have the possibility of complaining to the Financial Ombudsman Service (FOS), an alternative disputes resolution procedure established by FSMA[80] enabling retail clients to obtain awards of up to £150,000 against regulated firms. FSMA provides that Ombudsmen must decide complaints by reference to what is, in their 'opinion ... fair and reasonable in all the circumstances of the case'.[81] It has been confirmed[82] that the strict legal position, although clearly of some relevance,[83] is not determinative of the redress available. Hence, the FOS is unconcerned with the minutiae of what is technically actionable or not. So if 'in the opinion of the ombudsman' it is 'fair and reasonable'[84] to award compensation for a breach of Principle, the regulated firm is liable to pay it even if such an award would be unavailable as a matter of strict law.

Two of the three main arguments advanced by the BBA are of particular relevance.[85] The first was that, as a contravention of a Principle was clearly not actionable under FSMA, section 138D, it could not give rise to monetary redress to clients in some other way. This proposition was rejected: the only effect of rendering Principles non-actionable was 'to prevent a cause of action for breach of statutory

[78] See n 21 above. For a discussion of how reliance on the Principles in disciplinary proceedings in effect extends the scope of the market abuse regime, see Christa Band and Martyn Hopper, 'Market Abuse: A Developing Jurisprudence' (2007) *Journal of International Banking Law and Regulation* 231.

[79] 'Relevant requirement' is defined in s 384(7) and covers a 'requirement' imposed under FSMA (which an obligation imposed by a Principle (made under FSMA, s 137A) clearly is).

[80] See FSMA, Pt XVI and Financial Conduct Authority, *Dispute Resolution: Complaints* (FCA Handbook).

[81] FSMA, s 228(2).

[82] *R (on the application of Heather Moor and Edgecomb Ltd) v Financial Ombudsman Service Ltd* [2008] EWCA 642 (approving *IFG Financial Services Ltd v Financial Ombudsman Services Ltd* [2005] EWHC 1153 (Admin)). The rationale given by Rix LJ at para 89 was that 'an efficient and cost-effective and relatively informal type of alternative dispute resolution should not be stifled by the imposition of legal doctrine'.

[83] See FCA, *Dispute Resolution*, n 80 above, 3.6.4R: 'law and regulations' are but one relevant factor. Others are: (i) regulators' rules, guidance and standards, (ii) 'codes of practice' and (2) '(where appropriate) ... good industry practice at the relevant time'.

[84] Perhaps it is significant that there is no reference to 'just' in the test the FOS applies.

[85] The third argument was that the FSA was obliged to use the FSMA, s 404 CRS procedure (see above), which was confined to actionable breaches and provided other safeguards for regulated firms, and hence that it could not circumvent that procedure by purporting to use its more general powers. As a matter of statutory construction ('modestly' para 250 helped by FSMA, s 415A (which provides that any power conferred by any provision of FSMA 'is not limited in any way by any other power' it has under FSMA)), Ouseley J held that the existence of the CRS procedure did not preclude the FSA from acting in the alternative way that it did.

duty arising in respect of the Principles'.[86] There was no further impact on other consequences, in particular on other forms of redress.[87] This had to follow from the statutory provision that enables the FOS to decide redress on the basis of what the ombudsman considers is 'fair and reasonable'. Breaches of Principles alone, to that important extent,[88] may result in liability of firms to their clients irrespective of whether the breach is 'actionable' in law. Moreover, there is also the additional possibility of the regulators requiring firms to compensate for breach of a Principle under FSMA, section 384 or applying to court for a court order to the same effect under FSMA, section 382.

The second argument of the BBA was the more general one that, even if the Principles could give rise to redress, they should not be interpreted as 'augmenting' obligations imposed by the specific (ICOB) rules. Hence, once a firm complied with the specific rules, it could not be held to be in breach of a Principle. The sole role of the Principles was to aid interpretation of ambiguous rules[89] or to apply to cases not specifically covered by the rules. This argument brought into stark focus how the (non-actionable) Principles interrelated with the (actionable) specific rules. This argument also failed: in the words of the FSA Guidance cited above: the specific rules did not exhaust 'the implications of the Principles'. The starting point was not the specific rules, but any relevant 'overarching'[90] Principles that 'stood above' them.[91] The rules 'are but specific applications of [the Principles] to the particular requirements they cover'[92] and hence generally are not exhaustive of the obligations firms are under. It followed that compliance with the rules does not prevent a contravention of a Principle. Compliance with the rules does preclude a successful breach of statutory duty action in the courts, but this nevertheless leaves the possibility of other sanctions for contravention of a Principle, including the award of redress either by FOS or the regulator (under FSMA, section 384) or the court at the instigation of the regulator (under FSMA, section 382).

Hence, the fact that breaches of the Principles were *not* actionable, did not limit their legal impact in other respects, in particular their ability to give rise to redress to firms' clients by other means.

Unfair Relationship in the Event of Compliance

Some borrowers that were (mis-)sold PPI adopted another avenue for obtaining redress: the 'unfair relationship' provisions of the Consumer Credit Act (CCA)

[86] *British Bankers Association*, n 71 above, para 76.

[87] Including, most significantly, that available from FOS.

[88] As noted above, the FOS dealt with numerous PPI complaints.

[89] See *Saville v Central Capital Ltd* [2014] EWCA Civ 337: PRIN 6 and 7 invoked to determine if breach of ICOB 4.3.6(1) caused loss; hypothetical causation question to be asked 'openly and fairly' and not 'in a leading way'.

[90] *British Bankers Association*, n 71 above, para 161.

[91] The metaphors became somewhat mixed. Elsewhere (at para 162) the Principles were described 'as the ever present substrata to which the specific rules are added'.

[92] ibid para 162.

1974.[93] These enable the court to reopen a credit agreement and make a wide variety of orders (including the return of PPI premiums paid) if the court determines that the relationship between the creditor and debtor is 'unfair'. In deciding this question the court must take into account not only the credit agreement itself but also any 'related agreement' (as defined and including point-of-loan PPI)[94] and it must look not only at the terms of those agreements but also the pre- and post-contracting behaviour of the creditor and (sometimes)[95] persons acting 'on behalf of' the creditor. It is clear that the exercise by the creditor of its *rights* may nevertheless lead to 'unfairness'[96] and hence the strict legal position is not determinative of whether an 'unfair relationship' arises.

That litigation gave rise to the question whether compliance with ICOB/ICOBS could give rise to an 'unfair relationship' so as to enable the courts to order returns of the PPI premiums. The issue was eventually[97] settled at Court of Appeal level in *Harrison v Black Horse Ltd*.[98] In 2006 the defendant creditor advanced to the borrowers £60,000, repayable over 23 years, and simultaneously also sold the borrowers an optional PPI policy lasting only five years and costing £10,200,[99] the single premium being added to the loan amount. The creditor (who was not a fiduciary vis-à-vis the borrower) received an undisclosed commission of 87 per cent of the premium from the insurer, its associated company. As regards the undisclosed commission,[100] the sale of the policy had been effected in compliance with the ICOB which, as explained above, in these circumstances did not require disclosure either of the fact of or amount of commission. Tomlinson LJ, confirming the decision of HHJ Waksman QC at first instance,[101] said that if the creditor complied with the ICOB regime 'it is not easy to see from where unfairness in the relationship is to be derived'[102] and concluded that the 'touchstone must ... be the standard imposed by the regulatory authorities ... not resort to a visceral instinct that the relevant conduct

[93] CCA, ss 140A–140D, added on 6 April 2007 by the Consumer Credit Act 2006, s 20 and replacing the 'extortionate credit bargain' provisions (ss 137–140). Section 140D was repealed on 1 April 2014 by FSMA 2000 (Regulated Activities) (Amendment) (No 2) Order 2013, SI 2013/1881, art 20(40), when consumer credit regulation was transferred from the OFT to the FCA (which has corresponding powers under FSMA 2000).

[94] Defined in CCA 1974, s 140C(4). Optional PPI is a 'linked transaction' within CCA 1974, s 19(1)(b) and (c). See also *Link Financial Ltd v North Wilson* [2014] EWHC 252 (Ch): timeshare agreement financed by loan was 'related agreement' and its onerous terms rendered credit relationship 'unfair'.

[95] If CCA 1974, s 140A(1)(c) is being applied: 'any thing done (or not done) by, or on behalf of, the creditor'.

[96] CCA 1974, s 140A(1)(b).

[97] There was considerable county court litigation, much fuelled by claims management companies.

[98] *Harrison*, n 39.

[99] Evidence was given that equivalent stand-alone cover would only have cost £2,083.84 but the lender was only a vendor in relation to those particular single premium policies and hence not obliged under ICOB (and, it was held, under any other rule of law) to advise in relation to other policies available on the open market.

[100] Breaches of ICOB, 4.3.2(1) and 4.3.6(1) were found in relation to the fact that the PPI policy length was shorter than the term of the loan, but there was no evidence that this caused any loss (in particular, as the borrowers knew the length of the policy). Moreover, had breach of ICOB, 4.3.6(2) and 2.3.2(1) (in relation to the commission) been found, HHJ Waksman QC held that the borrower would have failed to recover because again he found no evidence of loss caused.

[101] [2010] EWHC 3152 (QB).

[102] *Harrison*, n 39 above, para 33.

is beyond the Pale'.[103] It would be 'anomalous' to use the discretion under the 'unfair relationship' provisions essentially to require creditors to make disclosures not required by their regulatory regime, which had been devised after extensive consultation and for cogently expressed reasons.[104] Hence this time ICOB was held as essentially exhaustive of the obligations on firms.

Subsequently, all three members of a differently constituted Court of Appeal in *Plevin v Paragon Personal Finance Ltd*[105] questioned the conclusion reached in *Harrison*[106] but felt the matter best left to the Supreme Court.[107] *R (on the application of the British Bankers Association) v Financial Services Authority*[108] was not cited,[109] although it would have drawn attention to the fact that FSMA already (through the FOS jurisdiction) enables recovery of PPI premiums if this is in the opinion of an ombudsman 'fair and reasonable', irrespective of the strict legal position, and hence on the face of it, it would not be so anomalous to interpret the 'unfair relationship' provisions (which also to some extent enable departure from the strict legal position) to reach a similar result. On the other hand, the fact remains that in contrast to the FOS, the courts do have to determine the *legal* position. There is nothing anomalous in having two parallel jurisdictions:[110] an informal ADR process with limited jurisdiction and powers (the FOS) where the matter will be determined on a 'fair and reasonable basis' and a formal court process which determines the strict legal position.

Whilst leaving the narrow issue in *Harrison* (whether non-disclosure of commission rendered the relationship 'unfair') for the Supreme Court, the Court of Appeal in *Plevin* did not regard ICOB as determinative of a different issue that arose in that case.[111] The issue was whether, for the purposes of the unfair relationship provisions,

[103] ibid para 58.

[104] ibid para 41. And see para 59: 'It is telling that in this heavily regulated market no ... obligation [to disclose commission] has been imposed'. And (as Tomlinson LJ also noted at para 62) non-disclosure of commission was not listed amongst the 15 'common failings' in the FSA's Policy Statement of August 2010 (see n 68 above). Such a disclosure obligation has not subsequently been imposed by either ICOBS (which can be amended at by the FCA any time) nor the Payment Protection Insurance Market Investigation Oder 2011 (see n 61 above), but presumably it is expected that the prohibition of the sale of PPI at the same time as the loan will result in the moderation of commission rates by the operation of market forces.

[105] *Plevin*, n 7 above.

[106] Briggs LJ at para 26 did not feel 'any sense of comfort' and 'regarded a visceral instinct ... as a persuasive starting point' in deciding unfairness. Beatson LJ 'share[d] the discomfort expressed' by his brethren (para 80) whilst Moses LJ agreed to follow *Harrison*'s 'dispiriting conclusion' (para 82) 'with reluctance' (para 81).

[107] At the time of writing, an appeal is pending.

[108] *British Bankers Association*, n 71 above.

[109] In that (earlier) case, Ouseley J had noted HHJ Waksman QC's first instance view in *Harrison*, n 101 above, that the common duty of care in tort could not 'go wider' so as to impose liability in cases where ICOB had been compiled with and said he disagreed, although he regarded HHJ Waksman QC's decision that negligence liability was not established as 'obviously right' on the facts.

[110] If the complainant chooses to go to FOS, s/he may choose whether to accept or reject the award: FSMA, s 228(5). The latter option leaves open court proceedings. The former forecloses further court proceedings; the complainant cannot 'top up' the award by commencing a court action after accepting the FOS award: *Clark v In Focus Asset Management & Tax Solutions Ltd* [2014] EWCA Civ 118.

[111] See also *Link Financial Ltd v North Wilson* [2014] EWHC 252 (Ch): compliance with Timeshare Act 1992 was immaterial as that legislation did not regulate the relevant issue (the terms of the timeshare agreement).

a broker who was not an agent (in the legal sense) of the creditor acted 'on behalf of' the creditor for the purpose of making the broker's actions (in breach of ICOB) relevant to the question of whether the creditor-debtor relationship was 'unfair'.[112] ICOB explicitly placed the relevant duties only on the person 'in contact' with the customer: the broker and not the creditor on the facts of that case. It was therefore argued that the creditor should not be responsible for the broker's breaches of ICOB and hence 'on behalf of' should be interpreted narrowly as requiring common law agency so as to render the broker's actions (in that case) irrelevant to the 'unfair relationship' issue. However, although ICOB was the relevant statutory regime, the creditor was a member of two trade associations that issued voluntary codes of conduct: FISA[113] and the FLA.[114] Both codes stated (albeit in rather vague terms) that creditors should monitor persons from whom they derived business. The court held that although ICOB clearly placed the duties it imposed squarely on the shoulders of the broker and not the creditor, 'on behalf of' should be interpreted broadly so that the creditor was nevertheless affected by the broker's breaches, at least to the extent that they could render his relationship with the borrower 'unfair'.[115] And even if 'on behalf of' were to be given its narrow 'agency' meaning, the court further held that ICOB did not 'wholly exonerate' the creditor from a share in responsibility for the actions of brokers from whom it received business as there was a residual obligation on creditors to undertake some monitoring of brokers. The fact that the creditor had subscribed to non-statutory codes that recognised that creditors were to monitor brokers supported this conclusion. The court emphasised that 'it was no part of the purpose' of the unfair relationship jurisdiction

> to limit the court's purview of conduct to that for which the creditor incurred some legal liability to the debtor, whether under the general law, or by means of statutory recourse under an enforceable regulatory code such as ICOB.[116]

CONCLUSION

The problem of accommodating regulatory regimes within the established common framework is not a new one. But the problem becomes more difficult when these regimes explicitly give rise to parallel remedies, especially actionably for their breach. An issue that has arisen in the context of PPI litigation is whether such explicit provision exhausts the legal consequences so that compliance with the regime assures protection from liability or whether the courts have residual discretion in effect to recognise additional obligations and hence additional liabilities. If the regulatory regime seems comprehensive and has been preceded by a process during which its

[112] Under CCA 1974, s 140A(1)(c).

[113] The Finance Industry Standards Association.

[114] The Finance and Leasing Association.

[115] The phrase 'on behalf of' is used extensively in the CCA 1974 (eg ss 49(2)(a), 56(3)(b), 57(3)(b), 61(1)(a), 67(1), 69(6)(b), 70(1)(c), 71(3), 77(1), 77A(2B), 78(1), (7B), 79(1), 102(1)(b), 103(1)(b), 105(4), 107(1)(c), 108(1)(c), 109(1)(c), 164, 185(1)(b), (6), 189(1) and 191(1)) and it seems clear that in those provisions it has its usual 'agency' meaning.

[116] Per Briggs LJ at para 54.

rationale has been consulted on and ultimately articulated with some precision, then in principle the courts should be reluctant to upset the balance stuck by the regulators and impose additional liabilities. This is especially so when regulated firms go to great lengths (and expense) to organise their affairs so as comply with the regime in the expectation that this will protect them from liability for breach.

However, it is also clear that actionability or non-actionability should not be the only relevant consideration. Even if there is an explicit decision not to impose the actionability sanction for breach of certain provisions, this does not mean that all further legal consequences of breach are necessarily foreclosed. This is evident from FSMA itself and is demonstrated in the BBA case.[117] Since the FOS (established under FSMA) can impose liability in circumstances where none arises at common law (if the ombudsman is of the opinion that such a result is 'fair and reasonable') then it must follow that just because FSMA actionability in a court of law does not arise, this cannot mean that the regulator cannot require the regulated to compensate customers in such cases. Moreover, if statutory provision (such as the 'unfair relationship' provisions in the CCA 1974) requires the courts to look beyond the strict legal rights and obligations in determining if the relationship is 'unfair', then clearly unfairness may arise even if there has been compliance with legal obligations. Hence, although there is an understandable reluctance in a court of law to be guided by 'visceral instinct', such instinct does have some relevance when the legislature itself has provided for mechanisms (such as the FOS jurisdiction or the 'unfair relationship' provisions) that can impose obligations (or, put more politically attractively, that create rights) going beyond the clear obligations that the courts generally recognise. But a court of law is still a very different dispute resolution forum to the FOS. Ultimately it must apply and develop legal rules and cannot (even when required by legislation to determine what is 'unfair') abandon its decision-making entirely to 'visceral instincts' alone. Lessons can be learnt from the history of the 'unfair prejudice' jurisprudence[118] where ultimately the House of Lords (as it then was) noted that a balance had to be struck between 'the breadth of the discretion given to the court and the principle of legal certainty'[119] and applied well established equitable principles. Those equitable principles may clearly support the imposition of obligations beyond those explicitly imposed by a regulatory regime.

[117] *British Bankers Association*, n 71 above.

[118] Petitions under Companies Act 2006, s 994 *et seq* and its predecessors.

[119] *O'Neill v Phillips* [1999] 1 WLR 1092, 1099 (per Lord Hoffmann).

5

Some Thoughts on Consumer Law Reform: Consolidation, Codification or a Restatement?

CHRISTIAN TWIGG-FLESNER

INTRODUCTION

IN THIS ESSAY, I would like to offer some thoughts on the process of law reform in the context of consumer law. Hugh Beale has, of course, written widely on this, and consumer law reform projects were also part of his remit during his time as a Law Commissioner. The primary focus of this chapter is on the reform of domestic consumer law within the United Kingdom.

Consumer law is a strange area of law, not least because it is incredibly complex. Whilst this is unlikely to trouble lawyers greatly, it does have implications for those who are directly affected by the law, ie both consumers and traders. Consumers are often unsure about what their rights are if they have encountered a problem, and it is not easy for them to discover these, should they make an effort to investigate their legal position. Similarly, traders often find it difficult to understand exactly what they are required to do for the same reason, which can mean that they inadvertently fail to honour the rights their customers have. Of course, both consumers and traders can seek legal advice, but this is rarely going to provide the clarity that is needed. There are various sources of advice in place, but complete and coherent advice can rarely be given in a quick answer because of the law's complexity. This complexity has been exacerbated by the adoption of consumer law in response to specific problems, combined with a similarly piecemeal evolution of consumer law at the European level. Indeed, the development of domestic and EU consumer law are now so closely intertwined that the resulting picture is a very complex one.

It is therefore unsurprising that there have been initiatives to reform and modernise consumer law both at the domestic and European levels. At the domestic level, following a call for evidence in 2008,[1] a White Paper was published in 2009[2] which gave a commitment to a thorough review of domestic consumer law. Following the

[1] Department for Business, Enterprise and Regulatory Reform, *Consumer Law Review: Call for Evidence* (Consumer White Paper, 08/624, 2008).

[2] HM Government, *A Better Deal for Consumers: Delivering Real Help Now and Change for the Future*, Cm 7669 (2009).

change of government in 2010, further policy papers followed setting out the new government's commitment to consumers,[3] which eventually resulted in a lengthy consultation document on a wide-ranging reform of domestic consumer law.[4] This culminated in the publication of the Draft Consumer Rights Bill in June 2013, and the introduction of the Bill into Parliament on 23 January 2014.

This flurry of activity at the domestic level was, in part, triggered by developments at the EU level. Over a 20-year period, the EU had adopted a number of Directives on aspects of consumer law, particularly consumer contract law. Initially, these all followed the so-called 'minimum harmonisation' approach, which left Member States free to introduce or maintain provisions in the field covered by a Directive which granted consumers a higher level of protection. More recent Directives shifted towards 'full' or 'maximum' harmonisation, essentially removing the discretion for Member States to have more protective domestic laws in the area, and this became the stated policy of the European Commission.[5] In 2005, it launched a process for reviewing the consumer *acquis*,[6] aiming to improve the quality of existing legislation whilst, at the same time, moving towards full harmonisation in those areas where there had previously only been minimum harmonisation. This process commenced with a research study to analyse how eight consumer law Directives were implemented into the domestic laws of the then 27 EU Member States. One of the conclusions of this study was that there continued to be significant variations between domestic consumer laws post-harmonisation.[7] Following on from this study, the Commission issued a *Green Paper on the Review of the Consumer Acquis* in February 2007.[8] This, in turn, led to the proposal for a Directive on Consumer Rights in October 2008.[9] This proposal would have introduced full harmonisation in respect of the areas it covered. It would have brought together the four existing Directives on doorstep selling, distance selling, unfair terms and consumer sales in one new measure, together with additional rules on delivery and risk. The academic debate both about the substantive changes to existing law and the policy shift towards full harmonisation was intense,[10] with few scholars supportive of the shift towards full harmonisation.[11] At best, it was suggested that there could be selective,

[3] Department for Business, Innovation and Skills, *Consumer Empowerment Strategy: Better Choices, Better Deals—Consumers Powering Growth* (Policy Paper, 11/749, 2011).

[4] Department for Business, Innovation and Skills, *Enhancing Consumer Confidence by Clarifying Consumer Law: Consultation on the Supply of Goods, Services and Digital Content* (Consultation Paper, 12/937, 2012).

[5] European Commission, *EU Consumer Policy Strategy 2007–2013*, COM(2007)99 final, p 7.

[6] See generally Marco Loos, *Review of the European Consumer Acquis* (Munich, Sellier, 2008).

[7] Published as Hans Schulte-Nölke, Christian Twigg-Flesner and Martin Ebers, *EU Consumer Law Compendium* (Munich, Sellier, 2008).

[8] European Commission, *Green Paper on the Review of the Consumer Acquis*, COM(2006)744 final.

[9] European Commission, Proposal for a Directive of the European Parliament and of the Council on consumer rights, COM(2008)614 final.

[10] See, eg Michael Faure, 'Towards Maximum Harmonization of Consumer Contract Law?!?' (2008) 15 *Maastricht Journal* 433; Peter Rott, and Evelyne Terryn, 'The Proposal for a Directive on Consumer Rights: No Single Set of Rules' (2009) 17 *Zeitschrift für Europäisches Privatrecht* 456.

[11] See, eg Ewoud Hondius, 'The Proposal for a European Directive on Consumer Rights: A Step Forward' (2010) 18 *European Review of Private Law* 103.

or targeted, full harmonisation of a few aspects.[12] After a turbulent progress through the legislative stages, political agreement on a Consumer Rights Directive was reached in June 2011. The final Directive[13] leaves the Directives on unfair contract terms and consumer sales untouched, and primarily standardises precontractual information duties and the right of withdrawal in 'off-premises' and distance' contracts.

In light of what once were quite ambitious plans by the EU to modernise the legislation adopted at the European level, the UK government committed to using the obligation of having to implement the Consumer Rights Directive as a vehicle for undertaking quite an extensive reform process, which has culminated in the introduction of the Consumer Rights Bill (although ironically, the Directive itself was implemented through separate regulations).[14]

Set against this context of intense activity to reform and modernise consumer law, this essay will take a step back and consider why the reform of consumer law has become a necessity, what the problems were (and to some extent still are and will continue to be in the future), and how reform could best have been achieved. This discussion will commence by considering the objectives of law reform in broad terms, before examining the particular difficulties that exist with the current state of UK consumer law.

OBJECTIVES OF LAW REFORM

The reasons for undertaking any law reform project might be quite diverse. Some will be the result of a particular policy decision significantly to change the law in a particular area (eg the extensive reforms in the field of company law leading to the Companies Act 2006), whereas others might be to simplify an area of law which has become too complex or where there is such an amount of conflicting case-law that it is difficult to work out exactly what the legal position is. Whatever the initial motivation for law reform might be, there are a number of objectives that could be pursued, as well several possible approaches to give effect to these objectives.

Simplification: simplification of the law may become necessary for two main reasons. First, the requirements imposed by the law to achieve a particular outcome may be regarded as too onerous and a simper procedure to achieve the same outcome could be established. This type of simplification may be termed 'substantive simplification' because the substance of the legal rules in question is amended so as to remove complexities which have become otiose. There are several possible reasons as to how such complexities might arise; for example, the law might initially have been drafted at a time when it was practically necessary to follow certain steps, but since then, technological advances such as the possibility to use electronic means might make it possible to have a simpler procedure in place (eg for the

[12] See, eg Hans-W Micklitz and Norbert Reich, 'Crónica de una muerte annunciada: The Commission Proposal for a "Directive on Consumer Rights"' (2009) 46 *Common Market Law Review* 471.

[13] Council Directive 2011/83/EU of 25 October 2011 on Consumer Rights [2011] OJ L304/64.

[14] Consumer Contracts (Information, Cancellation and Additional Charges) Regulations 2013, SI 2013/3134 (in force as of 13 June 2014).

registration of charges or other securities). A further reason might be that legislation has repeatedly been amended and that as a result, what was once a straightforward procedure has become too complicated. The latter, in particular, is an issue which has affected consumer law, as will be outlined below. Furthermore, the body of case-law which has emerged to interpret particular statutory provisions may have created complexity, eg by adopting an interpretation of a section which might not be immediately apparent from the literal wording of the section.[15]

Secondly, whilst the substance of the law itself might not be problematic (at least to those trained in law), the way the law is presented might be unnecessarily complex. Thus, a statute may be drafted in such a way that it becomes quite cumbersome easily to identify what exactly the law requires in a particular situation, or issues may be divided between different statutes. Also, the amendment of legislation could result in unwieldy statutes. Again, this is something which has affected domestic consumer law in several areas.

Ensuring coherence and consistency: allied with the idea of simplification, particularly in its substantive sense, is the objective of ensuring that the law is coherent and consistent. An area of law which has developed over time (whether through case-law or piecemeal legislation) may suffer from a lack of internal logic, with the effect that the different aspects of this area of law do not fit well together. Similar situations might be treated differently without there being a particular reason for this. In the field of consumer law, this has been particularly obvious in the way different transactions for the supply of goods were dealt with in separate statutes, with some common provisions (such as the implied terms regarding the quality and fitness of goods supplied), but some variations (eg the remedies available for breach).

Consolidation: simplification and making the law more coherent are objectives which can be attained in various ways. With a doctrine developed by the common law courts, the Supreme Court might be given, and take, the opportunity to review a complex body of case-law and provide a judicial restatement of the law. Legislation can be amended to ensure that provisions are coherent and consistent. However, in the case of an area of law which is governed heavily by statutes (such as consumer law) which have had to be amended for a variety of reasons (eg to respond to new issues identified nationally as well as the obligation to comply with EU law), in order to achieve the requisite levels of coherence and consistency, as well as simplification, it might be appropriate to consolidate separate pieces of legislation in one single new measure to ensure that matters which should be treated in the same way are all subject to one set of legal rules. Such an approach can also be useful to ensure that definitions used for key terms (such as the definition of 'consumer') are consistent.

Codification: any mention of the word 'codification' in the context of English/UK law will seem surprising, because unlike the civil law world, the idea of codification is still treated with some scepticism because it clashes with the problem-focused

[15] For example, Sale of Goods Act 1979, s 25 on an exception to the *nemo dat* principle has been interpreted by the courts in *Newtons of Wembley Ltd v Willliams* [1965] 1 QB 560 and *National Employers Mutual General Insurance Association Ltd v Jones* [1988] 2 All ER 425 (HL) in such a way that its literal meaning has been significantly restricted.

approach of the common law.[16] Nevertheless, in certain areas of law, particularly those which have a regulatory character, the idea of codification is perhaps not as far-fetched as it may seem. Moreover, the field of commercial law is one where there have been some instances of codifications of some areas, although thus far, the calls for a wider codification of commercial law[17] have gone unheeded.

Codification would go beyond simply consolidating and simplifying existing laws in one new single Act, and would be altogether more ambitious. In its broadest sense, it would result in a code which would include all the relevant provisions from existing legislation, but combine this, where appropriate, with common law rules which have not been reflected in legislation so far. For example, for a consumer contract, it would include all the rules required for the formation of a contract, performance, discharge, remedies and relevant vitiating factors. It would provide a single measure which would absorb both prior legislation and common law.

This brief discussion has sought to set out, in general terms, the objectives which might be pursued by law reform in any given area. The focus for the remainder of this chapter is on the potential reform of UK consumer law. Although a number of existing problems were already noted in passing above, the next section will set out in a little more detail why there is a real need to reform consumer law in the United Kingdom.

A BRIEF SKETCH OF CONSUMER LAW AND THE NEED FOR REFORM

It is first necessary to provide a brief overview of the various components of UK consumer law to appreciate its inherent complexity. From the outset, it has to be borne in mind that consumer law today is not purely a matter for domestic law; rather, it is a strange amalgam of domestic law and European Union law. It is well known that the European Union has, over the last three decades or so, adopted a string of Directives dealing with aspects of consumer law. In addition to these, there is a small body of case-law by the European Court of Justice (CJEU) on the interpretation of these Directives. These Directives take effect through national legislation adopted for this purpose. More recently, use has been made of directly applicable Regulations in some areas.

UK consumer law is a mixture of private law rules, administrative/regulatory provisions, as well as some criminal law rules. Taking the private law elements first, we have the cases and legislation in the areas of both contract and tort law applicable to all circumstances. One might refer to this as the 'general private law' because it is not confined to specific circumstances such as consumer transactions. Thus, in the field of tort law, general principles of negligence liability can be relied on by consumers in certain circumstances to seek redress, eg if they have suffered an injury.[18] Contract law principles govern the formation, performance and

[16] For an overview, see Reinhard Zimmermann, 'Codification' (2012) 8 *European Review of Contract Law* 367.

[17] Roy Goode, 'Removing the Obstacles to Commercial Law Reform' (2007) 123 *Law Quarterly Review* 602.

[18] *Donoghue v Stevenson* [1932] AC 562.

discharge of all contracts, and there is generally no distinction between consumer and non-consumer contracts in the case-law. Occasionally, one can identify circumstances where the application of particular principles may have been influenced by the fact that the contract in question could be described as a 'consumer contract',[19] but there is no separate system of consumer contract law. In addition, many of the statutes in the contract law field are of general application and are not restricted to consumer contracts. However, in some instances, it is possible to identify variations or particular provisions specifically aimed at consumer contracts. For example, the Unfair Contract Terms Act (UCTA) 1977 provides stricter controls over certain types of term in contracts where one party is 'dealing as a consumer'.[20]

Moreover, there are a number of statutory instruments dealing specifically with consumer contracts which were adopted in order to implement EU Directives. These statutory instruments either operate as free-standing measures, or amend existing legislation. Thus, alongside UCTA, the Unfair Terms in Consumer Contracts Regulations 1999, SI 1999/2083 (implementing Directive 93/13/EEC) provide greater scope for controlling unfair terms in consumer contracts. The existence of two parallel regimes for the control over contract terms, applying different tests, was long regarded as problematic, and one of the projects directed by Hugh Beale at the Law Commission was to recommend a consolidation of the two measures.[21] The proposals also included special provisions for business-to-business contracts and for contracts involving small and medium-sized enterprises, but these particular proposals were not implemented. In 2012, the Law Commission was asked to review its proposals for consumer contracts in light of case-law developments since 2005,[22] and its revised recommendations fed into the Consumer Rights Bill 2014.

The Sale and Supply of Goods to Consumers Regulations 2002, which implement the Consumer Sales Directive (99/44/EC) amended existing legislation in this area, notably the Sale of Goods Act 1979.[23] Whilst the requirement in article 2 of the Directive that goods must be 'in conformity with the contract' was regarded as already being covered by the terms implied by sections 13 and 14 of the Sale of Goods Act,[24] the performance-focused remedies in article 3 of the Directive were introduced as a new Part 5A into the Act. However, instead of limiting consumer remedies to those in Part 5A, it was decided at the time that the existing right to reject goods and terminate the contract should be retained, which meant that consumer remedies became incredibly complex. This matter was noted in a government

[19] *cf* John Adams and Roger Brownsword, *Understanding Contract Law*, 5th edn (London, Sweet & Maxwell, 2007).

[20] Defined in UCTA 1977, s 12 and related case-law: *R&B Customs Brokers Co Ltd v United Dominion Trust Ltd* [1988] 1 WLR 321 and *Feldaroll Foundry plc v Hermes Leasing (London) Ltd* [2004] EWCA Civ 747.

[21] Law Commission, *Unfair Terms in Contracts* (Law Com No 292, 2005).

[22] Law Commission, *Unfair Terms in Consumer Contracts: Advice to the Department for Business, Innovation and Skills* (Law Com, 2013).

[23] See generally, Robert Bradgate and Christian Twigg-Flesner, *Blackstone's Guide to Consumer Sales and Associated Guarantees* (Oxford University Press, 2003).

[24] Although an amendment to reflect the special emphasis on public statements in the Directive was made by adding s 14(2D)–(2F) to supplement the 'satisfactory quality' test.

review,[25] and once again, the Law Commission was asked to consider reform of this aspect of consumer law.[26]

Moreover, the process of contract formation for door-step and distance selling contracts is regulated in two separate statutory instruments[27] implementing the corresponding EU Directives, although both will be replaced with new regulations which took effect in June 2014.[28]

Finally, in the area of tort law, Part I of the Consumer Protection Act 1985 implements the EU Directive on Product Liability (85/374/EEC) and introduces a strict liability system for circumstances where defective products cause personal injury or damage. This supplements the common law's negligence liability scheme.

To this, one needs to add the body of case-law both from domestic courts and the CJEU which interpret these measures, although there are not that many cases coming through the domestic courts.[29]

In addition to legislation and case-law in the private law field, consumer law also includes important administrative law or regulatory provisions, again derived partly from domestic and partly from EU law. Historically, the key measure in this respect was the Trade Descriptions Act 1968, but this has now largely been replaced by the Consumer Protection from Unfair Trading Regulations 2008, SI 2008/1277, which in turn implement the Directive on Unfair Commercial Practices (Directive 2005/29/EC (UCPD)). In addition, there are some specific measures dealing with pricing, and a vast array of regulations dealing with the composition of products and labelling. Often, these regulatory measures are supplemented by criminal law provisions, which allow for their enforcement not only through administrative sanctions such as injunctions, but also through the prosecution particularly of persistent infringements of the relevant consumer law rules.[30]

As this short sketch demonstrates, consumer law consists of consumer-specific measures and those of general application, statute and case-law, and domestic and EU law. This is obviously not something that is unique to consumer law, but it seems that consumer law is a particularly extreme example of how so many different sources of law are put together to make up the full picture of this area of law. However, of itself, this might not be too much of a problem, provided that this amalgam of rules is internally consistent and non-contradictory. Unfortunately, one of the major deficiencies of UK consumer law is that it lacks coherence at times, and that there are quite illogical distinctions being drawn between different types of transactions.

[25] Neil Davidson, *Davidson Review: Implementation of EU Legislation* (London, HMSO, 2006).

[26] Law Commission, *Consumer Remedies for Faulty Goods* (Law Com No 317, 2009).

[27] Cancellation of Contracts Made in a Consumer's Home or Place of Work etc Regulations 2008, SI 2008/1816 and Consumer Protection (Distance Selling) Regulations 2000, SI 2000/2334, respectively.

[28] Consumer Contracts (Information, Cancellation and Additional Charges) Regulations 2013, SI 2013/3134.

[29] A rare exception being *Robertson v Swift*, a case on the Cancellation of Contracts Made in a Consumer's Home or Place of Work etc Regulations 2008, SI 2008/1816, which was heard by the Supreme Court in March 2014 (on appeal from [2012] EWCA Civ 1794).

[30] See, eg the provisions in Pt 3 of the Consumer Protection from Unfair Trading Regulations 2008, SI 2008/1277.

This sketch would not be complete without a few observations on the question of enforcement. One interesting feature of UK consumer law appears to be that only a small number of consumers will consider taking their claims to court. Out of those that do, almost all cases are dealt with in the county court on the small claims track, and hardly any cases make it to the High Court or beyond. This raises two matters of concern: (i) it becomes more difficult to figure out how the law works 'in action', ie how the courts interpret and apply the law; and (ii) more significantly, the vast majority of consumers will not involve the legal process at all when dealing with disputes.

The second issue is of relevance to this essay. If it is assumed that consumers generally do not involve the formal legal process when seeking redress, then that raises questions about the extent to which they are nonetheless able to enforce their legal rights. Research evidence suggests that most consumers will attempt to resolve any problems informally, and many will do so without necessarily seeking advice.[31] Those that do seek advice can obtain this from solicitors, as well as dedicated consumer advice services. However, the complexity and incoherence of consumer law can make it quite difficult to provide consumers with advice which is easy for them to understand and to act upon. In the drive to reform consumer law, it is crucial that sight is not lost of the fact that consumers largely resolve disputes on an informal, self-help, basis, and if their legal rights are to be utilised effectively, reform should facilitate this informal approach.

In addition to the factors influencing law reform outlined above, the nature of consumer disputes requires the addition of a further objective, and that is that law reform should ensure that an otherwise complex area of law is as accessible as possible to both users (consumers and traders) and advisers, to ensure that consumer rights are not just there on paper but have some bite and are utilised.

CONSUMER LAW REFORM IN THE UNITED KINGDOM: ANOTHER MISSED OPPORTUNITY?

The previous section sought to outline some of the key problems with UK consumer law. The first is its complexity, and consequent inaccessibility to anyone without a reasonable amount of expert knowledge. The second is the lack of coherence and the fact that there are inconsistencies in the law which seem difficult to justify. A related issue is that consumers faced with a particular problem will often only seek redress informally and will not obtain legal advice; most of those that do will still not pursue their claim through the courts. This might mean that many consumers are unable to enforce the rights given to them.

As noted, at the domestic level, the Department for Business, Innovation and Skills (BIS) published a White Paper in 2009 in which it promised to consider improvements to consumer law. As well as asking the Law Commission to consider improvements in particular areas of consumer law (unfair terms, remedies for faulty goods and misrepresentation), it also commissioned an academic research report

[31] See, eg Hazel Genn, *Paths to Justice* (Oxford, Hart Publishing, 1999).

focusing on the need for and feasibility of consolidation and simplification of UK consumer law.[32] The report recommended bringing together as many of the current statutes and statutory instruments as possible in one place and to consider removing as many as possible of the inconsistencies that currently exist. The overall purpose of this exercise would have been to simplify the law to make it easier for both consumers and traders to understand.

BIS accepted that consolidation and simplification was badly needed, although consolidation even as recommended in the academic report would only have gone so far in improving the state of UK consumer law. Whilst many of the consumer-specific measures that have been adopted in recent years through a variety of statutory instruments and primary legislation can be brought together in one new measure, this would fall short of a full codification of consumer law, as the rules of general contract and tort law (ie the common law) are not included in this exercise. So whilst an exercise in consolidation and simplification can remove many inconsistencies and some of the complexity of the law, thereby making the law more accessible, it would still not provide a complete picture of the law as it affects consumers.

The 2009 White Paper was followed by several further consultation documents and policy statements, before a Draft Consumer Rights Bill was presented in June 2013. The draft Consumer Rights Bill commenced its parliamentary journey in early 2014 and it is expected that it will be enacted by the end of 2014.[33] There are a number of things to note about this Bill. Most significantly, it falls a long way short of providing a full consolidation of even the main pieces of legislation which relate to consumer transactions. Thus, as already noted in the introduction, the Consumer Rights Directive (2011/83/EU) has already been implemented through separate free-standing regulations, and there is no indication that those provisions will become part of the Bill before it completes its legislative stages. But there are other concerns about this Bill in so far as it is presented as an exercise in consolidation and simplification, because whilst it does provide some simplification of the law, particularly with regard to the quality requirements of goods supplied to a consumer and the corresponding remedies, there are many aspects not included in this Bill. On the other hand, there are new provisions dealing with aspects which have not been subject to specific domestic rules, notably chapter 4 of Part 1 which deals with the supply of digital content. Crucially, this part mirrors the provisions relating to goods as much as possible, thereby maintaining the appropriate and necessary level of coherence.

The Bill itself is divided into three parts.[34] The first deals with some aspects of consumer contracts regarding the supply of goods, services and digital content. In essence, this brings together the implied terms regarding the quality and fitness of goods previously found in three separate Acts into one place. This is simplification and consolidation at its most basic and hardly revolutionary. There are also common provisions on remedies which apply the same set of remedies to all types of supply transactions with appropriate modification to allow for the type of contract

[32] Geraint Howells and Christian Twigg-Flesner (eds), *Consolidation and Simplification of UK Consumer Law* (London, BIS, 2010).

[33] At the time of writing, the Bill had passed its House of Commons stages and been introduced in the House of Lords.

[34] The following will only be a brief sketch, rather than a detailed analysis of the Bill.

in question (the right to a refund needs to be applied in different ways when it comes to contracts of sale and contracts of hire, for example). It is disappointing, however, that the recommendations made by the Law Commission have not been implemented in their entirety; greater simplification and coherence could have been achieved by adopting the analysis in the Law Commission's report about the distinct stages involved in exercising the right to reject the goods and the right to terminate the contract as they exist under the Sale of Goods Act 1979. In essence, the core of the Law Commission's approach was to say that a consumer who has bought goods which fall short of the statutory quality and fitness requirements has the right to reject the goods, which then opens up the remedies of repair, replacement or termination of the contract for a full refund of the purchase price as the three main options. In the Bill, the right to reject has been conflated with the right to terminate the contract for a refund, which leaves the law in a more complex and less coherent state than would be desirable, even if the section on remedies is a significant improvement compared to the state of the Sale of Goods Act 1979 after the implementation of the Consumer Sales Directive (99/44/EC).

The section on digital content is new and takes a similar approach to quality obligations and remedies as the section on goods. With regard to services, the basic standard of requiring a service to be performed with reasonable care and skill is retained, although new remedies are introduced—again, taking the remedies for the supply of goods as a template.

The Bill is a significant step forward in terms of simplification, consolidation and creating a more coherent law on the supply of goods, services and digital content, but so much more could have been done. For example, there are no provisions dealing with the transfer of 'ownership' (a new term introduced in the Bill but defined as corresponding to the notion of 'property' familiar from the Sale of Goods Act), and the Bill cross-refers to the archaic provisions in sections 16–18 of the Sale of Goods Act.

Part 2 is a further instance of simplification and consolidation, this time with regard to the rules on unfair terms in consumer contracts. It will remove the split between the Unfair Contract Terms Act 1977 and the Unfair Terms in Consumer Contracts Regulations 1999, and introduce a single set of rules.

Part 3 is headed 'Miscellaneous and General' and contains only a few sections. The substance of this Part can be found in the schedules, with improved provisions for the enforcement of consumer law, new measures allowing for collective redress ('enhanced consumer measures') and provisions providing for private actions in competition law.

Overall, the Bill does provide a degree of simplification, greater coherence and partial consolidation of consumer law, and will certainly improve the consumer law landscape. However, it could easily have gone further, particularly with regard to consolidating the main consumer law measures now in force. As already noted, the Consumer Contracts (Information, Cancellation and Additional Charges) Regulations 2013, SI 2013/3134, remain separate from the Bill (ironically so as the Regulations implement the Consumer Rights Directive) and important provisions dealing with information and the right to cancel distance and off-premises contracts are not part of the Bill. Moreover, the Consumer Protection from Unfair Trading Regulations 2008, which implement the EU's Directive on Unfair Commercial Practices (2005/29/

EU) and deal with the regulation of marketing and general trader behaviour at all stages of a consumer transaction also remain separate. Indeed, the 2008 Regulations will be amended with effect from 1 October 2014 to give individual consumers the right to 'unwind' a contract entered into as a result of an unfair commercial practice, or to be given a discount on the price paid. The Consumer Protection (Amendment) Regulations 2014[35] will do just that: 'amend' existing legislation by inserting new provisions into existing regulations. As the purpose of these regulations is to introduce new rights for consumers, it seems surprising, to say the least, that these were not introduced as part of the Consumer Rights Bill, and that the 2008 Regulations together with these new provisions are not a separate part in the Bill.[36] Whilst the introduction of the 2013 regulations might just about be understandable in view of the obligation under EU law to ensure the timely implementation of the Consumer Rights Directive, the same imperative does not apply to the 2014 Regulations as these deal with a matter on which there is no EU law at present. It runs against the idea of providing a simplified and more coherent consumer law to have three major measures being introduced in parallel, rather than in one Act of Parliament.

Looking beyond the changes to the law to be made by the Bill and the 2013 and 2014 Regulations, there are other major measures which are not included in this consolidation exercise. The obvious example is the Consumer Protection Act 1987, in particular Part I dealing with product liability. This Part contains key consumer rights, with a body of domestic and EU case-law now to be taken into account. Admittedly, the Product Liability Directive (85/374/EEC) was not included in the review of the consumer *acquis* and so it is perhaps excusable that the Consumer Protection Act was not taken into account as part of the domestic simplification and consolidation exercise; it is nevertheless regrettable that this has not happened.

A RESTATEMENT OF CONSUMER LAW?

The discussion so far has concentrated on the reform of the primary sources of consumer law, and has noted the practical difficulties which have been encountered as part of this process. As the volume of case-law from the CJEU continues to increase, the need to monitor and, if necessary, review consumer legislation to ensure it complies with EU law is an ever-pressing issue. In addition, there is the need to take into account the occasional ruling from the higher courts within the United Kingdom if these affect the interpretation of domestic law in a significant way. There are two main reasons for this need to keep the legislation under review: the first is to ensure that coherence and consistency is maintained in the light of relevant court rulings. That of itself might not be a sufficiently strong imperative, of course, because this is an issue which affects any area of law governed by legislation.

35 Consumer Protection (Amendment) Regulations 2014, SI 2014/870.

36 Even more ironically, the Consumer Protection (Amendment) Regulations 2014 are to come into force 'immediately before the coming into force of the Consumer Contracts (Information, Cancellation and Additional Charges) Regulations 2013'. The reason for this is that reg 9 of the 2014 Regulations *amends* the 2013 Regulations.

But the second reason might be more important: it is a trite observation that there is a very small amount of court action compared to the probable volume of instances where consumers have encountered a problem for which relevant legislation provides redress. Often, the value of the claim does not justify taking legal advice, nor does it seem that consumers are willing to risk court action without knowledge of the legal position. There are, of course, various sources of advice available, but the complexity of consumer law and its rather fast pace of evolution make it difficult for advisers to stay on top of developments.

So in addition to ensuring consumer law is simplified and made more coherent, something else is needed which will make the law more accessible to those directly affected by it, ie consumers, traders and those involved in advising consumers, in particular. A simplified law might go some way towards this, but even then, it will be difficult for most consumers to work out what their legal rights are simply by considering the relevant legislation. Nevertheless, law reform is an opportunity to attempt to make the law more accessible or user-friendly—if not for consumers and traders themselves, than at least to those who are going to provide advice and guidance to consumers and/or traders. This point was made by Hugh Beale:

> I do not believe it is realistic to expect that we can ever draft provisions that will be readily understandable to even the majority of consumers themselves. I think it would be realistic to aim at making it understandable to consumer advisors, many of whom are not legally qualified, and business people with some knowledge of contracting.[37]

Beale goes on to explain that any legislation will invariably have to deal with complex matters, which makes it largely impossible to provide a comprehensive statute which explains the full context in which any given provision operates. He suggests that use could be made of information technology to provide the text of the legislation with hyperlinks to related legislation and to commentaries.[38] Alternatively, there could be an official commentary, providing detailed explanations of the statute together with examples which illustrate how the law might operate in practice. But whilst this might assist in making consumer legislation more accessible, it would not do the same for the common law rules. Beale therefore concludes that:

> I have often wondered whether it would help consumer advisors and business people if we could produce an official, or at least semi-official code of consumer law that would include not only the legislative provisions, but also a restatement of the common law rules, using, needless to say, simple language and structures. This would not necessarily have to be in the form of legislation. I suspect that a semi-official restatement vetted by, say, a group of judges or by the Law Commission, would be accepted as 'the law' in almost all cases. Nor would it have to be enormously detailed. I have in mind something resembling the draft code of contract law written years ago for the Law Commissions by McGregor, or the Principles of European Contract Law.[39]

[37] Hugh Beale, 'The Draft Directive on Consumer Rights and UK Consumer Law: Where Now?' in Geraint Howells and Reiner Schulze (eds), *Modernising and Harmonising Consumer Contract Law* (Munich, Sellier, 2008) 299.

[38] ibid 300.

[39] ibid 302. The 'McGregor Code' was published as Harvey McGregor, *Contract Code, Drawn Up on behalf of the English Law Commission* (Milan, Giuffrè, 1993).

Although Beale uses the word 'code' here, he does not actually envisage the formal codification of consumer law. Rather, he is focusing on the possibility of utilising the 'restatement approach' for consumer law to make this area of law more accessible. The inspiration for this approach comes from the Restatements drafted by the American Law Institute in the United States (ALI), the UNIDROIT Principles of International Commercial Contracts, as well as the Principles of European Contract Law (PECL) and their successor, the Draft Common Frame of Reference (DCFR), and the Principles of Existing EU Contract Law (*Acquis* Principles).

The origins of the 'restatement' idea are with the American Law Institute, founded in 1923. In its Handbook for ALI reporters the notion of a 'restatement' is explained as follows:

> Restatements are addressed to courts and others applying existing law. Restatements aim at clear formulations of common law and its statutory elements or variations and reflect the law as it presently stands or might plausibly be stated by a court. Restatement blackletter formulations assume the stance of describing the law as it is.[40]

The crucial aspect of this description is that a restatement is concerned with providing an account of the law in its current state, and not to offer any suggestions for law reform or other improvement. It is intended to assist those charged with the task of applying existing law. Although its appearance is not dissimilar to a statute (or even a code), the intention of a restatement is to present the law in such a way as to 'reflect the flexibility and capacity for development and growth of the common law'.[41] Furthermore, although the focus is primarily on the common law, ie decisions by the courts, the restatements developed by the ALI can also take into account statutes, and provisions from such statutes can become part of a restatement alongside rules taken from the common law.[42] In short, therefore, a restatement can bring together in one place an exposition of the law as it stands, based on common law and relevant statutory provisions.

The fact that statutes are taken into account is important because much of consumer law is found in legislation, with some relevant case law both from the domestic courts and the CJEU. This complexity of sources makes the idea of a restatement rather appealing, not least because it will make the task of applying the law somewhat easier.

Prima facie, the idea of a restatement of some kind which expresses the entirety of consumer law, both statutes and cases, in one place in a more accessible manner sounds appealing. However, this idea merits further consideration. A number of questions would have to be considered. First, there is the fundamental issue as to whether such a 'restatement' would be feasible, ie can it actually be done? Secondly, assuming that the answer to the first question is positive, it would then have to be considered who might be best placed to produce such a restatement. Answering this question requires consideration of the likely form such a restatement might take.

[40] American Law Institute, *Capturing the Voice of the American Law Institute: A Handbook for ALI Reporters and Those that Review Their Work* (Philadelphia, PA, ALI, 2005) 4, available at www.ali.org/doc/StyleManual.pdf.

[41] ibid 5.

[42] See the discussion in American Law Institute, *Capturing the Voice*, n 40 above, 7–10.

Beale talks of a semi-official restatement which would 'not necessarily' have to be in the form of legislation. A restatement in the form of legislation would effectively be an attempt to codify the law, and would require parliamentary endorsement. This would entail the involvement of the Parliamentary Draftsman (Legislative Counsel), the use of parliamentary procedures, and it would result in a codifying statute. It seems unlikely that this would produce the accessible text in simple language and structures which seems necessary. Whilst some of the preparatory work might be undertaken by others, such as legal scholars, anything that will take the shape of legislation has to be adopted through the correct procedures. On the other hand, if this restatement is not in the form of legislation, then the pool of potential authors can be drawn more widely. Legal scholars would undoubtedly be central, as might practitioners and others with a direct interest in consumer issues, as well as business representatives. The composition of whichever group were to produce such a restatement could potentially have a significant impact on its overall content, which is something that would have to be borne in mind. This is, in fact, the approach adopted by the American Law Institute when drafting its restatements, where the intention is also to avoid using the language of legislation.

The third question is what would happen to the restatement once it has been produced, ie how could it be ensured that it will actually be used as intended? Beale seems to envisage some formal seal of approval, whether through judges or the Law Commission, which would then ensure that the restatement would be regarded as authoritative. But this raises the question whether formal approval of itself is likely to have that effect. Nils Jansen has recently sought to demonstrate that historical experience shows that the authority of non-legislative texts largely arises not from any kind of formal approval, but from a range of other factors, primarily through practical acceptance by those for whom the text was created.[43] This would suggest that whilst vetting by some official body might offer some form of validation, it would really only be the actual utilisation of the restatement primarily by consumer advisers and businesspeople that would give it any kind of authority.

If it is accepted that, in order for consumer law to be utilised, consumers and those advising consumers need an alternative to the relevant legislation itself that will provide them with an accessible, yet comprehensive statement of the law, then the obvious question is how this might be provided. What is needed is one place which brings together the diverse sources of consumer law (statutes and case-law, both domestic and European), and which can be kept up-to-date. Whilst a collection of legislative provisions with summaries of relevant cases would be a first step in this direction, it seems unlikely that this would provide a sufficient degree of accessibility for anyone without legal training.[44] Much of current consumer legislation is complex, which is partly due to the practice of parliamentary draftsmanship, and partly because of the need to reconcile requirements of EU Directives with domestic law. So a simple cut-and-paste exercise would not be sufficient.

[43] Nils Jansen, *The Making of Legal Authority* (Oxford University Press, 2010).

[44] Those trained in the law will find the 'Consumer Protection' title of *Halsbury's Laws of England* a useful starting point (*Halsbury's Laws*, 5th edn (2010) vol 21), but this is only updated at certain intervals and may therefore not be fully up-to-date.

Instead, it is suggested here that what would be needed is a 're-statement' of the law in clear language. Whilst it has proven difficult to draft legislation in plain and intelligible language,[45] this should not be as much of a problem for a restatement of the law. The kind of model envisaged here would adopt the features of other well-known restatements, notably the Principles of European Contract Law (PECL) and its successor, the Draft Common Frame of Reference, the *Acquis* Principles, the UNIDROIT Principles of International Commercial Contracts, and the American Restatements.

It may be asked why something like a restatement should be considered. The answer to this lies in the way legal material has been presented and supplemented in the various restatements mentioned. Thus, if the *Acquis* Principles are taken as an example, a restatement essentially comprises four elements:[46] first, a particular legal rule is stated. This might be quite a dense statement of the rule, although it need not be a verbatim statement of a particular statutory provision. Secondly, there is a commentary which expands on the meaning and purpose of the rule. This might explain in more detail what the purpose of the particular rule is, and also unpack its various elements to provide a better understanding of the rule. Thirdly, there are examples given as to how the rule operates in practice. These examples may be based on decided cases, or on common practical situations. Finally, there is an indication of the legal sources (legislation and cases) on which the particular rule is based.

There are clear advantages to presenting the law in this fashion. Key rules can be stated concisely and arranged in a logical fashion. The way matters are arranged in a statute does not always make it easy to figure out exactly what the scope of a particular rule of law is. Reading a statute and checking-up on related case-law requires considerable skill and experience, which neither consumers nor many consumer advisers necessarily possess. In a restatement, material can be arranged in a fashion that makes the law more accessible, and full account can be taken of any relevant case-law which interprets particular sections of a statute.

Furthermore, different sources of law can be combined in one place to present a more coherent and complete picture of the law. For example, there may be instances where common law rules and statutory provisions overlap, or at least coincide. A good example is the area of misrepresentation and the implied terms as to quality supplied by the Sale of Goods Act 1979. In a restatement of the law, these matters could be grouped together, and the respective overlaps and differences made clear in the commentary.

It might be queried whether a restatement is not very similar to a codification, ie an attempt to codify all of the law in one place. The purpose of codifying the law is generally to bring together legal rules which are scattered throughout different sources, or perhaps largely based on case-law, in one statute. To that extent, there is a parallel with the restatement idea considered here. However, a restatement should remain flexible and capable of further development, whereas a code is generally intended to be complete. As a codification would not only encompass the 'law as

[45] See Law Com No 292, n 21 above.

[46] The order in which these are given in the *Acquis* Principles is different from the one given here. There, the order is (i) Rule; (ii) Foundation in the *Acquis* (sources, development and political issues); (iii) Commentary (meaning and purpose; context; explanation); and (iv) Examples.

is', but also seek to determine how situations arising in the future should be dealt with, there is a risk that provisions in a code might end up being rather too general and insufficiently specific to be of value, or a wider principle might gloss over more diffuse case-law.[47]

Furthermore, any codification will be first and foremost a legally binding text, and will therefore have to be drafted accordingly. It will also lack the additional features provided by a commentary and examples. Although UK legislation is generally accompanied by Explanatory Notes which are useful in providing a basic indication of the purpose of a particular provision, they tend to be too superficial to offer a full and proper explanation of each provision. A restatement can offer much more by way of explanation.

Perhaps more crucially, a codification would be legally binding and would therefore have to be adopted through the appropriate legislative procedure. Should it become necessary to amend or update this text, either in light of further EU legislation, or developments in the case law, then this too would have to be done through formal procedures. As the experience of amending primary legislation to comply with EU obligations shows, this can often produce very complex amendments which do not necessarily fit into the existing text. Moreover, it will hardly be possible or appropriate to amend a codifying text in light of every case which may provide an interpretation or clarification of particular sections. A codification, assuming it was successfully done in the first place, would therefore only offer a snap-shot of the law at a particular point in time, but would in due course be overtaken by further developments. Indeed, any consolidation and simplification of the law that might be undertaken is at risk of being affected by subsequent legislative or judicial developments.

A restatement, on the other hand, would be a non-binding text. It would not be adopted by Parliament—indeed, Parliament would not even be required to approve the text. Instead, it would be drafted by a body of experts composed in a way most appropriate to the task.

Restatements have generally been undertaken by legal scholars, and whilst one would expect that legal scholars will make a significant contribution, representatives from other sections might equally have a role to play.[48] But irrespective of the composition, the advantage of a non-binding restatement of the law is that it can be updated more quickly and with greater ease than any parliamentary text. Case-law developments as well as changes made by legislation can be accommodated by amending the text, the commentary and the examples as appropriate. This would provide consumers and advisers with a much more accurate statement of the law than could be achieved through statutory consolidation.

[47] *cf* Andrew Tettenborn, 'From Chaos to Cosmos—or is it Confusion?' (2002) 2 *Web Journal of Current Legal Issues*.

[48] Some caution has been expressed about this process, particularly in the US context: see, eg Alan Schwartz and Robert E Scott, 'The Political Economy of Private Legislatures' (1995) 143 *University of Pennsylvania Law Review* 595, and Richard Hyland, 'American Private Legislatures and the Process Discussion' in Arthur Hartkamp, Martijn Hesselink, Ewoud Hondius, Chantal Mak and Edgar du Perron (eds), *Towards a European Civil Code*, 4th edn (Alphen aan den Rijn, Kluwer Law International, 2011).

Appropriate use of modern information technology can assist greatly in keeping the restatement current. It is conceivable that a major ruling by a court could be reflected in the text of the restatement within days if it were published online.

One major concern would, of course, be the question of how the initial creation and subsequent updating of any restatement could be resourced. It would require a significant amount of time and manpower to produce the initial restatement, together with the commentary and examples. As anybody who has had to edit or compile a single piece of work written by multiple authors will appreciate (not least the editors of the present volume), it can be a major task ensuring consistency between sections produced by different authors. And once the initial restatement has been completed, there would then be the need to keep it current, which would entail the allocation of further resources. The viability of this approach would therefore depend on an analysis of the costs incurred in creating the first restatement, and then the need for subsequent updating. This would have to be balanced against the cost savings that might be made by reducing the cost for business of seeking advice.

None of these observations suggest that it would not be worthwhile to pursue the idea of a restatement of consumer law in earnest. Such a project would have to be designed with some care in advance of its implementation, but a lot can be learned from the experience of the American Law Institute. The idea of a restatement therefore deserves to be considered seriously.

CONCLUDING THOUGHTS

This chapter has considered the process of law reform in the field of consumer law—a topic which has been the focus of a significant part of Hugh Beale's work, both as an academic and through his tenure as a Law Commissioner. With regard to the latter, Hugh once joked that he had a 100 per cent track-record as a Law Commissioner of not seeing any of the projects he was involved in leading to new legislation. Of course, since then, there have been a number of new measures, including, in the field of consumer law, the long-awaited consolidation of the law on unfair terms which will be part of the forthcoming Consumer Rights Act, although not all of the proposals from the original Law Commission report have been adopted.

However, the reform of consumer legislation, whilst badly needed, will only be one aspect of ensuring that consumers are adequately protected. It will be equally important that consumers and traders are aware of their respective rights and obligations, and that advisers are able to offer clear and swift advice on the legal position of both parties to a consumer transaction. In this regard, the idea of something like a restatement, as suggested by Hugh Beale, has some appeal, although its realisation would require some careful planning. But there can be little doubt that it would be a useful tool in ensuring that consumer law will be more than just legislation that is rarely enforced.

English Contract Law

6

Freedom to Exercise Contractual Rights of Termination

MICHAEL BRIDGE

INTRODUCTION

TERMINATION OF THE contract is a remedy that has received in the literature less attention than its importance warrants. Its impact on a broken-down contract may be severe, not merely because it arrests the transfer of assets but because of the impact of a damages award levied against a non-performing party in respect of future non-performance. There are also the non-performing party's investment costs to consider. In the case of executory, market-driven contracts of an instantaneous character, the consequences of termination may be limited to the rise or fall in the marketplace of the subject matter of the contract. But for any contract with significant start-up costs, especially one that is of a long-term character, the consequences of termination may prove to be drastic.

The character of the law in this area is revealed by a statement of Sumption SCJ in *Petroleo Brasiliero SA v ENE Kos 1 Ltd*, referring to the withdrawal from hire (that is, termination of a time charterparty) of a vessel for late payment by the charterer:

> There are no standards by which the owners' reasons may be judged, other than those to be found in the contract. There is no legal policy specific to termination rights restricting their availability or the consequences of their exercise more narrowly than does the language of the contract or the general law.[1]

These words amount to an uncompromising assertion that termination rights conferred by the contract may be exercised without let or hindrance. The particular context is the withdrawal of a time-chartered vessel from hire for untimely payment, but these words have a resonance for any market-driven contract. This assertion of contractual freedom is nevertheless subject to any limitations that might be imposed by the 'general law', which prompts a survey of the extent to which contractual termination rights are currently abridged or possibly under threat and of the methods used to abridge those rights at present and in the future. A realistic appraisal of where the law now is and where it is going had better be attentive to the type of contract under consideration, whether it is short-term or long-term, requires a

[1] *Petroleo Brasiliero SA v ENE Kos 1 Ltd* [2012] UKSC 17, para 7.

significant start-up investment or not, or is performed at arm's length or through a process of cooperation or interaction.

The availability of termination for breach of contract stems from a number of sources. First, it may arise from the commission of a repudiatory breach or, which comes to the same thing, a breach that goes to the root of the contract.[2] Secondly, it may derive from statute, the Sale of Goods Act 1979 being the prime example.[3] Thirdly, it may flow from the express language of the contract. Fourthly, it may be implied from the parties' intentions or from the character and setting of the contract.[4] The rigour of the radical (or repudiatory) breach test, and hence the rarity of the occasions on which the right to terminate arises by virtue of it, means that the exercise of the right in a given case on this basis is unlikely to be qualified by restrictions apart from those expressed or implied in the contract. But the three remaining cases, in different ways, call for an examination of the extent to which rights of termination are circumscribed. Two of these cases squarely raise the issue of contractual interpretation.

For both implied and express rights of termination, the mention made by Sumption SCJ of the language of the contract amounts to an invitation to line up termination rights with developments in the field of contractual interpretation. The torrent of case law on contractual interpretation that has poured forth since 1998 has had the reductive tendency to classify most important legal questions arising out of contract law as questions of interpretation. The movement away from literal interpretation in favour of a broader commercial interpretation has undoubtedly amplified the measure of judicial discretion in the interpretation of contracts. The restraint on judicial intervention imposed by *The Moorcock*[5] in the case of implied terms, resistant as it is to the implication of terms merely because they are reasonable,[6] may now be a thing of the past if judicial intervention may more freely be exercised in the form of interpretation. Faced with a choice to be made between different commercial interpretations displaying different degrees of business common-sense, courts have made it plain that they will select the interpretation that adheres more or most closely to business common-sense.[7] Yet who is to say where the line between business common-sense and perceived fairness falls?[8] Does the interest of the giver of a performance bond or a related instrument to minimise its exposure on the instrument adhere less to business common-sense than the promisee's interest in having full cover for its commercial exposure?[9]

[2] Intermediate stipulations are discussed below.

[3] Sale of Goods Act 1979, ss 12–15.

[4] *Maredelanto Cia Naviera SA v Bergbau-Handels GmbH (The Mihalis Angelos)* [1971] 1 QB 64.

[5] *The Moorcock* (1889) 14 PD 64.

[6] See, eg, *Liverpool City Council v Irwin* [1977] AC 239.

[7] See, eg, *Rainy Sky SA v Kookmin Bank* [2011] UKSC 50; [2011] 1 WLR 2900.

[8] The danger of imposing a fair solution is recognised by Moore-Bick LJ, referring to a clause reasonably capable of bearing two possible meanings, in *Procter and Gamble Co v Svenska Cellulosen Aktiebolaget SCA* [2012] EWCA Civ 1413, para 22: '[T]he starting point must be the words the parties have used to express their intention and in the case of a carefully drafted agreement of the present kind the court must take care not to fall into the trap of re-writing the contract in order to produce what it considers to be a more reasonable meaning'.

[9] ibid.

In this contribution, I propose to examine a number of instances where agreed or conferred rights of contractual termination may either be said to be at risk or undergoing a degree of transformation. These areas are: (a) the slight breach rule in section 15A of the Sale of Goods Act 1979; (b) the Unfair Contract Terms Act 1977; (c) the rule that in equity time is presumptively not of the essence; (d) the rule or rules against penalties and termination; and (e) the interpretation of an express termination clause.

SLIGHT BREACH AND SALE OF GOODS ACT 1979, SECTION 15A

According to section 15A, in the case of breaches of condition under sections 13–15 of the Sale of Goods Act 1979 occurring in non-consumer transactions, the buyer may not terminate where the breach is so slight that it would be unreasonable for him to do so. This provision departs from the orthodoxy that the right to terminate for a breach of condition is a pure question of law unaffected by the circumstances created by a breach of contract. It stems from a Law Commission report[10] that does not span the entire field of contract and does not make a case for treating these particular statutory conditions as a special case. Instead, section 15A sprang up between the working paper, which tentatively recommended that a seller have a right to cure non-conforming performance in non-consumer contracts, and a final report that substituted what became section 15A, by way of expedient or compromise, for this tentative recommendation. The origins of section 15A lie in an acute problem posed by the case of defective goods: what should be done about trivial defects in relation to the fitness for purpose and satisfactory quality implied terms? Excluding the application of the implied terms in such cases would compel a buyer to accept sub-standard goods; permitting rejection and termination for trivial breaches might in some cases allow buyers to act abusively.

To date, the impact of section 15A on the case-law has been slight and it is tempting to see the process of its enactment as an expression of legal aesthetics (because it is thought to be distasteful to sanction contractual termination for unmeritorious reasons) and as designed to have only a modest practical effect on sale of goods contracts. The argument has been advanced, nevertheless, that, taking account of the section 13 description reference in section 15A, the latter provision might be triggered where a buyer seeks to terminate a contract for late performance.[11] This is because the justification given for treating timely performance of commercial contracts as of the essence of the contract has been classically expressed in terms of description: a February cargo of Madras rice is not the same thing as a March cargo.[12] The argument, advanced tentatively and in a cautionary way, cannot be supported. Though description might lie at the heart of the timely performance rule in commercial sales, or at least sales in the commodity trades, the buyer invoking the rule does not rely on section 13. Section 15A is formalistic in its application: it applies to breaches of identified statutory conditions concerning the description,

[10] Law Commission, *Sale and Supply of Goods* (Law Com No 160, 1987).
[11] Ewan McKendrick (ed), *Sale of Goods* (London, Lloyd's of London, 2000) para 12-026.
[12] *Bowes v Shand* (1877) 2 App Cas 455, 468 (Lord Blackburn).

quality and fitness of goods.[13] A commercial buyer invoking the time of the essence rule need not plead section 13.

In commercial sale of goods contracts, it is more likely that contracts will be terminated for non-timely performance or for documentary breach than for breach of the statutory conditions of description, quality and fitness. It is common in the standard form commodity contracts for the right of termination to be excluded for breaches of sections 13–15[14] and for the buyer instead to be compensated by means of a price reduction. Yet, if the Law Commission and Parliament thought that termination for technical breaches in commercial contracts was to be dissuaded, it is not entirely clear why time and documentary breaches were left untouched. The reasons given for the reform by the Law Commission were of potentially general application: a terminating buyer could inflict a disproportionate loss on the seller; termination could upset the contractual allocation of commercial risk; and an opportunistic buyer was open to the charge of acting in bad faith. Admittedly, sections 13–15 are precise statutory targets of section 15A; equivalent common law rules dealing with time and documents would not be quite so easy to target. There exists, however, the unstated but entirely plausible reason that international sales exist in an unregulated world of their own, whose inhabitants are allowed to participate in the commercial equivalent of extreme sports. Termination for untimely performance and documentary non-conformity is very much a creature of international sales. In a similar way, the rules dealing with unreasonable clauses in the Unfair Contract Terms Act 1977 are disapplied for international sales.[15]

Although section 15A is narrowly confined in its scope, a civil lawyer might ask if it infects the remaining body of contract law so as to sanction or encourage the emergence of a general test at common law preventing unreasonable termination for breaches of condition.[16] In the common law tradition, we are not used to seeing statutes as having more than an irruptive effect on the common law and our response, therefore, is that section 15A is merely a piece of episodic statutory intervention fated not to germinate outside its defined limits.[17] Its birth was accidental and its impact lies between slight and non-existent.[18] Section 15A is unlikely to lend critical mass to other initiatives whose aim is to control termination for breach.

[13] This conclusion is supported by Law Com No 160, n 10 above, ch 4.

[14] A typical price allowance clause may also not include breach of the description condition in s 13 (eg Grain and Free Trade Association, *Contract for Shipment of Feeding Stuffs in Bulk* (No 100) cl 5: 'Difference in quality shall not entitle Buyers to reject …').

[15] Unfair Contract Terms Act (UCTA) 1977, ss 26–27.

[16] The transposition of the Consumer Sales Directive in German law created pressures compromising the structure and consistency of the BGB that led to a substantial revision some years later. As for whether the buyer's right to demand repair of non-conforming goods further to that same Directive would necessarily lead to a radical reappraisal of the availability of specific performance in English law, see Jürgen Basedow, 'Towards a Universal Breach of Contract: The Impact of the CISG' (2005) 25 *International Review of Law and Economics* 487, 493 ('breakthrough for specific performance in common law countries').

[17] *cf Timeload Ltd v British Telecommunications plc* [1995] EMLR 459, 468, discussed in text to nn 20–24.

[18] A rare instance of its application is *Filobake Ltd v Rondo Ltd* [2004] EWHC 695 (TCC) (a defective component in an industrial machine could be replaced).

UNFAIR CONTRACT TERMS ACT 1977

The relevant provision of the Unfair Contract Terms Act (UCTA) 1977 is section 3(2)(b), which applies where the parties contract on the basis of the written standard terms of one of them. It subjects to a standard of reasonableness any contract term giving rise to a 'claim to be entitled: (i) to render a contractual performance substantially different from that which was reasonably expected of [the proferens]; or (ii) in respect of the whole or any part of his contractual obligation, to render no performance at all'. Despite its title, UCTA 1977 is far from being a statute dealing with unfair contract terms in general, since it is largely confined to exclusion, limitation and indemnity clauses. Nevertheless, is there an argument that a party claiming the right to terminate on the basis of a standard clause is claiming to render no performance at all? This is not at first sight very promising ground. Claiming the right to render 'no performance' after exercising termination rights against a non-performing party may not be quite the same thing as claiming the right to render 'no performance at all'. Moreover, as far as the remainder of section 3(2)(b) goes, a party terminating a contract, although doing something that the other party might not reasonably expect, is hardly 'render[ing] a contractual performance', whether substantially different or otherwise.

The case-law on section 3(2)(b) is exiguous; the potential that the provision has for striking down unfair termination clauses may not have been sufficiently appreciated. In *Ilanchelian v Esso Petroleum Co Ltd*,[19] the court summarily dismissed an argument that section 3(2)(b)(i) (rendering substantially different performance) applied where a licensor invoked an option to terminate a contract by making a fixed sum payment instead of allowing the licensee of a filling station to work out the agreed notice period. In the light of the court's reaction, a more radical challenge to the exercise of any termination option at all, run more appropriately under section 3(2)(b)(ii) (rendering no performance at all), would surely have foundered, a fortiori if this had been a case of termination for breach. A more promising response comes from the Court of Appeal in *Timeload Ltd v British Telecommunications plc*,[20] which concerned a line rental agreement under which the customer had somehow managed to obtain a number,[21] giving it a significant advantage over other service providers, in order to run a telephone number inquiry service.

The agreed period of notice for the respondent to give was one month. Bingham MR stated that is 'was at least arguable' that a clause permitting the respondent to terminate the contract without cause was subject to section 3(2)(b)(i) of the Act, where the customer reasonably expected that the respondent would not invoke its termination right in the absence of a 'substantial reason'. This, of course, was before significant recent developments in the law of interpretation and implied terms, raising the plausible argument that business common-sense requires the wording of the clause not to be taken literally. The really intriguing feature of the case was the assertion that it was 'at least arguable that the common law could, if the letter of

[19] *Ilanchelian v Esso Petroleum Co Ltd*, 28 September 1998 (Rimer J).
[20] *Timeload*, n 17 above.
[21] 0800 192 192 (192 was the previous (uncompetitive) general inquiry number).

the statute does not apply, treat the clear intention of the legislature expressed in the statute as a platform for invalidating or restricting the operation of an oppressive clause in a situation of the present, very special, kind'.[22] The acceptance of a statutory stimulus to develop the common law is not avowedly the same thing as interpreting a statute in the same way that contracts are now being interpreted. Bingham MR's assertion was supported by reference to his own earlier statement in *Interfoto Picture Library Ltd v Stiletto Visual Programmes Ltd*[23] that the common law, while eschewing the adoption of a general principle of good faith, was capable of responding to demonstrated problems by means of piecemeal solutions. An argument of this sort (which incidentally invites a return to and reconsideration of the restrictive language of section 15A) is just as capable of being run, if sound, in the case of a clause that allows termination for breach for a wide variety of reasons, trivial and serious. Bingham MR did confine his dictum to 'very special' situations, but that may be seen as a conventional element of caution of the sort that accompanies a first decisive step. What sort of piecemeal solution exists at common law that might allow a court to build upon a statute without extending that statute, given the lack of identicality in statutory and case-law language? The continuing thread of this argument is here deferred since it runs into a discussion later in this contribution about the exercise of broad termination rights as a matter of controllable discretion against a background of good faith. Discretion and good faith have recently become the subject of intense judicial activity.

EQUITY AND TIMELY PERFORMANCE

A long-standing check on contractual termination rights comes from the equitable rule[24] that timely performance is presumptively not of the essence of the contract. Nevertheless, the parties are at liberty to make time of the essence by express provision or by necessary implication in their contract if they so wish.[25] Moreover, there is also the matter of one party serving on the non-performing other a notice making time of the essence. A useful entry point is Lord Simon's words in *United Scientific Holdings Ltd v Burnley Borough Council*, where he speaks of the service of a notice when *ex hypothesi* a reasonable time for performance has already elapsed:

> The notice operates as evidence that the promisee considers that a reasonable time for performance has elapsed by the date of the notice and as evidence of the date by which the promisee now considers it reasonable for the contractual obligation to be performed. It is only in this sense that time is made of the essence of a contract in which it was previously non-essential.[26]

Some little comfort for the view that the promisee may unilaterally vary the contract by serving a time notice, with the right to terminate following non-compliance,

[22] *Timeload*, n 17 above, at 468.
[23] *Interfoto Picture Library Ltd v Stiletto Visual Programmes Ltd* [1989] QB 433, 439.
[24] Or 'tendency': *Samarenko v Dawn Hill House Hotel* [2011] EWCA Civ 45, para 11; [2013] Ch 36.
[25] *Stickney v Keeble* [1915] AC 386, 416; *United Scientific Holdings Ltd v Burnley Borough Council* [1978] AC 904, 930; *Samarenko*, n 24 above.
[26] *United Scientific Holdings*, n 25 above, at 946.

may be derived from these words since Lord Simon refers to what was '*previously* non-essential' (emphasis added). Although Lord Simon goes on to make it plain that serving a notice does not introduce a new term into the contract,[27] doubt as to the meaning of this passage nevertheless remains: changing the status of a time obligation does not amount to introducing a new term. Moreover, Lord Simon lays emphasis upon the notice as evidencing what the promisee considers to be a reasonable further time for performance. What significance does the promisee's perception possess unless it has a transformative effect on the contract? What the promisee considers reasonable has no force in and of itself.

I shall now focus upon two features of the equitable doctrine concerning timely performance. The first, which may be called the variation feature of time notices, has just been outlined. The second and following feature concerns the extent to which, if at all, equity imposes its solution on the common law or, putting it another way, interferes with a party's rights of termination at common law.[28] I shall refer to these aspects of making time of the essence as the first and second features of the doctrine.

On the first feature, a conservative view of the effect of a time notice, at odds with any unilateral power of variation, came in a case where the failure to comply with the notice was held not to give rise to a repudiatory breach:[29] it would still need to be demonstrated that the breach went to the root of the contract.[30] This assumes, of course, that the term in question would not be a condition at common law. The limited effect thus ascribed by the conservative view to making time of the notice was challenged by counsel for the claimant in *Multi Veste 226 BV v NI Summer Row Unitholder BV*: if non-compliance with a served notice were not of itself treated as a repudiatory breach, then what was the point of serving the notice?[31] Counsel's argument, then, was that, if non-performance of a term would be repudiatory, the failure to perform the term on time, within the period set by the notice, should also be repudiatory. This bold argument, equating late performance with non-performance, commended itself to Lewison J in *Multi Veste*. Consequently, the possibility of unilateral contractual variation resurfaced.

More recently, the matter came before the Court of Appeal in *Samarenko v Dawn Hill House Ltd*.[32] Lewison LJ delivered the lead judgment, in the course of which he resiled from the proposition he adopted in *Multi Veste* that the giving of a time notice could convert a breach otherwise non-repudiatory into a repudiatory breach. In the case of a so-called innominate term or intermediate stipulation, the right to terminate would still depend upon whether the breach turned out to be repudiatory (or went to the root of the contract). One slight gloss that could be added concerns the weight of further delay in the period covered by a time notice: this may on the facts bring about a sufficient degree of additional prejudice for the promisor's

[27] ibid 946–47.

[28] Language in cases such as *Behzadi v Shaftesbury Hotels Ltd* [1992] ch and *Re Olympia & York Canary Wharf Ltd (No 2)* [1993] BCC 159.

[29] *Re Olympia*, n 28 above.

[30] *Dalkia Utilities Services plc v Celtech International Ltd* [2006] 1 Lloyd's Rep 599.

[31] *Multi Veste 226 BV v NI Summer Row Unitholder BV* [2011] EWHC 2026 (Ch), para 199; 139 con LR 23.

[32] *Samarenko*, n 24 above.

lateness as a whole to pass the repudiatory breach test. Apart from this, the outcome derived from *Samarenko*, therefore, is that equitable intervention does not *amplify* termination rights by converting, with the aid of a time notice, a breach otherwise non-repudiatory into a repudiatory breach. This is surely correct.

The second feature of the equitable doctrine, as stated above, concerns equitable interference with common law termination rights. In *Samarenko*, under the terms of a contract modified after the buyer had not obtained the type of planning permission that it had sought, the buyer was required to pay by way of deposit the amended sum of £450,000 by a stated date, which happened to be 60 days after the grant of the original planning permission. When the buyer failed to pay the deposit on the due date, the seller waited an extra six days before giving the buyer five more working days, stating that time was of the essence and that the seller would treat a failure to pay by that date as a repudiation of the contract. The buyer, awaiting the results of a soil survey, failed to pay by the extended date and the seller asserted by letter that the contract was terminated. The seller sought a declaratory judgment that the contract had been lawfully terminated and summary judgment to that effect was given by the trial judge, whose judgment was affirmed by the Court of Appeal.

The first point was that the duty to pay the deposit was a condition of the contract, so that the failure to pay by the contractually agreed date amounted to a repudiatory breach. Consequently, this was not a case where equity would interfere with the common law's treatment of the deposit term as a contractual condition.[33] One might fairly say, in this case, that timely payment was by necessary implication of the essence of the contract. Lest this reason did not stand up, however, Lewison LJ went on to consider the effect of a time notice in terms of equity's interference with common law termination rights. In so doing, Lewison LJ started with a view of nineteenth century contract law and its modern consequences that is oversimplified in two respects. The first respect is his belief that generations of lawyers overlooked the fact that contractual termination for breach did not exclusively depend upon the classification of the term as a condition or mere warranty and that this oversight found its way into the Sale of Goods Act 1979. The response to this is that quantity obligations are not classified as either conditions or warranties under the Act,[34] and that the test for discharge from a severable instalment contract is whether a breach concerning a particular instalment goes to the root of the contract.[35] The second respect, which flows from the first, is the proposition that there are three types of contractual term: conditions, warranties and intermediate stipulations. That view was persuasively inculcated by Diplock LJ in *Hongkong Fir Shipping Ltd v Kawasaki Kisen Kaisha*,[36] but the views of Upjohn LJ in the same case[37] and of

[33] To the same effect, see Rix LJ at para 59 and Etherton LJ at para 53, diminuendo at para 54, in the unusual case where the deposit is to be paid some considerable time after the formation of the contract.

[34] Sale of Goods Act 1979, s 30.

[35] ibid s 31(2). As for the common law of contract, consider *Jackson v Union Marine Insurance Co Ltd* (1875) LR 10 CP 125, which played a major part in the judgment of Diplock LJ in *Hongkong Fir Shipping Co Ltd v Kawasaki Kisen Kaisha* [1962] 2 QB 26, and the concept developed in that case of a frustrating delay.

[36] *Hongkong Fir*, n 35 above, at 69–70.

[37] ibid at 64.

Ormerod LJ in *Cehave NV v Bremer Handels GmbH*[38] more accurately state the position in the language of a two-term categorisation: conditions and remaining terms, subject to statutory intervention denying termination rights for a very small group of implied terms.[39] In other words, the test for a discharging or repudiatory breach is whether a breach goes to the root of the contract, save that it is open to the parties to designate a term as a condition, so that every breach is repudiatory.[40] If, which is unlikely, the contracting parties were to designate a term as a mere warranty, this should be treated as an attempt to contract out of termination rights and subject to the normal common law and statutory controls on exclusion clauses.

In *Samarenko*, Lewison LJ recognised that equity's treatment of time as not being of the essence, when it comes to the redemption of a land mortgage or the completion of a sale of land contract, was too well established now to be abandoned.[41] In so far as the supposed tripartite classification of terms means that in some cases equity is not interfering with rights of termination at common law, he is surely correct. In the present case, if it were only the common law that had recognised the deposit term as a condition, then at first sight it seems that the service of a time notice would have lifted the equitable bar to the termination of the contract at common law. This, however, is not the case: if the parties have expressly, or by necessary implication, treated the contractual term as a condition, equity would not intervene in the first place since the parties themselves have already made time of the essence.[42] Indeed, what business would equity have in interfering with contractually agreed rights of termination by insisting on the need for a time notice? Since the decision in *Hongkong Fir*, courts have shown an increasing reluctance to recognise contractual terms as conditions, sometimes even when dealing with time obligations in the commodities trades.[43] Given the state of the modern law of contract, is there any justification for retaining the equitable doctrine about making time of the essence? It seems to be redundant and has the capacity to mislead.[44] Even the most diehard opponent of the substantive fusion of law and equity should have to consider whether this equitable doctrine continues to serve a useful purpose. The common law and equity have already merged at this point and may have done so quite some time ago. They may also be said to have merged in respect of the general importance of timely performance: the common law would be unlikely to treat time as of the essence of completing a sale of land contract and equity equally unlikely to treat time as not of the essence in a commodities market. This is perhaps more a case of mutual jurisdictional withdrawal than of substantive merger.

[38] *Cehave NV v Bremer Handels GmbH* [1976] QB 44, 84. To similar but less explicit effect, see Roskill LJ (*passim*).

[39] Primarily Sale of Goods Act 1979, s 12(2) (the warranties of quiet possession and freedom from encumbrances).

[40] Even in the case of mere statutory warranties, such as those in ibid s 12(2), the parties would be free to elevate to the status of conditions those terms that were not already so.

[41] *Samarenko*, n 24 above, paras 29, 39.

[42] See n 25 above.

[43] See, eg *Bremer Handels GmbH v Vanden-Avenne Izegem PVBA* [1978] 2 Lloyd's Rep 109, and *The Honam Jade* [1991] 1 Lloyd's Rep 38.

[44] Rix LJ in *Samarenko*, n 24 above, had some additional misgivings about the equitable doctrine: para 64 *et seq*.

PENALTIES AND TERMINATION

Equitable relief against forfeiture, confined to cases where the non-performing party has a proprietary interest in the subject matter of the contract, is not available where time is of the essence. In such a case, equity will not proceed with specific performance of the contract by granting additional time to perform.[45] I do not propose to advance an argument that the scope of equitable relief should be extended beyond cases where the non-performing party has a proprietary interest. So far as equity will not intervene where timely performance has been made expressly or by necessary implication of the essence, this issue largely falls away.[46] Instead, I shall focus on the penalties doctrine and, in particular, on one aspect of the doctrine that came to the fore in *Lombard North Central plc v Butterworth*.[47] Does the treatment of a contractual clause as a condition indirectly offend the rule against penalties, in so far as the consequences of termination, expressed in an award of damages, bear down punitively on the non-performing party? Rotating the question slightly, is the autonomy of contracting parties in designating a term as a condition reduced when it comes to the consequences of termination? These questions fall within the scope of this chapter: the issue is whether the exercise of the right to terminate a contract for breach is inhibited by the way that the consequences of termination are treated in an ensuing damages award.

In *Lombard North Central*, the hirer (an accountant) of computer equipment had been late on a number of occasions in making payment. On the last of these occasions, the finance company exercised a right to terminate granted by the lease.[48] The lease further provided that timely payment was of the essence of the contract.[49] There was also a provision in the lease for the hirer, in these circumstances, to pay all accrued and future instalments, less an allowance for accelerated receipt.[50] Since no provision was made for reduction in respect of the value of the repossessed computer equipment, however, the provision was correctly regarded as a penalty. Indeed, the finance company had not pressed for recovery under the offending clause but sought damages that were ordered to be assessed.

The case centred on whether the finance company was entitled to recover, in a damages award, future instalments less deductions for accelerated receipt and resale value. This should have been a straightforward question. Mustill LJ correctly asserted that 'it is axiomatic that a person who establishes a breach of condition can terminate and claim damages for loss of the bargain'. In particular:

> [W]here a promisor fails to give timely performance of an obligation in respect of which time is expressly stated to be of the essence, the injured party may elect to terminate and recover *damages in respect of the promisor's outstanding obligations*, without regard to the magnitude of the breach. (emphasis added)

[45] *Steedman v Drinkle* [1916] 1 AC 275.

[46] I shall not deal here with the question whether monetary relief should be granted to the non-performing party in respect of any deposit or part payments made.

[47] *Lombard North Central plc v Butterworth* [1987] QB 527.

[48] In cl 6.

[49] In cl 2.

[50] In cl 6.

The problem for the court was that the Court of Appeal, in *Financings Ltd v Baldock*,[51] had earlier limited the finance company to accrued instalments and refused its claim for unpaid future instalments. It did so because it regarded the finance company as exercising a mere right of withdrawal from the contract, after the hirer had been late in making payments, in circumstances where the hirer was not guilty of a repudiatory breach. The drafting of hire purchase and similar contracts has always been torn between their artificial legal character and their economic reality. This accounts for the hirer's right of withdrawal and the presence of minimum payments clauses. It is decidedly odd, however, for a finance company to want a right of withdrawal corresponding to that of the hirer: the economic consequences of doing so, represented by loss of bargain and the recovery of depreciated goods, are so severe, as surely any accountant would understand. The withdrawal clause in *Baldock*, moreover, provided that if the hirer were ten days late in making payment 'the owner may by written notice and forthwith and for all purposes terminate the hiring'.[52] Despite this and numerous other references to termination in the agreement, the court held that the right to terminate the contract for breach, with the consequences flowing therefrom, was confined to breaches by the hirer of a repudiatory character, that is, breaches going to the root of the contract, which had not occurred in the present case. The finance company had therefore exercised a mere right of withdrawal.

The vital difference in *Butterworth* was that time was expressly made of the essence of the contract. It troubled the court that, in applying perfectly orthodox contract principles—and, one might add, in bringing hire purchase contracts back into the fold of general contract law—it was allowing the draftsman by a mere stroke of the pen to overturn the decision in *Baldock*.[53] Now, why should the application of orthodox contract principles cause such concern, unless hirers as a class are to be considered as a species deserving of protection even in cases where statute has not intervened? And is the court's concern likely to find a practical outlet in some future case approaching the issue from a different aspect?

The loss of bargain arising out of termination may be said in one sense to be due to the promisee's election to terminate the contract and not to the promisor's antecedent breach.[54] It would take a degree of boldness, nevertheless, to hold that the causal link had been severed by the exercise of a contractual right to terminate. Similarly, there is no scope for the doctrine of mitigation of damages, which does not qualify the right to terminate in a case of this nature[55] and would only apply to the extent that the promisee could alleviate adverse post-termination consequences. In practical terms, it would require only that the promisee strive to maximise the resale value of repossessed goods. Consequently, the outcome of *Butterworth*, that the penalties rule does not inhibit the exercise of termination rights by limiting

[51] *Financings Ltd v Baldock* [1963] 2 QB 104.

[52] In cl 8.

[53] *Lombard North Central v Butterworth* [1987] QB 527, 540 (Mustill LJ: 'not a result I view with much satisfaction'); 546 (Nicholls LJ: 'with considerable dissatisfaction').

[54] On recovering damages for loss arising out of the termination itself, see Marion Hetherington, 'Contract Damages for Loss of Bargain Following Termination: The Causation Problem' (1983) 6 *University of New South Wales Law Review* 211.

[55] *Tredegar Iron and Coal Co Ltd v Hawthorne Bros & Co* (1902) 18 TLR 716.

recoverable damages, may not be challenged on these grounds. Another approach, nevertheless, might be to require, on a 'business common-sense' interpretation of the clause,[56] that it be implemented by the promisee with a degree of restraint, possibly after repeated delays that do not have to amount to a repudiatory breach (which is the way finance companies in fact tend to implement such clauses, as the facts of *Butterworth* themselves attest). This possibility is pursued further in the next section of this contribution.

INTERPRETATION OF AN EXPRESS TERMINATION CLAUSE

Nearly 150 years ago, Blackburn J made the case for party autonomy in the contractual conferment of contractual termination rights when he said in *Bettini v Gye*: 'Parties may think some matter, apparently of very little importance, essential; and if they sufficiently express an intention to make the literal fulfilment of such a thing a condition precedent, it will be one'.[57] The intention has to be sufficiently expressed and one can take from the ensuing case law the conclusion that the sufficiency of that expression is directly proportional to the severity of the clause. In the well-known case of *Wickman Machine Tool Sales Ltd v Schuler AG*,[58] a contract, for the promotion of a German manufacturer's panel presses in the United Kingdom, required the promoter to adhere to a demanding schedule of visits of the major motor manufacturers and stipulated that it was '[a] condition' that the schedule be maintained. The House of Lords by a majority concluded that the parties did not understand the clause in question to be a promissory condition in the technical legal sense. Rather, the word signified that a failure to comply meant that a 'major' breach, for which provision in the contract had been made by means of a notice demanding compliance for the future within a stated period, had been committed. Had such provision not been made, affording the court an opportunity to make something of the termination clause, it would have had to be dismissed for adding nothing to the contract. Lord Wilberforce dissented, seeing no reason to substitute an easy-going tolerance for what the contract insistently demanded.

Nevertheless, both majority and minority may be said to have missed the real point, which is that the panel press manufacturer sought to have the means of putting an end to the promotional relationship at the point when it lost faith in the efforts and achievements of its United Kingdom promoter. It wished to have a contractual discretion to terminate a contract without having to give laborious, and no doubt contestable, reasons. It was not seeking the right to pounce upon a technical breach of condition so as to terminate the contract. Being tied to an unsuccessful promoter would stultify its efforts to expand its sales in the United Kingdom; putting a premature end to the relationship would be equally bad for business. If, taking the language of the termination clause at face value, the parties have agreed that the manufacturer has the power to do something that may not, if pushed to the limit, amount to business common-sense, should a problem of the sort that arose in

[56] See, eg *Rainy Sky SA v Kookmin Bank* [2011] UKSC 50; [2011] 1 WLR 2900.
[57] *Bettini v Gye* (1876) 1 QBD 183, 187.
[58] *Wickman Machine Tool Sales Ltd v Schuler AG* [1974] AC 235.

Wickman now be approached in the light of how the language of the clause might sensibly be read down in accordance with business common-sense? The same type of question might be asked in hire purchase cases like *Lombard North Central plc v Butterworth*.[59]

The question thus posed in relation to *Wickman* may be taken further in the similar case of *Rice v Great Yarmouth Borough Council*.[60] In that case, the outsourcing of park maintenance by a local authority led it to conclude with the same contractor two contracts on standard local authority terms providing for the maintenance of sports facilities and parks over a four-year period. After three months, the council served the first of numerous default notices requiring shortcomings to be rectified. Four months after that, apparently after discussion in its contracts committee and after taking counsel's opinion, the local authority purported to terminate the contracts in reliance on the following standard term:

> If the Contractor commits a breach of any of its obligations under the Contract ... the Council may, without prejudice to any accrued rights or remedies under the Contract, terminate the Contractor's employment under the Contract by notice in writing having immediate effect.[61]

It was clear, therefore, that the council's action was not ill-considered or precipitate. The facts of the case suggest too that the contractor, previously in quite a small way of business, might have over-extended itself.

The trial judge and the Court of Appeal were in agreement that, in a long-term contract of this nature involving substantial investment, the clause should be interpreted so as to be confined to repudiatory breaches. Influential in the court's decision was the following statement of Lord Diplock in *Antaios Compania SA v Salen Rederierna (The Antaios)*: '[I]f detailed semantic and syntactical analysis of words in a commercial contract is going to lead to a conclusion that flouts business commonsense, it must yield to business commonsense'.[62] Yet the clause in *Rice* was clear and simple and did not call for detailed semantic and syntactical analysis. *Rice* could hardly be said to be a case dealing with contested meanings of an intricate clause; it concerned whether a contracting party should have in the first place extensive rights of termination. The termination clause was interpreted by the court in a way consistent with some of the more extreme applications of the *contra proferentem* rule in exclusion clause cases. The interpretative process was in reality a cloak for the suppression of substantive unfairness.[63] That said, it was the clause itself that came under attack and not the use of it in the particular circumstances. The council

[59] *Butterworth*, n 47 above.

[60] *Rice v Great Yarmouth Borough Council* (2001) 3 LGLR 4. See also *Dominion Corporate Trustees Ltd v Debenhams Properties Ltd* [2010] EWHC 1193 (Ch).

[61] At cl 23.2.1.

[62] *Antaios Compania SA v Salen Rederierna (The Antaios)* [1985] AC 191, 201.

[63] To be contrasted with *Rice* is *TSG Building Services Plc v South Anglia Housing Ltd* [2013] EWHC 1151 (TCC), where the court considered a clause in a 'partnering' (not partnership) agreement for gas servicing and related services. The contracting parties were evidently of equal bargaining power. The agreement was expressed to run for four years but both parties had the right to give three months' notice to terminate the contract prematurely without cause. The clause was held to be clear and unqualified, either in itself or by the remaining language of the contract, and was not to be constrained by any implied duty of good faith. The housing authority was not required to give reasons for its decision to terminate.

did not invoke the clause in a capricious or peremptory fashion. Furthermore, any local authority, imagining itself to have acquired some measure of protection from the clause, would have every reason to feel dismayed on finding itself tied to an unsatisfactory contractor for four years while its parks and sports facilities (vitally important for a resort town) fell into decay. The demanding test of a repudiatory breach is hard to satisfy[64] and moreover would have applied if the contract had contained no provision at all dealing with termination for sub-standard performance. The Court of Appeal's interpretation meant that the clause served no purpose at all. As a measure of controlling the delinquencies of the contractor, and of asserting the interests of the council, by means less drastic than termination, the court was impressed by the provision for withholding moneys from the contractor when default notices were served. Yet this provision does not seem to have persuaded the contractor to mend its ways. Above all, the court was impressed by the way that the termination clause did not pick out particular performance clauses in the contract but visited the same 'draconian consequences' on all breaches of all clauses. One wonders what the court would have made of an open-ended contract that gave the council the right to terminate without cause on a relatively short period of notice. Clauses of this kind have been upheld.[65] The contractor would be hard pressed to gain traction from an argument that both parties factually expected the agreement to run for a longer period.[66]

The offending clause in the charterparty in *The Antaios* provided that 'on any breach of this charterparty, the owners shall be at liberty to withdraw the vessel'. This brings us back to Sumption JSC's words in *Petroleo Brasiliero SA v ENE Kos 1 Ltd*.[67] *The Antaios* did not concern the usual late payment of hire, rather, it concerned inaccurate charterers' bills of lading, but the shipowner's motive was the normal one, evident in the cases dealing with withdrawal for non-payment of hire, of seeking to recapture a rising market, which on numerous occasions has been held also not to disqualify termination for breach of commodity sale contracts.[68] The council's action in *Rice* was not in response to a single breach, as was the case in *The Antaios*, nor was it an attempt to recover a lost bargaining opportunity. This prompts an attempt to find a middle course between interpreting the clause at face value and interpreting it as having no meaning other than to state the default, repudiation-based, test for a discharging breach of contract. It may not be business common-sense to say that the termination clause allows the council to terminate for any breach, no matter how trivial and how early it comes in the four-year cycle, but it is hardly business common-sense to say that it adds nothing to the rest of the contract.

Is there a way of giving some effect to the clause whilst controlling its excesses? The remarks that follow are made in the shadow of the recent Court of Appeal decision in *Mid Essex Hospital Services NHS Trust v Compass Group UK and Ireland Ltd*, with particular reference to the following passage from Jackson LJ's

[64] Indeed, 'severe' according to the court in *Rice*, n 60 above.
[65] See *TSG Building Services*, n 63 above.
[66] See *Baird Textile Holdings Ltd v Marks & Spencer Plc* [2001] EWCA Civ 274; [2001] CLC 999.
[67] See p 87 above.
[68] Where it is at least as often the case of a buyer terminating on a falling market.

judgment referring to a line of cases on the exercise of a contractual discretion: 'An important feature of the above line of authorities is that in each case the discretion did not involve a simple decision whether or not to exercise an *absolute contractual right*. The discretion involved making an assessment or choosing from a range of options, taking into account the interest of both parties' (emphasis added).[69]

The exercise of a contractual right to terminate for breach would appear to involve the exercise of 'an absolute contractual right' and to be without reference to the interests of the party in breach. Thus understood, it would close off this line of cases as a means of controlling the intemperate use of excessively drawn termination clauses. Nevertheless, my argument is that the expectations arising between the parties, fuelled by the extravagant character of the clause, mean that the clause cannot be understood to confer an absolute right to terminate. It is not a case of controls over the exercise of a discretion being imposed by operation of law. Rather, that discretion, exercised in a particular manner, might be said to be agreed as a matter of business common-sense between the parties and grounded in the decision-making process. For this reason, the line of authorities on contractual discretion continues to merit consideration. The freedom of contracting parties is not being unjustifiably impeded. Instead, an attempt is being made to give effect to their intentions and to provide a purpose for a contractual clause that would otherwise be rendered nugatory. If a reasonable bystander were to ask whether the termination clause would be invoked for a first, technical breach, the candid response of the party with the right would probably be that the right would not be exercised without good reason.

An extravagantly drawn clause of the type in *Rice* might then be interpreted as vesting a discretionary power in the council, a power that is not to be exercised except where there exist good grounds to do so as perceived by a fair-minded contracting party. So, in what way does existing law circumscribe contractual discretion? The signs drawn from cases involving valuation suggest that the answer may not be quite enough to accord with commercial expectations of the kind fairly engendered in long-term contracts like those in *Wickman* and *Rice*. According to *Ludgate Insurance Co Ltd v Citibank NA*, the courts will not intervene in the exercise of a discretion 'provided that the discretion is exercised honestly and in good faith for the purposes for which it was conferred, and provided also that it was a true exercise of discretion in the sense that it was not capricious or arbitrary or so outrageous in its defiance of reason that it can properly be categorised as perverse'.[70] Referring to *Ludgate* and related cases, the court in *Socimer International Bank Ltd v Standard Bank Ltd London (No 2)* concluded that 'a decision-maker's discretion will be limited, as a matter of necessary implication, by concepts of honesty, good faith, and genuineness, and the need for the absence of arbitrariness, capriciousness, perversity and irrationality'.[71] This is far from being a duty of care and, as the

[69] *Mid Essex Hospital Services NHS Trust v Compass Group UK and Ireland Ltd* [2013] EWCA Civ 200, para 83; [2013] BLR 265 For a discussion of the exercise of contractual discretion, see Richard Hooley, 'Controlling Contractual Discretion' [2013] *Cambridge Law Journal* 65.

[70] *Ludgate Insurance Co Ltd v Citibank NA* [1998] Lloyd's Rep IR 221, para 35.

[71] *Socimer International Bank Ltd v Standard Bank Ltd London (No 2)* [2008] EWCA Civ 116 [2008] Bus LR 1304, para 66 (Rix LJ), with whom Lloyd and Laws LJJ agreed). See also *Paragon Finance plc v*

court observes, is not far removed from the test of *Wednesbury* unreasonableness in administrative law,[72] though the court itself did not favour the language of public law but instead preferred to express the test in terms of rationality.

Contracts like those in *Wickman* and *Rice* are not market driven contracts posing the sharp question whether the selfish capture of market gain justifies contractual termination for technical breaches of condition. Though involving close cooperation between contracting parties, neither do they give rise to fiduciary relations between the parties. The test put forward in *Socimer* was later explained in the same case as 'standard, for [it represents] the very essence of business, and other, relationships'.[73] Business necessity is also stated as performing a role in the emergence of this test, which suggests that, in line with the confluence of interpretation and implied terms in recent years, termination clauses of the broad kind that appear in cases like *Wickman* and *Rice* are to be read down in accordance with the business necessity (or efficacy) test, but only so far as is needed to comply with business necessity. This should be more demanding than the *Wednesbury* test or its private law counterpart of rationality. To the extent that it is, is there another route to pursue?

The recent decision of Leggatt J on the implication of a duty of good faith in the performance of a distributorship agreement, *Yam Seng Pte Ltd v International Trade Corp Ltd*,[74] makes a useful connection with the *Socimer* group of authorities and invites an analysis of the outcome in cases like *Rice* and *Wickman* in accordance with such implied duty of good faith.[75] As the case demonstrates, good faith has a range of meanings[76] stretching from honesty to fair dealing, a factor which represents not the least of the difficulties in creating space for its incorporation in English law. That said, Leggatt J was insistent that he was not proposing an overarching general principle imposed on the parties. Rather, it was a case of a genuine implied duty, sensitive to context, that, in accordance with the modern approach, could be seen as expressive of what the parties wished their contract to mean. (There is some slight slippage in the judgment where the intention of the parties becomes their presumed intention.) The core of Leggatt J's implied term, moreover, was honesty, which hardly suggests an implied term of ambitious reach. Although the *Mid Essex* case might be seen as rolling back the advance of good faith, the approach adopted in *Yam Seng* itself was referred to without criticism and an implied duty in 'certain categories' of case implicitly accepted.[77]

Good faith, so far as it transcends honesty, is not a notion that lends itself to exact meaning, even if its interpretation is limited to a particular context. The really hard question posed by a duty of good faith that transcends honesty is when it requires

Nash [2002] 1 WLR 685; *Abu Dhabi National Tanker Co v Product Star Shipping Ltd (The Product Star)* [1993] 1 Lloyd's Rep 397; *Horkaluk v Cantor Fitzgerald International* [2005] EWCA Civ 1287; [2005] ICR 402; *JML Direct v Freestar UK Ltd* [2010] EWCA Civ 34; *Barclays Bank plc v Unicredit Bank AG* [2012] EWHC 3655 (Comm) ('an objective standard of reasonableness') (affirmed [2014] EWCA Civ 302).

72 *Associated Provincial Picture House Ltd v Wednesbury Corporation* [1948] 1 KB 223.

73 *Socimer*, n 71 above, para 106.

74 *Yam Seng Pte Ltd v International Trade Corp Ltd* [2013] EWHC 111 (QB); [2013] 1 CLC 662.

75 Note, however, that the court in *The Product Star*, n 71 above, at 404, considered that the notion of fairness merely described the result arrived at by controlling a discretion in the manner stated above.

76 '[T]he content of a duty of good faith is heavily conditioned by its context': *Mid Essex*, n 69 above.

77 *Yam Seng*, n 74 above, para 105 (Jackson LJ).

the obligor to sacrifice self-interest in favour of the other party or the attainment of a shared objective, if such a thing exists in the particular case. This will surely depend upon the character of the contract and the proximity of the parties to each other. In a commodity sale, a duty not to take strategic advantage of a change in market conditions by pouncing on a breach of condition would, if it were ever recognised, involve a 180-degree turn from a line of authorities going back nearly a century and a half.[78] The judgment in *Yam Seng* provides little ammunition for those who would wish for such a change, given the nature of commodities markets and the nature of the relationships of those who operate in them. It was a key feature of *Yam Seng* that it concerned a long-term distribution agreement where overtones of joint venture and fiduciary relationships (a coat of many colours) begin to emerge.

Returning to *Rice*, the gardener in the brave new world of outsourcing might fairly expect the meaning of the termination clause to be encased in a spirit of some tolerance and patience, so that it would be 'improper' or 'commercially unacceptable' or even 'unconscionable' to pounce on a particular breach in order to terminate a contract for ulterior reasons, where, for example, the local authority does so because it believes that it can get a better quotation or even a higher standard of service from another gardener. That is, of course, far from what happened in *Rice* itself. If the termination clause were interpreted in accordance with the contractual context as amplified by a requirement of patience and reasonableness, a superior approach to a vague invocation of good faith, the court on facts like those in *Rice* would have the valuable option of recognising the exercise of termination rights pursuant to the clause on the facts as they existed at the time. The same flexibility is not present in the case of controls that might be exercised under UCTA 1977, section 3(2)(b): that provision does not allow the court to rewrite or 'rectify' the clause. And, of course, the modern dispensation in the area of contractual interpretation comes close to obliterating the distinction between interpretation and rectification.[79]

CONCLUSION

The modern approach to interpretation, folding into the process of interpretation the implication of contract terms, reductive as the process is, has the capacity to embrace the non-statutory issues discussed above. Equitable intervention to restrict common law rights of termination may well have had its day. Nor can there be a question of section 15A of the Sale of Goods Act being filtered through a common-sense interpretation of the contract: it may in any case already be said to represent common-sense to the limited extent of its application. As for UCTA 1977, section 3(2)(b), the bold approach suggested by Bingham MR may have been overtaken by the contemporary approach to contractual interpretation as recounted to a limited extent in the final substantive section of this chapter. Failing both a context-driven approach to interpretation in the contemporary fashion and Bingham MR's bold common law exploitation of a statutory provision, a *contra*

[78] *Bowes v Shand* (1877) 2 App Cas 455.

[79] See in particular *Investors Compensation Scheme Ltd v West Bromwich Building Society* [1998] 1 WLR 896.

proferentem approach to extravagantly drawn termination clauses, striking them down as though they were subject to UCTA 1977, will continue to prevail. This is inferior to a more nuanced, interpretative approach that gives some effect to a freely agreed clause.[80] Even so, the contemporary approach to contractual interpretation does not commend itself to those who continue to see merit in the compelling attractions of contractual certainty, which is one of the prized attributes of English law. The modern approach to contractual interpretation has come at the price of destabilising contract law, but it may prove to have some benefits in the area of contractual termination rights.

[80] There would then be less of a gap than now prevails between a termination for breach clause and a clause allowing 'termination for convenience' on notice being given, which is common in certain types of contract and has been upheld: *TSG Building Services Plc v South Anglia Housing Ltd*, n 63 above.

7

Regulating Unfair Terms

MINDY CHEN-WISHART*

INTRODUCTION

SINCE WRITTEN CONTRACTS are overwhelmingly in standard form,[1] regulating such contracts must be one of contract law's most important tasks. As Law Commissioner for England and Wales, Professor Beale brought his formidable scholarship, intellect and judgement to bear on the subject of unfair standard terms.[2] The Law Commission's avowed objective was to design a legislative regime that preserves the consumer protections currently afforded by both the Unfair Contract Terms Act 1977 (UCTA) and the Unfair Terms in Consumer Contracts Regulations 1999, SI 1999/2083 (UTCCR). This has borne fruit as part of the Consumer Rights Bill, currently before Parliament. However, while the substantive law embodied in UCTA and UTCCR is reasonably well settled, there has been relatively little theorising on the justification for the precise scheme of regulation contained therein.[3] Doing so is important in itself, for any law that demands obedience should also be justifiable. The task is also important to guide adjudication, to provide a basis for any critique of the current law, and to point the way of future reform.

At least three factors may have contributed to this situation. First, the basis for regulating unfair standard terms seems obvious, namely, that of 'unfair surprise' and 'harsh terms' buried in the fine print. But, while this explains the problems, it does not justify the particular responses contained in UCTA and UTCCR, in particular, the specific terms targeted and the precise mechanisms of regulation. Secondly, as

* The chapter is better for the helpful comments from my colleagues: thanks to Hugh Collins, Hugh Beale, Stephen Weatherill, Dorota Leczykiewicz and Sarah Green.

[1] W David Slawson, 'Standard Form Contracts and Democratic Control of Lawmaking Power' (1971) 84 *Harvard Law Review* 529; Robert Hillman and Jeffrey Rachlinski, 'Standard-Form Contracting in the Electronic Age' (2002) 77 *New York University Law Review* 429, 431; Russell Korobkin, 'Bounded Rationality, Standard Form Contracts, and Unconscionability' (2003) 70 *University Chicago Law Review* 1203, 1203–4.

[2] Law Commission and Scottish Law Commission, *Unfair Terms in Contracts: A Joint Consultation Paper* (Law Com CP No 166 and Scot Law Com No 119, 2002); Law Commission and Scottish Law Commission, *Unfair Terms in Contracts* (Law Com No 292 and Scot Law Com No 199, 2005).

[3] Eg Meryll Dean, 'Unfair Contract Terms: The European Approach' (1993) *Modern Law Review* 581, 585: 'At the heart of the test of unfairness is a desire to tackle the notion of unconscionability of unfair contract'; see also Law Commission and Scottish Law Commission, *Unfair Terms in Contracts*, (Law Com CP No 166 and Scot Law Com No 119, 2002) n 2 above, paras 2.5–2.9 referring to 'unfair surprise' and 'harsh terms'.

statutory (rather than common law) regulation, it is easier to regard them as 'public policy' implemented by a sovereign Parliament carrying out their Treaty mandate, and by the Council and the European Parliament, that does not demand the sort of legitimation (and so theorising) normally called for by common law doctrines. Thirdly, the proliferation of contract theory scholarship of the last 40 years[4] is very largely premised on the traditional paradigm of negotiated contracting and this translates poorly to the paradigm of non-negotiated contracting implicit in almost all contracts covered by UCTA and UTCCR. This last factor exposes the limitations of the orthodox contract paradigm in law-making and theorising, and the need to recognise multiple contract paradigms.

In the next section I contrast the negotiated and non-negotiated contract paradigms and examine the problems of questionable consent and unfair terms arising from the latter. In the third section I sketch the distinct tripartite pattern of control contained in UCTA and UTCCR; namely: (i) the types of dealing covered (consumer, standard form and standard form consumer contracts); (ii) the four types of terms controlled (exemptions of the trader's liability, reduction of the trader's obligations, increasing the customer's obligations, and increasing the customer's liabilities); and (iii) the method of control (invalidating some terms outright and subjecting others to a test of reasonableness or fairness). The fourth section then explores three possible justifications for this pattern of control (defective consent, market inefficiency and standard terms as defective product). These provide important insights, but not complete or satisfying justifications.

I then put forward and defend a justification for UCTA and UTCCR based on protecting the institution of contract. The primary purpose of this social institution is to expand valuable choices by providing the necessary security for exchange agreements that further each party's conception of the good. Mass market standard form contracting entails severe risks to constitutive features of the institution, namely, respect for voluntary choice; facilitation of mutually valuable exchange; and guarantee of legal redress. In practice, informed consent to the fine print is impossible, while the substance of the fine print tends to subvert the legitimate expectations based on the main subject matter and price terms, establish unacceptable power relationships, or destroy the right to meaningful redress. UCTA and UTCCR protect the institution of contract in contexts that pose the most acute dangers to it (accounting for (i) the type of dealings covered), by invalidating terms that unjustifiably (accounting for (iii) the method of regulation) undermine contract's underlying logic of voluntariness, reciprocity and right to redress (accounting for (ii) the type of terms targeted).

[4] Eg from Charles Fried, *Contract as Promise* (Cambridge, MA, Harvard University Press, 1981), to PS Atiyah, *The Rise and Fall of Freedom of Contract* (Oxford University Press, 1985), to Michael Trebilcock, *The Limits of Freedom of Contract* (Cambridge, MA, Harvard University Press 1997), to Dori Kimel, *From Promise to Contract: Towards a Liberal Theory of Contract* (Oxford, Hart Publishing, 2003), to Stephen Smith, *Contract Theory* (Oxford University Press, 2004), to Brian Bix, *Contract Law: Rules, Theory, and Context* (Cambridge University Press, 2012).

FROM NEGOTIATED TO NON-NEGOTIATED CONTRACTING

Negotiated Contract Paradigm

A general law of contract necessitates abstracting from the whole range of transactions, to a necessarily paradigmatic view of the contracting process. The orthodox paradigm of contracting is familiar enough: two parties with equal bargaining power freely, voluntarily and at arm's length, negotiating every aspect of their agreement, and then reducing their understanding to a writing intended to embody their whole agreement. This is the voluntary exchange envisaged by liberal and economic theories of contract; each party freely agreeing to give up something of hers to obtain something from the other that she values more, generating a contract satisfactory to both. Thus, contract presupposes *dealing* (manifesting the parties' free choice) as well as a *deal* (the product of that joint mutually enhancing creative process).

On this view, legal regulation of *procedural* unfairness is regarded as legitimate, while regulation for *substantive* unfairness is generally regarded as not. Accordingly, the orthodoxy is that contracts may be invalidated if there is no agreement on the objective test of intentions or if the complainant's consent is defective in ways recognised by the vitiating factors, especially if the party seeking to enforce the contract created, exacerbated or otherwise exploited this defective consent. However, regulation for substantive unfairness is rejected as unnecessary (because procedural unfairness guarantees substantive unfairness), undesirable (because it replaces the parties' autonomy with unjustified state paternalism), and impracticable (because courts are not competent to judge substantive unfairness, doing so will introduce excessive uncertainty and will backfire in the long run, and any justified redistribution should be left to the tax and welfare regime).[5] Nevertheless, substantive unfairness may be part of the burden of proof,[6] operate as evidence of procedural unfairness[7] (the complainant's defective consent[8] or the enforcer's unconscientiousness inducement).[9]

This justification for control of unfairness generated by this paradigm of contracting is ill-suited to the problems of unfairness arising from standard form contracting.

[5] See Hugh Collins, *Regulating Contracts* (Oxford University Press, 2002) 284; Richard Epstein, 'Unconscionability: A Critical Reappraisal' (1975) 18 *Journal of Law and Economics* 283, 305–15; Fried, *Contract as Promise*, n 4 above, chs 3, 7; Randy Barnett, 'A Consent Theory of Contract' (1986) 86 *Columbia Law Review* 269, 283–86; Michael Trebilcock, 'An Economic Approach to Unconscionability' in Barry Swan and John Reiter (eds), *Studies in Contract Law* (Oxford, Butterworth-Heinemann, 1980); Alan Schwartz, 'Justice and the Laws of Contract: A Case for the Traditional Approach' (1986) 9 *Harvard Journal Law and Public Policy* 107; Robert Nozick, *Anarchy, State and Utopia* (Oxford, Basil Blackwell, 1974) 64–65; Ludwig Von Mises, *Human Action,* 2nd edn (New Haven, CT, Yale University Press, 1963) 94–98, 242, 354, 727–30.

[6] Eg in finding an unconscionable bargain; for undue influence to be inferred, the transaction must 'call for an explanation'; the effect of infancy depends largely on whether the contracts are broadly beneficial to the infant.

[7] *Blomley v Ryan* (1956) 99 CLR 362, 405–6 (HCA).

[8] Eg *Credit Lyonnais v Burch* [1997] 1 All ER 144, 154, 155 (CA).

[9] Eg in respect of duress to the person, *Barton v Armstrong* [1976] AC 104 (PC) (appeal from New South Wales), and in respect of economic duress, *Huyton v Cremer* [1999] 1 Lloyd LR 620 (QB).

Non-negotiated Contract Paradigm

Standard form contracting does not involve 'bargain', 'negotiation' or 'consent' in any meaningful sense. A standard form contract is conventionally described as a printed document containing many terms purporting to be the contract; put forward by a commercial ('proffering') party who makes many contracts of the same type; presented explicitly or implicitly on a take-it-or-leave-it basis to the other ('adhering') party who enters few such contracts, and is generally unaware of and unable to assess their substance. The situation is aggravated by the rise and rise of electronic commerce (worth £100 bn to the UK economy in 2010; this was more than 7 per cent of national income, and nearly as big as the financial services sector),[10] and the associated use of the following:

— 'shrinkwrap' contracts (typically used in software contracts; they bind a party to terms contained therein even if these terms cannot be seen or agreed to until the product is bought and opened);
— terms sent after a contract is made over the telephone (eg in insurance or banking);
— 'clickwrap' (when parties are bound by clicking 'I agree' or equivalent online; reference may be made to dense text standard terms in a hyperlink, elsewhere on the site, offsite or even on a different website); and
— 'browsewrap' (where the terms for use of a website or downloadable product are posted on the website, typically as a hyperlink at the bottom of the screen, and the site user is bound by simply using the product, such as by entering the website or downloading software).

The non-negotiated paradigm generates different problems from those arising from negotiated contracting. First, the complainant suffers from no mental incapacity or mistake, which are the staple of the recognised vitiating factors. Indeed, most are perfectly competent by normal standards. Rather, the relevant weakness is situational, attaching to standard form contracting itself. Secondly, there is generally[11] no opportunity and no need for unconscientious conduct by the proffering party in the recognised senses of misrepresentation, duress, undue influence, unconscionable conduct, and so on. There is simply no negotiation for such conduct to 'bite' onto.[12] Thirdly, the concern with standard form contracts is not primarily about contractual imbalance in the sense of inadequacy of consideration. Rather, it is about the presence of terms that subvert the complainant's reasonable expectations based on the price and main subject matter of the contract, deprive complainants of default rights, or render such rights and obligations subject to the other party's discretionary power.

The non-negotiated paradigm is more akin to the imposition of the proffering party's will than of a mutually agreed arrangement; hence, its description as 'private

[10] See James Robinson, 'UK's Internet industry worth £100 bn: report', *The Guardian* (London), 28 October 2010, available at www.theguardian.com/technology/2010/oct/28/net-worth-100bn-uk.

[11] Of course, this is not ruled out. See Law Commission, *Consumer Redress for Misleading and Aggressive Practices* (Law Com No 332, 2012).

[12] Initiating standard form dealing cannot be regarded as unfair per se, see discussion at p 120 below.

legislation' and 'contracts of adhesion'.[13] The dangers of standard form contracts for the adhering party are indeed questionable consent and objectionable terms. But the important specifics of these problems contain the clues to the solutions contained in UCTA and UTCCR.

Problem of Consent

'Adhering' parties can realistically be taken to know and consent to the main subject matter and price terms of the contract. Beyond that, absent a lawyer at their elbow, adhering parties may not even know of the existence of the fine print. If they do know, reading will be deterred by the density and length of the fine print, the complicated and unintelligible language, the confusing layout, and the strong social pressure not to appear awkward or confrontational. One study found that even in an environment conducive to reading (the comfort of one's home or office) only one in every thousand retail software shoppers chooses to access the licence agreement for more than one second. And, those few spend too little time to have read more than a tiny portion of the text (the average time spent was 47.7 seconds and the median time was 29 seconds).[14] The *New York Times* reported that software from four major sellers 'were an average of 74,000-plus words, which is basically the length of the first Harry Potter book'.[15]

Lord Denning is thus vindicated in his assessment that 'no customer in a thousand ever read the conditions';[16] Lord Megaw anticipated the likely indignation of service providers if customers actually tried to read and understand the terms provided.[17] Indeed, there is much literature showing that an adhering party will be 'rationally ignorant' of such terms.[18] For, even if, freakishly, she invests the hours reading the terms, her comprehension and assessment of them will be significantly hindered by her lack of legal and financial literacy. One commentator concluded that 97 per cent of all American adults lack the basic literacy skills required to understand consumer

[13] Fredrich Kessler, 'Contracts of Adhesion: Some Thoughts about Freedom of Contract' (1943) 43 *Columbia Law Review* 629.

[14] This tracked the Internet browsing behaviour of 45,091 households with respect to 66 online software companies. Yannis Bakos, Florencia Marotta-Wurgler and David Trossen, *Does Anyone Read the Fine Print? Testing a Law and Economics Approach to Standard Form Contracts*, CELS Fourth Annual Conference on Empirical Legal Studies Paper (New York, 2009).

[15] See Alina Tugend, 'Those wordy contracts We all so quickly accept', *New York Times*, 12 July 2013, available at www.nytimes.com/2013/07/13/your-money/novel-length-contracts-online-and-what-they-say.html?pagewanted=1&src=me&_r=1&.

[16] *Thornton v Shoe Lane Parking Ltd* [1971] 2 QB 163, 169 (CA).

[17] ibid at 173.

[18] Melvin Aron Eisenberg, 'The Limits of Cognition and the Limits of Contract' (1995) 47 *Stanford Law Review* 211, 241, 243. Peter Alces, 'Guerrilla Terms' (2007) 56 *Emory Law Journal* 1511, 1529–30. ('[T]he "search" cost of discovering the higher price and greater risk is too great given the benefit the buyer imagines she would derive from discovering the cost'); Lucian Bebchuk and Richard Posner, 'One-Sided Contracts in Competitive Consumer Markets' (2006) 104 *Michigan Law Review* 827, 832 (arguing the cost imposed on consumers in gaining information may exceed the benefit, resulting in consumers' rational ignorance); Robert Prentice, 'Contract-based Defenses in Securities Fraud Litigation: A Behavioral Analysis' (2003) *University of Illinois Law Review* 337, 358–62 ('Personally, I neither read most of the contracts that I sign nor know anyone who does. I do not believe that this makes me unusually irrational, particularly stupid, or unreasonably lazy').

standard form contracts of even moderate complexity.[19] Aside from these limitations, the average person suffers from a long list of systematic cognitive biases[20] that inhibit her rational assessment of standard terms and their associated risks.[21] For example, most fine print terms lack salience; they usually deal with contingent (often highly contingent) events, which the bounded rationality of human beings will discount. Finally, anyone who has got as far as reading, understanding and objecting to any of the fine print would be told to 'take it or leave it'. If she then went to another supplier the result is likely to be the same.

A person today who refused to contract without being adequately apprised of the fine print would deny herself of most means of living in a modern society, or would lead a not very interesting or productive life. In reality then, the obstacles to giving informed consent to a standard form of any complexity is simply *insurmountable*. The fine print is for all intents and purposes invisible. This must inform the concept of the 'average consumer', which the Consumer Rights Bill defines as 'reasonably well-informed, observant and circumspect'.[22] Contract law should be responsive to what we know about human behaviour in respect of choice. After all, it is pervasively in the business of constructing the procedures and contexts for identifying choice, and for enforcing the choices made.[23]

Problem of Objectionable Terms

In any market where one party can unilaterally create most of the rules of the game by imposing its own terms, highly disproportionate contracts are likely to result. Whatever protection against unfairness a process of negotiation might give, standard form contracting gives no such protection. The problem is not primarily that of contractual imbalance between the main subject matter of the contract and

[19] Wayne Barnes, 'Toward a Fairer Model of Consumer Assent to Standard Form Contracts: In Defense of Restatement Subsection 211(3)' (2007) 82 *Washington Law Review* 227, 229–30, 261–62, citing Alan White and Cathy Lesser Mansfield, 'Literacy and Contract' (2002) 13 *Stanford Law and Policy Review* 233, 237–38, 233, 234.

[20] See, eg discussion in Anthony Ogus, *Costs and Cautionary Tales: Economic Insights for the Law* (Oxford, Hart Publishing, 2006) 232–38.

[21] See, in general, Cass Sunstein, 'Behavioral Analysis of Law' (1997) 64 *University of Chicago Law Review* 1175, and in particular Amos Tversky and Daniel Kahneman, 'Rational Choice and the Framing of Decisions' (1986) 59 *Journal of Business Law* (Supp) S251; Korobkin, 'Bounded Rationality, Standard Form Contracts, and Unconscionability', n 1 above; Lynn Baker and Robert Emery, 'When Every Relationship is Above Average: Perceptions and Expectations of Divorce at the Time of Marriage' (1993) 17 *Law and Human Behaviour* 439; Margaret Radin, *Boilerplate: The Fine Print, Vanishing Rights, and the Rule of Law* (Princeton, NJ, Princeton University Press, 2012) 26; Alces, 'Guerrilla Terms', n 18 above, 1523; Xavier Gabaix and David Laibson, 'Shrouded Attributes, Consumer Myopia, and Information Suppression in Competitive Markets' (2006) 121 *Quarterly Journal of Economics* 505; Shmuel Becher and Esther Unger-Aviram, 'The Law of Standard Form Contracts: Misguided Intuitions and Suggestions for Reconstruction' (2010) *DePaul Business and Commercial Law Journal* 199, 214; Ted Cruz and Jeffrey Hinck, 'Not My Brother's Keeper: The Inability of an Informed Minority to Correct for Imperfect Information' (1996) 47 *Hastings Law Journal* 635, 638–40; Eric Posner, 'Economic Analysis of Contract Law after Three Decades: Success or Failure?' (2003) 112 *Yale Law Journal* 829, 843; David Horton, 'The Shadow Terms: Contract Procedure and Unilateral Amendments' (2010) 57 *University of California at Los Angeles Law Review* 605, 647–48.

[22] Consumer Rights Bill 2013, cl 64(5).

[23] See generally, Cass Sunstein (ed), *Behavioral Law and Economics* (Cambridge University Press, 2000).

its price; even 'rationally ignorant' consumers bring their judgement to bear on these logically more transparent terms of the contract. The danger lurks in the 'invisible' fine print, for which there is no competitive market. The result is a 'race to the bottom'; a trend towards contracts characterised by low cost but harsh 'non-core' terms. The oft-stated concern about 'unfair surprise' in standard form contracting must be seen in this light. Fair surprises raise no concern. Thus, lack of knowledge or choice as to the non-core terms, while relevant, does not go to the nub of the problem

Objectionable terms are of four overlapping types. First, are terms that reduce or delete the remedial rights that the adhering party would otherwise have, leaving her with no or inadequate redress and allowing the proffering party to evade substantive legal oversight of the contract. Second which may amount to the same thing, are terms that reduce the proffering party's obligations against the baseline of the main subject matter term. Third are terms that inflate the adhering party's obligations against the price term. Fourth are terms that maximise protection of the proffering party's interests by imposing disproportionate or otherwise unfair burdens or liability on the adhering party.

STATUTORY CONTROL OF UNFAIR TERMS

Here, I sketch the types of contracts covered, the types of terms targeted, and the control mechanisms contained in UCTA and UTCCR, as a precursor to examining four justifications for this tripartite scheme.

Type of Contracts Targeted

UCTA operates in favour of both consumers (whether a natural person or a business acting as a consumer, and whether in standard form or not), *and businesses* (primarily those contracting on the other's standard form). UTCCR only protects *consumers who are natural persons in relation to non-negotiated terms*. Both UCTA and UTCCR operate only against businesses contracting for business purposes.

Type of Terms Targeted

UTCCR specifically immunises from challenge (a) negotiated terms, and (b) non-negotiated terms expressed in plain and intelligible language[24] that define the main subject matter or price.[25] Otherwise, UCTA and UTCCR together broadly target the four overlapping types of objectionable terms mentioned above (terms that shrink the proffering party's, or inflate the adhering party's, obligations or liabilities).[26] UTCCR also permits the review of any other non-negotiated non-core terms.

[24] Consumer Rights Bill 2013, cl 64(2) refers to 'transparent and prominent'.
[25] UTCCR, reg 6(2).
[26] They are discussed at p 121–24 below.

Mechanisms of Control

First, UTCCR requires all terms to be in plain and intelligible language on pain of *contra proferentem* construction and review for unfairness of otherwise immune core terms.[27]

Secondly, UCTA and UTCCR divide the targeted terms into two categories: black-listed terms are automatically invalid,[28] and grey-listed terms[29] are subject to the test of reasonableness under UCTA or fairness under UTCCR. Invalid terms are severed from the rest of the contract, which continues to bind the parties if possible.

The tests of reasonableness,[30] and of fairness[31] as contravention of good faith causing significant imbalance are very similar although not identical. *Chitty* concludes that any differences between them come down to the differences in the scope of the two pieces of legislation: the parties affected and types of terms tested.[32] Broadly speaking, the non-exhaustive factors relevant to the determination of validity of grey-listed terms fall into two overlapping categories. First, are factors that go to the quality of the adhering party's deliberation and so consent; this mirrors the common law's preoccupation with *procedural unfairness*. Thus, the court is directed to consider all the circumstances existing at formation, taking into account, inter alia, the parties' relative bargaining power, the availability of alternatives, and any pressure on the adhering party to conclude the contract or to do so in haste and without time to think about its significance, even if this pressure would not amount to duress or undue influence.[33] UCTA[34] and UTCCR[35] also direct the court to consider the adhering party's realistic opportunity to read, understand, consider and decide upon the challenged term.

[27] See UTCCR, reg 6(2) and 7.

[28] UCTA, ss 2(1), 5, 6(1), (2), 7(2), (3A)). These are discussed further at p 126–29 below.

[29] UCTA, ss 2(2), 3, 4, 6(3), 7(3), (4); terms listed in UTCCR, Sch 2 and other terms not going to the main subject matter or price of the contract (reg 6).

[30] Strictly speaking, three slightly different tests of reasonableness appear in UCTA: the general test in s 11(1); the test applicable to statutory implied terms falling within ss 6–7, detailed in Sch 2; and the test applicable to terms which limit rather than exclude liability referred to in s 11(4). However, the courts have made clear in *Rees Hough Ltd v Redland Reinforced Plastics Ltd* (1984) 2 Const LR 109, 151 (QBD); *Stewart Gill Ltd v Horatio Myer & Co Ltd* [1992] 1 QB 600, 608 (CA), that all the factors mentioned in the various guidelines are applicable to *all* cases in which they appear relevant. Moreover, these factors are neither exhaustive nor determinative; the court may take into account any other relevant circumstances. In practice, therefore, there is a single test of reasonableness.

[31] UTCCR, reg 5(1): a term is unfair if 'contrary to the requirement of good faith, it causes a significant imbalance in the parties' rights and obligations arising under the contract, to the detriment of the consumer'. This is supplemented by the guidance contained in reg 6(1) and in recital 16 of the originating Directive, and by the Sch 2 list of indicatively unfair terms.

[32] Hugh Beale (ed), *Chitty on Contracts*, 31st edn (London, Sweet & Maxwell, 2012) para 15-100.

[33] ibid para 15-084.

[34] UCTA, Sch 2, para (c) 'whether the customer knew or ought reasonably to have known of the existence and the extent of the term (having regard, among other things, to any custom of the trade and any previous course of dealing between the parties)'.

[35] UTCCR, Sch 2, para 1(i) lists as indicatively unfair a term which has the object or effect of 'irrevocably binding the consumer to terms with which he had no real opportunity of becoming acquainted before the conclusion of the contract'. See statement in Council Directive 93/13/EC of 5 April 1993 on unfair terms in consumer contracts [1993] OJ L095, recital 20 that 'the consumer should actually be given an opportunity to examine all the terms'.

Secondly, in a departure from the common law, the court must consider the *substance* of the challenged term. Thus, the court must specifically consider:[36] whether the customer received any inducement to accept the challenged term; the reasonableness of conditions imposed on claims; whether the goods were manufactured, processed or adapted to the customer's special order; and the profferring party's resources to meet or insure against likely claims.

UNDERSTANDING THE PATTERN OF CONTROL UNDER UCTA AND UTCCR

Here, I assess possible explanations for the pattern of control found in UCTA and UTCCR based on defective consent, market inefficiency, contract as product and protection of the institution of contract.

Defective Consent

The concern with defective consent of orthodox contract theory is consistent with some aspects of UCTA and UTCCR. First, it explains the type of contracts or dealing covered: broadly speaking, consumer, standard form and non-negotiated consumer contracts which entail particular risks of informational asymmetry and non-negotiability. Secondly, it explains why non-core terms in general are targeted (for which consent will be doubtful at best) while plain and intelligible core terms that will have been consented to are immune from review under UTCCR. Thirdly, it explains the requirement for all terms to be in plain and intelligible language.

However, defective consent does not readily explain the identity of the non-core terms that are specifically targeted; the automatic invalidity of some these terms; and the invalidity of others only if they are unfair and unreasonable, when consent is equally questionable in respect of *all* terms in the fine print. One rationale, used to justify common law rules on the enforceability of standard form contracts, is that the adhering party has given 'blanket consent'[37] to everything contained in the fine print that is not unfair or unreasonable, and that even those that *are* (the 'onerous or unusual' terms) are binding if the adhering party has received 'adequate notice' of them.

This explanation is problematic. First, the implicit assumption that it is up to the adhering party to read and understand the fine print (so that if she does not, that is her look-out) is unrealistic and premised on a 'world of make-believe which the law has created'.[38] Thus, Lord Denning returned repeatedly to the injustice of the signature rule (which he helped to create) in his extra-legal writings.[39] Secondly,

[36] UCTA, s 11(1), (4), and Sch 2.

[37] Karl Llewellyn, *The Common Law Tradition: Deciding Appeals* (Buffalo, NY, WS Hein, 1960) 370; Randy Barnett, 'Consenting to Form Contracts' (2002) 71 *Fordham Law Review* 627.

[38] *McCutcheon v David MacBrayne Ltd* [1964] 1 All ER 430, 436 (HL) (Lord Devlin).

[39] '[G]oing back to my junior days when I induced the Court of Appeal to uphold a most unrighteous clause in *L'Estrange v Graucob*'; Lord Denning, 'Foreword' (1986) 1 *Denning Law Journal* 1, 2; '[i]n those days I wasn't concerned so much with the rightness of the cause. I was concerned only … to win if I could', Lord Denning, 'This is My Life' (1986) 1 *Denning Law Journal* 17, 20; 'I thought I had done well by my clients, but since I have become a judge I have done everything I can to get that decision altered', Lord Denning, 'The Right Standards of Conduct' (1957) *Law Society's Gazette* 609, 610.

the idea that voluntary assent and personal autonomy are 'fixed' by disclosure is misguided because it ignores the evidence that people are not substantially more likely to read disclosures than the form terms themselves,[40] and that people's problems go well beyond ignorance.[41] Indeed, '[t]o the extent that one does not understand the terms of the agreement, requiring the same to be printed in bold letters is like yelling at a deaf man'.[42] Thirdly, the notice rule contradicts the well-justified rule that silence is no acceptance.[43] Fourthly, neither the notice nor the signature rules would satisfy the objective test of intention based on what a reasonable person in the position of the proffering party has reason to believe.[44] Such a person knows that adhering parties (unless relatively powerful businesses represented by lawyers) do not read standard terms and would not understand them if they did. In many, perhaps most, cases we might even infer that businesses intend this. The proffering party cannot even 'reasonably' understand adhering parties as consenting to its terms, just because they fail to object by the expiry of a 'cooling-off' period. If this is right for physical signatures of physical documents, how much more so in cases of 'clickwrap', 'shrinkwrap' or 'browsewrap' where the adhering party may not even know of the existence of the virtual terms.

More problematically, the defective consent thesis cannot easily accommodate UCTA and UTCCR's evident concern with substantive unfairness. Even accepting the evidential role of substantive unfairness, defective consent cannot readily explain why the black-listed terms are automatically invalid *irrespective* of adequate notice or the presence of untainted consent. Moreover, while defective consent is relevant, it is neither sufficient nor necessary to the invalidity of the grey-listed terms. It is insufficient because the court must also take into account the lengthy list of factors going to the substance of the terms, and UTCCR expressly requires 'significant imbalance' to find unfairness. It is unnecessary because invalidity under UCTA and UTCCR is not preconditioned on a finding of procedural unfairness.

Although the requirement of contravention of 'good faith' in UTCCR's test of unfairness looks like an invariable requirement of procedural unfairness, it is not. First, this is clear from the Schedule 2 list of indicatively unfair terms. These must, potentially at least, entail both 'significant imbalance' and 'contravention of good faith'. But, only one of the 17 terms listed focuses on procedural unfairness,[45] while the other 16 highlight substantive unfairness. The key lies in recital 16

[40] Shmuel Becher, 'Asymmetric Information in Consumer Contracts: The Challenge that is Yet to be Met' (2008) 45 *American Business Law Journal* 723, 757.

[41] Omri Ben-Shahar and Carl Schneider, 'The Failure of Mandated Disclosure' (2011) 159 *University of Pennsylvania Law Review* 647, 712.

[42] Jacqueline Baum, 'Note, Medical Malpractice Arbitration: A Patient's Perspective' (1983) 61 *Washington University Law Quarterly* 123, 148. In addition, disclosures can provide excessive information, resulting in cognitive overload and increased confusion, Becher, 'Asymmetric Information in Consumer Contracts', n 40 above, 758.

[43] *Felthouse v Bindley* (1862) 142 ER 1037 (Ct of CP).

[44] See *Hartog v Colin and Shields* [1939] 3 All ER 566 (KBD); *Investors Compensation Scheme Ltd v West Bromwich Building Society* [1998] 1 WLR 896, paras 912–13 (HL).

[45] UTCCR, Sch 2, para 1(i) a term which has the object or effect of 'irrevocably binding the consumer to terms with which he had no real opportunity of becoming acquainted before the conclusion of the contract'.

of the European Directive (which is implemented by UTCCR).[46] This defines 'contravention of good faith' not only in terms of failing to deal 'fairly and equitably' with the consumer, *but also* crucially of failing to take account of the consumer's 'legitimate interests'. From the character of the Schedule 2 terms, these legitimate interests can be understood in the substantive terms of: obtaining adequate redress; receiving the performance legitimately expected from the main subject matter term; avoiding an unreasonable inflation of the price term; and avoiding disproportionate liability for breach. Thus, Lord Steyn[47] concluded that the Schedule 2 terms 'convincingly demonstrate that the argument … that good faith is predominantly concerned with procedural defects in negotiating procedures cannot be sustained. Any purely procedural or even predominantly procedural interpretation of the requirement of good faith must be rejected'.[48]

Secondly, the European Court of Justice (CJEU) defined the 'requirement of good faith' in consent terms: whether the 'seller or supplier, dealing fairly and equitably with the consumer, could reasonably assume that the consumer would have agreed to the term concerned in individual contract negotiations'.[49] This is the objective test of intention, which I argued above must be presumptively answered in the negative[50] in standard form consumer dealing. The best that can be said is that the consumer *may* have agreed to the relevant term if it was *not unfair*.

Thirdly, Lord Steyn added that the very ability of 'qualifying bodies' to apply for injunctions against the future use of specific terms means that 'the primary focus of such a pre-emptive challenge is on issues of substantive unfairness'.[51] Logically, the issue must be determined without reference to any procedural unfairness that has occurred or might occur. And, once an injunction is granted, the term (and terms with like effect) is prohibited irrespective of the procedural safeguards surrounding its acceptance. It is the *term*, as opposed to the negotiating process, which must be in bad faith, in line with the policy of the European Directive to harmonise control of standard terms in consumer contracts.

Fourthly, any argument that UTCCR could not be aimed at substantive unfairness because clear and intelligible core terms are immune from review is unsustainable. It is true that UTCCR are not primarily concerned with inadequacy of consideration. However, recital 19 of the European Directive makes clear that the fairness of other terms can be challenged *in the light of these core terms*. In any case, retaining the core terms allows consumers to obtain the desired goods or services, shorn of the offending terms that produced the original significant and objectionable imbalance.

[46] Directive 93/13/EC, n 35 above. Hugh Collins, 'Good Faith in European Contract Law' (1994) 14 *Oxford Journal of Legal Studies* 229, 249–50, and see *Director General of Fair Trading v First National Bank* [2001] UKHL 52, paras 36–37; [2002] 1 AC 481, 499–500.

[47] ibid para 36; pages 499–500.

[48] While Lord Bingham explicitly links 'good faith' to procedural unfairness, his Lordship's description of it incorporates clear non-procedural elements (ibid para 17; page 494); 'Appropriate prominence should be given to *terms which might operate disadvantageously* to the customer … the supplier should not, whether deliberately *or unconsciously*, take advantage of the consumer's necessity, indigence, lack of experience, unfamiliarity with the subject matter of the contract, [and] *weak bargaining position*' (emphasis added).

[49] Case C-415/11 *Aziz v Catalunyacaixa* [2013] OJ C141, para 77.

[50] See text related to n 44 above.

[51] *Director General of Fair Trading*, n 46 above, para 33; pages 498–99.

Market Inefficiency

From the economic perspective, the adhering party's lack of informed consent to the fine print undermines contract as an aggregate welfare-maximising scheme based on mutual preference satisfaction. One legal response would be to impose information obligations on the proffering party and set aside the contract in the absence of a genuine expression of preference. Since informational asymmetry is the economic approach's equivalent of defective consent, the same problems identified there[52] (on its partial fit with the solution contained in UCTA and UTCCR) applies here.

A second response flows from the insight that invalidating contracts tainted by information failure would nevertheless, be inefficient. In their influential paper Calabresi and Melamed[53] argued that in certain circumstances, it would be more efficient to allow exceptions to the consent requirement as long as *compensation* is paid. That is, the 'property rules' that allow owners to choose whether and on what conditions to transfer their entitlements, should be degraded into 'liability rules' that tolerate the confiscation of the owners' entitlement without consent on payment of compensation. Thus, for example, where someone's building project mistakenly encroaches on another's land, it is more efficient to require her to pay compensation than to pull down the whole building. Analogously, unconsented to standard terms should be enforced if adhering parties are compensated. Here, supporters of standard form contracting point to the efficiency savings that are passed on in the form of lower prices. To align this with the orthodox paradigm of contract, the language of 'hypothetical consent' is sometimes deployed on the basis that a rational wealth-maximising adhering party 'would' or 'should' have consented to this arrangement.[54]

The routine criticism of the economic approach is that it adopts an over-simplistic view of incentive structures,[55] and rests on untested empirical assumptions.[56] In this context, it is unclear how the right amount of compensation should be calculated

[52] See p 113–16 above.

[53] Guido Calabresi and A Douglas Melamed, 'Property Rules, Liability Rules, and Inalienability: One View of the Cathedral' (1972) 85 *Harvard Law Review* 1089; see discussion in Emily Sherwin et al, 'Symposium, Property Rules, Liability Rules, and Inalienability: A Twenty-Five Year Retrospective' (1997) 106 *Yale Law Review* 2081.

[54] Eg Jason Scott Johnston, 'The Return of the Bargain: An Economic Theory of How Standard-Form Contracts Enable Cooperative Negotiation Between Businesses and Consumers' (2006) 104 *Michigan Law Review* 857, 862–63.

[55] Peter H Schuck, 'Legal Complexity: Some Causes, Consequences, and Cures' (1992) 42 *Duke Law Journal* 1, 37, comments that: 'any serious pursuit of efficiency … will often require complex rules. After all, the goals and constraints relevant to a given policy are likely to be numerous, and the legal rules, in order to be efficient, must take account of, and be tailored to, each of them. Accomplishing this may necessitate a system of multi-factored rules, complex defences, complex party structures, sequential burden shifting, and so on'.

[56] Posner, 'Economic Analysis of Contract Law after Three Decades', n 21 above, 880, famously observes that: 'Economics fails to explain contract law … And economics provides little normative guidance for reforming contract law. Models that have been proposed in the literature either focus on fine aspects of contractual behaviour or make optimal doctrine a function of variables that cannot realistically be observed, measured, or estimated. The models do give a sense of the factors that are at stake when the decisionmaker formulates doctrine, and might give that decisionmaker a sense of the trade-offs involved, but in the absence of information about the magnitude of these trade-offs—and the literature gives no sense of these magnitudes—the decisionmaker is left with little guidance'.

and it is impossible to verify the empirical assumption that businesses are passing on the right amount of their savings to the right people. Craswell[57] therefore refines this approach by leaving the 'liability' or 'compensation' to the courts rather than to the proffering party's unilateral determination. This may account for UCTA and UTCCR's review of non-core terms and the relevance in this review of efficiency factors (such as inducement; special order; the proffering party's ability to meet claims; and the availability and cost of insurance) in assessing the validity of terms.

However, it is not easy to equate the invalidation of unfair non-core terms with 'compensation' for being bound to non-core terms without consent, and it leaves other relevant considerations unexplained. Further, the assumption that any non-core term can be made binding for the 'right price' is contradicted by the black-listed terms. Most problematically, Craswell's theory is conditioned on courts having the institutional competence to determine the appropriate compensation, when there is general scepticism about the courts' competence in this respect.[58]

Even if these problems were surmountable, this approach may still lead to inefficient results. This is because the competitiveness and quality of products depend on the existence of at least a subset of well-informed and sophisticated adhering parties (on whom others free-ride) who can drive the appropriate structure of market demand.[59] This is unlikely to be true in respect of non-core standard terms. Indeed, even Alan Schwartz who came up with the thesis does not seem to believe in the existence of an informed minority any more, at least in the consumer context.[60] By ignoring the actual preference of adhering parties, enforcement of these contracts may not, after all, maximise aggregate welfare by moving commodities to highest valuers.

Standard Terms as Defective Product

A third approach is to treat non-core standard terms as part of the product being traded: the 'legalware' being bundled with the hardware.[61] The reasoning is that since dealing over the non-core standard terms is absent, the law is justified in

[57] Richard Craswell, 'Property Rules and Liability Rules in Unconscionability and Related Doctrines' (1993) 60 *University of Chicago Law Review* 1; Richard Craswell, 'Remedies When Contracts Lack Consent: Autonomy and Institutional Competence' (1996) 33 *Osgoode Hall Law Journal* 209; see also Radin, *Boilerplate*, n 21 above, 76–77.

[58] Note that the Consumer Rights Bill 2013, cl 71(2) and (3) require the court to consider the fairness of a term 'even if none of the parties to the proceedings has raised that issue', unless 'the court considers that it has before it sufficient legal and factual material to enable it to consider the fairness of the term'.

[59] See Alan Schwartz and Louis Wilde, 'Imperfect Information in Markets for Contract Terms: The Examples of Warranties and Security Interests' (1983) 69 *Virginia Law Review* 1387, 1391–92. Johnston, 'The Return of the Bargain', n 54 above, 862–63 ('Regardless of whether any particular consumer had ever read, understood, or bargained over the terms of the standard form, informed consumers generated a form of hypothetical market assent, which would bind all consumers').

[60] Ian Ayres and Alan Schwartz, *The No Reading Problem in Consumer Contract Law*, Yale Law School, Public Law Research Paper No 314 (2013), available at http://papers.ssrn.com/sol3/papers.cfm?abstract_id=2341840.

[61] See, eg *Hill v Gateway 2000, Inc*, 105 F 3d 1147, 1150 (7th Cir 1997). See Arthur Leff, 'Contract as Thing' (1970) 19 *American University Law Review* 131; Lewis A Kornhauser, 'Unconscionability in Standard Forms' (1976) 64 *California Law Review* 1151; Radin, *Boilerplate*, n 21 above, ch 6.

regulating the deal itself. This deftly sidesteps the issue of consent since non-core standard terms are transubstantiated into the product. Baird explains that:[62]

> The warranty that comes with your laptop computer is one of its many product attributes. The laptop has a screen of a particular size. Its microprocessors work at a particular speed … Just as I know the size of the screen, but nothing about the speed of the microprocessor, I know about some of the warranty terms that come with the computer and remain wholly ignorant of the others … To say that a product comes with boilerplate [standard form fine print] is to say that one of its attributes, along with many others, is partially hidden and is one over which there is no choice on the part of the buyer. But why should this raise any special concern? … Hidden product attributes over which sellers give potential buyers no choice are a commonplace, necessary and entirely unobjectionable feature of mass markets.

This new paradigm of manufacturer and end-user of a commodity opens up the possibility of direct regulation of the fine print by analogy to product liability law. The main problem is that it is unclear how the standards applied to products—of 'danger' or 'defect', 'fitness for purpose' or such like—can be applied to *terms*. In order to provide a point of reference, we need a theory of rights or legitimate expectations that should not be harmed. The idea of non-core terms as product provides little help in building such a theory. For this, I advance the fourth and preferred explanation for UCTA and UTCCR.

Preventing Abuse of the Institution of Contract

The state's justification includes the creation and maintenance of the institution of contract that makes possible a regime of private ordering. This institution is defined by its primary purpose of expanding valuable choices by providing the necessary security for (normally) exchange agreements. This generates three overlapping features that lie irreducibly at the heart of the institution. First, is the importance of voluntary choice about which much has already been said. Secondly, the institution of contract enhances the valuable choices of participants by normally requiring an exchange to further each party's conception of the ultimate good. This is supported by the idea of Kantian respect in our dealings with others. Each party should treat the other not merely as a means of enhancing her own ends, but also as an end which she simultaneously serves; this tracks the instinct of reciprocity as the mark of just dealing, and preserver of social stability.[63] Thirdly, the institution of contract enhances the reliability of voluntary exchanges, and bridges any gap in trust and sanctions between parties in the market domain, by guaranteeing redress for breach, backed up by the coercive power of the state. While bargains would still be struck without legal enforcement, parties would tend to regard each other with suspicion like participants of hostage swap, and adopt a 'you first!' stance. They would have to devise alternative enforcement schemes (think of the Mafia) or bias exchanges toward those that take place instantly, or toward persons with a reputation for

[62] Douglas Baird, 'The Boilerplate Puzzle' (2006) 104 *Michigan Law Review* 933, 939. And see Douglas Baird, *Reconstructing Contracts* (Cambridge, MA, Harvard University Press, 2013) 124–27, 133–34.

[63] See Mindy Chen-Wishart, 'In Defence of Consideration' (2013) *Oxford University Common Wealth Law Journal* 209.

keeping their promises. Thus, 'the supportive role of the law helps make contracts outside the framework of ongoing relations much more common',[64] and allows individuals to project their intentions into the future and plan actions that require concrete pre-commitments.

Accordingly, the legal infrastructure of the institution of contract should, very broadly speaking, enforce voluntary reciprocal agreements and not enforce involuntary or unreciprocated ones. The determination of voluntariness, reciprocity and redress for breach are *public* functions that safeguard the institution of contract. My thesis is that excessive privatisation of these public functions undermines the possibility of private ordering *by* contract. If you change the rules of a game of chess, you are no longer playing chess. Contracting out of contract's constitutive rules uses contract to destroy itself. This explains why the parties' ability to contract out of contract law's constitutive rules on formation (including the objective test of intention and the requirement of consideration), vitiation and the default remedies for breach is non-existent in most cases, and severely restricted in others.[65]

Standard form contracting subverts the institution of contract when it: (i) binds parties to unconsented to terms; (ii) undermines the reciprocity contained in the core terms; and (iii) shrinks the right to redress or otherwise ousts the court's remedial jurisdiction. Here, the adjective 'valuable' that qualifies the primary purpose of contract law in expanding individual choice comes to the fore. It signifies that contract law is not merely a mechanism for preference satisfaction; it facilitates valuable, and not worthless, choices.[66] While the value of autonomy itself requires a wide margin of tolerance in the law's conceptions of the worthwhile, eliminating the worst choices that do not contribute to the parties' worthwhile life plans actually increases people's chances of living good autonomous lives, whilst still leaving them plenty of sub-optimal options to choose from. This explains the refusal of the law to enforce contracts, on the grounds of illegality or contravention of public policy, that relate, for example, to babies, kidneys, human blood, slaves, sexual intercourse, love, endangered species of animals and human organs from living patients.[67]

Likewise, terms that unjustifiably derogate from the voluntariness, reciprocity and right to redress that are constitutive of the institution of contract are not valuable choices that the law should facilitate. They are 'defective' and not 'fit for purpose' in the language of non-core terms as product theory. The tripartite scheme of UCTA and UTCCR responds to these challenges in a nuanced way.

(a) Voluntariness: We have already seen that the concern with voluntariness provides a very partial justification for the scheme of control found in UCTA and UTCCR. It explains:[68] the types of dealing and the general non-core character of

[64] Joseph Raz, 'Promises in Morality and Law' (1981) *Harvard Law Review* 916, 934.

[65] Eg the parties cannot contract out of fraud or duress; the limit on forfeitures and penalties of money payments are well known; contract law also severely curtails the parties' power to agree specific performance. See Daniel Friedmann, 'Good Faith and Remedies for Breach of Contracts' in Jack Beatson and Daniel Friedmann (eds), *Good Faith and Fault in Contract* (Oxford, Clarendon Press, 1997).

[66] Joseph Raz, *Morality of Freedom* (Oxford University Press, 1988) 417; Hugh Collins, *The Law of Contract,* 4th edn, (London, LexisNexis Butterworths, 2003) ch 6.

[67] See Margaret Radin, 'Market-Inalienability' (1987) 100 *Harvard Law Review* 1849 and Margaret Radin, *Contested Commodities* (Cambridge, MA, Harvard University Press, 2001).

[68] See p 113 above.

the terms subject to invalidity, the factors going to invalidity that interrogate the quality of the adhering party's consent, and the requirement of plain and intelligible language. Most explicitly, UTCCR identifies as indicatively unfair and invalid a term with the object or effect of 'irrevocably binding the consumer to [other] terms with which he had no real opportunity of becoming acquainted before the conclusion of the contract'.[69] Such a term privatises the law's role in determining the presence of voluntary consent. It allows the proffering party to bind the adhering party to unknown terms by reference to some stipulated conduct (such as clicking a box, not clicking a box or entering a website). Agreeing to allow the proffering party to do that is not a valuable choice that the law should facilitate because it undermines the voluntariness feature of the institution of contract, the determination of which must remain with the court. The effect of invalidating this term is to release the consumer from those other terms.[70]

More broadly, it is arguable that standard form contracting *itself* has the effect, if not the object, of 'irrevocably binding the [adhering party] to terms with which he had no real opportunity of becoming acquainted before the conclusion of the contract'. This line of reasoning would invalidate the whole contract. This is because the orthodoxy on contract formation fuses the commitment question (whether the parties have committed to the contract) with the content question (what the parties committed to). This escalates defective consent to any term into defective consent to the whole contract. But an institution of contract that requires informed consent to every term of the fine print is too demanding and so too fragile, and not useful to fallible human beings. Autonomy is threatened not only by binding parties to terms that they have not consented to, but also by refusing to enforce the essential exchange that they *have* consented to and want. The general threat to voluntariness from being bound to unconsented-to fine print must be weighed against the threat to voluntariness from refusing to uphold the consented-to main subject matter and price terms.

Moreover, standard form contracting is not necessarily unfair; their wide use in *commercial* transactions 'facilitate the conduct of trade', while industry wide standard forms (eg bills of lading, charterparties, insurance policies and contracts of sale in the commodity market) have generally resulted from extensive negotiations by parties of roughly equal bargaining power.[71] In addition, any systematic refusal to enforce standard form contracts would cause massive disruption in today's market environment.[72] This takes account of the efficiency concern. Mass production has increased general welfare, and this demands mass distribution and mass contracting. Standard form contracting reduces transaction costs lowers prices,[73] and allows senior management in large operations to maintain control.

[69] UTCCR, Sch 2, para 1(i).

[70] Beale, *Chitty on Contracts*, n 32 above, para 15-113. Thus, UTCCR can indirectly impose more onerous notice requirements than the common law.

[71] *Macaulay v Schroeder Music Publishing Co Ltd* [1974] 1 WLR 1308, 1316 (HL).

[72] See, eg Brian Bix, 'Contracts' in Franklin Miller and Alan Wertheimer (eds), *In the Ethics of Consent* (Oxford University Press, 2010).

[73] See, eg Robert Hillman, 'Rolling Contracts' (2002) 71 *Fordham Law Review* 743, 747.

In practice, exceptions have always been made to the requirement of fully informed consent where it would make the institution of contract more valuable and robust (often couched in the language of 'certainty' and 'security' of contract). The rules on signature and incorporation are two examples (although these sometimes go too far). Other examples are: the legal bias towards the enforcement of so-called 'battle of forms' cases,[74] vague or incomplete contracts[75] and conditional agreements,[76] especially where the parties' commitment to the contract is clearly evinced by the commencement or completion of contractual performance. Analogously, an exception should be tolerated in the standard form context where the adhering party's exercise of autonomy in respect of the consented-to core terms outweighs her questionable consent in respect of the unconsented-to non-core terms. However, it would be as inappropriate to enforce the latter wholesale, as it would be to refuse to enforce them wholesale. Even the welfare claim for mass-market standard form contracting is only in the *aggregate*. Individual abuses can and do flow from the practice. Thus, an all-or-nothing approach must be rejected in favour of a more targeted approach. And, UCTA and UTCCR provide precisely that by subjecting non-core terms to nuanced legal oversight.

(b) Reciprocity and the protection of legitimate expectations: standard non-core terms entail a heightened risk of unjustifiable subversion of the reciprocity embodied in the contract's core terms. This explains two categories of non-core terms targeted by UCTA and UTCCR. On one side are terms that reduce or eliminate the proffering party's primary obligations. These prevent the adhering party from obtaining what was legitimately expected from the core terms. Thus, UCTA[77] targets 'terms and notices which exclude or restrict the relevant obligation or duty' in respect of liability in tort or breach of statutory implied terms, and stipulates that an adhering party's agreement to or awareness of a term purporting to exempt liability for negligence 'is not of itself to be taken as indicating his voluntary acceptance of any risk'[78] to pre-empt any argument that there was no duty to exclude. It also targets terms that allow a business to 'render a contractual performance substantially different from that which was reasonably expected of him', or 'render no performance at all' in respect of the whole or any part of his contractual obligation. Such terms also feature extensively on the Schedule 2 list of indicatively unfair terms in UTCCR and bear setting out; namely, those with the object or effect of:

(c) making an agreement binding on the consumer whereas provision of services by the seller or supplier is subject to a condition whose realisation depends on his own will alone; ...
(f) authorising the seller or supplier to dissolve the contract on a discretionary basis where the same facility is not granted to the consumer;

[74] Eg *Butler Machines v Ex-Cello Corp* [1979] 1 WLR 401 (CA).
[75] Eg *Hillas Ltd v Arcos Ltd* (1932) 147 LT 503 (HL).
[76] Eg *RTS Flexible Systems Ltd v Molkerei Alois Muller GMBH* [2010] UKSC 14; [2010] 3 All ER 1.
[77] UCTA, s 13(2) and s 3(2).
[78] UCTA, s 2(3).

(g) enabling the seller or supplier to terminate a contract of indeterminate duration without reasonable notice except where there are serious grounds for doing so; ...

(j) enabling the seller or supplier to alter the terms of the contract unilaterally without a valid reason which is specified in the contract;

(k) enabling the seller or supplier to alter unilaterally without a valid reason any characteristics of the product or service to be provided; ...

(m) giving the seller or supplier the right to determine whether the goods or services supplied are in conformity with the contract, or giving him the exclusive right to interpret any term of the contract;

(n) limiting the seller's or supplier's obligation to respect commitments undertaken by his agents or making his commitments subject to compliance with a particular formality; ...

(p) giving the seller or supplier the possibility of transferring his rights and obligations under the contract, where this may serve to reduce the guarantees for the consumer, without the latter's agreement.

The Consumer Rights Bill adds to the list a term that 'has the object or effect of permitting the trader to determine the characteristics of the subject matter of the contract after the consumer has become bound by it' (Schedule 2, Part 1, paragraph 12).

On the other side are terms that may inflate the adhering party's obligations against the core terms. Thus, UTCCR, Schedule 2 targets terms that have the object or effect of:

(h) automatically extending a contract of fixed duration where the consumer does not indicate otherwise, when the deadline fixed for the consumer to express his desire not to extend the contract is unreasonably early; ...

(l) providing for the price of goods to be determined at the time of delivery or allowing a seller of goods or supplier of services to increase their price without in both cases giving the consumer the corresponding right to cancel the contract if the final price is too high in relation to the price agreed when the contract was concluded; ...

(o) obliging the consumer to fulfil all his obligations where the seller or supplier does not perform his.

The Consumer Rights Bill adds to the list a term which has the object or effect of 'giving the trader the discretion to decide the price payable under the contract after the consumer has become bound by it, where no price or method of determining the price is agreed when the consumer becomes bound' (Schedule 2, Part 1, paragraph 14).

Shrinking the proffering party's obligations and inflating the adhering party's obligations can also result from terms that give the proffering party disproportionate and unilateral power to determine the scope of both parties' obligations and liabilities. All these terms have the potential to undermine the adhering party's legitimate (autonomy and welfare) interest in the stability of the contract derived from the consented to core terms.[79] Raz defended the objective test of intentions

[79] See further at *(d) Control mechanisms*, p 126 below and text attached to nn 101–04 below.

as necessary to protect the institution of contract: 'For if people were often to let it appear that they have promised when they have not, the currency of promises would be debased and their appeal and utility greatly diminished'.[80] The same applies to these targeted terms in UCTA and UTCCR. To allow the proffering party to do this constitutes potentially valueless choices that the law should not facilitate.

(c) Right to redress: what distinguishes contracts from promises is that contracts are enforceable by law and promises are not. Remedies are constitutive of a contract; they are *of its essence*. Indeed, the general right to legal redress is foundational to civil society and an integral feature of the rule of law. Any agreement between the parties to oust the jurisdiction of the courts, except as permitted by the Arbitration Act 1996 is unenforceable as contrary to public policy.[81] Likewise, article 6(1) of the European Convention on Human Rights and Fundamental Freedoms 1950 (ECHR) lays down the right to a fair hearing. The Human Rights Act 1998 requires national courts to observe the Convention in their adjudication, even between private parties. *The House of Lords has read down this right* as merely a procedural guarantee of access to the courts without guaranteeing 'any particular content for civil rights and obligations in the substantive law of the contracting states'.[82] However, a right of access to redress is empty if the background remedial rights can be deleted in the fine print, and all the worse, given the widespread use of such terms in the mass-market where consent is questionable. This is the mischief addressed by Lord Denning's ill-fated doctrine of fundamental breach as a rule of law.[83] The doctrine barred a party committing a 'fundamental breach' from relying on an exemption clause because a party simply cannot eliminate its own obligations in this way, irrespective of their intention. The doctrine was rejected by the House of Lords,[84] but substantially resurrected in UCTA and UTCCR.

Thus, UCTA specifically regulates exemptions for: negligence liability (section 2), breach of specific statutory implied terms (sections 6, 7) and breach of contract generally (section 3). UCTA also regulates exemptions of liability hidden in consumer 'guarantees' (section 5), and indemnity clauses, which may add insult to injury by requiring the consumer to indemnify the business for its liability to a third party (section 4). It also targets terms that make it more difficult for the adhering party to prove her case (section 13(1)) by:

(a) making the liability or its enforcement subject to restrictive or onerous conditions;
(b) excluding or restricting any right or remedy in respect of the liability, or subjecting a person to any prejudice in consequence of his pursuing any such right or remedy;
(c) excluding or restricting rules of evidence or procedure.

80 Raz, 'Promises in Morality and Law', n 64 above, 936.
81 *Lee v Showmen's Guild of Great Britain* [1952] 2 QB 329 (CA).
82 *Wilson v First County Trust Ltd (No 2)* [2003] UKHL 40, para 33; [2004] 1 AC 816, pages 834–35.
83 *Karsales (Harrow) Ltd v Wallis* [1956] 1 WLR 936 (CA), 943.
84 *Suisse Atlantique Société d'Armement Maritime SA v NV Rotterdamsche Kolen Centrale* [1967] 1 AC 361 (HL); *Photo Production Ltd v Securicor Transport Ltd* [1980] AC 827 (HL).

Likewise, Schedule 2 to UTCCR targets terms that have the object or effect of:

(a) excluding or limiting the legal liability of a seller or supplier in the event of the death of a consumer or personal injury to the latter resulting from an act or omission of that seller or supplier;
(b) inappropriately excluding or limiting the legal rights of the consumer vis-à-vis the seller or supplier or another party in the event of total or partial non-performance or inadequate performance by the seller or supplier of any of the contractual obligations, including the option of offsetting a debt owed to the seller or supplier against any claim which the consumer may have against him; …
(f) permitting the seller or supplier to retain the sums paid for services not yet supplied by him where it is the seller or supplier himself who dissolves the contract; …
(q) excluding or hindering the consumer's right to take legal action or exercise any other legal remedy, particularly by requiring the consumer to take disputes exclusively to arbitration not covered by legal provisions, unduly restricting the evidence available to him or imposing on him a burden of proof which, according to the applicable law, should lie with another party to the contract.

This is consistent with the invalidity of arbitration clauses that relate to claims for a 'modest amount'[85] and also of contract terms 'providing that a consumer bears the burden of proof in respect of showing whether a distance supplier or an intermediary complied with any or all of the obligations placed upon him resulting from the Directive' of 2002[86] concerning the distance marketing of consumer financial services.[87]

The proffering party can also usurp contract law's public function of determining fair redress by giving itself the power to inflate the adhering party's liabilities for breach. Other equitable doctrines assert contract law's jurisdiction to impose proportionate liability (eg rules controlling penalties, forfeitures and restraints of trade). Consistently, UTCCR subjects to review terms with the object or effect of:

(d) permitting the seller or supplier to retain sums paid by the consumer where the latter decides not to conclude or perform the contract, without providing for the consumer to receive compensation of an equivalent amount from the seller or supplier where the latter is the party cancelling the contract;
(e) requiring any consumer who fails to fulfil his obligation to pay a disproportionately high sum in compensation.

The Consumer Rights Bill adds to the list a term that has the object or effect of 'requiring that, where the consumer decides not to conclude or perform the contract, the consumer must pay the trader a disproportionately high sum in compensation or for services which have not been supplied' (Schedule 2, Part 1, paragraph 5).

[85] Arbitration Act 1996, ss 89, 90; Unfair Arbitration Agreements (Specified Amount) Order 1999, SI 1999/2167.

[86] Council Directive 2002/65/EC of 23 September 2002 concerning distance marketing of consumer financial services [2002] OJ L271/16.

[87] Financial Services (Distance Marketing) Regulations 2004, SI 2004/2095, reg 24, amending UTCCR, regs 3(1) and (5).

Chitty supports the 'indirect horizontal effect' of the Human Rights Act 1998[88] in relation to the tests of validity of terms under UTCCR[89] and UCTA.[90] That is, courts should legitimately take into account consistency with Convention rights (including that of the right to redress) when applying the reasonableness or unfairness tests.[91] This would merely reinforce the policy embodied in the statutory instruments to protect the adhering party's right to meaningful redress. EU rights to effective judicial protection against unfair terms go much further than the English interpretation of Article 6(1) ECHR.[92] This should encourage English courts to adopt a very robust and *substantive* (rather than purely formal) approach to evaluating terms that have the object or effect of depriving the adhering party of redress.

Terms that supplant the default remedy also have the potential to undermine equality before the law. Contracts both reflect and exacerbate existing inequalities because they distribute not only goods and services, but also power. Contracts can thus affect the kinds of relations we have with others. Equality before the law is degraded where adhering parties (as a class) are deprived of the right to meaningful redress, while proffering parties not only retain this right, but can also inflate it by exercising powers it has awarded itself. The adhering party is subject to the unaccountable rule of the proffering party rather than to the rule of law. This is only partly a problem of the adhering party's defective consent, for it also raises concerns about social justice and exploitation of unequal positions. It is no coincidence that at common law, courts have implied terms to restrain the dishonest, capricious, arbitrary or bad faith exercise of discretionary contractual power.[93] Common law

[88] Beale, *Chitty on Contracts*, n 32 above, para 1-079; see generally, Paul Craig, *Administrative Law*, 6th edn (London, Sweet & Maxwell, 2008) paras 18-027–18-028; Murray Hunt, 'The "Horizontal Effect" of the Human Rights Act' (1998) *Public Law* 423.

[89] Beale, *Chitty on Contracts*, n 32 above, para 1-083. The Preamble to Directive 93/13/EC, n 35 above, suggests at recital 16 that the function of the requirement of good faith is to ensure that a court makes 'an overall evaluation of the different interests involved', and it then refers to matters which appear to relate to the public interest.

[90] A similar argument could be run as regards the application of the reasonableness test under UCTA, s 11(1), though this test does not explicitly draw attention to the relevance of issues of public interest for its assessment.

[91] But not when interpreting contracts or implying terms since courts would be open to the charge of remaking the contract, Beale, *Chitty on Contracts*, n 32 above, paras 1-080 and 1-081.

[92] See, eg C-240/98 *Oceano Grupo Editorial SA v Roció Murciano Quintero*, 27 June 2000 (ECJ) and C-243/08 *Pannon GSM Zrt v Erzsébet Sustikné Gy rfi* [2009] ECR I-4713, where the CJEU held that it is not necessary for the consumer to contest the validity of an unfair term. Courts of the Member States have the power to evaluate whether a specific contract term is unfair of their own motion and a clause in a consumer contract conferring jurisdiction to the seller's seat may be considered unfair. And see C-473/00 *Cofidis SA v Jean-Louis Fredout* [2002] ECR I-10875, where it was held that a provision in the law of a Member State which prevents a national court from finding a contractual term in a consumer contract to be unfair after the expiry of a limitation period, is not compatible with the Unfair Terms Directive (Directive 93/13/EC, n 35 above).

[93] See Hugh Collins, 'Discretionary Powers in Contracts' in David Campbell, Hugh Collins and John Wightman (eds), *Implicit Dimensions of Contracts* (Oxford, Hart Publishing, 2003) 219; Terence Daintith, 'Contractual Discretion and Administrative Discretion: A Unified Analysis' (2005) 68 *Modern Law Review* 554. See *Lombard Tricity Finance Ltd v Paton* [1989] 1 All ER 918 (CA); *Paragon Finance Plc v Nash* [2001] EWCA Civ 1466; [2002] 2 All ER 248; *Horkuluk v Cantor Fitzgerald* [2004] EWCA Civ 1287; [2004] IRLR 942; *Socimer International Bank Ltd (in liq) v Standard Bank London Ltd* [2008] EWCA Civ 116; [2008] Bus LR 1304.

has also refused to enforce a contract for absence of consideration where one party's performance is agreed to be entirely at its own discretion.[94]

These concerns have been swept aside by those who argue that a proffering party's reputational concern would ensure that it exercises its discretion fairly and reasonably.[95] However, this is much more likely in the case of large, recurring and sophisticated customers (whose goodwill is more valuable) than in the case of weak, occasional and unsophisticated customers (whose goodwill is less valued). The concern to counter such unjustified preferential treatment in the exercise of discretionary power is evident elsewhere in contract law. It explains why the doctrine of frustration will not relieve a party from her obligations if the partial destruction of her supplies leaves her with an arbitrary choice as to which of her contracts she will perform. The frustration is said to be 'self-induced'[96] because preference can be given to the more profitable contract partners. The same concern explains why a harsh limitation clause in a contract to supply seeds was invalidated under UCTA when evidence showed, inter alia, that the seller had in many other cases agreed settlements exceeding the stated limitation.[97]

Even if the proffering party's exercise of discretion is even-handed, and indeed even if fair and reasonable, the very existence of excessive unaccountable power remains problematic. A term that amounts to a blank cheque, allowing the proffering party to do as it pleases once a dispute arises, makes adhering parties 'nothing more than supplicants'.[98] And, if successful, the adhering party's fair treatment will be by virtue of a favour bestowed, rather than a legitimate entitlement upheld. This undermines the rule of law and, paradoxically, the concept of contract as a regime of private ordering.

(d) Control mechanisms: It would be excessively heavy-handed to automatically invalidate all non-core terms. A flexible approach that invalidates a terms only if it derogates unjustifiably from the parties' core obligations or default liabilities enhances the utility of the institution of contract. UCTA and UTCCR adopt a four-toned approach. At one extreme are the black-listed terms. Here, the prohibition on exempting negligence liability causing personal injury or death[99] reflects individuals' legitimate interest in freedom from physical harm and the individual's responsibility to avoid causing such harm to others, usually expressed in tort law. The state should not abdicate its responsibility to give redress by allowing a proffering party to privatise the adhering party's right to safety and freedom from physical harm and immunise itself from negligently causing such harm. The adhering party is not permitted to waive this right, even with consent and for consideration. This is a worthless choice that the state should not facilitate. This right is 'market inalienable', as one's

[94] *Stabilad Ltd v Stephens and Carter (No 2)* [1999] 2 All ER (Comm) 651 (CA), 659–60.

[95] Bebchuk and Posner, 'One-Sided Contracts in Competitive Consumer Markets', n 18 above; Johnston, 'The Return of the Bargain', n 54 above.

[96] *J Lauritzen AS v Wijsmuller BV* ('The Super Servant Two') [1990] 1 Lloyds Rep 1 (CA).

[97] *George Mitchell (Chesterhall) Ltd v Finney Lock Seeds Ltd* [1983] 2 All ER 737 (HL).

[98] Todd Rakoff, 'The Law and Sociology of Boilerplate' (2006) 104 *Michigan Law Review* 1235, 1236.

[99] UCTA, s 2(1), and s 5 which invalidates a manufacturer's or distributor's liability in tort to a person injured by *goods proving defective in consumer use* where the exemption is contained in a 'guarantee' of the goods.

kidney and one's vote are.[100] As for the inalienability of the customer's right to title and satisfactory quality of the goods purchased,[101] these most basic expectations (implicit in the core terms) have been recognised by Parliament through the democratic process and made the subject of rights via statutory implied terms.[102] These represent the customer's legitimate interest when buying goods. They cannot be erased by standard form contracting. Indeed, the Consumer Rights Bill broadens the scope of such inalienable rights in consumer contracts for the supply of goods, digital content and services,[103] whether negotiated or non-negotiated.

At the other extreme are the white-listed terms that are immune from challenge. In consumer contracts, these are main subject matter and price terms expressed in plain and intelligible language[104] that will generally have received informed consent, and anyway, cannot be reviewed without undermining the most basic freedom of contract, and, if invalid, depriving consumers of the goods or services sought. In respect of commercial contracts, the concern to uphold contractual freedom also underlies the immunity from review of terms other than those exempting liability or having like effect. The various extensions of the scope of regulated 'exemption clauses'[105] reduce the scope of that immunity. Nevertheless, the wider immunity from review (and so lesser protection of businesses) is justified by the generally greater bargaining power of businesses to look after their own interests. Even so, small businesses may have little more bargaining power than consumers;[106] they may be just as affected by unfair surprise and lack of choice. And, unfairness attaches to many terms beyond those regulated by UCTA.[107] These legitimate concerns prompted the Law Commission to suggest extending the scope of review in favour of small businesses[108] to all non-negotiated non-core terms. But this has yet to be taken up.

In between the black- and white-listed terms are grey-listed terms of two shades that are subject to the tests of reasonableness or fairness. These terms lie along the inalienability spectrum attracting scrutiny of different severity and different burdens

[100] See Radin, 'Market-Inalienability', n 67 above; Michael Sandel, *What Money Can't Buy: The Moral Limits of Markets* (London, Penguin, 2013).

[101] UCTA, ss 6(1), (2) and 7(2)–(3A).

[102] Sale of Goods Act 1979, ss 12, 14.

[103] Consumer Rights Bill 2013, cls 31, 47, 57.

[104] UTCCR, reg 6(2), now 'transparent and prominent' under the Consumer Rights Bill 2013, cl 67.

[105] UCTA, ss 3(2)(b) and 13(1).

[106] Eg where it sells all its output to a major car-maker or a supermarket chain, or buys goods or services of relatively low volume or value.

[107] Eg a small business may be required to indemnify the larger business for losses not caused by its default, forfeit deposits or accept price variations; the larger business may reserve the right to terminate the contract at will, or for only a minor breach, while the small business is more rigorously bound by the contract.

[108] Law Com No 166 and Scot Law Com No 119, n 2 above, para 4.8. 'Small businesses' are those with nine or fewer staff: see UCTA, ss 11 and 27.

of proof. The non-core terms expressly nominated in UCTA[109] and UTCCR[110] entail clear risks to the institution of contract and are presumptively invalid. The burden is on the proffering party (under UCTA),[111] or *in practice* on the proffering party (under UTCCR)[112] to justify the terms' validity. In contrast, it is up to the consumer to prove the invalidity of non-core terms not expressly featured in Schedule 2 of UTCCR,[113] and of core terms not expressed in plain and intelligible language.

In applying the tests of validity (reasonableness and fairness), the court must again have regard to the voluntariness, reciprocity and redress dimensions of the contract. It must balance, on the one hand:

- the quality of the adhering party's consent (taking into account the transparency of any notice given of the potentially abusive term, any inducement received for it and any realistic alternative of contracting without it); and
- the extent to which the substance of the term derogates from the adhering party's legitimate expectations generated by the core terms and the background or default rules which would apply in the absence of the challenged term,[114] or reduces or destroys her default right to redress, whether directly or by subjecting her to the proffering party's unilateral, arbitrary and unaccountable power;

with, on the other hand:

- the economic necessity of the term for the proffering party's protection in view of the subject matter of the contract, the profferring party's resources to meet or insure against likely claims, and all the other terms of the contract and any other related contract.

[109] Indemnities against consumers (UCTA, s 4); exemptions of negligence liability causing loss other than personal injury or death (UCTA, s 2(2)); exemption of liability for breach of contract (UCTA, s 3); exemptions of liability for breach of implied terms relating to quality (the conformity of the goods with the description or sample, satisfactory quality and fitness for purpose) *against* non-consumers (UCTA, ss 6(3) and 7(3)); exemptions of liability in respect of contracts passing ownership or possession of goods (UCTA, s 7(4)).

[110] The terms listed in UTCCR, Sch 2 and other non-negotiated terms in consumer contracts *not* going to the main subject matter or price of the contract (reg 6).

[111] UCTA, s 11(5) places the burden of proving unreasonableness on the business seeking to enforce the term.

[112] It is arguable that the list of indicatively unfair terms in UTCCR, Sch 2 has the same practical effect. The Unfair Contract Terms Bill proposed in Law Com No 166 and Scot Law Com No 119, n 2 above, puts the burden on the business to prove the validity of a term that exempts liability for negligence causing loss other than personal injury or death, and for breach of contract (s 15). Section 16 puts the burden on the business to prove the validity of other non-core terms against consumers. Consumer Rights Bill 2013 does not mention the burden of proof apart from s 63(6): 'A term of a consumer contract must be regarded as unfair if it has the effect that the consumer bears the burden of proof with respect to compliance by a distance supplier or an intermediary with an obligation under any enactment or rule implementing the Distance Marketing Directive'.

[113] UTCCR, regs 5 and 6(2). But see Unfair Contract Terms Bill, ss 16–17 proposed in Law Com No 166 and Scot Law Com No 119, n 2 above, which restricts this to actions brought by (a) the Directorate General of Foreign Trade (DGFT) or other qualifying body; or (b) a 'small business', leaving the business to prove the validity of all non-core terms against consumers to the business.

[114] *Aziz*, n 49 above, para 77: '"significant imbalance" to the detriment of the consumer must be assessed in the light of an analysis of the rules of national law applicable in the absence of any agreement between the parties, in order to determine whether, and if so to what extent, the contract places the consumer in a less favourable legal situation than that provided for by the national law in force'.

Since a clause will be judged according to its *potential* unfairness, very widely drawn terms are more likely be invalidated as unreasonable or unfair for failing to take account of the adhering party's legitimate interests. A party's legitimate interests in contract can be described as that of: obtaining adequate redress; receiving the performance reasonably expected from the main subject matter term; avoiding an unreasonable inflation of one's own obligation; avoiding disproportionate liability for breach; and having a balanced power to determine the life of the contract.

A term which may look, prima facie, severely prejudicial to the rights of the adhering party may be fair if it is counterbalanced by a corresponding term to the adhering party's advantage. In the context of cancellation rights, for example, the Office of Fair Trading expressed the view that

> [f]airness and balance require that consumers and suppliers should be on an equal footing as regards rights to end or withdraw from the contract. The supplier's rights should not be excessive, nor should the consumer's be over-restricted. This does not, however, mean a merely formal equivalence in rights to cancel, but rather that both parties should enjoy rights of equal extent and value.[115]

Thus, for example, an exemption clause may be justifiable if the goods were manufactured, processed or adapted to the customer's special order, especially if it was brought to the customer's notice and she received an inducement to agree, or if the proffering party does not have the resources to meet potential claims and is unable to cover itself by insurance. A discretion to reduce the proffering party's, or increase the customer's, obligations may be justifiable if, for example, it is conditional on specified and warranted circumstances (eg significant rise in the price of raw materials or particular difficulties in performance), especially if the customer is empowered to withdraw from the contract without penalty. Again, a term requiring the customer to pay an apparently disproportionate sum on breach may be justifiable in the circumstances (eg a 75 per cent charge for a customer who cancels a world voyage by clipper may be fair given the importance of her commitment to the venture).[116] Lastly, standard terms between experienced and substantial businesses of equal bargaining power in terms of size and resources are presumptively valid because

> they may be taken to have had regard to the matters known to them. They should ... be taken to be the best judges of the commercial fairness of the agreement which they have made; including the fairness of each of the terms of that agreement.[117]

CONCLUSION

Standard form contracting presents an acute challenge to the social institution of contract as primarily a mechanism for expanding valuable choices by providing the necessary security for exchange agreements. The practical impossibility of informed

[115] Office of Fair Trading, *Unfair Contract Terms Guidance* (2008), para 6.1.1, available at www.oft.gov.uk/shared_oft/reports/unfair_contract_terms/oft311.pdf.

[116] *Clipper Ventures Plc v Boyde* 2013 SCLR 313; 2013 GWD 12-243.

[117] *Watford Electronics Ltd v Sanderson CFL Ltd* [2001] EWCA Civ 317; [2001] Build LR 143, para 63.

consent to the fine print, to which customers can only 'adhere', gives the proffering party a relatively free hand to smuggle in highly subversive terms. Faced with the undesirability of enforcing either all or none of the unconsented-to fine print, UCTA and UTCCR steer a middle path by encouraging conditions that increase the likelihood of informed consent, while directly targeting potentially harmful non-core terms and subjecting them to nuanced control.

This pattern of control cannot be fully explained by reference only to defective consent, or to market inefficiency, or by treating non-core terms as defective products, although all three provide important insights. UCTA and UTCCR strike down harmful terms that abuse the institution of contract, and those who rely on it, by unjustifiably undermining voluntariness, subverting the essential exchange embodied in the consented-to core terms, establishing unacceptable power relationships, or destroying the right to meaningful redress. UCTA and UTCCR refuse to allow the institution of contract to be used to degrade the underlying logic of the institution of contract. Using contract to destroy contract is a worthless choice that the law should not facilitate.

8

Time to Reflect on the Right to Reject

ERIC CLIVE

INTRODUCTION

ONE OF THE jewels in the crown of UK sale of goods law is supposed to be the buyer's 'right to reject'. In their *Report on Consumer Remedies for Faulty Goods* in 2009 the Law Commissions explained the right to reject as follows:

> Put simply, the consumer is entitled to reject faulty goods and terminate the contract. The consumer may then refuse to pay for the goods, or (if they have paid already) claim a full refund. We refer to this as 'the right to reject'.[1]

Later the Commissions explained that the consumer who had already paid had not just a right to *claim* a full refund but an actual right to a refund.[2] Still later they said:

> At least nine European jurisdictions currently have a 'right to reject' of some description. This means that consumers have a right to return goods, cancel the contract and obtain a refund for faulty goods as a remedy of first instance in those jurisdictions.[3]

There are slight differences between the formulations in different parts of the report but it is clear that the Commissions use the expression 'right to reject' in a wide sense to cover a right to reject the goods, a right to terminate the contract and a right to a refund of the price. This wide sense was also used in the Draft Consumer Rights Bill presented to the UK Parliament by the Secretary of State for Business, Innovation and Skills in June 2013.[4] Section 19(1) provided that:

> (1) A right to reject gives the consumer:
> (a) the right to reject the goods,
> (b) the right to treat the contract as at an end, and
> (c) the right to receive a refund from the trader …

The final Consumer Rights Bill which received its first reading on 28 January 2014 does not, however, include the right to a refund within the right to reject. It provides that the right to reject entitles the consumer to reject the goods and treat the

[1] *Report on Consumer Remedies for Faulty Goods* (Law Com No 317; Scot Law Com No 216, 2009) para 1.10.
[2] ibid paras 2.7 and 2.8.
[3] ibid para 3.22.
[4] Cm 8657.

contract as at an end.[5] Neither of these meanings, as will be shown, corresponds to the way the expression is used in the Sale of Goods Act 1979.

In this tribute to Hugh Beale, who values the precise use of language and uses language precisely, I will suggest that the use currently made of the expression 'right to reject' in UK sales law is confused, confusing and unnecessary.

First it is necessary to try to unpack the main elements of the so-called right to reject and consider how the notion of rejection is used in the Sale of Goods Act 1979.

UNPACKING THE ELEMENTS

What is Meant by a Right in this Context?

Drawing on the insights of Hohfeld, but without using his precise terminology, we can see that the word 'right' can be used in at least three ways in the present context.[6] First, it can be used in a strong sense, where the right of one party corresponds to an obligation of another. This is how it is used when it is said that a buyer has a right to a refund. The buyer's right to be repaid the price corresponds to the seller's obligation to repay it. The word would also be used in this sense if it was said that a buyer had a right to have goods taken back by the seller: this right would correspond to an obligation on the seller to take them back. Secondly, 'right' can be used in a weaker sense, where it does not correspond to a reciprocal obligation but merely signifies a legal freedom to do something. It is used in this sense when it is said that a buyer has a right to reject goods with the meaning that there is no duty to accept them or retain them; the buyer is legally free to reject them.[7] Thirdly, 'right' can be used of a power to bring about a change in the legal situation, for example, to terminate both parties' obligations under a contract or to bring about a retransfer of property. So we have:

(1) a right corresponding to an obligation on the other party;
(2) a right in the sense of a freedom from a duty;
(3) a right in the sense of a power to change the legal situation.

What is Meant by 'Reject' in this Context?

In ordinary language 'reject' can mean 'discard' or 'throw away'. For example, a recipe for making jam might begin by saying 'Reject any fruit which is mouldy or unsound'. This sense is not relevant for this chapter and will not be further considered. 'Reject' in ordinary language can also mean 'refuse to accept' or 'decline to accept', as in 'She rejected his offer'. This is more relevant.

[5] HC Bill 161, cls 19, 20.

[6] WN Hohfeld, 'Some Fundamental Legal Conceptions as Applied in Legal Reasoning' (1913) 23 *Yale Law Journal* 16.

[7] Normally there is an obligation on the buyer to accept the goods. Sale of Goods Act 1979, s 27 provides that 'It is the duty of the seller to deliver the goods, and of the buyer to accept and pay for them, in accordance with the terms of the contract of sale'.

In relation to contracts for the sale of goods, 'reject' can mean 'refuse to accept physical possession'. It might be used in this way where, for example, delivery is tendered and, before taking physical possession of the goods even for a moment, the buyer notices that there is something wrong with them and refuses to accept them. The buyer could be said to 'reject' the goods.

Where the buyer already has physical possession of the goods 'reject' can be used in the sense of 'throw back'. This does not necessarily imply actually returning the goods to the seller. The contract may require that to be done but otherwise the goods may be 'thrown back' by making them available for collection by the seller, with an indication in both cases that they are not accepted.[8] As 'throwing back' is rather a dramatic way of describing what is happening we could say that this meaning of 'reject' is 'return or make available for collection with an indication that not accepted'. There may be an implication that where the buyer has a right to reject in this sense the seller has an obligation to take the goods back but this is not provided for expressly in either the Sale of Goods Act 1979 or the Consumer Rights Bill 2014.

'Reject the goods' may also be used in the sense of 'intimate that the goods are not accepted' without there being any physical element of refusing delivery or returning the goods or making them available for collection. For example, a buyer who inspects the goods at the seller's premises before there is any question of delivery may find that they do not conform to contract and reject them in this sense.

'Reject' has also been used in relation to the contract. For example, in the first edition of Benjamin on the *Sale of Personal Property*[9] the author mentions the distinction between a breach of a condition and a breach of a warranty in English law and says that 'In the former case he may refuse to accept the goods and reject the contract, but not in the latter'. This sense is now, however, very unusual. 'Terminate the contract' or some other similar expression would now be used. This is considered below.

So we have three normal meanings of 'reject' which are relevant in the present context:

(1) refuse to accept physical possession;
(2) return or make available for collection with an indication that not accepted;
(3) intimate that not accepted.

The use of 'reject' in an abstract, intransitive sense, which does not answer the question of what is being rejected, is not normal.

[8] See the Sale of Goods Act 1979, s 36. The draft Consumer Rights Bill 2013 provided in cl 19(4) that 'To reject the goods the consumer must indicate to the trader that they are rejected, and (a) from that time, must make the goods available for collection by the trader; or (b) if there is an agreement to return rejected goods, must return them as agreed'. *cf* the Consumer Rights Bill 2014, cl 20(7)(b).

[9] JD Benjamin, *A Treatise on the Law on Sale of Personal Property* (London, H Sweet, 1868) 673.

'Terminate the Contract' and Related Expressions

The expression 'terminate the contract' is one of a remarkably large number of expressions which can be used in English legal language to denote the process whereby a party brings to an end, with prospective effect, the obligations of both parties under the contract with the exception of those, such as obligations relating to arbitration or the winding up of the contractual relationship generally, which are intended to survive termination.[10] Other expressions include: treat the contract as repudiated; treat the contract as at an end; treat the contract as discharged; rescind the contract; cancel the contract; determine the contract; repudiate the contract; terminate the contractual relationship; terminate the contractual obligations; and terminate the primary contractual obligations.[11]

The Sale of Goods Act 1979 generally uses 'treat the contract as repudiated'[12] but also uses 'rescind the contract'.[13] In one provision, added in 2002, it uses the more modern 'terminate the contract' for English law but the traditional 'treat the contract as repudiated' for Scottish law.[14] The Consumer Rights Bill 2014 uses 'treat the contract as at an end' but then provides that 'treating a contract as at an end means treating it as repudiated'.[15] This is rather an unfortunate usage. Not only does the 'treating as at an end' formula leave open the question whether the contract is actually at an end for both parties but also the reference to treating the contract as repudiated is legally unsophisticated. Treating a contract as repudiated can have no greater effect than if it is actually repudiated. If it is actually repudiated by one party the other has the option of terminating it: it is not automatically terminated. What is actually meant is 'terminate the contract'.

Right to a Refund

Although the termination of the contract will automatically extinguish any obligation to pay it will not, because it is prospective in effect, automatically give a right to a refund if the price has already been paid. This has to be provided by some other rule. Surprisingly, given the importance of this matter to buyers, the Sale of Goods Act 1979 provides no statutory right to a refund in this situation. The right to a refund is left to depend on the law of restitution or unjustified enrichment. The Consumer Rights Bill 2014 is better in this respect.[16]

[10] See the definition of 'terminate the contract' in art 8(1) of the Proposal for a Regulation on a Common European Sales Law, COM(2011)635 final (European Commission, Brussels).

[11] The UN Convention on Contracts for the International Sale of Goods even uses 'avoid the contract' but avoidance in UK law and European private law usually denotes a process with retrospective effect, treating the contract as void from the beginning because of some invalidity or defect in consent.

[12] See Sale of Goods Act 1979, ss 11, 15B, 31, 48D and 61.

[13] See ibid ss 48, 48A, 48C and 48E.

[14] ibid s 48D, added by the Sale and Supply of Goods to Consumers Regulations 2002, SI 2002/3045.

[15] Consumer Rights Bill 2014, cl 19(3).

[16] ibid cl 20(7)(a) gives an express right to a refund.

USE OF 'REJECT' IN THE SALE OF GOODS ACT 1979

The Sale of Goods Act 1979, as amended, is the major piece of legislation on the law on sale of goods in the United Kingdom.[17] It replaced the Sale of Goods Act 1893. It general it applies to all contracts for the sale of goods but some of the new rules apply only to business-to-consumer sales. The Consumer Rights Bill 2014 would replace many provisions of the 1979 Act for consumer sales, including the provisions on the 'right to reject', but leave it standing in other respects.

'Reject' is used 25 times in the Sale of Goods Act 1979 (if derivatives like 'rejected' or 'rejection' are included). It is used in different senses. It is not always clear in what sense it is being used.

Section 11 and its Scottish Equivalent

The expression 'a right to reject' first appears in section 11(3) which provides:

> Whether a stipulation in a contract of sale is a condition, the breach of which may give rise to a right to treat the contract as repudiated, or a warranty, the breach of which may give rise to a claim for damages but not to a right to reject the goods and treat the contract as repudiated, depends in each case on the construction of the contract.[18]

Section 11 does not apply to Scotland because Scottish law does not use the distinction between conditions and warranties. The equivalent Scottish section states that if the seller's breach of contract is material the buyer is entitled 'to reject any goods delivered under the contract and treat it as repudiated'.[19]

The 'right to reject the goods' here seems to refer to a right (in the sense of a freedom) to refuse to accept the goods if delivery is tendered or to return them or make them available for collection by the seller, with an indication that they are rejected, if they are already in the buyer's possession. Linguistically it could also refer to a freedom to intimate that the goods are not accepted but the legislature would hardly bother to say this. It makes some sense to say that a buyer is not under a duty to accept or retain the goods[20] but not much sense to say that a buyer is not under a duty to refrain from telling the seller something. In any event, the right to reject the goods is here clearly distinguished from the right to treat the contract as repudiated.

The next occurrence of the notion of rejection is in section 11(4) which, for England and Wales, provides that, subject to a later rule on partial rejection:

> where a contract of sale is not severable and the buyer has accepted the goods or part of them, the breach of a condition to be fulfilled by the seller can only be treated as a breach of warranty, and not as a ground for rejecting the goods and treating the contract as repudiated, unless there is an express or implied term of the contract to that effect.

[17] Important amendments were made by the Sale and Supply of Goods to Consumers Regulations 2002, SI 2002/3045.

[18] In this and all other cases I have added the emphasis.

[19] Sale of Goods Act 1979, s 15B(1) provides that, if the seller's breach is 'material', the buyer is entitled 'to reject any goods delivered under the contract and treat it as repudiated'.

[20] Normally there is a duty to accept the goods: ibid s 27.

Here 'rejecting the goods' cannot mean 'refusing to accept the goods' (because the buyer has already accepted them). It presumably means 'returning the goods or making them available for collection by the seller, with an indication that they are not accepted'.

The striking thing about the references to rejecting the goods in these provisions is that they are unnecessary: the rules would work equally well without them.

Section 15A

Matters become more complicated when 'reject' is next mentioned. This is in section 15A(1), which provides:

> (1) Where in the case of a contract of sale—
> (a) the buyer would, apart from this subsection, have the right to reject goods by reason of a breach on the part of the seller of a term implied by section 13, 14 or 15 above, but
> (b) the breach is so slight that it would be unreasonable for him to reject them, then, if the buyer does not deal as consumer, the breach is not to be treated as a breach of condition but may be treated as a breach of warranty.

Again, this section does not apply to Scotland but a similar effect is achieved by section 15B(2). At first sight 'reject' in section 15A would seem to have the same meaning as in section 11(3), ie 'refuse to accept' (if the buyer has not yet got physical possession of the goods) or 'return or make available for collection by the seller with an indication that the goods are rejected' (if the buyer has got physical possession). The reference is to rejection *of the goods* and nothing is said about termination of the contract. Elsewhere in the Act these two ideas are treated separately and it would do some violence to the wording and scheme of the Act to treat 'reject them' in section 15A(1)(b) as meaning 'reject them and terminate the contract'. The wording of the section follows the recommendation of the Law Commission quite closely. The Commission recommended (for English law):

(1) that in general the remedy for breach of one of the relevant statutory implied terms should be an absolute right to reject the goods and treat the contract as repudiated, and
(2) that this should be qualified in the case of the non-consumer buyer by preventing him from rejecting the goods and treating the contract as repudiated where the breach is so slight that it would be unreasonable to reject.[21]

Possibly the use of 'reject' on its own is just for the sake of brevity: adding 'and treat the contract as repudiated' would have been cumbersome. However, the result of the similar brevity in the statute is slightly strange because the reasonableness test in paragraph (b) does not apply well to rejection of the goods pure and simple. It would rarely be unreasonable for a buyer, generously, to return goods to the seller if the buyer does not want them and the seller could use them, even if the buyer has no

[21] *Report on Sale and Supply of Goods* (Law Com No 160; Scot Law Com No 104, 1987) para 4.25. The Scottish Law Commission made a separate recommendation for Scottish law.

right to terminate the contract or obtain a refund of the price. The reasonableness test should apply to termination not rejection.

This is not important because in almost all cases the right result would be achieved. Examples of the kind given above would be extremely rare. Nonetheless there must be a suspicion that the drafter, following the Law Commission, used 'reject them' in section 15A as a shorthand way of saying 'reject them and treat the contract as repudiated'. The section would work much better if it referred to, and only to, the right to treat the contract as repudiated.

Section 18

One of the rules in section 18, on the time when ownership of the goods passes, is that:

> When goods are delivered to the buyer on approval or on sale or return or other similar terms the property in the goods passes to the buyer: ...
>
> (b) if he does not signify his approval or acceptance to the seller but retains the goods without giving notice of rejection, then, if a time has been fixed for the return of the goods, on the expiration of that time, and, if no time has been fixed, on the expiration of a reasonable time.

Here, 'notice of rejection' seems to refer to an intimation that the goods are not accepted.[22] It has nothing to do with the physical possession of the goods or with the termination of the contract. There would not be termination of the contract because on the giving of a notice of rejection the contract would take effect according to its terms, including the terms on returning the goods.

Section 30

It is not so easy to decide how 'reject' is used in section 30 of the Act, on delivery of the wrong quantity. It provides as follows:

> (1) Where the seller delivers to the buyer a quantity of goods less than he contracted to sell, the buyer may *reject* them, but if the buyer accepts the goods so delivered he must pay for them at the contract rate.
>
> (2) Where the seller delivers to the buyer a quantity of goods larger than he contracted to sell, the buyer may accept the goods included in the contract and *reject* the rest, or he may *reject* the whole.
>
> (2A) A buyer who does not deal as consumer may not—
>
> (a) where the seller delivers a quantity of goods less than he contracted to sell, *reject* the goods under subsection (1) above, or
>
> (b) where the seller delivers a quantity of goods larger than he contracted to sell, *reject* the whole under subsection (2) above,
>
> if the shortfall or, as the case may be, excess is so slight that it would be unreasonable for him to do so.

[22] ie the third sense of 'reject' identified above.

Subsection (2A) does not apply to Scotland. The equivalent provision makes the test for rejection (in both consumer and non-consumer cases) whether the shortfall or excess is material.[23]

In 'reject the rest' in subsection (2) it is clear that 'reject' must refer simply to a refusal to accept the excess or, if delivery has already taken place, to return the excess or make it available for collection by the seller with an indication that it is rejected. The seller will have delivered the ordered quantity. There can be no question of termination of the contract. But what does 'reject' mean in subsection (1) and at the end of subsection (2) when it refers to rejection of all the goods, not just the excess? There are two possible views. One is that 'reject' has the same meaning as in 'reject the rest'. On this view there is no statutory conferral of a right to terminate the contract. So, if the buyer rejects all the goods because the quantity is less or more than was ordered the seller can still make a delivery of the correct quantity within the time left for performance. In support of this view it can be said that one would not expect the word 'reject' to be used in two different senses within one section—indeed within the same block of seven words—and that it leads to more reasonable results. Consider, for example, the following situations.

1. A buyer has ordered 20 printer cartridges, taking advantage of a special offer. Delivery is to be within five days. The seller, temporarily short of supplies but knowing that printer ink is sometimes required urgently and desiring to provide a good service, sends five by van on the day the order is placed. The driver explains that the rest will come the next day.
2. The facts are the same but the seller sends a pack of 30. The buyer notices this and refuses to accept it. The driver offers to phone his head office to ask whether he can open the pack and remove the excess.

It may be reasonable to allow the buyer to insist on getting what was ordered and to place on the seller or the seller's agent the burden (which might sometimes be a very light burden indeed, just removing a few items) of tendering the correct quantity and only the correct quantity. But it seems unreasonable to confer a right to terminate the contract. In support of this view it can also be noted that the situation where the seller delivers less than the contractual quantity without at the same time repudiating the obligation to deliver the whole quantity is very close functionally to a tender of delivery in instalments. Section 31 deals with instalment deliveries and provides in subsection (1) that:

> Unless otherwise agreed, the buyer of goods is not bound to accept delivery of them by instalments.

Here the focus is quite clearly on the factual situation. The buyer can refuse to accept delivery of an instalment but there is no suggestion that the mere tender of an instalment gives the buyer a right to terminate the contract.

The other view is that 'reject them' and 'reject the whole' in section 30 do indeed give a right to terminate the contract: the words should be read as 'reject them and treat the contract as repudiated' and 'reject the whole and treat the contract

[23] Sale of Goods Act 1979, s 30(2D).

as repudiated'. This would go beyond the words of the section and seems an inadmissible interpretation. Also, in Scotland the effect of this would be to give the buyer a right to terminate the contract for a material shortfall or material excess even if there was no material breach, eg because the seller was going to deliver the rest shortly or offered to remove the excess quantity there and then. This would be unprincipled. So the first meaning is to be preferred: rejection here just refers to a freedom from any duty to accept the goods at the time of delivery or, if delivery has already taken place, to return them or make them available for collection by the seller with an indication that they are rejected.[24] This reading of the section is now supported by the fact that the equivalent provision on wrong quantity in the Consumer Rights Bill 2014 states expressly that:

> Where the consumer is entitled to reject goods under this section, any entitlement for the consumer to treat the contract as at an end depends on the terms of the contract and the circumstances of the case.[25]

Section 31

Section 31 is interesting because it refers to treating the contract as repudiated without coupling this with rejection of the goods. Subsection (2) provides as follows:

> Where there is a contract for the sale of goods to be delivered by stated instalments, which are to be separately paid for, and the seller makes defective deliveries in respect of one or more instalments, or the buyer neglects or refuses to take delivery of or pay for one or more instalments, it is a question in each case depending on the terms of the contract and the circumstances of the case whether the breach of contract is a repudiation of the whole contract or whether it is a severable breach giving rise to a claim for compensation but not to *a right to treat the whole contract as repudiated.*

This provision cannot say 'reject the goods and treat the whole contract as repudiated' because it deals not only with the buyer's position but also with the seller's position. It would be inappropriate to refer to a rejection of the goods by the seller. What this demonstrates is that the sections of the Act which refer to rejecting the goods and treating the contract as repudiated could be shortened by simply omitting the references to rejecting the goods. It will be noted that section 31 leaves the question of partial termination of the contract (in relation to particular instalments) unresolved.

[24] This also seems to have been the view of the Law Commissions in their 1987 *Report on the Sale and Supply of Goods.* In commenting on the section as it was before the addition of subsection (2A) they noted that 'These rules do not form a complete code for dealing with cases of wrong quantity. In particular, they do not say when a contract may be treated as discharged for delivery of a wrong quantity'. *Report on Sale and Supply of Goods*, n 21 above, para 6.17.

[25] Consumer Rights Bill 2014, cl 25(4).

Section 35

Section 35 of the 1979 Act deals with acceptance of the goods. The importance of acceptance is that it precludes termination of the contract and leaves the buyer to rely on damages.[26] Section 35(4) provides that:

> (4) The buyer is also deemed to have accepted the goods when after the lapse of a reasonable time he retains the goods without intimating to the seller that he has rejected them.

Here 'has rejected them' seems to be used in the sense of 'does not accept them'. The section omits to add any reference to treating the contract as repudiated. On this view a buyer can keep open the right to terminate the contract by saying to the seller 'The goods are not conform to contract. I am rejecting them. I am considering whether to terminate the contract or to ask you to send conforming goods in replacement. I will let you know in the next few days'. It might be argued that 'has rejected them' should be read as meaning 'has rejected them and treats the contract as repudiated'. This interpretation would go far beyond the words of the section, however, and would lead to very strange results if the buyer rejects while expressly keeping open the option of not terminating the contract.

Section 35A

Section 35A deals with partial rejection. It provides:

> (1) If the buyer—
> (a) has the right to reject the goods by reason of a breach on the part of the seller that affects some or all of them, but
> (b) accepts some of the goods, including, where there are any goods unaffected by the breach, all such goods,
>
> he does not by accepting them lose his right to reject the rest.
>
> (2) In the case of a buyer having the right to reject an instalment of goods, subsection (1) above applies as if references to the goods were references to the goods comprised in the instalment.

Here, it seems at first sight that 'reject' is used in a factual sense. In the first reference to the right to reject it would be possible to replace 'reject the goods' by 'reject the goods and treat the contract as repudiated' but that would hardly be possible in the other two cases. It would be necessary, at the very least, to read in some such words as 'and treat the contract as repudiated in relation to the rejected goods'. In making the recommendations which led to the addition of these provisions the Law Commissions talked of 'rejection' and 'retention' of the goods without any reference to termination of the contract.[27] On the other hand, reading rejection here as relating only to the goods leaves unresolved the question of what happens to the contractual relationship so far as the rejected goods are concerned. The intention

[26] See Sale of Goods Act 1979, s 11(4) for English law and *Pollock v Macrae* 1922 SC (HL) 192 for Scottish law.

[27] *Report on Sale and Supply of Goods*, n 21 above, para 6.9.

presumably is that the buyer should be able to terminate the contract, and obtain a refund if the price has been paid, in relation to the rejected goods. But this is not stated.

Section 45

The next reference in the Act to rejection of the goods is in section 45 which deals with the duration of transit for the purposes of the seller's right of stoppage in transit. Subsection (4) provides that:

> If the goods are rejected by the buyer, and the carrier or other bailee or custodier continues in possession of them, the transit is not deemed to be at an end, even if the seller has refused to receive them back.

Here it seems clear that 'rejected' is used in the sense of not accepted. The opening words mean 'If the buyer has refused to accept physical possession of the goods'.

Section 48D

Section 48D provides that a consumer buyer who requires the seller to repair or replace the goods cannot resort to certain other remedies until the seller has had a reasonable time to effect the repair or replacement. These remedies include rejecting the goods and terminating the contract for breach of condition (England and Wales) or rejecting any goods delivered under the contract and treating the contract as repudiated (Scotland). 'Rejecting' here seems to mean refusing to accept physical possession of the goods or returning them or making them available for collection by the seller, but the result is very odd. A buyer who has required the seller to repair or replace the goods will already have rejected them. The provision is a fine illustration of the confusion which can arise from an unthinking assumption that rejection of the goods and termination of the contract always go together as a sort of composite remedy.

Conclusion on the Use of 'Reject' in the Sale of Goods Act 1979

The most important point to note is that the Sale of Goods Act 1979 does not contain a definition of 'right to reject'. It does *not* say that that the right to reject means a right to reject the goods and terminate the contract and obtain a refund. It never uses 'reject' in this tripartite sense. Nor does it use 'right to reject' to cover rejection of the goods and treating the contract as at an end. It consistently refers to rejection *of goods*, either all of the goods or some of them. In a few provisions there are grounds for suspecting that the drafter may have intended 'reject the goods' to be shorthand for 'reject the goods and terminate the contract' but the provisions cannot reasonably be interpreted as having that actual effect. In relation to goods the Act uses 'reject' in all three senses identified earlier: (1) refuse to accept physical possession; (2) return or make available for collection by the seller with an indication that not accepted; (3) intimate that not accepted.

Another conclusion is that those provisions which refer to a right to reject the goods and treat the contract as repudiated do not need to refer to the right to reject the goods and would be better if they did not. The return of the goods is better seen as an obligation of the buyer after termination of the contract, corresponding to the seller's obligation to refund the price.

USE OF 'REJECT' IN THE CONSUMER RIGHTS BILL

The draft Consumer Rights Bill of 2013 used 'right to reject' in a tripartite way to cover a right to reject the goods, terminate the contract and obtain a refund. This was very different from the right to reject of the Sale of Goods Act 1979. The Consumer Rights Bill of 2014 uses 'right to reject' in a bipartite way to cover a right to reject the goods and treat the contract as at an end. The seller's obligation to refund the price and the buyer's obligation to return the goods or make them available for collection follow from the exercise of the right to reject. This is better than the 2013 Bill but still different from the 1979 Act, and it leaves a question about what is meant by 'reject' in the expression 'reject the goods'.

The Bill gives a consumer buyer various remedies if goods do not conform to the contract. These vary depending on the nature of the breach but, basically, if the goods are defective because of a breach of the statutorily implied terms as to quality, fitness for purpose or description the consumer has, among other remedies, a 'short term right to reject' and a 'final right to reject'.[28] These are available at different times and different rules apply as to deduction for use but their essential nature is the same. The key provisions are in section 20, which provides as follows:

> (4) Each of these rights entitles the consumer to reject the goods and treat the contract as at an end.
> (5) The right is exercised if the consumer indicates to the trader that the consumer is rejecting the goods and treating the contract as at an end.
> (6) The indication may be something the consumer says or does, but it must be clear enough to be understood by the trader.
> (7) From the time when the right is exercised—
> (a) the trader has a duty to give the consumer a refund, subject to subsection (14), and
> (b) the consumer has a duty to make the goods available for collection by the trader or (if there is an agreement for the consumer to return rejected goods) to return them as agreed.

It will be noticed that rejection of the goods seems to be used in a different sense from that in which it is used in key provisions of the Sale of Goods Act 1979. There it often means 'throwing back' the goods, in a physical sense, by returning them or making them available for collection by the seller. In the 2014 Bill rejection seems to mean just intimating that they are not being accepted as conform to the contract. The physical 'throwing back' comes later and is seen, rightly, as a duty of the consumer rather than a right. This is a better and more logical structure but it is not clear why it is necessary to mention the indication of rejection at all. Consumers

[28] Consumer Rights Bill 2014, cl 19.

who are sold defective goods would naturally and correctly suppose that they have a right (freedom) to tell the seller that the goods are not conform to contract. Why say this in the Bill?

It is interesting to note that the Bill says nothing about the right to reject the goods in connection with the remedies of repair and replacement.[29] A consumer seeking those remedies would also tell the seller that the goods are not conform to contract but the Bill does not find it necessary to say this. Indeed, it says that a consumer who exercises the right to a repair or replacement cannot exercise the short-term right to reject until the seller has had a reasonable time to carry out the repair or replacement.[30] This is very odd in so far as the short-term right to reject includes rejection of the goods: the consumer will already have rejected the goods. The linking of rejection of the goods with the termination of the contract produces an unfortunate result.

Rejection and termination are not always linked in the Bill. In relation to partial rejection the Bill says that a consumer who rejects some of the goods has a right to a refund in relation to them, and a duty to return them or make them available for collection, but it says nothing about terminating the contract in part.[31] So the position of a consumer who has not paid in advance is not expressly covered. And a consumer who obtains a refund might still be liable to take, and pay for, conforming goods. In relation to delivery of a wrong quantity the Bill enables the consumer to reject all of the goods or the excess goods but expressly leaves termination of the contract to the general law.[32] In describing the other remedies which a consumer may have (eg for breach of an express term of the contract) the Bill mentions treating the contract as at an end but without linking this to rejection of the goods.[33]

CRITICISM OF THE COMPOSITE USE OF 'RIGHT TO REJECT'

By the composite use of 'right to reject' I mean either the bipartite way it is used in the Consumer Rights Bill 2014 (to cover rejecting the goods and treating the contract as at an end) and the tripartite way it is used by the Law Commissions (to cover those things and also a right to a refund).

Incoherent Law

It makes the law incoherent if 'right to reject' is used in two or three different ways.

[29] ibid cl 23.
[30] ibid cl 23(6) and (7).
[31] ibid cl 21(7)(a).
[32] ibid cl 25.
[33] ibid cl 19(11).

Inappropriate Use of 'Reject'

An obvious objection to using 'reject' in a bipartite sense (to cover rejection of the goods and termination of the contract) is that the word is not normally used in relation to the contract. Using the expression in a tripartite way to cover also a right to a refund is even more inappropriate. 'Reject' in the composite 'right to reject' seems to be used in a curious, intransitive, even meaningless, way. The unanswered question is 'Reject what?'. In fact 'reject' operates as a mere holder for what follows. Any word could be used. It also seems inappropriate to use the same word in two different ways in the same expression: in a concrete, transitive way in relation to the goods and in an abstract, intransitive way in the umbrella term. If an umbrella term for some of the consumer's remedies is needed at all, which it is not, then something which avoided 'reject' might have been preferable.

Inappropriate Use of 'Right'

Another objection is that the word 'right' has a density here which would have Hohfeld spinning in his grave. In the tripartite use of the expression the so-called 'right to reject' covers a right (in the sense of a freedom) to reject the goods, a right (in the sense of a power) to terminate the contract, and a right (in the strong sense of a right corresponding to an obligation) to a refund of the price. In the bipartite sense it covers a freedom and a power. It may also be intended to include a right to have the goods taken back corresponding to an obligation on the seller to take them back, although this is not stated. The composite 'right' to reject is not a single right at all: it is two or three different kinds of rights.

Inappropriate Focus

To call an umbrella term for some of the buyer's remedies a 'right to reject' inevitably invites a focus on the right (in the sense of a freedom) to reject the goods, something which is comparatively unimportant to buyers. Buyers do not need to be told that they can intimate to the seller that the goods are rejected. And most buyers are not greatly concerned about a right (freedom) to return the goods: they would not mind if the seller said they could keep the goods on providing adequate evidence of the faults and still get their money back.

It might be argued that the expression a 'right to reject', although technically suspect, is nonetheless a useful short formula which corresponds to ordinary usage and to what happens in real life. But this may be doubted. Sellers trying to reassure potential customers would not say 'Reject if not entirely satisfied'. This would leave far too many questions unanswered and would not be at all reassuring. They would say something like 'Money back if not entirely satisfied' or 'No quibble money back guarantee'. Buyers are not so much concerned with rejecting the goods as with getting their money back (if they have already paid) or being relieved of their obligation to pay (if they have not already paid). This was implicitly recognised in the Law

Commissions' *Report on Consumer Remedies for Faulty Goods*. In stating the views of consultees they used the right to reject when reporting on the views of professionals and organisations but when describing the views of consumers said that:

> Although consumers are generally unaware of their precise legal rights, most are aware that they have a legal right to a refund for faulty goods, and seek it in about 20% of cases where goods are faulty. In research, 94% of consumers said the right to a refund was important to them, and 89% thought it should be retained even though other remedies (repair and replacement) are available.[34]

It is significant that the 'right to reject' does not appear in this passage describing the views of consumers. The emphasis is all on the right to a refund.

If there is to be a focus on one element of the remedies of a buyer who wants to be finished with the contract and obtain a refund then it should be on the dominant element—the element from which other elements can be said to follow—and that, clearly, is the termination of the contract.

Another reason for preferring a focus on termination rather than rejection is that the latter is rather contract specific and party specific. It can be used of contracts for the sale or supply of goods but not, or at least not in the same way, for contracts where there is nothing to reject. It can be used of the buyer's remedies but not of the seller's remedies. This leads to unnecessary and undesirable fragmentation of the law.

Risk of Confusion

The fact that 'right to reject' can be used in different senses can lead to serious and harmful confusion. For example, when the European Commission proposed a wide-ranging Consumer Rights Directive on a 'maximum harmonisation' basis which would have left Member States with no option to give consumers more extensive remedies, there were complaints from the United Kingdom that this would mean the end of the right to reject.[35] The Commissioner in charge of the European project answered that there was no intention to affect the right to reject.[36] This was correct if the 'right to reject' was understood in a narrow sense but not if it was understood in a wide sense like that favoured by the Law Commissions. In the end the proposed Directive was cut down and did not affect the right to reject in either sense but the debate illustrated the great risk of confusion to which the United Kingdom's unfortunate 'right to reject' terminology can give rise.

[34] *Report on Consumer Remedies for Faulty Goods*, n 1 above, para 1.18.

[35] The Law Commissions in ibid said 'If the European Commission's proposed directive were adopted as published, on the face of it, the UK would have to repeal the right to reject' (para 1.17).

[36] Commissioner Kuneva at the IMCO Committee hearing on the Consumer Rights Directive, 2 March 2009, and at the 10th Anniversary European Consumer Day, 13 March 2009.

Rejection of the Goods and Termination of the Contract Do Not Always Go Together

The composite sense of 'right to reject' may give the impression that rejection of the goods and termination of the contract always go together. It is true that judges have occasionally assumed that this is the case. In one Scottish case, for example, Lord McLaren said that rejection of the goods by the buyer 'is in legal effect a rescission of the contract of sale on the ground of the seller's non-performance or imperfect performance of his obligations'.[37] In a later English case Lord Devlin said that 'A right to reject is after all only a particular form of the right to rescind the contract'.[38] These statements are, however, wrong. There can be rejection of the goods without termination of the contract.

For example, a consumer (C) may have ordered a bicycle wheel online with a delivery period of three to five days. On day three a carrier brings the wheel and asks C to sign for it. C notices, however, that the wheel is twisted and refuses to accept it, writing on the carrier's delivery note that the goods are rejected because the wheel was twisted on arrival. C then phones the sellers to explain what has happened. C still wants a wheel of the kind ordered and is glad when the sellers say that they will send another one by express delivery to arrive the next day.[39] C has rejected the goods but has not attempted to terminate the contract.[40]

Another example of rejection without termination occurs if a consumer (C) has taken delivery of the goods, then discovers that they are not conform to contract and would like repair or replacement. C has a right to reject the goods (ie indicate that they are not accepted as they are and return them or make them available for collection by the sellers) while requiring repair or replacement.[41] Again the contractual relationship is not terminated. C is, in effect, calling on the sellers to perform their contractual obligations and supply conforming goods.

Another well-known situation involving rejection without termination occurs when the seller delivers an excess quantity. The buyer can reject the excess, but clearly rejection in this case does not involve termination of the contract.[42]

A similar example is where there is partial rejection of a consignment of goods some of which do not conform to the contract. Under both the Sale of Goods Act 1979[43] and the Consumer Rights Bill 2014[44] it seems that the rejection of some of the defective goods can occur without termination of the contract. The question of partial termination is left unresolved by both instruments.

[37] Lord McLaren in *Electric Construction Co v Hurry and Young* (1897) 24 R 312, 321.

[38] *Kwei Tek Choo v British Traders & Shippers Ltd* [1954] 2 QB 459, 480.

[39] As C is a consumer the risk of damage in transit would be with the sellers: Sale of Gods Act 1979, s 20(4).

[40] Possibly this would not count as a rejection of the goods under cl 19(4) of the draft Consumer Rights Bill 2014 (see above) but it would under the existing law.

[41] Sale of Goods Act 1979, s 48B, added by the Sale and Supply of Goods Regulations 2002, SI 2002/3045, in implementation of Directive 1999/44/EC of the European Parliament and Council of 25 May 1999.

[42] Sale of Goods Act 1979, s 30(2); Consumer Rights Bill 2014, cl 25(4).

[43] See Sale of Goods Act 1979, s 35A and text to n 33 above.

[44] Consumer Rights Bill 2014, cl 21.

And in a 'sale or return' contract, rejection of the goods does not involve termination of the contract but rather the exercise of a contractual option and the performing of one of the main obligations under the contract, namely, the obligation to return the goods. As Phillips LJ observed in one modern case on this type of contract, the buyer's obligations after rejection depend on the contract, which may need to be interpreted in order to decide whether, for example, the buyer has to actually return the goods or just make them available for collection and, if so, how and when.[45] It is true that in the same case Auld LJ said that 'rejection determines the contract'[46] but that is clearly wrong. Rejection just ends the sale part of the contract: the return part remains in full force.

A very similar situation arises where the contract gives the buyer a right to a refund of the price if the goods are returned because of a fault within a certain period. A buyer who exercises the rights conferred by such terms would be exercising a right to reject but not terminating the contract. The buyer would be using the contract rather than ending it.

The Law Commissions in their report on faulty goods recognised that: 'The rejection of the goods and the termination of the contract are separate concepts. There are circumstances where the rejection of goods will not be followed by the termination of the contract'.[47] This recognition makes it all the more surprising that the Commissions should have used 'right to reject' to cover both concepts.

Same Rules Should Not Necessarily Apply to Rejection of the Goods and Termination of the Contract

Using 'right to reject' in a wide sense to cover both rejection of the goods and termination of the contract may give the impression that the same rules should always apply to both. This is not necessarily so.

For example, we have seen that if a seller delivers the wrong quantity, while making it clear that this is not a repudiation of the contract, it may be reasonable to give the buyer a right to refuse to accept delivery of any of the goods and to impose on the seller the (possibly very slight) burden of getting the quantity right but, as is now recognised in the Consumer Rights Bill 2014,[48] it may be unreasonable to give the buyer a right to terminate the contract for a slight and easily remedied difference in quantity. The same could be said for slight and remediable defects in quality: it is one thing to say that a buyer can insist on perfect tender; another to give a right to terminate the contract. To put this another way, some breaches of contract by the

[45] *Atari Corporation (UK) Ltd v Electronics Boutiques Stores (UK) Ltd* [1998] QB 539, 550.

[46] ibid 554.

[47] *Report on Consumer Remedies for Faulty Goods*, n 1 above, para 2.8. The Commissions repeated this point at para 3.111, saying that: 'the rejection of goods and the termination of the contract are two separate concepts. The rejection of goods (that is, the refusal to accept goods) is not necessarily followed by termination of the contract. For example, the consumer may reject goods and give the trader an opportunity to cure the fault'.

[48] Consumer Rights Bill 2014, cl 25(4).

seller may justify the buyer in withholding performance of his or her obligation to accept delivery without justifying termination of the contract.

Again it might be reasonable to say that a buyer loses the right to return the goods to the seller (and require the seller to take them back) if they suffer serious damage, for some reason unconnected with their original defect, while in the buyer's possession but retains the right to terminate the contract on paying the seller the monetary value which the goods would have had if not damaged in this way.

In short, to assume that the same rules must apply to both rejection of the goods and termination of the contract would be to cut down law reform options.

Unnecessary to Refer to Composite 'Right to Reject'

In the Consumer Rights Bill 2014 the references to the composite 'right to reject' could be replaced by references to a right to treat the contract as at an end without any loss of sense and with considerable gain in simplicity. An unfortunate feature of the Bill is that it provides one set of remedies for breach of some of the statutory implied terms and another for breach of express terms. The former includes, as we have seen, the composite 'right to reject': the latter includes the 'right to treat the contract as at an end' without any mention of rejection.[49]

ANOTHER APPROACH

The proposed Common European Sales Law shows that another approach is possible.[50] It is fitting to consider this as Hugh Beale played an enormously important role in its preparation, not only directly as a member of the Expert Group which prepared the draft text on which its rules are based, but also indirectly as a member of the Commission on European Contract Law (the Lando Commission) and of the Study Group on a European Civil Code, which respectively prepared the two texts which were most influential in the drafting of the Common European Sales Law (CESL).[51] Taking all these works together it is fair to say that no one played a more important role in the work culminating in the CESL.

It is a remarkable thing that, although the sales provisions of the Consumer Rights Bill 2014 and the CESL are both attempting to integrate the rules of certain EU Directives into a more general framework, the former uses 'right to reject' over 20 times and the latter once, and then only in describing a type of term which will be presumed to be unfair.[52] How can this be?

[49] ibid cl 19(11)(e).

[50] Proposal for a Regulation on a Common European Sales Law, n 10 above.

[51] O Lando and H Beale (eds), *The Principles of European Contract Law (Parts I and II)* (The Hague, Kluwer Law International, 2000) and O Lando et al (eds), *The Principles of European Contract Law (Part III)* (The Hague, Kluwer Law International, 2003); and C von Bar and E Clive (eds), *The Principles, Definitions and Model Rules of European Private Law (Draft Common Frame of Reference)* (Oxford University Press, 2010).

[52] In art 85(n) which says that a contract term is presumed to be unfair if it allows 'a trader, where what has been ordered is unavailable, to supply an equivalent without having expressly informed the consumer of this possibility and of the fact that the trader must bear the cost of returning what the consumer has received under the contract if the consumer exercises a right to reject performance'.

First, the CESL lists the buyer's remedies, without grouping some of them under an umbrella term. It does this in summary form in article 106, which provides as follows:

> In the case of non-performance of an obligation by the seller, the buyer may do any of the following:
> (a) require performance, which includes specific performance, repair or replacement of the goods or digital content, under Section 3 of this Chapter;
> (b) withhold the buyer's own performance under Section 4 of this Chapter;
> (c) terminate the contract under Section 5 of this Chapter and claim the return of any price already paid, under Chapter 17;
> (d) reduce the price under Section 6 of this Chapter; and
> (e) claim damages under Chapter 16.

The buyer's freedom to refuse to accept non-conforming goods at the point of delivery is covered by the rule in article 106(b) on withholding performance. The seller's obligation to deliver conforming goods and the buyer's obligation to accept delivery are reciprocal obligations and the buyer can refuse to accept delivery until conforming goods are tendered.

The question of returning goods for repair is left largely to the good sense of the parties, bearing in mind that they have an obligation to cooperate.[53] It is provided, however, that the buyer is entitled to have the repair done 'free of charge' which means that the seller has to bear the cost of getting the goods back for repair, repairing them and returning them to the buyer.[54] It is not necessary to provide that the buyer who is seeking repair has a 'right' (freedom) to return the goods to the seller or make them available for collection for that purpose: that goes without saying.

There is slightly more regulation of the return of the goods for replacement. Again the buyer is entitled to replacement 'free of charge'.[55] There is a danger here, however, that a seller might not want to take back a bulky defective item. So it is provided that

> [w]here the seller has remedied the lack of conformity by replacement, the seller has a right and an obligation to take back the replaced item at the seller's expense.[56]

So the buyer has a strong form of the right to reject the goods, although that actual expression is not used. The buyer also has an obligation to allow the seller to take back the item.

The return of the goods on termination of the contract is regulated in a different way. Here, the return of the goods (or the monetary equivalent in some cases) and the repayment of the price are seen as part of the restitutionary consequences of termination.[57] The buyer is obliged to return the goods and the seller is obliged to repay the price. There is quite detailed regulation of the obligation to return. This

[53] CESL, art 3.
[54] ibid art 110.
[55] ibid art 110.
[56] ibid art 112.
[57] ibid arts 172–77.

is a more realistic approach than focusing on the buyer's 'right' (freedom) to return the goods, as now seems to be recognised by the Consumer Rights Bill 2014.

The proposed Common European Sales Law shows that the use of the 'right to reject' is an unnecessary complication. The same or better results can be achieved without mentioning it at all.

CONCLUSION

The way in which the 'right to reject' is used in the sales law of the United Kingdom is confused, confusing and regrettable. It is confused because it mixes up different types of right and different types of rejection, uses words in inappropriate ways and focuses on the wrong element in the buyer's remedies. It is confusing because the 'right to reject' is used in two or three quite different senses. It is regrettable because it complicates the law and leads to incoherence and misleading assumptions. It is also quite unnecessary.

9

Universal Terms in Contract

MICHAEL FURMSTON

FOREWORD

HUGH BEALE AND I have connections which go back to before we ever met. We both read law at the same Oxford college (Exeter) and had the same tutor (Derek Hall). Exeter had long connections with the law of contract as Geoffrey Cheshire was the law fellow for 30 years. Derek Hall left Exeter in 1969 to become President of Corpus. After I returned to Oxford to teach in 1964, he was the first person I turned to for advice until his untimely death in 1975. One day in his study in Corpus (though I cannot now remember the context), he said 'you should look out for Hugh Beale'.

Hugh and I first met when I was an external examiner at Bristol in the mid 1970's, which was soon followed by my move to take up a chair. From then until Hugh's move to Warwick in 1987, we shared the teaching of contract and started an LLM course in Applied Contract. In those far off days Bristol only admitted 105 students a year and in contract there were 18 weekly tutorials in contract in groups of five as well as 40 lectures. Contract was taught as a second year subject which made it (perhaps) permissible to make the demands which we undoubtedly made of the class.

This period also saw the appearance of Beale, Bishop and Furmston in 1975.[1] I remember that Hugh did a great deal of the work. My clearest recollection is that I bought a secondhand word processor so large that I had to drive to London in my long wheel base Land Rover to collect it. Times have changed. The existence of the book has meant that we have kept fruitfully in contact.

INTRODUCTION

This essay started life some years ago in a talk to judges in New South Wales on the question whether, if there was a general rule that contracts contained an implied term that they should be performed in good faith, it was possible to exclude this

[1] Hugh Beale, William Bishop, and Michael Furmston, *Contract: Cases and Materials* (Oxford University Press, 1975). This book is now in its 5th edn, published 2007.

obligation. There are of course a number of New South Wales decisions which say that there is such an implied term[2] though the High Court of Australia has not yet expressed a view. Of course one might seek to sidestep this question by putting an obligation of good faith on a different basis but it did lead me to the broader question of whether there can be implied terms at common law which cannot be excluded. We are all of course familiar with statutory provisions which make implied terms mandatory but the conventional view is clearly that implied terms must yield to well drafted express terms. Reflection has led me to the view that this is not as obvious as it is generally believed to be.

FRAUD

It is orthodox law that a contracting party cannot exclude liability for deceit (though this is not usually explained on the basis of an implied obligation to be honest). Until recently, the leading authority for this proposition was *S Pearson & Son Ltd v Dublin Corporation,*[3] a decision by eight law lords on appeal from Ireland.

The appellant sued the respondent in deceit for a statement by the respondent's agent as to the nature of the works to be executed. A defence was run that the contract required the applicant to verify all representations for himself and not rely on their accuracy. The trial judge refused to leave any question to the jury and entered judgment for the respondent. The House of Lords held that there must be a new trial. Lord Loreburn LC said:[4]

> Now it seems clear that no one can escape liability for his own fraudulent statements by inserting in a contract a clause that the other party shall not rely upon them. I will not say that a man himself innocent may not under any circumstances, however peculiar, guard himself by apt and express clauses from liability for the fraud of his own agents. It suffices to say that in my opinion the clauses before us do not admit of such a construction.

In *Refuge Assurance Co Ltd v Kettlewell,*[5] the holder of a policy of life insurance was persuaded by the appellant's agents to continue the policy by a false representation that if she continued for five years she would receive a free policy. The company in due course refused to issue a free policy and the respondent sued for return of the premiums. The trial judge held that the company had ratified the unauthorised fraud of the agent by keeping the premiums. The House of Lords dismissed the appeal without giving reasons.

It will be seen that in both these cases the fraud was that of an agent. This was the case also in *HIH Casualty and General Insurance Ltd v Chase Manhattan Bank.*[6]

[2] See, eg, *Renard Construction (MFC) Pty Ltd v Minister for Public Works* (1992) 26 NS WLR 234 and in the Federal Court: *Hughes Aircraft Systems International v Air Services Australia* (1997) 146 ALR 1, and generally Elisabeth Peden, *Good Faith in the Performance of Contract* (Sydney, Lexis Nexis Butterworth, 2003).

[3] *S Pearson & Son Ltd v Dublin Corporation* [1907] 1 AC 351.

[4] ibid at 353–54.

[5] *Refuge Assurance Co Ltd v Kettlewell* [1909] AC 243.

[6] *HIH Casualty and General Insurance Ltd v Chase Manhattan Bank* [2003] 2 Lloyd Rep 61; [2003] 1 All ER (Comm) 349; see discussion by Ken Handley, 'Exclusion Clauses for Fraud' (2003) 119 *Law Quarterly Review* 537 and by Chris Nicoll, 'HIH Litigation' (2003) 119 *Law Quarterly Review* 572, 579.

Chase was the lead bank in a syndicate which provided finance for movies. This was clearly a high risk activity dependent not only on the success of the movies but also on the mysterious accounting practices of Hollywood. The loans would only be made if insurance was provided. HIH and other insurers provided financial contingency insurance for the scheme. Heath North America and Special Risks Ltd and Heath Insurance Broking Ltd (Heath) were brokers concerned in the negotiations.

The contract between Chase and HIH contained a 'truth of statement' clause which provided inter alia:

> 6. the Insured will not have any duty or obligation to make any representation, warranty or disclosure of any nature, express or implied (such duty and obligation being expressly waived by the insurers) and
> 7. shall have no liability of any nature to the insurers for any information provided by any other parties and
> 8. any such information provided by or non-disclosure by other parties including, but not limited to, Heath North American & Special Risks Ltd (other than Section I of the Questionnaire) shall not be a ground or grounds for avoidance of the insurers" obligations under the Policy or the cancellation thereof.

Preliminary issues were ordered. No allegations were made against Chase but non-disclosure and misrepresentation were alleged against Heath. The House of Lords held (Lord Scott dissenting) that clause 6 did not relieve Heath of its duty of disclosure and that clauses 7 and 8 should be read as excluding Chase's liability for Heath's negligence but not its liability for Heath's fraud if Heath were fraudulent.

The House was divided as to whether with sufficiently clear drafting Chase could exclude liability for Heath's fraud. It was clear that the contract had been carefully drafted for the particular transaction so as to reduce the liability of Chase.

On the facts there seem clear business reasons why Chase should wish to distance themselves contractually from Heath. There is no doubt that brokers sometimes act for the insured and sometimes for the insurer. It would seem that the most effective way for Chase to secure protection would have been to persuade HIH to agree to a provision that Heath was not an agent of Chase. It was clear that the existing contract did not have this effect. Of course, if Chase had made it adequately clear to HIH that it took no responsibility of any kind for anything said by Heath, HIH might have refused to insure the transaction. It would surely if prudent have demanded a larger premium and /or obtained adequate assurances from Heath.

The cases appear to support the proposition that a contracting party cannot exclude its own liability for fraud and (at most) can only exclude liability for its agent's fraud by the clearest words. The leading cases are all ones where the fraud alleged is clearly that of an agent but the defendants were all corporate bodies. There were therefore potential problems as to whose state of mind was relevant for the establishing of fraud. In the case of a large bank like Chase it is very unlikely that relevant decisions would be made at board level. In practice knowledge of untruth could often only be brought home to middle managers. This might be fraud by an agent rather than by the bank but it would surely be unacceptable for the bank to seek to contract on the basis that it took no liability for its staff.

I have, however, a problem. Some years ago I was engaged as an expert witness on English law on a contract made subject to English law by two American companies and litigated in the United States. Basically, one company had sold to the other an English subsidiary. The negotiations had been handled by two English firms of solicitors of the highest reputation. The contract ran to several hundred pages and contained a clause which said, in effect, that the buyer had relied only upon the information set out in the contract. The buyers now alleged deceit.

It seemed to me then and it still seems to me now that the allegation alone could not render the carefully drafted contract waste paper. To prove deceit one has to show not only a fraudulent statement but also that the person to whom it was addressed has relied on it. No doubt proof of the false statement will often support an inference of reliance but surely the wording of this contract would require the buyer to give evidence of reliance.

TERMS IMPLIED IN LAW

Today it is normal to distinguish between terms implied in fact and terms implied in law. This is not how the law was taught to me 50 years ago but somewhere in between it became the prevailing orthodoxy. On the other hand, 50 years ago I was taught that express terms trump implied terms.

For terms implied in fact this must usually be true. The express term will leave no room for the sort of arguments which would justify implication in fact.[7]

It is not difficult to find statements of the highest authority that express terms exclude terms implied in law, but this leaves some decisions which require explanation. A good starting point is *Johnstone v Bloomsbury Health Authority*.[8] The plaintiff was a junior hospital doctor. His contract of employment required him to work 40 hours a week and on average 48 hours a week more (the report does not indicate over what period the averaging was to be done). He argued that the contract was inconsistent with his employer's implied obligation to take reasonable care for his health and safety. Leggatt LJ took the orthodox position that the implied term was ousted by the express term. The majority of the Court of Appeal disagreed. Although their reasoning differs it is clear that both read the express and implied terms together. We all know that it is possible to work 88 hours a week without immediate danger to health. This still leaves 80 hours for sleep, eating and the occasional word with one's spouse. But to work 88 hours consecutively with no break for sleep, or to work 168 hours a week one week in four, is a different matter and the majority would not have read the contract as permitting this. In effect the express and implied terms are read together, qualifying each other. On the facts there was clearly an express term as to the hours to be worked and an implied term as to working conditions. These terms might be said to be interpenetrative; that is, the meaning properly to be given to each is substantially influenced by the other. This was in effect to anticipate Lord Hoffmann's view in *Attorney-General of Belize v Belize Telecom Ltd*[9] that the question of implication is part of the process of construction.

[7] As will be seen later I am not sure that this is always true.

[8] *Johnstone v Bloomsbury Health Authority* [1992] QB 333. See also *Gogay v Hertford Shire County Council* [2000] 1 RLR 703.

[9] *Attorney-General of Belize v Belize Telecom Ltd* [2002] 1 AC 408.

Sir Nicholas Browne Wilkinson said:[10]

> In my judgment there must be some restriction on the defendants' rights. In any sphere of employment other than that of junior hospital doctors, an obligation to work up to 88 hours in any one week would be rightly regarded as oppressive and intolerable. But even that is not the limit of what the defendants claim. Since the plaintiff's obligation is to be available 'on average' for 48 hours per week, the defendants claim to be entitled to require him to work more than 88 hours in some weeks regardless of possible injury to his health. Thus the plaintiff alleges that he was required to work for 100 hours during one week in February 1989 and 105 hours during another week in March 1989. How far can this go? Could the defendants demand of the plaintiff that he worked 130 hours (out of the total of 168 hours available) in any one week even if this would manifestly involve injury to his health? In my judgment the defendants' right to call for overtime under clause 4(b) is not an absolute right but must be limited in some way. There is no technical legal reason why the defendants' discretion to call for overtime should not be exercised in conformity with the normal implied duty to take reasonable care not to injure their employee's health.

One might attempt to draft the express term so as to prevent this form of construction. The Bloomsbury Health Trust might have said to junior doctors 'We care nothing for your health and safety and intend to proceed accordingly' but to go so far would probably have presented problems with the Unfair Contract Terms Act 1977 and would certainly have handed a blank cheque to any lawyer acting for a patient whose treatment was adversely affected.

Similar reasoning in a quite different context is to be found in the judgment of the Court of Appeal in *SSCF Employment v ASLEF*[11] where they had to consider whether a threat to work to rule would be a breach of contract.

Roskill LJ said:[12]

> Notwithstanding the skill with which the contrary view has been urged upon us, I regard it as self-evident that each party to each service agreement must, as rational beings, be taken to have assumed as a matter of course, when each service contract was entered into, that the employee would never seek so to interpret and act upon the rules as to disrupt the entire railway system. Accordingly, I have no hesitation in implying a term into the contract of service that each employee will not, in obeying his lawful instructions, seek to obey them in a wholly unreasonable way which has the effect of disrupting the system, the efficient running of which he is employed to ensure. I prefer to rest my decision that work to rule is a breach of contract on this ground rather than on the alternative ground, clearly equally tenable, advanced by the Solicitor-General, that work to rule involves a breach of the positive obligation of faithful service owed by employee to his master.

Such cases suggest that a mechanical 'express trumps implied' approach is too simple. There are significant cases where express qualifies implied and vice versa.

No cases of this kind seem yet to have reached the House of Lords. It is possible that the reasoning will be declared heterodox but in each case the result seems intuitively correct. I dare to suggest that in the long run it will be held that in certain circumstances implied in law terms can prevail over or at least qualify express terms.

[10] *Bloomsbury Health Authority*, n 8 above, at 351.
[11] *SSCF Employment v ASLEF* [1972] 2 QB 495.
[12] ibid at 508.

EQUITABLE LIFE V HYMAN

A central case in this argument is *Equitable Life v Hyman*,[13] though for reasons not immediately apparent from the judgment. In this case Equitable Life was a well-established insurance company which sold with profits insurance policies for use as pensions. Under the rules then operating, pensions enjoyed favourable tax treatment but as part of the package taxpayers were not allowed to take all the final payout in cash. Roughly speaking, if £100,000 was payable, a tax-free sum of £25,000 could be taken and £75,000 converted into an annuity. The insured could go into the market to buy an annuity but many would buy it from their insurer. From 1988 Equitable Life had been selling policies with a guaranteed annuity rate (GAR). In 1988 the GAR was below the market rate but from 1993 the market rate fell below the GAR. The case concerns the effect of this on the rights of the parties.

A central feature of 'with profits' policies was that the amount payable was not guaranteed. The deal was that the insured would share in the proceeds of the successful investment policy of the insurer but no one knew how successful the policy would be. This was dealt with by a system of bonuses. All the many insurers in the market would periodically (in the case of Equitable Life annually) declare bonuses. The bonus once declared would be guaranteed and added to the sum insured. Most companies in the market would declare larger terminal bonuses, that is, in the year when the policy matured.

It is a central feature of the system that the typical insured enters the market 20 or even 30 years ahead. Marketing by insurers tries to promote the perception that bonuses in year 30 will be like those in year 1. This is reinforced by the fact that the insured is usually not committed to the insurer for the whole term. Many insurers sold single premium policies but even if the insured contracts to pay £1,000 a year for 30 years, he will often choose to have a second policy for £5,000 with a different insurer in year 10. Promotion and inflation both make this likely.

This means that the insurer had to steer between two poles. On the one hand, generous bonuses this year will make policies attractive to next year's investors. On the other hand, next year may be a bad year for investment and it is desirable to have money in hand to avoid a sharp cut in the bonus level.

In the case of Equitable Life the position was controlled by article 65 which provides:

> (1) The directors shall, at such intervals as they may deem expedient, but at least once in every three years, cause an investigation to be made into the financial condition of the Society, including a valuation of its assets and liabilities, by the actuary. Provided that in the valuation of the assets the values thereof be not estimated beyond the market prices (if any) of the same, unless for reasons to be set out in the directors' report to the members upon the results of the valuation. After making such provision as they may think sufficient for such liabilities, and any special or other reserve they may think fit, the directors shall, at a special board meeting, declare what amount of the surplus (if any) shown by such valuation may, in their opinion, be divided by

[13] *Equitable Life v Hyman* [2002] 1 AC 408.

way of bonus, and they shall apportion the amount of such declared surplus by way of bonus among the holders of the participating policies on such principles, and by such methods, as they may from time to time determine. The directors may pay or apply the bonus so apportioned to each participating policy holder, either by way of reversionary bonus (that is to say, by way of addition to the sum assured when it shall become a claim), cash payment, reduction of premium for the whole of life or any less period, or in any other way they and any participating policy holder may agree.

(2) The directors (after obtaining such report or reports from the actuary as they may in their discretion consider to be necessary or desirable in the circumstances) may, in cases where participating policies become claims in the interval between two valuations, pay such interim or additional or special bonuses as they shall think fit.

(3) The amount of any bonus which may be declared or paid pursuant to paragraph (1) or paragraph (2) of this regulation and the amount (if any) to which any participating policyholder may become entitled under any mode of payment or application of any such bonus, shall be matters within the absolute discretion of the directors, whose decision thereon shall be final and conclusive.

It can be assumed that other companies selling with profits insurance have similar terms.

The discretion granted by clause 65 is clearly wide but it surely cannot be unlimited. There are many cases holding that apparently unlimited discretions are in fact limited.[14] It surely did not permit Equitable Life to give larger (or smaller) payments to Jews or old Etonians. The critical question was whether it permitted the payment of different bonuses to two policy-holders whose final pre-bonus entitlement was the same because one had a GAR and the other did not. The House of Lords held that it did not.

The core of the reasoning is to be found in the following passage from the speech of Lord Steyn:[15]

> It is necessary to distinguish between the processes of interpretation and implication. The purpose of interpretation is to assign to the language of the text the most appropriate meaning which the words can legitimately bear. The language of article 65(1) contains no relevant express restriction on the powers of the directors. It is impossible to assign to the language of article 65(1) by construction a restriction precluding the directors from overriding GARs. To this extent I would uphold the submissions made on behalf of the Society. The critical question is whether a relevant restriction may be implied into article 65(1). It is certainly not a case in which a term can be implied by law in the sense of incidents impliedly annexed to particular forms of contracts. Such standardised implied terms operate as general default rules: see *Scally v Southern Health and Social Services Board*.[16]

[14] There is much useful materials in Richard Hooley, 'Controlling Contractual Discretion' (2013) *Cambridge Law Journal* 65.

[15] *Hyman*, n 13 above. This reasoning is criticised in Anthony Grabiner, 'The Iterative Process of Contractual Interpretation' (2012) 128 *Law Quarterly Review* 41, 56–58. Lord Grabiner was leading counsel for Equitable Life.

[16] *Scally v Southern Health and Social Services Board* [1992] 1 AC 294.

If a term is to be implied, it could only be a term implied from the language of article 65 read in its particular commercial setting. Such implied terms operate as ad hoc gap fillers. In *Luxor (Eastbourne) Ltd v Cooper*,[17] Lord Wright explained this distinction as follows:

The expression 'implied term' is used in different senses. Sometimes it denotes some term which does not depend on the actual intention of the parties but on a rule of law, such as the terms, warranties or conditions which, if not expressly excluded, the law imports, as for instance under the Sale of Goods Act and the Marine Insurance Act ... But a case like the present is different because what it is sought to imply is based on an intention imputed to the parties from their actual circumstances.

It is only an individualised term of the second kind which can arguably arise in the present case. Such a term may be imputed to parties: it is not critically dependent on proof of an actual intention of the parties. The process 'is one of construction of the agreement as a whole in its commercial setting': *Banque Bruxelles Lambert SA v Eagle Star Insurance Co Ltd.*[18]

This principle is sparingly and cautiously used and may never be employed to imply a term in conflict with the express terms of the text. The legal test for the implication of such a term is a standard of strict necessity. This is how I must approach the question whether a term is to be implied into article 65(1) which precludes the directors from adopting a principle which has the effect of overriding or undermining the GARs.

The inquiry is entirely constructional in nature: proceeding from the express terms of article 65, viewed against its objective setting, the question is whether the implication is strictly necessary. My Lords, as counsel for the GAR policyholders observed, final bonuses are not bounty. They are a significant part of the consideration for the premiums paid. And the directors' discretions as to the amount and distribution of bonuses are conferred for the benefit of policyholders. In this context the self-evident commercial object of the inclusion of guaranteed rates in the policy is to protect the policyholder against a fall in market annuity rates by ensuring that if the fall occurs he will be better off than he would have been with market rates. The choice is given to the GAR policyholder and not to the Society. It cannot be seriously doubted that the provision for guaranteed annuity rates was a good selling point in the marketing by the Society of the GAR policies. It is also obvious that it would have been a significant attraction for purchasers of GAR policies. The Society points out that no special charge was made for the inclusion in the policy of GAR provisions. So be it. This factor does not alter the reasonable expectations of the parties. The supposition of the parties must be presumed to have been that the directors would not exercise their discretion in conflict with contractual rights. These are the circumstances in which the directors of the Society resolved upon a differential policy which was designed to deprive the relevant guarantees of any substantial value. In my judgment an implication precluding the use of the directors' discretion in this way is strictly necessary. The implication is essential to give effect to the reasonable expectations of the parties. The stringent test applicable to the implication of terms is satisfied.

In substantial agreement with Lord Woolf MR, I would hold that the directors were not entitled to adopt a principle of making the final bonuses of GAR policyholders dependent on how they exercised their rights under the policy. In adopting the principle of a differential policy in respect of GAR policyholders the directors acted in breach of article 65(1).

[17] *Luxor (Eastbourne) Ltd v Cooper* [1941] AC 108, 137.
[18] *Banque Bruxelles Lambert SA v Eagle Star Insurance Co Ltd* [1997] AC 191, 212 (Lord Hoffman).

It will be seen that Lord Steyn treats the implied term as one implied in fact and in principle capable of being excluded. Though I applaud the result I do not find it easy to accept the reasoning. The implied term did not depend on anything special about the relationship between Mr Hyman and Equitable Life. It applied to all 90,000 policy-holders who had bought GARS and to policy-holders with other with-profits insurers. It is basically a decision that the bonus discretion cannot be used to render worthless another promise made by the insurers. Surely this is a case where construction of the contract as a whole is decisive.

I am also not convinced that it would be at all easy to draft the contract so as to avoid this result. Surely Equitable Life could not in real life have said 'our guarantees are worthless' or 'we reserve the right to allocate bonuses on irrational grounds'. They were in a competitive market and their customers included many well-informed lawyers.

It is clear that the decision was a disaster for Equitable Life and for many of the policy-holders.[19] There have been a long series of reports into the behaviour of the company and of the regulators who were supposed to oversee it from which no one emerges well. It is natural to ask what Equitable Life should have done. It seems plausible that when it introduced GAR it should have sought to hedge or reinsure against the risk. It was apparently pursuing a high bonus policy which left it with relatively little in hand to meet downturns. It could and perhaps should have reduced everyone's bonus to a level at which it could honour the GARs, though this would clearly have had an effect on future sales. In retrospect it looks as if they relied for too long on their view of the width of the discretion as to the bonus.

GOOD FAITH

Consideration of *Hyman* leads me back to good faith. Of course, good faith is not mentioned in the case. It could be relied on both by those who think English law will come to embrace good faith and by those who think good results can be achieved without it. To my mind much the simplest explanation of the case is that good faith forbad Equitable Life from doing what it proposed.

It is clear that the American version of the common law has come to require good faith in the performance of contracts. In those contracts which are subject to the Uniform Commercial Code this is the result of section 1-203 which provides: 'every contract or duty within this act imposes an obligation of good faith in its performance or enforcement'.

Outside the statutory framework of the UCC, the second Restatement, section 1-205 lays down the same rule. This can be traced back to the famous judgment of Cardozo CJ in *Wood v Lucy, Lady Duff-Gordon*.[20]

[19] Much of the information in this paragraph comes from Wikipedia: 'Equitable Life Assurance Society v Hyman', www.en.wikipedia.org/wiki/Equitable_Life_v_Hyman.

[20] *Wood v Lucy, Lady Duff-Gordon* 222 NY 88 (1917).

It is clear that there are significant differences of view as to what good faith in fact requires[21] but no one suggests that the duty can simply be excluded. On the other hand, determining what good faith requires involves a careful reading of the contract. So, in *Kham and Nate's Shoes No 2 Inc v First Bank of Whiting*,[22] the plaintiffs first started banking with the defendants in 1981 when they took out a US$50,000 loan. A banking relationship continued for a couple of years and the plaintiffs then experienced cash flow problems. The bank suggested that the plaintiffs file for reorganisation under Chapter 11 of the Bankruptcy Code and the bank agreed to open a US$300,000 line of credit subject to cancellation on five days' notice. The plaintiffs drew down US$75,000 and about a month later the bank terminated. The Seventh Circuit Court of Appeal held that the bank had not broken their duty of good faith.[23]

It is surely clear that what good faith requires is heavily dependent on the particular contract. In *Hyman*, the policy-holders were signing up to pay money to the insurers over a very long period. They were totally dependent on the skill and judgement of the insurers. In general terms this faith was based on past performance. Equitable Life were the oldest player in the market; this gave them a substantial advantage over new entrants who offered exactly the same terms. Their obligations surely have to be read in the light of this.

[21] See Howard Hunter, 'The Growing Uncertainty about Good Faith in American Contract Law' (2004) 20 *Journal of Contract Law* 1.

[22] *Kham and Nate's Shoes No 2 Inc v First Bank of Whiting* 908 F 2d 1351 (7th Civ 1990).

[23] There is, of course, extensive literature on good faith. See, eg E Allan Farnsworth, 'Good Faith Performance and Commercial Reasonableness under the Uniform Commercial Code' (1962–63) 30 *University of Chicago Law Review* 666; Robert Summers, 'The General Recognition of Good Faith: Its Recognition and Conceptualisation' (1982) 67 *Cornell Law Review* 810; Steven Burton, 'Breach of Contract and Good Faith Performance of a Contract: A Reply to Professor Summers' (1984) 69 *Iowa Law Review* 497.

10

Some Thoughts on Undisclosed Agency

THOMAS KREBS

INTRODUCTION

HUGH HAS BEEN helping Louise Gullifer and me teach the Commercial Law course at Oxford for a number of years now, and both the students and his co-teachers have appreciated the gravitas and depth of understanding he brings to it. We normally take turns in leading seminars; there is only one, the seminar on assignment and agency, in which we share responsibility, with Hugh covering assignment before I take over the discussion of agency law. The combination makes some sense, of course, particularly if one regards agency, similarly to assignment, as an exception to privity. I have argued elsewhere that it is no such thing and that agency law obeys the same principles as the general law of contract: the agent brings about a contractual relationship between principal and third party, but both principal and third party have objectively manifested their consent to that relationship.[1] Hugh has always regarded this offer and acceptance model of agency with a certain amused, tolerant scepticism, and it is true that there is a formidable argument against it, namely, that undisclosed agency does not fit the model at all. English law allows an intermediary to bring about privity of contract between his principal and a third party without disclosing the existence of the principal to the third party. At no point is there an objectively manifested consensus *ad idem* between principal and third party that they are to be contractually bound to each other: undisclosed agency is therefore clearly a glaring exception to privity.

In this essay, I therefore propose to take a look at undisclosed agency with a view to establishing that the fact that it does not fit with general contractual principles is not fatal to an offer and acceptance model of agency law. I will try to show that attempts to explain the undisclosed principal's rights and obligations under the contract on the basis of the parties' consent are generally unproductive. Instead, one should regard undisclosed agency as a device that developed historically in order to manage the insolvency risk of intermediaries. In order to achieve this end, undisclosed agency borrows the vocabulary and framework of disclosed agency, but conceptually the two are entirely distinct. Undisclosed agency seeks to protect the 'real' parties to an economic transaction against the insolvency of someone who,

[1] Thomas Krebs, 'Agency Law for Muggles: Why There is no Magic in Agency' in Andrew Burrows and Edwin Peel (eds), *Contract Formation and Parties* (Oxford University Press, 2010) 205.

while acting in his own name, is in fact acting on somebody else's account. If the rules governing the relationship between undisclosed agent, third party and undisclosed principal are examined, they show that the differences between disclosed and undisclosed agency are so great that lumping them together as part of the same overarching legal category, agency, makes little or no sense. After a brief look at the purpose and history of undisclosed agency, this chapter will therefore examine the rules governing undisclosed agency from this perspective.

PURPOSE AND HISTORICAL DEVELOPMENT OF UNDISCLOSED AGENCY

The reasons why principals and agents might not want the third party to know whom they are really dealing with need not be objectionable. A principal may, for instance, wish to avoid extortionate behaviour on the part of third parties who might hope for a better price if they knew that they are really negotiating with a party of considerable financial resources, or with one to whom the transaction is of much greater subjective importance than may appear on the face of it.[2] The American case of *Senor v Bangor Mills Inc*[3] provides a good example. There the defendant was a heavy user of nylon yarn. It could only maintain its production levels by making substantial purchases in the secondary market, but because it was well known that it (a) had substantial financial resources, and (b) was dependent on a sustained supply of nylon yarn it was required to pay considerably over the odds in that market. It therefore employed an intermediary who bought yarn on its account but in his own name, enabling it to avoid this kind of strategic 'holding-out' behaviour on the part of the other market participants, preventing them from exploiting the effective monopoly they held vis-à-vis the principal. The intermediary might likewise not want it known that he is acting as an intermediary or 'middle-man'. He will have spent his own time, skill and resources in developing a distribution network, in creating goodwill, finding contacts, etc. He has a strong interest to keep the identity and perhaps even the very existence of his principal a secret, as otherwise his customers might be able to 'cut him out' and deal directly with the principal. However, it is highly questionable whether the concept of undisclosed agency is strictly necessary to achieve these goals. The crux of that concept is that undisclosed principal and third party end up in a contractual relationship where one of them, the third party, is unaware that the other even exists. The third party will, in other words, be liable to the principal on the contract and vice versa. It is not immediately obvious why this is necessary. Why should a principal, wishing to remain in the background, not simply ask the intermediary to act in his own name, giving rise to a contractual chain, so that in the event of the third party's breach the intermediary would claim against the third party and pass on the proceeds of that claim to the principal? There are two problems with such an arrangement, one conceptual and one practical.

[2] Tan Cheng-Han, 'Undisclosed Principals and Contract' (2004) 120 *Law Quarterly Review* 480, 483; Aharon Barak, 'On the Nature of Undisclosed Agency' (1976) 2 *Tel Aviv University Studies in Law* 45, 47.

[3] *Senor v Bangor Mills Inc* 211 F 2d 685 (3d Cir 1954).

The conceptual problem concerns the difficulty the agent might face of proving a loss when claiming from the third party. This is notoriously difficult given the narrow definition of loss which English contract law sometimes seems to adopt. Unfortunately, the House of Lords recently passed up an opportunity to clarify the law on the subject,[4] with the result that it is still unclear whether an agent who sues on a contract entered into on account of and for the benefit of a principal will be able to recover for losses effectively suffered by the principal. Undisclosed agency solves this problem in that it puts beyond doubt that the principal will be able to sue the third party directly and recover his loss.[5]

The practical problem with using a commission agency structure is the risk of the commission agent's insolvency. If the commission agent is regarded as a mere conduit pipe between the principal and the third party, there are arguments why the parties to the transaction should not be exposed to a greater insolvency risk than if they had been dealing directly with each other: though not acting in his principal's name, the commission agent is acting on his principal's *account*, he is not taking any risks with his own money and is, as the name implies, paid by way of commission rather than by generating profits from the transaction for himself. On the other hand, of course, the principal is using the commission agent for a reason, knowing that he may fail and choosing to use him anyway, while the third party does not even know that the commission agent is not acting on his own account. Preferring the principal and/or third party in the intermediary's insolvency is not a foregone conclusion: in other words, the arguments are finely balanced.

The problem, if indeed it is a problem, arises most acutely where the commission agent enters into a contract with the third party and fails before the third party performs. The trustee in bankruptcy cannot necessarily be relied on to enforce the contract on the principal's behalf and may, in fact, seek to retain any payments made by the third party for the benefit of the bankrupt estate. Conversely, if the third party grants the intermediary credit, while the principal may well be able to reap the benefits of the third party's performance, the third party will be hard pressed to get his money from the principal and may, for that reason, be unwilling to deal with the intermediary.

Some jurisdictions tackle this problem by statutory rules by which principal and third party are brought into a direct contractual relationship in such cases. One example of this can be found in the Principles of European Contract Law (PECL). Where an intermediary has become insolvent (or it is clear that he will not perform for some other reason), the principal may exercise any rights acquired by the intermediary against the third party on his behalf (article 3:302). By the same token, the third party may proceed directly against the principal and exercise any rights which he has acquired against the third party (article 3:303). In both cases, this is, of course, subject to defences which the third party could have relied on. These provisions are modelled on similar rules which may be found in a number of

[4] *Alfred McAlpine Construction Ltd v Panatown Ltd (No 1)* [2001] 1 AC 518.

[5] The problem does reappear, however, in that the undisclosed agent will, in order to protect the third party against *the principal's* insolvency risk, also be a party to the contract. He should therefore also be able to enforce the contract in his own right; however, it would appear that, given that the principal has his own independent claim, he will not be able to recover the principal's loss: see p 171 below.

jurisdictions, in particular the Netherlands, Belgium, Denmark, Sweden, Italy and Portugal.[6] A common law system, developing organically, cannot easily put in place similar rules. The common law therefore solved the problem by developing, very early on, a doctrine by which a contractual relationship between undisclosed principal and third party is brought about directly. The practical results will generally be indistinguishable from those reached in other jurisdictions.

The best historical account of the development of the doctrine of the undisclosed principal can be found in Stoljar's *The Law of Agency*. He very quickly and convincingly draws the link between the insolvency of factors and the development of the doctrine.[7] One such case, often credited in the literature with being the first recognising undisclosed agency, is *Scrimshire v Alderton*.[8] In fact, it is not at all clear from the report that the principal was undisclosed; rather, the case appears to be one of open commission agency, with the factor acting in his own right but it being known to all concerned that he was acting on a principal's account. Farmers were using a factor to sell their oats. Originally, the factor was paid 4 pence per quarter for this and would immediately tell the farmers who the buyer was and what quantities of oats he had bought at what price. As this was inconvenient for farmers in remote locations, a practice developed by which the factor was paid an extra 2 pence per quarter in consideration of taking the risk of non-payment by the buyer upon himself. When the factor failed, the plaintiff farmer gave immediate notice to the defendant buyer not to pay the factor but the farmer directly, which the defendant buyer ignored, paying the factor anyway. The Chief Justice, William Lee, thought that the buyer would have to pay again, and although the jury disagreed (twice), finding for the defendant buyer, the Chief Justice's view later prevailed, and soon the principal's right to sue the third party 'was completely settled'.[9] Yet it is not necessary to resort to undisclosed agency reasoning to explain the result desired by the Chief Justice; in fact, the report is silent on the issue whether the buyer thought he was buying directly from the factor as principal or as agent. The arrangement between factor and farmer, in any event, seems to have been internal to their relationship and did not really affect the third party at all. Nevertheless, the case is still widely regarded as the first reported case on undisclosed agency.

It would be overstating the case to argue that the institution of undisclosed agency is solely concerned with insolvency situations. There is no doubt that it can be useful, and commercially convenient, in other ways. What has to be understood, though, is that concern with the insolvency of intermediaries acting on another's account, though in their own name, was behind the historical development of undisclosed agency. It is for this reason that it does not fit the mould of agency law generally: it has different goals, different conceptual bases and, crucially, different *rules*.

[6] See Ole Lando and Hugh Beale (eds), *Principles of European Contract Law, Parts I and II* (The Hague, Kluwer, 2000) 222.

[7] Samuel J Stoljar, *The Law of Agency: Its History and Present Principles* (London, Sweet & Maxwell, 1961) 206.

[8] *Scrimshire v Alderton* (1742) 2 Strange 1182; 93 ER 1114.

[9] Stoljar, *The Law of Agency*, n 7 above, 208, citing *Drinkwater v Goodwin* (1775) 1 Cowp 251, 255; *George v Clagett* (1797) 7 TR 359.

PUTTING THE RULES IN CONTEXT

The broad rules pertaining to undisclosed agency were succinctly summarised by Lord Lloyd in the leading case of *Siu Yin Kwan v Eastern Insurance Co Ltd*:[10]

(1) An undisclosed principal may sue and be sued on a contract made by an agent on his behalf, acting within the scope of his actual authority.
(2) In entering into the contract, the agent must intend to act on the principal's behalf.
(3) The agent of an undisclosed principal may also sue and be sued on the contract.
(4) Any defence which the third party may have against the agent is available against his principal.
(5) The terms of the contract may, expressly or by implication, exclude the principal's right to sue, and his liability to be sued. The contract itself, or the circumstances surrounding the contract, may show that the agent is the true and only principal.

These rules represent a compromise between the commercial convenience of allowing an undisclosed principal to intervene in a contract made by an undisclosed agent, and the interest of the third party not to be prejudiced in any way by such intervention. What follows will examine the rules outlined by Lord Lloyd one by one, with a view to showing how they are in fact so far removed from the rules pertaining to agency proper that it makes little sense to regard undisclosed agency and disclosed agency to belong to the same legal category.

Agent Must Act Within the Scope of his Actual Authority

Where agency is disclosed, the principal may be entitled and bound by the contract made by his agent even where the agent has exceeded his actual authority in two situations: if he ratifies the agent's act and if he is bound by the agent's so-called 'apparent' authority. Lord Lloyd's first rule seems to rule both of these out where the principal is undisclosed.

Ratification

It is well established in English law that the undisclosed principal cannot ratify. The reason given for this rule by the House of Lords in the leading case, *Keighley, Maxsted & Co v Durant*,[11] is that 'civil obligations are not to be created by, or founded upon, undisclosed intentions'.[12] The editors of Bowstead and Reynolds criticise this reasoning, and the unavailability of ratification, as inconsistent with the very idea of undisclosed agency, which has as its foundations precisely the

[10] *Siu Yin Kwan v Eastern Insurance Co Ltd* [1994] 2 AC 199, 207.
[11] *Keighley, Maxsted & Co v Durant* [1901] AC 240.
[12] ibid at 247 (Lord Macnaghten).

agent's undisclosed intentions.[13] Section 4.03 of the Third American Restatement, following a number of American decisions,[14] and departing from the position taken by the Second Restatement (section 85(1)), abandons the rule altogether. Three more or less persuasive reasons are given for this departure from orthodoxy: first, it is said that 'the limitation is not necessary to prevent a person who is a stranger to a transaction from attempting to claim its benefit by ratifying. An undisclosed principal is not a stranger to the agent'.[15] This echoes the main criticism made by Bowstead and Reynolds. Secondly, the Restatement argues that 'whether to ratify is a choice an undisclosed principal should be free to make', given that his ratification creates rights and obligations for principal, third party and agent which are subject to the general limits applicable to undisclosed agency generally, designed to ensure that the third party is not prejudiced by the intervention of the undisclosed principal. Thirdly, it is said that it can be no objection to ratification by an undisclosed principal that the third party does not expect such an intervention any more than it is an objection to the general recognition of undisclosed agency. While the third argument seems to be no more than a variation of the first, the second argument merely asserts that ratification should be possible, without giving any reasons *why* it should be.

It is therefore the first argument, which is also endorsed by Bowstead and Reynolds, which needs to be addressed. I am going to put forward two counter-arguments, one on a practical and one on a conceptual level. The first argument, which was clearly strongly influential on the House of Lords in *Keighley v Durant*, is the danger of *ex post* fabrication. Granted, this danger exists in the context of undisclosed agency as well, and the whole doctrine of the undisclosed principal can be criticised on this ground. However, where an undisclosed agent acts with prior authority, any evidence that such authority was actually granted will clearly be more reliable than in the case of subsequent ratification. It will involve some sort of communication between the principal and the agent, possibly even in writing. On the other hand, the adoption of the contract by the principal in cases where the agent lacked authority at the time of the contract will be possible as long as the agent can credibly assert that, when entering into the contract, he intended to do so on the principal's account. This seems a much lesser burden than that of establishing antecedent authority, so that the danger of fabrication is correspondingly greater, with the result that the law would, in the words of Lord Shand, 'give one of two contracting parties in his option, merely from what was passing in his own mind and not disclosed, the power of saying the contract was his alone, or a contract in which others were bound with him'.[16]

If undisclosed agency can be explained on the basis that the undisclosed agent is acting on somebody else's account (as opposed to on his behalf), there is a good

[13] Peter Watts (ed), *Bowstead and Reynolds on Agency* 19th edn (London, Sweet & Maxwell, 2010) para 2-061.

[14] *Coyle v Smith* 300 So 2d 738 (Fla Dist App 1974); *Young & Rubicam, Inc v Ticket Holding Mktg, Inc* 1989 WL 4210 (ND Ill 1989); *Acuri v Figliolli,* 398 NYS 2d 923 (Dist 1977). See Reporter's Notes to s 4.03(b).

[15] Restatement of the Law Third, *The Foreign Relations Law of the United States* (American Law Institute, 1987) 322 ('Third Restatement').

[16] *Keighley*, n 11 above, at 250.

argument that the principal, who stands to benefit from the agent's contract, should also stand to lose from it. To extend the doctrine of the undisclosed principal by allowing the principal to ratify the acts of a person acting for himself, on the grounds that that person now professes to have formed an intention at the time to act on the principal's behalf, would subvert this rationale.

Reynolds finds it surprising that the rule applies even where it is sought to hold the ratifying principal liable, in other words, where obligations are imposed rather than rights conferred on him.[17] *Keighley v Durant* was itself such a case: the seller of wheat unsuccessfully sought to recover damages for non-acceptance from the alleged principal, which had privately agreed with its agent to take the contract on a joint account a day after it had been concluded in the agent's name alone, and in excess of the price at which he was authorised to buy on the joint account. The Third Restatement relies on a number of US cases which appear to contradict this result, but none of these appear to be particularly strong authority to support a departure from a rule well-established by English authority and accepted by the first two Restatements of Agency.[18] Two out of three of these cases involve alleged acts of ratification by undisclosed principals who accepted and retained money originating from the third party which was paid into their bank accounts.[19] The cases cited in the Restatement are, to some extent, consistent with the proposition that an undisclosed principal may well be bound by an act amounting to ratification where his liability arises in tort or unjust enrichment: neither cause of action depends on showing a consensus ad idem of any kind between principal and third party. Clearly, where the principal asserts the rights of an owner over property belonging to the third party, or retains a benefit at the third party's expense in circumstances which the law considers unjust, it is right and proper that he should be held liable accordingly, be he undisclosed or disclosed. This does not, however, change the general rule that neither he nor the third party will be bound in contract.

Apparent Authority and Watteau v Fenwick

Lord Lloyd's first rule insists that the undisclosed agent must act within the scope of his actual authority: the doctrine of apparent authority cannot apply. This makes sense, of course, given that apparent authority is founded on the principal's manifestation of assent to be bound. It might therefore be thought not to be worth mentioning that the doctrine cannot apply to cases in which the principal is undisclosed and has thus not even manifested his own existence, let alone his intention to be bound by the undisclosed agent's acts, to anyone other than the agent. The

[17] Hugh Beale (ed), *Chitty on Contracts*, 31st edn (London, Sweet & Maxwell, 2012) vol 2, 17, n 151.

[18] *Coyle v Smith*, n 14 above; *Young & Rubicam v Ticket Holder*, n 14 above and *Acuri v Figliolli* 91 Misc 2d 831, 398 NYS 2d 923 (NY Dist Ct 1977).

[19] In *Young & Rubicam v Ticket Holder*, n 14 above, the proceeds of a bill of exchange drawn on the third party were paid into the alleged principals' bank account. In *Acuri v Figliolli*, n 18 above, the alleged undisclosed agent had sold his mother's car, accepted a number of instalments in payment, which he had paid over to the mother, and later repossessed the car for alleged breach of contract. The third party's claim against the mother was for restitution of the instalments paid, and the action was in fact an action for money had and received.

difficult case of *Watteau v Fenwick*[20] is generally thought to contradict Lord Lloyd's first rule, in that it applies apparent authority reasoning in the undisclosed agency context. The facts were these: the defendants were brewers who had bought a public house from a Mr Humble, who stayed on to manage it on their behalf. His name remained above the door, and the licence remained in his name. It was part of the contract between Humble and the defendants that certain items, most importantly, of course, beer, but also cigars and Bovril, were to be supplied by the defendants and were therefore not to be procured from any other source. Humble breached this agreement by ordering cigars, on credit, from the plaintiffs. This had been going on for a number of years, and it was only when the plaintiffs discovered the true facts that they sued the owner in order to recover the price of the goods they had supplied (no doubt because Humble had been unable to pay, although the facts as reported are silent on this point). The case was argued squarely on the basis of undisclosed agency and apparent authority. The Divisional Court dismissed the owners' appeal from the decision of the county court to hold the owners liable for the price of the goods supplied. Wills J, with whom Coleridge CJ agreed, said:[21]

> Once it is established that the defendant was the real principal, the ordinary doctrine as to principal and agent applies—that the principal is liable for all the acts of the agent which are within the authority usually confided to an agent of that character, notwithstanding limitations, as between the principal and the agent, put upon that authority. It is said that it is only so where there has been a holding out of authority—which cannot be said where the person supplying the goods knew nothing of the existence of a principal. But I do not think so. Otherwise in every case of undisclosed principal, or at least in every case where the fact of there being a principal was undisclosed, the secret limitation of authority would prevail and defeat the action of the person dealing with the agent and then discovering that he was an agent and had a principal.

While many commentators acknowledge that this decision is 'eminently just',[22] the reasoning has been widely criticised, and the case has not been followed in Canada,[23] while it has been doubted in England[24] and Australia.[25]

The outcome is indeed difficult to disagree with. The owners had, after all, presumably benefited from Humble selling the goods in running the business, in that any profits from such sales accrued to them. Moreover, the suppliers were under the impression that Humble was the owner of a public house, and as such much less of a credit risk than the mere manager of a public house contracting on his own account. The conceptual difficulties are, however, equally undeniable. Apparent authority cannot help, given that the undisclosed principal cannot be said to make any representations about his agent's authority at all. Attempts to explain the case on the basis of a variant of the doctrine of apparent ownership and/or vicarious liability

[20] *Watteau v Fenwick* [1893] 1 QB 346.

[21] ibid at 348–49.

[22] John G Collier, 'Authority of an Agent: *Watteau v Fenwick* Revisited' (1985) *Cambridge Law Journal* 363.

[23] *McLaughlin v Gentles* (1919) 51 DLR 383; *Sign-o-Lite Plastics Ltd v Metropolitan Life Insurance Co* (1990) 73 DLR (4th) 541.

[24] *Rhodian River Shipping Co SA v Holla Maritime Corp (The Rhodian River)* [1984] 1 Lloyd's Rep 373, 379.

[25] *International Paper Co v Spicer* (1906) 4 CLR 739, 763.

are similarly unhelpful.[26] The former doctrine protects the bona fide purchaser of goods apparently belonging to the seller, effectively giving the purchaser a defence against the owner's conversion action in certain limited, defined circumstances. The doctrine is thus not concerned with obligations incurred on the strength of the other contracting party's perceived credit-worthiness. In other words, the 'cases on apparent ownership all concern the validity of disposals of property, rather than the creation of liability in the owner of it'.[27] Vicarious liability is similarly unsuited to explain the result of the case, given that it is primarily concerned with ensuring that accident victims receive compensation. Its application to voluntary transactions is limited; indeed, as Tettenborn deftly observes, outside that sphere, in the context of the economic torts of deceit and negligent misrepresentation, the rules of vicarious liability are closely aligned with the rules of actual and apparent authority in the law of agency.[28] Tettenborn's own explanation of *Watteau v Fenwick* is based on the doctrine of estoppel, but not in the way in which it is used in the context of agency. He regards the owners' actions of leaving Humble in charge of the hotel as amounting to a representation that Humble and the owner of the hotel are one and the same person, relied upon by the plaintiffs in agreeing to supply goods to Humble, which they would never had done had they known he was a man of straw. Tettenborn's explanation has much to commend it. The most striking point he makes is that, viewed in this way, *Watteau v Fenwick* has in fact nothing to do with agency at all.

This essay argues, of course, that undisclosed agency similarly has little in common with disclosed agency principles. While the contractual liability of a disclosed principal is based on consent, this is not the case for the contractual liability of the undisclosed principal. It could therefore be argued that it is not fatal to the reasoning in *Watteau v Fenwick* that it is clearly not based on consent. However, I argued above that the reason why the principal is made liable on a contract entered into on his behalf by an undisclosed agent is that the agent is acting on his account and at his risk. As the principal takes the benefit of the contract, he should also be exposed to the risks that go along with it. This is not the case where the agent is acting outside the scope of his mandate, ie without the principal's authority. In other words, it is arguable that the supposed rule in *Watteau v Fenwick* has nothing to do with the law of undisclosed agency, and even less with the law of agency proper. This also affirms Lord Lloyd's first rule, that the undisclosed agent must be acting within the terms of the authority conferred *on him* by the principal, ie that apparent authority is excluded. If the rule in *Watteau v Fenwick* remains good law, and there are good arguments that it should, it is a rule which is not based on agency principles.

[26] Both explanations are given short shrift by Andrew Tettenborn, 'Agents, Business Owners and Estoppel' (1998) 57 *Cambridge Law Journal* 274.

[27] ibid 276.

[28] ibid 277. *Cf Lloyd v Grace, Smith & Co* [1912] AC 716; *Kooragang Investment Property v Richardson & Wrench* [1982] AC 462.

Agent Must Intend to Act on the Principal's Behalf

In the law of contract, the true intentions of the parties entering into a contract are of comparatively little significance; what counts is how they have expressed these intentions, and they will therefore be held to what an objective observer in the other party's position would have understood them to mean by the words they used. This is no different where a contract is entered into through an agent: the agent will stipulate whether he is acting on behalf of a principal (named or unnamed), on his own account, or both on his own account and that of the principal. Where there is no express stipulation there may be difficulties of characterisation: did the agent imply that he was acting for a principal, or should this have been apparent to the third party based on an existing course of dealing or commercial custom?

For undisclosed agency to operate, the objective theory of contract has to be ignored; liability will depend not just on the agent's intentions, but on his *undisclosed* intentions. Of course, as we have seen above it must first be established that the agent was authorised to act on the principal's behalf, but the evidential difficulties will nevertheless be formidable, particularly where the agent is also in business for himself and sometimes acts on his own account as well as on behalf of others.[29] Where the supposed agent is himself available to give evidence, this will of course be helpful to whichever party, supposed principal or third party, is trying to establish undisclosed agency, particularly where this is corroborated by evidence relating to the contractual arrangements between the principal and the agent. It is, of course, entirely possible that there will be a dispute between the supposed agent and the principal, namely, where the principal seeks to take advantage of a good bargain entered into by the agent in circumstances which would have been within the scope of the agent's authority. Here, the principal will face an uphill battle to prove the subjective intentions of the agent in the face of the agent's own denial of such an intention.

Agent's Rights and Liabilities

In disclosed agency situations, the agent will normally 'drop out': he will not be liable on the contract entered into on behalf of the principal. This is because 'it is objectively apparent' that the contract does not confer rights and obligations on the agent, but only on the principal and the third party.[30] The agent is, of course, free to take on liabilities and/or rights under the contract if he wishes to do so, either by contracting alongside the principal, or by guaranteeing the third party's liabilities vis-à-vis the principal (which would make him a *del credere* agent).[31]

[29] *Cf National Oilwell (UK) Ltd v Davy Offshore Ltd* [1993] 2 Lloyd's Rep 582, 596–97 (Colman J) for examples of evidence which might be led.

[30] *Cf* Robert Stevens, 'Why Do Agents Drop Out?' (2005) *Lloyd's Maritime and Commercial Law Quarterly* 101.

[31] Watts, *Bowstead and Reynolds on Agency*, n 13 above, para 1-038. An agent may, of course, be liable in contract (if any) to his principal if he fails to perform his duties as agent, or to the third party (for breach of warranty of authority) if he purports to be acting within the scope of his authority but is not.

Where the principal is undisclosed, there are both conceptual and practical reasons why the agent should be personally liable on the contract. There are also conceptual reasons why he should acquire rights, but there are, as we shall see, considerable conceptual difficulties when it comes to the enforcement of any such rights.

The most obvious reason why the agent will be a party to the contract is simply that that is what he has objectively agreed to by contracting in his own name. The fact that he was also contracting on another's account is, by definition, undisclosed. There may be policy reasons why, particularly in the case of the agent's insolvency, the principal should also be obliged and entitled on the contract (as the case may be). The starting point must, however, be that, as far as the third party is concerned, he has contracted with the agent and nobody else.

Agent's Liability on the Contract

The practical reason for the rule that the agent himself will be liable to the third party is obvious. The third party, in entering into the contract, was in no position to assess the creditworthiness of the undisclosed principal, for the simple reason that the principal was undisclosed at that time. If the undisclosed agent 'dropped out' in the same way that disclosed agents commonly do, the third party might well be prejudiced by having to sue a less credit-worthy principal.

However, the third party will, at some stage, have to make up his mind. If he unequivocally chooses to sue the undisclosed principal, his right to sue the agent may well be lost. Again, it is not difficult to see the reason why. Once the principal has appeared on the scene, the third party can take his time to decide whether his chances of obtaining an enforceable judgment would be improved if he sued the principal. Once that decision has been made, the third party is in no worse a position than he would have been had the principal been disclosed from the start, and there is therefore no reason to protect him against the principal's insolvency risk by giving him another bite at the cherry by suing the agent.

The third party's right to choose between principal and agent as defendants is known as his right of election.[32] Once the right of election is exercised in favour of either the principal or the agent, the other will be discharged. In other words, principal and agent are severally, but not jointly, liable. The law is exactly the same as for all situations in which principal and agent are both liable on the same contract.

Agent's Rights Against the Third Party

Lord Lloyd assumes that the agent can sue the third party in exactly the same way as if he were the principal. This will be unproblematic as long as the existence of the principal remains undisclosed. However, once it has become clear that the agent was acting on behalf of a principal, it is difficult to see why the agent, rather than the principal, should bring the action. Of course, it is entirely possible for the agent to bring an action on the principal's behalf, this time as a disclosed agent. However,

[32] *Cf Muldoon v Wood* [1998] EWCA Civ 588.

where he brings the action in his own name, as Lord Lloyd assumes he is able to do, he may well encounter problems in establishing that he has suffered a loss. Although an action for breach of contract can be brought by a person who has not suffered any loss, such a person will only be awarded nominal damages.

The question to what extent and in what circumstances one person can sue for breach of contract and recover substantial damages in respect of losses suffered by another has exercised the courts relatively recently. The starting point is, of course, that in general only losses suffered by the contracting party himself can be claimed as damages. A number of different strategies have been developed over the years in order to deal with the 'legal black hole' problem that can arise where one party (A) has suffered loss but has no contractual claim against the contract breaker (D) (or does not wish to assert it due to procedural or tax disadvantages of doing so), while another (B) would have a contractual claim but has suffered no loss. One approach, which is generally traced back to the old shipping case of *Dunlop v Lambert*,[33] is to allow A to recover damages on behalf of B. This solution is essentially the creation of an exception to privity of contract. Lord Diplock in *The Albazero*[34] stressed that this exception would only be triggered if B at no stage possessed his own contractual claim against D. In that case, a vessel under charter had been lost at sea. A, a cargo owner who held a bill of lading, issued by the carrier, D, sought to sue D for the loss of the cargo but failed to do so within the one-year limit prescribed by the terms of the bill of lading (in compliance with the Hague Rules). His last ditch attempt to prevail notwithstanding was to procure the charterer of the vessel, B, to sue on the charterparty (which was still possible, the relevant limitation period being six years). B sought to rely on the *Dunlop v Lambert* exception, enabling him to recover substantial damages in respect of A's loss and then pass them on to A. Lord Diplock was adamant that, ingenious though this scheme was, it would not succeed, for the simple reason that A had, at one time, possessed his own perfectly valid claim on the bill of lading. If the limitation period on this claim had expired this was entirely A's fault. As such, no exception to privity was necessary or indeed desirable.

It is unlikely, therefore, that an undisclosed agent would be able to rely on the *Dunlop v Lambert/Albazero* exception and recover damages on behalf of the undisclosed principal: the principal will, by definition, have a right of his own to bring an action on the contract. However, when the *Dunlop v Lambert* exception was first applied in contexts other than shipping, in *Linden Gardens v Lenesta Sludge*,[35] Lord Griffiths put forward a wider definition of loss which might possibly be more helpful to an agent seeking to recover his principal's loss. His 'wider ground' should not be understood as an exception to privity at all, but rather as a more realistic and less mechanistic approach to identifying the loss suffered by a contractual party when such loss is not easily measurable in financial terms. However, unfortunately the status of the wider ground in *Linden Gardens* continues to be uncertain following *Alfred McAlpine Construction Ltd v Panatown Ltd*,[36] in which the issue fell to be reconsidered by the House of Lords. The claimants had contracted with the

[33] *Dunlop v Lambert* (1839) 6 Cl & F 600; 7 ER 824.
[34] *Owners of Cargo Laden on Board the Albacruz v Owners of the Albazero* [1977] AC 774.
[35] *Linden Gardens Trust Ltd v Lenesta Sludge Disposal Ltd* [1994] 1 AC 85.
[36] *Panatown*, n 4 above.

defendants to develop land belonging to another company in the claimants' group of companies. As part of the deal, the defendants had issued a duty of care deed which effectively settled them with negligence liability vis-à-vis the current owner of the site at any one time (the idea was that the developed site would be sold with the benefit of the duty of care deed). When problems with the development emerged, the claimants initiated an arbitration which eventually ended up before the House of Lords. The claim for breach of the main construction contract was resisted on the ground that the claimant had not suffered any loss, given that they were not the owners of the land in question. This argument was ultimately successful. Lords Goff and Millett fully endorsed Lord Griffiths' reasoning in *Linden Gardens* and argued in favour of a wider conception of loss in English law. They would have allowed the claimants to succeed. Lords Jauncey and Clyde, on the other hand, were not convinced that a wider definition of loss was the way forward. They would have applied the narrow ground, but this failed because the duty of care deed gave the owners of the site an independent, albeit less advantageous, claim. Lord Browne-Wilkinson thus effectively had the casting vote. While he generally agreed with Lords Goff and Millett that the broad ground had much to recommend it, he thought that, like the narrow ground, it was defeated by the existence of the duty of care deed. In effect, the claimants' performance interest extended, according to Lord Browne-Wilkinson, to giving the owner of the site an independent cause of action.

The ratio of *Panatown* is therefore rather unclear: no three of their Lordships agree on a sufficient numbers of reasons which are necessary for the decision. The authority of the case has subsequently been taken to be whatever Lord Browne-Wilkinson says it is. If this is correct, the broad ground is generally available, but only if the person who has suffered the 'immediate' loss does not possess an independent right of action against the defendant.

Where does this leave the undisclosed agent's right of action against the third party? He will be faced by the same problem as the claimants in *Panatown*, namely, that the person who has suffered the 'immediate' loss, the undisclosed principal, will by definition have his own cause of action against the third party. In any event, given that this is so, it is difficult to see why it would be necessary for the agent to bring the action in his own name, unless he has suffered losses over and above the losses suffered by the principal, in which case the problem would not arise in the first place.

Defences

I mentioned in the introduction that the undisclosed principal's position is not unlike the position of an assignee.[37] Lord Lloyd's fourth rule, that the undisclosed principal's rights are subject to the same equities and defences which the third party could rely on against the agent, is common to both. This is because the third parties' interests are exactly analogous: neither wants to end up in a worse relative

[37] But see *Siu Yin Kwan*, n 10 above, in which the analogy between undisclosed agency and assignment was rejected.

position to his contractual counterparty merely because the original counterparty has assigned his rights or because he turns out to have been acting on behalf of an undisclosed principal. Assignee and undisclosed principal thus step into the shoes of their assignor or undisclosed agent.

Logically, the law should draw a bright line between defences which arise before the principal is discovered, and defences which arise thereafter. This approach would focus on the position of the third party: so long as the third party does not know that a principal may intervene, the existence of such principal should not prejudice him.

Unfortunately, the authorities follow an approach focusing on the conduct of the principal rather than the position of the third party. This is due to a failure on the part of the courts to distinguish clearly between disclosed and undisclosed agency, demonstrating quite neatly the danger of categorising them both under the heading 'agency'. The problematic case is *Cooke & Sons v Eshelby*.[38] A firm of brokers sold cotton without disclosing that they were acting for a principal. However, the buyer was well aware that the brokers sometimes acted for their own account and sometimes as agents. As far as the sale of the cotton was concerned, it was found as a fact that the buyers had no particular belief as to whether the brokers were acting on their own account or on behalf of a principal. On the principal's intervention, the buyers were held to be unable to set off against the principal moneys they were owed by the brokers. The headnote of the report summarises the ratio of the case as follows:

> Where an agent sells in his own name for an undisclosed principal, and the principal sues the buyer for the price, the buyer cannot set off a debt due from the agent unless in making the contract he was induced by the conduct of the principal to believe, and did in fact believe, that the agent was selling on his own account.

It is, however, difficult to see how the buyer, who *ex hypothesi* is unaware of the principal's existence, can possibly be induced by the conduct of the principal to believe that the agent was selling on his own account. The headnote clearly confuses the categories of *undisclosed* principal on the one and *unidentified* principal on the other hand.

The practical issue in the case was whether the third party or the principal was to bear the agent's insolvency risk. The court decided that the loss occasioned by the agent's insolvency was to be borne by the third party rather than the principal. There are two possible explanations for this: the first focuses on the third party's position and the state of his knowledge and belief (and can easily be reconciled with the view here put forward). The second looks at the position of the principal and asks whether the principal has done anything to induce the third party to enter into the contract with the agent. This is the approach suggested by the headnote. It is necessary to look at the judgments to see whether the headnote accurately reflects them.

Lord Halsbury begins his speech by pointing out that, on the facts found by the judge and indeed admitted by the defendant third party, the third party 'had no

[38] *Cooke & Sons v Eshelby* (1887) 12 App Cas 271.

belief one way or the other whether they were dealing with principals or brokers'.[39] He then goes on to state the applicable principle as follows:

> The ground upon which all these cases have been decided is that the agent has been permitted by the principal to hold himself out as the principal, and that the person dealing with the agent has believed that the agent was the principal, and has acted on that belief.

The rest of the judgment focuses on the second part of this principle: whether the third party believed the agent to be acting as principal. It concludes:

> The selling in his own name by a broker is only one fact, and by no means a conclusive fact, from which, in the absence of other circumstances, it might be inferred that he was selling his own goods. Upon the facts proved or admitted in this case the fact of selling in the broker's name was neither calculated to induce nor did in fact induce that belief.[40]

Lord Watson's judgment stresses the importance of the business customs of the Liverpool cotton market, where brokers would buy and sell both for themselves and for principals, in the latter case 'sometimes in their own name without disclosing their agency, and at other times in the name of the principal'.[41] While Lord Watson makes a distinction between disclosed and undisclosed agency, there is, of course, a third possibility, namely, that the agent sells on behalf of a principal but without disclosing the identity of the principal (which he seems to ignore altogether). Although he then goes on to base his conclusion on the doctrine of estoppel, his analysis of the facts suggests a much more straightforward explanation, namely, that, on the true construction of the contract, the contract had been entered into on behalf of an unidentified principal, preventing the third party from relying on defences he would have been able to rely on had he been sued by the agent.

Lord FitzGerald's judgment focuses on the facts and their correct interpretation in the light of the customs of the Liverpool cotton market. His account of the 'ascertained facts' suggests very strongly that the case in reality concerned an unidentified as opposed to an undisclosed principal:

> Livesey & Co were extensive cotton brokers on the Liverpool Cotton Arrival Market. They also dealt in cotton arrivals on their own account as principals. Their position was well-known to Cooke & Co. Maximos employed Livesey & Co as brokers to sell for him the particular lots of cotton, and they did so, the contracts which they entered into, though in their own names, being in law contracts for and on behalf of Maximos. He also '*authorized* them not to give his name', which may be read as meaning not to give his name either in the contract notes or in answer to inquiries, his special object seeming to be to avoid the jealousies or solicitations of other brokers.[42]

It is clear from this passage that the concern was not so much that the third party not know that Livesey were selling as agents, but that he not know the identity of the principal. While Lord FitzGerald endorses the reasoning of the Court of Appeal, he expresses considerable doubt whether 'the decisions rest on the doctrine

[39] ibid at 275.
[40] ibid at 276.
[41] ibid at 277.
[42] ibid at 282.

of estoppel'.[43] While he does not expressly say so, he must be taken to base his decision on a construction of the contract under which the third party knew he was contracting with a principal, though he did not know the identity of the principal.

Based on this analysis of the judgments, it is suggested that *Cooke v Eshelby* does not in fact establish that the rule that a third party can rely on any defences he would have had available against the agent against an undisclosed principal is based on estoppel. On the better view, which can be supported by the findings of fact and the speech of Lord FitzGerald, everything depends on the position and state of knowledge of the third party. If the tripartite relationship is correctly analysed as one of undisclosed agency, the third party must not be put in any worse position by the intervention of the undisclosed principal than he would otherwise have been in. Where it is best analysed as one of disclosed agency in which the identity of the principal is withheld, the third party knew or should have known that he was contracting with a principal against whom any defences he may or may not have against the agent will be irrelevant.

To conclude: whether the third party can rely on defences he would have been able to assert against the intermediary should depend on whether he believes to be contracting with the intermediary as principal, in other words, whether the case involves an undisclosed principal. If the law on this is not clear, this is because undisclosed agency borrows the concepts and terminology of disclosed agency. While this is convenient, it can lead to confusion, particularly if the case involves an unidentified as opposed to undisclosed principal. Such confusion might be avoided by stressing the conceptual independence of undisclosed agency and by refusing to allow it to be dealt with as a branch of agency law.

Exclusion of Undisclosed Agency

There are a number of ways in which undisclosed agency can be excluded. These are as follows:

(1) exclusion by statute;
(2) express exclusion by contract;
(3) implied exclusion by contract.

Exclusion by Statute

Some statutes may provide that certain transactions may be entered into personally, or at any rate not by an agent acting on behalf of an undisclosed principal. In practice, the most important of these is likely to be section 2 of the Law of Property (Miscellaneous Provisions) Act 1989. This provides that contracts for the sale of land and certain similar contracts have to be in writing, signed by each party. It makes provision for signature by agents, but it requires that the signature be 'by or on behalf of each party to the contract'. This can give rise to problems where the

[43] ibid at 283.

principal is disclosed but unidentified, but these problems are rather more acute still where the principal is entirely undisclosed. It is arguable that the wording 'on behalf of' requires that the agent act in the principal's name. On the other hand, it can also be argued that an agent acts 'on behalf of' a principal whenever he acts with authority to act, intending to act for the principal. However, this would seem to run counter to the policy of the provision, which is that the full terms of the contract should be in writing.[44]

Express Exclusion by Contract

The contract between third party and agent may, of course, provide expressly that the intervention of an undisclosed principal shall be excluded. The consequence would then be that the principal would have to assert any claims against the third party through the agent. The principal would consequently be faced by the problem that he may not be able to recover anything from the third party in the event of the agent's insolvency (as any claims against the third party will be asserted by the liquidator or trustee in bankruptcy for the benefit of the general body of creditors, with the principal being merely one such creditor). Even a solvent agent may have difficulty in claiming substantial damages against a third party when it is clear that any proceeds of such an action will have to be paid over to a principal.[45] The third party may, of course, have good reasons to insert a clause excluding the intervention of an undisclosed principal. These reasons will be analogous to the reasons for inserting non-assignment clauses into contracts. Whether the inclusion of a non-assignment clause impliedly excludes undisclosed agency will be considered immediately below.

Implied Exclusion by Contract

A third party facing being sued by an undisclosed agent may argue that such intervention is excluded by the contract by necessary implication. The rules according to which terms are implied into contracts are no different here than in contractual construction generally: the implication may be so obvious as to be evident to an officious bystander, or may be necessary to give business efficacy to the contract.

Prohibitions of assignment are generally construed narrowly by the courts. In our Commercial Law seminars, Hugh expresses his deep dissatisfaction with two decisions, *Don King Productions Inc v Warren*[46] and *Barbados Trust Co Ltd v Bank of Zambia*,[47] which decided that a contractual prohibition of assignment did not prevent the creditor declaring himself trustee of the benefit of the contract; the reason given is that an assignment and a declaration of trust are different things—if a debtor wishes to prohibit a declaration of trust, he needs to say so. This is clearly wrong on at least two levels: first, it is in fact difficult to see why a declaration of trust of a contractual benefit should be seen as something different to an equitable

[44] Similarly, Watts, *Bowstead and Reynolds on Agency*, n 13 above, para 8-004.
[45] See *Senor*, n 3 above.
[46] *Don King Productions Inc v Warren* [2000] Ch 291.
[47] *Barbados Trust Co Ltd v Bank of Zambia* [2007] EWCA Civ 148; [2007] 1 Lloyd's Rep 494.

assignment, given that their result is the same: the assignor/trustee will continue to be the legal owner of the debt and will need to lend his name to any enforcement proceeding brought by the assignee/beneficiary. Secondly, even if the two were to be different legal (or rather, equitable) animals, the underlying contractual intention of a prohibition of assignment clause is not to be obliged to a person who is not the original contractor. To stay with the 'animal' metaphor for a moment, an occupier of premises erecting a sign prohibiting dogs from coming onto the premises must clearly be presumed to prohibit hyenas and other dangerous animals by necessary implication. As a matter of contractual construction, therefore, it would appear wrong, and unnecessarily literal, to say that a prohibition of assignment does not include a prohibition of a declaration of trust. By parity of reasoning, it should include the intervention of an undisclosed principal. The decision of the Privy Council in *Siu Yin Kwan v Eastern Insurance*,[48] however, is usually cited for the proposition that this does not follow. There, two seamen had drowned when their vessel capsized in a storm. Their estates sued their employer to judgment, but the employer was wound up before the judgment was satisfied. Their estates therefore attempted, under the relevant Hong Kong legislation, to proceed directly against the employer's indemnity insurance. The insurance company took the point that the insurance had been obtained by shipping agents without mentioning the employer's name upon whom they intended to be covered by the insurance, and that since insurance contracts were 'personal' contracts, the benefit of which was not assignable, the employer would not be able to intervene. This argument was rejected. While it is fair to say that the Board's advice cautions against drawing an analogy with the rules on assignment,[49] there is no finding that contracts of insurance (with the exception of marine and life insurance) are generally non-assignable—instead, there is a detailed and thoughtful discussion whether, for this particular contract, the identity of the employer was relevant to the risk insurance. True, there is an obiter dictum,[50] based on another Privy Council decision, *Browning v Provincial Insurance Co of Canada*,[51] to the effect that a provision in 'a contract which provides that it shall not be assignable ... does not preclude intervention by an undisclosed principal'. That case concerned an insurance certificate issued to the (undisclosed) agent of a baker who sought to insure a cargo of flour. The ship having been lost, the insurer took the point that only the person named on the certificate could sue. The certificate did indeed include a prohibition of assignment; however, this point was not relied on by the insurer and the Board's advice does not advert to it. Instead, the case was decided in favour of the undisclosed principal on the basis that, normally, an insurance policy would have been issued against the certificate which would have included a clause putting it beyond doubt that the insurance was taken out for the benefit of the principal, namely, the owner of the goods. As such, the case is less than perfect authority for the obiter dictum in *Siu Yin Kwan*. It must therefore still be arguable that the inclusion of an anti-assignment

[48] *Siu Yin Kwan v Eastern Insurance* [1994] 2 AC 199.
[49] ibid at 210.
[50] ibid.
[51] *Browning v Provincial Insurance Co of Canada* (1873) LR 5 PC 263, 273.

clause can be taken as a powerful indication that the parties also intended to exclude the intervention of an undisclosed principal.

There is another reason why *Siu Yin Kwan* is a problematic decision: it is very arguable, and acknowledged by the Board, that the case did not involve an undisclosed principal at all, but that it was objectively clear to the insurer that the shipping agent was procuring the insurance on behalf of the owner of the vessel and the employer of the crew. The judge had found as a fact that the insurers knew that the agents were shipping agents, and not the owners of the, or indeed any, vessel. He also found that the insurers had acted as agents for the owners when a hull policy in respect of the same vessel was taken out some years previously to the indemnity insurance. However, the judge was not satisfied that the insurers knew that the agent was not the employer of the crew, and therefore decided the case as one involving undisclosed agency. This was a surprising finding of fact, and one which certainly puzzled the members of the Privy Council.[52] Again, this confusion neatly illustrates the problems caused by undisclosed agency 'borrowing' the vocabulary and conceptual framework of agency: in this context as in others, entirely different facts have to be proved in order to establish one or the other. To show that the agent was indeed acting as an agent, it was necessary to show that the insurer knew that he was acting on behalf of somebody else, named or unnamed. In order to make an undisclosed principal entitled on the insurance contract, it was necessary to construe the contract with a view to excluding the intervention of anyone else. Conflating the two inquiries only can, and indeed did in *Siu Yin*, lead to confusion and muddled thinking.

In *Humble v Hunter*,[53] the claimant's son had entered into a charterparty with the defendant. In the charterparty he described himself as 'CJ.Humble, owner of the good ship or vessel called the Ann'. In fact, the owner of the ship was his mother, who subsequently sued the defendant for freight. The defendant objected that he never entered into any contract with the claimant. The claimant's argument that her son had contracted on her behalf, she being his undisclosed principal, was rejected. Patteson J said: 'If the contract had been made in the son's name merely, without more, it might have been shewn that he was an agent only, and that the plaintiff was the principal'.[54] However, as he had described himself as the 'owner' of the ship, he had impliedly contracted that no undisclosed principal would intervene on the contract. Parol evidence was not permissible to contradict the terms of the written contract. The reason for this was stated by Lord Denman CJ to be that '[y]ou have a right to the benefit you contemplate from the character, credit and substance of the party with whom you contract'.[55] It is not clear from the judgments or the recital of facts in the report in what way the defendant was put in a better position by being in a contractual relationship with the son (who had no ship) rather than the mother (who did). In any event, we know that an undisclosed agent will be personally liable on any contract he enters into on the undisclosed principal's behalf. There is very little reasoning in the judgments; the judges are mainly concerned about the

[52] *Cf Siu Yin*, n 48 above, at 207.
[53] *Humble v Hunter* (1848) 12 QB 310; 116 ER 885.
[54] ibid at 316.
[55] ibid at 317.

form of the contract, and they appear to be applying an absolute rule that where a party contracts giving himself 'any special description',[56] the intervention of an undisclosed principal is excluded. This does not, however, represent the ratio of the case, which must be restricted to a narrower principle that anyone who asserts title to property forming the subject matter of a contract will render inadmissible parol evidence contradicting this.[57] However, the more modern approach would be to say that the court concluded that, on the proper interpretation of the contract before them, the intervention of an undisclosed principal was excluded. Subsequent cases confirm this rather more flexible approach.[58]

In *Said v Butt*, a theatre critic had been banned from attending performances at the defendant's theatre. Well aware of this, he arranged for a ticket to a first night to be bought by his nominee, acting as his undisclosed agent. When he was refused admission he sued for breach of contract. The contract was held to be void for mistake. This justification appears strained. As is explained in *Bowstead and Reynolds*, it assumes that any contract would be between the principal and the third party; in reality, the contract would have been between the third party and the agent, with the principal able to intervene. If the relevant mistake was that the defendant was unaware of the principal's ability to intervene, it is suggested that this would not have been sufficiently fundamental to render the contract void. One interpretation of the decision which has been suggested is that since the first night was largely by invitation, this may have been a case where an implied exclusion of the, or any, principal was appropriate. However, this reasoning would allow, say, a football hooligan subject to a lifetime ban from a given stadium to gain access by procuring one of his friends to buy a ticket for him as undisclosed principal. Surely, the objective interpretation of contracts is too limited where the parties' actual *subjective* intentions are known or can be established by evidence. In *Said v Butt*, both principal and agent knew full well that the principal was not welcome in the theatre. Any contract entered into by the agent must be interpreted against this factual background. Looked at this way, the perceived difficulty in *Said v Butt* is eliminated.

CONCLUSION

I cannot claim to have 'solved' the conundrum that is undisclosed agency in this essay. What I tried to do is make a number of points which may help in making sense of some of the decisions. The first is that undisclosed agency has nothing to do with consent. It is a device designed to place the risk of loss on the same shoulders as the chance of profit. Once this is realised, cases like *Keighley v Durant* and the infamous *Watteau v Fenwick* may begin to make rather more sense.

The second point is that undisclosed agency, originally conceived in order to manage insolvency risks of intermediaries, has assumed a much greater scope than

[56] ibid at 315 (Wightman J).

[57] Roderick Munday, *Agency Law and Principles* (Oxford University Press, 2010) 248.

[58] *Cf Danziger v Thomson* [1944] KB 654 ('tenant'); *Fred Drughorn Ltd v Rederiaktiebolaget Trans-Atlantic* [1919] AC 203 ('charterer').

would have been necessary to that end: this may be bemoaned by doctrinal purists, but will generally be welcomed by commercial pragmatists.

The third and final point is that there are dangers in applying a set of concepts and terms of art developed in one area (agency proper) to an entirely different one (undisclosed agency), particularly if the latter pursues entirely different aims: it is easy to conflate the two, to apply precedents relating to one to the other and thus cause much confusion. It is hoped that this confusion will be reduced by realising how very distinct disclosed and undisclosed agency are.

11

Innominate Terms Revisited

EWAN MCKENDRICK

I FIRST READ Hugh Beale's book *Remedies for Breach of Contract* when I was a graduate student at the University of Oxford. It is a book that remains on my bookshelf in my study and I consult it on a regular basis. It has stood the test of time. The issues with which it grapples have not, however, been resolved and they continue to give rise to difficulties in the courts. The issue with which this essay is concerned is the entitlement of a party to a contract to terminate further performance of that contract on the occurrence of a breach by the other party of an innominate or an intermediate term of the contract. The category of innominate term was given new life in the modern law by the decision of the Court of Appeal in *Hongkong Fir Shipping Co Ltd v Kawasaki Kisen Kaisha Ltd.*[1] The essence of an innominate term is that the entitlement of the innocent party to terminate further performance of the contract depends upon the consequences of the breach of the term rather than the nature of the term itself. The flexibility which was thus introduced (or reintroduced)[2] into the law in *Hongkong Fir* has met with a mixed reception. For some, it has introduced unwelcome uncertainty into an area of the law where the rules of law should be clear and certain. For others, it is a welcome means by which courts can do justice on the facts of the individual case through confining the right to terminate further performance of the contract to the situation where that right is required, namely, when the consequences of the breach are sufficiently serious. The difficulty, of course, lies in ascertaining when for this purpose the consequences of the breach are 'sufficiently serious'. In *Hongkong Fir* itself, the analogy drawn by the Court of Appeal was with the doctrine of frustration which, given the narrow scope of the doctrine of frustration in English contract law,[3] suggests that the bar for the entitlement to terminate has been set at a very high level.

[1] *Hongkong Fir Shipping Co Ltd v Kawasaki Kisen Kaisha Ltd* [1962] 2 QB 26. For a recent assessment of the case and its reception in the modern law of contract see Donal Nolan, 'Hongkong Fir Shipping Co Ltd v Kawaski Kisen Kaisha Ltd, The Hongkong Fir (1961)' in Charles Mitchell and Paul Mitchell (eds), *Landmark Cases in the Law of Contract* (Oxford, Hart Publishing, 2008) 269.

[2] It can be argued that there was nothing particularly novel about the decision in *Hongkong Fir* and that it is consistent with the a line of authorities dating back into the nineteenth century: see further Nolan, 'Hongkong Fir Shipping Co Ltd v Kawaski Kisen Kaisha Ltd, The Hongkong Fir (1961)', n 1 above, 270–76.

[3] See, eg, *Davis Contractors Ltd v Fareham Urban District Council* [1956] AC 696 and *J Lauritzen AS v Wijsmuller BV (The 'Super Servant Two')* [1990] 1 Lloyd's Rep 1.

That this is so was recently confirmed by the Court of Appeal in *Ampurius Nu Homes Holdings Ltd v Telford Homes (Creekside) Ltd*,[4] the case which is the focus of this essay.

THE FACTS

In 2007 the defendant, Telford Homes (Creekside) Ltd, acquired the freehold of a site in London close to the south bank of the River Thames. The claimant, Ampurius Nu Homes Holdings Ltd, had acquired the adjoining site in 2005. The parties subsequently entered into a contract for the development of the site. The plan was an ambitious one but the timescale of its implementation was affected by the financial downturn which occurred in 2008 and 2009. The development consisted of four blocks (referred to as Blocks A, B, C and D). The blocks were designed to provide commercial accommodation on the ground, first and second floors, with residential accommodation on the floors above. In total there were to be 371 flats and two floors of underground parking.

The agreement which was the subject matter of the dispute between the parties was entered into on 7 October 2008. The parties described their contract as an 'Agreement for Lease' but in fact it encompassed both the construction to shell and core and the grant of long leases covering the commercial units on the ground and first floors of all four blocks, together with some car parking spaces. The defendant was named as the landlord and the claimant as the tenant. The defendant undertook responsibility for the construction of the property to shell and core. Under clause 2.3(vi) of the agreement the defendant agreed that it would procure that the landlord's works were carried out 'with due diligence' and in clause 2.4 it also agreed that it would 'use its reasonable endeavours to procure completion of the Landlord's works by the target date or as soon as reasonably possible thereafter'. The 'target date' for Blocks A and B was agreed to be 28 February 2011 and for Blocks C and D it was 21 July 2010. On the occurrence of the completion date for each block the defendant agreed to grant to the claimant a 999 year lease of the block and the claimant in turn agreed to pay the estimated purchase price less the deposit as apportioned to that block, subject to a proviso that the defendant could not serve a Certificate of Practical Completion in respect of Block C or D without the other or serve a Certificate of Practical Completion in respect of Block A or B without the other.

At the time at which the parties entered into this agreement, most of the excavation of the double storey basement and the foundation piling for the blocks had been completed. The works continued according to plan for the remainder of 2008 and into early 2009. However, in early March 2009 the first signs of significant difficulty began to emerge. The downturn in the housing market was beginning to hit the project hard, in the sense that little progress had been made in securing residential purchasers. At a meeting held on 23 March 2009, the defendant decided

[4] *Ampurius Nu Homes Holdings Ltd v Telford Homes (Creekside) Ltd* [2013] EWCA Civ 577; [2013] 4 All ER 377.

to stop works on Blocks A and B and to allow the programme for Block C to 'slip back' in order to 'assist with cash flow'. In accordance with this decision, work on Blocks A and B ceased in June 2009 subject to an exception in the case of Block A where work continued on the shell to the extent necessary for the delivery of the energy unit and car park entrance that would also be used by Blocks C and D. In July 2009, the defendant informed the claimant that the works on Blocks A and B were 'on hold' until the secured development finance had been released and that it was a condition that 85 pre-sales were made for the release of Phase II funding. At approximately the same time the defendant also managed to obtain an injection of cash which made it unnecessary for it to put back the works on Block C. The work on Blocks C and D therefore continued as planned.

In the period following the cessation of work on Blocks A and B there was extensive correspondence between the parties about the delay and its impact on the ability of the claimant to market the properties. In one of these letters lawyers acting for the claimant referred to the defendant's 'deliberate and ongoing breach ... of the terms of the contract' and stated that the claimant was 'currently considering whether to exercise its option to accept the repudiatory breach'. Nevertheless, the defendant continued throughout this period to work on Blocks C and D and to seek alternative sources of funds so that it could continue the work on Blocks A and B. Further, the defendant maintained that it had 'every intention of performing and completing the contract'. Initially, the defendant's hope was that it would be able to resume work on Blocks A and B in March 2010 but that hope was not fulfilled because of the continued absence of the required funds. Subsequently, in July 2010 it informed the claimant that the funding would be released in January 2011. In the event, the defendant was able to access the funding in October 2010 and it so informed the claimant in the course of rather heated exchanges in September 2010.

Accordingly, the defendant restarted the works on Blocks A and B on 4 October 2010. Although the claimant had been informed that such was the intention of the defendant, no one representing the claimant visited the site during this period and so the claimant was unaware of the fact that the work had indeed restarted. Then, on 22 October 2010, lawyers acting for the claimant sent to the defendant a letter in which, after referring to the fact that the defendant had not commenced work on Blocks A and B 'in any meaningful way' and to the assertion that the defendant was 'in fundamental breach of its obligations' concluded that 'our client is entitled to and does now accept the repudiatory breach'. The defendant denied that it had committed a repudiatory breach of contract and later asserted that it was entitled to terminate the contract on the ground of the claimant's repudiatory breach of contract in failing to pay the required deposit. The defendant continued with performance of the works. Blocks C and D were completed 'approximately nine months later than the Target Date'[5] and, if the claimant had not purported to terminate the contract between the parties, it was found that Block A and B would have been completed 'just under one year later than the Target Dates for those blocks'.[6]

[5] ibid para 31.
[6] ibid.

It was common ground between the parties that their contract had come to an end in late 2010. Further, it was agreed that, if the claimant was not entitled to terminate the contract on 22 October 2010, its letter of that date constituted a repudiatory breach such that the defendant was entitled to terminate the contract. Thus, the principal issue to be decided was whether the claimant had been entitled to terminate the contract on 22 October 2010.[7]

DECISION OF ROTH J

The case came before Roth J in the Chancery Division.[8] The first issue to be considered was whether or not the defendant had breached the contract between the parties. Roth J concluded that the defendant had breached the contract in two principal respects. First, he held that the defendant had breached its contractual obligation under clause 2.3(vi) to procure that the works were carried out 'with due diligence'. The defendant submitted that the reference to 'due diligence' required only that the work be done carefully. Roth J rejected this submission. He held that 'due diligence' was a 'familiar concept in construction contracts' and that it 'usually connotes both due care and "due assiduity/expedition"'.[9] On the facts of the case, he held that there was no justification for giving the words a 'restricted interpretation' of the type advanced by the defendant. This being the case, it was held that the deliberate cessation of all work on two of the four blocks was not consonant with the exercise of due diligence. While the lack of funding could explain the decision not to progress the works, it could not justify it, given the existence of the obligation to 'procure' the works with 'due diligence'.

Second, he held that the deliberate decision to put the works on Blocks A and B on hold and the delay created by that decision was a breach of clause 2.4. Although Roth J held that the defendant's obligation to use reasonable endeavours did not 'extend to matters antecedent or extraneous to the carrying out of the work, such as having the financial resources to do the work at all',[10] he concluded that the clause was designed to 'cover matters that directly relate to the physical conduct of the works'.[11] Although he held that it was 'not clear' that the defendant had breached this clause in March or June 2009 (because of the possibility of an early resumption of work which would enable a timely completion), he concluded that at some point thereafter (it not being necessary to identify the precise time at which this occurred) the defendant did commit a breach (and remained in breach) of this clause. The delay through to October 2010 was not consistent with the use of reasonable

[7] There was an alternative claim that the claimant was entitled to rescind the contract on the ground that it had been induced to enter into the contract by the defendant's misrepresentations regarding its access to funding for the development. This aspect of the case will not be considered further in this essay other than to note that Roth J held that the defendant had not made the misrepresentations upon which the claimant purported to rely. There was no appeal against that finding to the Court of Appeal.

[8] *Ampurius Nu Homes Holdings Ltd v Telford Homes (Creekside) Ltd* [2012] EWHC 1820 (Ch); [2012] BLR 387.

[9] ibid para 99.

[10] ibid para 100.

[11] ibid.

endeavours to procure completion of the works by the target date or as soon as reasonably possible thereafter.

Having decided that the defendant had breached the contract, the next question to be considered was whether the breach or breaches were repudiatory in character. Roth J held that the terms which had been broken were neither conditions nor warranties but were innominate terms so that the entitlement of the claimant to terminate further performance of the contract turned on 'the nature of the breach'.[12] He then noted the various tests which have been used in order to denote the circumstances in which a breach of an innominate term gives rise to an entitlement to terminate further performance of the contract (tests such as whether the breach goes 'to the root of the contract', 'frustrates the commercial purpose of the venture' or deprives thc innocent party of 'substantially the whole benefit which the parties intended he should derive from performance'). After noting that these 'established tests' were not 'particularly easy to apply',[13] Roth J held that 'at least by the end of 2009, if not before',[14] the defendant's ongoing breach of clause 2.3(vi) had become sufficiently substantial to amount to a repudiatory breach. At that stage the work had been halted for 'over five months' and the defendant had been unable to confirm when it might be in a position to resume the work. The fact that the defendant fully intended to resume the work as soon as funding became available did not prevent the breach from being a repudiatory breach. It was not sufficient for the defendant to assert that the claimant would ultimately obtain the performance for which it contracted and that it could be compensated in damages for any loss attributable to the delay. Given that the claimant had made it clear that it wanted delivery of all four blocks as close in time as possible, the continuing delay in relation to the completion of two of the blocks was held to have the consequence that the breach had become so substantial as to defeat the commercial purpose of the venture. Further, Roth J rejected the suggestion that it was necessary for the claimant to serve a notice making time of the essence before it could lawfully terminate the contract.[15] In relation to the breach of clause 2.4, Roth J concluded that it amounted to a repudiatory breach 'by at least July 2010'.[16] By July 2010 the work on Blocks A and B had been at a standstill for more than a year, by which time it was clear that the work would not be completed any time close to the target date.

In so far as the claimant submitted that the defendant's deliberate decision to cease work on Blocks A and B amounted to a renunciation of the contract, this submission was rejected by Roth J. This was not a case in which the defendant had stated its intention no longer to perform its contractual obligations. On the contrary, it had repeatedly asserted that it would continue to perform them. But it had nevertheless repudiated the contract as a result of its breaches of clauses 2.3(vi) and 2.4.

[12] ibid para 103.
[13] ibid para 107.
[14] ibid.
[15] ibid para 103.
[16] ibid para 110.

DECISION OF THE COURT OF APPEAL

The defendant appealed to the Court of Appeal. On appeal the defendant did not dispute that it had breached the contract; its case was that the breach or breaches were not repudiatory in character. The Court of Appeal allowed the appeal.

Lewison LJ commenced his consideration of whether or not the defendant had committed a repudiatory breach of contract with an extended analysis of the decision of the Court of Appeal in *Hongkong Fir*. He derived three propositions of law from the case.[17] First, the date or time which the court must examine when assessing whether a breach is repudiatory or not is the date of the purported termination of the contract. This is so whether the breach is actual or anticipatory in nature. Thus, on the present facts, the critical date was 22 October 2010, by which time, unknown to the claimant, the defendant had resumed the work on Blocks A and B. Secondly, when considering that position, the court must take into account any steps taken by the party in breach of contract to remedy any accrued breaches of contract. As we shall see, this is a more controversial proposition. Thirdly, the court must also 'take account of likely future events, judged by reference to objective facts as at the date of purported termination'.[18]

Turning to the test to be applied when deciding whether or not a breach is repudiatory, Lewison LJ noted an apparent discrepancy in the language used by the courts in the leading cases. In *Hongkong Fir*, Diplock LJ held that the breach must have deprived the innocent party of 'substantially the whole benefit' of the contract. This test 'sets the bar high'[19] because it requires the innocent party to satisfy 'the same test' as that applied by a court when considering whether or not a contract has been frustrated. In other cases, the test has been set out in what appears to be less stringent terms. Thus, Buckley LJ in *Decro-Wall International SA v Practitioners in Marketing Ltd*[20] stated that the breach must deprive the innocent party of a 'substantial part of the benefit to which he is entitled under the contract'.[21] However, the extent to which these differences in terminology are important in practice is difficult to discern. As Lewison LJ observed, the 'trouble with expressing important propositions of English law in metaphorical terms is that it is difficult to be sure what they mean'.[22] That said, it is at least possible to identify the factors to be taken into account by the courts when deciding whether a breach of an innominate term is repudiatory.

The first matter to be taken into account is the benefit which it was intended that the innocent party would obtain from performance of the contract.[23] This element was to prove to be an important aspect of the appeal because the Court of Appeal held that Roth J had failed to take sufficient account of it. The benefit which it was intended that the claimant would obtain from contractual performance was

[17] [2013] EWCA Civ 577; [2013] 4 All ER 377, para 44.
[18] ibid.
[19] ibid para 48.
[20] *Decro-Wall International SA v Practitioners in Marketing Ltd* [1971] 1 WLR 361.
[21] ibid at 380.
[22] *Ampurius Nu Holdings*, n 4 above, para 50
[23] ibid para 51.

'a leasehold interest of 999 years' duration in four blocks'.[24] Viewed against the backdrop of this very long-term benefit, the delay which occurred in completing the works did not seem to the Court of Appeal to be particularly significant. The error made by Roth J was to focus unduly on the impact of the delay on the marketing of the properties and so lose sight of the 'ultimate objective of the contract'[25] which was to grant the claimant a 999-year lease.

A second matter to be considered is the effect of the breach on the innocent party.[26] A number of factors are relevant here. These include the financial loss suffered by the innocent party as a result of the breach; the extent to which it has obtained the performance for which it contracted; the extent to which it can be adequately compensated by an award of damages; whether the breach was likely to be repeated; whether the guilty party would resume contractual performance; and whether the breach had fundamentally changed the value of future performance by the party in breach. Lewison LJ noted that this was not a case in which the claimant would only ever have obtained an interest in two of the four blocks. Rather, it was a case in which it would obtain the full promised performance but that performance would be delayed. Viewed against the backdrop of a 999-year lease, it could not be said that the delay which had occurred had deprived the claimant of a substantial part of the benefit of the lease of each of the four blocks. Further, it appeared that that delay had not itself caused any actual loss to the claimant as at the date on which the claimant purported to terminate the contract. Would the delay have caused the claimant loss in the future? This was an issue which Roth J did not, in fact, examine. Nevertheless, counsel for the defendant did attempt a calculation of that loss (which calculation was not challenged by counsel for the claimant) and that produced the sum of approximately £100,000 which, in the context of a purchase price of over £8 million and a total development cost in excess of £100 million, could not be said to be substantial. The effect of the breach on the claimant was therefore not sufficient to warrant a finding that the breach was repudiatory in nature.

A factor which weighed heavily with Roth J was the fact that the defendant was unable for a considerable period of time to state when works on Blocks A and B would re-start. While Lewison LJ acknowledged that 'uncertainty caused by delay is a commercial problem'[27] he concluded that Roth J had erred in considering the impact of the delay as at the end of 2009 or at some other point in 2009. The critical date was not the date of the defendant's breach but the date on which the claimant purported to accept the breach and terminate the contract. That date was 22 October 2010, by which time the work on Blocks A and B had recommenced. As at that date, Lewison LJ concluded that it was not possible to state that 'the actual and reasonably foreseeable effects' of the defendant's breaches were such as to deprive the claimant 'of a substantial part (let alone substantially the whole) benefit of the contract'.[28]

[24] ibid para 51.
[25] ibid.
[26] ibid para 52.
[27] ibid para 69.
[28] ibid.

Finally, the Court of Appeal upheld the finding of Roth J to the effect that the defendant had not renounced the contract. On the contrary, this was a case in which the defendant had maintained that it would perform its contractual obligations when the funding difficulties were resolved. So, in so far as the claimant submitted that the defendant had renounced the contract, its claim was rejected.

IMPLICATIONS

The conclusion of the Court of Appeal that the defendant had neither committed a repudiatory breach of the contract nor had renounced the contract is an important one for a number of reasons.

Setting the Bar High

First, it acknowledges that the test established by Diplock LJ in *Hongkong Fir,* namely, that the breach must have deprived the innocent party of substantially the whole benefit of the contract in order to give rise to a right to terminate further performance of the contract, 'sets the bar high',[29] a point further reinforced by the observation that the test to be applied is the 'same' (and not simply a similar) test as that applied by the courts when considering whether or not a contract has been frustrated. To the extent that the bar is indeed set at this high level, the fear that the recognition of a category of innominate terms will give rise to an unacceptable degree of uncertainty seems to be misplaced. While it may not be easy to formulate the applicable test with precision, the thrust of the approach is clear, namely, that termination for breach of an innominate term will be permitted only in cases where the consequences of the breach are extremely serious or, as it has been put by one set of commentators, 'where the consequences of breach are dire indeed'.[30]

Against this, it can be argued that this emphasis on certainty and on the need to 'set the bar high' has not been consistently applied by the courts, a factor recognised by Lewison LJ when he noted that the test applied by Buckley LJ in *Decro-Wall International SA v Practitioners in Marketing Ltd*[31] was 'more favourable'[32] to the innocent party. A similar point can be made in relation to the analogy drawn with the doctrine of frustration. Donal Nolan in his analysis of *Hongkong Fir* drew attention to the fact that the express link made by Diplock LJ between discharge by

[29] ibid para 48.

[30] John Carter, Gregory Tolhurst and Elisabeth Peden 'Developing the Intermediate Term Concept' (2006) 22 *Journal of Contract Law* 268, 272.

[31] *Decro-Wall*, n 20 above. Although Lord Wilberforce in *Federal Commerce & Navigation Co Ltd v Molena Alpha Inc (The Nanfri)* [1979] AC 757, 779 observed that the difference in expression did not in his view reflect any 'divergence of principle' but rather reflected the 'applications to different contracts, of the common principle that, to amount to repudiation a breach must go to the root of the contract'.

[32] [2013] EWCA Civ 577; [2013] 4 All ER 377, para 48.

breach and discharge by frustration 'seems so often to be overlooked today'.[33] Even those who acknowledge the link have in times sought to play it down. Thus, Hugh Beale has observed that

> whatever may be said in theory, in practice it is doubtful whether the same degree of seriousness is required when one party has failed to perform as when it is alleged that supervening circumstances have frustrated the contract.[34]

The decision of the Court of Appeal in the present case may herald a swing in the pendulum back in the direction of a more stringent test and a closer link with the doctrine of frustration. Some support for this proposition can be gleaned from the judgment of the Chancellor, Sir Terence Etherton, in *Urban I (Blonk Street) Ltd v Ayres*,[35] when he expressed his preference for the view that the test to be applied was whether the innocent party had been deprived of substantially the whole benefit of the contract rather than whether he had been deprived of a substantial part of the benefit of the contract.[36]

The application of this more stringent test will not, however, remove all of the uncertainty in this area of the law. While the court is not exercising a discretion when deciding whether or not the innocent party is entitled to terminate further performance of the contract, the exercise in which the court is engaged is 'fact-sensitive'[37] or 'involves a multi-factorial assessment'.[38] While the factors to be taken into account in this process can be identified at a high level of generality[39] the weight to be given to them and the balance to be struck between them very much depends upon the facts of the case. It is therefore important not to over-state the degree of certainty which has been provided by the Court of Appeal in the present case. To the extent that it has reaffirmed that the bar is 'set high' it has eliminated some of the uncertainty in relation to the circumstances in which a right to terminate further performance of the contract will arise. But it has not removed it entirely.

Delay

The second point of note which emerges from the decision of the Court of Appeal is that it seems to make it more difficult to establish that a breach is repudiatory where

[33] Nolan, 'Hongkong Fir Shipping Co Ltd v Kawaski Kisen Kaisha Ltd, The Hongkong Fir (1961)', n 1 above, 286.

[34] Hugh Beale, *Remedies for Breach of Contract* (London, Sweet & Maxwell, 1980) 45.

[35] *Urban I (Blonk Street) Ltd v Ayres* [2013] EWCA Civ 816; [2014] 1 WLR 756.

[36] ibid para 57.

[37] *Valilas v Janujaz* [2014] EWCA Civ 436, para 60 (Arden LJ).

[38] ibid para 53.

[39] The most complete list has been drawn up by Prof Carter, *Carter's Breach of Contract* (Oxford, Hart Publishing, 2012) para 6-57, in the following terms: (i) any detriment caused, or likely to be caused, by the breach; (ii) any delay caused, or likely to be caused, by the breach; (iii) the value of any performance received by or tendered to the party not in breach; (iv) the cost of making any performance given or tendered by the party in breach conform with the requirements of the contract; (v) any opportunity 'enjoyed' by the party in breach to remedy the discrepancies in its performance; (vi) the consequences of any prior breach of the contract by the party in breach and whether further breaches were a likely consequence of the breach at issue; and (vii) whether the party not in breach will be adequately compensated by an award of damages in respect of the breach.

the breach takes the form of delay in the performance of contractual obligations. As Lewison LJ observed:

> [I]t seems to me that (absent any attempt to make time of the essence) delay, even with its attendant uncertainties, will only become a repudiatory breach if and when the delay is so prolonged as to frustrate the contract.[40]

This link between delay that is sufficient to amount to a repudiatory breach and delay that will result in the frustration of a contract is not new. It was drawn by Mustill J in *The Hermosa*[41] and can be traced back as far as cases such as *Jackson v Union Marine Insurance Co Ltd*.[42] While the analogy is not precise,[43] it is firmly re-established. The effect of its invocation is likely to be to make it very difficult to prove that a delay in performance amounts to a repudiatory breach, particularly in the case where the party in breach maintains that it has not renounced its contractual obligations and intends to perform at some future time. Support for the latter proposition can be gleaned from the decision of the Court of Appeal in *Valilas v Januzaj*[44] where, by a majority, it was held that the withholding of payment was not a repudiatory breach, largely on the basis that the innocent party would ultimately receive the money to which he was entitled and that the delay in receipt could not be said to deprive him of substantially the whole benefit he was intended to receive from performance. While Underhill LJ in his dissenting judgment noted that there is no 'universal proposition that late payment cannot be repudiatory if eventual payment is assured',[45] the majority concluded that the innocent party had failed to demonstrate that the failure to make timely payment had serious consequences for him (other than the loss of use of the money which could be made good by an award of damages). This is not to say that late performance can never amount to a repudiatory breach of contract, but, in the absence of conduct by the party in breach evincing an intention no longer to be bound by the contract or a delay of very serious proportions, it is likely to be extremely difficult to establish that the delay amounts to a repudiatory breach and, for this reason, practitioners who wish to preserve a right of exit in the event of non-performance by the other party are likely to wish to make the time of performance a condition of the contract (or, which amounts to the same thing, to make 'time of the essence' of the contract) so that a breach of the time stipulation will give rise to a right to terminate further performance of the contract irrespective of the consequences of the breach.

[40] [2013] EWCA Civ 577; [2013] 4 All ER 377, para 69.

[41] *Chilean Nitrate Sales Corp v Marine Transportation Co Ltd (The Hermosa)* [1980] 1 Lloyd's Rep 638.

[42] *Jackson v Union Marine Insurance Co Ltd* (1874) 10 CP 125.

[43] Frustration operates automatically and discharges both parties from their obligations to perform in the future, whereas a repudiatory breach gives to the innocent party the right to terminate further performance of the contract if he or she wishes to do so and the party in breach remains liable to a claim in damages in respect of the loss caused by the non-performance.

[44] *Valilas*, n 37 above.

[45] ibid para 37.

Timing

This leads on to the third point of note to emerge from the decision of the Court of Appeal, namely, the identification of the date at which it is to be decided whether or not the breach is repudiatory. The choice of the date of the purported termination has significant consequences for the party who wishes to terminate further performance of the contract. It means that, at the date on which it purports to pull the trigger and terminate the contract, it must be in a position to demonstrate to a court, should the need arise, that the effect of the breach was such that it had been, or would be, deprived of substantially the whole benefit of the contract. If it does not have that evidence then it should not terminate (or, alternatively, should be aware of the fact that its termination may be held to be wrongful, thus exposing itself potentially to a substantial liability in damages). This was a point of direct relevance to the claimant on the facts of the present case. At the time at which it purported to terminate further performance of the contract, it was apparently unaware of the fact that the defendant had resumed work on Blocks A and B. The claimant complained that it had not been informed in writing of the defendant's intention to resume work and argued that it was reasonable for it not to have inspected the site before purporting to terminate. But these complaints got them nowhere. On 15 September the defendant had informed the claimant orally of its intention to resume work on 4 October and Roth J had made no finding that the claimant's state of ignorance was reasonable.[46] As Lewison LJ observed, Roth J had no need to make such a finding. It must be the responsibility of the party seeking to terminate further performance of the contract to ensure that it has established the facts before it takes the step of purporting to terminate the contract. A potentially peculiar aspect of the case on its facts was that the parties did hold a without prejudice meeting on 21 October,[47] the day before the claimant purported to terminate the contract. It seems odd that no mention was made at that meeting of the fact that works on Blocks A and B had resumed. But Lewison LJ noted that since Roth J had found that the claimant did not know that the works had been restarted, it was 'a fair inference that it was not told at that meeting' and it was 'an equally fair inference that it did not ask'.[48] Nonetheless, the practical lesson to learn is the need to get the facts together before deciding to terminate further performance of the contract.

What would have been the position if the claimant had purported to terminate the contract on 1 September 2010? The logic of the decision of the Court of Appeal is that the question of its entitlement to terminate further performance of the contract would then have to be assessed as at that date. As at that date work had been halted for approximately 14 months and the defendant's various representations to the effect that it hoped to be able to access funds had not been realised. This hypothetical raises in a rather stark form the practical difficulties that can arise in cases of delay. On the one hand, it seems paradoxical that the claimant could have improved its

[46] [2013] EWCA Civ 577; [2013] 4 All ER 377, para 66.

[47] The fact that the meeting was held on a 'without prejudice' basis is a complicating factor, although it is not necessary for present purposes to consider the question of whether the court should have had any regard to these discussions.

[48] [2013] EWCA Civ 577; [2013] 4 All ER 377, para 28.

case by purporting to terminate the contract at an earlier point in time. On the other hand, it is clear that the fact that the defendant had resumed work at the time at which the claimant did in fact purport to terminate the contract was a critical factor in persuading the Court of Appeal to conclude that the claimant had not been deprived of substantially the whole benefit of the contract. Had the defendant not resumed work at the time of the purported termination, could the claimant not have justified its decision to terminate the contract on the basis of the 14-month cessation of work combined with the continued uncertainty about when the work would be resumed? Given that the benefit which the claimant expected to obtain from performance was primarily a leasehold interest of 999 years duration in four blocks, a delay of 14 months does not of itself deprive the claimant of substantially the whole benefit of the contract. Therefore, on these facts, the critical factor would appear to be whether, assuming that the claimant had purported to terminate the contract on 1 September, the delay at that date appeared to be of such an indeterminate nature that the claimant could establish that it had been deprived of substantially the whole benefit of the contract. As has been noted, Lewison LJ stated that the court must take into account 'likely future benefits, judged by reference to objective facts as at the date of purported termination'.[49] The 'objective facts' as at 1 September 2010 could not include the fact that funding was subsequently obtained in October and that the work restarted on 4 October. It is the date of the purported termination that is critical and subsequent events should be irrelevant unless they shed light on the likelihood, as at the date of the purported termination, of the defendant obtaining the necessary funding.[50] Had the claimant been able to demonstrate that, as at 1 September, it had serious concerns about whether or not the defendant would be able to obtain the funding to complete Blocks A and B, it might have been able to persuade a court that the breach was sufficiently serious to entitle it to terminate the contract. Thus, it is possible that the claimant could have improved its position had it taken the decision to terminate the contract prior to the resumption of works on Blocks A and B. This is not to say that the claimant would necessarily have succeeded had it sought to terminate the contract at an earlier point in time. It is to state only that the fact that the work had not restarted, combined with the apparent inability of the defendant to state unequivocally when funding would be obtained, would have been factors which the claimant could have employed in support of its case that it was entitled to terminate the contract as at 1 September 2010.

[49] ibid para 44.

[50] The issue of whether a court should take account of subsequent events also arises in cases where the delay is alleged to have frustrated the contract between the parties. Although arguments have been made that the courts should take advantage of the benefit of hindsight (see Michael Howard, 'Frustration and Shipping Law' in Ewan McKendrick (ed), *Force Majeure and Frustration of Contract*, 2nd edn (London, Lloyd's of London Press, 1995) 129–38), the more orthodox view is that, while the parties may sometimes be expected to 'wait on events in order to see whether the delay already suffered and the prospects of further delay from that cause will make any ultimate performance of the relevant contractual obligations "radically different"' (*Pioneer Shipping Ltd v BTP Tioxide Ltd* [1982] AC 724, 752 (Lord Roskill)), this 'wait and see' is not equivalent to the use of hindsight. Rather, it is a postponement of the date on which the prospective analysis is conducted so that a contract may still be frustrated in the case where the delay which was anticipated to be substantial turned out to be unexpectedly short (*Bank Line Ltd v Arthur Capel & Co* [1919] AC 435).

Remedying the Breach

This leads on to the fourth point which relates to the statement of Lewison LJ that the court must 'take into account any steps taken by the guilty party to remedy accrued breaches of contract'.[51] Did the Court of Appeal conclude that the defendant's breach of contract was never repudiatory or did it hold that any repudiatory breach committed by the defendant had been remedied by the time that the claimant purported to terminate the contract? The answer to this question is not entirely clear. But it is clear that Lewison LJ used language which demonstrated that it was his opinion that 'a breach of contract, although serious, may be capable of remedy'.[52] He also observed that 'if it is remedied before the injured party purports to exercise a right of termination, then the fact that the breach has been remedied is an important factor to be taken into account'.[53] As Professor Carter has observed, the phrase remedying a breach 'is not very precise'.[54] The general rule in English law is that it is not open to one party unilaterally to remedy a repudiatory breach of contract.[55] As Sedley LJ observed, 'a completed breach, even if it can be compensated for, cannot be undone'.[56] Once the breach has been committed, 'all the cards are in the hands of the wronged party' and 'the defaulting party cannot choose to retreat'.[57] What it can do is 'to invite affirmation by making amends'.[58] The latter observation is of some significance in the present context because Roth J held that there had been no affirmation of the contract by the claimant[59] so that, if it was the case that all that the defendant could do was to invite affirmation, on the facts any such invitation had been declined.

Lewison LJ sought to find support for the proposition that a court must take into account any steps taken by the party in breach to remedy accrued breaches of contract in the decision of the Court of Appeal in *Hongkong Fir*. But, to the extent that the judges in *Hongkong Fir* made reference to the taking of remedial steps, they were made principally in the context of deciding whether or not a breach was repudiatory:[60] that is to say, a failure to remedy the breach may be evidence from which a court may infer that the innocent party was deprived of substantially the whole benefit of the contract, while the taking of steps to remedy the breach might prevent the breach from amounting to a repudiatory breach. The issue in *Hongkong*

[51] [2013] EWCA Civ 577; [2013] 4 All ER 377, para 44.
[52] ibid para 63.
[53] ibid.
[54] Carter, *Carter's Breach of Contract*, n 39 above, para 6–76.
[55] *Buckland v Bournemouth University Higher Education Corp* [2010] EWCA Civ 121; [2011] 1 QB 323.
[56] ibid para 43.
[57] ibid para 40.
[58] ibid.
[59] [2012] EWHC 1820 (Ch); [2012] BLR 387, para 123. He held that the fact that the claimant had engaged in prolonged negotiations with a view to finding a solution to the defendant's funding difficulties did not amount to an affirmation of the contract, given that these discussions had taken place without prejudice to the claimant's contention that it would be entitled to terminate the contract if no resolution was reached. It was also important that the breach was held to be of a continuing nature and that the effect of the breach became more serious with the passage of time. This was not a case in which the claimant had taken 15 months to decide what to do in relation to a one-off breach, where the effects of the breach had crystallised at the beginning of the period.
[60] *Hongkong Fir*, n 1 above, at 57, 72–73.

Fir was not whether a repudiatory breach ceased to be such as a consequence of the taking of remedial steps. But it may be that, in the context of the breach of an innominate term, it is possible to remedy what would otherwise be a repudiatory breach in the sense that the remedial steps taken may lessen the consequences of the breach so that the innocent party is no longer deprived of substantially the whole benefit of the contract. Given that the court must examine the entitlement of the innocent party to terminate further performance of the contract as at the date of the purported termination, the steps taken by the party in breach to alleviate the consequences of the breach prior to the date of the purported termination should be taken into account. This is not to say that the breach has thereby been remedied. On the facts of the present case the defendant had breached clauses 2.3(vi) and 2.4 and subsequent steps did not undo these breaches. But they could reduce the *consequences* of those breaches and, to the extent that the entitlement to terminate further performance of the contract depends upon the consequences of the breach, a court should take these remedial steps into account when deciding whether the consequences of the breach are sufficiently serious to entitle the innocent party to terminate. On this view there may be a difference between a breach of an innominate term (where the consequences of the breach can be reduced, and to an extent 'remedied', subsequent to the occurrence of the breach) and the breach of a condition where the entitlement to terminate arises at the time of breach so that subsequent remedial efforts should be irrelevant (at least in the absence of a waiver by the innocent party).

International Restatements

The final point to be made relates to international restatements of contract law. The test applied by the Court of Appeal, namely, whether the breach deprived the innocent party of substantially the whole benefit of the contract, is one which is reflected in various restatements of international and European contract law, to many of which Hugh Beale has made such a valuable contribution. Thus, it is to be found in the UNIDROIT Principles of International Commercial Contracts,[61] the Principles of European Contract Law,[62] the Draft Common Frame of Reference[63] and the proposed Common European Sales Law.[64] Thus, one might expect a court applying these international restatements to reach the same conclusion as that reached by the Court of Appeal in the present case. But it would be a mistake to infer from this that English law on termination for breach is identical to that to be found in these international restatements. There remain a number of differences, of which it suffices to point out two. First, English law permits contracting parties to agree to classify a term as a condition when that term would not otherwise be so classified. In short, freedom of contract prevails. If the parties wish to provide that

[61] UNIDROIT, *Principles of International Commercial Contracts* (Rome, 2010) (PICC), art 7.3.1 (2)(a).

[62] Lando Commission, *Principles of European Contract Law* (2002) (PECL), arts 8:103(b) and 9:301.

[63] Study Group on European Civil Code and the Acquis Group, *Draft Common Frame of Reference* (Dissen, Sellier, 2009) (DCFR), Book III, art 3:502, although it should be noted that the test is to be applied 'to the whole or relevant part of the performance'.

[64] Common European Sales Law, arts 114(1) and 87(2)(a).

any breach of a term is to give to the other party the entitlement to terminate further performance of the contract, they are free to do so and, provided that the court is satisfied that such was the intention of the parties, the court must give effect to that intention.[65] International restatements have tended to be more reticent about giving to the parties the unfettered right to decide what is or is not a breach that gives to the innocent party a right of termination.[66] The freedom which English law gives to contracting parties to define for themselves the circumstances in which a breach of contract will give rise to a right to terminate further performance of the contract is currently an important aspect of English contract law. Thus, the response of many English lawyers to the decision of the Court of Appeal in the present case may be to attempt to draft terms such as clause 2.3(vi) as conditions in order to give a clear right to terminate in the event of breach. Whether the other party will agree to the classification of such a term as a condition is, however, another matter which will ultimately turn on the bargaining power of the parties.

An alternative approach, and one in respect of which English lawyers might learn from the various international restatements of contract law, is to entitle the innocent party to terminate the contract after the expiry of an additional notice period given to the party in breach. The restatements referred to above all contain articles which provide that, in the case where the delay does not amount to fundamental non-performance, the innocent party may give to the non-performing party a notice fixing an additional period of time of reasonable length and that it may terminate the contract at the end of the notice period if performance has not been supplied.[67] Thus, had any of these restatements been applicable to the facts of the present case, the claimant could have given to the defendant a notice fixing an additional period of time of reasonable length for it to fulfil its obligations under clauses 2.3(vi) and 2.4 and, in the event of a failure by the defendant to comply with its terms, the claimant would have been entitled to terminate the contract. English law is less clear-cut on this point. While it is clear that, as a matter of English law, the claimant would have been entitled to serve such a notice on the occurrence of the breach by the defendant,[68] it is not so obvious that the claimant would have been entitled to terminate further performance of the contract in the event that the defendant failed to comply with the notice. While the international restatements provide in express terms that non-compliance with the notice gives an entitlement to terminate in respect of what is otherwise a non-fundamental breach, English law seems not to entitle a party unilaterally to alter the nature of a contract term. As the Chancellor, Sir Terence Etherton, stated in *Urban I (Blonk Street) Ltd v Ayres*,[69]

[65] *Lombard North Central plc v Butterworth* [1987] QB 527. The court must, however, be satisfied that this was the intention of the parties: *Schuler AG v Wickman Machine Tool Sales Ltd* [1974] AC 235.

[66] Different approaches to this issue are taken in the different international instruments. Greater autonomy appears to be given to the parties in PICC, art 7.3.1(2)(b) and PECL, art 8:103(a). Less flexible are DCFR, Book III, art 3:502, and art 87(2) of the proposed Common European Sales Law.

[67] See PECL, art 8:106(3); PICC, art 7.1.5(3); DCFR, Book III, art 3:503(1); and art 115 of the proposed Common European Sales Law. In the case of the PICC, the right to terminate does not arise where the obligation which has not been performed is only a minor part of the contractual obligation of the non-performing party: art 7.1.5(4).

[68] *Behzadi v Shaftesbury Hotels Ltd* [1992] Ch 1.

[69] [2013] EWCA Civ 816; [2014] 1 WLR 756.

'it is contrary to all principle for one party to be able unilaterally to transform one type of contractual provision (namely, an innominate term …) into something different (a condition in the strict sense)'.[70] To similar effect is the judgment of Rix LJ in *Samarenko v Dawn Hill House Ltd*,[71]when he observed:

> [I]f the underlying term in question is innominate only, I very much doubt that the service of a notice stipulating a time for performance, however reasonable, could, in itself, render failure to meet the time stipulated to be a repudiatory breach, although it could provide some evidence towards such a conclusion on the facts of any case.[72]

Given that clauses 2.3(vi) and 2.4 were found to be innominate terms, these observations are directly applicable to the present facts so that non-compliance with any notice would not of itself constitute a repudiatory breach.[73] The conclusion that non-compliance with such a notice does not amount to a repudiatory breach has been the subject of some criticism[74] and the issue may yet be reconsidered. In the event that it is, the adoption of the solution to be found in these international restatements might be a means of alleviating the position of a party who finds itself in the position of the claimant in the present case who is faced with a breach of an innominate term but is uncertain whether that breach is sufficiently serious to justify it in terminating further performance of the contract. Given that a wrongful termination will itself amount to a repudiatory breach (and so potentially result in an exposure to a claim for substantial damages), it may be preferable to give the claimant a means by which it can resolve the uncertainty caused by the continuing delay and permit it to fix an additional period of time for performance, at the end of which it is given a secure right to terminate the contract in the event of non-compliance with the terms of the notice.

[70] ibid 44.

[71] [2011] EWCA Civ 1445; [2013] Ch 36.

[72] ibid para 65.

[73] At most it would be evidence from which a court could infer a repudiatory breach. But, given that the defendant maintained throughout its intention to obtain finance and complete the works, it is difficult to see any basis on which it could be said that non-compliance with any notice would have given grounds to infer that the defendant had evinced an intention no longer to be bound by its contractual obligations.

[74] See John Carter, 'Deposits and "Time of the Essence"' (2013) 129 *Law Quarterly Review* 149. The criticisms relate principally to its consistency with existing precedent and the failure to attach sufficient weight to the fact that time 'becomes' of the essence on the giving of notice. In relation to the first point, the authorities are not easy to reconcile and it may be that a choice will have to be made between them (but that choice can be made in favour of the proposition advanced in the text). In relation to the second, although time may be said to have 'become' of the essence, the point is that it has 'become' of the essence as a result of the action of one party in sending a notice and, as noted in the text, it should not be open to one party unilaterally to make time of the essence in the absence of agreement to that step from the other contracting party.

12

Variation and Termination of Consumer Contracts

SIMON WHITTAKER

IN ENGLISH LAW the principle of the binding force of contracts gives effect to the exercise by the parties of their freedom of contract and provides the certainty seen as desirable for them in the planning of their future decision-making.[1] The law itself, of course, recognises a series of important qualifications on the binding force of contracts for a number of reasons, some affecting the contract as a whole (including many cases of illegality, invalidity for duress or undue influence, misrepresentation and mistake, termination for major breach of contract) and some merely a particular aspect of the contract or of one or more of its terms (including other cases of illegality, control of unfair contract terms and the rules on penalty clauses).

However, paradoxically, the binding nature of contracts as agreed is often qualified by the parties themselves in the contract, so that, in effect, one or more of the parties is not bound to perform in any real sense, or becomes no longer bound to perform as agreed either in certain circumstances or if one of the parties so elects. The range of contract terms which seek to have these different effects is very broad. Perhaps the most obvious example is a straightforward exemption clause which seeks to exclude liability for breach of contract which would otherwise arise in a party for its failure to perform: here, while the party may have an obligation to perform, the clause seeks to avoid any prejudicial legal consequences if he or she fails to do so: as the Law Commissions realised in recommending the control of such clauses, here the practical effect of promising is reduced almost to nothing.[2] Other contract terms (broadly known as *force majeure* or hardship clauses) provide for exceptions or qualifications on the binding force of the contract as agreed in the case of future contingencies of various types, and in particular to provide for changes in the factual or market circumstances on which performance by one or both of the parties depends, especially where performance is to take place over an extended period.[3] In common with exemption clauses, terms of this type may also be seen as allowing

[1] By stating the binding force of contracts in this way I do not intend to take a position on its proper remedial consequences nor on the theoretical question as to whether the binding nature of contract in the common law is truly obligational.

[2] Law Commission and Scottish Law Commission, *Exemption Clauses, Second Report* (Law Com No 69, SL Com No 39, 1975) para 139.

[3] Ewan McKendrick, 'Force Majeure Clauses: The Gap between Doctrine and Practice' in Andrew Burrows and Edwin Peel (eds), *Contract Terms* (Oxford University Press, 2007) ch 12.

one of the parties to take obliquely what the main contractual obligations appear to give directly and, for this reason, they may be subject to the same test of control as 'exemption clauses', but, even so, in a commercial context they are likely to be seen as reasonable and therefore held to be effective as a legitimate expression of contractual planning by the parties, at least where the parties enjoy roughly equal bargaining power.[4] Indeed, by making express provision for future changes in circumstances, terms of this sort can be seen to give to both parties greater contractual certainty, particularly when compared with the narrow and relatively uncertain ambit, and limited and discretionary remedial consequences, of the common law doctrine of frustration.[5]

Variation clauses can play a similar role by allowing the parties to build into their contract a degree of flexibility as to their future obligations and, as such, can play a useful role in the regulation of their relationship.[6] There are different kinds of variation clause.[7] Some provide for future agreement by *both* parties for changes in one or more aspects of their contract, often adding that the parties owe each other a duty to renegotiate in good faith. The courts have hesitated as to whether such a clause should be held effective, though recent dicta suggest a more liberal attitude.[8] Other variation clauses provide that one of the parties has a power under the contract to vary one or more of its aspects: a unilateral variation clause. In the case of consumer contracts, these differ considerably in practice according to whether it is the trader or the consumer who is granted the power of variation.[9]

Finally, contracts may include clauses which allow one or both parties to escape the contract. These are again of different types, but a broad distinction can be drawn between those which allow a party to terminate the contract on the ground of the other's breach of contract (typically in circumstances in which the general law of repudiatory breach would not otherwise allow)[10] and terms which allow one or both parties to terminate the contract on other grounds or in other circumstances.

[4] ibid 251, citing *Watford Electronics Ltd v Sanderson CFL Ltd* [2001] EWCA Civ 317; [2001] All ER (Com) 696; see especially par 55.

[5] ibid 238–43.

[6] In an earlier article I considered some of the issues in relation to price variation clauses: Simon Whittaker, 'Price Variation Clauses' in Muriel Fabre-Magnan, Jacques Ghestin and Patrice Jourdain (eds), *Etudes offertes à Geneviève Viney* (Paris, LGDJ, 2008).

[7] 'Anti-variation clauses' are also found, under which it is provided that the parties jointly cannot vary the terms of their contract, sometimes with an exception in the case of use of a formal procedure or documentation. It could be argued that such a clause cannot constrain the parties' future agreement to amend their contract, given that any such agreement could also disable *pro tanto* the anti-variation clause itself; conversely, the clause could be seen as requiring enforcement so as to reflect the binding force of contract. The position of the courts here is not yet settled: *United Bank v Asif* (2000) WL 456 (CA), paras 15–16; *World On-line Telecom Ltd v I-Way Ltd* [2002] EWCA Civ 413; (2002) WL 31173447, esp paras 10–12; *Spring Finance Ltd v HS Real Company LLC* [2011] EWHC 57 (Comm), para 53; *Globe Motors Inc v TRV Lucasvariety Electric Steering Ltd* [2012] EWHC 3134 (QB); (2012) WL 4888656, paras 33–36.

[8] Notably, *Petromec Inc v Petroleo Brasileiro SA Petrobras (No 3)* [2005] EWCA Civ 891; [2006] 1 Lloyd's Rep 121; see John Cartwright, 'Negotiation and Renegotiation: An English Perspective' in John Cartwright, Stefan Vogenauer and Simon Whittaker (eds), *Reforming the French Law of Obligations* (Oxford, Hart Publishing, 2009); Henry Hoskins, 'Contractual Obligations to Negotiate in Good Faith: Faithfulness to the Agreed Contract Purpose' (2014) 130 *Law Quarterly Review* 131.

[9] See pp 203–07; 208–20 respectively below.

[10] On these see Simon Whittaker, 'Termination Clauses' in Andrew Burrows and Edwin Peel (eds), *Contract Terms* (Oxford University Press, 2007) ch 13.

As regards the latter (with which I will be concerned here) the termination clause (or the contract more generally) often sets the consequences for the parties of the exercise of the power of termination as well as defining the circumstances in which this power exists. In this respect, the effect of termination may be retrospective (so as to deem the contract never to have been made and its obligations never to have existed, often providing also for secondary consequences such as the return or retention of deposits or the payment of 'penalties'); or the effect may be prospective (affecting only future obligations while leaving untouched obligations already accrued and/or performed, again often providing for secondary consequences of the decision to cancel such as the payment of a charge or penalty). Even though in contracts whose obligations arise and/or are performed over a period of time, and which do not specify expressly how long they are to remain in force, the courts have implied a right of termination in one or more party on reasonable grounds,[11] many contracts whose performance is to take place over a period of time (whether of definite or indefinite duration) include express provision for their prospective termination by one or other party, again usually at a cost for the party so acting.[12]

As I have said, the main purpose of many of these contract terms (exemption clauses, *force majeure* clauses, variation and termination clauses) is to qualify the practical force of what the parties have agreed; on the other hand, *ex hypothesi*, as terms of the contract, they form, or are taken by the law to form, part of the agreement of the parties. Paradoxically, therefore, the enforcement of these contract terms both gives effect to the agreement of the parties and qualifies its practical effect. At a theoretical level, this paradox can be resolved by refining the notion of the parties' agreement so as to include all the terms (including these incidental qualifying terms) as defining the ambit of the parties' obligations,[13] but this has not been the way of thinking informing the legislative control of unfair terms, whether under the Unfair Contract Terms Act (UCTA) 1977[14] or the Unfair Terms in Consumer Contracts Directive 1993 (the '1993 Directive'),[15] implemented very faithfully in UK law by the Unfair Terms in Consumer Contracts Regulations (UTCCR) 1999.[16] So, in the case of contractual liabilities in general,[17] following closely the recommendation of the Law Commissions, section 3 of UCTA 1977 subjects clauses

[11] H Beale (ed), *Chitty on Contracts,* 31st edn (London, Sweet & Maxwell, 2012) vol I, para 13-029.

[12] Where a contract term imposes such a monetary payment, it will not be seen as a penalty for the purposes of the rule at common law rendering penalty clauses invalid, as the duty to pay does not arise on breach of contract: *Export Credits Guarantee Department v Universal Oil Products Co* [1983] 1 WLR 399; Beale, *Chitty on Contracts*, n 11 above, paras 26-183–26-184.

[13] Brian Coote, *Exception Clauses* (London, Sweet & Maxwell,1964) ch 1.

[14] As Coote realised (Brian Coote 'Unfair Contract Terms Act 1977' (1978) 41 *Modern Law Review* 312), the Act being drafted on (for him) the false premise that 'exemption clauses do not affect the accrual of obligations but operate only as defences to accrued rights of action'.

[15] Council Directive 93/13/EEC of 5 April 1993 on unfair terms in consumer contracts [1993] OJ L95/21.

[16] Unfair Terms in Consumer Contracts Regulations 1999, SI 1999/2083. These Regulations revoked and replaced the Unfair Terms in Consumer Contracts Regulations 1994, SI 1994/3159. At the time of writing, these Regulations are likely to be revoked and the UK's implementation of the 1993 Directive replaced by the Consumer Rights Bill 2014 Part 2.

[17] The position as regards exclusion of liability for negligence (whether tortious or contractual) and for breach of the specified statutory implied terms differs, for here 'exemption clause' is defined more widely so as to extend to 'terms and notices which exclude or restrict the relevant obligation or duty': UCTA 1977, s 13(1), referring to ss 2 and 5–7 (thereby omitting the general treatment of the exclusion of contractual liability under s 3).

under which a trader claims 'to be entitled … to render a contractual performance substantially different from that which was reasonably expected of him' to the test of reasonableness to which it subjects exemption clauses proper.[18] And the UTCCR 1999 subject *all* contract terms in consumer contracts to a test of fairness, with the important exception of those which reflect their main subject matter and agreed contract price.[19]

The purpose of this chapter is to consider the incidence and legislative control of contract terms allowing the variation or termination (other than on the ground of breach) of consumer contracts. As will be seen, there is a close relationship between legislative and contractual rights of termination in consumers and contractual powers of variation in either consumers or in traders. So, some consumer contracts themselves provide that the consumer may vary the contract (or, typically, one or more aspect of the contract) and this advantage typically forms part of a wider, more expensive package within the range of contracts offered by the trader or available on the market more generally. Contracts may equally provide expressly that the consumer may terminate the contract either entirely or prospectively at will. Moreover, as regards many contracts concluded in particular ways and as regards some types of contract more generally, modern legislation has granted consumers rights of termination (called either withdrawal or cancellation) of their contract which they can exercise freely and without any need to provide justification or reason; where consumers possess such a right, they can simply terminate their contract and make another either with the same trader or with another trader rather than vary their original contract.[20] Whereas a power of variation in a party allows the party to keep the original bargain and change it, cancellation allows the party just to change it.

Conversely, while the law itself provides traders with a power to vary the terms of the contracts which they conclude with consumers only rarely,[21] many of the contracts which traders use to govern their contracts with consumers provide traders with the right to vary one or more aspect of the contract. Variation clauses of this type have long caused concern to law reformers and, since implementation of the 1993 Directive, have been subject to a very broad test of their fairness.[22] As we shall see, in assessing their fairness both the Directive itself and recent decisions of the European Court of Justice (CJEU) emphasise the relationship between a power of variation of the contract in the trader and a consequential right of cancellation in the consumer. In doing so, the CJEU has apparently nuanced its position as to the justification for the law's control of terms on the ground of their fairness.[23]

[18] UCTA 1977, s 3(2)(b)(i) and see below pp 210–11.

[19] UTCCR Regulations, reg 6(2), p 212 *et seq* below.

[20] See pp 204–06 below.

[21] An example may be found in the case of the power of landlords to vary the terms of certain residential tenancies, see pp 208–09 below.

[22] See p 210 *et seq* below.

[23] See p 213 *et seq* below.

VARIATION AND TERMINATION OF CONTRACTS BY CONSUMERS

At first sight, contract terms which allow consumers to vary the contract which they have made are hard to find. We certainly do not find—or at least we do not see in the law reports—contracts which empower the consumer to reduce the price in the light of changing market circumstances or to vary the standard terms on which they deal with traders! However, what we do find in the case of contracts for some types of goods or services is that the consumer may enjoy a power under the contract to vary the subject matter of what has been agreed.

A prominent example may be found in passenger travel by rail or air. In both contexts, carriers usually offer different types of tickets with different fares, and while these different types of ticket may relate to different 'classes' of travel (apparently with different levels of comfort or ancillary services), they often also attract different rules governing the possibility of changes to travel by the consumer. So, for example, in the case of travel by rail from London to Paris and other continental destinations by Eurostar, there are three classes of travel: two ('Standard' and 'Standard Premier') have two variants: 'non-flexible', which is 'non-exchangeable and non-refundable', and, at a higher price, 'semi-flexible', which is 'exchangeable and refundable on payment of a fee and the difference in price with the next available fare if required'; the third and most expensive class of travel ('Business Premier') is 'fully flexible' and therefore fully exchangeable or refundable before or up to two months after the date of departure.[24] Airlines often make similar distinctions between their classes of fare, with premium categories of ticket allowing the passenger to change the timing of their flights, their destination or even to obtain a full refund without cost.[25] In this way, consumers are able to choose between a cheaper fare which allows no variation in the subject matter of the contract (notably, when or where they are travelling) and more expensive fares which allow them a degree of choice to allow the alteration of their travel plans, either with or without payment of a further charge.

These examples also illustrate the relationship of a contractual right to vary the subject matter of the contract and a right to cancel the contract altogether and obtain a refund. For if a consumer has the possibility of cancelling their booking and obtaining a refund without charge (often expressed as 'without penalty'), then, if they wish to change their travel plans they can simply cancel their original 'booking' (in law, contract) and then immediately or at a later date conclude a second contract reflecting their changed travel requirements either with the original trader or with another trader. As earlier noted, from this perspective, a right to cancel or to terminate a contract in a consumer without the need to point to any justification is, from the point of view of the consumer, functionally very similar to a right to vary the subject matter of their contract. The main difference is that a new contract

24 See www.eurostar.com/uk-en/travel-information/service-information/eurostar-fares/fares-to-paris-brussels-lille-and-calais.

25 A clear example can be found in easyJet's distinction between two categories of fare: 'standard' fares (which do not allow date changes) and 'Flexi' fares (which do). In addition, for both categories of fare, a person contracting with the airline can vary certain other aspects of their booking (notably, transferring the flight into the name of a different passenger) on the payment of a separate fee: see www.easyjet.com/en/fees-and-charges.

may not be available except at a higher price than the earlier one, either because the market in question has changed or because, for example, the date of travel is closer and therefore the fare is for this reason higher.[26] But the possibility of variation or cancellation allows consumers to change their mind.

Moreover, as I also have noted, many consumer contracts attract short-lived legislative rights of cancellation in the consumer without the need to give any reason and without the possibility of exclusion by the terms of the contract, most of these rights resulting from implementation of EU Directives. So, in principle, consumer contracts concluded off the premises of the trader[27] or by 'distance contract' (that is, notably, by post, telephone, the Internet or email)[28] attract a right of cancellation in the consumer 'without giving any reason';[29] though this general position possesses a string of exceptions for particular types of consumer contract, notably, contracts for 'the creation of immovable property or rights in immovable property' or for the rental of residential accommodation[30] and (in the case of distance contracts) contracts for passenger transport services[31] and contracts for goods or services (other than the supply of water, gas, electricity or district heating) for which the price is dependent on fluctuations in the financial market which cannot be controlled by the trader and which may occur within the cancellation period, and contracts for the supply of perishable goods.[32] This right of cancellation normally lasts for 14 days after receipt of the goods or, in the case of service contracts from the date of the contract,[33] though this may be extended to sanction a failure in the trader to provide information.[34] On cancellation, the trader must reimburse to the consumer all payments other than sums representing the enhanced cost of delivery beyond the least expensive delivery offered by the trader.[35] The trader must not make any deductions from the sums to be restored to the consumer (notably, by way of an administrative charge), though in the case of contracts of sales of goods, he may deduct an amount to the extent to which the value of goods is diminished as a result of the consumer's

[26] *cf* p 206 below.

[27] Consumer Contracts (Information, Cancellation and Additional Charges) Regulations 2013, SI 2013/3134 ('2013 Regulations'), reg 5 (off-premises contract) and Pt 3. These Regulations implemented in UK law Council Directive 2011/83/EU of 25 October 2011 on consumer rights ('Consumer Rights Directive') [2011] OJ L304/64 and replaced earlier UK Regulations implementing earlier Directives, notably Council Directive 85/577/EEC of 20 December 1985 to protect the consumer in respect of contracts negotiated away from business premises [1985] OJ L372/31 and Council Directive 97/7/EC of 20 May 1997 on the protection of consumers in respect of distance contracts [1997] OJ L144/19.

[28] 2013 Regulations, reg 5 (distance contract) and Pt 3. In the case of contracts for the provision of financial services, similar rights of cancellation of *distance* contracts (but not off-premises contracts) are provided by the Distance Contracts (Financial Services) Regulations 2004, SI 2004/2095, implementing Council Directive 2002/65/EC of 23 September 2002 concerning the distance marketing of financial services [2002] OJ L271/16. Contracts for financial services are excluded from the scope of the Consumer Rights Directive: art 3(3)(d).

[29] 2013 Regulations, reg 29(1).

[30] ibid reg 6(1)(b), (c), (d).

[31] ibid reg 27.

[32] ibid regs 27(1)(c), 28(1)(a), (c).

[33] ibid reg 30.

[34] ibid reg 31.

[35] ibid reg 34(1), (2).

handling of them 'beyond what is necessary to establish the nature, characteristics and functioning of the goods'.[36]

Other EU legislation has provided for general rights of cancellation in the consumer (usually termed rights of withdrawal) in particular types of contract. This is true of most consumer credit agreements in respect of an amount under £60,260[37] and contracts for timeshare and similar contracts, such as contracts for membership of 'holiday clubs'.[38] By contrast, in the case of contracts for package travel, package holidays or package tours (whose regulation goes back to a Directive of 1990), the consumer holiday-maker's right of cancellation is restricted to the situation where the trader (the holiday 'organiser') has exercised its express contractual power of variation.[39] So, the Directive provides that the trader's power to revise the price must be based on an express term which 'states precisely how the revised price is to be calculated' and it then restricts effective variations under such an express term to those based on changes in transportation costs, dues, taxes or fees chargeable or relevant exchange rates.[40] Where the holiday organiser 'finds that before the departure he is constrained to alter significantly any of the essential terms, such as the price, he shall notify the consumer as quickly as possible' and the consumer may choose either to accept these changes or 'withdraw from the contract without penalty'.[41] As will be seen, an effective variation of the price in these contracts must be based on a term which explains the basis of any variation and restricts the grounds on which variations may be made and, even here, allows the consumer to cancel if the power is exercised.

The justifications for these various legislative rights of cancellation in consumers differ according to context:[42] so, for example, in timeshare contracts, the right is provided so as to give the consumer the 'opportunity of fully understanding their rights and obligations under the contract'[43] given the high-pressure sales techniques associated with the conclusion of many timeshare contracts; in distance contracts, on the ground that 'the consumer is not able to see the goods before concluding the

[36] ibid regs 34(1), 9 and 10.

[37] Consumer Credit Act 1974, s 66A implementing and to some extent extending the Council Directive 2008/48/EC of 23 April 2008 on credit agreements for consumers [2008] OJ L133/66, art 14 (right of withdrawal). Consumer Credit Act 1974, ss 67 and 68 further provide that agreements not subject to this 'right of withdrawal' may by cancelled by the debtor in certain circumstances. These rights are in addition to a right of early discharge (either wholly or in part) by the consumer of its obligations under a regulated consumer credit agreement (known as early repayment or early settlement): Directive 2008/48/EC, art 16; Consumer Credit Act 1974, s 94 (as amended).

[38] Timeshare, Holiday Products, Resale and Exchange Contracts Regulations 2010, SI 2010/2960 (as amended) implementing Council Directive 2008/122/EC of 14 January 2009 on the protection of consumers in respect of certain aspects of timeshare, long-term holiday product, resale and exchange contracts [2009] OJ L33/30 ('Timeshare Directive').

[39] Council Directive 90/314/EEC of 13 June 1990 on package travel, package holidays and package tours [1990] OJ L158/59 implemented in UK law by the Package Travel, Package Holidays and Package Tours Regulations 1992, SI 1992/3288 ('1992 Regulations').

[40] Directive 90/314/EEC, art 4(4)(a); 1992 Regulations, reg 11. No changes to the price shall be made during the 20 days prior to the departure date: Directive 90/314/EEC, art 4(4)(b) and 1992 Regulations, reg 11(3), respectively.

[41] Directive 90/314/EEC, art 4(5); 1992 Regulations, reg 12.

[42] Directive 2008/48/EC, recital 34 merely stating that its procedure should be harmonious with the right of withdrawal under Directive 2002/65/EC.

[43] Timeshare Directive, recital 11.

contract';[44] and in off-premises contracts 'because of the potential surprise element and/or psychological pressure'.[45] Whatever the justification, where a consumer has a legal (and mandatory) right of cancellation, while it lasts he or she does not need a right of variation of the contract, but can simply cancel his or her original contract and conclude a new one to suit his or her changed requirements.

I have noted earlier that some contractual packages (typically at an enhanced price) allow consumers to vary or cancel their contract,[46] but I should also note that some major retailers of goods have long adopted a policy of allowing their customers to return unwanted goods and obtain a refund outside or apart from the conditions of any legislative rights of cancellation. This is famously true of Marks and Spencer and John Lewis, both of which allow their customers to return most types of goods purchased either by distance contract (on-line or by telephone) or in person at their stores well beyond the periods required by the relevant legislation.[47] These possibilities for consumers to change their mind are granted to them at no extra cost; from the retailers point of view, such a 'returns policy' is clearly used as a way of positioning themselves in the market (returns policy forming part of wider 'customer service') and as a way of encouraging customers to feel more free to purchase goods on the basis that they can always return them if they have second thoughts; consumers who do not feel that they are committed to their purchases are more likely to buy more goods, only some of which they will later return: here, then, *not* binding the consumer may have commercial advantages to a trader.

However, quite apart from these rights or possibilities of cancellation in consumers, contractual practice has generated other possibilities of variation by consumers of the goods or services for which they contract, but they are not expressed in terms of the variation of the subject matter of the contract or the performance of the contract by either party; instead, the contract is structured so as to allow the consumer to draw down from the trader the goods or services which they require and to pay for them accordingly. So, for example, contracts for the domestic supply of gas or electricity are concluded on the basis that the consumer pays only for what he or she consumes, without having any minimum or maximum number of units which they undertake to consume (and therefore to pay for), although there may be other, additional charges.[48] Here, after conclusion of the contract (which sets the general terms and conditions of supply and which will set the price of supply per unit),[49] the consumer remains able to choose how much they consume and, therefore, how much they will have to pay. In this way, the consumer retains control over two central aspects of 'performance' of the contract, without the need to vary the contract itself.

The bases on which mobile telephone services are available also illustrates that consumer choice regarding consumption and payment of services may be available without the need for variation of the contract under which they are supplied. While

[44] Consumer Rights Directive, recital 37.

[45] ibid recital 37.

[46] See pp 203–04 above.

[47] See www.johnlewis.com/customer-services/information-about-ordering-and-returning-products, and http://help.marksandspencer.com/support/returns-and-refunds/clothing-homeware.

[48] For a helpful guide see www.moneysupermarket.com/gas-and-electricity/bills/.

[49] The price per unit may be subject to variation either by the trader or by reference to a third party standard.

there are thousands of contractual packages available, there are broadly two main types: 'pay-as-you-go' and 'contract'. Under 'pay-as-you-go', the consumer uses his or her own telephone handset and buys credits ('top-ups') from a telecom provider and these credits are then drawn on to pay for calls or text-messaging. Here, the consumer pays only for what he or she uses and, having used up the credit purchased, can either buy more or can change or end the arrangement with the telecom provider. This gives the consumer considerable flexibility, but the cost of calls may be higher than under a 'contract', the consumer must provide his or her own handset and buying top-ups may be inconvenient.[50] By contrast, under a 'contract' the trader provides a handset either free or at a reduced cost with a number of inclusive minutes of call-time and text-messages each month. There is a wider choice of packages of this sort, but a standard feature is that the consumer is tied for a period (known as the 'minimum contract period' and typically between 18 and 24 months) during which he or she must continue to pay the monthly charge, this charge and the minimum contract period being related to the type of handset which the consumer chooses. If a consumer goes beyond the allowance of call or text-messages, the cost of any further use can be expensive (these are known as 'out of bundle costs').[51] So, under 'contracts' the benefits of flexibility of use for the consumer and the advantages of a better or more up-to-date telephone have to be balanced against the consumer being tied to a particular provider and/or package and the risk of higher out of bundle costs. Clearly, though, the extent of the consumer's likely use of the service is of crucial importance in deciding which package to choose. Under pay-as-you-go, as its name implies, a consumer can simply pay according to the service actually used as he or she chooses to use it; under a 'contract', the consumer pays for the *availability* of the service (up to a certain number of units) per month, whether or not he or she actually uses the service; here, therefore, consumers cannot vary their use of the service in a way which affects its cost. In this situation, the possibility of escaping the contract during the minimum contract period (and therefore being able to buy some other, more suitable or advantageous package) becomes more significant. This being the case, the period during which the consumer is tied to a contract without the possibility of termination plays a significant element in the decision-making of the well-informed consumer, who can take advantage of information provided on the terms of the various packages on price-comparison websites.[52] Certainly, though, the nature of the contractual package under which the consumer enjoys a mobile telephone service should be relevant to the fairness of contract terms which seek to constrain or penalise its early termination.[53]

[50] Ofcom, 'How to get the best mobile phone deal: time to switch, or stay put and haggle?', available at http://consumers.ofcom.org.uk/2010/05/how-to-get-the-best-mobile-phone-deal/.

[51] ibid.

[52] ibid, which recommends two such sites which it has accredited: BillMonitor (www.billmonitor.com) and Mobilife (www.mobilife.com), though there are many others. For an example of comparison of 'pay-as-you-go' deals, see http://compareuk.net/products/Card+Payg+Sim/.

[53] Ofcom review of additional charges; see 'Annex 1: Guidance on Unfair Terms in Contracts for Communications Services' (undated), paras A1.58–A1.62, available at http://stakeholders.ofcom.org.uk/binaries/telecoms/policy/addcharges.pdf.

VARIATION OF CONTRACTS BY TRADERS AND TERMINATION BY CONSUMERS

Contract terms which allow traders to vary aspects of their contracts with consumers have become a regular feature of contractual practice. Traders may reserve to themselves a power to change (and typically to increase) the price or other charges to be paid by the consumer, or to change the specifications of the goods or services to be supplied, the timing of their supply or the standard terms on which they are supplied. While not restricted to this context, contractual powers of variation of these types are particularly prevalent in contracts whose performance takes place over a longer period,[54] such as contracts for the provision of credit or other financial services.

The existence and exercise of unilateral powers in traders to vary their contracts with consumers has long caused concern, not least because they mirror and can reinforce the imbalance of power between the contracting parties already existing between traders and consumers: consumers need protection from the abuse of power by traders in the course of performance of contracts as well as their conclusion. How then has the law reacted to unilateral variation clauses? We can identify three possible techniques of control of the possible abuse of terms, only one of which is of major importance in English law.

The most stringent technique is for the law to provide that variation (or certain types of variation) of a contract by the trader can be effected only within powers provided by mandatory legal rules. A rare example of this in English law may be seen in relation to public sector residential tenancies under the Housing Act 1985.[55] This Act provides that the terms of a secure tenancy of a dwelling-house may be varied in a series of ways set out by the legislation 'and not otherwise'.[56] Apart from variation by agreement of the parties, the terms of such a tenancy may be varied 'to the extent that the variation relates to rent or to payments in respect of rates, council tax or services, by the landlord or the tenant in accordance with a provision in the lease or agreement creating the tenancy, or in an agreement varying it'.[57] Outside these two cases, variations can be made by the landlord by a notice of variation served on the tenant.[58] In *Rochdale BC v Dixon*, the local authority landlord sought to vary its secure tenancies, including with the defendant tenant, so as to include payment of annual water charges within the tenants' weekly payment of rent.[59] The Court of Appeal held that the proper procedure for variation of the terms of these tenancies by the landlord as required by the Act had been followed

[54] *cf* powers of variation of the price in the organisers of package holidays, discussed at p 205 above. In that situation the contract itself is not performed over a particularly long period, but there may be a considerable lapse of time between the conclusion of the contract (booking the holiday) and its performance (when the consumers go on holiday).

[55] The characterisation of a public sector tenancy as a consumer contract may appear strange but it has been accepted by the Court of Appeal for the purposes of UTCCR 1999: *London Borough of Newham v Khatun* [2004] EWCA Civ 55; [2005] QB 37 (contract of tenancy concluded by local authority pursuant to its duty to house homeless persons under Pt VII of the Housing Act 1996).

[56] Housing Act 1985, ss 102, 103.

[57] ibid s 102(1)(b).

[58] ibid s 103(1)(c).

[59] *Rochdale BC v Dixon* [2011] EWCA Civ 1173; [2012] HLR 6.

and, in particular, the notice of variation had substantially specified the effect of the proposed variation, that is, that non-payment of the water charge could lead to eviction of the tenant.[60] Here, therefore, the landlord's power to vary was contained in the legislation which set out the procedure required for its effective exercise. The Court of Appeal further held that where the landlord had exercised such a power of variation, the *resulting* term was not unfair within UTCCR 1999, on a number of grounds but not least because 'a term which is expressly authorised by a statutory power … is unlikely to be unfair'.[61]

A second possibility is for a court to imply into an express contractual power of variation some substantive qualification. For example, in *Paragon Finance plc v Nash*,[62] a mortgage lender possessed a power expressed in very general terms to vary the interest rates of a contract of consumer credit. Drawing on analogies from public law, the Court of Appeal held that this power was 'not completely unfettered'[63] and implied a term that 'it should not be exercised dishonestly, for an improper purpose, capriciously or arbitrarily'.[64] While the court was prepared to go as far as to imply a term that the interest rate would not be set in a way that 'no reasonable lender, acting reasonably, would do', this was not the same as saying that the lender could not impose unreasonable rates.[65] On the other hand, in *Paragon Finance plc v Pender*,[66] it was held that use of an implied term in this way should not mean

> that a lender may not, *for a genuine commercial reason*, adopt a policy of raising interest rates to levels at which its borrows generally, or a particular category of its borrowers, may be expected to consider refinancing their borrowings at more favourable rates of interest offered by other commercial lenders. Save as otherwise expressly agreed with its borrowers, a commercial lender is … free to conduct its business in what it genuinely believes to be its best commercial interest.[67]

While, therefore, English courts remain free to qualify the ambit of a contractual power of variation by construction or by implication in the context, there is little evidence that they have chosen to use this technique widely to control the exercise of contractual rights of variation. In my view, this reluctance is related to the absence of a general legal principle of good faith or general doctrine of abuse of rights in English law,[68] as this absence reflects a sense that contractual rights (including powers of variation of the contract) should not generally be constrained by reference to an external standard of behaviour imposed by the courts. Certainly, in other laws which contain a general doctrine of abuse of rights or principle of good faith

[60] *Paragon Finance plc v Pender* [2011] EWCA Civ 1173, paras 52–58.

[61] ibid para 68 (Rix LJ). *cf* Beale, *Chitty on Contracts*, n 11 above, para 15-047 on the question whether such a term is excluded from review as reflecting statutory provisions under UTCCR 1999, reg 4(2)(a).

[62] *Paragon Finance plc v Nash* [2001] EWCA Civ 1466; [2002] 1 WLR 685.

[63] ibid para 30 (Dyson LJ).

[64] ibid para 32.

[65] ibid para 40.

[66] *Pender* [2005] EWCA Civ 760; [2005] 1 WLR 3412.

[67] ibid para 120 (Jonathan Parker LJ) (original emphasis).

[68] On which see Beale, *Chitty on Contracts*, n 11 above, para 1-036 *et seq*.

governing contracts, control of the exercise of a contractual power is intimately linked to control of the fairness of the terms which grant that power.[69]

Thirdly, English contract law may subject the contract term which permits the trader to vary the contract to a test of reasonableness or fairness. Such a power can be seen first in the UCTA 1977 and has become particularly prominent in relation to consumer contracts under UTCCR 1999. Indeed, over the last few years, the proper approach to the assessment of the fairness of variation clauses has been subject to considerable discussion in the CJEU.

Variation Clauses as a Form of Exemption Clause

The controls imposed by UCTA 1977 are generally restricted to exemption clauses (which it defines broadly),[70] but they extend to other types of clause which were seen by the Law Commissions in the Report which led to the Act as sufficiently similar in function.[71] In this respect, the Law Commissions noted a term which seeks to allow a business to vary its *own* obligations, pointing to a case in which a shipowner had agreed with a travel agent to provide a cruise for a party of tourists on a particular vessel on a particular route, but later claimed to be entitled under the contract to change the vessel.[72] In the view of the Law Commissions, the potential for unfairness in such a case lies in the supplier of goods or services inducing their customers into thinking that they are getting a more valuable right than they are, and so the operation of the contract term could disappoint the customers' legitimate expectations, in a similar way to the case where a supplier makes promises in wide terms but then cuts them down in practice by means of exclusions of liability.[73] Section 3(2)(b) of UCTA 1977 reflects this way of thinking, providing that, as against a person 'dealing as consumer' or on the other's written standard terms of business, a trader[74] may not claim to be entitled:

(i) to render a contractual performance substantially different from that which was reasonably expected of him; or
(ii) in respect of the whole or any part of his contractual obligation, to render no performance at all, except in so far as … the contract term satisfies the requirement of reasonableness.[75]

[69] Simon Whittaker, 'Contractual Control and Contractual Review in England and France' (2005) 13 *European Review of Private Law* 757, which explains that in French law the expression used to describe unfair contract terms (*clauses abusives*) evokes the general doctrine of the abuse of rights, here, the abuse of the contracting party's freedom of contract.

[70] UCTA 1977, s 13.

[71] Law Com Report 1975, n 2 above, paras 143–46. UCTA 1977 also controls indemnity clauses and non-contractual notices: ss 2 and 4.

[72] *Anglo-Continental Holidays Ltd v Typaldos Lines (London) Ltd* [1967] 2 Lloyd's Rep 61, given by the Law Com Report 1975, n 2 above, para 146.

[73] Law Com Report 1975, n 2 above, paras 139, 143–46.

[74] Technically, the controls in s 3 apply only to 'business liability': UCTA 1977, s 1(3).

[75] ibid s 3(2)(b). If enacted, the Consumer Rights Bill 2014 would disapply the controls in s 3 UCTA as against persons 'dealing as consumer', following its general approach of protecting consumers under its own provisions, leaving UCTA for the control of other cases: see Consumer Rights Bill 2014 cl 75; sch 4 para 5.

For this purpose, the better view is that the court should assess the reasonable expectations as to contractual performance by the trader of the party seeking to avoid the effect of the variation without reference to the existence of the variation clause itself.[76] As Lord Bingham of Cornhill CJ (giving judgment for the Court of Appeal), expressed it, the question as to what contractual performance a person can reasonably expect 'cannot be answered by saying that the [relevant party] had no reasonable expectation of any contractual performance above or beyond what the contract on a proper construction provided that it should have', as such an interpretation would 'frustrate the purpose of the legislature, which is to relieve a party in the position of the [relevant party] from the effect of the unreasonable or unfair contractual provisions'.[77] So the Act requires courts to distinguish between the performance (normally, the actual provision of goods or services) which the party reasonably expected of the trader given what was agreed, on the one hand, and the strict position of the parties under all the terms of the contract as properly construed, on the other. The *application* of the test of reasonableness is then made contingent on there being a substantial difference between what the person so expected and the performance which the trader seeks to provide by way of application of the contract term, or on the trader seeking thereby to escape performance altogether 'in respect of the whole or any part of his contractual obligation'.[78]

As a result, a contract term which entitles a trader to vary its own obligations or performance to a consumer may be subject to assessment on the ground of its reasonableness; on the other hand, a contract term which entitles a trader to vary the obligations of the *consumer* would not.

Before leaving UCTA 1977, it is interesting to recall the rationale for the restriction of these controls on unfair terms excluding, restricting or affecting (in the way just described) contractual liability in general. This power was restricted to situations where a trader seeks to rely on a contract term as against a person 'dealing as consumer' or another person dealing on that person's 'written standard terms of business'.[79] Here, the Law Commissions' discussion in relation to their various recommendations makes clear that as regards consumer contracts, control of contract terms is justified because consumers may not understand their implications and, even if they do, they may not have sufficient bargaining strength to prevent their inclusion in the contract.[80] In their view, in many cases business parties are in a similar position to a consumer, as in the case of a small shopkeeper contracting to advertise his goods in a magazine: subjecting exclusion clauses and related clauses to a test of reasonableness does not represent 'too high a degree of interference with freedom of contract', where 'one party requires the other to accept terms which the former has decided upon in advance as being generally advantageous to him, and the customer must either accept those terms or not enter the contract, ie a standard

[76] *Zockoll Group Ltd v Mercury Communications Ltd (No 2)* [1999] EMLR 385, 395–96; Beale, *Chitty on Contracts*, n 11 above, para 14-073.

[77] ibid para 395.

[78] UCTA 1977, s 3(2)(b)(ii).

[79] ibid s 3(1).

[80] Law Com Report 1975, n 2 above, para 147.

form contract'.[81] While the lack of negotiation of standard terms is 'the essential element' justifying intervention, this should not be set as the distinguishing feature under the Act, as there may be negotiation of some terms, but not others.[82]

Variation Clauses in Consumer Contracts More Generally

Under the 1993 Directive and, in the United Kingdom, UTCCR 1999, in principle all consumer contract terms which have not been subject to 'individual negotiation' may be reviewed on the ground of their fairness.[83] There are just two exceptions: terms which reflect 'mandatory statutory or regulatory provisions'[84] and what are often known as core terms, that is, 'terms which describe the main subject matter of the contract' or which set the price at which the consumer contracts, subject to a proviso that these terms are in plain, intelligible language.[85] The test of unfairness in the 1993 Directive is a composite test, with a basic test that a term 'contrary to the requirement of good faith' 'causes a significant imbalance in the parties' rights and obligations under the contract, to the detriment of the consumer' being supplemented by a range of considerations which a court is directed to take into account for this purpose (including the nature of the contract and all the circumstances in which it was concluded) and an 'indicative list' in its Annex of terms which *may* be unfair.[86]

In principle, therefore, contract terms under which a trader purports to reserve to itself a power to vary either its own obligations or the obligations of the consumer or, indeed, any other aspect of their contractual relationship (for example, by amendment of the standard terms and conditions to include an arbitration clause) are subject to control. This is confirmed by the presence in the 'indicative list' (which by its nature contains examples of terms which fall under the test of fairness) of several examples of variation clauses: terms which allow the business to vary the terms of the contract 'unilaterally without a valid reason which is specified in the contract'; to vary 'unilaterally without a valid reason any characteristics of the product or service to be provided'; or to vary the price (either by providing for it to be determined on delivery or to be increased) 'without ... giving the consumer the corresponding right to cancel the contract if the final price is too high in relation to the price agreed when the contract was concluded'.[87] Given the merely indicative nature of the list and the fact that the 1993 Directive requires only minimum harmonisation, it is perhaps surprising to see the second part of the Annex appearing to rescue some of these terms from the charge of unfairness in particular contexts or circumstances.

[81] ibid para 148.
[82] ibid para 156.
[83] For these propositions see Beale, *Chitty on Contracts*, n 11 above, paras 15-016–15-038, 15-040.
[84] 1993 Directive, art 1(2); 1999 Regulations, reg 4(2).
[85] 1993 Directive, art 4(2); 1999 Regulations, reg 6(2). This description of the position is controversial, there being, in particular, differences of view as to whether art 4(2) of the Directive excludes 'core terms' or 'core issues' from the assessment of fairness: my reasons for the position as stated in the text are set out in Beale, *Chitty on Contracts*, n 11 above, paras 15-047–15-070.
[86] 1993 Directive, arts 3(1), (3), 4(1), Annex; 1999 Regulations, regs 5(1), 5(5), 6(1) and Sch 2.
[87] 1993 Directive, Annex, para 1(j), (k), (l), respectively.

So, for example, the inclusion in the list of a term under which the business can vary the terms of the contract 'is without hindrance' to terms

> under which a supplier of financial services reserves the right to alter the rate of interest payable by the consumer or due to the latter, or the amount of other charges for financial services without notice where there is a valid reason, provided that the supplier is required to inform the other contracting party or parties thereof at the earliest opportunity and that the latter are free to dissolve the contract immediately.[88]

The inclusion of such a variation clause is also 'without hindrance' to terms

> under which a seller or supplier reserves the right to alter unilaterally the conditions of a contract of indeterminate duration, provided that he is required to inform the consumer with reasonable notice and the consumer is free to dissolve the contract.[89]

Here, therefore, the Directive indirectly explains the particular elements which it sees as likely to be relevant to the fairness of variation clauses.

In *Invitel*[90] and *RWE Vertrieb AG*,[91] the CJEU has recently given considerable guidance on the way in which national courts should understand and apply the test of fairness in the Directive to variation clauses contained in longer-term contracts.[92]

In *Invitel*, a term in a contract for the supply of land-line telephone services provided for payment of invoices by the consumer by 'money order', without specifying how these fees would be calculated, with the result, according to the CJEU, that 'the consumer pay[s] fees which had not initially been agreed between the parties'.[93] The Court referred to various examples of terms in the Directive's Annex earlier noted,[94] these examples providing 'an essential element on which the competent court may basis its assessment of the unfair nature of that term'.[95] According to the Court, in the case of a price variation clause

> the possibility for the consumer to foresee, on the basis of clear, intelligible criteria, the amendments, by a seller or supplier, of the [general business conditions] with regard to the fees connected to the service to be provided is of fundamental importance.[96]

It was therefore relevant to the fairness of a term whether it provided reasons for any variation of the fees; whether it explained the method of their calculation; and whether it provided the consumer with the right to terminate the contract on

[88] 1993 Directive, Annex, para 1(j), qualified by para 2(b) first sentence.

[89] 1993 Directive, Annex, para 1(j), qualified in para 2(b) second sentence.

[90] C-472/10 *Nemzeti Fogyasztóvédelmi Hatóság v Invitel Távközlési Zrt*, 26 April 2012.

[91] C-92/11 *RWE Vertrieb AG v Verbraucherzentrale Nordrhein-Westfalen e.V*, 21 March 2013 (CJEU).

[92] In giving this guidance the CJEU was careful to maintain its formal position that while it may itself interpret the criteria of fairness under the 1993 Directive and provide guidance on its application, its application remains for national courts in the factual and legal context before them: 237/02 *Freiburger Kommunalbauten GmbH Baugesellschaft & Co KG v Hofstetter* [2004] ECR I-3403, paras 21–22; *Invitel*, n 90 above, para 22; *RWE Vertrieb AG*, n 91 above, para 66. See similarly 26/13 *Kásler v OTP Jelzálogbank Zrt* of 30 April 2014 (which concerned a contract term under which the amount payable by the consumer under a contract of loan varied according to changes in international currency exchange rates).

[93] *Invitel*, n 90 above, para 17.

[94] 1993 Directive, Annex, para 1(j), (l), p 212 above.

[95] *Invitel*, n 90 above, para 26.

[96] ibid para 28.

variation of the fee by the business.[97] More generally, the actual opportunity of the consumer to examine the terms and their consequences and the plainness and intelligibility of terms were also relevant.[98]

The CJEU took a similar approach in *RWE Vertrieb AG* to a standard term in a consumer gas supply contract which allowed the supplier unilaterally to vary the price without indicating the grounds, conditions or scope of such a variation.[99] The Court emphasised the importance in assessing the fairness of this term of the information provided to the consumer before the contract was made, for '[i]t is on the basis of that information in particular that he decides whether he wishes to be bound by the terms previously drawn up by the seller or supplier'.[100] It considered that, while the Annex to the Directive acknowledges that in contracts of indeterminate length the supplier has a legitimate interest in being able to alter the charge for the service,[101] any lack of information for the consumer before contract 'cannot, in principle, be compensated for by the mere fact that consumers will, during the performance of the contract, be informed in good time of a variation of the charges and of their right to terminate the contract if they do not wish to accept the variation'.[102] In this way, the strict requirements as to the provision of information for consumers and the acceptance of the possibility of a right in the seller unilaterally to vary the terms of the contract 'correspond to a balancing of the interests of the two parties'.[103] But pre-contractual information to the consumer is not enough: the contract should provide the consumer with a right to terminate the contract if the charges are in fact altered[104] and it is 'of fundamental importance … that the right of termination given to the consumer is not purely formal but can actually be exercised' and, for this purpose, various circumstances should be taken into account, including whether or not the market concerned is competitive.[105] A real ability to switch suppliers may therefore contribute to the fairness of a term under which a consumer's present supplier can vary its charges.

So, in the context of variation clauses (in these cases varying the consumer's payment obligations), there are two particular elements to be taken into account in the assessment of their fairness: first, the consumer must be able to appreciate not merely the possibility of variation by the trader, but also the reasons for which and the method by which any changes can be made. This follows the general concern of EU consumer contract law with the informed nature of consumer decision-making as reflected, in particular, in its imposition of many pre-contractual information requirements,[106] but its practical effect will be to encourage traders to specify these grounds and methods in their own variation clauses so as to give support to their

[97] ibid para 26.
[98] ibid para 27.
[99] *RWE Vertrieb AG*, n 91 above.
[100] ibid para 44.
[101] ibid para 40, referring to 1993 Directive, Annex, paras 1(j), 2(b), and also to Council Directive 98/30/EC of 26 June 2003 concerning common rules for the internal market in natural gas, art 3(3), Annex A, paras (a), (b) [2003] OJ L204/12.
[102] *RWE Vertrieb AG*, n 91 above, para 51.
[103] ibid para 53.
[104] ibid paras 48–49.
[105] ibid para 43.
[106] Eg the wide duties of information contained in Consumer Rights Directive, arts 5–8.

effectiveness. This in turn will provide consumers with a further ground of challenge: not to the fairness of the variation clause, but rather to the exercise of the power which it provides. For if a variation clause sets out the grounds and methods by which a variation can be made, a consumer may be able to argue that either these grounds were not present or these methods were not followed in relation to his or her own contract. Secondly, a contract which provides for a power of variation in a trader should also provide for a right of termination in the consumer on the exercise of that power so as to allow the latter, in effect, to choose whether or not to keep the contract as varied by the trader, for in the absence of such a right of termination the variation clause may itself be unfair and so the variation ineffective. Most interestingly, in *RWE Vertrieb AG*, the CJEU considered that the presence of a mere formal right of termination may not be enough if market circumstances rendered its exercise impractical.[107]

While not concerned with variation clauses, this discussion would not be complete without mentioning the decision of the CJEU in *Aziz*, which explained the application of the test of unfairness in relation to three terms in a contract of loan secured by a mortgage of residential property to be repaid over 33 years and, in doing so, also explained its legal rationale.[108] Following earlier pronouncements, the Court declared that the system of protection introduced by the Directive is 'based on the idea that the consumer is in a weaker position vis-à-vis the seller or supplier, as regards both his bargaining power and his level of knowledge'; according to the Court, the Directive's provision that unfair terms are not binding on the consumer 'aims to replace the formal balance which the contract establishes between the rights and obligations of the parties with an effective balance which re-establishes equality between them'.[109] Accordingly, the national court's assessment whether a term causes a 'significant imbalance' in the parties' rights and obligations arising under the contract should start by considering what rules of national law would apply in its absence and comparing the consumer's position with and without the term.[110] However, the Court continued:

> With regard to the question of the circumstances in which such an imbalance arises 'contrary to the requirement of good faith', having regard to the sixteenth recital in the preamble to the directive ..., the national court must assess for those purposes whether the seller or supplier, dealing fairly and equitably with the consumer, could reasonably assume that the consumer would have agreed to such a term in individual contract negotiations.[111]

[107] See p 214 above.

[108] C-415 *Aziz v Caixa d'Estalvis de Catalunya, Tarragona i Manresa*, 14 March 2013 (CJEU). The terms were: an acceleration clause (under which the lender was entitled to call in the totality of a long-term loan where the consumer borrower failed to pay an instalment or interest on time); a term fixing the level of default interest at 18.75% (treated by the court as falling within the example in the 'indicative list' in para 1(e) of a term setting a consumer's obligation to pay compensation for non-performance at a 'disproportionately high sum'; and a term under which the lender under a long-term contract of loan secured by a mortgage of residential premises was able unilaterally to determine the amount of debt unpaid.

[109] *Aziz*, n 108 above, paras 44–45, referring to C-618/10 *Banco Español de Crédito, SA v Calderón Camino*, 14 June 2012 (CJEU) paras 39–40.

[110] *Aziz*, n 108 above, para 68.

[111] ibid para 69.

The CJEU therefore requires national courts to make a hypothetical judgement as to what the *business could reasonably assume* as to the agreement of the consumer. This approach links the assessment of the fairness of contract terms with the condition for its application that the term in question was *not* individually negotiated[112] and which sees the court's control as a substitute for the consumer's own decision-making. At first sight the idea of a judicial substitution of the consumer's decision-making (if open to the charge of fiction) looks harmless, but the particular formulation used by the Court could lead to national decision-making too restrictive of the consumer's protection. For national courts are not invited to consider whether the consumer would have agreed to the term in question in individual negotiations, but rather whether the business 'dealing fairly and equitably with the consumer, could reasonably assume' that he would have done so. While the fairness of a term should not turn on what a consumer (or consumers generally) would actually agree (as their decision-making may well be unreasonable, irrational or 'ignorant'), nor should it turn on the business's reasonable assumption of what an ('average'?) consumer may or may not agree. The practical danger of the Court's approach here may be seen in the opinion of Advocate General Kokott on which the Court relied, as she suggested that a court should consider for this purpose whether a term is common or surprising, whether it has an 'objective reason' and 'whether, despite the shift in the contractual balance in favour of the user of the term in relation to the substance of the term in question, the consumer is not left without protection'.[113] While the last of these is fully justified, the relevance of the customary nature of a contract term or the fact that the business has a good ('objective') reason for it could encourage a national court to hold that, despite a significant imbalance in the rights and obligations of the parties to the detriment of the consumer, the term is fair as it was customary and/or entirely justified from the business's point of view. It is not surprising that, understood in this way, Advocate General Kokott considered that the test of fairness allows 'the principle of contractual freedom [to be] observed', it being 'recognised that in many cases parties have a legitimate interest in organising their contractual relations in a manner which derogates from the statutory provisions'.[114]

Of more general significance are the CJEU's observations which reveal its understanding of the rationale for subjecting terms in consumer contracts to a test of fairness. The Court's continuing reference to the 1993 Directive's protection of consumers as 'weaker parties' strongly suggests that it lies in the risk of abuse by businesses of their stronger contractual power and of the substantive unfairness which may result from it. But if this is true and businesses may impose unfair terms on consumers whether or not these terms are 'individually negotiated', then the ambit of the Directive's controls are too restrictive.[115] On the other hand, the Court's continuing emphasis on the quality of information to the consumer about

[112] 1993 Directive, art 3, esp art 3(2).

[113] *Aziz*, n 108 above, Advocate General Kokott's Opinion, para 75.

[114] ibid para 73.

[115] This sort of argument has convinced some Member States to implement the Directive in a way which extends its controls to the terms of consumer contracts, whether or not they are individually negotiated: see, eg French law: Code de la consommation, art L132-1 al 4; Gilles Paisant, 'Les clauses abusives et la présentation des contrats dans la loi no 95-96 du 1er février 1995' *Recueil Dalloz Sirey* 1995 *Chronique* 99, paras 19, 20. See similarly Consumer Rights Bill 2014 cl 62.

contract terms (even those not subject to negotiation) does not fit readily with this rationale, for if a term is imposed on a consumer by way of exercise of the business's superior market power, why should it matter whether the consumer was in a position to understand its significance? To adapt the classic language of the traditional private lawyer, the consumer's consent is undermined not by mistake or ignorance, but by (market) duress.

Despite my criticisms of its particular formulation, perhaps most interesting, though, is the possible connection made in *Aziz*[116] between the requirement of good faith and the restriction of the test of fairness to terms which are not individually negotiated,[117] with the result that a national court should consider whether the business 'dealing fairly and equitably with the consumer, could reasonably assume that the consumer would have agreed to such a term in individual contract negotiations'.[118] This observation may be highly significant at a theoretical level. At one level, it merely invites a court to make a somewhat Rawlsian hypothetical assessment of how parties in the position of the actual contracting parties would have agreed, a nice formula to help a court to assess what would have been fair in order to compare it with the term as concluded. On the other hand, its introduction of hypothetical individual negotiation to the assessment of fairness may be thought to suggest that it is this lack of negotiation which is the fundamental problem which the Directive is concerned to address. As we have seen, a party's inability to negotiate in relation to another's standard terms may be thought merely to reflect a difference in bargaining power, a very traditional basis for intervention in consumer contracts and, indeed, a potential justification for imposing some controls on unfair terms in commercial contracts in some circumstances.[119] However, it could be thought instead to give a degree of support to the argument that the proper justification for the judicial control of contract terms which have not been individually negotiated lies in the fact that parties to contracts acting rationally in relation to another business's standard contract terms avoid the disproportionate costs of obtaining the necessary information and negotiating contracts on more favourable terms, given that these costs are out of proportion to the advantages to be gained.[120] This rationale for judicial review of the fairness of contract terms justifies its extension to *all* contracts, commercial, consumer and even between two persons acting outside the course of any business, and has found particular favour with many German lawyers whose courts have long taken on such a role in the control of standard contract terms.[121] And while the 1993 Directive is necessarily restricted to the review of unfair terms in consumer contracts, the question whether it is right for the law to

[116] See p n 108 above.

[117] See pp 215–16 above.

[118] *Aziz*, n 108 above, para 69 (quoted above).

[119] See, notably, Law Commission and Scottish Law Commission, *Unfair Terms in Contracts* (Law Com No 292, Scot Law Com No 199, 2005) Pt 5.

[120] Hein Kötz and Axel Flessner, *European Contract Law*, vol I, *Formation, Validity, and Contract of Contracts: Contracts for Third Parties* (Tony Weir (trans), Oxford University Press, 1997) 139, 144.

[121] Reinhard Zimmermann, *The New German Law of Obligations: Historical and Comparative Perspectives* (Oxford University Press, 2005) 176. See also Michael Schillig, 'Directive 93/13 and the "Price Term Exemption": A Comparative Analysis in the Light of the "Market for Lemons" Rationale' (2011) 60 *International and Comparative Law Quarterly* 933.

empower courts to review terms that are not individually negotiated in *commercial* contracts forms a central point of controversy in relation to the proposed Common European Sales Law, whose controls on unfair terms apply to contracts between two business parties, as long as one of them is a small or medium-sized business and subject to a condition that the terms are not 'individually negotiated'.[122]

Variation Clauses, Restrictions on Termination and the 'Core Term' Exclusion

Most variation clauses in consumer contracts will clearly fall under the test of fairness required by the 1993 Directive, as the examples set out in its indicative list of terms which may be unfair make clear.[123] However, some variation clauses may come within the exception made by the Directive for 'core terms'[124] and so, as long as they are plain and intelligible, outside the test of fairness.

This can best be illustrated from contractual practice in relation to loans by building societies or banks taken out to finance the purchase of residential property secured by mortgage, for in this context the presence of a power of variation in a trader may form a significant part of the consumer's decision to conclude the contract. There are here, of course, a wide range of contractual packages available, but broad distinctions can be made between contracts where the interest is variable either following a third party rate ('tracker rate', the Bank of England's base rate often being used) or in the discretion of the lender ('standard variable rate') and contracts where the interest payable is fixed for a particular period (at the end of which the lender will move the borrower to another rate, typically the lender's own standard variable rate); a further distinction can be made between 'interest-only mortgages' (where the borrower pays interest for the loan but does not repay the principal) and 'repayment mortgages' (where the borrower repays the principal by instalments as well as interest accruing). In all these cases, the loan contract may contain provisions allowing the borrower to terminate the contract by paying what is owed (a power which allows the borrower to refinance the loan on a different basis and, if need be, with a different lender), but in the case of fixed-rate interest loans (but not standard variable rate loans) the exercise of such a power will typically attract a financial penalty (called an 'early repayment charge').[125] We can see in practice here a similar relationship between the inclusion or exclusion of a power of variation in a trader (the lender) and the possibility of a consumer (the borrower) escaping the contract and concluding a different contract on more advantageous terms, as we saw in the case-law of the CJEU in *Invitel* and *RWE Vertrieb AG*.[126] Whether it is to the actual advantage of a borrower to take a mortgage loan at a fixed rate or at one or other variable rate depends both on the situation

[122] European Commission, Proposal for a Regulation of the European Parliament and of the Council on a Common European Sales Law, COM(2011)635 final, Annex I, ch 8, esp art 86.

[123] See pp 212–13 above.

[124] 1993 Directive, art 4(2); 1999 Regulations, reg 6(2).

[125] See www.moneyadviceservice.org.uk/en/articles/mortgage-interest-rate-options. The Money Advice Service is an independent advisory service, set up by the UK government.

[126] See pp 213–15 above.

of the individual borrower (and, in particular, on the security of their own income intended to cover the interest payments) and on the state of interest rates more generally: where interest rates generally are likely to increase, a mortgage loan at an interest fixed for a period is more attractive, but such a loan is less attractive if interest rates are likely to decrease.

In the case of a contract of loan of this type, it could be argued that the term which allowed the lender to vary the interest in a loan at a 'standard variable rate' could fall within the exception for 'core terms' found in article 4(2) of the 1993 Directive (subject to its being plain and intelligible') on the ground that this term gave expression to the main subject matter of the contract, even from the perspective of the average consumer.[127] Conversely, in a contract of loan at a fixed rate over a definite period, a term which allows the consumer borrower to escape the contract only on payment of a (considerable) early repayment charge could also be seen as falling within this exception.[128] In both these cases, the terms governing (respectively) variation or cancellation describe (if but in part) the main subject matter of the contract and, at least in this particular market context, this may be appreciated by the 'average consumer'. On the other hand, instead of applying the exclusion found in article 4(2), a court could prefer to take into consideration in its assessment of the fairness of such a variation or termination clause its central element in the nature of the contract. In doing so, it could also take into account the sort of considerations outlined by the CJEU in *Invitel* and *RWE Vertrieb AG*, so that, notably, a term allowing a lender to vary the interest rate entirely in its own discretion without providing the grounds on which or methods by which it could do so could be held unfair, an approach which has, indeed, been taken recently by the UK public regulator responsible for the financial services industry.[129] In my view, such an approach can be reconciled with the exclusion in article 4(2) of the Directive by holding that a variation clause which does not specify the grounds of or methods

[127] On the significance of the average consumer for this purpose, see Beale, *Chitty on Contracts*, n 11 above, paras 15-033, 15-064.

[128] *cf Office of Fair Trading v Ashbourne Management Services Ltd* [2011] EWHC 1237 (Ch); [2011] ECC 31, where Kitchin J held that terms which set a minimum duration of one year for membership of a gym with either no or only a very limited possibility of cancellation without liability did concern the main subject matter of the agreements in question: [2011] EWHC 1237 (Ch), para 152. As a result, even though the terms in question were, in Kitchin J's view, in plain intelligible language (ibid paras 154–161) his view that the exclusion in reg 6(2)(a) of the 1999 Regulations excluded a category of issues rather than a category of terms allowed him to assess their fairness, holding them unfair on the ground that they locked consumers into the minimum period when they have overestimated the use they will make of their memberships and failed to appreciate that unforeseen circumstances may make their continued use of a gym impractical or their memberships unaffordable. As I have argued elsewhere, a better view of these facts would have been to hold that the failure of the gym owners sufficiently to bring to the attention of consumers the practical consequences of the minimum period of membership rendered the terms in question not 'plain and intelligible'. This would have meant that the terms would not have satisfied the proviso to reg 6(2) and would as a result have been assessable for their fairness without any exclusion of their main subject matter or price/quality ratio: Beale, *Chitty on Contracts*, n 11 above, para 15-067. See also the interpretation of the 'main subject matter of the contract' in art 4(2) of the 1993 Directive in 26/13 *Kásler v OTP Jelzálogbank Zrt* of 30 April 2014 at paras 49–50 where the CJEU distinguished between terms 'that lay down the essential obligations of the contract and, as such, characterise it' and 'terms ancillary to those that define the very essence of the contractual relationship'.

[129] Financial Conduct Authority: see, eg, *Notice of Undertaking made by Cheshire Mortgage Corporation Limited* (5 March 2012), available at www.fca.org.uk/static/pubs/other/cmc-undertaking.pdf.

by which a variation is to be made is not 'plain and intelligible' and therefore falls within the proviso to the exclusion in article 4(2): so even if such a term were held to describe the main subject matter of the contract, it would still fall to be reviewed on the ground of its fairness.

CONCLUDING OBSERVATIONS

By way of conclusion, I would wish to draw attention to three features of this discussion.

First, the possibility of variation of consumer contracts may be structured by the contract in a number of ways. Some contracts start by setting out the rights and obligations of the contracting parties and then include a contract term (a variation clause) which allows one or other of them to vary either their own or the other's obligation or performance. On the other hand, other contracts are structured in a way which allows the consumer to determine during the life of the contract the actual extent to which he or she wants to consume the trader's goods or services, paying for these according to their actual consumption. Here, therefore, there is no need for a variation clause; instead, performance by the trader as required by the consumer triggers the consumer's obligation to pay.

Secondly, the possibility of the consumer escaping the contract (whether this is expressed in terms of cancellation, termination or otherwise) is relevant in three distinct ways. (1) In certain contracts a consumer may enjoy a right to escape the contract either by law (typically for a short period), by contract (as in the case of premium travel tickets), or by concession (as in the case of many retailers under their 'returns policy'). Where consumers can do so, then they do not usually have any need to vary the contract which they have concluded, but can instead simply escape that contract and conclude a new contract with different subject matter, terms or trader. (2) Where a trader seeks to vary its own or the consumer's obligations under an express contract term, the fairness and, therefore, effectiveness of that term will turn at least in part on the contract's also providing for the possibility of the consumer terminating the contract on the trader exercising its power to vary. (3) Conversely, where consumers conclude a contract, such as a loan to purchase residential property at a fixed rate of interest for a determined period, the nature of this contract may lead either to a finding that review of the fairness of a term which restricts early termination of the contract is excluded or, if not excluded, that the term is itself fair.

Thirdly, the decisions of the CJEU in *Invitel*, *RWE Vertrieb AG* and *Aziz*[130] demonstrate that it has become willing (somewhat late in the day), to give specific advice as to the application of the test of fairness to particular terms in consumer contracts. In doing so, it has emphasised the importance of the indicative list of terms in the 1993 Directive as a source of elements which point in favour or against the fairness of terms, even if the term before the national court is not directly matched by a term in the list. Moreover, the Court's guidance reflects a desire to

[130] *Invitel*, n 90 above; *RWE Vertrieb AG*, n 91 above; *Aziz*, n 108 above.

ensure that consumers are in a position, before the conclusion of the contract, to understand not merely the meaning of the words used by the standard terms with which they are faced, but also their likely significance to their own position. This is, in my view, the significance of the Court requiring that the trader should enable consumers to foresee any variation made under the contract by setting out the grounds on which and methods by which it may do so.

Finally, and on a very different note, I very much hope that this discussion will be thought appropriate as a token of the esteem in which I hold Hugh Beale and his work, especially given the important contributions which he has made to the development of the law on unfair contract terms as an academic lawyer, as a Law Commissioner and as a member of successive expert groups drafting the bases of a future European contract law.

European Contract Law

13

Unfair Prices in the Common European Sales Law

MARTIJN W HESSELINK*

INTRODUCTION

AT ITS PLENARY session of 26 February 2014 in Strasburg, the European Parliament voted in favour of the Common European Sales Law (CESL).[1] The legislative resolution, which was adopted by a large majority, includes two amendments which significantly extend the protection of consumers against unfair terms, not only to individually negotiated terms but also to core terms, including price terms. The combined effect of these two amendments is that contract prices, including individually negotiated prices, in consumer contracts would become subject to unfairness control. So, if these amendments will be supported by the European Commission and the Council, this will bring a major increase in consumer protection compared not only to the Commission's proposal, but also to the minimum level of protection that the Directive on unfair terms in consumer contracts (Unfair Terms Directive 93/13/EEC) currently requires the Member States to maintain in their national laws. In this contribution, I will argue that both these amendments make good sense and that there are good reasons for the Council and the Commission to endorse them so that they can become part of the optional European sales law. My argument is organised as follows: first, I will briefly introduce the exclusion from unfairness control of individually negotiated and core terms in the Unfair Terms Directive and the Commission proposal for a CESL. Then, I will argue that the prohibition of unfair core terms would be fully in line with the main objectives of both the Unfair Terms Directive and the proposed CESL. Subsequently, I will discuss and reject the main objections against the unfairness control of

* This essay was written in honour of Hugh Beale with whom it has been such a pleasure to collaborate, for almost two decades, on the Casebook, in the Study Group on a European Civil Code and the European Commission Expert Group, and as a colleague at the University of Amsterdam, and from whom I have learned so much.

[1] European Parliament Legislative Resolution of 26 February 2014 on the Proposal for a Regulation of the European Parliament and of the Council on a Common European Sales Law, COM(2011)0635, C7-0329/2011, 2011/0284(COD) (P7_TA-PROV(2014)0159). There were 416 votes in favour, 159 against and 65 abstentions. *cf* European Commission MEMO/14/137, *Optional European Sales Law Receives Strong Backing by the European Parliament* (Strasbourg, 26 February 2014).

core terms. Finally, I will conclude that the amendments should be supported. Throughout, the focus will be primarily on excessive prices.[2]

PERMISSION OF UNFAIR CORE TERMS

Pursuant to the Unfair Terms Directive, Member States must ensure that unfair terms are not binding on consumers (article 6).[3] A contract term must be regarded as unfair if, 'contrary to the requirement of good faith, it causes a significant imbalance in the parties' rights and obligations arising under the contract, to the detriment of the consumer'.[4] However, not all terms that are unfair in this sense are covered by the unfairness control. The Directive contains two important and well-known limitations. First, the required control extends only to contractual terms which have not been individually negotiated.[5] Secondly, the 'definition of the main subject matter of the contract' and 'the adequacy of the price' do not have to be subject to an unfairness assessment (as long as these terms are written in plain intelligible language).[6] Thus, the Directive explicitly permits a significant imbalance in the parties' rights and obligations arising under the contract as long as it relates to the *main* obligations of the parties, such as the obligation to pay an excessive contract price, not merely ancillary ones.

A significant number of Member States decided not to introduce these limitations when transposing the Directive into their national laws.[7] For example, the

[2] Just like the European Parliament's amendments, this contribution will focus primarily on consumer contracts. However, as I have argued elsewhere, when it comes to the control of unfair terms there is no convincing reason to draw a general distinction between business to consumer ('B2C') contracts and business to business ('B2B') commercial contracts. See my 'Unfair Terms in Contracts between Businesses' in J Stuyck and R Schulze (eds), *Towards a European Contract Law* (Munich, Sellier European Law Publishers, 2011) 131–48. Individually negotiated terms and core terms are not different in this respect, but I will not further develop that point here. It suffices, perhaps, to refer to art 3.2.7 (gross disparity) of the UNIDROIT Principles of International Commercial Contracts (Rome, Unidroit, 2010), pursuant to which 'a party may avoid the contract or an individual term of it if, at the time of the conclusion of the contract, the contract term unjustifiably gave the other party an excessive advantage', without any limitation (in B2B!) to non-individually negotiated or non-core terms.

Another subject that I will not address is the remaining role for CESL, art 51 (unfair exploitation). Obviously, that role would be diminished with the introduction of an unfairness control of individually negotiated terms and core terms under Chapter 8 of CESL. However, that would not make the article obsolete. For example, cases where the advantage taken cannot easily be (or should not) be monetised, or cases like the *Bürgschaft* case (BVerfGE 89, 214, *NJW* 1994, 36), which are, of course, beyond the current substantive scope of the CESL, could probably be dealt with more satisfactorily under CESL, art 51.

Finally, I will not discuss the cases where the price (or other core term) is unfair against the seller. Such cases may occur, not only in B2B contracts but also in B2C. There is no reason in justice to exclude such cases from control (nor is there a reason relating to the legal basis, now TFEU, Art 114).

[3] Council Directive 93/13/EEC of 5 April 1993 on unfair terms in consumer contracts, art 6 [1993] OJ L95/29 ('Unfair Terms Directive').

[4] ibid art 3(1).

[5] ibid art 3(1).

[6] ibid art 4(2).

[7] According to Hans Schulte-Nölke, Christian Twigg-Flesner and Martin Ebers (eds), *Consumer Law Compendium: The Consumer Acquis and its Transposition in the Member States* (Munich, Sellier, 2008) 383 (see also 353–54), in 10 Member States the unfairness control extends also to individually negotiated terms, in some (eg the Nordic countries) also, in principle, to core terms.

Nordic countries kept their famous general clause (article 36), which also covers individually negotiated core terms, even, in principle, in commercial contracts.[8] The Member States are allowed to maintain or introduce such more protective provisions, because the Directive only aims at minimum harmonisation.[9]

With regard to the control of unfair terms in consumer contracts, the European Commission's proposal for a Common European Sales Law of 2011 substantially followed the Unfair Terms Directive.[10] In particular, the CESL-proposal contains the same exclusions as the Directive, for price and other core term and for individually negotiated terms.[11] This in spite of the fact that the Commission Expert Group on European Contract Law had proposed to extend the unfairness control in business to consumer ('B2C') contracts to individually negotiated terms—a rare deviation by the Commission from the Expert Group's draft.[12]

In its Statement on the CESL proposal, the European Law Institute (ELI) pointed out that the protection of consumers against unfair clauses that have been individually negotiated needs to be improved.[13] It therefore proposed to add to CESL, article 51 (unfair exploitation) a presumption of an unfair exploitation whenever the terms of a consumer contract are such as to create a grossly unfair imbalance of the parties' rights and obligations to the detriment of the consumer.[14] However, in the ELI's proposal, price and other core terms remain explicitly excluded from the presumption of unfairness and the protection provided by it.[15]

PROHIBITION OF UNFAIR CORE TERMS

In its amendments in first reading, the European Parliament goes an important step further. Not only does Amendment 155 remove the exclusion of individually negotiated terms from unfairness control, thus essentially following the Expert Group's proposal, in addition Amendment 153 also eliminates the exclusion of price and other core terms from scrutiny.[16] The combined effect of these two amendments is that under the CESL, as adopted in first reading by the European Parliament, price

[8] See Thomas Wilhelmsson, 'Private Law in the EU: Harmonised or Fragmented Europeanisation?' (2002) 10 *ERPL* 77.

[9] See Unfair Terms Directive, art 8.

[10] Proposal for a Regulation of the European Parliament and of the Council on a Common European Sales Law, COM(2011)635 final. The most significant differences are the inclusion of black and grey lists containing terms that are, respectively, deemed and presumed to be unfair (arts 84 and 85), and the inclusion of some (rather limited) unfairness control also in B2B contracts (art 86).

[11] See CESL, art 80 (exclusions from unfairness test), art 80(2) (for B2C) and (3) (for B2B), respectively and art 83 (meaning of 'unfair' in contracts between a trader and a consumer).

[12] See Commission Expert Group on European Contract Law, *Feasibility Study for a Future Instrument in European Contract Law* (3 May 2011) art 81. For reasons of transparency, I declare that I was a member of that Expert Group.

[13] Statement of the European Law Institute on the Proposal for a Regulation on a Common European Sales Law, COM(2011)635 final (S-2-2012) 15.

[14] See ibid art 52(2).

[15] See ibid art 52(2), last sentence.

[16] More precisely it deletes the provision in the Commission's proposal (art 80(2)) according to which 'Section 2 [of CESL, Chapter 8] does not apply to the definition of the main subject matter of the contract, or to the appropriateness of the price to be paid in so far as the trader has complied with the duty of transparency set out in Article 82'.

terms and other core terms can be controlled for unfairness, even if these terms have been individually negotiated by the parties.

These amendments by the European Parliament to the Commission's CESL proposal make good sense, because the main reasons for the control of unfair terms apply equally to individually negotiated terms and even a fortiori to core terms. The prevention of injustice, the protection of consumers as weaker parties, and consumer confidence in cross-border shopping are all likely to benefit much more significantly from the control for unfairness of core terms than from an unfairness control which is limited merely to ancillary terms.

Contractual Injustice

Contract terms normally create more contractual unfairness to the extent that they are the more important terms of the contract. For that reason, the core terms, and in particular the contract price, are the ones that matter most from the perspective of contractual justice. Therefore, if the aim is for the European Union to prevent injustice against citizens in their role of consumers,[17] then clearly it should ban the terms that are most likely to make the entire contract become significantly imbalanced, and therefore unfair, ie the core terms. In particular, they should target excessive prices.

It is important to clarify at this point that we are talking here about preventing the *introduction* of injustice by the law, not the removal of an already existing injustice. If the law grants legally binding force to agreements that are unfair then to that extent the law creates an unjust situation that did not exist before: someone becomes entitled to something that they should not be entitled to. Moreover, if the law refuses to enforce certain contracts or contract clauses because of their unfairness then (absent provisions of criminal or administrative law to the contrary) parties remain free to conclude and voluntarily perform such agreements. The only difference is that these unfair contract terms fail to create legal obligations and can therefore not benefit from the apparatus of remedies and state supported enforcement which come with legally binding force. The concept of 'freedom of contract' is somewhat misleading in this regard: when we 'limit the freedom of contract', the only thing we do in reality is to refuse to require the contracting parties to comply with the agreement, and consequentially we prevent public officials from forcing people to perform unfair contracts, eg to pay excessive contract prices, against their will.

So, the moral argument in favour of unfairness control actually operates a fortiori when it comes to the unfairness of the most important terms in the contract. The moral force (or the logic) of the argument that it is acceptable for contract terms to be unfair as long as they are the important terms, while unfair terms must not be binding on consumers as soon as it comes to the unimportant terms, is rather doubtful.

[17] *cf* the preliminary recitals to the Unfair Terms Directive.

Interestingly enough, the preliminary recitals in the proposed Regulation announce quite generally that the CESL should govern 'the assessment and consequences of unfairness of contract terms',[18] while the heading of Chapter 8 is also very generally entitled 'Unfair contract terms', rather than 'Unfair non-core contract terms'. They are already fully in line with—indeed better than—the European Parliament's amendments.

Weaker Party Protection

Another reason for unfair terms control, and one of the objectives of the proposed regulation, is the protection of consumers as weaker parties. Pursuant to article 1(3) (Objective and subject matter), the consumer protection rules contained in the CESL are meant to ensure a high level of consumer protection (as required by the Treaty on the Functioning of the European Union (TFEU), Articles 114(3) and 169(3)). However, there is little doubt that the negative impact of weak bargaining power is likely to be strongest, and have the most serious consequences, with regard to price and other core terms.

The following considerations were set out with regard to the Unfair Terms Directive by the European Court of Justice (CJEU) in the *Mostaza Claro* case in 2006 and were repeated subsequently in several other cases:[19]

> The system of protection introduced by the Directive is based on the idea that the consumer is in a weak position vis-à-vis the seller or supplier, as regards both his bargaining power and his level of knowledge. This leads to the consumer agreeing to terms drawn up in advance by the seller or supplier without being able to influence the content of those terms.
>
> [Article 6(1) of the Directive] is a mandatory provision which, taking into account the weaker position of one of the parties to the contract, aims to replace the formal balance which the latter establishes between the rights and obligations of the parties with an effective balance which re-establishes equality between them.
>
> Moreover, as the aim of the Directive is to strengthen consumer protection, it constitutes, according to Article 3(1)(t) EC, a measure which is essential to the accomplishment of the tasks entrusted to the Community and, in particular, to raising the standard of living and the quality of life in its territory.

If the system of protection against unfair terms in the Directive and the CESL is indeed based on the idea that the consumer is in a weak bargaining and informational position, then is there any reason to expect the consumer's position to be any better with regard to negotiations concerning the core terms of the contract? Will a consumer with weak bargaining power be able to substantially influence the main terms of the contract including the price? And can the equality between the parties ever be restored, by replacing the formal balance between the rights and obligations

[18] CESL, recital 26.

[19] C-168/05 *Elisa Maria Mostaza Claro v Centro Móvil Milenium SL* [2006] ECR I-10421, Considerations 25 and 36, 37 (references omitted); the first consideration was already present in C-240/98–C-244/98 *Océano Grupo Editorial SA v Roció Murciano Quintero and Others* [2000] ECR I-04941, para 25.

of the parties, as established by the contract, with an effective balance, if this operation only includes the less important terms of the contract? Finally, if the protection of consumers against unfair terms constitutes a measure which is essential to the European Union's fulfilment of its task to raise the standard of living and the quality of life, then will the EU not be much more successful in fulfilling its task if it bans unfair core terms, especially unfair prices, rather than concentrating merely on combating unfairness in contract terms of lesser importance? In sum, if the aim of unfair terms control is weaker party protection, then core terms should definitely be included, if not the prime target.

Consumer Confidence in Cross-border Shopping

According to the preliminary recital to the proposed CESL regulation, the consumer protection rules 'should guarantee a high level of consumer protection with a view to enhancing consumer confidence in the Common European Sales Law and thus provide consumers with an incentive to enter into cross-border contracts on that basis'.[20] Such an increased consumer confidence in cross-border shopping, it seems, can also much more easily be achieved if the protection against unfair terms is indeed extended to individually negotiated terms and core terms. Consumers are more likely to be put off from cross-border buying by the risk of encountering unfair core terms, including unfair prices, than by unfair ancillary terms. So, if consumers are currently afraid to buy from foreign sellers and if a high level of consumer protection in the CESL can enhance consumer confidence and can thus contribute to an increase in cross-border sales, especially on-line (which indeed seems plausible, although probably on a smaller scale than the Commission expects), then protection as regards core terms and individually negotiated terms is likely to be much more effective than mere protection in relation to unfair non-core non-individually negotiated terms, simply because the level of consumer protection would be significantly higher.

OBJECTIONS

In sum, the main reasons for unfair terms control all seem to apply just as much, or even more, to individually negotiated terms and core terms. Indeed, on its own terms, ie in light of its objectives and internal logic, there is every reason for the CESL to extend its control of unfair terms also to individually negotiated terms and to price and other core terms. Are there any valid reasons against extending unfair terms control beyond non-individually negotiated non-core terms? If we can refer apocalyptic scenarios ('road to serfdom' style) and the related warnings against 'socialism' to the Cold-War age where they belong,[21] the two main reasons that need

[20] CESL, recital 11. See also CESL, art 1(3) (objective and subject matter): 'to enhance consumer confidence in the internal market and encourage consumers to shop across borders'.

[21] The Brandner and Ulmer article, cited at n 25 below, although written in 1991, was still full of Cold-War rhetoric.

to be considered here are a moral objection based on party autonomy and pragmatic objection based on impracticability.[22]

Personal Autonomy

The original Commission proposal of 1990 for a Directive on unfair terms in consumer contracts did not exclude individually negotiated terms and core terms from the unfairness control.[23] These limitations were only introduced by the Council. Of course, we can only speculate about the reasons for the introduction of these restrictions since Council meetings, at the time as much as today, take place behind closed doors,[24] but a crucial role seems to have been played by a critical article in the *Common Market Law Review* by Brandner and Ulmer.[25] In that article the authors argued that 'individually negotiated terms' (as opposed to standard terms)[26] and 'terms specifying the principal obligations and ... prices in relation to the value of goods or services provided' should be excluded from control.[27] The similarity, even in the wording, with the two exclusions in the final text of the Directive is striking. The authors made their argument primarily in the name of 'individual autonomy', 'the contracting parties' right of self-determination' and 'the principle of a free market autonomy'. The core idea is that the control of individually negotiated terms and core terms by courts (ie the state) means an inadmissible interference with the individual freedom on which our national societies (and, it is often argued, the European Union) is based.

[22] Another classical objection against the introduction of unfair price rules is the idea of a division of labour between competition law, on the one hand, and consumer protection law and general contract law, on the other. However, this argument provides no reason in justice why a monopolist, who somehow escaped the enforcement of competition law, should be facilitated by the law in extorting excessive prices. On the contrary, off-market contracts (ie contracts that are not concluded on a reasonably competitive market) are among the classical cases (think eg of rescue cases) where unconscionability and unfair exploitation doctrines have been applied uncontroversially. Interestingly, the recent Proposal by the European Commission for a Directive on certain rules governing actions for damages under national law for infringements of the competition law provisions of the Member States and of the European Union, COM(2013)404 final (Strasbourg, 11 June 2013), by introducing (or rather codifying: see the CJEU in Joined Cases C-295/04 to C-298/04 *Vincenzo Manfredi v Lloyd Adriatico Assicurazioni* [2006] ECR I-6619) a 'right to full compensation' (art 2), which includes compensation for a 'loss of profit', de facto comes very close to introducing a fair price rule if a fair price is defined as the price on a reasonably well-functioning market (see below). The main difference would be the remedy, ie invalidity of the contract versus the (much further going) conversion (de facto) of the unfair contract price into a fair one. In other words, the unfairness control of contract prices not only would not undermine competition law, it would actually support it, in particular its 'private enforcement'.

[23] Commission Proposal for a Council Directive on unfair terms in consumer contracts, COM(90)322 final, SYN 285 (90/C 243/02) [1990] OJ C243/2.

[24] See Deirdre Curtin, 'Challenging Executive Dominance in European Democracy' (2014) 77 *Modern Law Review* 1, who points out that the Council of Ministers 'still behaves as if legislation is largely a matter of "diplomatic" negotiation behind closed doors among representatives of the Member States'.

[25] Hans Erich Brandner and Peter Ulmer, 'The Community Directive on Unfair Terms in Consumer Contracts: Some Critical Remarks on the Proposal Submitted by the EC Commission' (1991) 28 *Common Market Law Review* 647.

[26] ibid 651.

[27] ibid 655.

The argument from party autonomy is unconvincing for a number of reasons none of which, however, have to do with downplaying the importance of individual autonomy. On the contrary, most of us will agree that personal autonomy is of central value for the possibility of human flourishing and that respect by the state for the autonomy of its citizens, as free and equal, is an indispensible precondition for a just society.[28] However, this is not the same as arguing that it should be the task of the state, through its private law, to uphold and enforce prices and other core terms, even when these can be shown to be unfair. There is a simple question: if we accept the moral importance of private autonomy and individual self-determination through contracts, then must we also accept a moral entitlement to the legal enforcement of contracts containing an unfair price or another unfair core term?

A first reply to that question could be the observation that an unfair individually negotiated or core term is simply an impossibility. The mere fact that the term is a price term or other core term, or was individually negotiated, makes it a fair term for that reason: 'qui dit contractuel dit juste'.[29] At first sight, this argument may seem to be nothing more than a *parti pris*. However, it can easily be transformed into a political argument: freedom is justice; there is nothing more to justice than freedom, formally understood, and also formal freedom of contract is all that matters for contractual justice. On this view, there is nothing wrong with exploiting one's bargaining power to the most with a view to obtaining the best possible deal. Bargaining power, unless obtained through fraud or threats, is just a consequence or aspect of entitlement, including what Nozick calls 'self-ownership', and if the state tries to 'replace the formal balance ... with an effective balance which re-establishes equality', as the CJEU put it in *Mostaza Claro*,[30] in the name of fairness, then that amounts to plain theft.[31] However, it is not generally accepted that freedom formally understood, ie without going into the question what the freedom is valuable for (eg as a precondition for human flourishing), is of any value at all. It has been suggested that if freedom has pure non-instrumental value, we might as well strive to double the population in order to increase freedom.[32] In any case, it is not at all clear that in our pluralist society the state should enforce contracts in the name of such a sectarian and controversial notion of liberty.[33] Moreover, the libertarian view is clearly not compatible with the way in which unfairness is understood in the Unfair Terms Directive or the CESL proposal. The wordings of both the Directive and the CESL express that core terms and prices may very well be unfair; the courts are simply not allowed to verify the unfairness or attach any consequences to it.

[28] Still, not everyone will regard personal autonomy as a fundamental value. Therefore, in a pluralist society, the government should not give binding force to contracts *in the name of* the ideal of an autonomous, self-authored life. It should rely on a thinner, more political notion of individual autonomy. See, generally, John Rawls, *Political Liberalism*, expanded edn (New York, Columbia University Press, 2005 [1993]).

[29] A Fouillée, *La science sociale contemporaine* (Paris, Hachette, 1880) 410.

[30] See p 229 above.

[31] Robert Nozick, *Anarchy, State and Utopia* (Oxford, Blackwell Publishing, 2006 [1974]).

[32] See Will Kymlicka, *Contemporary Political Philosophy: An Introduction* 2nd edn (Oxford University Press, 2002).

[33] Rawls, *Political Liberalism*, n 28 above.

As article 80 puts it, core terms are excluded from the unfairness test. So, core terms may be unfair; we are just not going to test them.

If we believe that there exists contractual justice beyond mere formal individual liberty, then the question will have to be addressed whether private autonomy requires the law to enforce individually negotiated or core contract terms that we know to be unfair,[34] any more than non-individually negotiated and non-core terms, that will not bind consumers. What value is there, in terms of human flourishing or other, in the possibility for one contracting party to enforce an unfair contract against another contracting party? And if there is some value in that possibility then is it of such importance that the state's authority and public resources should be put at the disposal of traders who want to extort significantly unbalanced deals from their customers? Is there a task for the state to encourage the conclusion of unfair contracts by granting them legally binding force? As Shiffrin puts it, '[e]ven were respect for autonomy to require non-interference with voluntary, but unconscionable, agreements, it would not necessitate assistance in making and implementing them'.[35] It is a mistake to think that unfair terms control is paternalistic.[36] If the state refuses to make unfair terms legally binding it is not telling private parties that it is in their best interest not to include unfair core terms in their contracts. It merely tells these parties that it sees no good reason for using public resources and the authority of the state for supporting significantly unbalanced contracts, whatever interests the parties may see in their voluntary performance. In sum, the state does not interfere with anyone's autonomy if it refuses to make unfair core terms become binding on consumers.

This also explains why the fact that a term was individually negotiated cannot be decisive. Not only is the libertarian argument that a term that was individually negotiated is, for that reason, a fair one, unconvincing; also, the fact that in light of the preceding individual negotiation it is more likely that both parties actually wanted the clause cannot be decisive, because we have no right to the unconditional support of our projects by the state.[37] The state remains free to decide that certain contract clauses, even if they were individually agreed to by the parties, will not be granted legally binding force, because the state sees no task for itself in promoting and upholding unfair contract terms.

Finally, even if it were true that freedom of contract must be understood in a formal sense or that the unfairness control of core terms amounts to intolerable paternalism, then clearly this does not apply to the CESL, because it is optional. The CESL will only become applicable to parties that choose it. Sellers who wish to charge excessive prices or include other unfair core terms into their contracts remain entirely free not to opt into the CESL. Of course, it could be argued that thus fewer sellers will opt into the CESL, which might impair the economic objective ('justice

[34] The feasibility of determining unfairness in practice will be addressed below.

[35] Seana Valentine Shiffrin, 'Paternalism, Unconscionability Doctrine, and Accommodation' (2000) 29 *Philosophy and Public Affairs* 205.

[36] ibid.

[37] ibid.

for growth') of increased cross-border shopping.[38] However, it is not clear that we should care. Maybe we should accept the risk of a slightly smaller economic growth in order to be able to live in a decently just society (justice for justice). The black and grey lists may also put off some sellers who want to include unfair non-core terms in their standard terms, but that is the price we are prepared to pay. Moreover, it is not even clear, as an empirical matter, that unfairness control of individually negotiated and core terms would in fact have such a negative economic effect. If the CESL can contribute to an increase in cross-border sales by increasing consumer confidence, as the Commission claims, then clearly protection against unfair prices and other core terms is much more effective than protection against the unfairness of less important terms. So, following the Commission's own reasoning, the cross-border demand could even significantly increase as a result of the Parliament's amendments. Moreover, on the supply side a choice by a seller for the CESL with unfairness control for prices and other core terms seems an ideal way for sellers to signal that they are confident that their prices and other core terms are entirely fair: 'Trust me, I sell under the CESL'. It may well be that the number of sellers who hoped to opt into the CESL in order to be able to charge unfair prices is outweighed by the number of bona fide sellers who would like to submit their fair cross-border sales conditions and prices to the CESL.

Practicability

Under the Unfair Terms Directive and the proposed CESL, the test for unfairness, as we saw, is whether the term 'causes a significant imbalance in the parties' rights and obligations arising under the contract, to the detriment of the consumer, contrary to good faith and fair dealing'.[39] The way the test is phrased suggests that a significant imbalance in the rights and obligations of the parties under the contract is not a sufficient condition for unfairness since it may still not be contrary to good faith. However, in practice such cases, if they exist at all, will be very rare.[40] This means that for all practical purposes the unfair test can be regarded as one that concentrates on the equilibrium of the contractual obligations, in particular their relative value. If the test is extended to individually negotiated terms and price terms, this means that courts will have to determine whether there is a significant imbalance between the main obligations of the parties. For sales contracts (to which the CESL's scope of application is almost exclusively limited), this means that the contract is unfair when there is a significant imbalance between the contract price and the value of the goods (or the digital content). Can courts determine whether prices are unfair in this sense? This is not the question of whether the control by courts of

[38] See Vice-President Reding's 'Justice for Growth Agenda'. *cf* 'Speech: Justice for Growth Makes Headway at Today's Justice Council', available at http://europa.eu/rapid/press-release_SPEECH-13-29_en.htm?locale=en.

[39] See CESL, art 83 and Unfair Terms Directive, art 3.

[40] Pursuant to CESL, art 2(b): '"good faith and fair dealing" means a standard of conduct characterised by honesty, openness and consideration for the interests of the other party to the transaction or relationship in question'.

price and other core terms would not amount to an illegitimate interference with the autonomy of the parties, that was discussed above. The question here is whether it can be done, as a practical matter, without leading to intolerable legal uncertainty.

It is true that it may sometimes be difficult for courts to determine whether a certain contractual term causes a significant imbalance in the parties' rights and obligations arising under the contract, as they are currently expected to do under the national laws based on article 3 of the Unfair Terms Directive. However, surely this task is *easier* when it comes to price and other core terms than to terms of minor importance. The economic value of jurisdiction clauses, exemption clauses and other non-core terms may indeed be difficult to estimate, and the question whether their presence is fairly reflected in the rights and obligations of the buyer (eg a lower price) may be quite difficult to answer. However, according to the CJEU this can nevertheless be done. In the *Freiburger Kommunalbauten* case in 2004, the Court held as follows:[41]

> It is true that in [*Océano*] the Court held that a term, drafted in advance by the seller, the purpose of which is to confer jurisdiction in respect of all disputes arising under the contract on the court in the territorial jurisdiction of which the seller has his principal place of business, satisfies all the criteria necessary for it to be judged unfair for the purposes of the Directive. Nevertheless, that assessment was reached in relation to *a term which was solely to the benefit of the seller and contained no benefit in return for the consumer.* Whatever the nature of the contract, it thereby undermined the effectiveness of the legal protection of the rights which the Directive affords to the consumer. It was thus possible to hold that the term was unfair without having to consider all the circumstances in which the contract was concluded and without having to assess the advantages and disadvantages that that term would have under the national law applicable to the contract.

The reasoning of the Court is not entirely satisfactory. Of course, most terms are entirely to the benefit of either the seller (eg the term that requires payment of the price) or the buyer (eg the term that requires delivery of the goods). Taken on its own, almost any contract term is one-sided. However, on its own, no term can cause a significant imbalance in the parties' rights and obligations arising under the contract. The rights and obligations following from the term will always have to be compared with the other rights and obligations arising under the contract, in order to be able to determine whether the clause causes a significant imbalance. Especially for a term of minor importance, it will often not be easy to determine what exactly the customer got in return for it. Rather, the term will usually be regarded by consumers as part of the package, as one of the terms that she had to sign or click for if she wanted to obtain the goods.

However, that task, it is submitted, is much easier when it comes to the core terms because these spell out the parties' main rights and obligations. A significant imbalance in the main obligations (in particular an unfair price) is usually much easier to establish. This is especially the case when the parties operate on a functioning

[41] Consideration 24 (emphasis added).

market.[42] With regard to the price terms, the competitive market price will provide the reference price: it can safely be assumed that prices that significantly deviate from the market price are unfair.[43] This presumption can then be rebutted by establishing the relevance of specific, untypical circumstances relating to the contractual relationship and the parties at hand.

Presumptions are a well-known practical mechanism that we are already familiar with also in the context of unfair terms control. Indeed, the CESL-proposal contains a grey list of contract terms that are presumed to be unfair.[44] The presence of the grey list in the CESL proposal (and the successful functioning of similar lists in several Member States) also suggest that is possible to compare contract terms which benefit one party with what the other party obtains in return for its presence: typically a lower price. It is submitted that what can be done for non-core terms should certainly be possible also for core terms. There is no reason to expect a reduction of legal certainty.

CONCLUSION

In conclusion, the amendments to the CESL extending unfairness control to individually negotiated terms and core terms, including price terms, as adopted by the European Parliament at first reading, make good sense, and there is good reason for the Council and Commission to support them. Extending the unfairness control in the CESL to individually negotiated terms and core terms, including price terms, contributes to avoiding injustice, increasing consumer protection and consumer confidence. At the same time, the control of individually negotiated terms and core terms does not represent an interference with private autonomy, not even if personal freedom is understood in a purely formal libertarian sense, since no one will be obliged to opt into the CESL. Nor is the unfairness control of core terms impracticable or is it likely to lead to legal uncertainty. It will even be easier, in most cases, to assess the unfairness of the contract price, and to predict the assessment, than in the case of non-core terms, since the price on a reasonably well-functioning market will be available as a reference price.

[42] If it is true that prices are best set by markets, not by courts, then why should it be the task of courts to enforce a price term that substantially deviates from the market price, in the absence of any plausible contextual justification? Contracts for a price that substantially differs from an existing market price are for that reason (ie by definition) concluded off-market and there is nothing against conducing them back to the market. See Melvin Aron Eisenberg, *Foundational Principles of Contract Law* (Oxford University Press, 2014) ch 4.

[43] Similarly, James Gordley, *Foundations of Private Law: Property, Tort, Contract, and Unjust Enrichment* (Oxford University Press, 2006) ch 17; Eisenberg, *Foundational Principles of Contract Law*, n 42 above; Brigitta Lurger, *Grundfragen der Vereinheitlichung des Vertragsrechts in der Europäischen Union* (Vienna and New York, Springer, 2002) 294; Florian Rödl, 'Contractual Freedom, Contractual Justice and Contract Law (Theory)' (2013) 76 *Law and Contemporary Problems* 57. See also my 'Fair Prices in the Common Market: On Commutative and Distributive Justice in European Contract Law' in Guido Alpa and Remo Danovi (eds), *Diritto privato europeo; Fonti ed effetti; Materiali del Seminario dell' 8–9 Novembre 2002* (Milan, Giuffrè Editore, 2004) 245–54.

[44] CESL, art 85.

14

CISG and CESL: Simplicity, Fairness and Social Justice

OLE LANDO

HUGH BEALE JOINED the Commission on European Contract Law in 1987. He was a member of the group of four members that prepared the texts for adoption by the full Commission. He was the co-editor of the Principles of European Contract Law (PECL) Part I, which was published in 1995, and of Part I and II combined and revised, which appeared in 2000.[1]

For a continental lawyer it is a treat to work with a common lawyer. One gets fascinated by the way in which the common law is developed by the courts. He who has learned to deduce from principles established in statutes, discovers how the law can be created from case to case; how the experience gained from a case can become a rule; and how the scope and operation of the rule is tried and refined again and again in the cases.

With his eminent knowledge of the English cases Hugh could often tell us when the rule we proposed was inappropriate due to the experience of the English courts. I do not exaggerate when I state that Hugh Beale is one of the most talented lawyers I have ever met. Without him, the Principles of European Contract Law would not have attained the same scholarly standing.

The Principles covered the general part of contract law. My idea was that they should become part of a Contract Code for the European Union to be adopted as a EU Regulation, but I knew already from the outset that several of the members of the Commission did not share this vision, and that Hugh was one of them. This, however, did not prevent them from participating with enthusiasm and giving the Principles a shape which made it possible for this instrument to be adopted as part of an EU Regulation.

Later, Hugh joined the Study Group on a European Civil Code, which together with the Research Group on EC Private Law (the *Acquis* Group) prepared the Draft Common Frame of Reference (DCFR),[2] which in part is based on a revised version

[1] See now O Lando and H Beale (eds), *Principles of European Contract Law, Parts I and II, prepared by the Commission on European Contract Law* (The Hague, 1999) and O Lando, E Clive, A Prüm and R Zimmermann (eds), *Principles of European Contract Law, Part III* (The Hague, 2003).

[2] Christian von Bar and Eric Clive (eds), *Principles, Definitions and Model Rules of European Private Law: Draft Common Frame of Reference*, full edn, prepared by the Study Group on a European Civil Code and the Research Group on EC Private Law (Acquis Group) (Munich, 2009) vols 1–6.

of the Principles of European Contract Law. In this work, Hugh was one of the leading scholars. The DCFR covers contracts, torts, unjustified enrichment, *negotiorum gestio*, acquisition and loss of ownership of goods, security rights in movable assets and trusts. It is only meant to be soft law but it has all the ingredients of the patrimonial parts of a Civil Code, which the Study Group originally planned to call it. The EU Commission and Council would not hear of a Civil Code. So it got the castrated title Common Frame of Reference.

When by a Decision of 26 April 2010, the EU Commission set up an Expert Group with the task of developing a 'Feasibility Study on a Possible Future European Contract Law', Hugh Beale was appointed one of its members. The Feasibility Study was published a year later, and the Commission used it as a tool-box for its Proposal of 11 October 2011 for a Regulation on a Common European Sales Law (CESL).[3] Hugh Beale has accepted an offer by the Commission to prepare a Commentary on the rules of this proposed Regulation.

So it may confidently be asserted that Hugh Beale has been and is a leading figure in the development of a European Contract Law.

The subject for this article is the CESL, which I will compare with the UN Convention on the International Sale of Goods (CISG) and with the soft laws, the PECL, the DCFR and also the UNIDROIT Principles of International Commercial Contracts (PICC),[4] which came into being during the same period as PECL, and which also deal with the general part of contract law.

I will primarily treat the business to business ('B2B') contracts.

The CISG covers the international sale of goods and excludes consumer sales. It applies when the parties have their places of business in contracting states, and when the rules of private international law lead to the application of the law of a contracting state. It is not concerned with the validity of the contract. Parties may exclude the application of the CISG or derogate from or vary the effect of any of its provisions.

The CESL covers sale of goods, the supply of digital contents and related services. It applies to cross-border transactions between a trader and a consumer and between a trader and a small and medium-sized enterprise (SME). It only applies when the parties agree on its application.

The CESL is the first EU proposal for a Common European Sales Law and in spite of the criticism to be made below, I consider it to be an important step forward.

ADVANTAGES OF CESL OVER CISG

The CISG has been a success. When it was adopted at a UN Conference in 1980 it had been in the melting pot for over 50 years with several conferences and drafts behind it, and that may account for its high quality. In July 2014, it had been adopted by 81 countries.

[3] COM(2011)635 final.

[4] UNIDROIT Principles of International Commercial Contracts 2010 (UNIDROIT, International Institute for the Unification of Private Law, 2011).

The CISG has, however, some weaknesses which the drafters of the soft laws and of the CESL have avoided. The CESL contains rules that I regard to be improvements on the CISG.

Good Faith

Article 7(1) of the CISG provides that 'in the interpretation of this Convention, regard is to be had to ... the observance of good faith in international trade'. The duty to observe good faith is limited to the interpretation of the CISG. The majority of the delegates at the UN Conference feared that when applying such a vague concept national courts would be influenced by their own legal traditions with the result that the provision would be interpreted differently in the different countries. However, as has been pointed out, this narrow scope of the principle is neither fair nor practicable.[5] When applying the CISG, several courts[6] and among them the German Supreme Court have imposed upon the parties a general duty to act in accordance with good faith and fair dealing when concluding, interpreting, performing and enforcing the contract,[7] and that is what PICC, article 1.7, PECL, article 1:201, DCFR, article III.-1:103 and CESL, Annex I, article 2 provide. In addition, PECL, article 1:202, PICC, article 5.1.3, DCFR, article III.-1:104 and CESL, Annex I, article 3 provide that the parties have a duty to cooperate with each other for the performance of the contract.

Price

Article 14(1) of the CISG requires the offer and therefore also the contract to fix or make provision for determining the price. Article 55 presupposes that a contract has been validly concluded without expressly or implicitly fixing or making provision for determining the price. The majority of legal systems[8] do not require the price to be a necessary condition for the conclusion of a contract. Several of them provide rules similar to article 55. The commentators on the CISG have capered about to suggest tenable solutions to the unsolvable antinomy[9] between article 14(1) and article 55.

PECL, article 2:201, DCFR, article II.-4:201, PICC, article 2.1.2 and CESL, Annex I, article 31 do not require that the offer contains a proposal to fix or make provision for determining the price.

[5] See P Schlechtriem (ed), *Commentary on the UN Convention on the International Sale of Goods*, 2nd edn (Oxford, Clarendon Press, 1988) (Herber) 63 and *J von Staudingers Kommentar zum Bürgerlichen Gesetzbuch mit Einführungsgesetz und Nebengesetzen: Wiener UN-Kaufrecht (CISG) Berlin 2005* (Neubearbeitung von Ulrich Magnus), art 7, comment no 10, 170.

[6] UNILEX lists courts in Australia, Germany, Belgium, Italy and the Netherlands.

[7] BGH, 31 October 2001, NJW 2002, 370.

[8] See UCC § 2:204, and on European law, notes to DCFR, art II.-4:201, vol I, 294 and to DCFR, art II.-9:104, 596.

[9] See Schlechtriem, n 5 above, (Schlechtriem) 108; P Schlechtriem and I Schwenzer (eds), *Commentary on the UN Convention on the International Sale of Goods (CISG)*, 3rd edn (Oxford, 2010) (Schroeter) 267 and Magnus, n 5 above, art 14, comments nos 27–35.

Offer Made Irrevocable

Article 16(2) of the CISG lays down that an offer cannot be revoked, if it indicates *whether by stating a fixed time for acceptance or otherwise*, that it is irrevocable. This rule was the result of a compromise. Depending on the circumstance, the common lawyers may regard the fixing of a time for acceptance as not making, whereas civil lawyers will regard it as making, the offer irrevocable. PECL, article 2:202(3)(b), DCFR, article II.-4:202(3)(b) and CESL, Annex I, article 31(3)(b) avoid this double speak. They provide that an offer is irrevocable if it states a fixed time for its acceptance.

Battle of Forms

The CISG does not address the so-called 'battle of forms', the situation where the parties have reached agreement except that the offer and the acceptance refer to conflicting general conditions. CISG, article 19(1) provides that if the conditions of the answer do not materially change the conditions of the offer, they will conclude the contract, unless the offeror objects without undue delay.[10] If he does not so object, the terms of the contract are the terms of the offer with the modifications contained in the acceptance. If the terms of the answer materially alter the terms of the offer, there is no contract, unless by his conduct the offeror accepts the terms of the counter-offer, for instance by performing the contract, see article 18(1). It appears to be a widespread view that in that case, the terms of the party who answers last, who 'fires the last shot', will prevail.[11]

However, experience shows that even if the terms of the answer materially alter the terms of the offer, the parties wish to have a contract. They should therefore be bound before the contract has been performed. Furthermore, the 'last shot' solution described above depends upon factors that are coincidental.

The German case law, PECL, article 2:209, DCFR, article II.-4:209, PICC, article 2.1.22 and CESL, Annex I, article 39 provide that the contract is concluded on the basis of the terms that are common in substance, unless one party has indicated in advance and not by way of general conditions that he will not be bound by a contract that alters his terms, or if without delay he informs the other party that he will not be bound by such contracts. In most cases, the 'stop gap' rules of the law will apply to the issue(s) covered by the conflicting general conditions which this rule 'knocks out'.

Interpretation and Contents

CESL, Annex I, Chapter 6 on interpretation and Chapter 7 on contents and effects provide useful rules that the CISG does not have. Thus, the CISG has no rule on

[10] See Schwenzer, n 9 above, (Schroeter) 346, art 19, comments nos 31–51.

[11] See the comment in Schlechtriem, n 5 above, 143. Schwenzer, n 9 above, (Schroeter) 347, 350 prefers the 'knock out' rule, and some courts agree.

terms implied in fact, such as CESL, Annex I, article 68 (on terms derived from pre-contractual statements), and CESL, Annex I, article 69 (on merger clauses); see also CESL, Annex I, articles 72 and 73 (on determination by a third party).

CISG has No Provision on Hardship

It has been argued that CISG, article 79 dealing with 'exemption' stands somewhere between the very tough French rule on *force majeure* governing civil contracts and the more lenient § 313 of the German BGB on *Störung der Geschäftsgrundlage*.[12] The rules in CESL, Annex I, article 89 on change of circumstances (hardship) are similar to the German rule. PECL, article 6:111, DCFR, article III.-1:110 and PICC, Chapter 6, Section 2 also have provisions on hardship.

Interests

Article 78 of the CISG provides that if 'a Party fails to pay the price or any other sum that is in arrears, the other Party is entitled to interest on it, without prejudice to any claim for damages recoverable under article 74'. Article 78 does not provide when the interest accrues nor does it set the rate of interest. CESL, Annex I, article 168 on interest on late payments states the rate of interest and its accrual.

Kaufmännische Bestätigungsschreiben

It would have improved the CESL if it had included a rule on a professional's written confirmation like the German rule on the *kaufmännische Bestätigungsschreiben*. PECL, article 2:210 provides that if professionals have concluded a contract but have not embodied it in a final document, and one without delay sends the other a writing which purports to be a confirmation of the contract but which contains additional or different terms, such terms will become part of the contract unless (a) the terms materially alter the terms of the contract, or (b) the addressee objects to them without delay.

DFCR, article II.-4:210 and PICC, article 2.1.12 have similar provisions. The rule applies in Austria, Denmark, Estonia, Finland, Germany, Norway, Poland, Turkey, Switzerland and Sweden.[13]

[12] See Schlechtriem, n 5 above, (Stoll) 618, note 40.

[13] See for Austria, Germany, Estonia, Poland, Turkey, Denmark, Sweden and Finland, DCFR, vol I, 315.

CESL AND SIMPLICITY

One of the demands one can make of any regulation is that it is easily accessible for the reader. Unfortunately, the CESL does not live up to this demand in some respects.

Systematic

The Commission's Proposal contains an Explanatory Memorandum, a Regulation, Annex I and Annex II to the Regulation. The Regulation is an 'Introductory Law' laying down the objective and subject matter of the CESL, definitions, the scope of the CESL and its optional character. The substantive provisions of the CESL are in Annex I.[14]

This system is confusing. The Regulation and its Annex I should be merged.

Why Exclude Big Traders?

The CESL applies to business to consumer ('B2C') and to B2B contracts, where at least one of the parties is an SME but, unless a contracting state provides otherwise, not to contracts between traders none of which are SMEs; see CESL, articles 7(1) and 13(b). Article 7(2) provides that:

> For the purposes of this Regulation, an SME is a trader which:
> (a) employs fewer than 250 persons; and
> (b) has an annual turnover not exceeding EUR 50 million or an annual balance sheet total not exceeding EUR 43 million, or, for an SME which has its habitual residence in a Member State whose currency is not the euro or in a third country, the equivalent amounts in the currency of that Member State or third country.

Contracts between traders none of which are SMEs are excluded from the scope of the CESL, probably because these traders do not need rules for the protection of the SMEs.

This exclusion complicates matters. It may be difficult for a trader to find out whether his contracting party is an SME or not. And why are traders none of which are SMEs not permitted to select the CESL if they so wish?

The mandatory rules protecting the SMEs are not so radical that they unreasonably limit the freedom of the big traders, and there are traders who lack the specialised knowledge about the product and the terms of their supplier. A big law firm buying a computer system is often, as the French say, '*en dehors de sa compétence professionelle*'. In such situations both big and small traders are in need of protection.

[14] Annex II is a Standard Information Notice.

Why Exclude Domestic Contracts?

Unless a contracting state decides to make the CESL apply to domestic contracts it applies only to cross-border transactions. CESL, article 4(2) provides that:

> For the purposes of this Regulation, a contract between traders is a cross-border contract if the parties have their habitual residence in different countries of which at least one is a Member State.

It may, however, be preferable for a supplier to have all his contracts, whether cross-border contracts or not, governed by the same rules. The fact that a trader has to deal with two different sales laws may dissuade him from choosing the CESL.

Too Many Definitions

Article 2 of the Regulation brings a list that defines 23 concepts that are used in the Regulation and Annex I. Definitions are necessary, where the drafters feel compelled to use words the meaning of which deviates from their usual meaning, and when the meaning of the words they use is unclear. The long list of definitions, however, makes the use of the Regulation and Annex I cumbersome for the reader. For each article he must check whether its words are defined in article 2. And do the definitions of 'consumer', 'contract', 'standard contract terms', 'damages', 'price', 'customer', 'business premises', 'debtor', 'creditor' and 'obligation' tell the readers any novelties?

CESL AND SOCIAL JUSTICE

When addressing the legal values of the DCFR, the European Parliament asked:

> Does the DCFR perceive contract law only as a tool for regulating private law relations between equally strong parties or does it contain elements of 'social justice' in favour of consumers, victims of discrimination, small and medium sized enterprises and other possibly weaker parties to contracts?[15]

The question reveals the ongoing debate in the European Union between the liberals and the partisans of social justice. By mentioning social justice in favour of weak parties to contracts the Parliament indicates that not only consumers may need protection.

The drafters of the CESL have been torn between the neo-liberalists who feared a 'massive reduction of private autonomy' and the advocates of social justice, who feared 'a law for big business'.

[15] Here quoted from Martijn W Hesselink, *CFR and Social Justice* (Munich, 2008) 1.

Is the Protection of SMEs Offered by CESL Sufficient?

The CESL gives SMEs some protection, but, as will be shown, many of its rules only protect consumers, and several rules that are mandatory in favour of the consumer are non-mandatory in contracts between traders.

The consumer generally does not read the supplier's general conditions. Even if she does, she often does not understand them, and even if she understands them, she is generally optimistic as regards the contingencies and risks dealt with in the standard form contracts. Should she see the dangers, she is too weak to have the conditions changed in her favour.

In favour of not granting SMEs the same protection as that afforded to the consumers it is argued that an SME is not as careless, ignorant, optimistic and weak as the consumer. The trader is more likely than the consumer to read the other party's general conditions, and he may be less optimistic as regards the contingencies and risks dealt with in the other party's standard form contracts. However, the situation of the 'small' trader, the farmer, the fisherman, the shopkeeper, the artisan, etc is mostly the same as that of the consumer; he may have the same difficulties in understanding the terms of the stipulator's general conditions, and he is as weak as she is, when it comes to negotiating better terms. A dependence on the stipulator, to whom he owes money or who is his main customer, may make him put up with the stipulator's terms when concluding the contract.

In favour of limiting the protection to the consumer it is also argued that she belongs to an easily defined group of weak parties, whereas it may be doubtful whether an SME is a weak party. For instance, is the farmer who went to college and who has a middle-sized farm in the same situation as the owner of a small farm who only had six or seven years of schooling? This uncertainty, it is argued, will cause unpredictability in business relations.

The SME need not be protected against all those terms against which the consumer is guarded,[16] but an increased protection of the SME should not be given up because it is difficult to determine who is weak. The decision on which traders to protect should be left to the courts. Any trader needs protection against behaviour by the other party that is unfair.

Good Faith

The duty to act in accordance with good faith and fair dealing is provided in CESL, Annex 1, article 2(1). Its place at the front as one of the general principles indicates that it is meant to be an overarching principle.

CESL, Annex I, article 2(2) provides that breach of this duty may preclude the party in breach from exercising or relying on a right, remedy or defence which that party would otherwise have, or may make the party liable for any loss thereby caused to the other party.

[16] See, eg on price-index adjustment clauses, Palandt, *Bürgerliches Gesetzbuch*, 64th edn (Munich, 2005) § 309 note 9 (Heinrichs).

I understand this rule to mean that a violation of the duty to act in accordance with good faith has only two consequences. You many lose a right, remedy and defence you would otherwise have and you may be liable in damages. But breach of the duty does not give you a right or remedy other than damages. If, for instance, the seller delivers goods that are in conformity with the buyer's order but which he knows that the buyer cannot use for his purpose, the buyer cannot refuse to take the goods and terminate the contract.[17]

If this is the case, it is a help to the hardnosed trader which is absent from PECL, article 1:201. As Martijn Hesselink writes in connection with the DCFR, in which the role of good faith is also narrower than in the PECL, 'the role of good faith as an undisputed legal basis for judge-made law should be restored'.[18]

Duty to Cooperate

The same is true of CESL, Annex I, article 3. PECL, article 1:202 states: 'Each party owes to the other a duty to co-operate in order to give full effect to the contract'. CESL, article 3 reads: 'The parties are obliged to co-operate with each other to the extent that this can be expected for the performance of their contractual obligations'. Do the words 'to the extent that this can be expected' mean that there are situations where you cannot expect cooperation, where some parties are considered to be adversaries and not cooperating companions?

Statements by Earlier Links

CESL, Annex I, article 69 is about terms derived from certain pre-contractual statements. Paragraph 3 on a statement made by a person in earlier links of the chain of transactions reads:

> (3) Where the other party is a consumer then, for the purposes of paragraph (1), a public statement made by or on behalf of a producer or other person in earlier links of the chain of transactions leading to the contract is regarded as being made by the trader unless the *trader*, at the time of conclusion of the contract, did not know and could not be expected to have known of it. (emphasis added)

Why is a supplier in a B2B relationship not liable for statements given by someone in an earlier link? Is it not up to the supplier rather than to the customer to carry the risk for misrepresentations made in the earlier link? As a supplier to a consumer, the trader is liable for statements made by his supplier, but cannot hold his supplier responsible for statements by the latter's supplier? It would have a sobering effect upon business

[17] See Preamble, para 31: 'The principle of good faith and fair dealing should provide guidance on the way parties have to cooperate. As some rules constitute specific manifestations of the general principle of good faith and fair dealing, they should take precedent over the general principle. The general principle should therefore not be used as a tool to amend the specific rights and obligations of parties as set out in the specific rules'.

[18] Hesselink, *CFR and Social Justice*, n 15 above, 86.

if the rules in CESL, Annex I, article 69(3) were extended to B2B relationships. The similar rules in the Nordic Sale of Goods Act, article 18 and the German BGB, § 434(3) on sales apply to B2B contracts, and so does PECL, article 6:101(3) on statements giving rise to contractual obligations.

Individually Negotiated Terms

Chapter 8 in Annex I on unfair contract terms deals with non-individually negotiated terms. Rules on individually negotiated terms that are unfair are not provided in the Regulation. Individually negotiated terms that are unfair may be held invalid if the rule in CESL, Annex I, article 51 on unfair exploitation applies. Terms, however, may be unfair also when there was no unfair exploitation. PECL, article 4:110 is limited to terms not individually negotiated, but individually negotiated terms may be held invalid under the principle of good faith and fair dealing in PECL, article 2:201. CESL, Annex I, article 2(2) seems to exclude this possibility, see above.

Under CESL, Annex I, article 4(2), these issues are to be settled in accordance with the objectives and the principles underlying the CESL and all its provisions without recourse to the national law that would be applicable in the absence of an agreement to use the Common European Sales Law or any other law. The validity of individually negotiated terms may be issues within the scope of the CESL that are not expressly settled by it. This, however, is uncertain, and it would be preferable if the CESL also dealt with individually negotiated terms.

Transparency and Traders

The rules in CESL, Annex I, Chapter 8, Section 3 on unfair terms in contracts between traders are more lenient to the trader than the rules in Section 2 on unfair terms in contracts between a trader and a consumer.

CESL, Annex I, article 82 (in Section 2 on duty of transparency in terms not individually negotiated) provides:

> Where a trader supplies contract terms which have not been individually negotiated with the consumer … it has a duty to ensure that they are presented in an accessible and comprehensible way.

A similar provision is not provided in Section 3 on contract terms with a trader.

Why does this provision not apply to B2B contracts? Should suppliers be permitted to use convoluted language and hide their terms vis-à-vis their business customers?

PECL, article 2:104 (on terms not individually negotiated) provides.

> (1) Contract terms which have not been individually negotiated may be invoked against a party who did not know of them only if the party invoking them took reasonable steps to bring them to the other party's attention before or when the contract was concluded.
> (2) Terms are not brought appropriately to a party's attention by a mere reference to them in a contract document, even if that party signs the document.

This provision applies to B2C and to all B2B contracts.

Why Graduate Unfairness?

CESL, Annex I, article 83 gives the meaning of 'unfair' in contracts between a trader and a consumer. A non-individually negotiated term is unfair *if it causes a significant imbalance in the parties' rights and obligations arising under the contract to the detriment of the consumer contrary to good faith and fair dealing*. This language is similar to that of PECL, article 4:110, which applies both to B2B and B2C contracts. The PECL have borrowed their language from article 5 of Council Directive 93/13/EC on Unfair Terms in Consumer Contracts.[19] CESL, Annex I, article 86 provides that a non-individually negotiated term in a B2B is unfair: 'if it is of such a nature that its use grossly deviates from good commercial practice contrary to good faith and fair dealing'. This gives the supplier of the term more freedom than the trader in a B2C relationship.

It is submitted that this differential treatment of B2B and B2C contract terms is unjustified. There is no reason to tolerate more unfairness in a B2B contract than in a B2C contract. The similar general clauses of the German Civil Code, § 307, the Nordic Contract Act, § 36, the Dutch BW, article 6:248(2) and the US Uniform Commercial Code, § 2:302 apply both to B2B and to B2C contracts.[20]

The difference between the B2B and the B2C contract term is not that a term may be more unfair in a B2B than in a B2C contract. The difference is that in B2B contracts, terms are fair that are not fair in B2C contracts. In a B2B contract, a term may exclude the remedies available to the customer against the supplier when the parties have agreed that the risk that the digital content does not possess the qualities that the buyer may expect is to be borne by the customer. The same term is unfair in a B2C relationship. The PECL definition of an unfair term should be used for both B2C and B2B contracts.

Why Exclude the Unfair Price?

Council Directive 93/13/EC, article 4(2) and PECL, article 4:110(2) provide that the article does not apply to a term which defines the main subject matter of the contract, provided the term is in plain and intelligible language; or to the adequacy in value of one party's obligations compared to the value of the obligations of the other party. Similarly, CESL, Annex I, article 80 provides that Section 3 (ie article 86 on unfair terms in B2B contracts) does not apply to the definition of the main subject matter of the contract or to the appropriateness of the price to be paid.

In my view, it is unreasonable that agreements on unconscionable prices cannot be set aside or the price be reduced. Council Directive 93/13/EC, article 4(2) has been omitted in the provisions implementing the Directive in Austria, Denmark,

[19] Directive 93/13/EC, art 5 is modelled on § 9 of the former German Law on General Conditions of Contracts 1976 which is now § 307 of the German Civil Code, as amended in 2001. It applies to B2B and B2C contracts.

[20] See Hesselink, *CFR and Social Justice*, n 15 above, 37, who also advocates a unitary fairness test for B2B and B2C contracts.

Greece, Latvia, Luxembourg, Romania, Slovenia, Spain and Sweden.[21] The US Uniform Commercial Code, § 2:302 on unconscionable contracts or clauses has also been applied to agreements on an unfair price, where the mark-up of the seller was unconscionably high.[22]

Black and Grey Lists and Traders

CESL, Annex I, article 79 provides that a 'contract term which is supplied by one party and which is unfair under Sections 2 and 3 of this Chapter is not binding on the other party'. Article 84 (in Section 2 on unfair terms in contracts between businesses and consumers) lists 12 'black' terms, which are always unfair, and article 85 lists 22 'grey' terms, which may be unfair. Article 86 (in Section 3 on the meaning of 'unfair' in contracts between traders) does not provide lists of unfair terms.

The CESL does not mention that courts may find inspiration in the lists when applying articles 79 and 86 to B2B contracts. This should be done.

Incorrect Installation

CESL, Annex I, article 104 treats incorrect installation under a consumer sales contract:

> (1) Where goods supplied under a consumer sales contract are incorrectly installed, any non-conformity resulting from the incorrect installation is regarded as a non-conformity of the goods if:
> (a) the goods were installed by the seller or under the seller's responsibility; or
> (b) the goods were intended to be installed by the consumer and the incorrect installation was due to a shortcoming in the installation instructions.
>
> (2) The parties may not, to the detriment of the consumer, exclude the application of this Article or derogate from or vary its effects.

Why does article 104(1) not apply to B2B contracts as well? It could be made a non-mandatory rule.

Other examples of rules reflecting a more individualistic attitude in the CESL than in the PECL could be mentioned.[23] On several points, the CESL tolerates a more thick-skinned behaviour in B2B relationships than the PECL, and this in spite of the fact that the CESL was prepared to cater for SMEs, who were not in the foreground of the minds of the Commission on European Contract Law. A more individualistic attitude also prevailed in the Study Group preparing the DCFR[24] and among the experts who prepared the Feasibility Study.

[21] Hans Schulte-Nölke et al (eds), *EC Consumer Law Compendium: Comparative Analysis* (February 2008) 345, 393. Here quoted from Hesselink, *CFR and Social Justice*, n 15 above, 63.

[22] See White and Summers, *Uniform Commercial Code*, 4th edn (1996) 218.

[23] Compare eg CESL, art 72 on merger clauses with PECL, art 2:205; and CESL, art 75(2), (4) on a grossly unreasonable price determined by a third party with PECL, art 6:105.

[24] See Hesselink, *CFR and Social Justice*, n 15 above, passim.

A Graduation of Protection is Appropriate, But the Big Trader Should Also be Protected

Weakest and in need of most protection is the consumer, followed by the 'small' trader, the farmer, the fisherman, the shopkeeper, the artisan, etc; then comes the trader who lacks knowledge about the product and the terms of his supplier, and finally other big traders.

The small trader needs the same protection against the onerous standard terms of the supplier as the consumer but should not have the consumer's right to withdraw in distance and off-premises contracts. The trader who lacks the specialised knowledge about the other party's performance needs the protection of some but not all the rules protecting the consumer. He should, for instance, be able to rely on public statements made by or on behalf of a producer or other person in earlier links, as provided in CESL, Annex I, article 69(3)(c).

One may ask why the representatives of business wished to exclude the contracts between big traders from the scope of the CESL, and why they wished to offer such a moderate protection for SMEs? As suppliers, traders wish for freedom and abhor intervention. As customers, the big traders feel strong enough to avoid the unfair terms and other manifestations of unfair behaviour on the part of their suppliers.

However, although he is big and well-informed, the trader needs protection against behaviour by the other party that is unfair. Traders often do not study the standard terms of their contracting parties, but if they do they will object to most of the contract terms listed in CESL, Annex I, articles 84 and 85, which protect consumers. To hold them bound by these terms is in my view to let them pay too high a price for their negligence. Protection relieves the traders from the trouble of studying and negotiating about the unfair standard terms of the other party.[25]

FINAL REMARKS

The CESL has avoided some of the flaws of the CISG, but the division of the Commission's Proposal into a Regulation and Annexes I and II, and the many definitions in article 2 of the Regulation, are confusing. The exclusion of big traders and domestic contracts from its scope of application is not well-founded. The CESL gives SMEs some protection and contains some *esprit collectif*, but it is hard to see why much of the protection it accords to consumers should not be bestowed on SMEs.

[25] See also Hein Kötz, *Der Schutzzweck der AGB Kontrolle* (2003), in Hein Kötz, *Undogmatisches* (Tübingen, 2005) 221; and see Hesselink, *CFR and Social Justice*, n 15 above, 37.

15

The Law of Assignment in European Contract Law

WOLF-GEORG RINGE

INTRODUCTION

I HAD THE pleasure of working together with Hugh Beale on a highly interesting research project, where we looked at policy proposals to create a common European law on assignments, as part of the ambitious plan for a (draft) Common Frame of Reference (DCFR).[1] As is commonly known, the DCFR did not materialise in its full shape. All that made it to the legislative process is the proposed Common European Sales Law (CESL), which is much reduced in scope, and crucially leaves out the law of assignment. We emphasised in our earlier work that this decision is regrettable.[2]

Thus, at the present time, cross-border assignments in Europe are still governed by a fragmented collection of legal rules, involving a variety of mostly national contract laws, elements of the law of property and personal security, and, to some extent, by harmonised provisions on private international law. The present system is complex and far from perfect. This essay takes stock of the development and seeks to explore perspectives for the optimal way forward in a European framework for cross-border assignments.

Assignments are multiparty transactions that frequently occur in a cross-border context. They are an inherent part of modern trade: for example, the entire factoring sector is based on them. The intangible character of an assignment operation allows international actors to transfer rights around the globe in no time and with very low transaction costs.[3] From a legal perspective, however, assignments are a very complex matter involving at least three parties and frequently multiple national legal systems. Jurisdictions differ in this field with regard to their doctrine and

[1] H Beale and WG Ringe, 'Transfer of Rights and Obligations' in G Dannemann and S Vogenauer (eds), *The Common European Sales Law in Context: Interactions with English and German Law* (Oxford University Press, 2013) 521–61.

[2] Beale and Ringe, 'Transfer of Rights and Obligations', n 1 above, 521.

[3] EM Kieninger, 'General Principles on the Law Applicable to the Assignment of Receivables in Europe' in J Basedow, H Baum and Y Nishitani (eds), *Japanese and European Private International Law in Comparative Perspective* (Tübingen, Mohr Siebeck, 2008) 153; EM Kieninger, 'Das Abtretungsrecht des DCFR' [2010] *Zeitschrift für Europäisches Privatrecht (ZEuP)* 724; S Leible and M Müller, 'Die Anknüpfung der Drittwirkung von Forderungsabtretungen in der Rom I-VO' (2012) 32 *Praxis des Internationalen Privat- und Verfahrensrechts (IPRax)* 491.

substantive rules.[4] Examples are proprietary aspects and substantive requirements for an assignment. Legal rules should aim at ensuring that such cross-border transactions run smoothly, and law-makers have long attempted to find appropriate solutions for this complex cross-border subject.

Academic literature and policy-makers have developed two general approaches to ease cross-border assignments over the past decades. Although both developed in parallel at the same time, their doctrinal background is fundamentally different.

The first approach is to create a common European *private international law* for assignments (see below). Private international law (PIL) or 'conflict of laws' is a form of 'meta law'. It classifies legal issues into groups, provides a 'connecting factor' and determines appropriate rules of national law to apply to the situation. The basic idea of a harmonised PIL approach is to foster legal certainty for cross-border situations. A clear connecting factor, eg the place of residence of a contracting party, allows parties to determine which national law applies to their situation. In theory, harmonised private international law ensures the application of the same law tailor-made for every individual case regardless of which court hears the case. In early times, the Hague Conference on Private International Law[5] attempted to create harmonised PIL rules with respect to marriage and civil procedure, as early as the beginning of the twentieth century.[6] The Rome Convention[7] from 1980 and the Rome I Regulation[8] from 2009 were the first harmonised PIL rules for European contract law. Inter alia, both instruments contain conflict of laws rules for cross-border assignments.

The second approach seeks to harmonise *substantive law itself* across countries (see below). The idea of developing an independent international code for contracts has a certain charm. Such an international rulebook could apply to international situations without recourse to private international law. The proponents of unitary law view the method of PIL, ie referring to different national laws, as inappropriate to fulfil the demands of a modern economy. The divergences in national laws would increase transaction costs.[9] As a result, most consumers and businesses would refuse cross-border activity. Ernst Rabel and UNIDROIT had already attempted to unify the international law of sales of goods back in 1929.[10] In 1980, a number of

[4] H Kötz, 'Rights of Third Parties: Third Party Beneficiaries and Assignment' in A von Mehren (ed), *International Encyclopedia of Comparative Law*, vol VII, *Contracts in General* (Tübingen, Mohr Siebeck, 1992) ch 13.

[5] Commonly abbreviated HCCH, for Hague Conference/Conférence de La Haye.

[6] Convention of 12 June 1902 relating to the Settlement of the Conflict of the Laws concerning Marriage, available at www.hcch.net/index_en.php?act=text.display&tid=13; Convention of 17 July 1905 relating to Civil Procedure, available at www.hcch.net/index_en.php?act=text.display&tid=16.

[7] Convention 80/934/EC on the Law applicable to Contractual Obligations opened for signature in Rome on 19 June 1980 [1980] OJ L266/1. Today, the Convention still remains applicable for all contracts relating to Denmark, which is not bound by the Rome I Regulation.

[8] Regulation (EC) 593/2008 of the European Parliament and of the Council of 17 June 2008 on the law applicable to contractual obligations [2008] OJ L177/6 ('Rome I Regulation').

[9] Eg European Commission, *Europe 2020: A Strategy for Smart, Sustainable and Inclusive Growth*, COM(2010)2020 final, 21; European Commission, 'Single Market Act: Twelve Levers to Boost Growth and Strengthen Confidence: Working Together to Create New Growth, COM(2011)206, 19; European Commission, Proposal for a Regulation of the European Parliament and of the Council on a Common European Sales Law of 11 October 2011, COM(2011)635, 2–4.

[10] SdN UDP 1929, Etudes: IV Vente, Doc 1, Observations concernant l'utilité de l'unification, au point de vue des besoins de commerce internationale, par ME Rabel, available at www.unidroit.org/work-in-progress-studies/studies/international-sales/188-study-iv-international-sale-of-goods.

countries concluded the UN-based Convention on Contracts for the International Sale of Goods (CISG) in Vienna.[11] It is now applicable in 81 different nations. More recently, the European Union has published a proposal for a Common European Sales Law (CESL).[12] These examples show that the concept of unitary law is already common practice for several areas of law.

Even though assignments are of high practical relevance for international trade, there is no such harmonised international instrument to deal with it. At this stage, only a few non-binding initiatives exist on the supra- and international levels.[13] These rules do not have legal force, but serve as a type of 'soft law'. However, it is possible that today's soft law may be a blueprint for binding rules in the future.

This article explores the current situation of the law of assignment against the background of the two mentioned strategies, legal unification and private international law, and advances suggestions for its future development. The second section takes stock with the *acquis* of European assignment law, explaining the different instruments already dealing with the subject matter. The third section then seeks to develop the essential differences and economic functions that both legal strategies seek to accomplish, and maps these onto the necessities of an effective cross-border law of assignment for Europe. Essentially, I suggest a combination of both strategies as a way forward: an optional unitary instrument, coupled with coherent private international law rules, will be the best strategy for the future development of this area of law. The fourth section then concludes.

STATUS QUO

The current *acquis* of European assignment law is characterised by a high degree of heterogeneity of legal instruments. Law-makers and international working groups have worked on a range of instruments, but there is no master plan to develop all of these into a coherent shape. The following describes that current state of play in terms of the two most prominent strategies: private international law and substantial harmonisation.

Private International Law

Under the law as it stands today, international contracts of assignment are governed by article 14 of the Rome I Regulation. This regime is applicable to contracts which were concluded after 17 December 2009.[14] Contracts that were concluded before this date fall under its predecessor, the Rome Convention of 1980.

[11] United Nations Convention on Contracts for the International Sale of Goods (CISG), opened for signature 11 April 1980, Vienna, available at www.uncitral.org/pdf/english/texts/sales/cisg/V1056997-CISG-e-book.pdf.

[12] European Commission, Proposal for a Regulation of the European Parliament and of the Council on a Common European Sales Law of 11 October 2011, COM(2011)635.

[13] Eg European initiatives: Principles of European Contract Law; Draft Common Frame of Reference; international initiatives: UNIDROIT Principles of International Commercial Contracts; United Nations Convention on Assignment of Receivables in International Trade.

[14] Rome I Regulation, art 28.

Rome Convention 1980

The Rome Convention is an international treaty, operating under the roof of the European Union, but legally independent from it.[15] The Convention harmonised Member States' PIL rules on contracts for the first time. Before that, most national jurisdictions had hardly any conflict of law rules for contractual obligations. The few existing rules were based on customer protection.[16] The only instrument that existed were common rules for determining the appropriate forum for international conflicts, based on a 1968 Convention.[17] This so-called Brussels Convention allowed parties to choose a particular forum for their contract. In the absence of harmonised rules on the applicable law, the Brussels Convention thereby facilitated the possibility of forum shopping. For example, a party with a strong bargaining position could insist on the selection of a forum that would have a more advantageous law for its purposes. In order to avoid such forum shopping, all EU Member States concluded a separate treaty on private international law, the Rome Convention, which aimed at assuring the application of the same substantive law regardless of the hearing court.[18] Incidentally, this Convention was also supposed to increase legal certainty for cross-border contracts by providing a common connecting factor for the applicable law.[19] New consolidated versions were published in 1998 and 2005.[20] At these times, new EU Member States had acceded to the Convention.

The Rome Convention dealt with the law of cross-border assignments in Article 12:

Article 12. Voluntary assignment

1. *The mutual obligations of assignor and assignee under a voluntary assignment of a right against another person ('the debtor') shall be governed by the law which under this Convention applies to the contract between the assignor and assignee.*
2. *The law governing the right to which the assignment relates shall determine its assignability, the relationship between the assignee and the debtor, the conditions under which the assignment can be invoked against the debtor and any question whether the debtor's obligations have been discharged.*

[15] JF Morrissey and JM Graves, *International Sales Law and Arbitration: Problems, Cases and Commentary* (Kluwer Law International, 2008) 62.

[16] Report on the Convention on the Law applicable to Contractual Obligations [1980] OJ C282/1, 8.

[17] Brussels Convention on Jurisdiction and the Enforcement of Judgments in Civil and Commercial Matters [1972] OJ L299/32. This Convention has been replaced by Brussels I Regulation in 2002: Council Regulation (EC) 44/2001 of 22 December 2000 on jurisdiction and the recognition and enforcement of judgments in civil and commercial matters [2001] OJ L12/1.

[18] European Commission, *Green Paper on the Conversion of the Rome Convention of 1980 on the Law applicable to Contractual Obligations into a Community Instrument and its Modernisation*, COM(2002)654 final, 9.

[19] Commission Opinion 80/383/EEC of 17 March 1980 concerning the draft Convention on the Law applicable to Contractual Obligations [1980] OJ L94/39.

[20] Convention 98/C27/02 on the Law applicable to Contractual Obligations (consolidated version); First Protocol on the Interpretation of the 1980 Convention by the European Court of Justice (consolidated version); Second Protocol Conferring on the CJEU Powers to Interpret the 1980 Convention (consolidated version) on 26 January 1998 [1998] OJ C27/34; Convention 2005/C334/01 on the Law applicable to Contractual Obligations (consolidated version); First Protocol on the Interpretation of the 1980 Convention by the European Court of Justice (consolidated version); Second Protocol Conferring on the CJEU Powers to Interpret the 1980 Convention (consolidated version) on 30 December 2005 [2005] OJ C334/1.

The first paragraph applies to the relationship between assignor and assignee. It depends on the law which governs the contract they concluded. Article 3 of the Rome Convention allows them to choose this law. In the absence of a choice, the applicable law will be determined objectively by specific rules in Articles 4 to 8.

The second paragraph refers to the law that governs the 'right to which the assignment relates'. The purpose of this rule is to ensure that the debtor's obligations and security are the same compared to his previous situation. An assignment must not affect or change his position.[21]

Article 12 already covers many questions regarding the law of assignment. Nevertheless, it is incomplete in some ways. For example, an explicit rule for proprietary aspects of the assignment is missing. In other words, Article 12 does not cover the proprietary relationship between assignor and assignee, nor does it cover the effectiveness of the assignment against third parties (eg the assignor's insolvency administrator or other creditors). In order to fill this gap, academic commentators and case-law have long discussed whether the aspects between assignor and assignee were to be governed by the first paragraph of Article 12,[22] its second paragraph[23] or rather national conflicts law.[24] These different views are of high practical relevance, since they lead to different applicable laws for an important implication of the assignment. These laws vary in their substantial requirements for the effectiveness of an assignment. It might occur that an assignment is void under one jurisdiction and valid under another one. As a consequence, the identical problem might be solved differently, depending on the court ruling on the case. Moreover, Article 12 does not offer a solution for the effectiveness of assignments against third parties. This lack of legal clarity stands in stark contrast to its original purpose.

Rome I Regulation

In 2009, the Rome I Regulation replaced the Rome Convention for two reasons. As we have shown, practice revealed several loopholes in the Rome Convention. For that reason, the Rome I Regulation intended to modernise certain parts of the Convention. Changing the Convention itself would have required complicated negotiations, as it is a multilateral treaty.[25] All contracting states would have had to agree to every single change. Instead, a Regulation is directly applicable and automatically takes effect in all EU Member States.[26] Consequently, it was the easiest way to apply identical rules in all EU Member States. The second reason goes

[21] F Garcimartin Alférez, 'Assignment of Claims in the Rome I Regulation: Article 14' in F Ferrari and S Leible, *Rome I Regulation: The Law applicable to Contractual Obligations in Europe* (Munich, Sellier, 2009) 217, 228, with further references.

[22] Eg 16 May 1997, Rechtspraak van de Week 126; NJ 1998, 585; H Verhagen and S van Dongen, 'Cross-border Assignments under Rome I' (2010) 6 *Journal of Private International Law* 1, 13 and 17.

[23] BGH, Judgment of 8 December 1998, XI ZR 302/97, para 21.

[24] Garcimartin Alférez, 'Assignment of Claims in the Rome I Regulation: Article 14', n 21 above, 234, with further references.

[25] Opinion of the European Economic and Social Committee on the Proposal for a Regulation of the European Parliament and of the Council on the law applicable to contractual obligations (Rome I) [2006] OJ C318/56.

[26] TFEU, art 288(2).

back to the context of the general legal development at that time.[27] First of all, the Brussels I Regulation was adopted in 2001, modernising cross-border jurisdiction of courts. In a second step, the Rome II Regulation[28] harmonised private international law for non-contractual obligations, in 2007. The Rome Convention, Rome II and Brussels I were seen as 'an indissoluble set of Community rules of private international law relating to contractual and non-contractual obligations [in] civil and commercial matters'.[29] They developed a uniform European private international law in a broad coverage. The main difference between these instruments was the legal nature of the Rome Convention. For this reason, EU law-makers sought to bring it into line with the two other existing instruments.[30]

In substance, the basic content of the convention was broadly maintained. A few attempts to update the existing rules concerned, inter alia, the law of assignment. New article 14 of the Rome I Regulation now deals with voluntary assignments and contractual subrogation:

> *Article 14*
>
> 1. *The relationship between assignor and assignee under a voluntary assignment or contractual subrogation of a claim against another person (the debtor) shall be governed by the law that applies to the contract between the assignor and assignee under this Regulation.*
> 2. *The law governing the assigned or subrogated claim shall determine its assignability, the relationship between the assignee and the debtor, the conditions under which the assignment or subrogation can be invoked against the debtor and whether the debtor's obligations have been discharged.*
> 3. *The concept of assignment in this Article includes outright transfers of claims, transfers of claims by way of security and pledges or other security rights over claims.*

Comparing this to the Convention, it becomes apparent that the first paragraph's text has changed. Furthermore, a new third paragraph has been added. This paragraph defines the assignment itself, as well as the scope of it. It covers all contractual claims, claims by way of security and pledges or other security rights over claims. Since the Rome II Regulation does not contain its own assignment rules, Article 14 also covers the transfer of non-contractual claims. However, obligations arising under bills of exchange, cheques and promissory notes and other negotiable instruments, and claims determined by company law are excluded from the scope of the Rome I Regulation.[31]

Besides clarifying the scope, the Commission needed to deal with one particular topic. As we have mentioned above, the Rome Convention did not deal with proprietary aspects of assignments and thus created uncertainty and confusion. As recital 38 emphasises, the Regulation sought to address this problem. The change

[27] F Garcimartin Alférez, 'The Rome I Regulation: Much Ado about Nothing?' (2008) 2 *European Legal Forum* I-62.

[28] Regulation (EC) 864/2007 of the European Parliament and of the Council of 11 July 2007 on the law applicable to non-contractual obligations [2007] OJ L199/40 (Rome II Regulation).

[29] European Commission, Proposal for a Regulation of the European Parliament and the Council on the law applicable to contractual obligations (Rome I), COM(2005)650 final, 2.

[30] ibid 3.

[31] Rome I Regulation, art 1(2)(d), (f).

of wording from 'obligations' to 'relationship' in the first paragraph should imply that article 14 also covers the proprietary aspects of the contract between assignor and assignee. Nevertheless, it is still controversially discussed whether and how far article 14 covers these.[32] Furthermore and worse, the question concerning third party rights has been omitted. During the drafting process of the Regulation, previous article 13 of the (proposed) Regulation was supposed to deal with this problem. It contained a rule for third party rights in its paragraph 3, referring to the law of the habitual residence of the assignor.[33] The solution was inspired by the UN Convention on the Assignment of Receivables in International Trade of 2001.[34] However, the proposal caused heated and controversial discussions. Proponents of the different positions were not able to agree on a compromise solution.[35] As a result, the European institutions decided to omit the controversial text. Instead, they included a review clause in article 27(2), mandating a report on the 'question of the effectiveness of an assignment or subrogation of a claim against third parties and the priority of the assigned or subrogated claim over a right of another person', to be submitted by the Commission by 2010.[36] The British Institute for International and Comparative Law (BIICL) in London was commissioned to draft such a report, which it published in 2011.[37] This study offers a number of different solutions to the problem, but does not speak out in favour of one. Since the publication of the BIICL report, law-makers have not further addressed the question.

Harmonisation Approach

It is interesting to note that EU law-makers, at the same time as they developed common PIL rules, also initiated preparatory work for a substantial common contract law on the EU level. Article 3 and recital 13 of the Rome I Regulation demonstrate

[32] The different opinions are similar to the arguments put forward in the context of the Rome Convention. See Verhagen and van Dongen, 'Cross-border Assignments under Rome I', n 22 above, 19, 20, who hold that the first paragraph covers the property aspects. In addition, they offer the alternative that property aspects can be solved by the law governing the assigned right, plus the possibility to choose the assignor's domestic law. Contrast this with T Hartley, 'Choice of Law regarding the Voluntary Assignment of Contractual Obligations under the Rome I Regulation' (2011) 60 *International and Comparative Law Quarterly (ICLQ)* 29, 34, who states that the first paragraph covers all the property aspects between assignor and assignee, but no preliminary questions. See also EM Kieninger, 'General Principles on the Law applicable to the Assignment of Receivables in Europe' in J Basedow, H Baum and Y Nishitani (eds), *Japanese and European Private International Law in Comparative Perspective* (Tübingen, Mohr Siebeck, 2008) 153, 171.

[33] Commission Proposal, n 29 above, art 13.

[34] ibid.

[35] Leible and Müller, 'Die Anknüpfung der Drittwirkung von Forderungsabtretungen in der Rom I-VO', n 3 above, 494.

[36] 'By 17 June 2010, the Commission shall submit to the European Parliament, the Council and the European Economic and Social Committee a report on the question of the effectiveness of an assignment or subrogation of a claim against third parties and the priority of the assigned or subrogated claim over a right of another person. The report shall be accompanied, if appropriate, by a proposal to amend this Regulation and an assessment of the impact of the provisions to be introduced.'

[37] BIICL, *Study on the Question of Effectiveness of an Assignment or Subrogation of a Claim against Third Parties and the Priority of the Assigned or Subrogated Claim over a Right of Another Person: Final Report* (2011), available at http://ec.europa.eu/justice/civil/files/report_assignment_en.pdf.

that the European law-makers were aware of this dual process, while they were drafting the Regulation. Recital 13 emphasises that the parties may choose a non-state body of law as well as international conventions. In addition, the European Economic and Social Committee stated in its opinion on the proposed Rome I Regulation:

> *If an optional instrument/26th regime ever comes into being, this would then claim to be the best of all possible systems of civil law. If it were agreed to apply this instrument rather than a national system of law, there would logically no longer be any need to align it with national laws or allow interference on the grounds of national mandatory rules.*[38]

This statement demonstrates the Committee's general preference for the harmonisation approach. The European Commission shares this preference for unitary law, as it explains in the recently proposed Common European Sales Law: arguably, the heterogeneity of national private laws makes cross-border trades too complex.[39] A high degree of heterogeneity creates information costs for business participants and thereby high transaction costs. We will revisit this discussion below. At this stage, we first need to look at various other attempts in recent history where initiatives or law-makers have promulgated the adoption of unitary law. This will allow us to compare the two concepts of PIL and unitary law and to explore the right way forward for the law of assignment.

Principles of European Contract Law (PECL)

A private, voluntary association of legal academics, the so-called Lando Commission, developed the so-called Principles of European Contract Law[40] during the time from 1982 to 2002. They did not officially represent the European Union.[41] Their main purpose was to draw up a neutral set of principles for European contract law. Thereby, these principles intended to mirror the common core of European national contract systems.[42] The Lando Commission was influenced by existing harmonisation approaches, namely, the Uniform Commercial Code (UCC) and the UNIDROIT Principles.[43] The UCC is unitary law for different US American states. The UNIDROIT Principles, on the other hand, were an attempt to create worldwide uniformity in contract law. Especially the latter was the most important source of inspiration for the Lando Commission.[44]

[38] Commission Proposal, n 29 above, note 9.

[39] European Commission, Proposal for a Regulation of the European Parliament and of the Council on a Common European Sales Law, COM(2011)635, 2–3, 8.

[40] Reprinted in O Lando and H Beale (eds), *Principles of European Contract Law* (Kluwer Law International, 2000).

[41] W Hesselink, 'The Principles of European Contract Law: Some Choices Made by the Lando Commission' in MW Hesselink and GJP de Vries, *Principles of European Contract Law; Preadviezen uitgebracht voor de vereniging voor Burgerlijk Recht* (Deventer, Kluwer, 2001) 5.

[42] JM Smits, 'The Principles of European Contract Law and the Harmonisation of Private Law in Europe' in A Vacquer (ed), *La Tercera Parte de Los Principios de Derecho Contractual Europeo* (Valencia, Tirant, 2005) 567, 568.

[43] Hesselink, 'The Principles of European Contract Law', n 41 above.

[44] ibid 8.

The Principles of European Contract Law are an ambitious and influential set of rules, which, however, do not have any legal force as such. Being soft law, contracting parties can opt for the application of the PECL by agreement.[45] In that case, national law will not be applicable, except for its mandatory rules.[46] It has been criticised that the PECL are too general in order to ensure full legal certainty.[47] Nevertheless, they have certainly brought one big advantage: a common basic language for contract law. Martijn Hesselink has described this as 'meta-language'.[48] Legal scholars and practitioners were able to use the same terms to describe international legal affairs. It simplified the international debate and reduced uncertainties resulting from different designations in various languages.

The law of assignment is regulated in Chapter 11. It covers the assignment of rights from existing and future contracts as well as other transferable claims.[49] The scope also covers the transfer of security rights. The PECL exclude transfers assuming an entry in in the register or an endorsement.[50] They do not require a special form for the effectiveness of an assignment. The assignment takes effect at the time of the agreement to assign, or if agreed at any other moment afterwards.[51] The assignment transfers all the assignor's rights to performance and the accessory rights to the assignee.[52] The debtor may set up against the assignee all substantive and procedural defences to the assigned claim which the debtor could have invoked against the assignor.[53]

PECL, article 11:401 deals with priority and third party rights. This article gives priority to the assignment that was first notified to the debtor, except where he knew or ought to have known of an earlier assignment. In the case of breach of a contractual prohibition, the assignment will not be effective against the debtor.[54] However, this prohibition does not infringe the proprietary *erga omnes* effect of the assignment, which remains effective.[55] The liability only refers to the contractual relationship between assignor and assignee.

UNIDROIT Principles of International Commercial Contracts

The International Institute for the Unification of Private Law (UNIDROIT) has adopted two Conventions which refer to the topic at hand. UNIDROIT is a private foundation which works without any governmental order. The Conventions have universal character.

[45] PECL, art 1:101.
[46] ibid art 1:103.
[47] Smits, 'The Principles of European Contract Law and the Harmonisation of Private Law in Europe', n 42 above, 12.
[48] Hesselink, 'The Principles of European Contract Law', n 41 above, 14.
[49] PECL, arts 11:102(2), 11:101.
[50] ibid art 11:101(3).
[51] ibid arts 11:104, 11:202.
[52] ibid art 11:201.
[53] ibid art 11:307.
[54] ibid art 11:301.
[55] Kieninger, 'Das Abtretungsrecht des DCFR', n 3 above, 733.

In 1988, the UNIDROIT Convention on International Factoring was signed in Ottawa. It deals only with the law of international factoring. Its application has priority over the Rome I Regulation.[56] The background for creating this Convention was the importance the authors attributed to the factoring sector in the commercial and financial world. They emphasised the existing legal uncertainty because of the differences in substantive national laws. The Factoring Convention is a set of key principles to create a minimum standard of legal certainty and therefore to reduce transaction costs. It was furthermore limited in its scope. Detailed questions like priority were left to established rules of private international law.[57]

Six years later, UNIDROIT adopted the Principles of International Commercial Contracts (PICC).[58] These were introduced with the reason that the existing soft-law texts were fragmented in character or might end up as dead letter.[59] While developing the rules, UNIDROIT has been influenced by the UCC and the CISG. These two instruments only deal with a limited area of law. In contrast, the PICC cover a very broad field of international contract law. The first version did not deal with the law of assignment. A second, extended version was published in 2004. The foreword to this edition introduced five new chapters. Amongst others it contained the law of assignment. These new chapters were integrated because they were deemed 'of interest to the international legal business communities'.[60]

Chapter 9 deals with the assignment of rights (Section 1). The principles cover the assignment of obligations to money or to render other performance.[61] Future rights can be assigned as well.[62] In the case that the assigned right has an 'essential personal character', the PICC require the debtor's consensus for a valid assignment.[63]

Furthermore and similar to the DCFR, the assignment has to be notified to the debtor, otherwise he will be discharged for paying either to assignor or assignee.[64] An effective assignment transfers all the assignor's rights to payment or other performance, as well as all rights securing performance of the right assigned.[65] The debtor is as well protected as in the other codes. He may assert all the defences against the assignee which he could assert against the assignor.[66] Furthermore, the priority solutions are quite similar. The only difference is that the debtor will be discharged for paying to the assignor, even though he knew about an earlier assignment. This requires that he did not receive a notice about the transfer.[67] The authors wanted to make sure that the assignor/assignee will notify the transfer to the obligee.[68]

[56] Rosch, *Juris Praxiskommentar BGB*, art 14 Rom I-VO, para 8.

[57] UNIDROIT Secretariat, Explanatory Note, UNIDROIT Convention on International Factoring, 1–2, available at www.unidroit.org/english/conventions/1988factoring/explanatorynote-e.pdf.

[58] On this in detail see S Vogenauer and J Kleinheisterkamp (eds), *Commentary on the UNIDROIT Principles of International Commercial Contracts* (Oxford University Press, 2009).

[59] UNIDROIT Secretariat, Explanatory Note, PICC, Introduction to the 1994 Edition, available at www.unidroit.org/english/principles/contracts/principles2010/integralversionprinciples2010-e.pdf.

[60] PICC, Foreword to the 2004 Edition.

[61] PICC, art 9.1.1.

[62] PICC, art 9.1.5, Comment 3: 'retroactive effect'.

[63] PICC, art 9.1.7.

[64] ibid art 9.1.10.

[65] ibid art 9.1.14.

[66] ibid art 9.1.13.

[67] ibid art 9.1.11.

[68] PICC, art 9.1.11, Comment 1.

By dealing with contractual prohibition of assignments the PICC distinguish between the assignment of a right to pay a monetary sum and the assignment of other rights and performances.[69] The assignor can transfer rights to pay a monetary sum, but he will be liable to the debtor. Other rights may not be assigned, with the exception that the assignee did not know the contractual prohibition or ought to have known it. In this case, the assignor is liable to the debtor.

United Nations Convention on Assignment of Receivables in International Trade

Yet another example is the Convention on Assignment of Receivables in International Trade (CARIT), negotiated under the auspices of the United Nations Commission on International Trade Law (UNCITRAL), and adopted in 2001. It is not in force yet, and it is doubtful whether it ever will.[70] However, this Convention has already influenced other international legislation. The Association of the Bar of the City of New York even describes it as 'foundation for future development in this area of law'. One current example was the above-mentioned proposal for the Rome I Regulation. It adopted the conflict of laws rule from the Convention with respect to third party rights.

UNCITRAL developed the Convention to promote the availability of capital and credit at more affordable rates across national borders.[71] In other words, they wanted to increase the amount of cross-border assignments. The Preamble explains that international trade is fraught with uncertainties caused by diverging legal provisions. The Convention's purpose is to facilitate the law for cross-border receivables in financing transactions.[72] As a result, the Convention is only applicable for transfers of a monetary sum.[73] It covers the transfer of future rights and security rights. A further act of assignment is not necessary for its effectiveness.[74]

UNCITRAL excluded several rights from the scope of this Convention. Some were excluded for the reason that there is no market for them.[75] Several rights were excluded because other codes deal with them. Furthermore, some rights were so special that the Convention could not develop a solution for them.[76]

CARIT harmonises several aspects, eg the relationship between assignor and assignee. These rules are not binding and the parties can diverge from them by agreement.[77] However, party autonomy is limited where it affects third parties, and

[69] PICC, art 9.1.9.

[70] Hartley, 'Choice of Law regarding the Voluntary Assignment of Contractual Obligations under the Rome I Regulation', n 32 above, 52.

[71] UNCITRAL Secretariat, Explanatory Notes on the United Nations Convention on the Assignment of Receivables in International Trade, No 2, available at www.uncitral.org/pdf/english/texts/payments/receivables/ctc-assignment-convention-e.pdf.

[72] ibid No 1.

[73] CARIT, art 2.

[74] ibid arts 8 and 10.

[75] ibid art 4(1); Explanatory Notes on United Nations Convention on the Assignment of Receivables in International Trade, No 11.

[76] CARIT, art 4(2); Explanatory Notes on United Nations Convention on the Assignment of Receivables in International Trade, No 11.

[77] CARIT, arts 6, 11.

the debtor may not waive certain defences.[78] UNCITRAL policy-makers could not come to a uniform agreement on several aspects. These were left to autonomous conflict of law rules in Chapter 5. For example, Article 22 refers to the assignor's domestic law for priority conflicts. This displays the doctrinal pattern of CARIT. Harmonised rules govern basic questions. More complex issues are governed by clear conflict of law rules.[79]

Draft Common Frame of Reference

The Draft Common Frame of Reference (DCFR) was published in 2009. Legal scholars who work in the field of international private law, comparative law and EU law have developed this comprehensive piece of codification over some years.[80] Its content has been strongly influenced by the Principles of European Contract Law.[81] The DCFR is a result of the Action Plan on a More Coherent European Contract Law, which was published in February 2003.[82] This action plan aimed to advance the harmonisation of European private law by developing a so-called 'Common Frame of Reference' (CFR). The European Commission sought to facilitate cross-border trade with the CFR. It intended to strengthen legal certainty and make cross-border trade less costly. The DCFR is only an academic proposal and must not be confused with the CFR.[83] It is soft law based on principles, definitions and model rules.[84] Contracting parties can choose its application by agreement. The DCFR deals with the law of assignment in Chapter III, Book 5.[85] These provisions are intended to facilitate assignments and guarantee a high standard of debtor protection.[86] The official comments on the DCFR stress the economic importance of assigned rights as major tradable assets.[87]

DCFR, article III.-5:101 defines the scope of assignable rights: contractual and non-contractual claims can be assigned, as well as future rights.[88] Claims that need an entry in a register or anything comparable are excluded from the assignment, likewise the PECL. The DCFR names five requirements for an effective assignment in article III.-5:103: the right must exist; the right must be assignable; the person purporting to assign the right has the right or authority to transfer it; the assignee has to be entitled as against the assignor to the transfer by virtue of a contract or

[78] Explanatory Notes on United Nations Convention on the Assignment of Receivables in International Trade, Nos 22, 30.

[79] ibid No 5.

[80] Study Group on a European Civil Code and Research Group on the Existing EC Private Law (Acquis Group), *Draft Common Frame of Reference: Principles, Definitions and Model Rules of European Private Law* (Munich, Sellier European Law Publishers, 2009) Intr 4, 6.

[81] DCFR, Intr 8.

[82] European Commission, Communication from the Commission to the European Parliament and the Council: A More Coherent European Contract Law: An Action Plan [2003] OJ C63/1.

[83] DCFR, Intr 1.

[84] ibid Intr 24.

[85] For more detail on this, see H Beale and WG Ringe, 'Transfer of Rights and Obligations' in G Dannemann and S Vogenauer (eds), *The Common European Sales Law in Context: Interactions with English and German Law* (Oxford University Press, 2013) 521.

[86] DCFR, art III.-5:101, Comment E.

[87] ibid.

[88] DCFR, art III.-5:106.

other juridical act, a court order or a rule of law; and there must be a valid act of assignment to the right. This is a mentionable academic difference to the PECL and other regulations. None of them contains comparable requirements for an effective assignment. The transfer of future rights depends on their coming into existence. A further act of assignment is not required.[89] This illustrates a further doctrinal difference to the PECL. The DCFR distinguishes between the contractual reason for the assignment and the valid proprietary act of assignment.

The assignment is effective as soon as the five requirements are fulfilled.[90] The assignment of a future right will be retroactively regarded as having taken place at the moment in which all requirements except for those depending on the existence of the right were satisfied.[91] Any further formal requirements are not necessary.[92]

The DCFR protects the debtor in a similar way as the PECL. The debtor may set up against the assignee all substantive and procedural defences to the assigned claim which the debtor could have used against the assignor.[93] The only difference is that the assignor or assignee has to send a notice about the transfer to the debtor. Otherwise, he will be discharged for paying to the assignee, as well as to the assignor.[94] There are no differences worth mentioning to the PECL regarding the questions of priority conflicts and contractual prohibition of the assignments.[95]

Summary

The law of international assignments has been partially regulated by a number of different international instruments, conventions and EU legislation. In terms of legal strategy, it is interesting to note that both approaches, harmonising private international law and adopting common instruments of unitary law, have been pursued largely in parallel. Both strategies advance similar justifications: both claim to ensure legal certainty for cross-border assignments.

Attempts to harmonise private international law for assignments has formally been more successful, at least on the European level. Unfortunately, the Rome I Regulation did not close all loopholes in essential areas, especially with respect to third party rights.

The different efforts to draft international unitary standards have been more difficult to agree, both for governmental and for non-governmental initiatives. All of these instruments emphasise that they will overcome the obstacles of diverse national legal provisions. Their purposes are to create legal certainty and to reduce transaction costs. The essence of their substantial rules does not diverge remarkably. They all deal with key areas, such as the coming into existence of rights and their

[89] DCFR, art III.-5:106, Comment A, 1027: 'general acceptance that an act of assignment can cover future rights and that the rights will then be transferred without the need for any new act of transfer once they come into existence'.

[90] DCFR, art III.-5:104.

[91] ibid art III.-5:114.

[92] ibid arts III.-5:104 and III.-5:110 set out the exclusive requirements for an effective assignment.

[93] ibid art III.-5:116.

[94] ibid art III.-5:119.

[95] ibid arts III.-5:121, III.-5:108.

effects concerning third parties. The main advantage they brought can be seen in harmonising legal terms and language. Nonetheless, these codes do not (yet) have legal force. As we have seen, most working groups and commissions have been strongly influenced by their predecessors and previous attempts. It is therefore likely that future attempts at harmonising international standards on assignment law will refer back to the existing soft law texts.

FUTURE DIRECTION FOR ASSIGNMENT IN EUROPEAN CONTRACT LAW

The previous section introduced two regulatory approaches, PIL and unitary law, and discussed the respective law-makers' motivations for developing them. The paper now turns to a normative question: which of the two strategies is the more promising for the future development of the European law on cross-border assignments?

The following section attempts to provide some guidelines to help answer this question. I will revisit some of the economic foundations of both approaches, and discuss experiences with both strategies as they have been pursued in other areas over recent years. We will see that unitary law tends to increase transaction costs in the beginning, but has certain advantages over a longer timeframe. Optional unification can be a helpful tool to overcome obstacles caused by different legal provisions. Against this background, the section develops a possible way forward for the law of assignment, claiming that the legal nature of assignments makes them more likely for an optional standardisation than other areas of law.

Economic Background

It is generally accepted that markets can maximise welfare only on the basis of a legal system.[96] Going back to the fundamental insights discovered by Ronald Coase, the main objective of legal rules is to reduce transaction costs. To see why, Coase starts from the assumption of a world without transaction costs. In such a world, and under the condition that trade in externalities is possible, the so-called Coase Theorem states that bargaining between the parties will always lead to an efficient outcome—regardless of the initial allocation of property rights.[97] There would, accordingly, be no original need for legal rules.[98]

However, as Coase points out, this theoretical perspective does not hold true in much of the real world, where transaction costs are pervasive. Moreover, reality has shown that human beings are cognitively not able to fully understand all externalities.[99] Usually, contracting parties are at a different stage of information. A clear allocation

[96] R Kirstein and D Schmidtchen, *Ökonomische Analyse des Rechts*, CSLE Discussion Paper No 2003-04 (2003) 1, 46, available at www.econstor.eu/handle/10419/23035.

[97] The term 'Coase theorem' goes back to GJ Stigler, *The Theory of Price*, 3rd edn (New York, Macmillan, 1966).

[98] R Coase, 'The Problem of Social Cost' (1960) 3 *Journal of Law and Economics* 1.

[99] RA Heiner, 'Imperfect Decisions and the Law: On the Evolution of Legal Precedent and Rules' (1986) 15 *Journal of Legal Studies* 227.

of property rights is important to minimise costs of bargaining. Harold Demsetz went on to show that negotiation costs increase with the number of owners.[100] These factors limit efficient bargaining. They even limit trade.[101] Therefore, national private laws have the objective of minimising these obstacles.[102] Their *raison d'être* is to serve as an instrument to facilitate and increase the efficiencies of bargaining.

International situations add to the complexity of the situation. Each jurisdiction has a different system of property rights. It defines the formation, protection and transfer of such rights.[103] Statutory law usually ties the application of property rights to a national territory. However, international trade crosses borders and therefore frequently involves different legal systems. Jurisdictions have different requirements for the coming into existence of property rights. They further establish different types of rights. In consequence, the involvement of different property rights is prone to creating ambiguities. Contracting parties usually have different levels of knowledge about these laws. By applying one single national law, at least one party is at a disadvantage, since he would be less familiar with it. The uncertainty also extends to administrative procedures and enforcement by way of litigation. Therefore, parties have to devote great efforts to familiarise themselves with foreign laws. As can be seen, limiting factors are considerably more pronounced in an international context compared to domestic trades. Most participants therefore refuse to sell across borders and concentrate on the domestic market.[104]

As we have seen, a well-designed legal framework is a necessary tool for the functioning of trade. Legal rules have an even greater importance in an international context. This is the reason for the existence of private international law (PIL). These 'meta-rules' detect international conflicts between different legal systems claiming to apply to the same situation and determine the appropriate national law for their solution. However, since each jurisdiction has its own PIL rules, the system is far from offering a coherent solution to cross-border trade, and many scholars have characterised it as insufficient to overcome its fundamental problems.[105] Therefore, in a further step, the European Union has begun to *harmonise* its Member States' private international law rules, for example concerning the rules on contracts, with the above mentioned Rome I Regulation.

An alternative strategy would be to agree on *identical substantive rules* across countries, so-called unitary law. The benefits of such a system would be obvious. One could imagine a mandatory European contract law with a harmonised jurisprudence. Contracting parties would not have to invest time and money in finding out about provisions of other Member States' legal systems, since the law is identical

[100] H Demsetz, 'Toward a Theory of Property Rights' (1967) 57 *American Economic Review* 347, 357.

[101] R Coase, 'The Nature of the Firm' (1937) 4 *Economica* 386.

[102] R Cooter and T Ulen, *Law and Economics*, 5th edn (New York, Pearson Education, 2008) 1, 217.

[103] G Rühl, *Statut und Effizienz: ökonomische Grundlagen des internationalen Privatrechts* (Tübingen, Mohr Siebeck, 2011) 1, 34.

[104] A Common Sales Law for Europe, Factsheets: Benefits for Business and Consumers at a Glance: at European Level and for Each EU Country, General Factsheet, available at http://ec.europa.eu/justice/contract/document/index_en.htm.

[105] HJ Schmidt-Trenz, *Außenhandel und Territorialität des Rechts: Grundlegung einer neuen Institutionenökonomik des Außenhandels* (Baden-Baden, Nomos, 1990) 1, 297; D Schmidtchen, 'Territorialität des Rechts, Internationales Privatrecht und die privatautonome Regelung internationaler Sachverhalte' (1995) 59 *Rabels Zeitschrift für ausländisches und internationales Privatrecht (RabelsZ)* 56, 89.

for everyone. This would minimise information costs and avoid uncertainties caused by different legal provisions. However, such a unified legal system would reduce the scope for private autonomy, and it would clash with principles of national sovereignty.

Both approaches were developed to facilitate international trade. In a nutshell, the principle of 'choice' of law, as enshrined in PIL, grants a higher level of party autonomy. On the other hand, explicit unitary rules seem to overcome obstacles caused by different legal provisions.

At this point, it becomes clear that both law-making strategies, PIL and unitary law, have their respective costs and benefits. In what follows, I will assess both approaches with regard to their contribution to eliminating obstacles for trade. Bearing the above-mentioned explanations in mind, I assume that the most appropriate legislative framework will minimise obstacles in international trade (namely, transaction costs and information asymmetries), but at the same time maintain the greatest level of private autonomy possible.

Transaction Costs

We start with an examination of transaction costs. Advocates of unitary law hold that it will reduce transaction costs more efficiently than PIL.[106] In accordance with Coase, reduced transaction costs would be a strong argument for parties to choose unitary law to govern their relationship; this would support efforts of international cooperation to draft unitary standards of law. In private international law, by contrast, parties have the freedom to choose the applicable law. Nevertheless, they have to negotiate and inform themselves about different provisions to find the most advantageous law for their purposes. As a consequence, in the European context, it is possible that they have to inform themselves about up to 28 different national laws.

Consider the example of drafting the CESL. In this context, the European Union estimated that current costs for businesses of obtaining legal advice per each new legal system amount to over EUR 10,000.[107] Accordingly, the 'general fact sheet' for introducing the CESL states that almost 99 per cent of small businesses are effectively barred from selling across borders due to prohibitively high information costs. These costs would be much reduced if the parties were able to apply a common, unitary legal framework, which would be identical for both parties.[108] Especially SMEs would benefit from such a system.[109] By reducing these costs with the help of unitary rules, the law could create incentives for businesses to engage in more cross-border business activity. Furthermore, firms would be able to sell into

[106] European Commission, Action Plan, n 82 above, paras 29, 30, 32; European Commission, *A Common European Sales Law to Facilitate Cross-border Transactions in the Single Market*, COM(2011)636 final, 1, 8–9.

[107] A Common Sales Law for Europe Factsheets, n 104 above.

[108] W Kerber and S Grundmann, 'An Optional European Contract Law Code: Advantages and Disadvantages' (2006) 21 *European Journal of Law and Economics* 215, 230.

[109] JJ Ganzua and F Gomez, 'Optional Law for Firms and Consumers: An Economic Analysis of Opting into the Common European Sales Law' (2013) 50 *Common Market Law Review* 29, 50.

a greater variety of countries. This would ultimately contribute to the European internal market.

This argumentation provoked notable objections in literature. The first argument against unitary law refers to the risk of diverging jurisprudence. National courts would have to interpret the substantive rules until a standardised jurisdiction were to be developed by the European Court of Justice (CJEU). The legal understanding of national courts is influenced by their national law. As a result, they are likely to interpret the same rules in different ways.[110] In a worst case scenario, one could imagine 28 different interpretations of the same legal text. These 28 interpretations would be in addition to the 28 national private laws. As a consequence, a myriad of different legal rules and interpretations would be created, and contracting parties would have to face high information costs to understand these different interpretations.[111] In other words, the underlying purpose of unitary legal rules—to achieve legal certainty—may not be realised.

In contrast, national case-law and practice on domestic private law have developed over a long time. Businesses and consumers can rely on a wide range of established judgments, interpreting the different provisions. Thus, it could be argued that a diverse, Member-State based private law system would provide much greater legal certainty than an unknown unitary EU instrument. As a result, transaction costs, especially information costs, may increase instead of decrease when parties apply unitary law.

Eric Posner introduces a further interesting dimension. His claim is that the mere existence of another layer of legal rules will as such already increase transaction costs. The reason is that a party, seeking to maximise profits, will always compare the different rules on offer for its proposed contract and choose the most advantageous for their purposes.[112] An additional, harmonised legal system will thereby increase their negotiation costs, as they have to consider three instead of two legal systems, irrespective of which they are going to choose in the end.

Private Autonomy

Besides transaction costs, we need to have a closer look at the guarantee of private autonomy in both approaches. For that purpose, we will use the Rome I Regulation as an example of harmonised PIL. Article 3 of the Rome I Regulation principally allows parties to choose the applicable law for a transaction. Recital 13 emphasises that they may even choose soft-law texts. The Rome I Regulation thereby creates a menu of possible legal regimes. Contracting parties can compare different options on offer and choose the most appropriate for their purposes. This general principle is only limited in order to protect constituencies that may be affected by this choice.

[110] D Schmidtchen, 'Vereinheitlichung des Vertragsrechts in Europa—eine Lösung auf der Suche nach dem Problem? Die Sicht der Neuen Institutionenökonomik' in T Eger and HB Schäfer (eds), *Ökonomische Analyse der europäischen Zivilrechtsentwicklung* (Tübingen, Mohr Siebeck, 2007) 1, 22.

[111] E Posner, 'The Questionable Basis of the Common European Sales Law: The Role of an Optional Instrument in Jurisdictional Competition' (2013) 50 *Common Market Law Review* 261, 271.

[112] ibid 266.

For example, in consumer contracts, article 6 applies principally the law of the consumer's habitual residence. But this rule is not mandatory. Parties can deviate by agreement, as long as the consumer is as well protected as in the law of his residence. This system seems to strike a good balance between party autonomy and protection of weaker parties.[113] Overall, it is fair to say that the Rome I Regulation grants a high level of private autonomy and simultaneously develops a strong level of protection.

At the other end of the spectrum, we could imagine a mandatory, unified European law on contracts, not allowing for private choice. This is not currently on the agenda, but was discussed prior to the consideration of the CESL.[114] Such an instrument would dramatically reduce the scope for private autonomy. The European institutions could hardly justify such an intrusion into economic freedom.

But unifying law does not have to follow an 'either-or principle'. The CISG and the proposed CESL offer two different approaches. We will explain both texts more in detail below. At this point, we just need to have a look at their legal nature. The CISG is directly applicable for international sales contracts between businesses from contracting states (opt-out instrument).[115] It thereby supersedes PIL in the areas that it covers. If the parties intend to deselect the CISG, they have to explicitly mention this in their contract. Likewise, parties can also explicitly choose the application of the CISG in situations where it would not apply by default. This availability and the possibility to opt out makes this instrument more 'private autonomy friendly' than mandatory solutions.

The proposed CESL offers another strategy. It operates as an opt-in (and not opt-out) instrument.[116] It stands as a second national law regime besides national private law.[117] Parties have to choose its application explicitly via their PIL's choice of law. This solution extends the existing 'legal menu', since it grants contracting parties a greater variety to choose from and thereby increases the possibility to find an appropriate bargain between the parties. This point is reinforced by the consideration of heterogeneity of preferences and problems in international business transactions.[118] The European sales law will be available for a number of different economic situations. It will cover both business to business ('B2B') and business to consumer ('B2C') contracts. The variety of these different fields of application demonstrates the need for legal rules that can accommodate very heterogeneous

[113] FJ Garcimartin Alferez, 'The Rome I Regulation: Exceptions to the Rule on Consumer Contracts and Financial Instruments' (2009) 5 *Journal of Private International Law* 85.

[114] European Commission, Communication from the Commission to the Council and the European Parliament on European Contract Law, 11 July 2001, COM(2001)398 final, Option IV; European Commission, *Impact Assessment accompanying Proposal for a Regulation of the European Parliament and of the Council on a Common European Sales Law*, Staff Working Paper, COM(2011)635 final, SEC(2011)1166 final.

[115] CISG, arts 1 and 6.

[116] Hesselink, 'The Principles of European Contract Law', n 41 above, 203–4.

[117] S Whittaker, 'The Proposed "Common European Sales Law": Legal Framework and the Agreement of the Parties' (2012) 75 MLR 578, 587.

[118] Kerber and Grundmann, 'An Optional European Contract Law Code: Advantages and Disadvantages', n 108 above, 11.

preferences. Thereby, it is impossible to create a single law which satisfies all needs.[119] It can thus be seen that a relatively large number of different options serve the heterogeneity of preferences and problems best.

Against this background, a mandatory European Civil Code would eliminate every possibility of choice, hence not be advantageous. In a rational, economic perspective, an opt-out solution would be as advantageous as an opt-in instrument. It is an additional legal offer which expands the catalogue of choices available to the parties. In theory, negotiations will lead contracting parties to the application of the most advantageous law for their purposes. If the opt-out instrument is not the most advantageous, parties will negotiate and find another bargain.

However, insights from behavioural economics suggest that this assumption is flawed. Economists have empirically demonstrated that the existence of default rules influences the parties' decision-making. In other words, default rules bias the preferences of contracting parties in favour of choosing the default rule instead of contracting around it.[120] This 'stickiness of the default' is irrespective of whether the rule is efficient for their purposes or not.[121] Scientists attribute this phenomenon to the 'endowment effect' (also called 'divestiture aversion' or 'status quo bias').[122] This effect describes 'the principle that people tend to value goods more when they own them than when they do not'.[123] Translated to contract law, this means that contracting parties are less willing to give up a legal position which has been previously determined by law (which they literally 'own'), instead of when they have to reach it through negotiations.[124]

We can generalise these findings to the legal nature of opt-out instruments. The situation that contracting parties have to become active if they want to choose another law instead of the opt-out instrument, is equivalent to the previous allocation of a default rule. As a consequence of the endowment effect, contracting parties will be less likely to apply another law, even though this law might be more advantageous for them. By contrast, when it comes to an opt-in instrument, parties have to actively select its application within the PIL's choice of law framework. Literally, they do not 'own' any applicable law beforehand. It follows that contracting parties will react differently in this situation. They might be more likely to reach an individual bargain, since no 'sticky' standard is provided in advance. This shows that an opt-in instrument in combination with PIL's choice of law is less paternalistic than an opt-out instrument, it hence grants a greater level of private autonomy.

[119] R Epstein, 'Harmonization, Heterogeneity and Regulation: CESL, the Lost Opportunity for Constructive Harmonization' (2013) 50 *Common Market Law Review* 207, 213.

[120] WG Ringe, 'Menügesetzgebung im Privatrecht' (2013) 213 *Archiv für die civilistische Praxis (AcP)* 98, 120.

[121] RB Korobkin, 'The Endowment Effect and Legal Analysis' (2003) 97 *Northwestern University Law Review* 1227, 1270.

[122] R Thaler, 'Toward a Positive Theory of Consumer Choice' (1980) 1 *Journal of Economic Behavior and Organization* 39; Ringe, 'Menügesetzgebung im Privatrecht', n 120 above, 119; D Kahneman, JL Knetsch and RH Thaler 'Experimental Tests of the Endowment Effect and Coase Theorem' in R Thaler (ed), *Quasi Rational Economics* (New York, Russell Sage Foundation, 1994) 167; E Hoffman and ML Spitzer, 'Willingness to Pay vs Willingness to Accept: Legal and Economic Implications' (1993) 71 *Washington University Law Quarterly* 59.

[123] Korobkin, 'The Endowment Effect and Legal Analysis', n 121 above, 1228.

[124] Ringe, 'Menügesetzgebung im Privatrecht', n 120 above, 120; Kahneman, Knetsch and Thaler, 'Experimental Tests of the Endowment Effect and the Coase Theorem', n 122 above, 169, 184–86.

Furthermore, it should be noted that an opt-in instrument is less intrusive to national sovereignty. Where an opt-out instrument (like the CISG) very frequently overrules national legal systems, an opt-in instrument would only apply if the parties deliberately select it—and thereby actively deselect their otherwise applicable national law. An opt-in instrument is therefore more palatable from a political economy perspective, and would also be more in line with the principle of subsidiarity, as enshrined in the European Treaties.[125]

Unification Instead of Private International Law

What then drives the drafters of unitary law? The following discusses a number of examples where law-makers preferred unification over private international law. We will see that the main motivation for this type of law-making appears to be very much in line with the basic law & economics framework sketched out above: the goal is most notably to lower transaction costs for cross-border contracts.[126] It is, however, very much an open question whether these objectives are in fact achieved.

CISG

The most prominent example is the United Nations Convention on Contracts for the International Sale of Goods (CISG) of 1980. This international treaty was concluded in Vienna, Austria. First attempts to unify the international law of sales of goods go back to 1929 by Ernst Rabel and UNIDROIT. These early attempts were interrupted due to the Second World War and only finalised in 1964 with the adoption of two Conventions, ULFIS and ULIS.[127] These attempts show that the approach of harmonising private law has a long tradition. The CISG has been a role model for other instruments of harmonised commercial law and has influenced in particular the PICC, the PECL and the DCFR.[128]

At the present time, the CISG has been ratified and is applicable in 81 states.[129] It was created to remove barriers in international trade.[130] The barriers were seen in complexity of different contract laws and in uncertainty of conflict of laws rules.[131] The CISG's advocates emphasise its practical advantages. They mention

[125] See Treaty on European Union, art 5(3).

[126] See p 266 above.

[127] Convention relating to a Uniform Law on the Formation of Contracts for the International Sale of Goods 1964 (ULFIS), text available at www.cisg.law.pace.edu/cisg/text/ulf.html; Convention relating to a Uniform Law on the International Sale of Goods 1964 (ULIS), text available at www.cisg.law.pace.edu/cisg/text/ulis.html.

[128] I Schwenzer and P Hachem, 'The CISG: A Story of Worldwide Success' in J Kleinemann (ed), *CISG Part II Conference* (Stockholm, Stockholm Centre for Commercial Law, 2009) 119, 123, with further references.

[129] See www.uncitral.org/uncitral/en/uncitral_texts/sale_goods/1980CISG_status.html.

[130] CISG, Preamble, para 3.

[131] L Spagnolo, 'The Last Outpost: Automatic CISG Opt Outs, Misapplications and the Costs of Ignoring the Vienna Sales Convention for Australian Lawyers' (2009) 10 *Melbourne Journal of International Law* 141, 143.

the uniformity of applicable law, neutrality and simplicity in the choice of law.[132] In accordance with our theoretical framework sketched out above, the CISG intends to reduce transaction costs,[133] foster efficient bargaining and thereby increase the effectiveness of international trade.[134]

The CISG is a useful instrument for analysing the success of the harmonisation approach, as it has since become the paradigm example of successful legal unification and has influenced many other instruments of international trade law. For the purpose of this essay, it is of interest to find out how much use the market makes of the CISG. If unification is as beneficial as the drafters of the CISG claim, we would expect that most parties do indeed make use of it in practice; otherwise, we would expect a large number of opt-outs.

There is ample research on this empirical question. The results are as diverse as the surveys. For example, a study by Martin Koehler relied on a questionnaire which was sent to lawyers and in-house jurists. Koehler came to the conclusion that 70.8 per cent of American and 72.2 per cent of German lawyers who participated in the survey principally or preponderantly opted out of the CISG.[135] By contrast, Schwenzer and Kee determined that only 13 per cent of lawyers who participated in their survey usually opted out of the CISG, with a further 32 per cent doing so sometimes.[136] Fitzgerald found that even 56 per cent of those lawyers who are familiar with the CISG specifically opted out.[137] De Ly's results contrast with these studies. He drew the conclusion that there was no empirical evidence for preponderantly opting out of the CISG.[138]

This is not the place to analyse the reasons for the different results. I further do not intend to take a position in favour of an individual result. The point to make is how the authors explain their results. The arguments are very similar at their basis. Especially, two interlinked reasons are always mentioned. Martin Koehler described it as a 'divergence between theory and practice'.[139] The first reason is that lawyers are not familiar with the CISG. As a result they prefer using choice of

[132] ibid 149.

[133] F De Ly, 'Sources of International Sales Law: An Eclectic Model' (2005) 25 *Journal of Law and Commerce* 1, 2; R Knieper 'Celebrating Success by Accession to CISG' (2005) 25 *Journal of Law and Commerce* 477, 478; Schwenzer and Hachem, 'The CISG: A Story of Worldwide Success', n 128 above, 128, 140.

[134] CISG, Preamble, note 3.

[135] MF Koehler, *Survey regarding the Relevance of the United Nations Convention for the International Sale of Goods (CISG) in Legal Practice and the Exclusion of its Application* (2006), available at www.cisg.law.pace.edu/cisg/biblio/koehler.html.

[136] I Schwenzer and C Kee, 'Global Sales Law: Theory and Practice' in I Schwenzer and L Spagnolo (eds), *Towards Uniformity: The 2nd Annual MAA Peter Schlechtriem CISG Conference* (The Hague, Eleven International Publishing, 2011) 155, 159.

[137] PL Fitzgerald, 'An Empirical Study of the Value and Utility of the United Nation's Convention on the International Sale of Goods (CISG) and the UNIDROIT Principles of International Commercial Contracts to Practitioners, Jurists, and Legal Academics in the United States' (2008) 27 *Journal of Law and Commerce*, Annex Pt II, 'Specific Questions for Practitioners No 11'.

[138] De Ly, 'Sources of International Sales Law', 4 note 7, referring to F De Ly, 'The Relevance of the Vienna Convention for International Sales Contracts: Should We Stop Contracting it Out?' (2003) 3 *Business Law International* 241; F De Ly, 'Opting Out: Some Observations on the Occasion of CISG's 25th Anniversary' in F Ferrari (ed), *Quo vadis CISG? Celebrating the 25th Anniversary of the United Nations Convention on Contracts for the International Sale of Goods* (Brussels, Bruylant, 2011) 25.

[139] Koehler, *Survey*, n 135 above.

law clauses within their domestic law.[140] Becoming familiar with the CISG involves time and money. Thus, the second argument is start-up costs for lawyers themselves and their clients.[141] Harry Flechtner distinguished these costs into short-term costs and long-term costs. He argued that the short-term costs are worthwhile to invest and that they will amortise over several years.[142] Whether this will happen, is at least doubtful. The CISG has one structural disadvantage compared to European unitary law: there is no worldwide authority, no court having the power to define the terms used in the Convention and to ensure that they are applied in a consistent manner. As said above, it will take a long time until a harmonised European jurisdiction will develop. A harmonised jurisdiction on substantive rules worldwide seems almost impossible. As we have shown above, this fact reduces legal certainty and increases information costs. These two reasons contrast the main idea behind the approach: costs savings and legal certainty.

CESL

The Common European Sales Law (CESL) is the result of a long discussion on the harmonisation of contract law that began in Europe in 2001. The European Commission published a legislative proposal in 2011.[143] The CESL is located in Annex I to that proposal. Its text is influenced by the DCFR and the PECL.[144] It is limited in its scope of application and covers only contracts for sale, supply of digital content and the supply of related services.[145] Thereby, it is applicable to both B2B and also B2C contracts.

The Commission argues that the possible application of many different national laws make cross-border sales more complex and costly than domestic trades.[146] Uniform rules shall therefore simplify the legal aspects of international trades. This is seen as a necessary step to improve the establishment and functioning of the internal market.[147] The basic idea for harmonising European sales law is thus similar to what we saw above for other harmonisation attempts and in line with the concept of transaction costs.

[140] Eg Koehler, *Survey*, n 135 above; L Spagnolo, 'A Glimpse through the Kaleidoscope: Choices of Law and the CISG (Kaleidoscope Part I)' (2009) 13 *Vindobona Journal of International Commercial Law and Arbitration* 135, 137; Schwenzer and Hachem, 'The CISG: A Story of Worldwide Success', n 128 above, 125; Fitzgerald, 'An Empirical Study of the Value and Utility of the CISG', n 137 above, 25.

[141] Eg JS Ziegel, 'The Future of the International Sales Convention from a Common Law Perspective' (2000) 6 *New Zealand Business Law Quarterly* 336, 345; HM Flechtner, 'Changing the Opt-out Tradition in the United States' (2007) *UNCITRAL Modern Law for Global Commerce Congress* 249, 250; Spagnolo, 'A Glimpse through the Kaleidoscope', n 140 above, 140.

[142] Flechtner, 'Changing the Opt-out Tradition in the United States', n 141 above, 250; C Mak, 'Unweaving the CESL: Legal-economic Reason and Institutional Imagination in European Contract Law' (2013) 50 *Common Market Law Review* 277, 295.

[143] European Commission, Proposal for a Regulation of the European Parliament and of the Council on a Common European Sales Law of 11 October 2011, COM(2011) 635 final.

[144] MW Hesselink, 'How to Opt into the Common European Sales Law? Brief Comments on the Commission's Proposal for a Regulation' (2012) 20 *European Review of Private Law* 195.

[145] CESL, art 5.

[146] Commission Proposal, n 143 above, 3.

[147] ibid 4.

Nevertheless, the CESL has a different focus of protection when compared to the CISG. It specifically seeks to bring benefits to consumers and SMEs.[148] The European Union has published fact sheets about possible effects of the CESL. They draw the conclusion that the actual situation leads to a loss of EUR 26 billion in trade. These numbers are derived from the fact that companies do not sell as much as they could.[149] Furthermore, they state that consumers do not benefit from the internal market as much as they could. Each year, around 3 million consumers are affected by companies refusing to sell to consumers living abroad.[150]

These data lead us to the question whether the CESL can achieve its predicted aims. We will concentrate on consumer protection. The question is whether the CESL, as an opt-in instrument, achieves its objective of better consumer protection. The survey Eurobarometer[151] states that finding out about different consumer protection rules is at least a minimal obstacle for 38 per cent of businesses.[152] The CESL seeks to address this problem by developing a harmonised standard of consumer protection. The idea is that businesses and consumers can rely on the same conditions for each contract regardless of their place in Europe. Thereby, they will save money because they no longer have to find out about foreign provisions. However, this conclusion is not fully accurate and leaves some aspects out of consideration. For example, article 6 of the Rome I Regulation would still apply, mandating a comparison between the selected law (eg the CESL) and the law of the habitual residence of the consumer, and giving preference to the stronger consumer protection standard.[153] Secondly, the choice of the CESL will only be effective if the parties deliberately opt in. In most B2C contractual negotiations, however, the business side will have a stronger bargaining position, and it is an open question whether it will accept the high consumer protection standards in the CESL.

Societas Europaea

The final example is the European Company, Societas Europaea (SE).[154] This is a pan-European corporate form, in force since 2004, which public companies can choose for their legal organisation. Existing companies which were formed under different national laws in Europe can reincorporate as an SE.[155]

Again, the fathers of this piece of unification point out that many companies operate internationally in different legal systems but have to choose the application

[148] ibid 5–6.

[149] A Common Sales Law for Europe General Factsheet, n 104 above.

[150] Factsheet for United Kingdom, n 104 above.

[151] Gallup Organization, *Flash Eurobarometer #321: Business Attitudes towards Cross-border Business-to-Consumer (B2C) Transactions and the Usefulness of a European Contract Law* (2011), available at http://ec.europa.eu/public_opinion/flash/fl_321_en.pdf.

[152] ibid 19.

[153] On the relationship in detail, see G Dannemann, 'Jurisdiction and Choice of Law' in G Dannemann and S Vogenauer (eds), *The Common European Sales Law in Context: Interactions with English and German Law* (Oxford University Press, 2013).

[154] Regulation (EC) 2157/2001 of the Council of 8 October 2001 on the Statute for a European Company (SE) [2001] OJ L294/1.

[155] ibid art 2.

of a single national company law.[156] They regarded this situation as a gap between the economic and political reality.[157] The SE was therefore intended to remove barriers to international corporate activities and, ultimately, to promote the internal market.[158] This pattern of argumentation is again similar to the other two examples given above.

Does the SE live up to the goals that it was set to fulfil? Empirical data are still sparse. One study, conducted by Eidenmüller and co-authors, analysed stock price reactions to the announcement of a company's decision to change its legal status to an SE. The study is ultimately inconclusive and does not establish a positive reaction between the reorganisation decision and the occurrence of any abnormal positive returns.[159] Another study by Lamp confirms this result.[160]

In fact, from what we know about the actual use of the SE, it appears that it is mostly used for reasons that are fundamentally different from the ones that its drafters expected. The vast majority of SEs are incorporated in Germany and the Czech Republic, two countries with high employee involvement standards.[161] This suggests that some arbitrage around mandatory employee representation on the board may have played a role in the decision to become an SE. In fact, the SE in practice does not allow for an explicit reduction of employee rights, but does permit indirect ways to mitigate their influence.[162] For example, the size of the supervisory board can be reduced in comparison with the otherwise strict standards found in the German public company (AG). Secondly, an SE allows employee standards under national law to be 'frozen', typically under a certain threshold, when the company converts into an SE, avoiding the mandatory expansion of employees' board representation as the number of total employees continues to grow and to cross the line.[163]

On the other hand, the SE has a number of other advantages that may contribute to its attractiveness.[164] For example, the SE offers the possibility to move the seat of the company across borders, and to engage in cross-border mergers. A further plus is the possibility to choose between a one-tier and a two-tier structure to organise the company's board of directors. These aspects may also play a role in companies' decisions whether or not to become an SE, and they are definitely more in line with the expected benefits that a centralised company structure may bring to European firms.

[156] ibid recital 3.

[157] ibid recital 4.

[158] ibid recitals 1 and 29.

[159] H Eidenmüller et al, 'How Does the Market React to the Societas Europaea?' (2010) 11 *European Business Organization Law Review (EBOR)* 35.

[160] F Lamp, *Value Creation and Value Destruction in the Societas Europaea: Evidence from the New Legal Form*, Working Paper (2011), available at http://ssrn.com/abstract=1728162.

[161] SE Europe and ETUI, data on SE Incorporations, January 2014, available at http://de.worker-participation.eu/var/ezwebin_site/storage/images/media/images/folie0318/96771-1-eng-GB/Folie03.jpg.

[162] H Eidenmüller et al, 'Incorporating under European Law: The Societas Europaea as a Vehicle for Legal Arbitrage' (2009) 10 *EBOR* 1, 6.

[163] ibid 11, 27–28.

[164] See J Armour and WG Ringe, 'European Company Law 1999–2010: Renaissance and Crisis' (2011) 48 *Common Market Law Review* 125, 158.

Summary

Our analysis has so far shown that legal instruments seek to facilitate transactions and thereby minimise costs. Both strategies examined here, unitary law and private international law, contribute to this objective. However, it seems that unitary substantive law initially *increases* transaction costs rather than lowers them, as the transition costs to a new and uncertain legal instrument are high as long as no established case-law or practice exist. Furthermore, it appears that harmonisation can have unexpected side-effects. These are good arguments for preferring a harmonised PIL strategy.

On the other hand, the problems of unitary law may be mitigated if the unitary law instrument is made *optional*. An optional instrument allows the market to test the new instrument and to explore its strengths over a longer timeframe: disruptions will thus be minimised. Further, it appears that an optional instrument should then be combined with reliable and ideally harmonised rules on private international law. This would ensure a predictable selection of national laws for situations where parties prefer not to use the optional instrument. Such a combination of an optional unitary instrument and harmonised PIL may be particularly helpful in areas where parties have very heterogeneous preferences: as explained above, the combination model offers more choice than the pure unification model and is less intrusive into private autonomy. On the other hand, it combines the possibility of private bargaining with the attractiveness of an optional transnational instrument.

Implications for the Law of Assignments

At this point, we need to return to the law of assignment. The insights gained from the general reflections on the benefits of legal unification will help us to develop a concept for the future direction of assignment law in Europe.

In the language of Coase, we need to ask which approach best increases legal certainty and thereby minimises transaction costs for cross-border assignment contracts. To answer this question, it might be beneficial to have a closer look at the legal nature of assignments. Assignments are multiparty transactions that deal with the transfer of intangible rights and frequently occur in a cross-border context. They have a high practical importance for different economic areas. This combination of factors poses a number of specific requirements that are different when compared with other areas of law.

It is commonly accepted that ex ante certainty is of particular importance for financial transactions. Practice has shown that different national property law provisions led to uncertainties with respect to performance, priority and other effects of transfer. The crucial point about transferring intangible rights is that the heterogeneity of law is obviously more pronounced in the field of property law in international transactions. But a clear allocation of property rights is necessary to reduce transaction costs. So it is not surprising that former policy-makers already dealt with conflict of law problems in the (neighbouring) field of international payments. In this area, several Treaties and Conventions sponsored by the League of Nations entered into force in the 1920s and 1930s. It is fascinating to note that they created unitary substantive law rules as well as unitary conflict of law rules. These Conventions and Treaties dealt with bills of exchange and promissory notes, cheques and maritime liens and mortgages.[165] The existence of international, uniform laws in fields so similar to assignments already illustrate the markets' urgent need for unambiguous legal rules with respect to intangible rights. However, to date, there is still no binding unitary law dealing with assignments in general. Article 14 of the Rome I Regulation refers questions on cross-border assignments to national law. It is generally accepted that this article does not, however, deal with the property law aspects of an assignment. As a consequence, legal uncertainty appears to increase instead of being eliminated as contracting parties have to invest information costs to find out which national law applies and how it deals with the proprietary aspects of their transaction. This determination will vary in almost every case. Besides, a consequence of referring to national law is that an assignment might be effective under one jurisdiction and void under another because of different property law provisions. Since the trade in intangible rights occurs faster and more cheaply than in corporeal goods, the volume of transferred rights tends to be relatively high. In many cases, the owner of the right, as well as the legal system, will change.

This system creates a complex symbiosis of different international and national instruments, partly applying to the contractual and partly to the proprietary sides of an assignment transaction. The implication is that the ex ante certainty decreases for involved parties, and information costs tend to be high. Legal certainty will be even lower for bulk assignments and assignments of future rights, which are very important as collateral in the factoring sector. If a unitary system could be agreed in this field, it would provide predictable solutions with respect to the requirements for perfection, priority and other effects of transfer. Especially, predictability about the effectiveness of an assignment will decrease transaction costs.

This last point is even more pronounced when we consider that assignments are typically multiparty transactions. At a minimum level, three parties are involved. It also happens that more parties become involved. Such a multiparty arrangement can rapidly increase the number of potentially involved jurisdictions. This will exacerbate the potential problems and complicate the transaction further. For example, proprietary rules might jeopardise the effectiveness and priority of an assignment. A conceivable outcome is that an assignment turns out to be void and that the right still belongs to the assignor's assets. As we have mentioned above, a clear allocation of property rights is important to minimise costs of bargaining. A strong unitary law could create standard rules for property questions. As a consequence, it would be ex ante, as well as ex post, easier to find out for all involved parties if an assignment in a row of assignments was valid or not. This is because parties do not have to find out about different legal provisions of foreign property law, but can examine all

[165] Eg International Convention for the Unification of Certain Rules relating to Maritime Liens and Mortgages (Brussels, 1926); Convention providing a Uniform Law for Bills of Exchange and Promissory Notes (Geneva, 1930); Convention for the Settlement of Certain Conflicts of Laws in connection with Bills of Exchange and Promissory Notes (Geneva, 1930); Convention providing a Uniform Law for Cheques (Geneva, 1931); Convention for the Settlement of Certain Conflicts of Laws in connection with Cheques (Geneva, 1930).

assignments with the same instrument. As a result, this would dramatically reduce the costs of contracting.

Another point to consider is that assignments are of great importance for different economic areas. These areas differ in their requirements and in their aims for economic tools. It follows that the heterogeneity of problems that might occur and the preferences of parties are considerably more pronounced than in other areas of law. We have already mentioned that this divergence makes it impossible to create a single law which can satisfy all needs. From that point of view, mandatory full harmonisation does not make sense for assignments. A choice of law framework offers contracting parties various solutions to find the most beneficial law for their purposes.

How can we combine the advantages of both strategies? The answer is obvious: a combination of an (optional) unitary instrument with a solid and harmonised PIL framework would yield best results. Such a combination would harness the advantages of a predictable, common framework that parties can select for cross-border transactions. As it wouldn't be mandatory, the transition period would be smooth, and parties could decide to trust this new instrument over time, once a substantial body of case-law and practice has built up. Were this to be combined with a harmonised and complete PIL instrument, it would allow parties to tailor-make a solution for their contract that would deviate by simply opting for another legal system. Whether the optional instrument should have an opt-out character (like the CISG) or an opt-in mechanism (like the CESL) is debatable. Both would have respective advantages.

CONCLUSION

The law of assignment in European contract law is a hazy field. The current status quo is characterised by uncertainties in essential areas. Especially, loopholes in the Rome I Regulation with respect to property law provisions decrease ex ante and ex post legal certainty. This paper urges European lawmakers to consider the BIICL proposal and to address the unsolved problem of cross-border assignments.

The obvious avenue to consider is to design an optional instrument of substantive assignment law as a possible future solution for the field of assignments. This is based on the recognition that the fast transfer of intangible rights involves a considerable number of different owners and legal systems in a short time. Thereby, it often affects third parties. For that reason, especially property law provisions are crucial to create ex ante and ex post certainty of a transaction. Harmonised PIL might be inappropriate to solve this problem, since it does not overcome the heterogeneity of national property laws. In my opinion, this obstacle can only be removed by standardised, clear provisions for the effectiveness and priority of an assignment.

In light of considerations from behavioural scholarship and the principle of subsidiarity, I would recommend the usage of an *opt-in* instrument for unification. Such an optional instrument would expand the legal menu and thereby not clash with the heterogeneity of problems and preferences. It should be coupled with a reliable and complete private international law framework. The Rome I Regulation fulfils this role only partly today: Article 14 would have to be expanded and completed.

It is fair to say that an optional unitary law does not overcome the problem of different national jurisdictions on single rules in the short term. Thereby, we have to admit that the costs of switching will increase at first. To be sure, international rules always have to deal with these problems and costs in the beginning. The non-mandatory character of the proposed instrument would soften its impact, and parties could choose it as soon as they feel that it has a reliable body of case-law and practice. Furthermore, the existence of a common court, the CJEU, raises the possibility that time will help to create a harmonised body of interpretation guidelines.

Finally, I need to emphasise that the proposal made here does not claim to be the ideal solution. The purpose was to illustrate a few guidelines for the current discussion. The law of assignment might be a more likely candidate for harmonisation than other areas of law. An optional harmonisation with respect to property law provisions will increase legal certainty. Thereby, it seems possible that the transition costs will amortise over the years. An optional unitary European law of assignment would have the chance to develop its benefits in the long run. It might not be the ideal solution, but it is a step in the right direction.

16

Unfair Terms in Consumer Contracts

JACOBIEN W RUTGERS

> Since 1913, an Act of Congress has protected hogs, sheep and cattle against the marketing of worthless drugs. It is time, we gave men, women and children the same protection.[1]

JOHN F KENNEDY spoke these words on 15 March 1962 when he addressed the US Congress to announce his plans for consumer protection. Consumer policy, which is now laid down in Treaty on the Functioning of the EU (TFEU) Article 169, has not always been included in the Treaties governing the European Union. The Treaty establishing the Economic European Community of 1957 did not mention consumer policy.[2] Ten years after Kennedy's speech to the US Congress, consumer policy was discussed at the Paris Summit in 1972.[3] Nearly seven years later, the European Court of Justice (CJEU) mentioned consumer protection as one of the overriding mandatory requirements when the CJEU introduced the rule of reasons in *Cassis de Dijon*, which could justify an infringement of the free movement of goods.[4] In the Maastricht Treaty (1992), consumer policy was mentioned for the first time. However, already within the context of the internal market, the first consumer, product liability and doorstep selling Directives were adopted in 1985.[5]

Within this context, Directive 93/13/EC on unfair terms in consumer contracts[6] ('Unfair Terms Directive') was adopted on 5 April 1993. It had to be implemented into the national legal systems of the Member States of the then European Economic Community by 21 December 1994.

[1] See jfklibrary.org/Asset-Viewer/Archives/JFKPOF-037-028.aspx.

[2] See about the development of consumer policy in the European Union, S Weatherill, 'Consumer Policy' in P Craig and G de Búrca (eds), *The Evolution of EU Law*, 2nd edn (Oxford University Press, 2011) 837.

[3] [1975] OJ C92/1.

[4] 120/78 *Rewe-Zentral v Bundesmonopolverwaltung für Branntwein (Cassis de Dijon)* [1979] ECR 649.

[5] Council Directive 85/374/EEC of 25 July 1985 on the approximation of the laws, regulations and administrative provisions of the Member States concerning liability for defective products [1985] OJ L210/29; Council Directive 85/577/EEC of 20 December 1985 to protect the consumer in respect of contracts negotiated away from business premises [1985] OJ L372/31.

[6] Council Directive 93/13/EEC of 5 April 1993 on unfair terms in consumer contracts [1993] OJ L95/29. For a comparative overview of the transposition of the Directive in French, German and English law, see H Beale et al (eds), *Cases, Materials and Text on Contract Law*, Ius Commune Casebooks for the Common Law of Europe, 2nd edn (Oxford, Hart Publishing, 2010) 780.

It has been suggested[7] that this Directive does not only concern unfair terms, but 'goes to the heart of contract law'.[8] In *Océano*, the CJEU handed down the first decision regarding this Directive, in 2000.[9] This decision resulted in an essential change as to how the courts should deal with general conditions and the notion of avoidance in many Member States. This is just one example of the effect of the Unfair Terms Directive on contract law. The question which I will address in this chapter is whether this Directive has gone to the heart of contract law. To do so, I will discuss the case-law of the CJEU and try to place the cases in a broader perspective.

As is well known, the Unfair Terms Directive aims at the protection of the consumer. This is stated in the recitals to the Directive and the CJEU referred to this repeatedly:

> [T]he system of protection implemented by the Directive is based on the idea that the consumer is in a weak position vis-à-vis the seller or supplier, as regards both his bargaining power and his level of knowledge.[10]

The Directive only applies to business to consumer ('B2C') contracts. The consumer is a natural person who acts outside his business, trade or profession, whereas the seller or supplier is a either a natural or a legal person who acts within his business, trade or profession (Unfair Terms Directive, article 2(b), (c)). Moreover, the Directive concerns minimum harmonisation. This implies that Member States are allowed to have more stringent rules to protect the consumer (article 8).[11] According to the general scheme of the Directive, an unfair term in a B2C contract which is not individually negotiated, is not binding. However, contract terms that constitute the core of the contract do not have to pass the fairness test, provided they are in plain and intelligible language. The Directive gives general indications when a term is considered to be unfair. In addition, a term must be in plain and intelligible language (article 5). Hereafter, I will discuss in particular the recent case-law of the CJEU as to whether the Unfair Terms Directive goes to the heart of contract law.

UNFAIR TERMS

Preliminary Remarks

To assess whether a contract term is unfair, it must first be established whether the challenged contract term falls within the scope of the Unfair Terms Directive, which concerns a non-individually negotiated term in a B2C contract (Unfair Terms

[7] E Hondius, 'The Reception of the Directive on Unfair Terms in Consumer Contracts by Member States' (1995) *ERPL* 242.

[8] See also titles of books concerning this Directive: H Collins (ed), *Standard Contract Terms in Europe: A Basis and a Challenge to European Contract Law* (The Hague, Kluwer Law International, 2008). See also in this respect H Collins, 'Good Faith in European Contract Law' (1994) 14 *OJLS* 253.

[9] C-240/98–C-244/98 *Océano Grupo Editorial SA v Roció Murciano Quintero; Salvat Editores SA v José M. Sánchez Alcón Prades, José Luis Copano Badillo, Mohammed Berroane, Emilio Viñas Feliú* [2000] ECR I-4941.

[10] C-472/11 *Banif Plus Bank Zrt v Csaba Csipai and Viktória Csipai*, 21 February 2013 (CJEU, nyr).

[11] See, eg also C-484/08 *Caja de Ahorros y Monte de Piedad de Madrid v Asociación de Usuarios de Servicios Bancarios (Ausbanc)* [2010] ECR I-4785.

Directive, art 3(1)).[12] Moreover, the unfairness of a term that belongs to the core terms of the contract, provided that they are in plain and intelligible language, cannot be challenged (article 4(2)). The CJEU has held that this exemption does not apply in the case of mechanisms that amend/change the price of either the services or the goods.[13]

Within English case-law and literature there is a discussion as to which terms belong to the core of the contract and how this must be established.[14] I will not discuss English law, but I would like to address one element of that discussion. In this respect references are made to the average or typical consumer. It has been argued that, as to whether a term relating to the price of the service or the good is a core term of the contract, the term at stake must be considered through the eyes of the typical or average consumer.[15] This was dismissed by Lord Mance in *Office of Fair Trading v Abbey National*, who held that this would not fit within the scheme of the Directive, since it introduced too complicated a test.[16]

The notion of the average consumer is taken from European law. In this respect, Directive 2005/29/EC on unfair commercial practices[17] and the CJEU ruling in *Gut Springenheide*[18] are mentioned. Whittaker argues that for the sake of uniformity in European law, the notion of the average consumer should be used.[19] He refers to a number of CJEU decisions, but does not distinguish as to the subject matter of the case. Does it concern free movement or, for instance, is it a case concerning harmonisation of the labelling or marketing of eggs, which was the situation in *Gut Springenheide*?[20] This notion, however, has also been criticised.[21] Thus, opinions differ as to whether the consumer to be protected under the Unfair Terms Directive is the average consumer. Unberath and Johnston have pointed out that, in the case of consumer protection, the CJEU case-law has a double face.[22] In their view, a distinction must be made between the case-law relating to the free movement of

[12] *Cf* Weatherill, 'Consumer Policy', n 2 above, 858; S Whittaker in H Beale (general ed), *Chitty on the Law of Contracts*, vol I, *General Principles* 31st edn (London, Sweet & Maxwell, 2012) para 15–053.

[13] C-472/10 *Nemzeti Fogyasztóvédelmi Hatóság v Invitel Távközlési Zrt*, 26 April 2012 (CJEU, nyr) para 23.

[14] *Office of Fair Trading v Abbey National plc* [2009] UKSC 6; *Chitty on the Law of Contracts*, n 12 above, para 15-033; S Whittaker, 'Unfair Contract Terms, Unfair Prices and Bank Charges' (2011) 74 *MLR* 114. *Cf* M Kenny, 'The Law Commissions' 2012 Issues Paper on Unfair Terms: Subverting the System of Europeanized Private Law' (2013) *ERPL* 871.

[15] *Chitty on the Law of Contracts*, n 12 above, para 15-033; Whittaker, 'Unfair Contract Terms, Unfair Prices and Bank Charges', n 14 above. See further in respect of the average consumer T Wilhelmsson, 'Cooperation and Competition regarding Standard Contract Terms in Consumer Contracts' (2006) *EBLR* 52.

[16] *Office of Fair Trading v Abbey National plc* [2009] UKSC 6, para 102. *Cf* Beale et al, *Cases, Materials and Text on Contract Law*, n 6 above, 809.

[17] Directive 2005/29/EC on unfair commercial practices [2005] OJ L149/22.

[18] C-210/96 *Gut Springenheide GmbH and R Trusky v Oberkreisdirektor des Kreises Steinfurt and Amt für Lebensmittelüberwachung* [1998] ECR I-4657.

[19] Whittaker, 'Unfair Contract Terms, Unfair Prices and Bank Charges', n 14 above.

[20] *Chitty on the Law of Contracts*, n 12 above, para 15-033; C-210/96 *Gut Springenheide GmbH*, n 18 above.

[21] Collins, 'Good Faith in European Contract Law', n 8 above; E Macdonald, 'Bank Charges and the Core Exemption: Office of Fair Trading v. Abbey National Plc' (2008) 71 *MLR* 990.

[22] H Unberath and A Johnston, 'The Double-headed Approach of the ECJ concerning Consumer Protection' (2007) 44 *CML Rev* 1237. *Cf* H-W Micklitz et al (eds), *Cases, Materials and Text on Consumer Law* (Oxford, Hart Publishing, 2010) 38.

goods and consumer protection, on the one hand, and the case-law relating to Directives harmonising consumer law, on the other.[23] As to the free movement cases, a national rule can be challenged if it is contrary to the free movement of goods. Nevertheless, if an impediment to the free movement of goods is established, a national rule can be justified, inter alia, because of consumer protection, provided the other requirements of the rule of reason are also met.[24] In these instances, only national rules which protect the confident, circumspect and well-informed consumer may justify an infringement; more protection for the consumer is dismissed by the CJEU. Many of these free movement cases concern national rules on advertising or marketing.

In the case of positive integration, harmonisation of rules relating to consumer transactions, another type of consumer is protected, Unberath and Johnston have argued.[25] Among those Directives, the Directive on unfair commercial practices[26] is the odd one out, because it provides explicitly that the consumer to be protected under that Directive is the average consumer. This notion has been taken from the case-law on free movement as regards advertising law.[27] Taking into account the distinction between the two types of cases, as Unberath and Johnston have pointed out, it does not seem obvious that the notion of the average consumer should be used to determine the core terms of the contract.

Thus, if a term is not individually negotiated and does not belong to the core of the contract, a court can establish whether a term is unfair.

Unfair

A term is 'unfair if, contrary to the requirement of good faith, it causes a significant imbalance in the parties' rights and obligations under the contract to the detriment of the consumer' (Unfair Terms Directive, article 3(1)). Assessing this significant imbalance contrary to good faith, 'all the circumstances attending the conclusion of the contract and ... all the other terms of the contract or of another contract on which it is dependent' must be considered, as well as 'the nature of the goods or services for which the contract was concluded' (article 4(1)). From the CJEU case-law it can be inferred which circumstances must be considered. In *Freiburger Kommunalbauten*, the CJEU held that 'the consequences of the term under the law applicable to the contract must also be taken into account. This requires that consideration be given to national law'.[28] The case concerned Mr and Mrs Hofstetter, who had bought a parking space in a car park which had still to be built. According to the contract, they had to pay the price before the building was finished and the builder had to provide them with a bank guarantee. They refused to pay the price,

[23] Unberath and Johnston, 'The Double-headed Approach of the ECJ', n 22 above.
[24] ibid. *Cf* Weatherill, 'Consumer Policy', n 2 above, 842.
[25] Unberath and Johnston, 'The Double-headed Approach of the ECJ', n 22 above.
[26] See n 17 above.
[27] Micklitz et al, *Cases, Materials and Text on Consumer Law*, n 22 above, 38.
[28] C-237/02 *Freiburger Kommunalbauten GmbH Baugesellschaft & Co KG v L Hofstetter and U Hofstetter* [2004] ECR I-3403, para 21. Note by MW Hesselink, (2006) 2 *ERCL* 366; C-76/10 *Photovost' SRO v Iveta Korčkovská* [2010] ECR I-11557.

whereas the builder had done what he had to do. The builder started proceedings against the couple and claimed payment of the price. Mr and Mrs Hofstetter argued that the clause according to which they had to pay the full price before the building was finished was unfair. Under German law, the clause was fair, because the builder had to provide a bank guarantee and had done that.

In addition, the other circumstances to be considered are all the other terms of the contract[29] and information included in a term which can be considered an unfair commercial practice.[30] There is a list of clauses which could be considered unfair (article 3(3)). Thus, the test to be applied as to whether a clause is unfair is whether there is a significant imbalance to the detriment of the consumer contrary to good faith, considering all the circumstances during the conclusion of the contract and the other terms of the contract.[31]

Significant Imbalance Contrary to Good Faith

In *Aziz*, the CJEU discussed what pertains to a significant imbalance in the rights and obligations to the detriment of the consumer.[32] In that case, Mohammed Aziz had borrowed EUR138,000 from a Catalan bank, Catalunyacaixa, to pay off another loan, which he had used to buy his family home in Spain. The loan was secured by a mortgage which was vested in the family home. At the moment he borrowed the money, 19 July 2007, Aziz had a monthly income of EUR1,341. Until 30 January 2008, he had to pay a fixed amount of interest of EUR701.04. After that date, the interest was variable. From May 2008, Aziz failed to pay the monthly instalments. The general conditions of the loan agreement stipulated that if a debtor failed to pay, he had to pay an interest rate of 18.75 per cent. Aziz had accrued a debt of EUR139,764.76 when the bank started enforcement proceedings against Aziz to sell the house. In the end, the family home was sold for 50 per cent of its value and Aziz was forced to leave the house on 21 January 2011. In the meantime, Aziz had also started proceedings in which he asked for a declaratory judgment that clauses in his loan contract were unfair. Under Spanish procedural law, the enforcement proceedings could not be deferred until a decision on whether the stipulations concerning the interest rate were unfair was given.

To assess whether there is a significant imbalance to the detriment of the consumer, the CJEU held that a court must make a comparison between the situation where the contract was concluded and the situation where there is no contract.[33] The latter refers to the situation where a court will apply the national rules as if there is no

[29] C-472/11 *Banif Plus Bank Zrt v C Csipai and V Csipai*, n 10 above, para 41. *Chitty on the Law of Contracts*, n 12 above, para 15-86.

[30] C-453/10 *J Pereničová and V Perenič v SOS financ spol SRO*, 15 March 2012 (CJEU, nyr), Note by B Keirsblick, 'The Interaction between Consumer Protection Rules on Unfair Contract Terms, and Unfair Commercial Practices: Pereničová and Perenič' (2013) 50 *CML Rev* 247; *Chitty on the Law of Contracts*, n 12 above, para 15-077.

[31] See C-137/08 *VB Pénzügy Lízing v F Schneider* [2010] ECR I-10847.

[32] Case C-415/11 *M Aziz v Caixa d'Estalvis de Catalunya, Tarragona I Manresa (Catalunyacaixa)*, 14 March 2013 (CJEU, nyr).

[33] ibid para 68.

contract. A court can then assess whether and to what extent the consumer will be in a worse position. If so, there is a significant imbalance. In a subsequent judgment, *Menéndez Álvarez*, the CJEU observed that the assessment of a significant imbalance is not restricted to a quantitative economic evaluation.[34] In that case, Menéndez Álvarez had bought a house. According to the sale contract, he was responsible for payment of an urban tax, which he paid, whereas it was the legislator's intention that this tax should be borne by the seller. The question arose whether this clause was unfair, because the buyer had to pay a tax for which he was not liable. The CJEU considered that an impairment of the legal situation sufficed. The CJEU referred to three types of impairment: a restriction of rights; a constraint on the exercise of such rights; an imposition on the consumer of additional obligations.

Apart from the significant imbalance, the contract term must also be contrary to good faith to qualify as unfair. In *Aziz*, the CJEU elaborated on this.[35] The test to be applied is whether 'the seller or supplier, dealing fairly and equitably with the consumer, could reasonably assume that the consumer would have agreed to such a term in individual contract negotiations'.[36]

Annex to Unfair Terms Directive

Another important element to assess as to whether a clause is unfair is the list provided in the Annex to the Unfair Terms Directive. According to article 3(3) of the Directive, these clauses may be considered unfair. The CJEU was asked repeatedly what the meaning of these terms are and in which situations they apply.[37] In general, the CJEU held that inclusion of a term on the list is an essential element to assess whether a clause is unfair.[38] In other words, inclusion is a strong indication that a term is unfair. Further, where necessary, the terms listed in the Annex must be interpreted in the light of articles 3 and 4 of the Directive.[39] This line of reasoning of the CJEU seems to deviate from its ruling in *Océano*, where it held that a forum choice for the seller's place of business was an unfair term, because these terms were included in paragraph 1(q) of the Annex.[40]

Apart from the general meaning of the Annex, the CJEU also discussed specific terms of the Annex. As already stated, in *Océano*, the CJEU held that a forum choice for the place of business of the seller fell within the scope of paragraph

[34] C-226/12 *Constructora Principado SA v José Ignacio Menéndez Álvarez*, 16 January 2014 (CJEU, nyr) para 24.

[35] C-415/11 *M Aziz v Caixa d'Estalvis de Catalunya*, n 32 above, para 68.

[36] ibid para 69. A different test seems to be proposed in *Chitty on the Law of Contracts*, n 12 above, para 15-074, where good faith is 'to ensure that the test of "significant imbalance" ... is not applied in any sense mechanically'.

[37] C-415/11 *M Aziz v Caixa d'Estalvis de Catalunya*, n 32 above, para 74.

[38] C-472/10 *Nemzeti Fogyasztóvédelmi Hatóság v Invitel Távközlési Zrt*, n 13 above; C-488/11 *DF Asbeek Brusse and K de Man Garabito v Jahani BV*, 30 May 2013 (CJEU, nyr) para 55. In an earlier decision, C-243/08 *Pannon GSM Zrt v E Sustikné Győrfi* [2009] ECR I-4713, para 43, the CJEU applied a more lenient test.

[39] C-243/08 *Pannon GSM Zrt v E Sustikné Győrfi*, n 38 above.

[40] C-240/98–C-244/98 *Océano Grupo Editorial SA v Roció Murciano Quintero*, n 9 above.

1(q) of the Annex and the CJEU itself held that it was an unfair term.[41] This was nuanced in later decisions.[42] In *Pannon*, also a forum choice for the place of the seller's business was included.[43] The forum was 275 km from the place where the buyer, who received an invalidity benefit, lived. Moreover, there was no direct train or bus connection, as a result it was very difficult for the consumer to reach the court chosen. The CJEU did not consider itself whether the clause was unfair, but held that it was for the national court to do so taking into account all the circumstances described above.[44]

Another term listed in the Annex is the term according to which a consumer must pay a disproportionately high sum in compensation (paragraph 1(e)). In a number of cases, where especially Spanish courts had referred cases for a preliminary ruling, the CJEU considered paragraph 1(e) in connection with paragraph 1(g) and paragraph 2(a).[45] One element of the tests which the CJEU explicitly referred to in connection with articles 3 and 4 is that the national court must compare the statutory interest with the interest laid down in the contract. The CJEU applied the rule which it expressed as to the meaning of significant imbalance.

Another issue which the CJEU confirmed was that in long-term contracts, the supplier or seller has a legitimate interest to change the price unilaterally. If he does so, he must meet the requirements of transparency, balance and good faith. This all follows from paragraph 2(b) second sentence and (d) of the Annex.[46] Crucial is whether 'the reason for and the mode of a change of costs are specified in a transparent way in the contract', so that the consumer may expect the cost increases. Moreover, in the case of a price increase, the consumer must have the possibility of ending the contract.

To sum up, from the case-law it follows that to assess whether a term is unfair, all the circumstances at the moment of conclusion of the contract are relevant, as well as the other terms of the contract. Moreover, to assess whether there is a significant imbalance to the detriment of the consumer, it does not suffice to assess whether the economic situation of the consumer is worse. Reference must also be made to the legal situation. To assess whether this is the case, a comparison must be made between the situation as if no contract had been concluded and the situation under the contract. In addition, under the case-law of the CJEU, the notion of good faith refers to the situation where a seller or supplier could reasonably expect a consumer to enter into a contract with those terms if the consumer had negotiated about the contract terms individually. The Annex (referred to in Unfair Terms Directive,

---

41 ibid; *Chitty on the Law of Contracts*, n 12 above, para 15–106.

42 See, eg C-243/08 *Pannon GSM Zrt v E Sustikné Györfi*, n 38 above; C-137/08 *VB Pénzügy Lízing v F Schneider*, n 31 above.

43 C-243/08 *Pannon GSM Zrt v E Sustikné Györfi*, n 38 above.

44 It must be noted that arguably it follows from the holding in C-413/12 *Asociación de Consumidores Independientes de Castilla y León v Anuntis Segundamano España*, 5 December 2013 (CJEU, nyr), that in the case of consumer organisations, a forum choice for the habitual residence of the seller is permitted.

45 C-415/11 *M Aziz v Caixa d'Estalvis de Catalunya*, n 32 above, para 74; C-537/12 and C-116/13 *Banco Popular Español SA v Maria Teodolinda Rivas Quichimbo and Wilmar Edgar Cun Pérez; Banco de Valencia SA v J Valldeperas Tortosa and MÁ Miret Jaume*, 14 November 2013 (CJEU, nyr).

46 C-92/11 *RWE Vertrieb AG v Verbraucherzentrale Nordrhein-Westfalen eV*, 21 March 2013 (CJEU, nyr).

article 3(3)) is an essential element, together with those mentioned in articles 3 and 4, to establish whether a clause is unfair.

ADDITIONAL REQUIREMENTS

The Unfair Terms Directive provides that unfair contract terms are non-binding. In addition, article 5 of the Directive also provides that a term must be in plain and intelligible language. The Directive does not provide a remedy where a contract includes an incomprehensible term.[47] It only provides the *contra proferentem* rule, which implies that in case of doubt the most favourable interpretation for the consumer must be taken.

Together with recital 20 of the Directive, the CJEU has also inferred from this provision that the information on contract terms must be available before the conclusion of the contract.[48] This is 'of fundamental importance to the consumer'.[49] In practice, this results in an obligation for the seller or supplier to provide the consumer with the contract terms before the conclusion of the contract, otherwise the consumer is not able to read the contract terms before entering into it. Thus, the CJEU presumes that the consumer reads the terms of the contract if they are provided to them before entering into the contract. The underlying idea is that the consumer understands the contract terms if he reads them before the conclusion of the contract and consequently he can take a well-informed decision about entering into the contract.[50] However, this idea is questioned, because in daily life a consumer does not read general terms.[51] A consumer does not read the general conditions before he buys a train ticket, because '[r]eading is boring, incomprehensible, alienating, time-consuming, but most of all pointless. We want the product, not the contract',[52] as Ben-Sahar writes.

In this respect, the question is raised whether the duty to provide the information before the conclusion of the contract should not be abandoned, because it does not reflect empirical evidence and should be replaced by other means, for instance ranking of companies.[53]

Where the supplier or seller fails to provide the general conditions before the conclusion of the contract, the case-law does not indicate what the remedy should be, albeit, it is provided that it does not suffice to provide the information during the contract.

[47] Collins, 'Good Faith in European Contract Law', n 8 above.

[48] C-472/10 *Nemzeti Fogyasztóvédelmi Hatóság v Invitel Távközlési Zrt*, n 13 above, para 27; C-92/11 *RWE Vertrieb AG v Verbraucherzentrale Nordrhein-Westfalen eV*, n 46 above; C-226/12 *Constructora Principado SA v JI Menéndez Álvarez*, 16 January 2014 (CJEU, nyr) para 24.

[49] C-472/10 *Nemzeti Fogyasztóvédelmi Hatóság v Invitel Távközlési Zrt*, n 13 above, para 27; C-92/11 *RWE Vertrieb AG v Verbraucherzentrale Nordrhein-Westfalen eV*, n 46 above; C-226/12 *Constructora Principado SA v JI Menéndez Álvarez*, n 48 above, para 24.

[50] *Cf* O Ben-Sahar, 'The Myth of the Opportunity to Read in Contract Law' (2009) *ERCL* 1.

[51] ibid; O Ben-Sahar and CE Schneider, 'The Failure of Mandated Disclosure' (2011) 159 *University of Pennsylvania Law Review* 647.

[52] Ben-Sahar, 'The Myth of the Opportunity to Read in Contract Law', n 50 above.

[53] O Bar-Gill and O Ben-Shahar, 'Regulatory Techniques in Consumer Protection: A Critique of European Consumer Contract Law' (2013) 50 *CML Rev* 119.

UNFAIR CLAUSES: NON-BINDING

An unfair clause is non-binding (Unfair Terms Directive, article 6). This is a mandatory provision which aims 'to replace the formal balance which the contract establishes between the rights and the obligations of the parties with an effective balance which re-establishes equality between them'.[54] Non-binding is not a technical legal term. In some legal systems of the Member States, a distinction is made between nullity and avoidance. Non-binding means nullity rather than avoidance within the meaning of the Directive.[55] Also, other questions arise in this respect, for instance, whether a court may declare the whole contract non-binding if the consumer is better off that way. The CJEU held that this is not the legal consequence which the Directive attaches to an unfair clause, but since the Directive concerns minimum harmonisation, national legal systems can include that remedy in their legislation.[56]

Another question is whether the non-bindingness of a clause in one particular case also has consequences for other cases. In *Invitel*, the CJEU said 'no'.[57] However, in a recent decision, *Banco Popular Español*, the CJEU explicitly referred to its previous decision in *Aziz* and its conclusion in that decision. In that sense, there is an informal way of dealing with precedents.[58] The situation occurs most frequently when there are frequently used general conditions in a particular field. In practice, it is very likely that a court will follow an earlier decision, but it will result in costs for the litigating parties.

The notion of non-bindingness is not only important with respect to the remedy, but also concerns rules of civil procedural law. Now, I will deal with the latter consequences.

In *Océano*, the CJEU held, in answer to a preliminary question of a Spanish court, that a court has to apply the national rules transposing the rules laid down in the Unfair Terms Directive, by its own motion.[59] The reasoning is that the Directive aims at the protection of the consumer vis-à-vis the supplier or the seller, because the consumer is in a weaker position than the creditor. To make sure that the consumer will have the protection he is entitled to under the Directive, a court must apply the rules of its own motion. A considerable number of preliminary questions, in which national courts sought guidance, followed *Océano*.[60] The CJEU ruled in a similar vein. However, a few qualifications were made. To apply a rule of its own motion, a court must have sufficient factual and legal information.[61] Moreover, a court cannot

[54] See, eg C-76/10 *Photovost' SRO v Iveta Korčkovská*, n 28 above, para 38.

[55] V Trstenjak, 'Procedural Aspects of European Consumer Protection Law and the Case Law of the CJEU' (2013) *ERPL* 459.

[56] C-453/10 *J Pereničová and V Perenič v SOS financ spol SRO*, n 30 above.

[57] C-472/10 *Nemzeti Fogyasztóvédelmi Hatóság v Invitel Távközlési Zrt*, n 13 above.

[58] C-537/12 and C-116/13 *Banco Popular Español SA v MT Rivas Quichimbo*, n 45 above.

[59] *Cf Chitty on the Law of Contracts*, n 12 above, para 15–130; V Trstenjak and E Beysen, 'European Consumer Protection Law: *Curia Semper Dabit Remedium?*' (2011) 48 *CML Rev* 119; Trstenjak, 'Procedural Aspects of European Consumer Protection Law', n 55 above; Weatherill, 'Consumer Policy', n 2 above, 859.

[60] See, eg C-137/08 *VB Pénzügy Lízing v F Schneider*, n 31 above; C-76/10 *Photovost' SRO v Iveta Korčkovská*, n 28 above.

[61] *Chitty on the Law of Contracts*, n 12 above, para 15–131.

declare a term unfair if a consumer opposes this.[62] In addition, a court must inform the parties that it will apply of its own motion the rules concerning unfair terms, and invite the parties to express their view on it.[63] The CJEU referred in this respect to the right to a fair trial as laid down in Article 47 of the Charter of Fundamental Rights, which includes, amongst other things, the principle of *audi alterem partem.*

This is an effective way of preventing consumers being bound by unfair terms and the use of unfair terms by traders in contracts with consumers, the CJEU held.[64] It also elaborated why the consumer does not raise the unfairness of the term. It could, for instance, be that the consumer is not aware of his rights or he does not appear in the proceedings because of the costs which those proceedings would involve.[65]

Whether a court must apply a rule of its own motion is generally considered to belong to the ambit of civil procedural law. This is not the only example of the way the Unfair Terms Directive affects national civil procedural law. If national rules of civil procedural law render the enforcement of consumer rights which stem from European law practically impossible, such national rules cannot be applied.[66] To come to this conclusion, the CJEU has used the doctrine of effective judicial protection. It applies in situations where the matter at stake has not been harmonised (in the words of the CJEU: it is a matter for the Member States), but these national rules prevent or render the enforcement of rights to which a person is entitled under European law more difficult or even impossible. If that is the case, the national rule cannot be applied in that situation.[67] To test whether the national rules render the enforcement of rights derived from European law more difficult, the CJEU uses the principles of effectiveness and equivalence.[68] The latter refers to the situation where there is a similar rule under national law. In those instances, the European situation must be treated in the same way as the national one. If not, the national rules cannot be applied. This was at stake in *Asbeek Brusse*.[69] Under Dutch civil procedural law, a court must apply rules of public policy even on appeal and even if the parties have not mentioned the issue in their complaints. However, on appeal a court is not allowed to raise issues which fall outside the complaints concerning the decision at first instance. The CJEU held that the rules laid down in the Unfair Terms Directive are comparable to rules which have a public policy character within the national legal system. As a consequence, since a court must apply national rules of a public policy character of its own motion on appeal, it

62 C-243/08 *Pannon GSM Zrt v E Sustikné Györfi*, n 38 above.

63 C-472/11 *Banif Plus Bank Zrt v C Csipai and V Csipai*, n 10 above.

64 C-76/10 *Photovost' SRO v Iveta Korčkovská*, n 28 above, para 41.

65 ibid para 43.

66 *Chitty on the Law of Contracts*, n 12 above, para 15–131; M Dougan, 'The Vicissitudes of Life at the Coalface: Remedies and Procedures or Enforcing Union Law before the National Courts' in P Craig and G de Búrca (eds), *The Evolution of EU Law*, 2nd edn (Oxford University Press, 2011) ch 14, 411. See, eg C-76/10 *Photovost' SRO v Iveta Korčkovská*, n 28 above; C-413/12 *Asociación de Consumidores Independientes de Castilla y León v Anuntis Segundamano España*, n 44 above.

67 *Cf* Trstenjak and Beysen, 'European Consumer Protection Law', n 59 above, 96.

68 See, eg C-473/00 *Cofidis* [2002] ECR I-10875; C-488/11 *DF Asbeek Brusse and K de man Garabito v Jahani BV*, n 38 above; C-537/12 *Banco Popular Español SA v Maria Teodolinda Rivas Quichimbo*, n 45 above; and C-116/13 *Banco de Valencia SA v Joaquín Valldeperas Tortosa*, n 45 above. *Cf* Trstenjak, 'Procedural Aspects of European Consumer Protection Law', n 55 above.

69 C-488/11 *DF Asbeek Brusse and K de Man Grabito v Jahani BV*, n 38 above.

should also apply rules of a European origin that have a public policy character, of its own motion.

The principle of effectiveness applies when the national rule 'makes the application of European Union law impossible or excessively difficult'.[70] In *Aziz*, Spanish rules of civil procedure resulted in the impossibility of applying the rules included in the Directive, since it was not permitted to defer the enforcement proceedings relating to the mortgage until another judge had decided whether it concerned an unfair clause.

Thus, the notion of non-bindingness does not only concern the remedy for an unfair term, but also affects national civil procedural law, as follows from the CJEU case-law. National rules which make it practically impossible to render an unfair clause not binding, cannot be applied under CJEU case-law.

CONCLUSION

The CJEU case-law on the Unfair Terms Directive deals with daily life situations: loan contracts which people enter into because they want to buy a car, a house; subscriptions to gyms; sale contracts to buy a parking lot or an encyclopaedia; rent contracts. By obliging the national court to apply of its own motion the rules in the Directive in so far as there are sufficient legal and factual grounds and, moreover, setting aside national rules according to which this is impossible, the CJEU has shown an activist side, which not only goes to the heart of contract law but also of other areas, for instance civil procedural law. In addition, in answer to preliminary questions, the CJEU has referred to the specific consequences in a particular case; for instance, in *Aziz*, Aziz was expelled from his home regardless of whether the terms were considered. Moreover, the CJEU has given guidance on how to interpret the notions of significant imbalance and good faith. This all leads to the conclusion that, because of the activist approach of the CJEU with respect to the Directive, the Unfair Terms Directive's reach is beyond mere contract law.

Hugh, I first met within the framework of the Study Group on a European Civil Code. Hugh was one of the members of the drafting committee and I worked within the Amsterdam Team that drafted rules on commercial agency, franchising and distribution. Hugh came to the meetings we had with our advisors as a member of the drafting committee. Subsequently, Hugh invited me to work on the second edition of the *Casebook on European Contract Law*, together with Denis Tallon, Bénédicte Fauvarque Cosson and Stefan Vogenauer. I have really fond memories of working together on the *Casebook* in Leamington and the other times we met. We not only discussed law but also, with Jane and Mark, the novels we had read and films we had seen. I hope that we will continue to do so.

[70] C-415/11 *M Aziz v Caixa d'Estalvis de Catalunya*, n 32 above; joined cases C-537/12 and C-116/13 *Banco Popular Español SA v Maria Teodolinda Rivas Quichimbo*, n 45 above; and *Banco de Valencia SA v Joaquín Valldeperas Tortosa*, n 45 above.

17

'General Principles' of Contract Law in Transnational Instruments

STEFAN VOGENAUER

INTRODUCTION

SOME 20 YEARS ago, the Lando Commission issued the first part of the Principles of European Contract Law (PECL).[1] The publication was co-edited by Hugh Beale, one of the most influential drafters of the instrument. Professor Beale, to whom this contribution is dedicated, was also heavily involved in the drafting of the second part of the PECL.[2] Moreover, he contributed to the making of two further instruments within the broader framework of the European Commission's 'European contract law initiative':[3] the 2009 Draft Common Frame of Reference (DCFR)[4] and the 2011 Feasibility Study (FS) of the so-called 'Expert Group'.[5] Both of these were based on the PECL and, to a lesser extent, the 2007 Principles of Existing EC Contract Law, or 'Acquis Principles' (ACQP).[6] The Feasibility Study provided the blueprint for the 2011 Commission Proposal for a Regulation on a Common European Sales Law (CESL).[7]

[1] O Lando and H Beale (eds), *The Principles of European Contract Law, Part I: Performance, Non-Performance and Remedies* (Dordrecht, Martinus Nijhoff, 1995).

[2] O Lando and H Beale (eds), *Principles of European Contract Law, Parts I and II Combined and Revised* (The Hague, Kluwer, 2000).

[3] For the broader political context, see G Dannemann and S Vogenauer, 'Introduction: The European Contract Law Initiative and the "CFR in Context" Project' in G Dannemann and S Vogenauer (eds), *The Common European Sales Law in Context: Interactions with English and German Law* (Oxford University Press, 2013) 1.

[4] C von Bar, E Clive and H Schulte-Nölke (eds), *Principles, Definitions and Model Rules of European Private Law: Draft Common Frame of Reference (DCFR). Outline Edition*, prepared by the Study Group on a European Civil Code and the Research Group on EC Private Law (Acquis Group) (Munich, Sellier, 2009).

[5] European Commission, *A European contract law for consumers and businesses: Publication of the results of the feasibility study carried out by the Expert Group on European contract law for stakeholders' and legal practitioners' feedback*, 3 May 2011, available at http://ec.europa.eu/justice/contract/files/feasibility_study_final.pdf, Annex IV; revised version: European Commission, *European Contract Law: Work in Progress, Version of 19 August 2011*, available at http://ec.europa.eu/justice/contract/files/feasibility-study_en.pdf.

[6] Research Group on the Existing EC Private Law (Acquis Group), *Principles of the Existing EC Contract Law (Acquis Principles): Contract II* (Munich, Sellier, 2009).

[7] European Commission, Proposal for a Regulation of the European Parliament and of the Council on a Common European Sales Law, 11 October 2011, COM(2011) 635 final.

All of these texts have one feature in common, which they share with another transnational instrument in the field of general contract law, the UNIDROIT Principles of International Commercial Contracts (PICC).[8] At the same time, it distinguishes these documents from most national private law codifications and the major international treaty in the field of contract law, the Vienna Convention on Contracts for the International Sale of Goods (CISG):[9] the PECL, the ACQP, the DCFR, the FS and the PICC all spell out a number of 'fundamental', 'general' or 'underlying principles' of contract law.[10] The exact number and the precise content of these principles differ across the instruments. However, all of the texts deal, in one way or another, with at least some of the five principles that I will discuss in this contribution: freedom of contract; the binding effect of contracts; good faith and fair dealing; freedom from formalities; and the duty to co-operate. More often than not, these principles are given particular prominence by being laid down at the very outset of the respective instrument. The very first three articles of the CESL, for example, concern 'freedom of contract', 'good faith and fair dealing' and 'co-operation'.

The general contract law principles in transnational contract law instruments have not received much attention in the academic literature to date.[11] It is the purpose of this contribution to highlight some of the issues pertaining to the five principles mentioned in the previous paragraph. The concern is not so much with their substantive content. I will rather explore whether such principles should be codified at all and, if so, how they can be given the fullest possible effect. In order to do so, I will first sketch the background against which the drafters of the PECL and the other instruments worked, ie the earlier national and transnational approaches to codifying general principles of contract law. Thereafter, I will analyse the relevant provisions in the PECL and the subsequent transnational instruments, so as to identify the difficulties encountered in, and the benefits that can be derived from, the codification of general contract law principles in transnational contract law regimes. I will

[8] UNIDROIT, *UNIDROIT Principles of International Commercial Contracts 2010* (Rome, UNIDROIT, 2010).

[9] United Nations Convention on Contracts for the International Sale of Goods (Vienna, 11 April 1980).

[10] I will not discuss a further instrument, the so-called 'Gandolfi-Code', which contains provisions on freedom of contract (art 2), good faith and fair dealing (arts 6 and 32(b)(1)) and the binding force of contracts (art 42), while freedom from form is only implied (arts 34–38): Académie des Privatistes Européens (ed), *Code européen des contrats: Avant-projet* (Milan, Giuffrè, 2001).

[11] This is in marked contrast to the abundant literature on the 'general principles' of 'private' and 'civil' law postulated by the Court of Justice of the European Union: see, among others, J Basedow, 'The Court of Justice and Private Law: Vaccillations, General Principles and the Architecture of the European Judiciary' (2010) 18 *European Review of Private Law* 443; S Weatherill, 'The "Principles of Civil Law" as a Basis for Interpreting the Legislative Acquis' (2010) 6 *European Review of Contract Law* 74; A Hartkamp, 'The General Principles of EU Law and Private Law' (2011) 75 *Rabels Zeitschrift für ausländisches und internationales Privatrecht* 241, 255–57; MW Hesselink, 'The General Principles of Civil Law: Their Nature, Roles and Legitimacy' in D Leczkiewicz and S Weatherill (eds), *The Involvement of EU Law in Private Law Relationships* (Oxford, Hart Publishing, 2013) 131; and, despite the title, K Purnhagen, 'Principles of European Private or Civil Law? A Reminder of the Symbiotic Relationship Between the ECJ and the DCFR in a Pluralistic European Private Law' (2012) 18 *European Law Journal* 844.

finally attempt to make some structural and formal suggestions for the codification of such principles with the aim of maximising their impact.

EARLIER APPROACHES TOWARDS THE CODIFICATION OF GENERAL CONTRACT LAW PRINCIPLES

The explicit and comprehensive codification of general contract law principles is a recent phenomenon. As one might expect, there has never been much sympathy for laying down such principles in the common law jurisdictions. With regard to legislation, this would have been at odds with the casuistic, fragmentary and rule-bound tradition of statutory drafting. With regard to case-law, common law judges have been equally suspicious of broad and sweeping pronouncements, one of the rare exceptions being the famous statement of Jessel MR that captured both freedom and the binding force of contract:

> [I]f there is one thing which more than another public policy requires it is that men of full age and competent understanding shall have the utmost liberty of contracting, and that their contracts when entered into freely and voluntarily shall be held sacred and shall be enforced by Courts of justice.[12]

To this day, the most systematic overview of the 'fundamental principles of contract law' in England, notably of the 'the principles of freedom of contract and the binding force of contracts' and the absence of a 'principle of good faith of general application', can be gathered from the first chapter of *Chitty on Contracts*.[13]

Contrary to what one might believe, the codification of general principles of contract law is not a long-standing feature of the civil law tradition either. Modern legislation in this area began with the great continental codifications in the tradition of natural law and the law of reason. The codes of the late eighteenth and the early nineteenth century normally set forth rules on general contract law in a separate part of the codification before going on to lay down provisions for specific types of contract. The respective passages typically spelt out definitions in a textbook-like manner and were prone to give legislative force to doctrinal distinctions, such as the ones between different types of contract or different types of obligations.[14] However, these codes did not attempt to legislate for the kind of 'general principles' of contract law that prevail in modern transnational instruments.

If at all, the existence of such principles tended to be presupposed and was only implicitly alluded to. For example, the earliest three codes from this period, the Bavarian Code of 1756, the Prussian General Law of the Land of 1794 and the West Galician Code of 1797, did not contain a specific provision spelling out the

[12] *Printing and Numerical Registering Co v Sampson* (1875) 19 Eq 462, 465, CA.

[13] SJ Whittaker, 'Introductory' in HG Beale (ed), *Chitty on Contracts*, 31st edn (London, Sweet & Maxwell, 2012) paras 1-027–1-053 (Section 3 of the chapter, with the heading 'Fundamental principles of contract law'); the quotation in the text is from para 1-039. Freedom from form is covered later in the same chapter (para 1-095).

[14] See, eg Bürgerliches Gesetzbuch für Westgalizien III, 1, § 3 on the distinction between contract and delict, towards the beginning of its part 'On Contracts in General' (Dritter Theil, Erstes Hauptstück: 'Von Verträgen überhaupt').

binding effect of contracts. Yet, in the Bavarian Code it could be inferred from the heading of the relevant chapter, 'Of conventions and the obligations resulting from them (*obligationibus personalibus*) in general',[15] as well as from the first two provisions in the chapter, according to which a contract entailed 'duty and obligation'[16] while a mere unilateral promise, as a general rule, did not.[17] In the Prussian[18] and the West Galician Codes, the principle of binding force also had to be inferred from rules that stipulated the lack of bindingness of unilateral promises[19] and explained the distinction between unilateral and bilateral contracts.[20]

Sometimes, of course, a particular fundamental principle was not codified for the simple reason that it was not yet fully recognised. Looking for general principles of good faith or cooperation in these early continental codifications would be as fruitless as it is in modern English law. The principle of freedom from form was not universally accepted either; the rigid formal requirements inherited from Roman law were only gradually overcome.[21] The Prussian Code, for example, still laid down more than 60 provisions on formalities in the law of contract. The very first of them made it clear that compliance with statutory requirements of form was as essential for the validity of the contract as the parties' meeting of the minds.[22] The following provisions then contained a long list of contracts that were subject to formalities.[23] The Bavarian provision in question recognised the principle of freedom from form but did so in such a reluctant fashion that it might as well have gone unnoticed. It first warned that, for evidentiary reasons, it was 'advisable' to fix agreements in writing, and only then proceeded to say that this was 'not necessary', unless specifically required by statute.[24] Towards the end of the century, the West Galician Code was much more explicit: one of its provisions on contractual invalidity proclaimed that it was irrelevant for the bindingness of a contract whether the agreement had been made orally or in writing, in court or out of court.[25]

The early nineteenth century saw the enactment of two influential private law codifications that are still in force today, the French Civil Code of 1804 and the Austrian Civil Code of 1811. Their approach to general contract law principles was

[15] Codex Maximilianeus Bavaricus Civilis, Vierter Theil Kap 1: 'Von der Convention und denen hieraus entspringenden Pflichten (Obligationibus personalibus) überhaupt'.

[16] Codex Maximilianeus Bavaricus Civilis IV 1, § 1.

[17] Codex Maximilianeus Bavaricus Civilis IV 1, § 2.

[18] Allgemeines Landrecht für die Preußischen Staaten, Erster Theil, Fünfter Titel: 'Von Verträgen'.

[19] Allgemeines Landrecht für die Preußischen Staaten I, 5, § 109: 'Bloße Gelübde haben, als bloß einseitige Versprechen, nach bürgerlichen Gesetzen keine Verbindlichkeit'.

[20] Bürgerliches Gesetzbuch für Westgalizien III, 1, § 9.

[21] For an overview, see R Meyer-Pritzl, '§§ 125–129. Form der Rechtsgeschäfte' in M Schmoeckel, J Rückert and R Zimmermann (eds), *Historisch-kritischer Kommentar zum BGB*, vol I, *Allgemeiner Teil §§ 1–240* (Tübingen, Mohr Siebeck, 2003) paras 5–24.

[22] Allgemeines Landrecht für die Preußischen Staaten I, 5, § 109: 'Zur Gültigkeit eines Vertrags gehört, außer der wechselseitigen Einwilligung, auch die Beobachtung der in den Gesetzen vorgeschriebenen Form'.

[23] Eg, for all contracts of sale exceeding a certain sum: Allgemeines Landrecht für die Preußischen Staaten I, 5, § 131.

[24] Codex Maximilianeus Bavaricus Civilis IV 1, § 6: 'Daß man geschlossene Handlungen zu Papier bringe, ist zwar 1mò der leichteren Prob und Gedächtnuß wegen rathsam, nicht aber nothwendig, ohne wo solches 2dò sub Pœna Nullitatis specaliter bedungen'.

[25] Bürgerliches Gesetzbuch für Westgalizien III, 1, § 26: 'Ob ein Vertrag mündlich oder schriftlich, ob er vor Gerichte, oder außer demselben errichtet worden sey, dieses macht in Ansehung der Verbindlichkeit keinen Unterschied'.

only slightly less patchy than that of their predecessors. The Austrian Code merely followed its West Galician ancestor, with a broadly similar provision on freedom from form.[26] Freedom of contract and the binding force of contracts were simply presumed; good faith was not even referred to. At first sight, attitudes seemed to change with the French Code. Its drafters famously inserted the iconic phrase that equates the effect of contracts with that of legislation at the very beginning of the chapter 'Of the effect of contracts': 'Agreements lawfully entered into take the place of the law for those who have made them'.[27] This provision, article 1134(1) of the Code, has been seen as embodying the 'principle' of the binding force of contract (*force obligatoire du contrat*) ever since.[28]

Yet, the other four general principles of contract law mentioned at the outset of this contribution figured much less prominently in the Code. Article 1134 also stipulated that contracts 'must be performed in good faith'[29] but it only did so in the third paragraph of the provision. The very position of the rule in article 1134(3) for a long time prevented the acceptance of good faith as a general principle of contract law: the drafters had ostensibly subordinated good faith to the principle of binding force, so there seemed to be little room for good faith to qualify contractual rights and obligations. In fact, good faith was widely understood as merely underscoring the idea that the parties must keep to their agreement.[30] Although good faith is today widely regarded as a principle of contract law in France,[31] French lawyers remain ambivalent about its role.[32]

Moreover, the Code had no provisions guaranteeing freedom of contract, freedom from form and the duty to cooperate. The latter two were not yet fully acknowledged: the Code stipulated an evidential form requirement to the effect that written evidence was required in order to prove any contract above a relatively modest sum;[33] the duty to cooperate only developed in France during the twentieth century (where it was increasingly linked to the principle of good faith).[34] Freedom of contract (*liberté contractuelle*), while fully accepted as a general principle of French contract law today,[35] still has to be attached 'somewhat fictitiously' to articles 6 and 1123 of the Code,[36] two provisions that *limit* freedom of contract in cases where the agreement would contravene public policy or was affected by the

[26] According to the first sentence of Allgemeines Bürgerliches Gesetzbuch, § 883, a 'contract can be made orally or in writing; in court or out of court; with or without witnesses' ('Ein Vertrag kann mündlich oder schriftlich; vor Gerichte oder außerhalb desselben; mit oder ohne Zeugen errichtet werden').

[27] Code civil, art 1134(1): 'Les conventions légalement formées tiennent lieu de loi à ceux qui les ont faites'.

[28] F Terré, P Simler and Y Lequette, *Droit civil: les obligations*, 11th edn (Paris, Dalloz, 2013) paras 23, 25, 438.

[29] Code civil, art 1134(3): 'Elles [les conventions] doivent être exécutées de bonne foi'.

[30] S Whittaker and R Zimmermann, 'Good Faith in European Contract Law: Surveying the Landscape' in R Zimmermann and S Whittaker (eds), *Good Faith in European Contract Law* (Cambridge University Press, 2000) 7, 33–34.

[31] Terré, Simler and Lequette, *Droit civil: les obligations*, n 28 above, para 43.

[32] Whittaker and Zimmermann, 'Good Faith in European Contract Law', n 30 above, 37–39.

[33] Code civil, art 1341.

[34] Terré, Simler and Lequette, *Droit civil: les obligations*, n 28 above, paras 439, 441.

[35] ibid paras 23–24.

[36] R Cabrillac, *Droit européen comparé des contrats* (Paris, LGDJ, 2013) 31.

incapacity of one of the parties; the French Constitutional Court found yet another route and deduced the principle from article 4 of the 1789 Declaration of Rights of Man and the Citizen, according to which '[l]iberty consists in the freedom to do everything which injures no one else'.[37]

The German Civil Code of 1900 is widely regarded as particularly coherent and principled, and the preparatory materials reveal that its drafters perceived of general principles as key elements of their work. However, they deliberately shied away from the textbook-style doctrinal statements that had characterised the eighteenth and nineteenth century codes in the German-speaking world. They were also hostile, as a matter of legislative technique, to the explicit codification of general principles: these were self-evident, and any legislative enactment of obvious statements would have been inefficient and superfluous.[38] Accordingly, the Code contains no provisions stipulating freedom of contract and the binding force of contracts. Today's lawyers tend to deduce freedom of contract from the constitutional 'right to free development of one's personality' which article 2(1) of the 1949 Basic Law grants to every person. The idea of binding force is normally simply referred to as the 'principle of *pacta sunt servanda*' and thus grounded in the medieval and early modern scholarly writings of the European *ius commune* from which it originated.[39] If it is at all attempted to relate the principle to the text of the Code, it is pegged to the first provision in the Code's second Book on the 'Law of Obligations', according to which 'by virtue of an obligation the creditor is entitled to claim performance from the debtor'.[40] An explicit provision on freedom from form was envisaged in the first draft of the Code but ultimately discarded as a self-evident and thus dispensable statement.[41] As enacted, the Code only implies the principle in a rule which stipulates that a 'legal transaction which lacks the form prescribed by statute is void'.[42] The duty to cooperate is today mostly regarded as flowing from the principle of good faith, the only general principle of contract law that was explicitly laid down in § 242 of the Code. But on a literal reading even the famous § 242 ('The debtor is bound to perform in accordance with the requirements of good faith, taking into account ordinary usage')[43] with its very prominent position towards the beginning of the Code's second Book is not the broad and sweeping statement that German lawyers made of it later in the twentieth century: the drafters limited good faith

[37] Conseil constitutionnel DC, 13 January 2000 (2000-437), *Juris-classeur périodique, La semaine juridique* 2001.I.261, no 17.

[38] J Rückert, 'vor § 1. Das BGB und seine Prinzipien: Aufgabe, Lösung, Erfolg' in Schmoeckel, Rückert and Zimmermann, *Historisch-kritischer Kommentar zum BGB*, n 21 above, paras 31–32, 35–36, 44; B Mertens, *Gesetzgebungskunst im Zeitalter der Kodifikationen: Theorie und Praxis der Gesetzgebungstechnik aus historisch-vergleichender Sicht* (Tübingen, Mohr Siebeck, 2003) 312–25.

[39] P Landau, '*Pacta sunt servanda*: Zu den kanonistischen Grundlagen der Privatautonomie' in M Ascheri, F Ebel and M Heckel (eds), *Ins Wasser geworfen und Ozeane durchquert: Festschrift für Knut Wolfgang Nörr* (Cologne etc, Böhlau, 2003) 457.

[40] Bürgerliches Gesetzbuch, § 241(1)(1): 'Kraft des Schuldverhältnisses ist der Gläubiger berechtigt, von dem Schuldner eine Leistung zu fordern'. For an overview, see M-P Weller, *Die Vertragstreue: Vertragsbindung—Naturalerfüllungsgrundsatz—Leistungstreue* (Tübingen, Mohr Siebeck, 2009) 36–38.

[41] For references, see Meyer-Pritzl, '§§ 125–129', n 21 above, para 22.

[42] Bürgerliches Gesetzbuch, § 125(1): 'Ein Rechtsgeschäft, welches der durch Gesetz vorgeschriebenen Form ermangelt, ist nichtig'.

[43] Bürgerliches Gesetzbuch, § 242: 'Der Schuldner ist verpflichtet, die Leistung so zu bewirken, wie Treu und Glauben mit Rücksicht auf die Verkehrssitte es erfordern'.

to the manner in which performance must be rendered, and they even felt it was necessary to enact a separate provision on the role of good faith in contractual interpretation.[44]

The Swiss Civil Code of 1912 followed German law in enacting a good faith clause in a prominent position. Its article 2 requires that '[e]veryone has to act according to good faith in exercising his rights and in performing his duties'.[45] Moreover, article 11(1) of the contemporaneous Swiss Code of Obligations made it clear that '[t]he validity of a contract only requires compliance with a particular form if this is provided for by statute'. Apart from these provisions, the Swiss legislator was silent on general principles of contract law. Meanwhile, however, a different approach had begun to emerge in the Romanistic tradition. The Spanish Civil Code of 1889 explicitly spelt out some general principles, and the new Civil Codes of Italy (1942) and Portugal (1967) followed suit. Freedom of contract figured prominently in all these codifications. For example, the first provision in the Italian Code's Title on 'Contracts in General' was given the heading 'Contractual autonomy'; it unequivocally stipulates that '[t]he parties can freely determine the content of the contract within the limits imposed by law'.[46] The Portuguese Code contains a very similar provision on 'contractual freedom' that is placed in an equally eye-catching position.[47] In the Spanish Code, the first provision of the chapter 'On the effectiveness of contracts' spells out that '[c]ontracts are binding, whatever the form under which they have been entered into',[48] so it links the principles of binding force and freedom from form. The latter principle was also expressly codified in Portugal[49] and even in the Greek Civil Code of 1940,[50] which is otherwise firmly grounded in the Germanic tradition.

The move towards the codification of general contract law principles particularly affected the issue of good faith. The Greek Code adopted a verbatim translation of the German good faith provision which was inserted at the same place within the

[44] For the comparatively narrow scope of the rule in § 242 and its later development in German case law, see Whittaker and Zimmermann, 'Good Faith in European Contract Law', n 30 above, 18–32. The rule on contractual interpretation is in Bürgerliches Gesetzbuch, § 157.

[45] Schweizerisches Zivilgesetzbuch, art 2(1): 'Jedermann hat in der Ausübung seiner Rechte und in der Erfüllung seiner Pflichten nach Treu und Glauben zu handeln'; Schweizerisches Obligationenrecht, art 11(1): 'Verträge bedürfen zu ihrer Gültigkeit nur dann einer besonderen Form, wenn das Gesetz eine solche vorschreibt'.

[46] Codice civile, art 1322(1): 'Autonomia contrattuale. (1) Le parti possono liberamente determinare il contenuto del contratto nei limiti imposti dalla legge'. See already Código civil español, art 1255: 'Los contratantes pueden establecer los pactos, cláusulas y condiciones que tengan por conveniente, siempre que no sean contrarios a las leyes, a la moral ni al orden público'. ('The contracting parties may establish any covenants, clauses and conditions deemed convenient, provided that they are not contrary to the laws, to morals or to public policy.')

[47] Código civil português, art 405: '(Liberdade contratual). (1) Dentro dos limites da lei, as partes têm a faculdade de fixar livremente o conteúdo dos contratos, celebrar contratos diferentes dos previstos neste código ou incluir nestes as cláusulas que lhes aprouver'.

[48] Código civil español, art 1278: 'Los contratos serán obligatorios, cualquiera que sea la forma en que se hayan celebrado, siempre que en ellos concurran las condiciones esenciales para su validez'. See also the opening words of art 1258 (n 53 below).

[49] Código civil português, art 219: '(Liberdade de forma). A validade da declaração negocial não depende da observância de forma especial, salvo quando a lei a exigir'. ('The validity of the declaration of intent does not depend on the observance of a special formality, unless this is required by statute.')

[50] Greek Civil Code, art 158: 'Compliance with a formal requirement is only necessary in those cases prescribed by statute'.

structure of the Code.[51] A very similar rule found its way into the Italian Code.[52] The Spanish Code, in its original version of 1889, envisaged only a relatively limited role for good faith.[53] However, when it was revised in 1974, a strikingly general provision was inserted at the very outset of the Code. Its new article 7(1) stipulated without any qualification that '[r]ights must be exercised in accordance with the requirements of good faith'.[54] In 1992, an even more sweeping good faith clause was introduced in the new Dutch Civil Code.[55] The good faith principle even made an inroad into non-binding contract law instruments in the common law world. In the United States, both the Restatement Second Contracts and the Uniform Commercial Code (UCC), while resisting the express codification of any other of the five principles,[56] contain good faith clauses that are broadly comparable to the provisions in Germany and Italy.[57] Indeed, the idea of good faith and fair dealing is seen as 'a basic principle running throughout the Uniform Commercial Code',[58] it is codified and defined towards the beginning of the Code's first Article which sets out 'General Provisions',[59] and it is even made mandatory.[60]

The drafters of the CISG resisted the trend towards the codification of general principles of contract law. To some extent, this was a question of substance. The drafters surely did not intend to establish a general duty of the parties to cooperate with each other. Even the suggestion to insert a general good faith clause was, as is well known, rejected by a majority. The result was a botched compromise in article 7 CISG, according to which the 'observance of good faith in international trade' is

[51] ibid art 288.

[52] Codice civile, art 1375: 'Esecuzione di buona fede. Il contratto deve essere eseguito secondo buona fede'.

[53] However, Código civil español, art 1258 linked the notion of good faith to the idea of implying terms by inserting a reference to good faith in a provision resembling Code civil, art 1135: 'Los contratos se perfeccionan por el mero consentimiento, y desde entonces obligan, no sólo al cumplimiento de lo expresamente pactado, sino también a todas las consecuencias que, según su naturaleza, sean conformes a la buena fe, al uso y a la ley'. ('Contracts are perfected by mere consent, and from then on bind the parties, not just to the performance of the matters expressly agreed therein, but also to all consequences which, according to their nature, are in accordance with good faith, custom and law.')

[54] Código civil español, art 7(1): 'Los derechos deberán ejercitarse conforme a las exigencias de la buena fe'.

[55] Burgerlijk Wetboek, art 6:2: '(1) Schuldeiser en schuldenaar zijn verplicht zich jegens elkaar te gedragen overeenkomstig de eisen van redelijkheid en billijkheid. (2) Een tussen hen krachtens wet, gewoonte of rechtshandeling geldende regel is niet van toepassing, voor zover dit in de gegeven omstandigheden naar maatstaven van redelijkheid en billijkheid onaanvaardbaar zou zijn'. ('(1) Debtor and creditor must act against each other in accordance with the requirements of good faith. (2) Any rule derived from statute law, custom or legal transactions does not apply to the extent that it is, in the given circumstances, inappropriate according to the requirements of good faith.') The provision is amplified by art 6:248 of the Burgerlijk Wetboek.

[56] With regard to freedom from formalities, there is a substantive reason in that the Statute of Frauds still has a wide application in the contract laws of the United States; see Restatement Second Contracts (1981), §§ 110–50; UCC 2013, § 2-201. With regard to freedom of contract, the Official Comment to the UCC claims that the Code is 'stating affirmatively at the outset that freedom of contract is a principle of the Uniform Commercial Code' (UCC 2013, § 1-302 Official Comment 1); however, the principle can only be inferred from the rule in UCC 2013, § 1-302(a), according to which parties are free to derogate from the UCC, unless otherwise provided.

[57] Restatement Second Contracts (1981), § 205.

[58] UCC 2013, § 1-304 Official Comment 1.

[59] UCC 2013, § 1-304: 'Every contract or duty within the Uniform Commercial Code imposes an obligation of good faith in its performance and enforcement'; with statutory definition of the notion of 'good faith' in §1-201(b)(20).

[60] UCC 2013, § 1-302(b).

one of the factors to be regarded in the interpretation of the Convention. The precise meaning of this provision is still far from clear.[61] In contrast, the CISG certainly subscribes to the other general principles, yet it does so in a decidedly low-key fashion. That freedom of contract prevails can only be gathered from article 6 CISG. The provision is tucked away in the chapter of the Convention that deals with its 'Sphere of Application' and provides that the parties are free to derogate from, or vary the effect of the provisions of the CISG.[62] The binding effect of contracts is not explicitly spelt out either. The applicability of the principle is usually inferred from the Convention's rules on the remedies for breach and from the narrow scope of the only notable exemption from contractual liability that the CISG provides for, ie the *force majeure*-type rule in article 79.[63] Freedom from form, finally, is laid down expressly and comprehensively in article 11 CISG. However, its impact is somewhat diminished by its being placed towards the end of the Convention's chapter on 'General Provisions'. More importantly, the general principle is overshadowed by the two articles that immediately follow article 11: article 12 creates a broad exception by allowing contracting states to declare a reservation with the effect that national requirements as to form may apply in a contract governed by the CISG; article 13 contains a definition of the notion of 'writing' which is, as such, trivial but directs the attention of the reader away from the general principle and towards those cases where the parties specifically agreed to deviate from the principle and make their contract in writing.

A NEW WAVE OF TRANSNATIONAL CONTRACT LAW INSTRUMENTS

The preceding section shows that the drafters of the transnational contract law instruments covered in this contribution were not able to fall back on a uniform approach towards the codification of general principles of contract law. As a result, they faced difficult choices as to which, if any, of the principles they should lay down and how much prominence they ought to give them. This section explores, in chronological order, how the different instruments reflect this challenge.

UNIDROIT Principles

The first version of the PICC was published in 1994,[64] and the provisions that are relevant for the purposes of this contribution have not changed since. They codify all our five general principles of contract law. The drafters gave particular prominence

[61] For a concise account of the issues, see EA Farnsworth, 'Duties of Good Faith and Fair Dealing under the UNIDROIT Principles, Relevant International Conventions and National Laws' (1995) 3 *Tulane Journal of International and Comparative Law* 47, 55–57.

[62] For a similar argument with regard to the UCC, see n 56 above.

[63] I Schwenzer, P Hachem and C Kee, *Global Sales and Contract Law* (Oxford University Press, 2012) para 45.87, refer to *pacta sunt servanda* as a 'foundation principle of contract law' but discuss it only in the context of hardship (paras 45.87 and 45.88) and, very much in passing, in the context of the remedies of specific performance (para 43.06) and damages (para 44.31).

[64] UNIDROIT, *UNIDROIT Principles of International Commercial Contracts* (Rome, UNIDROIT, 1994). The following references are all to the most recent edition of the PICC with its Official Comments (n 8 above).

to three of them by laying them down at the very outset of the black letter rules. Chapter 1 on 'General Provisions' contains rules that apply to all the following chapters of the PICC. It dramatically opens with an article on 'Freedom of contract' (article 1.1) which pithily pronounces that '[t]he parties are free to enter into a contract and to determine its content'. This is immediately followed by 'the principle that the conclusion of a contract is not subject to any requirement as to form'[65] (article 1.2: 'No form required') and 'another basic principle of contract law, that of *pacta sunt servanda*'[66] (article 1.3: 'Binding character of contract').

Somewhat less prominence is given to 'the principle of good faith and fair dealing'[67] (article 1.7: 'Good faith and fair dealing'). Although the drafters made it clear that they considered this principle, too, 'to be one of the fundamental ideas underlying the [PICC]'[68] and thus phrased it very broadly, they squeezed it in at a less conspicuous place, ie between articles on the role of mandatory rules (article 1.4), the default character of the PICC (article 1.5) and the interpretation of the PICC (article 1.6) on the one hand, and further provisions on issues of general concern for the application of the PICC as a whole on the other hand, inter alia, the role of usages and practices (article 1.9), the definition and effect of notices (article 1.10), some further definitions (article 1.11) and rules on the computation of time (article 1.12).[69] Things became even more muddled in the second edition of the PICC, published in 2004, which introduced a new article 1.8 on 'Inconsistent behaviour'. This provision covers scenarios of the kind that national legal systems tend to tackle with doctrines of estoppel or *venire contra factum proprium*. It is designed as 'a general application of the principle of good faith and fair dealing'[70] or, as the drafters had it, as the most important 'direct ... application' of that principle[71] which is in turn 'reflected in other more specific provisions of the [PICC]'.[72]

Thus, the PICC seem to envisage a complex structure of, first, top level principles ('fundamental', 'basic' or 'general' principles); secondly, intermediate or subordinate principles as 'direct applications' of the former; and, finally, ordinary and specific black letter rules that are, at best, 'indirect' applications of the first group.

While the current position of article 1.7 only mildly detracts from the force of the principle of good faith and fair dealing, the attention of the reader is much less drawn to the duty of the parties to cooperate with each other. The relevant article (article 5.1.3: 'Co-operation between the parties') is placed between textbook-style provisions on express and implied obligations (articles 5.1.1 and 5.1.2) and the duties of best effort and to achieve specific results (articles 5.1.4 and 5.1.5). The provision could not have been hidden more effectively than by placing it in Section 5.1 of the PICC, a rag-bag of articles that could not be dealt with anywhere else and

65 PICC 2010, Comment 1 to art 1.2 (9).
66 ibid Comment 1 to art 1.3 (11).
67 ibid Comment 1 to art 1.7 (19).
68 ibid Comment 1 to art 1.7 (19).
69 Article numbers in the text refer to the 2010 version of the PICC. In the original version of 1994, the current arts 1.9–1.12 were numbered 1.8–1.11. For the new art 1.8, see the text at nn 70–71 below.
70 PICC 2010, Comment 1 to art 1.8 (22).
71 ibid Comment 1 to art 1.7 (19).
72 ibid Comment 1 to art 1.8 (22).

were lumped together under the bland title of 'Content'.[73] More importantly, the duty of each party to cooperate with the other is immediately qualified since it only exists 'when such co-operation may reasonably be expected for the performance of that party's obligations'. The Official Comment confirms the relatively low status that the drafters attached to the duty of cooperation. Although the provision is seen as 'related to the principle of good faith and fair dealing ... which permeates the law of contract', cooperation is not referred to as a 'principle' in its own right.[74]

Principles of European Contract Law

Part I of the PECL was first published in 1995. The original version codified three of our five principles in Chapter 1 which dealt with 'General Provisions'. However, most of them were figuring much less prominently than in the PICC. This is particularly the case for freedom of contract. Like in article 6 CISG, the principle was only implicit in a rule dealing with the '[e]xclusion or modification of the [PECL]' (ex-article 1:102). Moreover, the provision was eclipsed by the lengthy ex-article 1:101 on the '[a]pplication of the [PECL]' (an issue that the drafters of the PICC had elegantly relegated to a Preamble) and the subsequent provisions which dealt with vastly different subjects, ie the role of usages and practices and the interpretation of the PECL (ex-articles 1:103–1:105). These were followed by an article on '[g]ood faith and fair dealing' (ex-article 1:106). This principle was spelt out clearly although it was limited to the exercise of contractual rights and performance of contractual duties. In contrast, the following article (ex-article 1:107) stipulated a '[d]uty to co-operate' which was not only placed in a more prominent position than the corresponding provision in the PICC but was also broader and less circumscribed: it simply provided that '[e]ach party owes to the other a duty to co-operate in order to give full effect to the contract'. The final three provisions of Chapter 1 dealt with the notion of 'reasonableness', imputed knowledge and intention, and notices (ex-articles 1:108–1:110). It is difficult to see why the provisions on good faith and the duty to cooperate were positioned as they were rather than having them inserted right after the article on freedom of contract.

It seems that the drafters were not content with this structure either. In the following years, they overhauled Chapter 1, and a revised version was published, together with Part II of the PECL, in 2000.[75] The new Chapter 1 with its 'General Provisions' opened with a Section 1 on the 'Scope of the Principles', followed by Section 2 on 'General Duties' and Section 3 on 'Terminology and Other Provisions'. The

[73] For criticism of the structure and content of Section 5.1 (originally 'Chapter 5: Content') by one of the drafters, see M Fontaine, 'Content and Performance' (1992) 40 *American Journal of Comparative Law* 645, 645–46.

[74] PICC 2010, Comment to art 5.1.3 (150).

[75] Lando and Beale, *Principles of European Contract Law, Parts I and II*, n 2 above. The following references to articles of the PECL and the Official Comments with their comparative Notes are to this version.

latter Section merely mirrored articles 1.10–1.12 PICC and spelt out a number of statutory definitions as well as rules on notices and the computation of time.[76]

The new Section 1 contained a provision on 'Freedom of Contract' (article 1:102). While the second paragraph merely repeated the rule that the parties may derogate from or vary the effects of the PECL, the first paragraph set out the principle much more clearly. However, the principle came across less forcefully than in article 1.1 PICC. First, the reader of article 1:102 PECL was explicitly reminded that, while the parties 'are free to enter into a contract and to determine its contents', this was 'subject to the requirements of good faith and fair dealing, and the mandatory rules established by [the PECL]'. Secondly, the provision remained much less eye-catching than article 1.1 PICC because it was still placed somewhat forlornly between the rule on the application of the PECL (article 1:101) and the remainder of the new Section 1 which covered issues that had nothing to do with general contract law principles, such as the role of mandatory rules, usages and practices and the interpretation of the PECL (articles 1:103–1:107). Thirdly, retaining the rule on variations and derogations in the second paragraph directed the reader's eye away from the actual principle in the first paragraph. Fourthly, and perhaps most importantly, article 1:102 suffered from its vicinity to the first article in the Section. It is obvious that the potential applications of the PECL set out in article 1:101 only represented lofty ambitions of the drafters. They were, as has been said with regard to the corresponding rules in the Preamble of the PICC, 'merely aspirational: they suggest possible uses of the [instrument] but cannot and do not prescribe them'.[77] As a result, the pallor of article 1:101 affected the proclamation of freedom of contract in article 1:102, which immediately raised suspicion that it had as little bite as the former. Interestingly, and perhaps inadvertently, the drafters, in their Official Comment, did not expressly elevate freedom of contract in the context of the PECL to the status of 'principle', but referred to it as a 'rule'.[78]

This was in marked contrast to 'Good Faith and Fair Dealing' which was immediately introduced as 'a basic principle running through the [PECL]'.[79] The eponymous provision (article 1:201) was one of the 'General Duties' spelt out in Section 2 of the new Chapter 1, the second being the 'Duty to Co-operate' (article 1:202). The good faith clause was broadened vis-à-vis the original version: the limitation to the exercise of contractual rights and performance of contractual duties was dropped. The duty to cooperate remained unamended and thus retained its sweeping nature. Yet, the drafters did not refer to it as a 'principle' in their Official Comment,[80] although they acknowledged that in some continental systems the duty was 'derived from the principle of good faith and fair dealing'.[81]

[76] PECL, arts 1:301–1:304; however, art 1:303 with its definition of 'reasonableness' represents a significant innovation.

[77] R Michaels, 'Preamble I' in S Vogenauer and J Kleinheisterkamp (eds), *Commentary on the UNIDROIT Principles of International Commercial Contracts (PICC)* (Oxford University Press, 2009) para 2.

[78] PECL, art 1:102 Comment (99); however, with regard to its application in national laws, freedom of contract is explicitly referred to as a 'basic principle': art 1:102 Notes (100).

[79] ibid art 1:201 Comment A (113).

[80] ibid art 1:202 Comments A to D (119–21).

[81] ibid art 1:202 Notes (121).

Both in the original and the revised version of the PECL the rule that contracts are not subject to formal requirements was much less visible than in the PICC. Although it was framed equally broadly and the drafters also regarded it as a 'principle',[82] it was not even accorded its own article and was tucked away in the second paragraph of article 2:101, which outlined the 'Conditions for the Conclusion of the Contract' and was placed in Section 1 ('General Provisions') of Chapter 2 on 'Formation of Contracts'. The first paragraph of the article set forth the fundamental requirements for making a contract under the PECL, ie an agreement of the parties and their intention to be legally bound. At the same time it explicitly spelt out that no 'further requirement' existed. This was meant to clarify that the additional requirements of some legal systems, eg valid consideration in the common law or *cause* in many of the Romanistic jurisdictions, did not apply in the case of the PECL. Formal requirements might be regarded as 'further requirements' of a similar kind, so it would seem that they were already covered by the first paragraph,[83] and the second paragraph almost appeared like an afterthought.

As opposed to the PICC, the PECL did not contain a specific provision on the bindingness of contract. The existence of the principle could be gathered from the article on change of circumstances[84] and, like under the CISG, from the rules on the availability of remedies for non-performance and the excuses that might apply.[85]

Principles of the Existing EC Contract Law

The 'Acquis Principles' did not set forth a specific rule on the binding force of contracts either; nor did they codify the principle of freedom of contract. The requirement to act in accordance with good faith was mentioned in a number of contexts, such as pre-contractual negotiations and performance.[86] However, the drafters deliberately refrained from a more sweeping solution because of their conviction that the 'acquis does not provide a solid base for an overarching principle of good faith'.[87] In contrast, they spelt out the principle of 'Freedom of form' (article 1:304) in a crystal clear and undiluted version[88] and referred to the 'Duty to co-operate' (article 7:104) as a 'general principle',[89] although they (re)introduced the qualification of reasonableness that was first found in article 5.1.3 PICC and then dropped from article 1:202 PECL.[90]

[82] ibid art 2:101 Comment F (138) and Notes (142).
[83] ibid art 2:101 Comment D (138) seems to say as much.
[84] ibid art 6:111(1): 'A party is bound to fulfil its obligations even if performance has become more onerous'.
[85] ibid arts 8:101(1) and 8:108.
[86] ACQP, arts 2:101 and 7:101.
[87] ibid art 2:101 Comment A.2 (para 8) (103).
[88] 'Unless provided otherwise, no form needs to be observed in legal dealings'.
[89] ACQP, art 7:104 Comment A.2 (para 3) (353).
[90] ibid art 7:104: 'The debtor and the creditor must co-operate with each other to the extent that this can reasonably be expected for the performance of an obligation'.

Draft Common Frame of Reference

The DCFR differed from the other instruments discussed in this contribution, to the extent that it did not only set forth rules for contracts but also for non-contractual obligations, property and other matters.[91] The contract law rules were contained in Book II of the instrument. They were mostly based on the PECL, as were the Official Comments accompanying them.[92] This was also the case for the general principles of contract law although some of them differed markedly from the respective provisions in the PECL.

The first of these concerned the article on freedom of contract which was laid down as the second provision of Book II in article II.-1:102, right after the definition of 'contract'. The provision was given a broader heading ('Party autonomy') but the Official Comment made it clear that the provision codified the 'principle of freedom of contract as a key principle'.[93] Again, this was a deviation from the PECL which did not use the notion of 'principle' in this context. In the 2008 'Interim Outline Edition', a kind of pre-publication of the black letter rules of the DCFR, the relevant text of article II.-1:102 was almost identical to that of article 1:201 PECL. Freedom of contract was granted, but only 'subject to the rules on good faith and fair dealing and any other applicable mandatory rules'.[94] This was widely criticised as too strong a qualification of the actual principle; the drafters apparently disagreed but they acknowledged that the reference to good faith had 'given rise to confusion' and therefore deleted it from the revised and final version of the instrument.[95] Thus, according to article II.-1:102 in its amended form, freedom of contract was only subject to the applicable mandatory rules.[96] As with its precursor in the PECL, the power of the principle in the first paragraph of article II.-1:102 was somewhat diluted by a lengthy rule on variations and derogations in the second paragraph, with an even more complex new third paragraph added.

Article II.-1:103 was affected by a similar weakness, although its first paragraph, in contrast to the PECL, explicitly spelt out the principle of '[b]inding effect', and did so in a beautifully concise manner: 'A valid contract is binding on the parties'. However, this was followed by two longer paragraphs, one on the bindingness of unilateral promises and another one on modification and termination of contractual rights. Although the Official Comment enthusiastically referred to the binding effect

[91] While some of the provisions of the PECL and the PICC might also be used to apply in the context of extra-contractual obligations, they were not specifically designed to be used for this purpose.

[92] C von Bar, H Beale, E Clive and H Schulte-Nölke, 'Introduction' in C von Bar, E Clive and H Schulte-Nölke (eds), *Principles, Definitions and Model Rules of European Private Law: Draft Common Frame of Reference (DCFR). Outline Edition*, prepared by the Study Group on a European Civil Code and the Research Group on EC Private Law (Acquis Group) (Munich, Sellier, 2009) 1, 30 (para 49).

[93] DCFR, art II.-1:102 Comments (130).

[94] C von Bar, E Clive and H Schulte-Nölke (eds), *Draft Common Frame of Reference (DCFR): Interim Outline Edition*, prepared by the Study Group on a European Civil Code and the Research Group on EC Private Law (Acquis Group) (Munich, Sellier, 2008) art II.-1:102(1): 'Parties are free to make a contract or other juridical act and to determine its contents, subject to the rules on good faith and fair dealing and any other applicable mandatory rules'.

[95] von Bar et al, 'Introduction', n 92 above, 19, para 28.

[96] DCFR, art II.-1:102(1): 'Parties are free to make a contract or other juridical act and to determine its contents, subject to any applicable mandatory rules'.

of contracts as 'one of the most fundamental and general principles of European contract law'[97] the principle was in danger of being overlooked because of the verbosity and the love of detail that characterised the DCFR as a whole.[98]

In another notable departure from the PECL, the DCFR unambiguously spelt out the principle of freedom from form in the first paragraph of article II.-1:106.[99] Yet, once again, its power was diminished by the lengthy second paragraph of the provision that covered non-compliance with particular formal requirements. It would also have added force to the principle had it been mentioned right away after freedom of contract and binding effect rather than inserted after the rules on the effect of usages and practices (article II.-1:104) and the imputation of knowledge (article II.-1:105).

The remaining two general principles that were identified at the outset of this contribution were codified in Book III of the DCFR which dealt with both contractual and non-contractual obligations (*cf* article III.-1:101). Chapter 1 of this Book laid down a broad rule on good faith and fair dealing in performance (article III.-1:103),[100] and designated it as 'a basic principle' in the Official Comment.[101] The following article dealt with 'Co-operation' (article III.-1:104) which the drafters did not refer to as a 'principle' but rather as 'a particular application of the duty of good faith and fair dealing'.[102]

Finally, the black letter rules (or 'model rules') of the DCFR were preceded by an elegant 'self-contained' essay of 40 pages length which was authored, amongst others, by Hugh Beale and 'set out four underlying principles underpinning the DCFR'.[103] This veritable *discours préliminaire* was a direct response to a French research project that had been published between the Interim Outline Edition and the revised and final version of the DCFR. The French scholars had been working under the auspices of the Association Henri Capitant and the Société de Législation Comparée. Their aim was a revision of the PECL that would be confined to contract law and not include rules on non-contractual obligations and property. As an integral part of this project, the French scholars produced an elaborate set of 'guiding principles of European contract law' (*Principes directeurs du droit européen du contrat*).[104] These 'principles' were not designed as legal principles in the ordinary

[97] DCFR, art II.-1:103 Comment A (132).

[98] S Vogenauer, 'Common Frame of Reference and UNIDROIT Principles of International Contracts: Coexistence, Competition, or Overkill of Soft Law?' (2010) 6 *European Review of Contract Law* 143, 164–69.

[99] 'A contract or other juridical act need not be concluded, made or evidenced in writing nor is it subject to any other requirement as to form.'

[100] There is a specific rule on good faith and fair dealing in contractual negotiations in DCFR, art II.-3:301. For a definition of the notion of good faith and fair dealing, see DCFR, art I.-1:103.

[101] DCFR, art III.-1:103 Comment A (676). See also DCFR, art I.-1:103 Comment B (90): 'principle of good faith and fair dealing'.

[102] ibid art III.-1:104 Comment B (685).

[103] von Bar et al, 'Introduction', n 92 above, 5, para 2.

[104] B Fauvarque-Cosson and D Mazeaud (eds), *Projet de Cadre Commun de Référence: Principes Contractuels Communs*, prepared for the Association Henri Capitant des Amis de la Culture Juridique Française and the Société de Législation Comparée (Paris, Société de Législation Comparée, 2008) 21-209; an English translation was published as B Fauvarque-Cosson and D Mazeaud (eds), *European Contract Law: Materials for a Common Frame of Reference. Terminology—Guiding Principles—Model Rules* (Munich, Sellier, 2008) 419–572.

sense. They were supposed to be the 'philosophical underpinnings' or 'values of European contract law', and these values would then 'underlie the different types of legal proposals in any future CFR, whether these legal proposals are in the form of principles, rules or even definitions'.[105] They would also be available as 'a guide for the interpretation and application' for a European contract law instrument.[106]

The *principes directeurs* were published in the form of 11 draft articles, some of them directly borrowed from the PECL, others making explicit ideas that had been implicitly expressed in the PECL, and again others based on a comparison of domestic contract laws of European jurisdictions. These articles were meant to give 'concrete content' to the three 'pillars' or 'ideas' of 'freedom of contract, contractual certainty and contractual fairness'.[107] Amongst themselves, they spelt out all the five fundamental principles discussed in this contribution: the article on the '[f]reedom of the parties to enter into a contract' stipulated that each party 'is free to contract and choose the other party' as well as 'to determine the content of the contract', and it also mentioned the freedom of the parties 'to determine ... the rules of form which apply to it' (article 0-101(1) and (2)). The '[p]rinciple of binding force' was placed at the head of the Section on 'Contractual certainty' (article 0-201) and the Section on 'Contractual fairness' spelt out a '[g]eneral duty of good faith and fair dealing' (article 0-301) and a '[d]uty to cooperate' (article 0-303).

The essay preceding the black letter rules of the DCFR equally aimed to provide an 'overview of the guiding principles underlying the model rules'.[108] Its authors had 'drawn heavily on the *Principes directeurs*' although these had been slightly adjusted in order to align them with the scope of an instrument that was not confined to contract law.[109] Overall, the essay identified four 'all-pervasive'[110] principles that 'underlie the whole of the DCFR'.[111] This list was much shorter than that of 15 'underlying' or 'fundamental' principles that had been mooted in the Interim Outline Edition of the instrument and that had included 'core aims' and 'values' such as consumer protection, solidarity, social responsibility, protection of human rights and the promotion of the internal market.[112] In the revised and final version,

[105] B Fauvarque-Cosson and D Mazeaud, 'Preface' in B Fauvarque-Cosson and D Mazeaud (eds), *European Contract Law: Materials for a Common Frame of Reference. Terminology—Guiding Principles—Model Rules* (Munich, Sellier, 2008) xxvii, xxvii and xxviii.

[106] G Wicker and J-B Racine, 'Introduction to the Guiding Principles and Revised Principles of European Contract Law' in B Fauvarque-Cosson and D Mazeaud (eds), *European Contract Law: Materials for a Common Frame of Reference. Terminology—Guiding Principles—Model Rules* (Munich, Sellier, 2008) xxxi, xxxiii.

[107] ibid xxxiii, xxxiv.

[108] von Bar et al, 'Introduction', n 92 above, 6, para 5; *cf* ibid 18–19, para 26.

[109] C von Bar, H Beale, E Clive and H Schulte-Nölke, 'The Underlying Principles of Freedom, Security, Justice and Efficiency' in C von Bar, E Clive and H Schulte-Nölke (eds), *Principles, Definitions and Model Rules of European Private Law: Draft Common Frame of Reference (DCFR). Outline Edition*, prepared by the Study Group on a European Civil Code and the Research Group on EC Private Law (Acquis Group) (Munich, Sellier, 2009) 60, para 1; see also von Bar et al, 'Introduction', n 92 above, 5 and 12, paras 2 and 13.

[110] von Bar et al, 'Introduction', n 92 above, 13, para 14.

[111] von Bar et al, 'The Underlying Principles of Freedom, Security, Justice and Efficiency', n 109 above, 60, para 1.

[112] C von Bar, H Beale, E Clive and H Schulte-Nölke, 'Introduction' in C von Bar, E Clive and H Schulte-Nölke (eds), *Draft Common Frame of Reference (DCFR): Interim Outline Edition*, prepared by the Study Group on a European Civil Code and the Research Group on EC Private Law (Acquis Group) (Munich, Sellier, 2008) 1, 13–18, paras 22–36.

these items, now relabelled as '"overriding principles" of a high political nature',[113] were not codified, and only the 'underlying principles' of 'freedom', 'security', 'justice' and 'efficiency' were retained. The introductory essay presented each of them and showed how they operated in the areas of contract law, non-contractual obligations and property, respectively.

With regard to contract law, the first guiding principle of 'freedom' easily translated into 'freedom of contract' which was said to be 'the starting point' in the law of contract.[114] Interventions in freedom of contract were only legitimate when justified, for example, in cases of defective consent or discrimination, but they would have to be limited to the minimum.[115] The second guiding principle of 'security' (apparently nothing else but the old fashioned value of legal certainty)[116] became, with regard to contract law, 'contractual security'. Its 'ingredients'[117] included, among others, the binding force of contract, the availability of adequate remedies and 'the approach' of *favor contractus*.[118] The protection of reasonable reliance and expectations was another 'aspect of security'.[119] Like freedom of contract, the 'principle of binding force'[120] might have to be 'qualified', as in the case of consumer withdrawal rights or the change of circumstances.[121] The third guiding principle, 'justice', was referred to as 'an all-pervading principle within the DCFR'.[122] In the contractual context, there were 'several aspects to justice',[123] such as treating like cases alike, protecting the vulnerable and not allowing people to rely on their own unlawful, dishonest or unreasonable conduct.[124] The actual rules of the DCFR were conceived as 'manifestations', 'examples', 'concretisations', 'reflections' or a 'recognition' of one of these 'aspects' of the guiding principle of justice. For example, the rules on discrimination were 'the most obvious manifestation' of the aspect of justice that like cases are to be treated alike.[125] The rule spelling out a duty to negotiate in accordance with good faith and fair dealing was one of the 'examples' of the aspect of justice that people were not allowed to rely on their own unlawful, dishonest or unreasonable conduct, and it was possible to see other specific provisions in the DCFR as 'concretisations' of the same 'idea'.[126] In a similar way, the fourth guiding principle of 'efficiency' had a variety of 'aspects', such as the

[113] von Bar et al, 'Introduction', n 92 above, 14, para 16.

[114] von Bar et al, 'The Underlying Principles of Freedom, Security, Justice and Efficiency', n 109 above, 62, para 3.

[115] ibid 65–68, paras 6–11.

[116] ibid 71, para 16: 'the uncertainty of outcomes' as the opposite of 'security'; *cf* the equation of 'security' and 'certainty', ibid 83, para 36.

[117] ibid 72, para 17.

[118] ibid 72, para 18.

[119] ibid 73, para 19.

[120] ibid 74, para 20.

[121] ibid 74, para 20.

[122] ibid 84, para 40.

[123] ibid 84, para 40.

[124] ibid 85–89, paras 41–46.

[125] ibid 85, para 41.

[126] ibid 85 and 86, para 42. For a rule being an 'explicit recognition' of one of the aspects of justice, see ibid 87, para 43.

imposition of 'minimal formal and procedural restrictions', and freedom from form was mentioned as an 'example' of this 'aspect'.[127]

The essay therefore envisaged a kind of hierarchy, with four 'guiding' or 'all-pervading' principles on top, a number of 'aspects' or 'ingredients' of each principle at the intermediate level and a host of rules as 'manifestations', 'examples', 'reflections', etc of these intermediate principles. Our five principles were not all accorded the same status in this scheme although it is not quite clear whether this was a deliberate choice: freedom of contract and the binding force of contract were mentioned at the intermediate level; freedom from form and good faith were only classified as lower-level 'manifestations', and this probably also applied to the duty of cooperation which was touched upon in the context of legal certainty without its status being made explicit.[128]

Importantly, the authors made it clear that, while in 'normal situations' there would be 'no incompatibility' between the four principles,[129] they might sometimes 'conflict' and would 'have to be balanced'.[130] In other cases the principles might 'overlap' to the extent that a black letter rule might be regarded as an expression of two different principles.[131] 'Therefore', they concluded, 'the principles can never be applied in a pure and rigid way'.[132] In any event, the four principles were not of equal value: efficiency was 'less fundamental than the others'.[133] The propensity of the four principles to overlap and conflict was also advanced as a reason for not incorporating them into the black letter rules of the DCFR. The rules were meant to show the operation of the underlying principles in practice, with all the necessary qualifications and exceptions; for the presentation of the principles, a discursive essay was deemed to be more appropriate.[134]

Although the introductory essay touched on fundamental issues of European private law, it elicited much less discussion than the black letter rules of the DCFR. It was, of course, hard to disagree with the relevance of any of the four guiding principles. To an innocent observer, they might have appeared to be the legislative equivalent of 'motherhood and apple pie'. However, they were strongly criticised for being not inclusive enough. Some observers argued that, in particular, in comparison to the set of broader values laid down in the Interim Outline Edition, they were a reactionary attempt to depoliticise European contract law, if not an outright conspiracy to impose a market-focused ideological agenda.[135] At a more formal

[127] ibid 94, para 55.

[128] ibid 77, para 24.

[129] ibid 62–63, para 3, for freedom of contract, on the one hand, and justice or efficiency, on the other.

[130] ibid 60, para 1; see, eg ibid 84, para 40 for the principle of justice.

[131] ibid 61, para 1.

[132] ibid 61, para 1; eg good faith and cooperation were said to promote both 'contractual security' and justice: ibid 76 and 77, paras 23 and 24.

[133] ibid 60, para 1.

[134] von Bar et al, 'Introduction', n 92 above, 12–13, para 13.

[135] MW Hesselink, 'If You Don't Like Our Principles We Have Others—On Core Values and Underlying Principles in European Private Law: A Critical Discussion of the New "Principles" Section in the Draft Common Frame of Reference' in R Brownsword, H-W Micklitz, L Niglia and S Weatherill (eds), *The Foundations of European Private Law* (Oxford, Hart Publishing, 2011) 59, 65–69; L Niglia, 'The Question Concerning the Common Frame of Reference' (2012) 18 *European Law Journal* 739, 751–53.

level, the idea of setting out the guiding principles in a document that would be separate from the model rules and yet an integral part of a European contract law instrument did not meet with universal acclaim: unless the principles were not included in the model rules, it was suggested, there was bound to be considerable debate on the relationship between the 'higher order principles' in the essay and the 'lower order principles' in the black letter rules.[136]

Feasibility Study

The Feasibility Study did not only 're-contractualise' the DCFR by removing the rules on non-contractual obligations and property and narrowing the scope of application down to sales and related services contracts. It also abandoned the introductory essay. General contract law principles were dealt with in the black letter rules alone. The first version of the FS provided for '[f]reedom of contract' (article 7), '[g]ood faith and fair dealing' (article 8) and '[n]o form required' (article 9), and it did so in the second Section ('General principles') of 'Chapter 1: General'. This Section was sandwiched between Section 1 with its articles on the 'Application of the instrument', mostly general rules on interpretation and definitions (articles 1–6), and the third Section with its 'Other general rules' on notices (article 10), computation of time (article 11) and unilateral statements and conduct (article 12). The duty of '[c]o-operation' was spelt out at the very beginning of Part IV of the FS which dealt with the obligations and remedies of the parties (article 89). The principle of binding force was only implicitly addressed: the heading of Part II of the instrument dealing with formation signalled that this was all about 'Making a binding contract'; equally, certain unfair terms were said to be 'not binding on the other party' (articles 77, 88, 109, 172, 185).

The second and revised version of the FS did not make substantive changes with regard to our five principles. Binding force remained implicit in the heading of Part II and a number of articles providing for the lack of bindingness of unfair terms (articles 72, 80, 168, 171). The provisions setting out the other four principles merely underwent some minor linguistic amendments. However, they were reshuffled once again. The first Chapter of the instrument was now entitled 'General principles and application of the rules', and the order of the first two Sections was reversed accordingly. Section 1 dealt with 'General principles' (articles 1–3) before Section 2 set out its provisions on the 'Application of the rules' (articles 4–13). As a result, the general principles were given much more punch than in the first version. The relevant Section still set out the principles of '[f]reedom of contract' (article 1) and '[g]ood faith and fair dealing' (article 2). 'Co-operation' was now moved to this Section as well (article 3), thus replacing the '[n]o form required' provision which was somewhat inexplicably moved to Section 2 of the Chapter where it ended up in a rather inauspicious place between a number of statutory definitions of key terms (article 7).

136 Vogenauer, 'Common Frame of Reference and UNIDROIT Principles of International Contracts', n 98 above, 171.

Proposal for a Common European Sales Law

The CESL fully replicates the relevant provisions of the revised version of the FS, again with some very minor linguistic changes. Thus, freedom of contract, good faith and fair dealing and cooperation make up the first Section on 'General principles' (articles 1–3). Freedom from form (article 6) remains in the second Section on 'Application' (articles 4–12). The binding effect of contracts continues to be presumed by the heading of Part II.

CODIFYING GENERAL PRINCIPLES IN TRANSNATIONAL INSTRUMENTS: PROBLEMS

Terminology and Classification: Languages and Systems of 'Principles'

The provisions discussed in this contribution are often referred to as 'general principles' of contract law. However, a comparison of the various instruments shows that the term 'principle' is not used uniformly. Part of the confusion stems from the fact that some of the instruments in question, such as the PICC and the PECL, refer to themselves as 'Principles' in their title. This is intended to highlight their non-binding or 'soft law' character. Only some of the provisions in these instruments are, however, 'principles' in the jurisprudential sense, ie standards that guide, but do not necessarily determine the outcome of a given case and that can be outweighed by countervailing principles.[137] From the perspective of legal theory, the majority of the articles of the PICC and the PECL are straightforward 'rules' that do not possess such a specific 'dimension of weight', but more or less dictate the outcome of a given case in an 'all-or-nothing' fashion.[138]

Whether all the five 'general principles' discussed in this contribution are really 'principles' in the jurisprudential sense is open to debate. For example, a provision stipulating freedom from form is clearly of fundamental importance. However, its application, together with other provisions on formalities in the respective instrument, will normally yield a very definite answer as to whether a formality is required in a given case. The provision rather appears to represent a kind of 'general rule' which permits for certain (narrow) exceptions. Many of the instruments seem to use the notion of 'principle' in this sense. The Official Comment to article 1.1 PICC, for example, boldly asserts that the 'principle of freedom of contract is of paramount importance in the context of international trade'. It then immediately proceeds to say that there are 'of course'(!) a 'number of possible exceptions to the principle laid down in this Article'.[139] In a similar fashion, it is said that the 'principle *pacta sunt servanda*' permits of 'exceptions'.[140] This kind of use of the concept of 'principle'

[137] For the jurisprudential distinction between rules and principles, see R Dworkin, *Taking Rights Seriously* (London, Duckworth, 1977) 22–28.

[138] For these characteristics of rules, see Dworkin ibid.

[139] PICC 2010, Comments 1 and 2 to art 1.1 (8).

[140] PICC 2010, Comments 1 and 2 to art 1.3 (11). With regard to the no-form requirement, exceptions are not mentioned; however, it is said in PICC 2010, Comment 3 to art 1.2 (10) that the 'principle of no requirement as to form may of course be overridden by the applicable law'.

is even more palpable in the PECL and their successor instruments which were promoted by the Commission within the framework of its 'European contract law initiative'.[141] Here, for example, freedom of contract was right from the outset made 'subject to' the requirements of good faith and fair dealing and/or any applicable mandatory rules. As the Official Comment to the DCFR pointed out, this was 'just a reminder that party autonomy is not absolute'.[142] The idea of a legal principle as a general rule to which other provisions stipulate exceptions also seemed to be reflected in the statement that interventions in the principle of freedom of contract were only legitimate when 'justified'.[143]

Perhaps it is for this reason that the drafters of the DCFR did not refer to the respective provisions as 'principles' but rather as 'rules which are of a more general nature, such as those on freedom of contract or good faith'.[144] They reserved the notion of 'principle' for the four 'fundamental', 'deep-rooted' and 'underlying principles' or 'basic values' that they identified in their introductory essay.[145] Sometimes they used the concept of 'basic idea' as a synonym.[146] But this attempt at terminological purity did not filter through to the Official Comment, where the notion of 'principle' was used much more loosely and inconsistently. 'Good faith and fair dealing', for example, was presented as an 'example' of one of the 'aspects' of the 'guiding principle' of 'justice' in the introductory essay. The Official Comment variously referred to it as a 'basic principle' or a 'duty'.[147]

Overall, it does not seem to make much of a difference whether a given 'principle' is referred to as such. Sometimes this designation is expressly used in the black letter rules of the instrument[148] or in a chapter heading,[149] sometimes only in the Official Comment or the accompanying Comparative Notes. Sometimes one or the other of our five 'principles' is not styled a 'principle' at all.[150]

Differences also exist with regard to the systematisation or categorisation of the principles. As has been seen, the PICC seem to assume a hierarchy of top level 'general principles', eg 'good faith and fair dealing', intermediate level 'applications' of these general principles, eg the rule on inconsistent behaviour, and the lower level black letter rules.[151] A similar, but not identical tripartite order is envisaged by the introductory essay of the DCFR, with its four top level 'guiding' principles, their intermediate level 'aspects' and the black letter rules as 'examples' of these 'aspects'.[152]

[141] European Commission, 'Annex I: Possible Structure of the CFR' in European Commission, Communication from the Commission to the European Parliament and the Council: European Contract Law and the Revision of the acquis: The Way Forward, Brussels, 11 October 2004, COM(2004) 651 final, 14, speaks of 'common fundamental principles of European contract law and exceptions for some of these principles, applicable in limited circumstances'. In a similar vein, see p 11 of the Communication.

[142] DCFR, art II.-1:102 Comments (130).

[143] See text at n 115 above.

[144] von Bar et al, 'Introduction', n 92 above, 9, para 10.

[145] ibid 10, para 11.

[146] von Bar et al, 'The Underlying Principles of Freedom, Security, Justice and Efficiency', n 109 above, 77, para 26.

[147] See text at nn 101, 102, 126 above.

[148] Eg Principes directeurs, art 0-201.

[149] Eg Chapter 1 of the CESL.

[150] Eg the duty of cooperation in the PICC: see text at n 74 above.

[151] See text at nn 70–72 above.

[152] See text at n 128 above.

Of the five principles that are of interest to us, some are placed at the top level, others at the intermediate level; and, more disconcertingly, the instruments do not always place one and the same principle at an identical level.

Arguably, the inconsistencies in terminology and categorisation conceal an underlying uncertainty about the actual content of the notion of 'general principles' and, more particularly, 'general principles of contract law'. The notion of 'principle' that identifies a general rule which only allows for narrow exceptions resembles the traditional German conception of *allgemeine Rechtsgrundsätze* which has no precise terminological equivalent in the English and the French legal language and is thus normally translated as 'general principles' or *principes généraux*.[153] Yet, the latter concepts have their own distinctive meanings in their domestic legal systems. More recently, German legal theorists have been particularly influenced by the Dworkinan theory of legal principles and have begun to use the notions of *allgemeiner Rechtsgrundsatz* and *Rechtsprinzip* more or less synonymously.[154] It is by no means clear whether this is meant to reflect a change in the substantive understanding of legal principles.[155]

Perhaps the notion of 'general principles' suffers from the same problem that besets legal terminology in general: some concepts cannot be properly translated from one legal language into another; others are typical 'false friends' that look deceptively similar but carry significantly different meanings. German lawyers, for example, would expect that the designation of a legal precept as a 'general principle of contract law' would bring with it certain consequences with regard to the place of this precept within the overall scheme, structure and hierarchy of contract law rules and, more generally, private law as a whole. In contrast, for an English lawyer, 'such a designation does not have a technical legal significance'.[156] A transnational instrument that must be understood and applied by lawyers from different national backgrounds would do well to avoid this problem and refrain from using the language of 'general principles' in its black letter text. This would entail a return to the earlier instruments discussed in this contribution: the PICC, the PECL and the DCFR placed the relevant articles in Chapters or Sections with the title 'General provisions'. The shift to Chapter and Section headings on 'General principles' only appeared in the FS and was maintained in the CESL. If the main purpose of such Chapters and Sections is to single out the most important provisions the respective heading might also be 'Fundamental provisions'.

[153] See, eg the perceptive account of JM Kelly, *A Short History of Western Legal Theory* (Oxford University Press, 1992) 407.

[154] See, eg KF Röhl and HC Röhl, *Allgemeine Rechtslehre*, 3rd edn (Cologne etc, Heymanns, 2008) 283, and the index of B Rüthers, C Fischer and A Birk, *Rechtstheorie mit Juristischer Methodenlehre*, 7th edn (Munich, CH Beck, 2013) 594: 'Prinzipien (Rechtsgrundsätze)'.

[155] For accounts of the terminological confusion of German law in this area, see Röhl and Röhl, *Allgemeine Rechtslehre*, n 154 above, 288–90; Rüthers et al, *Rechtstheorie mit Juristischer Methodenlehre*, n 154 above, 447–52.

[156] Whittaker, 'Introductory', n 13 above, para 1-027.

Indeterminacy

One thing that most of the 'general principles' discussed in this contribution have in common is their indeterminate and open-textured nature.[157] Their language is highly abstract and general rather than specific and concrete. It is virtually impossible, for example, to give a precise definition of the notion of 'good faith and fair dealing' or to set out exactly what the 'duty to cooperate' entails. 'Bindingness of contracts' can mean dramatically different things to different people: for lawyers from the civil law tradition it almost inevitably seems to entail that specific performance must be the primary remedy;[158] in the common law it was famously said that the 'duty to keep a contract at common law means a prediction that you must pay damages if you do not keep it'.[159] 'Freedom of contract' may be invoked as a moral principle promoting private autonomy as well as a vehicle for the facilitation of market transactions. Specific contract law doctrines and rules may differ greatly, depending on which of these two visions of contractual freedom is adopted.[160]

The advantages and disadvantages of the use of vague language in legislative drafting are well known. On the one hand, they promote flexibility and often allow for fairer outcomes on the basis of a case-by-case analysis. On the other hand, they are bound to make the law less predictable and thus less certain.[161] As a result, any decision on the question whether general principles of contract law ought to be codified will depend on the prevailing outlook on the two competing fundamental legal values at play: those decision-makers who are particularly concerned about legal certainty will be more reluctant to enact provisions of this kind than those who place a premium on substantive justice and fairness of outcomes.

Under- and Over-inclusiveness

Any list of 'general principles' in a contract law instrument will be subject to criticism that it includes either too many or too few principles. Arguably, reasonable minds will differ with regard to the question whether cooperation of the parties is indeed a fundamental principle of general contract law.[162] There is also room for disagreement

[157] This is also conceded with regard to the 'guiding principles' underlying the DCFR: von Bar et al, 'The Underlying Principles of Freedom, Security, Justice and Efficiency', n 109 above, 84, para 40: 'Justice is hard to define, impossible to measure and subjective at the edges'.

[158] For a comparative overview of the issues arising, see P Hachem, 'Die Konturen des Prinzips *Pacta Sunt Servanda*' in A Büchler and M Müller-Chen (eds), *Private Law: National, Global, Comparative. Festschrift for Ingeborg Schwenzer* (Bern, Stämpfli, 2011) 647.

[159] OW Holmes, 'The Path of the Law' (1897) 10 *Harvard Law Review* 457, 462.

[160] See, among others, SJ Whittaker, 'The Optional Instrument of European Contract Law and Freedom of Contract' (2011) 7 *European Review of Contract Law* 371, 372–77; C Herresthal, 'Constitutionalisation of the Freedom of Contract in European Union Law' in K Ziegler and P Huber (eds), *Current Problems in the Protection of Human Rights: Perspectives from Germany and the UK* (Oxford, Hart Publishing, 2013) 89, 96–97.

[161] For an overview of the issues in the context of European contract law, see S Vogenauer, 'Drafting and Interpretation of a European Contract Law Instrument' in Dannemann and Vogenauer (eds), *The Common European Sales Law in Context*, n 3 above, 82, 94–99.

[162] Answered in the positive by, inter alia, H Schulte-Nölke, 'Article 3' in R Schulze (ed), *Common European Sales Law (CESL): Commentary* (Munich and Oxford, CH Beck and Hart Publishing, 2012) para 2.

with regard to the '[p]rinciple of non-discrimination in contract law' which was explicitly advanced by article 3:101 ACQP, morphed into a '[r]ight not to be discriminated against' in article II.-2:101 DCFR[163] (where it was later mentioned on a par with good faith and cooperation),[164] and was dropped entirely from the FS and the CESL. Others, particularly those from the Romanistic tradition, might suggest that the need to uphold public policy, *bonnes moeures*, *gute Sitten*, etc is a general principle of law.[165] Moreover, many would argue that it is a fundamental structural principle of contract law that a contract only produces effects between the two parties to the agreement. This 'relative effect of contracts' (*effet relatif des contrats*) has iconic status in French law, as well as in English law where it tends to be referred to as 'privity of contract'.[166] Unsurprisingly, when the DCFR was published, 'the curious *absence* of a legal principle which is recognised by all the laws of contract of the Member States' was noted with disapproval.[167] As a matter of fact, neither of the instruments discussed in this contribution spells out the principle. The drafters of the DCFR deliberately excluded it because it was 'taken as self-evident'; they only thought it worthwhile to set forth the exceptions, such as agency or contracts for the benefit of third parties.[168] They equally did not think it necessary to codify the 'principle',[169] cherished by French lawyers, that the parties may invoke their contract against third parties (*opposabilité*).[170] Finally, as was pointed out above, some of the instruments do not expressly codify the principle of binding force of contract, surely a fundamental principle of contract law.

Limitations and Inconsistencies

It is one thing to enunciate a 'general principle'; it is another to agree on its limitations. As has been shown above, all the principles are subject to qualifications if these can be justified. These qualifications are made in the black letter rules of the respective instruments. Only after all these limitations have been factored in will the true scope and content of the principle be apparent. If the qualifications are too

[163] DCFR, art II.-2:101 Comments (165–76): not referred to as a 'principle'.

[164] DCFR, art III.-1:105, following art III.-1:103 on good faith and art III.-1:104 on cooperation. DCFR, art III.-1:105 Comments (689) speak of 'the principle of non-discrimination' when referring to DCFR, art II.-2:101.

[165] Eg art 4 of the so-called *Projet Terré*, a proposal for the reform of French contract law: F Terré (ed), *Pour une réforme du droit des contrats* (Paris, Dalloz, 2009).

[166] For a comparative overview, see S Vogenauer, 'The Effects of Contracts on Third Parties: The *Avant-projet de réforme* in a Comparative Perspective' in J Cartwright, S Vogenauer and S Whittaker (eds), *Reforming the French Law of Obligations: Comparative Reflections on the* Avant-projet de réforme du droit des obligations et de la prescription *('the* Avant-projet Catala*')* (Oxford, Hart Publishing, 2009) 235, 235–39. See also Principes directeurs, art 0-102 ('Respect for the freedom and rights of third parties').

[167] S Whittaker, *The Draft Common Frame of Reference: An Assessment, Commissioned by the Ministry of Justice, United Kingdom* (November 2008) 60 (emphasis in the original).

[168] von Bar et al, 'The Underlying Principles of Freedom, Security, Justice and Efficiency', n 109 above, 63, para 4.

[169] See Cass civ (1), 17 October 2000, Bull civ I no 246: 'principe d'opposabilité des conventions aux tiers'. See also Principes directeurs, art 0-203 ('Rights and duties of third parties').

[170] von Bar et al, 'The Underlying Principles of Freedom, Security, Justice and Efficiency', n 109 above, 73, para 18.

numerous and too broad the principle is reduced to a *quantité negligeable*. It is, for example, perfectly possible to state that freedom of contract is 'the starting point' in contract law, on the one hand, and to enact a raft of restrictions of contractual freedom on the other.[171] Arguably, this inconsistency lay at the heart of much of the criticism directed against the DCFR. While the instrument professed to promote freedom of contract it seemed to curtail the principle in an unprecedented fashion by subjecting it to one restriction after the other.[172] In a similar vein, the grand proclamation of the binding force of contract in the DCFR had a quasi-totemic quality, given that there were so many black letter rules which carved out exceptions—with the result that ultimately not much of the principle was left. As was observed at the time, 'the difficulty lies here not with these statements of principle as with their qualifications or exceptions ... it is the subject-matter and extent of these qualifications which give rise to concern'.[173] With regard to freedom from form it is almost ironic if article 6 CESL proclaims that no form is required although in the vast majority of cases in which the instrument potentially applies, ie in consumer contracts, it can only apply if most intricate and complex formalities are complied with.[174]

CODIFYING GENERAL PRINCIPLES IN TRANSNATIONAL INSTRUMENTS: BENEFITS

Despite the problems encountered in the codification of general principles the exercise remains worthwhile.[175] At the very least, these provisions can guide the interpretation of other articles in the same instrument, even so as to extend their scope to instances that are not covered by their wording.[176] Even more importantly, they can serve as programmatic statements that define the spirit and set the tone for the subsequent application and development of the entire instrument. Their nature may be largely symbolic and pedagogical.[177] However, they send out a signal as to what kind of contract law this particular instrument wants to lay down. It is no coincidence that of all the instruments analysed in this contribution it is the PICC,

[171] For the different limitations of freedom of contract in the various transnational instruments, see H Unberath, 'Freedom of Contract' in J Basedow, KJ Hopt and R Zimmermann (eds), *Max Planck Encyclopedia of European Private Law* (Oxford University Press, 2012) 751, 754–55.

[172] See only Whittaker, *The Draft Common Frame of Reference*, n 167 above, 54: 'there are an extraordinary number of qualifications of freedom of contract in the DCFR which are given little or no proper justification'.

[173] ibid 56.

[174] See arts 8(2) and 9 of the Regulation giving effect to the CESL (requiring the trader to provide a written Standard Information Notice and/or confirmation of the agreement on the use of the CESL 'on a durable medium').

[175] Despite the title of her contribution, B Fauvarque-Cosson, 'The Need for Codified Guiding Principles and Model Rules in European Contract Law' in R Brownsword, H-W Micklitz, L Niglia and S Weatherill (eds), *The Foundations of European Private Law* (Oxford, Hart Publishing, 2011) 73, does not make a case for codifying such principles, apart from the fairly abstract proposition that this would help 'to promote a European legal culture' (at 82).

[176] See PICC, art 1.6; PECL, art 1:106; DCFR, art I.-1:102; FS, art 1; CESL, art 4.

[177] C Aubert de Vincelles, 'Les principes généraux relatifs au droit des contrats' in F Terré (ed), *Pour une réforme du droit des contrats* (Paris, Dalloz, 2009) 113.

with their commercial focus, which set out freedom of contract in the crispest form and give the greatest prominence to bindingness of contract. At the other end of the spectrum, the ACQP, with their roots in the *acquis communautaire* and their focus on consumer protection, codify neither of these two principles. They rather set great store by two other principles: cooperation of the parties, which plays a comparatively minor role in the PICC, and non-discrimination, which is not even contemplated by the PICC. The other instruments which try to cater for both consumer and commercial contracts are somewhere in between. Even where they profess to promote the principle of freedom of contract they subject it to much greater qualifications than the PICC and therefore give it a more limited scope. Again, it is no coincidence that the CESL does not explicitly set forth the principle of bindingness: given the extensive withdrawal rights for consumers, the paradigm contract that would be governed by the CESL may not be properly binding for more than a year.

General principles of contract law at the outset of these texts help us better understand the general nature of the instruments. Their presence or absence, their exact formulation and their position within the overall context of a given instrument provide us with an idea as to how their black letter rules will attempt to strike the balance between freedom and social justice. Such guideposts are particularly useful in a transnational context where there is no shared background legal culture, as it exists in national jurisdictions. In the past, as this contribution has shown, general principles of contract law were not codified when they were either not yet fully established or so well-established that they were regarded as self-evident and their codification would have seemed superfluous, if not ridiculous. This is precisely not the case with the transnational instruments discussed in this contribution. They will be applied by lawyers with very different understandings of the role and function of contracts in law, society and the economy. In these circumstances, there are no self-evident or obvious solutions, and laying down a number of fundamental provisions will help them in gradually finding common ground.

EIGHT GUIDELINES FOR THE CODIFICATION OF GENERAL PRINCIPLES OF CONTRACT LAW

As has been seen, the codification of general principles of contract law in a transnational environment is desirable but difficult. Drafters of such provisions can learn from the experiences of the existing transnational contract law instruments. The following guidelines might help them succeed in giving their provisions on general contract law principles full force.

First, 'general principles' of contract law should be codified in transnational contract law instruments. These principles are important guideposts in the application of the instrument and have the potential for 'setting the overall tone' with regard to how the instrument will work in practice. This is particularly so in the transnational context, which as yet lacks a shared background legal culture and 'self-evident' and 'obvious' solutions.

Second, the provisions codifying general principles should not refer to these principles as 'general principles' but rather as 'fundamental provisions'. This avoids the confusion that flows from the inconsistent use of the enigmatic term 'principle' across different jurisdictions.

Third, the number of general principles that is codified should be relatively small. If it is too big, the principles will seem unexceptional and thus not particularly important. As a consequence, they will have much less force.

Fourth, the respective provisions should be integrated in the black letter rules of the instrument and not set out in a separate document. Separating them from the black letter rules is bound to create confusion as to the status of the general principles vis-à-vis the black letter rules. In a genuine legislative act of the European Union it may be possible to move the general principles to the Recitals; however, even this will increase the complexity of their relationship with the black letter rules.

Fifth, the provisions on general principles should be placed in a particularly prominent position in the instrument, ideally at its very outset or at least at the beginning of individual Chapters. The more eye-catching they are, the more attention they receive and the more powerfully they will operate.

Sixth, the general principles should be isolated from other, less fundamental provisions, so that they do not suffer from being associated with banal and trivial issues.

Seventh, the general principles should be set forth without qualifications. Ideally, they should come across as a set of 'self-evident truths'. It is clear that they have to be subject to exceptions. However, the place to lay down these exceptions is in other black letter rules further below in the text of the instrument. Immediate restrictions only detract from the force of the principle.

Eighth, restrictions of the general principles should be kept to an absolute minimum in order to avoid inconsistencies. There is no point in proclaiming a general principle and at the same time emasculating it by a raft of limitations.

OUTLOOK: TRANSNATIONAL INSTRUMENTS AS MODEL CODES

Codifications of general principles of contract law are here to stay. The transnational instruments discussed in this contribution served as 'model codes' for many national legislators who reformed their contract laws in the past two decades.[178] Some of these jurisdictions drew inspiration from the transnational provisions spelling out 'general principles' of contract law.[179] Others have been more reluctant, for example, a recent reform proposal for the Swiss Law of Obligations.[180]

The influence of the relevant provisions is particularly evident in the latest proposals for a far-reaching reform of French contract law. The first of these, the

[178] For overviews, see Michaels, 'Preamble I', n 77 above, paras 118–39; S Vogenauer, 'The DCFR and the CESL as Models for Law Reform' in Dannemann and Vogenauer (eds), *The Common European Sales Law in Context*, n 3 above, 732.

[179] For a detailed analysis of the reception in the 2001 Lithuanian Civil Code of the provisions on freedom of contract and good faith in the PICC and the PECL, see T Zukas, *Einfluss der 'Unidroit Principles of International Commercial Contracts' und der 'Principles of European Contract Law' auf die Transformation des Vertragsrechts in Litauen* (Berne, Stämpfli, 2011) 52–63, 94–109.

[180] C Huguenin and RM Hilty (eds), *Code des obligations suisse 2020: Projet relative à une nouvelle partie générale* (Zurich etc, Schulthess, 2013).

so-called *Avant-projet Catala* of 2006,[181] still adhered to the traditional style of the French Code civil. It did not set forth 'guiding principles' and was criticised on this ground.[182] In contrast, the draft of the Ministry of Justice that was finalised two years later[183] contained a Chapter II on 'Principes directeurs' which laid down freedom of contract (article 15),[184] bindingness of contract (article 17) and a broad good faith clause (article 18). An academic draft of 2009, the so-called *Projet Terré*,[185] did not have an entire Chapter dedicated to guiding principles. However, it suggested the codification of freedom of contract at the very outset of the Title on contracts (article 3), almost immediately followed by a provision on good faith (article 5); the first provision in the Section on formalities stipulated that, 'as a rule' (*en principe*), contracts were concluded simply by agreement, and only 'exceptionally' (*par exception*) certain formal requirements would apply (article 68(1) and (2)); the first provision on the effects of contracts laid down the principle of binding force (article 91(1)); and only the duty to cooperate was not codified because it was seen as an aspect of good faith.[186] The most recent Ministry draft[187] is even more comfortable with the idea of codifying general principles. It has a Chapter with 'Preliminary Provisions' (*dispositions préliminaires*) at the very outset which codifies two 'principles' which are expressly designated as such in the headings of the relevant articles, ie the *principe de liberté contractuelle* (article 2) and the *principe de bonne foi* (article 3). The first provision on formalities (article 79) sets out the 'principle' that mere consent suffices for the formation of a valid contract and the exceptions therefrom (*principe du consensualisme et exceptions*); the first paragraph makes clear that, as a general rule, no formalities are required. At the beginning of the Chapter on the effects of contracts, the *force obligatoire* of contracts is highlighted (article 102(1)).

The transnational provisions that codify general principles of contract law are bound to remain an important part of the debate both at the European and the national level. It is hoped that Hugh Beale will continue to guide those working in the field, and even more so after his retirement from full-time teaching at the University.

181 P Catala, *Avant-projet de réforme du droit des obligations et de la prescription* (Paris, La Documentation française, 2006).

182 For references, see Aubert de Vincelles, 'Les principes généraux relatifs au droit des contrats', n 177 above, 114.

183 Ministère de la Justice, *Projet de réforme du droit des contrats* (July 2008).

184 This was further defined in art 16(1); art 16(2) clarified that the principle was subject to public policy and public morality.

185 Terré, *Pour une réforme du droit des contrats*, n 165 above.

186 Aubert de Vincelles, 'Les principes généraux relatifs au droit des contrats', n 177 above, 117.

187 Bureau de droit des obligations and Ministère de la Justice, *Avant-projet de réforme du droit des obligations: Document de travail* (23 October 2013).

18

Interest for Delay in Payment of Money

REINHARD ZIMMERMANN

INTRODUCTION

OVER THE PAST 20 years I have met Hugh Beale on many different and memorable occasions. Once in Brussels, at a very early stage of the development ultimately leading to the creation of a European Law Institute, we even had to share a bedroom in a rather second rate hotel. I was then reminded of my days as a school boy during a class outing: even after the light had been turned off, the conversation continued for a long time. I remember an intensive week at Goodhart Lodge with Hugh and the other members of the 'drafting group' working on Part III of the Principles of European Contract Law (PECL),[1] and I remember our collaboration, always stimulating, pleasant and fruitful, during the plenary sessions of the Lando Commission in Regensburg, Edinburgh and Graz. Some years later, we had a long discussion in Oxford on the Draft Common Frame of Reference (DCFR)[2] and on the process, set in motion by the Commission of the European Union in a sequence of Communications,[3] of harmonising European contract law. One of our last meetings, so far, was at the conference of the Society of Legal Scholars in Edinburgh in September 2013; Hugh gave a talk about the future of contract law, and I spoke on the three provisions in the proposed Common European Sales Law dealing with the limitation of liability for damages.[4] This sparked off a lively discussion on the desirability of supplementing the 'black letter' rules of that document with comments (an enterprise Hugh, as a member of the Commission Expert Group on European Contract Law,[5] had been charged with, as I was then

[1] O Lando, E Clive, A Prüm and R Zimmermann (eds), *Principles of European Contract Law*, Part III (The Hague, Kluver Law International, 2003). Not very long after the meeting in Cambridge Hugh resigned from the Lando Commission because he had been appointed to the Law Commission of England and Wales.

[2] C von Bar, E Clive and H Schulte-Nölke (eds), *Principles, Definitions and Model Rules of European Private Law: Draft Common Frame of Reference*, Outline Edition (Munich, Sellier, 2009); Christian von Bar and Eric Clive (eds), *Principles, Definitions and Model Rules of European Private Law: Draft Common Frame of Reference,* Full Edition (Munich, Sellier European Law Publishers, 2009).

[3] For details, see Reinhard Zimmermann, 'European Contract Law: General Report' in *Fourth European Jurists' Forum* (Vienna, Manz, 2008) 185–204, 195.

[4] R Zimmermann, 'Limitation of Liability for Damages in European Contract Law' (2014) 18 *Edinburgh Law Review* 193–224.

[5] That group had produced the so-called Feasibility Study for a future instrument in European Contract Law, 3 May 2011, easily accessible in R Schulze and R Zimmermann (eds), *Europäisches Privatrecht: Basistexte*, 4th edn (Baden-Baden, Nomos, 2012) III.30.

told by him) and of elucidating its comparative and historical background by means of a comparative, genetic and critical commentary (a project Nils Jansen and I had embarked upon, together with a number of friends and colleagues).

It thus appears to be quite natural to contribute to this volume in Hugh's honour a small piece attempting to lay the foundations for such commentary with regard to Chapter 16, Sections 2 and 3 of the proposed Common European Sales Law (CESL)[6] on 'interest on late payments' (Articles 166–171). Thematically, the present essay is related to the three rules to which my lecture in Edinburgh was devoted, for they form part of Chapter 16, Section 1, on Damages. Hopefully, it will lead to an equally lively exchange of ideas and may perhaps even prompt those in charge of critically examining the CESL within the legislative process in Brussels to rethink and redraft these provisions. In view of the fact that the CESL is not likely to enter into force before the second half of 2015,[7] there may still be time for such rethinking and redrafting. My comments are based on the text of the CESL as published on 11 October 2011;[8] in order to facilitate the understanding of what follows it will be reprinted below on pp 325–27. At the end of the essay a proposal for a revision will be made. It should be emphasised that I am not questioning the basic policy choices made by the European legislature; for this reason the two Late Payment Directives[9] have been taken as a point of departure for my comments. My concern is, essentially, an academic one: I am interested in consistency, in the coherence of the ideas pursued, and the devices chosen to implement those ideas, in rational justifications for legal rules,[10] and, of course, in 'better regulation'.[11] In addition, this essay (and the commentary project mentioned above) is based on the idea that the provisions in the CESL need to be assessed, and can often only properly be understood, against the background of the respective provisions in the national legal systems and of the many layers of text preceding the CESL:[12] from

[6] 'Proposal for a Regulation of the European Parliament and of the Council on a Common European Sales Law'. The provisions of the Common European Sales Law (CESL) constitute Annex I to the Regulation itself (PR CESL). For comment see, eg, H Eidenmüller, N Jansen, E-M Kieninger, G Wagner and R Zimmermann, 'The Proposal for a Regulation on a Common European Sales Law: Deficits of the Most Recent Textual Layer of European Contract Law' (2012) 16 *Edinburgh Law Review* 301–57, and the contributions to G Wagner and R Zimmermann (eds), 'Sondertagung der Zivilrechtslehrervereinigung zum Vorschlag für ein Common European Sales Law' (2012) 212 *Archiv für die civilistische Praxis* 467–852.

[7] See HP Mayer and J Lindemann, 'Zu den aktuellen Entwicklungen um das Gemeinsame Europäische Kaufrecht auf EU-Ebene' (2014) 22 *Zeitschrift für Europäisches Privatrecht* 1–8, 6.

[8] COM(2011)635 final. The text of these provisions does not appear to have been affected by the proceedings up to and including the first reading of the CESL in the European Parliament on 26 February 2014, even if the numbering has been changed.

[9] On which, see p 324 below.

[10] The same approach has previously been adopted by H Eidenmüller, F Faust, HC Grigoleit, N Jansen, G Wagner and R Zimmermann, *Revision des Verbraucher-acquis* (Tübingen, Mohr Siebeck, 2011); for a summary in English see the same authors, 'Towards a Revision of the Consumer *Acquis*' (2011) 48 *Common Market Law Review* 1077–123.

[11] This is a catchword often used by the European Commission; see, eg, the brochure *Better Regulation: simply explained* (2006). According to José Manuel Barroso in his Foreword, better regulation is 'one of our [ie the European Commission's] core priorities'.

[12] See R Zimmermann, 'Textstufen in der modernen Entwicklung des europäischen Privatrechts' (2009) *Europäische Zeitschrift für Wirtschaftsrecht* 319–23; N Jansen and R Zimmermann, 'Contract Formation and Mistake in European Contract Law: A Genetic Comparison of Transnational Model Rules' (2011) 31 *Oxford Journal of Legal Studies* 625–62.

the United Nations Convention on Contracts for the International Sale of Goods (CISG) via the Principles of European Contract Law, and the UNIDROIT Principles of International Commercial Contracts (PICC),[13] the *Acquis* Principles (ACQP)[14] and the *Principes Contractuels Communs* (PCC)[15] to the DCFR and the Feasibility Study (FS). These texts will often be referred to over the following pages, but due to lack of space they cannot be reprinted here.

INTEREST ON LATE PAYMENT: GENERAL BACKGROUND

From Fixed Rates to Flexibility

Economic life in the Middle Ages was characteristically shaped by a rule, originating in Canon law, which prohibited the charging of interest.[16] It was abandoned only in the early modern period when it was replaced by a policy, already pursued in Roman law,[17] of imposing statutory maximum rates in order to combat the exploitation of borrowers. The rates differed from city to city, and from region to region,[18] but from the seventeenth century onwards, the statutory rate of five per cent laid down by Imperial legislation[19] came to be accepted very widely.[20] The German Civil Code, in line with other codifications in force at the time, retained the policy of fixing a specific rate, though the rate was reduced to four per cent (five per cent for commercial transactions in terms of the Commercial Code).[21]

Fixed statutory interest rates, however, do not reflect the reality of fluctuating capital markets.[22] If the rate at which money can be invested is higher than the statutory rate, the latter provides insufficient compensation for the creditor and, at the same time, constitutes an incentive for the debtor to delay his payment; if

13 UNIDROIT (ed), *UNIDROIT Principles of International Commercial Contracts* (1994, 2004, 2010).

14 Research Group on the Existing EC Private Law (ed), *Principles of the Existing EC Contract Law, Contract I* (2007); *Contract II* (2009).

15 Association Henri Capitant des Amis de la Culture Juridique Française and Société de Législation Comparée, *Principes Contractuels Communs* (2008) (constituting a proposed revision of the PECL).

16 See, eg, JT Noonan, *The Scholastic Analysis of Usury* (Cambridge, MA, Harvard University Press, 1957); F Wittreck, *Geld als Instrument der Gerechtigkeit* (Paderborn, Schöningh, 2002) 111–39; and the overviews in R Zimmermann, *The Law of Obligations: Roman Foundations of the Civilian Tradition* (Oxford, Clarendon Press, 1996) 170–72; F Dorn, in M Schmoeckel, J Rückert, and R Zimmermann (eds), *Historisch-kritischer Kommentar zum BGB* (Tübingen, Mohr Siebeck, 2007) vol II/1, §§ 246–48, para 13.

17 Zimmermann, *The Law of Obligations*, n 16 above, 166–70; Dorn, n 16 above, §§ 246–48, para 10.

18 Zimmermann, *The Law of Obligations*, n 16 above, 799; S Lohsse, in M Schmoeckel, J Rückert and R Zimmermann (eds), *Historisch-kritischer Kommentar zum BGB* (Tübingen, Mohr Siebeck, 2007) vol II/1, §§ 286–92, para 30.

19 *Reichsdeputationsabschied* of 1600, § 139.

20 See, eg, B Windscheid and T Kipp, *Lehrbuch des Pandektenrechts*, 9th edn (Frankfurt aM, Rütten & Loening, 1906) § 280, 1.

21 German Civil Code (BGB) of 1900, § 246; (German) Commercial Code (HGB), § 352; for background, see P Kindler, *Gesetzliche Zinsansprüche im Zivil- und Handelsrecht: Plädoyer für einen kreditmarktorientierten Fälligkeitszins* (Tübingen, Mohr, 1996).

22 For a comprehensive historical analysis of interest rates see S Homer and R Sylla, *A History of Interest Rates*, 4th edn (Hoboken, NJ, John Wiley & Sons, 2011); for a general overview on the problem of floating interest rates, see B Coyle, *Introduction to Interest-Rate Risk* (Kent, Global Professional Publishing, 2001) paras 23–53.

it is lower, the creditor is over-compensated.[23] This is the reason why more recent legislation has aimed to achieve greater flexibility:[24] either by introducing a regime according to which it is the task of the government, from time to time, to fix the interest rate,[25] or by linking the interest rate to a reference rate.[26] The methods of determining the reference rate vary considerably.[27] Broadly speaking, the interest rate can either be linked directly to the market rate,[28] or to a rate fixed by a central bank which both takes account of, and influences, the market rate. In the latter case, the statutory interest rate is often set at the reference rate *plus* a certain number of percentage points (referred to as 'the margin').[29] The two Late Payment Directives have subscribed to this policy, and they have fixed particularly big margins[30] which are clearly not just intended to approximate the market rate but to have a preventive effect.[31] They are constituent elements of '[a] decisive shift' towards 'a culture of prompt payment' envisaged by the European Union and of reversing a situation, prevailing in many Member States prior to 2002, in which late payments had tended to become financially attractive to debtors.[32] In addition, the Late Payment Directives have fixed the European Central Bank's refinancing rate as the relevant reference rate.

UN Sales Law

The CISG is unhelpful, in the present context, in view of the fact that while it establishes a duty to pay interest in cases of late payment, it does not determine any statutory rate.[33] Compared to Article 83 Uniform Law on the International

[23] See eg, J Basedow, 'Die Aufgabe der Verzugszinsen im Recht der Wirtschaft' (1979) 143 *Zeitschrift für das gesamte Handels- und Wirtschaftsrecht* 317, 321–27.

[24] Generally on this tendency, see ibid 327–34; Kindler, *Gesetzliche Zinsansprüche im Zivil- und Handelsrecht*, n 21 above, 225–56, 321–45.

[25] Art 6:120 BW; this was also the system in France between 1959 and 1975 where, however, it did not work properly.

[26] See Art 3(d) of the Late Payment Directive 2000/35/EC, and Art 2(7) Late Payment Directive 2011/7/EU; for France, see Art L313-2 Code monétaire et financier; for the Netherlands, see Art 120(2) BW; for Austria, see § 456 UGB; for England, see H McGregor, *McGregor on Damages*, 18th edn (London, Sweet & Maxwell, 2009) paras 15-104–15-118; for Germany, see §§ 247, 288 BGB (in force since 2002). The German rule is strangely drafted in that the first sentence of its first paragraph ('The basic interest rate is 3.62 %') is meaningless, precisely because the interest rate is flexible. As from December 2012 the interest rate stood at - 0.13 per cent, ie it was negative. For comment, see C Coen, 'Der negative Basiszinssatz nach § 247 BGB' (2012) *Neue Juristische Wochenschrift* 3329.

[27] For a comparative overview, see I Schwenzer, P Hachem and C Kee, *Global Sales and Contract Law* (Oxford University Press, 2012) paras 46.85–46.94.

[28] See, eg, PECL 9:508; PICC 7.4.9(2).

[29] For background, see Basedow, 'Die Aufgabe der Verzugszinsen im Recht der Wirtschaft', n 23 above, 317, 332 f; Kindler, *Gesetzliche Zinsansprüche im Zivil- und Handelsrecht*, n 21 above, 328–31.

[30] 'plus at least seven percentage points' (Directive 2000/35/EC); 'and at least eight percentage points' (Directive 2011/7/EU).

[31] See, in the context of a broadly based investigation, G Wagner, 'Prävention und Verhaltenssteuerung durch Privatrecht—Anmaßung oder legitime Aufgabe?' (2006) 206 *Archiv für die civilistische Praxis* 352, 368–88. See also Schwenzer, Hachem and Kee, *Global Sales and Contract Law*, n 27 above, para 46.120 (over-compensation accepted for the sake of deterrence).

[32] Recital 16 Directive 2000/35/EC; Recital 12 Directive 2011/7/EU.

[33] Arts 78, 84 CISG.

Sale of Goods (ULIS), [34] this is a step backwards, resulting from the fact that it proved impossible, at the conference in Vienna, to reach agreement on this issue.[35] The (lack of) regulation in Articles 78 and 84 CISG constitutes an unsatisfactory compromise;[36] after all, some delegations did not want to make provision for any claim for interest at all. This attitude reflects experiences and traditions different from those of the modern civilian systems. Thus, in particular, Islamic law still recognises a general prohibition to charge interest[37] strongly reminiscent of the prohibition in the other two Abrahamitic religions.[38]

English Law

English law, in turn, has also, for a surprisingly long time, been under the influence of 'the stigma attached by the religion and thought of an earlier day to the taking of usury',[39] for its law on interest has developed 'in a fragmentary and unsatisfactory manner'.[40] Until very recently, no general common law duty was recognised to pay interest in cases of late payment.[41] A discretionary power to include interest in any sum for which judgment is given was first granted to the courts in 1833; it was extended in 1934 and is now contained in section 35A of the Senior Courts Act 1981 and section 69 of the County Court Act 1984.[42] Furthermore, there is a right to 'statutory interest' concerning commercial debts under the Late Payment of Commercial Debts (Interest) Act 1998.[43] Apart from that, the parties have been (and still, of course, are) able to rely on a term in their contract, express or implied. However, the landmark decision in *Sempra Metals Ltd (formerly Metallgesellschaft Ltd)*

[34] Art 83 ULIS: the seller is entitled to interest 'at a rate equal to the official discount rate in the country where he has his place of business or, if he has no place of business, his habitual residence, plus 1 %'.

[35] See P Schlechtriem, *Einheitliches UN-Kaufrecht: das Übereinkommen der Vereinten Nationen über internationale Warenkaufverträge—CISG* (Tübingen, Mohr, 1981) 93 f; F Faust, 'Zinsen bei Zahlungsverzug [im UN-Kaufrecht]' (2004) 68 *RabelsZ* 511, 515 f); C Fountoulakis, in I Schwenzer (ed), *Schlechtriem and Schwenzer: Commentary on the UN Convention on the International Sale of Goods (CISG)*, 3rd edn (Oxford University Press, 2010) Art 84, para 1; Schwenzer, Hachem and Kee, *Global Sales and Contract Law*, n 27 above, para 46.02.

[36] It has given rise to a vigorous dispute as to how the rate of interest is to be determined (are we dealing with an internal gap so that a uniform approach can be adopted, or is it necessary to refer to the applicable national law?); see K Bacher in I Schwenzer (ed), *Schlechtriem and Schwenzer: Commentary on the UN Convention on the International Sale of Goods (CISG)*, 3rd edn (Oxford University Press, 2010) Art 78, paras 27–39; U Magnus, in J von Staudinger, *Kommentar zum Bürgerlichen Gesetzbuch*, revised edn (Berlin, Sellier-de Gruyter, 1994) art 78, paras 12–18; Faust, 'Zinsen bei Zahlungsverzug [im UN-Kaufrecht]', n 35 above, 511–27; Schwenzer, Hachem and Kee, *Global Sales and Contract Law*, n 27 above, paras 46.100–46.110.

[37] See Qur'an 2:278, 3:275 f, 278; also see M Rohe, *Das islamische Recht*, 3rd edn (Munich, Beck, 2011) 112 f.

[38] For Jewish law, see *Exodus* 22, 24; *Leviticus* 25, 35–38; *Deuteronomium* 23, 20 f; for medieval Canon law, see n 16 above.

[39] McGregor, *McGregor on Damages*, n 26 above, para 15-001.

[40] *Westdeutsche Landesbank Girozentrale v Islington Borough Council* [1996] AC 669 (HL) at 682.

[41] See, eg, *Page v Newman* (1829) 9 B&C 378; for details, see McGregor, *McGregor on Damages*, n 26 above, paras 15-005–15-011.

[42] For details see McGregor, *McGregor on Damages*, n 26 above, paras 15-030–15-059.

[43] On which, see E Peel, *Treitel: The Law of Contract*, 13th edn (London, Sweet & Maxwell, 2011) para 20-064.

v Commissioners of Inland Revenue,[44] has now led to an 'almost total abolition' of the 'anomalous' common law rule.[45] It has 'brought English law more in line with the proposed CESL and the DFR by establishing that it is always, in principle, open to a creditor to plead and prove the actual interest losses ... caused by late payment of a debt'.[46]

Late Payment Directives and the Structure of the CESL's Rules on Interest

In their Directive 2000/35/EC, the European Parliament and the Council have made clear their intention to combat 'late payment in commercial transactions'. The rules contained in that (first) Directive have been duly implemented by the Member States;[47] and they have now been further entrenched, with a number of (minor) amendments,[48] in the new Late Payment Directive 2011/7/EU.[49] According to a Press Release from the European Commission of 5 October 2012, 57 per cent of businesses in Europe claim to have problems with liquidity due to late payments: 'Every day across Europe, dozens of small and medium sized enterprises go bankrupt as their invoices are not paid'.[50] The provisions in Section 3 of the CESL's

[44] *Sempra Metals Ltd (formerly Metallgesellschaft Ltd) v Commissioners of Inland Revenue* [2008] 1 AC 561.

[45] Peel, *Treitel: The Law of Contract*, n 43 above, para 20-061.

[46] M Chen-Wishart and U Magnus 'Termination, Price Reduction, and Damages' in G Dannemann and S Vogenauer (eds), *The Common European Sales Law in Context: Interactions with English and German Law* (Oxford University Press, 2013) 682. But they rightly point out that the proposed CESL and DCFR (and most civilian systems) still provide for a more generous recovery in view of the fact that the creditor need not prove the requirements for a damages claim. For details of the legal position after *Sempra Metals*, see McGregor, *McGregor on Damages*, n 26 above, paras 15-060–15-072; on the relationship between the common law after *Sempra Metals* and statute, see Peel, *Treitel: The Law of Contract*, n 43 above, para 20-066. For a concise overview of the position relating to interest on damages in England, see also E Bueren, 'Die Berücksichtigung der Anspruchsentwertung im Zeitablauf bei Schadensersatz wegen Verstößen gegen EU-Kartellrecht' (2013) 77 *RabelsZ* 514; and see the historical account in Schwenzer, Hachem and Kee, *Global Sales and Contract Law*, n 27 above, paras 46.25–46.28.

[47] For general background (including details of the transposition), see M Schmidt-Kessel, 'Zahlungszeit (§§ 269 bis 271 BGB) und Verzug (§§ 280 Abs. 1 und 2, 286, 288 BGB)' in M Gebauer and T Wiedmann (eds), *Zivilrecht unter europäischem Einfluss: die richtlinienkonforme Auslegung des BGB und anderer Gesetze*, 2nd edn (Stuttgart, Boorberg, 2010) 143–72; for an assessment, see U Huber, 'Das Gesetz zur Beschleunigung fälliger Zahlungen und die europäische Richtlinie zur Bekämpfung von Zahlungsverzug im Geschäftsverkehr' [2000] *Juristenzeitung* 957.

[48] More important changes, however, relate to transactions between undertakings and public authorities (which are notoriously slow to pay): Art 4 Late Payment Directive 2011/7/EU.

[49] The new Late Payment Directive had to be transposed into the national legal systems by the middle of March 2013; for Austria: see §§ 455-460 UGB; France: Art L441-6 Code civil, as amended by Art 121 of loi no 2012-387 of 22 March 2012 and Art 20 of loi no 2012-1270 of 20 November 2012; Italy: decreto legislativo no 231 of 19 October 2002, as amended by the decreto legislativo no 192 of 9 November 2012; the Netherlands: Arts 119a, 120(2) BW; England: Late Payment of Commercial Debts (Interest) Act 1998, as amended by the Late Payment of Commercial Debts Regulations 2013, SI 2013/395. In Germany the new Directive is scheduled to be transposed into national law in the course of June or July 2014; for details, see C Wendehorst, 'Das neue Gesetz zur Umsetzung der Verbraucherrechterichtlinie' (2014) *Neue Juristische Wochenschrift* 577.

[50] See also Recital 3 Directive 2011/7/EU (pointing to liquidity problems and to the negative effects of late payments on the competitiveness and profitability of undertakings). Similarly, a British *Report from the All Party Inquiry into Late Payments in Small and Medium-Sized Enterprises* released in July 2013 states that late payments to small and medium-sized enterprises 'are a real issue. SMEs report that this is the most important issue for them after access to finance' (4). So far, the EU initiatives focusing on late

Chapter 16 (as well as those in Section 4 of Chapter 17 in the FS) are modelled on the new Directive, just as ACQP 8:406(f) and DCFR III.-3:710(f) were modelled on the old one. The changes are not substantial, so that there is very considerable correspondence between the respective provisions in the five documents. The PECL and the PICC had adopted a different approach: they did not incorporate special provisions on late payments in commercial transactions, but merely had one general provision on 'Delay in payment of money' (PECL) and 'Interest for failure to pay money' (PICC), respectively.[51] Chapter 16, Section 2, in turn contains two 'general provisions' on late payments, one of them entitled 'Interest on late payments', the other 'Interest when the debtor is a consumer'. The significance of the latter provisions only becomes clear when they are read together with those contained in Section 3. It is therefore advisable to look at Articles 168–71 CESL before turning to Articles 166 and 167 CESL.[52] Moreover, it has to be asked to what extent the Late Payment Directives have established, or should be taken to have established, a more general pattern for the regulation of late payments.

PROVISIONS OF THE CESL

Section 3 Late Payments by Traders

Article 168 Rate of interest and accrual

1. Where a trader delays the payment of a price due under a contract for the delivery of goods, supply of digital content or provision of related services without being excused by virtue of Article 88, interest is due at the rate specified in paragraph 5 of this Article.
2. Interest at the rate specified in paragraph 5 starts to run on the day which follows the date or the end of the period for payment provided in the contract. If there is no such date or period, interest at that rate starts to run:
   (a) 30 days after the date when the debtor receives the invoice or an equivalent request for payment; or

payment, such as the Late Payment Directive, appear 'not to have proven a big hit' (*European Payment Index 2012*, 85); this is why the implementation of the new Late Payment Directive is accompanied by an information campaign. The campaign 'puts particular importance on ensuring that SMEs know the new rights conferred by the directive and how to exercise these rights' (European Commission, Press Release, 5 October 2012).

[51] PECL 9:508; PICC 7.4.9.

[52] That the structure of the provisions concerning interest on late payments is hardly 'user-friendly' (user-friendliness is an attribute regarded as specifically desirable for the CESL by the EU) has been noted by many commentators: Eidenmüller, Jansen, Kieninger, Wagner and Zimmermann in (2012) 16 *Edinburgh Law Review* 301, 343; E-M Kieninger, 'Allgemeines Leistungsstörungsrecht im Vorschlag für ein Gemeinsames Europäisches Kaufrecht' in H Schulte-Nölke, F Zoll, N Jansen and R Schulze (eds), *Der Entwurf für ein optionales europäisches Kaufrecht* (Munich, Sellier, 2012) 205, 221 f; D Looschelders, 'Das allgemeine Vertragsrecht des Common European Sales Law' (2012) 212 *Archiv für die civilistische Praxis* 581, 667; see also the European Law Institute in its Statement on the Proposal for a Common European Sales Law, Remark to Section 4: 'The rules on interest for late payment must be made much simpler and more user-friendly'; J Baeck, in I Claeys and R Feltkamp, *The Draft Common European Sales Law: towards an alternative sales law? A Belgian Perspective* (Cambridge, Intersentia, 2013) para 32.

(b) 30 days after the date of receipt of the goods, digital content or related services, if the date provided for in point (a) is earlier or uncertain, or if it is uncertain whether the debtor has received an invoice or equivalent request for payment.

3. Where conformity of goods, digital content or related services to the contract is to be ascertained by way of acceptance or examination, the 30 day period provided for in point (b) of paragraph 2 begins on the date of the acceptance or the date [when] the examination procedure is finalised. The maximum duration of the examination procedure cannot exceed 30 days from the date of delivery of the goods, supply of digital content or provision of related services, unless the parties expressly agree otherwise and that agreement is not unfair according to Article 170.
4. The period for payment determined under paragraph 2 cannot exceed 60 days, unless the parties expressly agree otherwise and that agreement is not unfair according to Article 170.
5. The interest rate for delayed payment is:
   (a) where the creditor's habitual residence is in a Member State whose currency is the euro or in a third country, the interest rate applied by the European Central Bank to its most recent main refinancing operation carried out before the first calendar day of the half-year in question, or the marginal interest rate resulting from variable-rate tender procedures for the most recent main refinancing operations of the European Central Bank, plus eight percentage points;
   (b) where the creditor's habitual residence is in a Member State whose currency is not the euro, the equivalent rate set by the national central bank of that Member State, plus eight percentage points.
6. The creditor may recover damages for any further loss.

Article 169 Compensation for recovery costs

1. Where interest is payable in accordance with Article 168, the creditor is entitled to obtain from the debtor, as a minimum, a fixed sum of EUR 40 or the equivalent sum in the currency agreed for the contract price as compensation for the creditor's recovery costs.
2. The creditor is entitled to obtain from the debtor reasonable compensation for any recovery costs exceeding the fixed sum referred to in paragraph 1 and incurred due to the debtor's late payment.

Article 170 Unfair contract terms relating to interest for late payment

1. A contract term relating to the date or the period for payment, the rate of interest for late payment or the compensation for recovery costs is not binding to the extent that the term is unfair. A term is unfair if it grossly deviates from good commercial practice, contrary to good faith and fair dealing, taking into account all circumstances of the case, including the nature of the goods, digital content or related service.
2. For the purpose of paragraph 1, a contract term providing for a time or period for payment or a rate of interest less favourable to the creditor than the time, period or rate specified in Articles 167 or 168, or a term providing for an amount of compensation for recovery costs lower than the amount specified in Article 169 is presumed to be unfair.
3. For the purpose of paragraph 1, a contract term excluding interest for late payment or compensation for recovery costs is always unfair.

Article 171 Mandatory nature

The parties may not exclude the application of this Section or derogate from or vary its effects.

Section 2 Interest on Late Payments: General Provisions

Article 166 Interest on late payments

1. Where payment of a sum of money is delayed, the creditor is entitled, without the need to give notice, to interest on that sum from the time when payment is due to the time of payment at the rate specified in paragraph 2.
2. The interest rate for delayed payment is:
   (a) where the creditor's habitual residence is in a Member State whose currency is the euro or in a third country, the rate applied by the European Central Bank to its most recent main refinancing operation carried out before the first calendar day of the half-year in question, or the marginal interest rate resulting from variable-rate tender procedures for the most recent main refinancing operations of the European Central Bank, plus two percentage points;
   (b) where the creditor's habitual residence is in a Member State whose currency is not the euro, the equivalent rate set by the national central bank of that Member State, plus two percentage points.
3. The creditor may recover damages for any further loss.

Article 167 Interest when the debtor is a consumer

1. When the debtor is a consumer, interest for delay in payment is due at the rate provided in Article 166 only when non-performance is not excused.
2. Interest does not start to run until 30 days after the creditor has given notice to the debtor specifying the obligation to pay interest and its rate. Notice may be given before the date when payment is due.
3. A term of the contract which fixes a rate of interest higher than that provided in Article 166, or accrual earlier than the time specified in paragraph 2 of this Article is not binding to the extent that this would be unfair according to Article 83.
4. Interest for delay in payment cannot be added to capital in order to produce interest.
5. The parties may not, to the detriment of the consumer, exclude the application of this Article or derogate from or vary its effects.

LATE PAYMENT BY TRADERS

Basis of the Claim for Interest

Are Higher Rates Permissible?

Article 168(1) CESL provides the basis for a claim for interest. It has precursors in the ACQP, DCFR and FS. The respective rules in these four documents are largely identical, apart from differences in terminology and scope of application. There is, however, one significant difference between ACQP 8:406(1) and DCFR III.-3:710(I), on the one hand, and FS 173(1) and Article 168(1) CESL, on the other: the phrase 'unless a higher rate is applicable' has been deleted.[53] This must be due to the passing of the new Late Payment Directive on 16 February 2011, an event that could only

[53] See, eg, ACQP 8:406(1): 'If a business delays the payment of a price for goods or services owed to a business without being excused under Article 8:401 (Right to damages), interest is due at the rate specified in paragraph (4), unless a higher rate is applicable'.

be taken into account by the drafters of the FS and CESL. A higher interest rate can only be applicable as a result of an agreement by the parties. In that respect, the old Late Payment Directive had stated that the parties were free to specify an interest rate other than the statutory rate in their contract.[54] Such agreements, in so far as they were to the disadvantage of the creditor, were subject to a fairness control.[55] The ACQP and the DCFR, therefore, dealt with agreements for a lower interest rate in their provisions on unfair terms,[56] while agreements concerning higher interest rates were only subject to the general limits of contractual freedom. Directive 2011/7/EU no longer specifically affirms the non-mandatory character of the statutory interest rate; but the provision on unfair terms appears to proceed from the assumption that the parties are still allowed to fix a higher rate of interest.[57] Such agreement would, indeed, further the aims pursued by the Directive even more effectively than the statutory rate. Nothing should, therefore, be read into the deletion of the phrase 'unless a higher rate is applicable' in FS 173(1) either. A dramatic change, however, may result from the introduction of Article 171 CESL (which does not have any parallel in the previous texts).[58] The statutory interest rate would thus appear to be of a mandatory character, with the result that a higher interest rate can no longer be specified in the contract. Policy-wise, that can hardly be right.

Commercial Contracts Only?

Another significant difference between the four texts relates to the type of transaction to which they apply. ACQP 8:406(1) clearly states that a business must have delayed the payment of a price for goods or services 'owed to a business'. The rule is, therefore, dealing with interest in commercial contracts. This is also stated in the heading and is in line with both Late Payment Directives. In DCFR III.-3:710(1), the words 'owed to a business' have been deleted. Yet, the heading 'Interest in commercial contracts' has been retained. Since the provision is said to be modelled on the Late Payment Directive,[59] it may be assumed that the phrase 'owed to a business' has either been dropped inadvertently, or because it was thought to be self-evident. Article 173, however, has a changed heading and neither here nor in the heading of Chapter 17, Section 4 ('Provision Combating Late Payments by Commercial Debtors') refers to 'commercial contracts'. The same is true for the CESL. It must therefore be assumed that Article 168(1) CESL no longer merely refers to transactions between traders but also to transactions where the debtor is a trader and the creditor is a consumer. This is supported by a phrase contained in a 'synthesis' of the Expert Group on a Common Frame of Reference, according to which 'the consumer creditor must be protected by the same rules as the business creditor'.[60]

[54] Art 3(1)(d) Late Payment Directive 2000/35/EC.
[55] ibid Art 3(3).
[56] ACQP 8:407(1); DCFR III.-3:711(1).
[57] Art 7(1) Late Payment Directive 2011/7/EU.
[58] See p 338 below.
[59] DCFR III.-3:710, Comment A (957).
[60] *Synthesis of the Tenth Meeting, 17–18 February 2011* (Brussels, 14 March 2011) 6. But see, eg, D Možina, in R Schulze (ed), *Common Frame of Reference and Existing EC Contract Law* (Munich, Sellier, 2008) Art 168, para 1.

Delay not Excused

Doctrinally the most interesting feature of all four texts is the fact that interest is due only if the delay in payment is not excused in terms of Article 88 (and its predecessor provisions). Article 168(1) thus differs from the approach adopted by the general rules on interest in cases of delay in payment of money in the PECL and the PICC,[61] and subsequently also in the DCFR;[62] but it corresponds to the provision contained in both Late Payment Directives, according to which the creditor cannot claim interest if 'the debtor is not responsible for the delay'.[63] In view of the fact that inability to pay money is never an excuse for failure to pay on due date,[64] Article 88 can only be resorted to where unforeseeable impediments affect the payment process. This will occur but very rarely. An example mentioned in the Official Comment to PICC 7.4.9 is that the debtor is prevented from obtaining the sum due by reason of the introduction of new exchange control regulations.[65]

Interest as Damages

In developed economies 'the interest-bearing use of ready money is common to such an extent, that it may unhesitatingly be assumed ... that every sum of money, big or small, can for any period of time be used in a way that it bears interest'.[66] This is the justification for a general rule to the effect that whoever is unjustifiably deprived of the use of money is entitled to interest. Very widely, over the centuries, this claim for interest was taken to be a convenient way of allowing the creditor to recover the damages he had typically suffered, without the need specifically to prove them.[67]

[61] PECL 9:508, Comment B; PICC 7.4.9(1).

[62] DCFR III.-3:708(1). For comparative background, see Schwenzer, Hachem and Kee, *Global Sales and Contract Law*, n 27 above, para 46.51.

[63] Art 3(1)(c)(ii) Late Payment Directive 2000/35/EC; Art 3(1)(b) Late Payment Directive 2011/7/EU. This is in line, eg, with Dutch law (see H Schelhaas, in D Busch, E Hondius, H van Kooten, H Schelhaas and W Schrama (eds), *The Principles of European Contract Law and Dutch Law: A Commentary* (Nijmegen, Ars Aequi Libri, 2002) 425), Italian law (see L Mari, in L Antoniolli and A Veneziano (eds), *Prinicples of European Contract Law and Italian Law* (The Hague, Kluwer Law International, 2005) 468), and German law (§§ 286(4), 288(1) BGB); in England, too, the normal rules on damages apply.

[64] GH Treitel, *Remedies for Breach of Contract: A Comparative Account* (Oxford, Clarendon Press, 1988) para 17 ('The principle is so much taken for granted that it is not expressly stated in the codes'); J Kleinheisterkamp, in S Vogenauer and J Kleinheisterkamp (eds), *Commentary on the UNIDROIT Principles of International Commercial Contracts (PICC)* (Oxford University Press, 2009) art 7.1.7, para 18 ('basic assumption underlying all contracts').

[65] PICC 7.4.9, Comment 1; see also A Flessner, 'Geldersatz bei Zahlungsverzug—Eine Skizze zum Europäischen Vertragsrecht' in J Gerkens (ed), *Mélanges Fritz Sturm* (Liège, Editions Juridiques de l'Université de Liège, 1999) 1165, 1177, drawing attention to the fact that in Europe today this situation is hardly likely to arise in view of the European monetary system. But see W Ernst and R Sethe, 'Zivilrechtliche Folgefragen der Finanz- und Währungskrise' (2013) 21 *Zeitschrift für Europäisches Privatrecht* 691, 698, referring to a 'rediscovery' of breach of contract relating to monetary obligations.

[66] FC von Savigny, *System des heutigen Römischen Rechts* (Berlin, Veit, 1847) vol 6, 133; *cf*, eg, *Reichsdeputationsabschied* of 1600, § 139; F Mommsen, *Beiträge zum Obligationenrecht*, vol III, *Die Lehre von der Mora nebst Beiträgen zur Lehre von der Culpa* (Braunschweig, CA Schwetschke & Sohn, 1855) 245.

[67] See the references in Lohsse, n 18 above, §§ 286–92, paras 22, 29 f (but *cf* para 11, where Lohsse points out that originally, in Roman law, the duty to pay interest had a punitive function; it was supposed to provide an incentive for the debtor to pay); Savigny, *System des heutigen Römischen Rechts*, n 66 above, 134–38; Art 1153 (2) Code civil ('Ces dommages et interêts sont dus sans que le créancier soit tenu de justifier d'aucune perte').

In a way, therefore, it can be seen as a further instance[68] of an abstract assessment of a damages claim: since the creditor has been unable to use the money 'in an interest-bearing way', the average interest rate at which he could have invested the money represents the damages he has suffered in any event.[69] This is the perspective adopted, eg, in § 288(1) BGB.[70] According to Article 1153 Code civil in obligations which are limited to the payment of money 'les dommages-intérêts résultant du retard' never consist of anything but interest at the statutory rate.[71]

Disgorgement of Gain?

But there is also a different way of looking at the situation: the creditor's interest claim can be seen as an attempt, in a generalising manner, to skim off the gain the debtor has made by having a sum of money available which he should have paid to the creditor; for he has, or could typically have, used the money in an 'interest-bearing' manner—just as much as the creditor could have done had he received the money when it was due.[72] The right to claim interest, from this point of view, is akin to a right to claim unjustified enrichment: it constitutes an abstract way of assessing the debtor's gain. This argument is plausible only for interest that immediately starts to run from the due date, without the further requirements traditionally established by the rules on *mora debitoris*, as is the case, in a number of legal systems, in the field of commercial law.[73]

Concept of CESL

Article 168 CESL is clearly based on the 'interest as damages' idea. Indicative of this are (i) that no interest has to be paid when the delay in payment is excused in terms of Article 88 CESL;[74] (ii) that the duty to pay interest does not run from due date but that the debtor only has to pay after the lapse of a certain period of time;[75] (iii) that it is the interest rate at the creditor's rather than the debtor's habitual

[68] Generally, see Art 76 CISG; PECL 9:507; PICC 7.4.6; DCFR III.-3:707; Art 165 CESL.

[69] U Huber, *Leistungsstörungen*, vol 2, *Die Folgen des Schuldnerverzugs, die Erfüllungsverweigerung und die vom Schuldner zu vertretende Unmöglichkeit* (Tübingen, Mohr, 1999) 68.

[70] See the references in Lohsse, n 18 above, §§ 286–92, para 44; Huber, *Leistungsstörungen*, n 69 above, 68 f.

[71] Art 1153 (1) Code civil; for the Netherlands, see Art 6:119 BW; for Italy (*danni-interessi moratori*), see Art 1224 Codice civile; for Austria, see § 1333(1) ABGB. On the notion of *dommages et intérêts moratoires*, in comparative perspective, see B Fauvarque-Cosson and D Mazeaud (eds), *European Contract Law: Materials for a common frame of reference: terminology, guiding principles, model rules* (Munich, Sellier, 2008) paras 303–7; generally on 'interest as damages', see Treitel, *Remedies for Breach of Contract*, n 64 above, paras 159–62.

[72] See H Koziol, *Österreichisches Haftpflichtsrecht* (Vienna, Manz, 1973) vol I, 250 (but see also K-H Danzl, in H Koziol, P Bydlinsky and B Bollenberger (eds), *Kurzkommentar zum ABGB*, 3rd edn (Vienna, Springer, 2010) § 1333, para 1); Basedow, 'Die Aufgabe der Verzugszinsen im Recht der Wirtschaft', n 23 above, 323; Kindler, *Gesetzliche Zinsansprüche im Zivil- und Handelsrecht*, n 21 above, 138–49 and *passim*.

[73] For Germany, see § 353 HGB ('Fälligkeitszins'); for the historical and comparative background Kindler, *Gesetzliche Zinsansprüche im Zivil- und Handelsrecht*, n 21 above, 11–59 (Germany), 60–87 (Italy), 88–93 (Austria).

[74] See p 329 above.

[75] See p 331 below.

residence that matters;[76] (iv) that the creditor is allowed under Article 168(6) CESL to recover damages 'for any further loss'; and (v) the systematic position of the rule within a Chapter on 'Damages and Interest'.[77] The question concerning the legal nature of the damages claim is not a purely theoretical one. Thus, for example, if the interest claim in Article 168(1) CESL is classified as being in the nature of damages, based on an abstract assessment of the creditor's loss, it does not, arguably, bar a claim for interest as compensation for the debtor's gain: provided, of course, such gain can be proven by the creditor.[78]

'Accrual' of Interest

The traditional civilian requirements for *mora debitoris* and its consequences (including the duty to pay interest) are: the due date must have lapsed without the debtor having paid; the debtor must have received a reminder; and the debtor must have been responsible for the non-performance.[79] Traditionally, also, a reminder is regarded as dispensable if the contract has specified a time for performance (*dies interpellat pro homine*).[80] The international instruments no longer recognise a specific type of breach of contract called *mora debitoris*; the umbrella concept on which the debtor's liability hinges is called non-performance. As far as the duty to pay interest in cases of late payment is concerned, the Late Payment Directives have introduced a new set of requirements which has been adopted by the ACQP, DCFR, FS and CESL. In the first place, the date for payment agreed upon by the parties is relevant. This corresponds to the policy underlying the maxim *dies interpellat pro homine*. The date does not have to be determined or to be determinable with reference to the calendar; it suffices if the parties refer to a specific event.[81] If there is no such agreement, a 30-day period begins to run from the date of receipt of an invoice or an equivalent request for payment, or from the date of receipt of the goods, digital content or related service. The latter period is only relevant if the date of receipt of an invoice is earlier or uncertain, or if it is uncertain whether the debtor has received an invoice or equivalent request for payment. Article 168(2) (in line with ACQP 8:406(2); DCFR III.-3:710(2); and FS 173(2)) formulates the respective rules contained in the Late Payment Directives more succinctly, and in a more user-friendly way. Nonetheless, it could be brought out more clearly, that the first crucial date for the debtor is normally that of receipt of the goods, digital content

[76] Art 168(5) CESL.

[77] *Cf*, as far as the CISG and PICC are concerned, Schwenzer, Hachem and Kee, *Global Sales and Contract Law*, n 27 above, para 46.06. For a critical assessment of the 'interest as disgorgement of gain' idea in general, see Flessner, 'Geldersatz bei Zahlungsverzug', n 65 above, 1175–77.

[78] See, in this context, PICC 7.4.9, Comment 1. Such claim might arguably be based on Art 4 CESL and the general principle that where a person keeps something that is due to another, the natural and legal fruits of what is kept are also to be allocated to the latter person; see Art 172(2) CESL. *Cf* Schwenzer, Hachem and Kee, *Global Sales and Contract Law*, n 27 above, para 46.09.

[79] H Coing, *Europäisches Privatrecht* (Munich, Beck, 1985) vol I, 435–37; Zimmermann, *The Law of Obligations*, n 16 above, 790–800.

[80] Today see, eg, § 286(2) BGB; Art 1219 Codice civile; but see, for France, P Malaurie, L Aynès and P Stoffel-Munck, *Les Obligations*, 5th edn (Paris, Defrénois, 2011) para 973.

[81] See also Možina, n 60 above, Art 168, para 5.

or related services (which is also, according to Article 126(1) CESL, the due date for payment of the price).[82] Generally speaking, therefore, *traditio* is supposed to remind the debtor that he has to pay. It is only when the debtor receives the goods, digital content or related services before he receives an invoice that the receipt of the invoice triggers the 30-day period. The second sentence of Article 168(2) CESL might thus be reformulated in the following way:

> If there is no such date or period, interest at that rate starts to run: (a) 30 days after the date of receipt of the goods, digital content or related services; or (b) 30 days after the date of receipt of an invoice or equivalent request for payment, if that date is later than the one set out under (a).

Acceptance or Examination Procedure

The rule contained in the first sentence of Article 168(3) CESL takes account of the fact that often conformity of the goods, digital content or related services will have to be ascertained by way of acceptance or an examination procedure. It is based on the Late Payment Directives and is in line with them, provided that the term 'examination' must be taken to mean the same as 'verification'.[83] The relationship with the 30-day period set out in Article 168(2) could be made clearer by integrating the rule into the second sentence of Article 168(2). The second sentence of Article 168(3) was first formulated by the Expert Group responsible for the FS, has been taken over into the CESL, and is based on Article 3(4) Late Payment Directive 2011/7/EU. It is badly drafted in that it frames what must be a normative statement in ontological terms.[84] Moreover, the word 'maximum' does not appear to be in the right place, for the 30-day period is obviously intended as a maximum for the duration of the examination (and also acceptance!) procedure. The rule laid down here probably attempts to ensure that normally no more than 60 days may pass between the date of delivery of the goods, and the date when interest starts to run: 60 days, after all, is also the maximum envisaged in Article 3(5) Late Payment Directive 2011/7/EU and Article 168(4) CESL. However, under Article 168(4) the maximum period between delivery of the goods and the finalisation of the examination or acceptance can be 90 days (30 days' examination or acceptance procedure plus 60 days' payment period). This is hardly in line with the purpose pursued by both the Late Payment Directive and the CESL. But that result would only be avoided if the 60-day period in Article 3(5) Late Payment Directive 2011/7/EU and in Article 168(4) CESL could be taken as an absolute cap which, at least as far as the CESL is concerned, is obviously not what is intended: after all, its Article 168(4) refers only to paragraph (2) and not also to paragraph (3).

[82] The duty to pay interest presupposes, of course, that the payment is due; see Art 168(1) CESL ('payment of a price due under a contract'); *cf* Možina, n 60 above, Art 168, para 7; W Ernst, in *Münchener Kommentar zum Bürgerlichen Gesetzbuch*, 6th edn (Munich, Beck, 2012) vol II, § 286, para 70.

[83] Both terms are, indeed, translated into German as 'Überprüfung'.

[84] This is corrected in the German translation ('Die Überprüfung darf sich …').

Maximum Period for Payment

Article 168(4) CESL raises a number of problems. In the first place, 'cannot exceed' is not what its draftsmen obviously wanted to say.[85] The phrase has to be read as 'must not exceed'. Secondly, the provision does not state from what moment the 60-day period has to be counted. Clearly, Article 168(4) is modelled on Article 3(5) Late Payment Directive 2011/7/EU. There, it does not matter that no starting date for the 60-day period is mentioned, since we are dealing with 'the period for payment fixed in the contract'. The starting date will also, therefore, normally have been fixed in the contract, either expressly or by implication. In case of doubt, the 60-day period will presumably have to be counted from due date. The drafters of the FS (and subsequently the CESL) have changed the wording of the rule; Article 168 (4) CESL refers to '[t]he period for payment determined under paragraph 2'. This can be taken to relate to the two 30-day periods determined under (a) and (b) of paragraph 2, second sentence; and the 60-day period can then either constitute a relative maximum (counting from the dates set out in (a) and (b)), or an absolute maximum (counting from the due date). Since this is unclear, it may be better to assume that those who drafted the FS and the CESL did not really want to deviate from the Late Payment Directive. But then the wording of the Directive should be reinstated, in order to avoid any misunderstanding.

The emphasis in the part of Article 3(5) Late Payment Directive 2011/7/EU and Article 168 CESL which starts with 'unless' lies on the word 'expressly'. Otherwise, what is said here could easily have been covered by an extension, possibly even by an extensive interpretation, of Article 170 CESL. Requiring that terms deviating from Article 168(3) and (4) (as opposed to terms deviating from other provisions in Article 168) must be express, adds an unnecessary level of complexity to the provision on late payments by traders.

Interest Rate

Reference Rate and Margin

Traditionally, as was pointed out above,[86] most civilian systems have subscribed to a policy of establishing fixed statutory interest rates. In the last decades of the twentieth century, however, there has been an increasingly strong tendency towards greater flexibility.[87] The Late Payment Directive 2000/35/EC reflects this tendency. It defines the 'statutory rate' as the sum of the 'reference rate' and a 'margin'. The reference rate is the interest rate applied by the European Central Bank to its most recent refinancing operation before the first calendar day of the half-year in question. The focal point is thus the interest rate charged by the European Central Bank for

[85] Once again, this has been corrected in the German translation ('darf ... nicht überschreiten').
[86] See p 321 above.
[87] See p 321–22 above.

money fed into the market, ie lent to the banking sector of the Eurozone.[88] Such 'refinancing operations' occur on a weekly basis.[89] The interest rate (also referred to as prime rate) is changed, from time to time, by the European Central Bank depending on the development of the financial markets and on what signals the European Central Bank, in turn, intends to send to the financial markets. At the moment (ie in February 2014) it stands at 0.25 per cent. For reasons of convenience the reference rates in force on 1 January and 1 July of a given year, respectively, apply for the following six months. For Member States 'not participating in the third stage of economic and monetary union', ie which have not introduced the euro and for whose monetary policy the European Central Bank is not, therefore, responsible, the equivalent rate set by their national bank applies as reference rate.

The 'margin' is supposed to bridge the gap inevitably existing between the reference rate and the market rate, at which traders can obtain money from their bank. But it can also serve as an extra incentive to motivate debtors to pay in time. This is the case if the margin is as high as 'at least' seven per cent (Late Payment Directive 2000/35/EC), seven per cent (ACQP and DCFR), eight per cent (FS and CESL) or 'at least' eight per cent (Late Payment Directive 2011/7/EU).[90]

Textual Differences

ACQP 8:406 is modelled on the respective provision in the Late Payment Directive 2000/35/EC except that the last sentence has been dropped, probably because it is redundant. From DCFR III.-3:710(4) onwards, the phrase 'unless otherwise specified in the contract' has disappeared, probably because it was taken to be self-evident that the statutory rate is not of a mandatory character.[91] It would only be as a result of Article 171 CESL that that deletion could acquire considerable significance.

For some time, the European Central Bank has either provided the banking system with liquidity at specific rates, fixed from time to time, or in terms of a 'variable-rate tender procedure'.[92] This is reflected in the text of the FS, the CESL and the Late Payment Directive 2011/7/EU (even though the European Central Bank has not used the variable-rate tender procedure for the past five years).[93] Apart from that, the FS, the CESL and the Late Payment Directive 2011/7/EU refer to 'the most recent main refinancing operation' rather than just 'the most recent refinancing

[88] See U Bindseil, KG Nyborg and IA Strebulaev, *Bidding and Performance in Repo Auctions: Evidence from ECB Open Market Operations*, Nota di Lavoro, Fondazione Eni Enrico Mattei, No 92.2005 (London, Centre for Economic Policy Research, 2005) 1.

[89] See, eg S Ejerskov, C Moss and L Stracca, *How Does the ECB Allot Liquidity in Its Weekly Main Refinancing Operations?: A Look at the Empirical Evidence*, European Central Bank Working Paper Series No 244 (2003) 5; Bindseil, Nyborg, and Strebulaev, *Bidding and Performance in Repo Auctions*, n 88 above.

[90] See nn 30 and 31 above.

[91] DCFR III.-3:710, Comment C.

[92] On which see U Bindseil, *Monetary Policy Implementation: Theory, Past, and Present* (Oxford University Press, 2004) para 5.6.2; E Apel, *Central Banking Systems Compared: The ECB, The Pre-Euro Bundesbank and the Federal Reserve System* (Abingdon, Routledge, 2003) 84.

[93] The official interest rate tables issued by the European Central Bank reveal that a variable rate tender procedure was utilised from 28 June 2000 until 9 July 2008, whilst a fixed rate tender procedure was implemented prior to that period (1 January 1999–9 June 2000) as well as since 15 October 2008.

operation'. There does not appear to be any difference in meaning. Moreover, in all three texts the margin has been raised by one percentage point.

Textual Differences Continued

The Late Payment Directive 2011/7/EU, contrary to all other texts, refers to the European Central Bank's 'most recent main refinancing operations' (rather than 'operation'). It is not clear what the plural is supposed to indicate. It can hardly mean that the main refinancing operations of the past couple of weeks must be taken into account: after all, it is not specified how far back one will have to go. Apart from reverting to the singular 'operation' again, Article 168 fixes the statutory rate in accordance with the Late Payment Directive 2011/7/EU.[94]

The most significant deviation between the texts lies in the fact that the CESL specifically determines in which cases the reference rate set by the European Central Bank, or the equivalent rate set by a national bank, applies. The decisive factor is the creditor's habitual residence. This is in line with the general regime for the payment of interest: it is the interest rate prevailing for the contractual currency of payment at the place where payment is due,[95] and that is the creditor's place of business.[96] Since Article 168 refers not only to cases where the creditor is a trader but also where he is a consumer, the creditor's habitual residence rather than the place of business was chosen.[97] If the creditor's habitual residence is in an EU Member State whose currency is not the euro, it was obviously thought inappropriate to apply to his claim for interest a rate fixed by a central bank not responsible for that state's currency and monetary policy. That explains the recourse to the equivalent rate set by the national central bank. Somewhat strangely, at first blush, the rate set by the European Central Bank is not only applicable if the creditor's habitual residence is in a Member State whose currency is the euro, but also if it is in a third country, ie a country not belonging to the European Union. This can only be explained by fears that debtors within the European Union might be prejudiced by inappropriately high equivalent rates set by national banks, lacking independence, in distant parts of the world, beset by high inflation rates.

Damages for Further Loss

The Late Payment Directives merely deal with interest and compensation for recovery costs. But they do not wish to prevent the creditor from claiming compensation for any further loss he may have suffered as a result of the late payment. In that

[94] Concerning the 'variable-rate tender procedure' all texts use the plural 'operations'. It is unclear why this is so. Whether or not we are dealing with a variable- or fixed-rate procedure, the matter can be looked at from the point of view of the European Central Bank (singular) or from the point of view of the market participants receiving the European Central Bank's money (plural).

[95] *Cf*, eg PECL 9:508(1); PICC 7.4.9(2); DCFR III.-3:708(1); Art 166(2) CESL.

[96] *Cf*, eg PECL 7:101(1)(a); PICC 6.1.6(1)(a); DCFR III.-2:101(1)(a); and see Art 125(1) CESL.

[97] See also Art 4 of the CESL Regulation. No distinction is drawn between a party's habitual residence and its place of business in the Rome I and II Regulations; for an autonomous definition of habitual residence, see Art 19 Rome I Regulation, Art 23 Rome II Regulation; and Recital 39 of the Rome I Regulation.

respect, the national laws apply and many of them do, indeed, allow the creditor to claim such further loss.[98] The same position has been adopted in the *general* provisions on late payment contained in the international instruments.[99] Obviously, therefore, the ACQP, DCFR, FS and CESL have also included this rule in their *special* provisions on late payments by traders. The claim for further loss is subject to the normal rules on damages.

Recovery Costs

The interest claim in Article 168 CESL constitutes a convenient way for the creditor to obtain compensation for damages that he has typically suffered. It is a form of abstract assessment of his loss, or of a typical part of it.[100] The same is true of the claim under Article 169. It relates to the costs the creditor often, or perhaps even typically, has incurred in order to recover the money that is due to him. In addition, just like the rules on interest, the rule in Article 169 is regarded 'as necessary to discourage late payment'.[101] It is supposed to put the debtor under pressure and it thus has a regulatory component. Systematically, this rule is positioned in an odd place, for the recovery costs also fall under the 'any further loss' provision immediately preceding it. Article 169(1) CESL, however, allows the creditor to claim a lump sum without having to prove whether he has incurred recovery costs and, if so, to what extent.[102] Article 169(2) allows him to claim recovery costs exceeding the fixed sum, provided he can prove that they have been incurred 'due to the debtor's late payment'. Foreseeability does not, apparently, play a role in this respect. The creditor's claim will often, therefore, consist of four components: interest under Article 168(1)–(5); lump sum under Article 169(1); recovery costs exceeding the lump sum under Article 169(2); and, in the last resort, any further loss under Article 168(6). This is a more complex system than in any national law prior to the transposition of the Late Payment Directive 2011/7/EU. It would be more easily comprehensible, if Article 168(6) were to be placed after Article 169.

[98] § 288(4) BGB; § 1333(2) ABGB (also applicable to the regulation on interest in §§ 455–460 UGB); Art 1224(2) Codice civile (for details, see Mari, n 63 above, 468); Art 1153(4) Code civil (only in cases of *mauvaise foi;* the requirements have, however, been relaxed by the Cour de cassation: see Malaurie, Aynès and Stoffel-Munck, *Les Obligations*, n 80 above, para 970. No additional damages can, at least in principle, be claimed in Dutch law; see Schelhaas, n 63 above, 426–27. *cf* the overviews in DCFR III.-3:708, Note IV, and Schwenzer, Hachem and Kee, *Global Sales and Contract Law*, n 27 above, paras 46.122–46.125.

[99] On Art 78 CISG ('without prejudice to any claim for damages recoverable under article 74'), see Magnus, n 36 above, para 19; the same applies with respect to the interest claim under Art 84(1) CISG; Magnus, n 36 above, art 84, para 11; I Schwenzer, in I Schwenzer (ed), *Schlechtriem and Schwenzer: Commentary on the UN Convention on the International Sale of Goods (CISG)*, 3rd edn (Oxford University Press, 2010) Art 84, para 14 f; see further PECL 9:508(2); PICC 7.4.9(3); DCFR III.-3:708(2). See also Art 83 ULIS ('in any event').

[100] See text to n 68 above.

[101] Recital 19 Late Payment Directive 2011/7/EU.

[102] The lump sum has been fixed at EUR40. The English Late Payment of Commercial Debts (Interest) Act 1998 (as amended by the Late Payment of Commercial Debts Regulations 2013, SI 2013/395) has put in place a graded system: EUR40 for a debt less than £1,000; EUR70 for a debt of £1,000 or more, but less than £10,000; EUR100 for a debt of £10,000 or more.

Unfair Contract Terms

The provision on unfair terms relating to interest for late payment (Article 170 CESL) has four remarkable features. First, it covers not only non-individually negotiated terms, but contract terms in general.[103] Why it was thought necessary to establish such general fairness control is not quite clear. Contract terms relating to the date or the period of interest are hardly more dangerous or burdensome for the creditor than contract terms deviating from other non-mandatory provisions of the CESL. A possible explanation may be the public interest component inherent in the interest rate,[104] as well as the strong desire to combat economic distress arising from late payments.[105]

Secondly, while all previous texts (including FS 175(1)!) only related to contract terms deviating from the provisions on interest for late payment to the detriment of the creditor (with the result that contract terms more favourable to the creditor would have been subject to the ordinary fairness control under Chapter 8), Article 170 CESL introduces a fairness control that operates both ways. The reason for this extension is unclear, for it is not required by the protective purpose of the Directive.[106] Only the second and third subparagraphs continue specifically to envisage the protection of the creditor.

Thirdly, the general standard for policing contract terms relating to interest for late payment is captured by the word 'grossly unfair' in the two Late Payment Directives and 'unfair' in all the other texts (ACQP, DCFR, FS, CESL). This is irritating in view of the fact that it does not, probably, entail any difference: after all, a crucial issue under the Late Payments Directive 2011/7/EU, as well as under the DCFR, FS and CESL, is whether the contractual term in question 'grossly deviates from good commercial practice, contrary to good faith and fair dealing'. In addition, the Late Payment Directive 2011/7/EU and the CESL (but not the ACQP, DCFR and FS) contain an exhortation to consider 'all circumstances of the case'. Once again, however, the factors specifically mentioned by way of example differ slightly. It should also be noted that the standard chosen in Article 170(1) CESL is, in principle, identical with that for the policing of non-individually negotiated contracts between traders, even though the factors mentioned in Article 86 CESL (conclusively, ie not merely by way of example) are again somewhat different.

Fourthly, on the analogy of Articles 84 and 85 CESL, Article 170 draws a distinction between specific contract terms which are presumed to be unfair (paragraph 2) and which are always unfair (paragraph 3). This distinction is also drawn in Article 3(2) and (3)

[103] See also ACQP 8:407, Comment B.3; DCFR III.-3:711, Comment B; Možina, n 60 above, Art 170, para 3. But see Baeck, n 52 above, para 49, proceeding from the assumption that Art 170(1) merely repeats the provisions of Chapter 8 on unfair contract terms and is therefore superfluous. On the unfair terms provision in the Late Payment Directive 2000/35/EU, see S Cerina, *Die Missbrauchsklausel der Zahlungsverzugsrichtlinie* (Baden-Baden, Nomos, 2009); J Kessel, *Die Missbrauchsklausel der Zahlungsverzugsrichtlinie* (Baden-Baden, Nomos, 2011); A Gorski, *Die Umsetzung der Missbrauchsklausel der Zalungsverzugsrichtlinie* (Dresden, TUDpress, 2011) (this latter work also deals with the new Directive 2011/71/EU).

[104] See n 31 above.

[105] See text to n 50 above.

[106] 'The Directive should prohibit abuse of freedom of contract to the disadvantage of the creditor': Recital 28 Late Payment Directive 2011/7/EU.

Late Payment Directive 2011/7/EU. Interestingly, however, Article 170 CESL tightens up the approach adopted in the Directive in two respects: any contract term deviating from the date or period of payment, or the rate of interest for late payment specified in Article 168, or the amount of compensation for recovery costs, to the detriment of the creditor, however small, is presumed to be unfair; and a contract term excluding compensation for recovery costs is always unfair (as opposed to presumed to be unfair under the Directive). There does not appear to be any good reason to restrict contractual freedom (among traders!) even further than under the recently enacted Late Payment Directive.[107]

Mandatory Nature

To the extent that it goes beyond making the fairness control under Article 170 CESL mandatory, this provision contradicts Article 170: for Article 170 presupposes that the parties *are* actually allowed to deviate from the time or period for payment, the rate of interest for late payment, and the compensation for recovery costs specified in Article 168(f) (though not to an extent that such deviation would be 'unfair'). There is very little else in respect of which parties to a contract might want to deviate from Article 168. Even if, eg, the parties have introduced, in their contact, a requirement that the debtor must receive a notice to pay before the interest starts to run, this would have to be regarded as a 'contract term relating to the date of payment'. Conceivably, the parties might want to make sure that interest is due, no matter whether the non-payment is excused or not. But why should such contractual arrangement, which would be even more in line with the policy pursued by the Late Payment Directive 2011/7/EU and the drafters of the CESL than Article 168(1), and which would, moreover, reflect the general statutory regime established by Article 166(1) CESL, not be permitted? In view of the fact that Article 171 lacks any plausible rationale, appears to bring about consequences that are quite unintended, that it is contrary to what was taken for granted by all previous texts, and is taken for granted by just about all national legal systems,[108] and that there is an unresolved tension with Article 170, it needs to be deleted.[109] Arguably, this may even be a case of perplexity, and Article 171 may therefore be taken to be *lex non scripta*.

[107] See also Kieninger, 'Allgemeines Leistungsstörungsrecht im Vorschlag für ein Gemeinsames Europäisches Kaufrecht', n 52 above, 223; Možina, n 60 above, Art 170, para 12. Austria (§ 459 UWG), France (Art L441-6 Code de Commerce), Italy (decreto legislativo no 192 of 9 November 2012), England (Art 14(2) Late Payment of Commercial Debts (Interest) Act 1998 as amended by the Late Payment of Commercial Debts Regulations 2013) and the Netherlands (Arts 6:119a f and 6:231–48 BW) have not gone beyond the restrictions imposed by the Directive.

[108] Schwenzer, Hachem and Kee, *Global Sales and Contract Law*, n 27 above, para 46.33: 'Today contractual agreements on the obligation to pay interest are enforced in the vast majority of legal systems'.

[109] See also Kieninger, 'Allgemeines Leistungsstörungsrecht im Vorschlag für ein Gemeinsames Europäisches Kaufrecht', n 52 above, 233; Možina, n 60 above, Art 171, para 1 (approach adopted in Art 171 'cannot coexist' with that of Arts 168–170); Baeck, n 52 above, para 50.

INTEREST ON LATE PAYMENT: GENERAL PROVISIONS

Range of Application

In order to assess this 'general' provision concerning interest on late payments, it has to be examined to which situations it applies. It does not apply to obligations on the part of traders to pay the price under a contract for the delivery of goods, the supply of digital content, or the provision of related services, no matter whether the creditor is also a trader or whether he is a consumer: for such 'regular' payment obligations the CESL has the special rule of Article 168. Essentially, therefore, Article 166 applies to obligations on the part of traders that can be termed 'irregular': obligations to pay damages; to pay an agreed sum in case of non-performance; to return money received under a contract that has subsequently been avoided or terminated[110] or otherwise been brought to an end;[111] to recover part of the price after having exercised a right to reduce the price,[112] etc. Apart from that, all (regular and irregular) obligations on the part of a consumer, no matter whether the creditor is a trader or also a consumer, would fall under Article 166, had special rules for those obligations not been laid down in Article 167. The range of exclusive application of Article 166, therefore, is very limited: to irregular obligations on the part of traders.

Comparison with Article 168 CESL

Obviously, those who drafted Article 166 CESL have asked themselves to what extent the legal regime for late payments established by the Late Payment Directives can be generalised. Thus, indeed, as far as the statutory interest rate is concerned, they have used the same approach: reference rate plus margin. The reference rate is identical, while the margin was reduced from 8 to 2 percentage points.[113] Apart from that, however (and, apart from Article 166(3) which is identical with Article 168(6)) they have put in place a different regime which is inspired by PECL 9:508, DCFR III.-3:708 and, indirectly, Article 78 CISG; it is also in line with PICC 7.4.9. The main reason for this must be that the dates specified in Article 168(2)(a), (b) and (3) are not normally appropriate for irregular obligations. Another starting date for the running of interest is thus required.[114] This can either be the due date or the receipt of a warning (or notice to pay). The drafters of Article 166 CESL opted for due date.[115] That is in line

110 Art 172 CESL.

111 ibid Art 44 (relating to the consequences of withdrawal).

112 ibid Art 120(2).

113 ibid Art 166(2).

114 For a general, broad-ranging comparative overview, see Schwenzer, Hachem and Kee, *Global Sales and Contract Law*, n 27 above, paras 46.50–46.76.

115 The words 'without the need to give notice' are, strictly speaking, redundant. They are not contained in Art 78 CISG, PECL 9:508(1), PICC 7.4.9(1), and DCFR III.-3:708(1). Their addition in the FS and CESL is without substantive significance: interest starts to run from due date.

with what is recognised in a number of legal systems generally[116] and in others for commercial contracts.[117] In the present context, however, the question arises why traders under Article 166 should be worse off, in this respect, than under Article 168: their obligation being an irregular rather than a regular one arising from a contract they have concluded, they have not fixed a date or period for payment; nor are they alerted to their obligation to pay by either an invoice or an equivalent request for payment, or the receipt of a counter-performance, and then granted a 30-day moratorium. In addition, the drafters of Article 166 CESL have also imported from the general rules on late payment contained in the previous texts the idea that it does not matter whether the non-payment is excused or not. This is in conflict with Article 168(1), for there is no reason why for a delay in payment of a price, but not for a delay in payment of another payment obligation, it should be relevant that the non-payment is excused.[118]

We are, therefore, faced with a strange discrepancy of regimes,[119] with the trader under Article 166 being treated partly more strictly and partly much more leniently (six per cent interest less!) than the trader under Article 168. Taking the regime established in the Late Payment Directives, and also entrenched in Article 168, as point of reference, it would be preferable to tie the running of interest to the receipt of a notice.[120] In addition, Article 166(1) will have to be brought in line with Article 168(1) as far as the excuse under Article 88 is concerned. The need for a special rule protecting consumers would, at least in one respect, also be obviated.[121] That, in turn, would make it possible to formulate a general *chapeau* rule for all provisions relating to interest on late payments, and it would also avoid any possible confusion resulting from the fact that the words 'whether or not the non-performance is excused', still contained in DCFR III.-3:708(1),[122] had to be deleted.[123]

[116] See the references in Schwenzer, Hachem and Kee, *Global Sales and Contract Law*, n 27 above, paras 46–51.

[117] See n 73 above. It must be kept in mind that the provisions on interest in the CISG and PICC also only relate to commercial contracts.

[118] The point is also made by the European Law Institute in its Statement on the Proposal for a Common European Sales Law, Remark 2 to Art 166; see also Baeck, n 52 above, para 52.

[119] This has also been noted by Možina, n 60 above, art 168, para 16 (who refers to 'incoherent results' produced by having two different interest rates for different categories of payment from the same contract). In order to reduce this incoherence, he suggests a 'broad interpretation' of the term 'payment of a price due under a contract for the delivery of goods' in Art 168(5).

[120] This would also obviate the problems outlined in Schwenzer, Hachem and Kee, *Global Sales and Contract Law*, n 27 above, paras 46.56–46.66 on determining the due date with regard to damages and restitution claims.

[121] See also Možina, n 60 above, Art 167, para 17.

[122] *Cf* PICC 7.4.9(1); as far as PECL 9:508(1) is concerned, see Comment B: 'Interest is owed whether or not non-payment is excused under Article 8:108'.

[123] This is due to the fact that under art 167(1), ie in cases where the debtor is a consumer, interest is due only when non-performance is not excused. See also Kieninger, 'Allgemeines Leistungsstörungsrecht im Vorschlag für ein Gemeinsames Europäisches Kaufrecht', n 52 above, 221. Možina, n 60 above, art 166, para 13 appears to proceed from the assumption that even under Art 166 interest is only due when non-performance is not excused.

Rate of Interest and Damages for Further Loss

Article 166(2) CESL is identical with Article 168(5), and thus follows the model established in the Late Payment Directives,[124] except that the 'margin' is six per cent lower. That is easily understandable as far as obligations by consumers are concerned. It is less plausible for obligations on the part of traders. Is a 'culture of prompt payment'[125] here less desirable than with regard to obligations to pay a price? On the other hand, it may be argued that irregular obligations are more likely to give rise to reasonable doubt than regular ones; and that it would thus be unfair to impose the penalty of a supracompensatory interest rate on all persons refusing to discharge an obligation to pay damages, or to render restitution.

The rule contained in Article 166(3) is identical with Article 168(6) and thus, what has been said there, also applies here. Deletion of the words 'in addition' contained in the previous texts (including the FS) is probably without significance.

Interest When the Debtor is a Consumer

Comparative Assessment

The provisions concerning interest on late payments are intended to protect the creditor: the debtor must be discouraged from behaviour that might jeopardise the creditor's liquidity, or even solvency.[126] Article 167 CESL, in a way, counteracts this rationale: it is aimed to protect the debtor, as long as he is a consumer. A specific provision protecting consumers was not thought to be necessary in the PECL, ACQP, and not even in the DCFR: it was introduced by the Expert Group in charge of drafting the FS and from there taken over into the CESL. The national legal systems also normally apply to consumers the general rules on delay in payment (*mora debitoris*) contained in their civil codes. Here, the requirements of fault and of a warning[127] can be taken to provide a sufficient degree of protection. The specific problem with the general regime envisaged in Article 166 CESL is that it is based on the concept of interest running from due date (*Fälligkeitszins*): a concept traditionally implemented with regard to commercial contracts. That was, probably, thought to be unduly harsh for a consumer who does not keep track of his payment obligations in the same way as a trader does (or should). Hence the special rules in Article 167.

Interestingly, in some respects, these special rules resemble the regime relating to late payments of regular payment obligations by traders. For, as under Article 168(1) CESL, interest is due only when the non-payment is not excused by virtue of Article 88.

[124] See text to n 29 above. For comment on the approach adopted in the PECL, PICC, DCFR, PCC and FS (floating commercial interest rate), see Schwenzer, Hachem and Kee, *Global Sales and Contract Law*, n 27 above, paras 46.92–46.94.

[125] Recital 12 Late Payment Directive 2011/7/EU.

[126] See n 50 above.

[127] See § 286 BGB; §§ 1298, 1334 ABGB; Art 1146 Code civil; Arts 1218, 1224 *Codice civile*; for the Netherlands, see Schelhaas, n 63 above, 425 f. The warning, however, is only necessary as long as the modern equivalents of the maxim *dies interpellat pro homine* do not apply.

In addition, the debtor must have received a notice; this is structurally similar to the way in which traders, unless a date or period of payment has been specified in the contract, are alerted to their obligation to pay by either an invoice or equivalent request for payment, or by the receipt of counter-performance. And, as under Article 168(2), consumers are granted a 30-day period after having received the notice. Article 167(2) goes further than Article 168(2) and the general rules in the national civil codes, by requiring the notice specifically to draw the debtor's attention to his obligation to pay interest as well as to the rate of interest. This presupposes that consumers typically do not know about the 'interest-bearing use' that can be made of ready money and of which a creditor who is not paid is thus deprived. That is a questionable assumption. But it ties in with the general approach prevailing in modern consumer protection legislation that consumers must be comprehensively informed about their rights and duties by their contractual partner.[128] On the other hand, Article 167(2) specifically states that the notice may be given before the date when payment is due. In such cases, the 30-day period available for consumers may be considerably shorter than the one available to traders, which is counter-intuitive.

Consumer Protection?

The wisdom of special rules for the protection of consumers is questionable. Thus, the 30-day period 'is not exactly a message encouraging timely payments by consumers';[129] nor does it contribute to the 'culture of prompt payment' envisaged by those responsible for EU legislation.[130] And late payment by consumers will sometimes be as detrimental for the liquidity of small and medium-sized enterprises[131] as late payment by traders. At the same time, however, it would hardly be right if consumers would have to pay interest immediately in situations where traders would have a 30-day period available without even having to pay interest at a compensatory rate.

Damages for Further Loss

Whether the creditor may, under Article 167 CESL, recover damages for any further loss, is unclear. Since, contrary to Articles 166 and 168,[132] Article 167 does not contain a special provision to that effect, it may be argued that he cannot claim

[128] See Eidenmüller et al, *Revision des Verbraucher-acquis*, n 10 above, 193–265.

[129] Možina, n 60 above, Art 167, para 18; see also Kieninger, 'Allgemeines Leistungsstörungsrecht im Vorschlag für ein Gemeinsames Europäisches Kaufrecht', n 52 above, 224; B Koch, in C Wedehorst and B Zöchling-Jud, *Am Vorabend eines Gemeinsamen Europäischen Kaufrecht: Zum Verordnungsentwurf der Europäischen Kommission vom 11.10.2011 KOM (2011) 635 endg* (Vienna, Manz, 2012) 239 f (referring to the view of the Austrian Ministry of Justice that 'even of consumers it can be expected that they pay interest from due date'); Baeck, n 52 above, para 37 (noting an overprotection of the consumer); European Law Institute, Statement on the Proposal for a Common European Sales Law, Remark to Art 167: 'There is no real justification for consumers only to be liable for interest on late payment 30 days after receipt of notice'. The problem with this view is that under the rules introduced by the Late Payment Directives not even traders are expected to pay interest from due date.

[130] Recital 12 Late Payment Directive 2011/7/EU.

[131] See ibid recital 3.

[132] Arts 11(3), 168(6) CESL.

damages for any further loss. On the other hand, Article 166 may be seen as a general provision which also covers transactions where the debtor is a consumer, unless Article 167 contains special rules deviating from Article 166. The Expert Group appears to have taken the former view (even though it failed to act accordingly).[133] Why a consumer-debtor should not have to pay for the loss suffered by the creditor as a result of his late payment is not obvious. At least, it should be open to the creditor to claim such loss if he has alerted the debtor in his notice to that possibility.

Fairness Control

Article 167(3) CESL resembles Article 170(2), except that it operates the other way round: contractual provisions deviating from the statutory interest rate, or from the statutory starting date for such interest, to the detriment of the consumer are subject to a fairness control, no matter whether they have been individually negotiated or not. Of course, the general fairness test of Article 83 rather than the one tailored for traders under Article 86 is applicable. Certain deviations of formulation are less easy to explain.

Drafting

Throughout the entirety of Article 167 CESL it is obvious that it has been drafted without much concern for the text of other rules in Sections 2 and 3 of Chapter 16: 'when performance is not excused' (Article 167(1)) as opposed to 'without being excused by virtue of Article 88' (Article 168(1)); '[a] term of the contract' (Article 167(3)) as opposed to '[a] contract term (Article 170(1)); 'rate of interest higher than that provided in Article 166, or accrual earlier than the time specified in paragraph 2 of this Article' (Article 167(3)) as opposed to 'time or period for payment or a rate of interest less favourable to the creditor than the time, period or rate specified in Articles 167 or 168' (Article 170(2)); 'to the extent that this would be unfair' (Article 167(3)) as opposed to 'to the extent that the term is unfair' (Article 170(1)). Article 167(3) introduces the term 'accrual' for what Articles 167(2) and 168(2) describe as 'starts to run'.[134]

Capitalisation of Interest

Article 167(4) CESL prohibits the capitalisation of interest (or, compound interest). Oddly, it is the only rule relating to that topic in the entire set of provisions on interest on late payments. What this means for interest to be charged under Articles 166

[133] *Synthesis of the Tenth Meeting, 17–18 February 2011*, n 60 above, 6: 'It would be necessary to provide that when interest is paid, no other damages can be recovered by a business against a consumer debtor'. No such provision is, however, contained in Art 167.

[134] On the latter point, see also Možina, n 60, Art 167, para 18 *in fine* ('[does] not contribute to the clarity of the provision').

and 168 is unclear. On the one hand, it may be argued that since compound interest is specifically prohibited under Article 167, it must be allowed under Articles 166 and 168. A remark by the Expert Group may be quoted in support of this.[135] On the other hand, both the PECL and the DCFR did contain a general rule allowing the capitalisation of interest and specifying the details.[136] That rule was not received into the FS and the CESL. This may be taken to mean that the drafters of the latter two instruments either wanted to rule out the capitalisation of interest or did not want to take '[a] stand on the question'.[137] It is also of interest, in this context, that the Late Payment Directive 2011/7/EU provides that interest 'should be calculated … as simple interest' (ie not be compounded with the capital),[138] and that the drafters of FS Articles 173–75 and Articles 168–170 CESL have followed the Late Payment Directive very closely.[139] The matter should therefore be clarified.

Mandatory Nature

Article 167(5) CESL must be qualified in the light of Article 167(3): from the latter provision it follows that the parties may in fact deviate, to the detriment of the consumer, from the statutory interest rate and the statutory date when interest starts to run.[140] Mandatory in the sense of Article 167(5) are, therefore, the requirement of giving notice, specifying the obligation to pay interest and its rate, and the rule on compound interest (Article 167(4)).

ONCE AGAIN: CAPITALISATION OF INTEREST

It has just been stated that Article 167(4) CESL on the capitalisation of interest is inconclusive as far as contracts are concerned where the debtor is not a consumer.

Anatocism

Under the *ius commune* the capitalisation of interest was prohibited. This followed from an enactment by Justinian,[141] tightening up earlier restrictions from classical Roman law.[142] The prohibition of *anatocismus* or *anatocismus coniunctus*, as it was

[135] *Synthesis of the Tenth Meeting, 17–18 February 2011*, n 60 above, 6: 'It was agreed that the instrument should not allow the capitalisation of interest when the debtor is a consumer'.

[136] PECL 17:101; DCFR III.-3:709.

[137] See PICC 7.4.10, Comment; and see E McKendrick, in S Vogenauer and J Kleinheisterkamp (eds), *Commentary on the UNIDROIT Principles of International Commercial Contracts (PICC)* (Oxford University Press, 2009) Art 7.4.9, para 15.

[138] Recital 15 Late Payment Directive 2011/7/EU; and see Art 2(6) of that Directive.

[139] Možina, n 60 above, Art 166, para 24, therefore indeed concludes that the approach of the Late Payment Directive is also the approach of the CESL.

[140] But see Baeck, n 52 above, para 39 ('inconsistent with Article 167(5) CESL').

[141] C 4.32.28; see also C 7.54.3 pr.

[142] Ulp D 12.6.26; Mod D 42.1.27; Zimmermann, *The Law of Obligations*, n 16 above, 169; Dorn, n 16 above, §§ 246–48, para 12.

called,[143] continued to be recognised, down to the end of the nineteenth century, in pandectist literature.[144] It was designed to protect the debtor from being burdened by an ever-increasing avalanche of interest. Moreover, the exact extent of that burden is usually not easy to calculate.[145] Some of the codifications in force at that time, however, recognised certain exceptions, or modifications.[146] Thus, the Prussian code allowed the creditor to claim interest on interest which the debtor had been found liable to pay by a court of law.[147] Under Article 1154 French Code civil, the creditor was (and still is) allowed to claim compound interest on the basis of 'une demande judiciaire' and provided that interest has accrued for at least one year.[148] An Austrian statute of 1868 permitted interest to be claimed on interest that had fallen due, provided an action had been brought for the latter and from the moment of bringing such action.[149] Franz Philipp von Kübel, who prepared the first draft of the German Civil Code, also proposed to relax the prohibition on compound interest[150] but he remained unsuccessful in that respect; § 289 BGB eventually entrenched the traditional, restrictive attitude.[151]

Modern Approach

That attitude, however, is highly questionable. If a creditor does not receive a sum of money that is due to him he is deprived of the 'interest-bearing use'[152] he would normally be able (or can perhaps even be expected) to make of that money. That is the basis for his claim for interest. Interest, however, is *also* a sum of money, and if the creditor does not receive it in time, he is deprived of the possibility to earn interest on it: 'Delay in [the] payment of interest deprives the creditor of a [benefit that is due to him] as much as delay in the payment of the capital itself'.[153] English law, therefore, following the decision of *Sempra Metals Ltd (formerly Metallgesellschaft Ltd)*

[143] *Anatocismus coniunctus* because the interest was added to the capital. In the case of *anatocismus separatus* (which, of course, was also prohibited) the interest was regarded as a new, or separate, capital which bore interest.

[144] Windscheid and Kipp, *Lehrbuch des Pandektenrechts*, n 20 above, § 261, 1; CF Glück, *Ausfürliche Erläuterung der Pandecten nach Hellfeld* (Erlangen, Palmische Verlagsbuchhandlung, 1820) vol 21, 115–26; Dorn, n 16 above, §§ 246–48, para 24; K Schmidt, 'Das Zinseszinsverbot' (1982) *Juristenzeitung* 829 f.

[145] Dorn, n 16 above, §§ 246–48, para 41.

[146] For a modern comparative overview, see PECL 17:101, Notes 1–7; DCFR III.-3:709, Notes 1–18; see also Schwenzer, Hachem and Kee, *Global Sales and Contract Law*, n 27 above, paras 46.111–46.118

[147] § 821 I 11 PrALR.

[148] See also Art 1283 Codice civile (fixing a period of six months rather than a year).

[149] Today, see § 1000(2) second sentence ABGB.

[150] See Dorn, n 16 above, §§ 246–48, para 30.

[151] And see, for commercial transactions, § 353 second sentence HGB.

[152] See n 66 above.

[153] PECL 17:101, Comment C (= DCFR III.-3:709, Comment C); see also, eg FP von Kübel, 'Entwurf eines bürglerlichen Gesetzbuches für das Deutsche Reich, Recht der Schuldverhältnisse' in W Schubert (ed), *Die Vorlagen der Redaktoren für die erste Kommission zur Ausarbeitung des Entwurfs eines Bürgerlichen Gesetzbuches, Recht der Schuldverhältnisse* (Berlin/New York, de Gruyter, 1980) vol I, 897. For the modern economic view of compound interest (from the point of view of the time value of money), see, eg SA Ross, R Westerfield and BD Jordan, *Corporate Finance Fundamentals* (New York, McGraw-Hill Higher Education, 2008) 121–26.

v Commissioners of Inland Revenue,[154] now includes compound interest in an award of interest for the late payment of money;[155] and the most modern of the Western European civil codes also, quite rightly, no longer has the traditional inhibitions concerning compound interest: always at the end of one full year the amount on which the statutory interest is calculated is increased by the interest that has fallen due within that year. This is what Articles 119(2) and 119a(3) BW determine, both for commercial and for other contracts, and it is clearly the basis for the rules subsequently adopted in the PECL and the DCFR. There is no reason why such rule should not be included in the CESL. To the contrary: if it is a priority of the European Union to bring about a 'decisive shift [towards] a culture of prompt payment',[156] the capitalisation of interest would appear to be entirely in line with it.[157] The authors of the PECL even regarded it as 'an effective sanction because of its gradually increasing effect'.[158] However, just as the claim for interest, the claim for compound interest is nothing but an abstract assessment of a loss typically suffered by the creditor.

Party Agreement

Under the *ius commune*, the parties were not allowed to contract out of the prohibition on anatocism: any agreement to the contrary was void.[159] This is the one issue on which the BGB took at least a somewhat more liberal line: The parties are allowed to agree on compound interest, though they are not allowed to do so 'in advance'.[160] In this respect the draftsmen of the BGB followed a number of contemporary codifications; many of them, however, had fixed a certain period of time that had to have elapsed since interest had fallen due.[161] Interest 'par une convention spéciale' was

[154] *Sempra Metals Ltd (formerly Metallgesellschaft Ltd) v Commissioners of Inland Revenue* [2008] 1 AC 561, para 100.

[155] McGregor, *McGregor on Damages*, n 26 above, para 15-069; Bueren, 'Die Berücksichtigung der Anspruchsentwertung im Zeitablauf bei Schadensersatz wegen Verstößen gegen EU-Kartellrecht', n 46 above, 520. Compound interest is thus part of the 'interest as damages' claim which means that the creditor has to prove the normal requirements for such damages claim. This is the position under the common law; interest under the two statutes mentioned above (text to n 42) can only be awarded as simple interest.

[156] See text after n 31 above.

[157] It is, therefore, surprising to see that the Late Payment Directive 2011/7/EU defines 'statutory interest' as 'simple interest' and does not envisage compounding. But, according to Art 13(3), this is just a minimum standard; the Member States may maintain or bring into force provisions which are more favourable to the creditor than the provisions necessary to comply with the Directive.

[158] PECL 17:101, Comment C (= DCFR III.-3:709, Comment C).

[159] Marci D 22.1.29; Windscheid and Kipp, *Lehrbuch des Pandektenrechts*, n 20 above, § 261 (83); Dorn, n 16 above, §§ 246–48, para 24.

[160] § 248(2) BGB; on which see Dorn, n 16 above, §§ 246–48, paras 34 and 41; Schwenzer, Hachem and Kee, *Global Sales and Contract Law*, n 27 above, para 46.44.

[161] See, eg § 819 I 11 PrALR (two years); Art 1154 Code civil (one year). For modern comparative overviews, see PECL 17:101, Note 5; DCFR III.-3:709, Notes 11 and 12; Schwenzer, Hachem and Kee, *Global Sales and Contract Law*, n 27 above, paras 46.43–46.47.

thus treated in the same way as 'par une demande judiciaire'.[162] But there are also legal systems where the parties are allowed to agree on compound interest without restrictions.[163] This is also, essentially, the line taken by the authors of PECL 17:101(2), even though it is implicit, rather than explicitly stated, in that rule: the parties are free to make their own arrangements as far as interest upon delay in the payment of money is concerned; but the fact that 'the parties have addressed themselves to the question of interest means that it is up to them to provide for capitalization if they so wish'.[164] The rule in PECL 17:101(1) does not, therefore, apply. The logic of this argument is unexceptionable.

Consumer Protection: Usage

The consumer protection envisaged by Article 167(4) CESL may be preserved.[165] It should be made clear that consumers can neither be under a statutory nor under a contractual duty to pay compound interest.

Some countries recognise usage as a separate source for allowing compound interest; Article 1283 Codice civile provides a prominent example ('[i]n mancanza di usi contrari'). According to the Corte di cassazione, such usage to claim interest exists in the relationship between credit institutions and their customers.[166]

PROPOSAL FOR A REVISION OF ARTICLES 166–171 CESL

The following proposal for a revision of the CESL's rules on interest for delay in the payment of money is based on the preceding analysis. At the same time it can be read as a summary.

[162] This is still the position today: Art 1154 Code civil. The same is true for Italy (Art 1283 Codice civile) except that the period there is six months. French courts have, incidentally, regarded agreements as valid which, though made in advance, relate to the interest that has fallen due after the lapse of one year from due date: Cass 3e civ, 26 February 1974, Bull civ III, no 91; Cass com, 20 October 1982, Bull civ IV, no 323; Cass 1re civ, 12 March 1991, Bull civ I, no 89; 7 January1992, *pourvoi* no 89-11.894; 22 November 1994, *pourvoi* no 92-19.554 ; Cass 3e civ, 8 March 1995, Bull civ III, no 77. For Italy, see A Zaccaria, in G Cian and A Trabucchi (eds), *Commentario breve al codice civile,* 10th edn (Padova, Cedam, 2011) Art 1283, I and III.

[163] For Austria, ABGB, see § 1000(2) first sentence (agreement must be 'express'); for the Netherlands, see Schelhaas, n 63 above, 276; for England (and the United States), see the references in Schwenzer, Hachem, and Kee, *Global Sales and Contract Law*, n 27 above, para 46.46 (agreement may be implicit). In the other systems, current account agreements are usually taken as an implicit justification for the capitalisation of interest, without the normal restrictions; see, for Germany, § 355(1) HGB; for references concerning other systems, see PECL 17:101, Note 6 (= DCFR III.-3:709, Note 13).

[164] PECL 17:101, Comment D (= DCFR III.-3:709, Comment D).

[165] But see Baeck, n 52 above, para 38.

[166] See Zaccaria, n 162 above, Art 1283, IV. In a similar vein, § 248(2) BGB exempts credit institutions from the prohibition to agree on compound interest 'in advance'.

Revision

Article 166 Interest for Delay in Payment of Money

If payment of a sum of money is delayed, interest on that sum is due at the rate specified in Article 167, unless the non-payment is excused by virtue of Article 88.

Article 167 When Interest Starts to Run

(1) If payment of a price due under a contract for the delivery of goods, supply of digital content or provision of related services is delayed, interest at the rate specified in Article 167 starts to run on the day which follows the date or the end of the period for payment provided in the contract. If there is no such date or period, interest at that rate starts to run:
   (a) 30 days after the date of receipt of the goods, digital content or related services;
   (b) if conformity of the goods, digital content or related services to the contract is to be ascertained by way of acceptance or examination, 30 days after the date of acceptance or finalisation of the examination procedure; or
   (c) 30 days after the date of receipt of an invoice or equivalent request for payment, if that date is later than the dates set out under (a) and (b).
(2) The period for payment provided in the contract must not exceed 60 days. Where conformity of goods, digital content or related services to the contract is to be ascertained by way of acceptance or examination, that procedure must not exceed 30 days from the date of delivery of the goods, supply for digital content or provision of related services.
(3) In other cases of delay in the payment of a sum of money, interest at the rate specified in Article 167 starts to run when the creditor has given notice to the debtor.

Article 168 Rate of Interest

(1) The interest rate for delayed payment is:
   (a) if the creditor's habitual residence is in a Member State whose currency is the euro, or in a third country, the interest rate applied by the European Central Bank to its most recent refinance operation carried out before the first calendar day of the half-year in question, or the marginal interest rate resulting from variable-rate tender procedures for the most recent refinancing operations of the European Central Bank, plus two percentage points;
   (b) if the creditor's habitual residence is in a Member State whose currency is not the euro, the equivalent rate set by the national central bank of that Member State plus two percentage points, or plus two percentage points.
(2) If a trader delays payment of a price due under a contract for the delivery of goods, supply of digital content or provision of related services, another six percentage points are added to the rate determined by paragraph (1).

Article 169 Compensation for Recovery Costs

The creditor may recover damages for any further loss, including his recovery costs. If the debtor is a trader, the creditor is entitled to a lump sum of 40 euros for his recovery costs; this does not prevent him from claiming damages for recovery costs exceeding that sum and damages for other loss.

Article 170 To What Extent these Rules are Mandatory

If the debtor is a consumer, the parties may not, to his detriment, exclude the application of this section or derogate or vary its effects.

Article 171 Capitalisation of Interest

(1) Interest payable according to Articles 166–168 is added to the outstanding capital every 12 months.
(2) Paragraph (1) of this Article does not apply if the parties have provided for interest upon delay in payment.
(3) If the debtor is a consumer interest may neither be added to the outstanding capital under paragraph (1) of this Article nor by agreement of the parties.

Security and Financing

19

The Assignment of Pure Intangibles in the Conflict of Laws

ROY GOODE

IT WAS WITH the greatest pleasure that I received an invitation to contribute to this collection of essays in honour of our friend and colleague Professor Hugh Beale. Hugh is a man of many parts. A scholar of international repute and one of this country's leading experts on contract law and on the law of personal property security, he has played a central role in the move towards a common European contract law through his membership of the Lando Group which produced the Principles of European Contract Law and of the Study Group on a European Civil Code. He has also performed a valuable service in inculcating an awareness of European contract law among law students through his various publications with others on European contract law. It was under Hugh's direction as a Law Commissioner that the Law Commission produced its fine consultative report on company security interests, one of the main sources consulted when Jersey undertook a reform of its security interests law. Despite the various honours conferred on him, including appointment as an honorary Queen's Counsel and the conferment of an honorary doctorate from the University of Antwerp, Hugh remains modest and unassuming, a lively colleague and a good friend. It is very much to be hoped that his retirement will be a purely notional one.

INTRODUCTION

Despite the growing volume of international conventions designed to harmonise substantive rules of commercial law, it is clear that private international law continues to flourish. In the case of the transfer of goods the rules governing the applicable law have been tolerably well worked out.[1] It is necessary to describe these briefly

[1] Some 50 years ago one of Canada's leading commercial lawyers, Prof Jacob Ziegel, teamed up with me to write a comparative survey of hire-purchase and conditional sales law of which one chapter was devoted to the conflict of laws. In this we took issue with several leading scholars on what was then thought to be established doctrine on the effect of a change of *situs*. Half a century later our analysis, which was well received, still seems to hold good. See Roy M Goode and Jacob S Ziegel, *Hire-Purchase and Conditional Sale: A Comparative Survey of Commonwealth and American Law* (London, British Institute of International and Comparative Law, 1965) Part V. The subject was further developed by Ziegel in 'Conditional Sales and the Conflict of Laws' (1967) 45 *Canadian Bar Review* 284. However, the traditional *lex situs* rule is not well-suited to mobile equipment regularly moving across national borders and makes no sense at all when applied to pure intangibles. See p 355 below.

in order to highlight the problems involved in seeking to apply the same principles to the assignment of intangible movables, a topic the subject of extensive literature only a very small selection of which can be noted here.

LAW APPLICABLE TO DEALINGS IN GOODS

The general rule applicable to dealings in goods[2] is that the validity of a transfer of goods, including a security interest, is governed by the *lex situs* (*lex rei sitae*) of the goods at the time of the relevant dealing. This applies not only to security interests in the traditional sense but also to reservation of title under conditional sale agreements, which has given rise to a good deal of case-law.

Validity as between the parties is not to be confused with efficacy against third parties. Where, for example, D grants C1 a security interest in goods while they are in Ruritania, under the law of which a security interest must be registered in order to be effective against a subsequent secured creditor, this perfection requirement is entirely irrelevant to the validity of the security interest as between D and C1. It comes into play only if there is a further dealing in the goods by D, as by granting a second security interest, to C2, while they are still in Ruritania, and then it is a question not of validity but of priorities. An English court would recognise C1 as having a valid security interest but one which, if C1 had failed to register under Ruritanian law, would be subordinated to the security interest of C2. The same applies where S agrees to sell goods situated in Ruritania to B, who wrongfully disposes of them to T while they are still in Ruritania. If under Ruritanian law a title reservation is ineffective against a subsequent purchaser unless registered and S failed to register, an English court would hold that T acquires an overriding title under Ruritanian law.

Things become a little more complex where there is a change of *situs*, as where D, instead of granting a second security interest to C2, takes the goods to Urbania and sells them to T, a bona fide purchaser for value, or where B does the same in relation to the goods acquired from S. Here the rule of the law of last dealing applies. An English court will treat the perfection requirements of Ruritanian law as of no relevance to a dealing in the goods after they have left Ruritania. So the court will look to Urbanian law to determine the impact of the sale on C1's security interest or on S's reservation of title. If under Urbanian law T acquires an overriding title, no reference to Ruritanian law is necessary. If, on the other hand, Urbanian law applies the principle *nemo dat quod non habet*, then T will be considered by an English court as taking the goods subject to C1's security interest validly created, or S's title validly reserved, under the law of Ruritania.

The rule of the last dealing also applies to a wrongful double sale by the seller and, indeed, to theft. So in *Winkworth v Christie, Manson & Woods Ltd*,[3] certain works of art were stolen from the plaintiff in England and taken to Italy where they were sold to the second defendant, who subsequently delivered them for sale to the

[2] For this purpose, documentary intangibles such as documents of title, negotiable instruments and negotiable securities are equated with goods, so that the *lex situs* is the location of the document of title, negotiable instrument or negotiable bond or certificate at the time of the relevant dealing.

[3] *Winkworth v Christie, Manson & Woods Ltd* [1980] Ch 496.

first defendants, auctioneers in England. The plaintiff claimed the works of art as his property but the second defendant successfully established his overriding title under the Italian law, being the law of the new *situs*, as a purchaser in good faith without knowledge of his vendor's defect in title.

In general the *lex situs* rule, though not immune from criticism,[4] works well enough for tangible movables. It is, however, unsatisfactory when applied to goods in transit or to dealings in mobile equipment of a kind regularly moving from one jurisdiction to another, as in the case of aircraft. The location of an aircraft at any given time may be quite unrelated to the state with which it has its closest connection. For example, in the famous *Blue Sky* case,[5] the dispute concerned the validity of mortgages of two aircraft, one of which was registered in the United Kingdom but grounded at Schiphol airport in the Netherlands at the time of execution of the mortgage. The mortgage was valid under English law but invalid under Dutch domestic law. However, a Dutch court would have applied English law as the *lex registri*[6] and it was argued that this was more satisfactory than the *lex situs* because it would mirror the position under Article 1 of the 1948 Geneva Convention on the International Recognition of Rights in Aircraft. This was rejected by Beatson J on the ground that the application of the *lex situs* was well established and that reference to the *lex registri* would not by itself secure uniformity, because the conflict rules of other jurisdictions might be different. Further, the reference back to English law under Dutch conflict of laws rules would involve resort to *renvoi*, a doctrine which is nowadays rejected by the English conflict of laws in most situations. The mortgage was therefore invalid as being contrary to Dutch domestic law.

It was this kind of problem that led to the 2001 Convention on International Interests in Mobile Equipment and its associated Protocols, which establish an international legal regime for international interests (security interests and interests held by conditional sellers and lessors) in aircraft objects, railway rolling stock and space assets, with a set of basic default remedies, an International Registry for the registration of such interests, and priority largely determined by the order of registration.[7]

[4] Primarily on the ground that the parties will not necessarily know where the goods are situated. The most detailed analysis is by Janeen M Carruthers, *The Transfer of Property in the Conflict of Laws* (Oxford University Press, 2005) chs 8 and 9. Dr Carruthers concluded that 'the legitimate interests of the law of the *situs* must be protected' in order to preserve predictability but with exceptions to allow flexibility in appropriate cases, eg where the transfer of property issue concerns only the parties themselves (paras 9.48–9.49).

[5] *Blue Sky One Ltd v Mahan Air PK Airfinance US Inc* [2010] EWHC 631 (comm).

[6] The judgment adopts the language of counsel in referring throughout to the *lex registrii*, though it is not clear where the second 'i' comes from. The word 'registrum' does not feature in classical Latin, in which the word for 'registry' is *tabularium*, but it is found in mediaeval Latin.

[7] The Convention and Aircraft Protocol are the only ones yet in force. There have so far been 61 ratifications of the Convention and 55 of the Aircraft Protocol, with ratifications to come from Australia in 2014 and the United Kingdom in the same year or 2015.

LAW APPLICABLE TO ASSIGNMENTS OF NON-DOCUMENTARY INTANGIBLES: GENERAL CONSIDERATIONS

Assignment by Way of Security and Absolute Assignments

The common use of title reservation clauses in contracts for the sale of goods, coupled with the requirements in many jurisdictions of registration of chattel mortgages, has led to a focus on rules for the recognition and displacement of security and quasi-security devices in goods. Where title is reserved to the seller, the buyer acquires neither legal nor equitable ownership of the goods. By contrast there are many agreements for the assignment of non-documentary intangibles where the transfer of legal title by a statutory assignment is deferred, and indeed may never take place at all, but beneficial ownership vests in the assignee from the outset. Moreover, despite the well-understood distinction between security assignments and outright assignments of debts, it is not always easy to distinguish the economic effects of the two types of transaction and in a number of jurisdictions registration and priority rules apply alike to outright and security assignments.

Consistently with this, article 14(3) of the Rome I Regulation[8] is expressed to cover both security and outright assignments, while the UNCITRAL legislative guide on secured transactions explains in detail why, exceptionally, its proposals as to creation, third-party effectiveness and priorities apply equally to security assignments and absolute assignments of receivables.[9] None of the suggested changes to the Rome I Regulation is based on a distinction between outright and security assignments of non-documentary intangibles and no distinction is drawn between the two in the analysis which follows.

Decline and Fall of the *Lex Situs*

Attempts to determine the law applicable to the proprietary effects of a security assignment of non-documentary (or 'pure') intangibles have mainly led to confusion. So strong has been the influence of the *lex situs* rule that conflict of laws lawyers have been driven to ascribe an artificial *situs* to intangibles, namely, the location of the debtor, being the place where the debt can be recovered. This, however, meets difficulties as soon as it is sought to be applied to particular facts. In the first place, non-documentary intangibles have no physical location, so what is provided is a purely legal construct which is not axiomatic but needs justification. Secondly, the appropriate applicable law depends on the relationship under examination and cannot sensibly be ascertained by reference to a single determinant, the *lex situs*.[10] Thirdly, since the notional *situs* varies according to the type of intangible under consideration, reference to the *lex situs* does not serve as an organising principle at all. That is why our conflict textbooks, having gone to some trouble to define the

[8] Regulation No 593/2008 of the European Parliament and of the Council of 11 July 2007 on the law applicable to contractual obligations ('Rome I Regulation') [2008] OJ L/177/6.

[9] At para 25.

[10] See p 372 below.

situs of intangibles, then tend to avoid applying it except in relation to documentary intangibles. This exposes the futility of the *lex situs* approach, which has, indeed, been disavowed by more recent decisions.[11] Why go through the two-stage process of designating the *lex situs* as the applicable law and then seeking to determine the *situs* of a particular pure intangible? Why not simply lay down a direct rule appropriate to the type of relationship under consideration? It is therefore not surprising that the *lex situs* has been discredited as a choice of law rule for the assignment of debts, contract rights and other pure intangibles, and that the various options put forward by the BIICL consultees[12] did not include the *lex situs* rule, which accordingly now serves no useful function except in relation to documentary intangibles.

Special Cases

There are certain rights in respect of which the problem either does not arise at present, namely, recorded rights to financial collateral, or will cease to arise once the Space Protocol to the Cape Town Convention is in force, namely, recorded assignments of rights to payment or other performance due to a debtor by any person with respect to a space asset ('debtor's rights').[13]

Financial Collateral

For financial collateral the right to which is recorded in a register or account located in a Member State of what is now the European Union, the ordinary conflict rules in Rome I Regulation are displaced by the Financial Collateral Directive,[14] article 9(2) of which applies the law of the place where the register or securities account is maintained.

The 2006 Hague Convention on the Law applicable to Intermediated Securities initially adopted the same approach but moved away from this because of the perceived problem that the functions of maintaining securities accounts were often distributed among different offices of the same bank situated in different jurisdictions. The Explanatory Report[15] gave as an illustration an account initially opened

[11] *Macmillan Inc v Bishopsgate Invesatment Trust plc (No 3)* [1996] 1 All ER 585, 598; *Raffeisen Zentralbank Österreichv Five Star General Trading LLC* [2001] 2 WLR 1344; Carruthers, *The Transfer of Property in the Conflict of Laws*, n 4 above, chs 8 and 9. See to similar effect the *UNCITRAL Legislative Guide on Secured Transactions* (Vienna, United Nations 2010) para 20: 'as intangible assets are not capable of physical possession, adopting the *lex situs* as the applicable conflict-of-laws rule would require the development of special rules and legal fictions for the determination of the actual location of various types of intangible asset. For this reason, the *Guide* does not consider the location of the asset as being the appropriate connecting factor for intangible assets and favours an approach generally based on the law of the location of the grantor'.

[12] For details of the consultation by the British Institute of International and Comparative Law, see pp 366 *et seq* below.

[13] See p 358 below.

[14] Council Directive 2002/47/EC of 6 June 2002 on financial collateral arrangements as regards linked systems and credit claims [2002] OJ L168/43 as amended by Council Directive 2009/44/EC of 6 May 2009 [2009] OJ L146/37.

[15] Roy Goode, Hideki Kanda and Karl Kreuzer, assisted by Christophe Bernasconi, *Hague Securities Convention: Explanatory Report* (Leiden, Koninklijk Brill NV, 2005) 20 ('Explanatory Report').

in Tokyo, where the first credit to the account was effected; the dispatch of all account statements from an office in Dublin; the administration and remittance of dividends from an office in Hong Kong; the obtaining of advice as to the ongoing status of the account from an office near the client's main office in Singapore; and the backing-up and monitoring of each securities account by two computer systems run from the bank's New Delhi and San Francisco offices, respectively. Accordingly the solution adopted was to select as the law governing all issues except purely contractual or purely personal issues[16] the law expressly provided by the account agreement to govern that account agreement or, if the account agreement expressly provided for the application of another law, that law,[17] provided that in either case the relevant intermediary had at the time of the agreement a qualifying office in the designated state.[18] The Convention is not yet in force.

Assignments of 'Debtor's Rights'

The Space Protocol to the Cape Town Convention provides a regime under which a creditor holding a registered international interest in a space asset may, either at the time of that registration or subsequently, record against the registration an assignment of debtor's rights to the creditor. Of the three categories of equipment covered by the Cape Town Convention, space assets are unique in that once launched they cease to be readily susceptible to the exercise of default remedies, though it is possible for an enforcing creditor to exercise some control, for example, by taking control of the command codes or by exercising a contractual right to terminate the debtor's access to the space asset and blocking such access. But the value of these remedies is limited. Greater importance is attached to the provision of debtor's rights as additional collateral, since these may be enforced against the account debtors (the debtor's debtors). In other words, funding for space assets is considered to be more in the nature of project finance than asset-based finance.

However, security interests in debtor's rights cannot be registered in isolation, because the registration system is based on the registration of interests in physical assets and requires that each asset be uniquely identified and registered separately. Debtor's rights, by contrast, are intangible and incapable of any standard system of unique identification. The Space Protocol overcomes this problem by allowing the creditor to protect this additional collateral by recording the assignment against the linked registered international interest, a recorded assignment having priority over a subsequently recorded assignment and over an unrecorded assignment.[19]

[16] Hague Convention 2006, Art 2.

[17] ibid Art 4(1).

[18] This was the shorthand expression used by the authors of the Explanatory Report (n 15 above) to denote an office fulfilling the requirements of Art 4 as to the maintenance of securities accounts in the designated state. See the Explanatory Report, n 15 above, p 68 *et seq*. Where the requirements of Art 4 are not fulfilled then one of the cascade of fall-back rules in Art 5 has to be applied.

[19] UNIDROIT, Protocol to the Convention on International Interests in Mobile Equipment on Matters specific to Space Assets ('Space Protocol') (Berlin, UNIDROIT, 2011), Art XIII. For a full analysis see the writer's Official Commentary on the Convention and Space Protocol (Rome, UNIDROIT, 2013) paras 3.45 *et seq*, 5.54 *et seq*.

Ordinary Non-documentary Intangibles

Matters Affecting the Debtor: The General Rule

When we come to ordinary non-documentary intangible movables (term loans, sale, lease and credit card receivables, mortgage debts, contract rights, intellectual property rights, and the like) certain things are clear. In general, anything that affects the debtor, such as the assignability of the debt vis-à-vis the debtor (including the effect of a no-assignment clause),[20] defences to the creditor's claim, rights of set-off and other grounds of discharge of the debtor, is governed by the law applicable to the debt, for the obvious reason that the debtor ought not to have its position affected by an assignment to which it is not a party. This is expressly provided by Rome I Regulation, article 14(2). On the other hand, the effect of a prohibition against assignment on the efficacy of the assignment as between assignor or its liquidator and assignee is of no concern to the debtor and will be governed not by article 14(2) but by the law applicable to the assignment agreement under Rome I Regulation, article 14(1), as a matter going to performance.[21]

What if the purported assignee is asserting an assignment that was never made? The issue here is whether a debtor who pays a purported assignee obtains a good discharge. That is undoubtedly a matter governed by the law applicable to the debt, not, however, because of article 14, which is plainly inapplicable, but under article 12(1)(b).[22]

Proprietary Effects as Between Assignor and Assignee

To the above rule there is one qualification. It is now generally accepted that as article 14 stands, the proprietary effects as between assignor and assignee as well as contractual effects are governed by the law applicable to the contract between

[20] Certain assignability issues do not concern the debtor. For example, a legal system might treat an assignment as void if it is by way of security or relates to future debts. The law applicable to this issue is that governing the contract of assignment (art 14(1)).

[21] See below and Francisco Garcimartin Alférez, 'Assignment of Claims in the Rome I Regulation: Article 14' in Franco Ferrari and Stefan Leible (eds), *Rome I Regulation: The Law Applicable to Contractual Obligations in Europe* (Munich, Sellier, 2009) 217, 231.

[22] So far as English law is concerned, the position of a debtor who in good faith pays a person wrongfully claiming to be an assignee is remarkably obscure. The question is which of two innocent parties should bear the risk, the creditor or the debtor. One of the few scholars to address the issue considers the risk is on the debtor, See Greg Tolhurst, *The Assignment of Contractual Rights* (Oxford, Hart Publishing, 2006) 387. This is almost certainly the position under English law. See to similar effect, from an American law perspective, Grant Gilmore, *Security Interests in Personal Property* (Boston, MA and Toronto, Little Brown & Co, 1965) 393, while drawing attention to what is now art 9-416(c) of the Uniform Commercial Code, which entitles the debtor to ask the assignee for reasonable proof of the assignment and, if this is not provided, to pay the assignor. Article 9.1.12 of the UNIDROIT Principles of International Commercial Contracts and art 11:303(2) of the Principles of European Contract Law do not allow payment to the assignor, merely a right to withhold payment to the assignee, while PECL, art 11:304 also entitles the debtor who pays the supposed assignee to a discharge unless the debtor could not have been unaware that such person was not the person entitled to performance. See to similar effect Dutch Civil Code, art 6:34. The prudent course for a debtor who is unsure of the status of the person claiming to be an assignee is to consult the creditor and, if the latter denies there has been a valid assignment and calls for payment, to interplead.

them,[23] a principle embodied in recital 38 of the Regulation. That is no doubt why the rule in Dicey, Morris and Collins, *The Conflict of Laws*[24] is not formulated in property terms at all but refers merely to the mutual *obligations* of assignor and assignee. This rule applies even though the debtor is affected as well as the intended assignee in that the debtor is not obliged to recognise an assignment which is invalid under the law applicable to it. This is not a true exception, because in proceedings against the debtor the validity of the assignment is a preliminary question which has to be answered by reference to the law governing the assignment.[25]

A rather different case is where it is asserted that the assignment is invalid because the assignor never acquired the title to the assigned claim in the first place. This is not a matter for the law governing the agreement to assign, rather it is a preliminary question which has to be answered by reference to its own applicable law.[26]

It has to be said that this focus in Rome I Regulation, article 14(1) on the *contract* between assignor and assignee is wholly illogical. It is possibly predicated on the mistaken assumption that an assignment depends on the validity of the underlying contract, but a more likely explanation is that the predecessor of article 14(1), namely, Article 12(1) of the Rome Convention, was conceived as purely contractual in character, and when recital 38 was introduced into the Rome I Regulation to encompass proprietary effects there was no corresponding change from the contract of assignment to the assignment itself in what is now article 14(1).

The fallacy of ascribing proprietary effects to a contract that does not also constitute a conveyance was convincingly demonstrated many years ago by Mark Moshinsky.[27] It is necessary to distinguish an agreement for transfer from the transfer itself. Where the assignment is effected by a distinct act, as where an agreement to assign is subsequently followed by an assignment, or where in a given legal system there is a notional, abstract transfer distinct from the contract, the assignment is in no way dependent on the validity of the contract[28] and, indeed, may be governed by its own distinct law. Further, it is perfectly possible to have an assignment with no underlying contract to assign, a point made by Professors Hugh Beale and Wolf-Georg Ringe in a discussion of assignment in the context of the proposed European sales law.[29]

It is interesting that in the case of a transfer of tangible movables, eg under a sale, the textbooks distinguish sharply between the contractual and the proprietary effects, the latter being governed by the *lex situs*. Why this distinction should be ignored in the case of intangible movables is not explained. But since the rule is confined to relations between assignor and assignee and does not engage third parties, the point is of little importance in practice, and anyway it falls outside the

[23] Namely, the law chosen by the parties (Rome I Regulation, srt 3(1)) or in the absence of choice the law determined by the applicable rule in art 4.

[24] Lawrence Collins (gen ed), *Dicey, Morris and Collins: The Conflict of Laws*, 15th edn (London, Sweet & Maxwell, 2012) rule 135(a).

[25] Trevor Hartley, 'Choice of Law regarding the Voluntary Assignment of Contractual Obligations under the Rome I Regulation' (2011) *International and Comparative Law Quarterly* 29, 36–37.

[26] ibid 34.

[27] 'The Assignment of Debts in the Conflict of Laws' (1992) 108 *Law Quarterly Review* 591.

[28] See Garcimartin, 'Assignment of Claims in the Rome I Regulation', n 21 above, 225.

[29] 'Transfer of Rights and Obligations' in Gerhard Danneman and Stefan Vogenauer (eds), *The Common European Sales Law in Context* (Oxford University Press, 2013) 524.

remit given by the European Commission to the BIICL Study Group[30] and is not discussed further.

Third Party Issues

Among the relationships not covered by article 14 are disputes between an assignee and (a) the assignor's trustee or liquidator where occupying the position of a third party;[31] (b) an attachment creditor of the assignor; (c) a competing assignee. Moreover, competing claims to proceeds which are not the subject of a contractual provision in the assignment agreement are governed not by the Rome I Regulation but by the Rome II Regulation.[32]

Some years ago, the European Commission proposed a sensible new rule that would subject these third party issues to the law of the assignor's habitual residence. The proposal received strong support but also determined opposition, particularly from UK lawyers acting in securitisation arrangements, who favour the law applicable to the assigned debts, while others favoured freedom of choice of the parties to the assignment.

In view of this division of opinion, the European Commission invited the British Institute of International and Comparative Law to prepare a study on the question of the effectiveness of an assignment or subrogation of a claim against third parties and the priority of the assigned or subrogated claim over a right of another person. The BICCL team, coordinated by Dr Eva Lein of BICCL and Professor Andrew Dickinson then of the University of Sydney, undertook a major programme of comparative research, drawing on national rapporteurs from 12 European countries and working with an expert group of academic and practising lawyers and representatives of ISDA and AFME. The Final Report,[33] presented to the Commission in December 2011, contains a wealth of statistical, empirical and legal analysis. Its recommendations are discussed a little later in this chapter.

SPECIFIC PRIORITY ISSUES

Assignee versus Assignor's Liquidator

In an excellent article some three years ago,[34] Professor Trevor Hartley made the point that where the assignor (the creditor) goes into liquidation it is necessary to distinguish cases where the liquidator is not asserting rights greater than those of the

[30] See p 366 below.

[31] See below.

[32] Council Regulation (EC) 864/2007 of 11 July 2007 on the law applicable to non-contractual obligations ('Rome II Regulation') [2007] OJ L 199/40. See p 366 below.

[33] British Institute of International and Comparative Law, *Study on the Question of Effectiveness of an Assignment or Subrogation of a Claim against Third Parties and the Priority of the Assigned or Subrogated Claim over a Right of Another Person: Final Report* (London, British Institute of International and Comparative Law, 2011) ('BIICL Final Report'), available at www.ec.europa.eu/justice/civil/files/report_assignment_en.pdf.

[34] Hartley, 'Choice of Law regarding the Voluntary Assignment of Contractual Obligations under the Rome I Regulation', n 25 above.

creditor (the assignor) and cases where he is invoking an overriding right by virtue of a rule of insolvency law, for example, avoidance of the assignment as a preference or a transaction in fraud of creditors. In the former case the liquidator simply stands in the shoes of the insolvent assignor and is not a third party for the purpose of any proposed new rule, and the liquidation is of no significance in determining the applicable law, which is the law governing the assignment. By contrast, if the liquidator is asserting an overriding right by virtue of insolvency law then he is a third party[35] and the applicable law will be the *lex concursus* and, where the assignor's centre of main interests is in an EU Member State and the insolvency proceedings are brought in a Member State other than Denmark, the EC Insolvency Regulation.[36] In this situation there seems no scope for the operation of any addition to article 14.

The interrelationship between the Rome I Regulation and the Insolvency Regulation is not free from difficulty but the position would appear to be as follows. In the case mentioned above, the effects of insolvency, for example, grounds of avoidance of a transaction, are governed by the *lex concursus* under article 4 of the Insolvency Regulation but, subject to this, rights *in rem* acquired by the assignee which are situated within the territory of another Member State at the time of opening of the insolvency proceedings are not affected.[37] For this purpose an assigned debt is situated in the Member State within the territory of which the obligor has its centre of main interests.[38] Article 5(1) of the Insolvency Regulation is attracted if this is anywhere outside the Member State in which the insolvency proceedings are opened. However, this does not necessarily mean that the law of that Member State governs the efficacy of the assignment. Article 5(1) does not lay down a conflict of laws rule; the applicable law remains determined by the conflict of laws rule of the forum,[39] which in a case within Rome I Regulation, article 14(1) leads to the law applicable to the agreement to assign.

The following example illustrates the points made above:

> A, an English factoring company, enters into a factoring agreement with B for the purchase of B's ongoing stream of receivables arising from export transactions, these to vest automatically in A on coming into existence. The agreement, which is expressed to be governed by English law, provides for advance payments to be made to B by A. B's centre of main interests is in the Netherlands but the receivables are or will become due from customers in England. Various receivables arising from contracts already concluded at the time of the factoring agreement come into existence. B then goes into liquidation in the Netherlands. The liquidator challenges A's title to the receivables on the ground that (a) the formalities prescribed by Dutch law for perfection of an assignment of receivables were not observed; and (b) the assignment of some of the receivables was a fraudulent conveyance for the purposes of Dutch insolvency law.

35 ibid 38.

36 Council Regulation (EC) 1346/2000 of 29 May 2000 on insolvency proceedings ('Insolvency Regulation') [2000] OJ L160/1, as amended. For this purpose, references to 'debtor' in the Regulation denote the insolvent assignor, not the account debtor under an assigned claim, who to avoid confusion is here labelled the 'obligor'.

37 Insolvency Regulation, art 5(1).

38 ibid art 2(g).

39 Roy Goode, *Principles of Corporate Insolvency Law*, 4th edn (London, Sweet & Maxwell, 2011) para 15-88.

Here, ground (a) is based on the general law, not on some overriding provision of insolvency law, so that the liquidator is not a third party but stands in the shoes of the assignor, the validity of the assignment is governed by English law under Rome I Regulation, article 14(1), and A's claim is not affected by the insolvency proceedings against B in the Netherlands, the assigned debts being situated in England.[40] Ground (b), however, is a special rule of insolvency law, as regards which the liquidator is a third party, and the issue of fraudulent preference is in any event governed by Insolvency Regulation, article 4(2)(m), and is not excluded under article 13. The assignment will therefore be invalid if constituting a fraudulent conveyance under Dutch insolvency law.

Another example, given by Hartley, of an overriding right in the liquidator is avoidance of an assignment against insolvency creditors for want of the registration required by statute.

Assignee versus Assignor's Attachment Creditor

This case is more complex in that it depends on the basis of the attaching debtor's claim. If this is based on the invalidity of the assignment, that is a claim governed by the law applicable to the assignment. If the attachment is sought in the mistaken belief that the assignor is still the owner of the claim, it should be refused. Where, on the other hand, the question is whether the claim can be attached even against an assignee, the question is one of priorities. The distinction is well brought out in the decision of the Court of Appeal in *Raiffeisen Zentralbank Österreich AG v Five Star Trading LLC*,[41] a decision on the 1980 Rome Convention on the Law applicable to Contractual Obligations. In that case:

> Five Star borrowed money from RZB to finance the purchase of a ship, the loan being secured by a mortgage of the ship and an assignment of an insurance policy covering it and issued by French insurers, the insurance policy and the assignment being governed by English law. The assignment was notified to the insurers by fax, a mode of notification valid under English law but not under French law.
>
> Subsequently the ship was involved in a collision. Among the claimants were cargo owners, who contended that they were entitled to attach the insurance policy as being an asset of Five Star. They were granted a provisional attachment by the Paris Tribunal de Grande Instance de Commerce, stayed to await the outcome of proceedings in England brought by RZB as assignee of the policy claiming a declaration of its entitlement, the cargo owners being subsequently joined in the proceedings.
>
> RZB argued that the question was whether the claim was validly assigned to it, this being a contractual matter governed by English law. The cargo owners contended that the issue was one of priority as between them and RZB and fell outside the Convention, being

[40] The application of Insolvency Regulation, art 5(1) does not, however, depend on this; it suffices if the assigned debts are situated anywhere outside the Netherlands. So if, for example, they were due from obligors having their centres of administration in France this would suffice to ensure the application of art 5(1) but the law governing the efficacy of the assignment as between assignor and assignee would be English law, not French law. See Goode, *Principles of Corporate Insolvency Law*, n 39 above.

[41] *Raiffeisen Zentralbank Österreich AG v Five Star Trading LLC* [2001] 2 WLR 1344.

a property law issue governed by the *lex situs* of the debt, ie French law. The Court of Appeal applied English law, holding that the question whom the insurer had to pay was a contractual matter governed by English law[42] and that the notified assignment was binding on the insurers.[43]

If the question had truly been one of priority, as contended by the cargo owners, then under English conflict of laws rules French law would have been applied to determine whether the attachment overrode RZB's title. But the evidence indicated that the French court had proceeded on the basis that the insurance policy was an asset of Five Star, whereas by reason of the assignment (governed by English law) it was not. So the issue was not a priority issue at all. As Hartley puts it, since the attachment creditors were not invoking a priority rule but only attaching on the basis that the asset was still vested in the assignor, they stood in no better position than the assignor itself. The position would have been otherwise if under French law the attachment had the effect of overriding the assignee's title.

A Competing Assignee

It may be necessary to distinguish the assignment of a single debt from an assignment of multiple debts or future debts. This distinction is drawn by Dicey, Morris and Collins in *The Conflict of* Laws,[44] which, however, does not address the former in the Comment and simply provides in rule 135 that, *semble*, 'the validity and effect of an assignment may be governed by the law with which the right assigned has its most significant connection'. That is as far as the guidance goes and it makes no specific mention of any of the three specific priority issues identified above. Cheshire, North and Fawcett, *Private International Law*,[45] at least propound a rule, albeit a controversial one:

> The law governing the right to which the assignment relates is the most satisfactory system by which to determine the ranking of competing claimants where the creditor has made more than one contractual assignment.

[42] This is questionable. An assignment does not make the assignee a party to the contract and it is not by virtue of the contract that the assignee acquires rights against the assignor's counterparty but by virtue of the assignment itself. The issue is whether at a given time the contractual rights belonged to the assignor or to the assignee. That is a question of property. The fact that the subject matter of the assignment consists of contractual rights is not to the point. But on the facts of the case this characterisation made no difference, the assignment being expressed to be governed by English law, under which it was valid, so that title to the policy moneys passed to RZB, with the result that they were no longer an asset of Five Star. Mance LJ concluded that in any event Rome Convention, Arts 12(1) and (2) plainly covered the situation. It is now clear from recital 38 to what is now the Rome I Regulation that in the relations between assignor and assignee there is no distinction between contractual and proprietary aspects, both being governed by the law applicable to the agreement to assign. See further Michael Bridge, 'The Proprietary Aspects of Assignment and Choice of Law' (2009) 125 *Law Quarterly Review* 671, esp 687, where Prof Bridge also takes the view that the assignee's acquisition of ownership of the contractual right to the insurance moneys was a matter of property, not merely of contract.

[43] Presumably the Tribunal de Commerce then discharged the provisional attachment but I have not been able to verify this.

[44] *Dicey, Morris and Collins: The Conflict of Laws*, n 24 above, para 24-079.

[45] James Fawcett, Janeen Carruthers and Peter North (eds), *Cheshire, North and Fawcett: Private International Law*, 14th edn (Oxford University Press, 2008) 1234.

As will be seen from the BIICL study,[46] this view receives support from a substantial proportion of the securitisation industry who responded to the consultation paper, but is opposed by the factoring and invoice discounting industry and by some securitisers.

Cheshire, North and Fawcett do admit an exception, where both assignments are governed by the same law, in which case, they say, it is that law that should determine priorities. The problem with this apparently reasonable solution is that it lacks transparency vis-à-vis third parties; there is no external connecting factor, merely a couple of internal governing laws which themselves may result from an express choice of law. It is not without significance that this did not feature as an option in the responses of consultees to the BIICL study.

Finally, by the time the dispute between the competing assignees surfaces the debt may no longer exist; it may have been collected by one of the assignees, so that the dispute now concerns title to the proceeds. There is obviously no sense in applying the law governing a debt which has ceased to exist.[47]

What, then, should be the law governing the priority of competing assignments? Addressing this issue was one of the main tasks of the BIICL Study. The resulting report is discussed below.

Treatment of Proceeds

As Between Assignor/Assignor's Liquidator and Assignee

In invoice discounting and other forms of non-notification finance, the account debtor is not notified of the assignment and it is left to the assignor to collect in the assigned debts and account for them to the assignee. In English assignment agreements, it is customary to include a provision that the assignor will hold the proceeds on trust for the assignee until handing them over and this suffices to protect the assignee from the effects of the assignor's insolvency, since the proceeds will not form part of the assignor's assets; indeed, this would be so even without an express trust provision. Assuming that the agreement to assign is governed by English law, either because of an express provision to that effect or because of the rules in the Rome I Regulation,[48] the rights of the assignee in regard to the proceeds will be governed by English law as the law of the contract governing the assignment.[49]

[46] See to similar effect Carruthers, *The Transfer of Property in the Conflict of Laws*, n 4 above, para 6.40.

[47] See below.

[48] Rome I Regulation, art 4(1) and (2) states that in general the law applicable to the sale of goods or the supply of services is governed by the law of the country where the seller or service provider has its habitual residence. However, art 4 is curiously silent as to the law applicable to a contract for the assignment of intangible movables. In most cases this is likely to be the law of the habitual residence of the assignor, either by analogy with the sale of goods or the supply of services (art 4(1)(a), (b)) or because it is the assignor whose performance is characteristic of the contract (art 4(2)).

[49] Rome I Regulation, art 14(1). It may be noted that an express trust of proceeds contained in the assignment agreement is governed by the Rome I Regulation, not by the Rome II Regulation, art 1(2)(e) of which excludes non-contractual obligations arising out of the relations between the settlors, trustees and beneficiaries of a trust created voluntarily. It is thought that proceeds held on trust by an assignor under a trust provision in an assignment do not constitute 'assets placed under the control of a trustee'

Where, however, the contract makes no provision for the application of proceeds, the Rome I Regulation does not apply and the case falls within the Rome II Regulation as a claim based on unjust enrichment.[50] Article 10(1) of the Rome II Regulation applies the law governing a closely connected pre-existing relationship between assignor and assignee, namely, the relationship established by the agreement to assign. So the result under the Rome II Regulation is the same as where there is an express proceeds clause governed by the Rome I Regulation.

As Between Competing Assignees

Where there are successive assignments to A and B and the proceeds are collected by B, any claim by A against B will normally be based on unjust enrichment. If both parties have their habitual residence in the same country it is the law of that country that will determine priority.[51] If their habitual residence is in different countries, then the law of the country in which the unjust enrichment took place will apply,[52] or, if the unjust enrichment claim is manifestly more closely connected with another country, that country.[53] It is for the applicable law to determine whether A's claim is proprietary, in which case it will survive B's insolvency, as under English law,[54] or is purely personal, in which event A will simply be an unsecured creditor, as under German law. There is much controversy as to these provisions and space does not allow them to be explored here.[55]

BIICL REPORT

The BIICL Study, though handicapped by a very disappointing response rate, was a major research undertaking which included a collection of statistical data; an

so as to fall within the 1986 Hague Convention on the Law applicable to Trusts and their Recognition, implemented in the United Kingdom by the Recognition of Trusts Act 1987; but even if the Convention applies, the trust is governed by the law chosen by the parties (Art 6), which is that governing the contract as a whole, including the trust provision, so that the applicable law is the same as under Rome I Regulation, art 14(1). For a detailed analysis see Andrew Dickinson, *The Rome II Regulation: The Law Applicable to Non-Contractual Obligations* (Oxford University Press, 2008) chs 3 and 4 and *Updating Supplement* (2010).

[50] However, the BIICL Final Report, n 33 above, 18, 379, 382, 406, advocates extension of the Rome I Regulation to cover claims in unjust enrichment arising from a contractual relationship. The question has long been controversial. See, eg Stephen Pitel, 'Rome II and Choice of Law for Unjust Enrichment' in John Ahern and William Binchy (eds), *The Rome II Regulation on the Law Applicable to Non-Contractual Obligations* (Leiden, Martinus Nijhoff Publishers, 2009) 231, 239 and Andrew Scott, 'The Scope of Non-Contractual Obligations' in the same volume at 57.

[51] Rome II Regulation, art 10(1).

[52] ibid art 10(3).

[53] ibid art 10(4).

[54] To similar effect is art III 5.122 of the (European) Draft Common Frame of Reference, which provides that where the debtor who pays the assignor is discharged 'the assignee's right against the assignor to the proceeds has priority over the right of a competing claimant so long as the proceeds are held by the assignor and are reasonably identifiable from the other assets of the assignor'.

[55] For detailed analyses see Dickinson, *The Rome II Regulation*, n 49 above; Pitel, 'Rome II and Choice of Law for Unjust Enrichment', n 50 above, 246–53; *Dicey, Morris and Collins: The Conflict of Laws,* n 24 above, paras 36-037–36-045.

EU-wide empirical analysis of practical problems encountered in different market sectors in cross-border assignment and subrogation cases; a legal analysis based on national reports from 12 EU Member States; and a comprehensive examination of the arguments for and against a new conflict of laws solution. The study was opposed to special rules for special types of transaction on the ground that this was likely to result in more uncertainty and characterisation issues.[56] However, it considered that the transfer of intermediated securities should be excluded as being governed by special rules.[57]

Some 80 per cent of responding stakeholders expressed a need for new legislation on the law applicable to third party effects of an assignment. Of the various possible solutions, only three came into serious consideration, namely, the law applicable to the contract between assignor and assignee (11 per cent), the law applicable to the assigned claim (30 per cent), and the law of the assignor's habitual residence (44 per cent). As regards the second and third of these, the securitisation industry largely favoured the law of the assigned claim while the factoring and invoice discounting industries were equally strongly supportive of the law of the assignor's habitual residence. The securitisers were content that if the general rule adopted was the law of the assigned claim there should be an exception for factoring and invoice discounting in favour of the law of the assignor's habitual residence.

Solution 1: Law Applicable to the Contract Between Assignor and Assignee

The Study describes the advantages and disadvantages as follows:[58]

Advantages

- flexibility for the different sectors;
- no evidence of abuse in practice in the Netherlands, where the solution has been implemented;
- avoidance or reduction of the need for sector-specific rules;
- synergy, reduction of applicable laws and of complexity;
- suitability for the assignment of future claims.

Disadvantages

- possible prejudice to third parties, however reduced by the suggested limited party autonomy approach;
- risk of the avoidance of publicity requirements.

[56] At p 364.
[57] ibid. See above, p 357.
[58] pp 385 *et seq*.

Solution 2: Law Applicable to the Assigned Claim

The BIICL Study sets out the perceived advantages and disadvantages of the law applicable to the assigned claim as follows[59]:

Advantages

— consistency of the connecting factor;
— synergy and cost-effectiveness;
— suitability for financial claims.

Disadvantages

— unsuitability for future claims;
— complexity and inefficiency for bulk assignments;
— uncertainty as to the law applicable to the claim assigned.

Solution 3: Law of Assignor's Habitual Residence

The BIICL Study summarises the advantages and disadvantages of the law of the assignor's habitual residence in the following terms:[60]

Advantages

— single connecting factor;
— suitability for bulk assignments, and for assignments of receivables under contracts not yet in existence;
— synergies with the Insolvency Regulation and the UN Convention on the Assignment of Receivables in International Trade;
— suitability for factoring transactions;
— suitability to resolve conflicts between competing right-holders.

Disadvantages

— problems in defining 'habitual residence' as the connecting factor;
— increased transaction costs, complexity;
— conflict of connecting factors;
— problems in practice, in particular in Belgium and Luxembourg;
— unsuitability for financial claims;
— inflexibility.

[59] pp 390 *et seq.*
[60] pp 394 *et seq.*

Recommendations

The Study Group advanced all three possible solutions without stating a preference but on the basis that (a) the law applicable to the contract of assignment should apply only where chosen by the parties and then only if the chosen law was that of the assigned claim or the law of the country in which the assignor has its habitual residence; and (b) whichever solution was adopted the selected law should govern all property aspects of an assignment without distinguishing between whether they arise in the relationship between assignor and assignee or against third parties, with consideration being given to a moderate use of sector-specific rules.[61]

REFLECTIONS ON THE RECOMMENDATIONS IN THE BIICL REPORT

Overview

The BIICL Study Group engaged in Herculean efforts to produce its report and is to be congratulated on its compilations of statistical data, its national reports on the applicable law and its laying out of the issues. But at the end of the day one is left with a sense of disappointment. Asked to come up with a report providing the basis for a new conflict of laws solution on third party aspects of assignment, the BIICL felt unable to put forward an unequivocal set of rules because of differences of opinion among the members of the Expert Group and consultees. Instead, the Institute found itself with no alternative but to present to the Commission with three options and no indication of preference, coupled with a recommendation that whichever option was adopted the conflict rule should govern all proprietary aspects regardless of the relationship under consideration.

There are three comments that can be made on these proposed alternative solutions.

First, solution 1 (law applicable to the contract of assignment) is not really a solution at all, it simply gives the parties a choice whether to adopt solution 2 (law of the assigned claim) or solution 3 (law of the assignor's habitual residence). But these alternatives are far apart. Why should it be open to the parties to an assignment to dictate third party effects under a choice of law that will not be visible to third parties? Moreover, as the Report points out,[62] competing assignments may specify different laws. For example, assignment 1 specifies the law applicable to the assigned claim while assignment 2 designates the law of the assignor's habitual residence. The Report refers to the 'last event' rule as one way of resolving the problem but then goes on to say that it would seem preferable to have a single connecting factor, which seems to suggest a rule that is not based on party choice at all but on the second option, the third option or some other unstated option.

Secondly, the alleged merits and demerits of each of the remaining alternatives could have received rather more critical examination than they did. Instead, they

61 BIICL Final Report, n 33 above, 402–3.

62 ibid 388–89.

are reproduced without significant comment.[63] Where the Report does offer some independent thinking, as instanced by its proposed 'super conflict' rule to deal with cases where the primary rule is that of the assignor's habitual residence and the assignor changes its habitual residence between the first and the second assignments, the rule proposed makes little sense either in commercial or in conceptual terms.[64]

Thirdly, some of the conclusions of the Report do not match the preceding analysis. For example, the factors and invoice discounters want the habitual residence rule; the securitisers and their lawyers want the law governing the assigned claim but are not opposed to a carve-out for the factoring and discounting industry.[65] So there is general agreement that if the general rule were to be in favour of the law of the assigned claim there should be a factor-specific exception. Yet the Report suggests exactly the opposite, stating that only one company representing 3 per cent of stakeholders supported a sector-specific solution and that the overwhelming majority advocated a single rule for all sectors,[66] and it goes on to set out what it sees as the *disadvantages* of such a carve-out which the factors and invoice discounters want and to which the securitisers do not object. The overwhelming consideration seems to be to have a single law governing all proprietary aspects without differentiation.

It is worth looking in a little more detail at the primary ground on which a substantial part (but by no means all) of the securitisation industry wanted a conflict of laws rule based on the law of the assigned claim and opposed the European Commission's proposal that the applicable law for third party issues should be the law of the habitual residence of the assignor, and the perceived disadvantages of such a rule.

Claimed Advantage of Applying the Law of the Assigned Claim

The primary advantage claimed is that there would be a reduction in the number of laws applicable to the assignment, with a consequent reduction in cost. As the evidence submitted to the Study Group shows, it is the practice of securitisers, as part of their legal due diligence, to analyse each individual debt to seek to determine the applicable law; the formalities prescribed by that law; the assignability of the claims; the proprietary effects of the assignment and the effectiveness of the assignment as between assignor and assignee; the enforceability of the assignment against the debtor; and its enforceability against third parties.[67] Accordingly, the securitisers say that selection of the law of the assignor's habitual residence to govern third party effects would simply add one more legal system to those already examined as

[63] For example, a disadvantage of the rule applying the law of the assignor's habitual residence is said to be that it is inflexible, yet it is a key recommendation of the Report that whichever rule is selected to determine the law applicable to third party effects that law should govern *all* relationships.

[64] See p 364 below.

[65] BIICL Final Report, n 33 above, 117–18.

[66] ibid 400.

[67] See, eg the response of an unidentified French company reproduced in BIICL Final Report, n 33 above, Annex, file 1.PDF. See also Joanna Perkins, 'Proprietary Issues arising from the Assignment of Debts: A New Rule?' (2010) 6 *Journal of International Banking and Financial Law* 333.

part of the legal due diligence. As will be seen,[68] this is a misconception; far from adding to the number of legal systems to be consulted on proprietary effects, the application of the law of the assignor's habitual residence reduces them. Securitisers are also concerned at what they see as the lack of legal certainty in determining the habitual residence of the assignor as defined in Rome I Regulation, article 19. The Report addressed this concern by proposing that Rome I Regulation, article 19(2) and (3) should be disapplied, leaving only the place of central administration as regards other bodies, corporate or unincorporated.

Different Viewpoints of the Two Main Industries

When one examines the advantages and disadvantages perceived for each of the two primary alternatives, it is clear that they reflect the different needs and practices of the securitisation industry, on the one hand, and the factoring and invoice discount industry, on the other. As stated above, securitisers examine each assigned contract and check the applicable law and its effects as regards all relationships;[69] factors and invoice discounters are not geared up to do so, so that for the latter the application of the law of the assigned claim would entail a substantial additional burden, particularly since under a whole turnover agreement the assignment may cover debts not notified to the factor. So, for factors and discounters the law of the assignor's habitual residence provides a single law which is known at the outset without the need to examine individual assigned contracts and which, moreover, can be applied to the assignment of future debts arising under contracts not yet concluded and whose governing law will therefore not be known.[70] The Report concedes[71] that for such assignments the solution does not work and it would be necessary to specify that the relevant date for ascertaining each such future debt would be the date it came into existence. One would think that this solution is far from simple. In any event, there are other serious objections to the selection of the law of the assigned claim to govern priority between competing assignees. These are set out below.

Report's Final Conclusions

The Report sensibly concludes that no general solution is perfect. There are in fact only two solutions receiving significant support and the third, the law applicable to the assignment, should be dropped, as suggested earlier. The Report does not indicate any preference for one solution over the others but strongly advocates a single rule covering *all* third party proprietary interests, regardless of the relationship involved.

[68] See p 375 below.

[69] This legal due diligence is partly driven by the demands of rating agencies for information that will enable them to assess the rating of the notes or bonds issued on the market.

[70] See Garcimartin, 'Assignment of Claims in the Rome I Regulation', n 21 above, 249, arguing that the law-of-the-assignor approach offers an adequate solution for future and bulk assignments and one which should in principle be acceptable to the securitisation industry.

[71] BIICL Final Report, n 33 above, 391.

In other words, the same rule should apply to proprietary effects as between assignor and assignee, assignee and attachment creditors, assignee and the assignor's insolvency trustee or liquidator and competing assignees. That is a major change from existing conflict of laws rules and one would have thought should receive extended reasoning. Instead, this proposal is justified in just two sentences.[72] The first states simply that there would be only one applicable rule governing the proprietary aspects of assignment and the number of potentially applicable laws could be reduced from the outset. The second asserts that 'the current artificial distinction between property aspects as between assignor and assignee and as against third parties could be removed'. Neither of these arguments is in the slightest convincing.

'One Rule': The Law of the Assigned Claim

It would no doubt be feasible to apply the law of the assignor's place of business to all third party relationships where a single debt is assigned. But if the law applicable to the assigned claims were to be adopted as the conflict of laws rule in relation to bulk assignments there would not be a single law at all but a potential plethora of laws varying according to the law governing each particular assignment. In that scenario, only a preoccupation with legal tidiness could justify the argument in favour of applying the same law to proprietary effects regardless of the relationship under consideration and even without consideration of the question of what constitutes a third party. As between the assignor and the assignee, the effect of a valid assignment is to transfer ownership of the assigned debts to the assignee, a matter of great importance to the assignee if the assignor should become insolvent after collecting in the debts but before accounting for them to the assignee. What possible justification can there be for subjecting the efficacy of the assignment as between assignor and assignee, a matter of no concern to the debtor, to the law applicable to each assigned claim? What can be the rationality of a rule that would require a liquidator or trustee in bankruptcy of the assignor to examine every one of what may be hundreds or even thousands of contracts, identify the applicable law and then determine whether the collected proceeds of the assigned debts belong to the assignee or remain part of the assignor's estate? As we have seen, unless asserting an overriding right under insolvency law, a liquidator is not a third party but stands in the shoes of the assignor, so that an assignment effective as between assignor and assignee should be equally effective against the assignor's liquidator, subject to any overriding legislation of the *lex concursus*.[73]

The argument for the application of the law of the assigned claim may be based on the common misconception that the obligor's duty is to pay the assignee with

[72] ibid 402.

[73] For example, where a company registered in the United Kingdom grants a security assignment or charge which is registrable under Companies Act 2006, s 859A but is not registered, the assignment or charge is void against the liquidator, an administrator and a creditor in UK insolvency proceedings (Companies Act 2006, s 859H(3)) regardless of the law otherwise applicable to the assignment or charge.

the best title to the debt.[74] That is certainly not the case under English law. If the assignee fails to give the debtor notice of assignment, the debtor obtains a good discharge by paying the assignor, and the fact that as between assignor and assignee it is the latter who has best title to the debt is irrelevant.[75] Similarly, where there are two successive assignments the debtor is entitled to pay the assignee who first gives notice of assignment and has no obligation to investigate which assignee has priority. Let us assume, for example, that under two assignments governed by English law, C assigns first to A1 and then to A2 a debt due from D, A2 purchasing the debt with knowledge of the prior assignment to A1 but being the first to give written notice of assignment to D. It is clear that D obtains a good discharge on paying A2,[76] but it is equally clear that the best title to the debt is vested in A1, who has a proprietary claim for any moneys received from D by A2. In other words, priority between competing assignees has no necessary connection with the question whether the debtor obtains a good discharge by paying one creditor rather than another and is not the debtor's concern.[77]

It would be hard to think of a more impracticable rule than that which applies the law of the assigned claim. The point was made with great clarity many years ago in a comprehensive article by Professor Catherine Walsh:[78]

> However, in modern financing practice, the assignment of multiple and future receivables in a single transaction is commonplace, whether the assignment involves the outright sale of receivables as in a factoring or securitization arrangement, or their assignment merely

[74] That seems to have been the thinking behind the approach taken by the Bank of England's Financial Markets Law Committee. See *Issue 121: European Commission Final Proposal for a Regulation on the Law Applicable to Contractual Obligations ('Rome I')* (April 2006, para 9.4; October 2006, 5), which stated that 'Article 13(3) arguably ignores the important principle of debtor protection'; Joanna Perkins, 'A Question of Priorities: Choice of Law and Proprietary Aspects of the Assignment of Debts' (2008) *Law and Financial Markets Review* 238, 240. However, in its later paper *Issue 137: European Commission Review of Article 14: Assignment* (March 2010), the FMLC recognised the need to reach a compromise between the law of the assigned obligation and the law of the assignor's habitual residence (by exceptions in favour of the factoring and related industries and assignments by consumers), while still maintaining that the habitual residence rule 'would unfairly prejudice the interests of the underlying debtor' and that it 'is important for several reasons for the underlying debtor to be able to identify the person entitled to lay claim to the debt in priority to other assignees' (para 2.1.3).

[75] *Bence v Shearman* [1898] 2 Ch 582. See to the same effect *Principles of European Contract Law, Part 3* (The Hague, Kluwer law International, 2003) art 11:303(1), (3); *UNIDROIT Principles of International Commercial Contracts 2010* (Rome, UNIDROIT, 2010) art 9.1.10.

[76] The reasoning is the same, namely, that in the absence of notice from the first assignee the debtor is entitled to assume from the second assignee's notice of assignment that the debt has become vested in the second assignee. See to the same effect the UNIDROIT Principles, n 75 above, art 9.1.11, which states that the debtor is discharged if he pays the first assignee to give notice.

[77] In the illustration given by Perkins the obligor receives notices from both assignees. In that situation, contrary to what is suggested, it is not necessary for the debtor to work out which of the assignees has priority. If he pays the second assignee before receiving notice of the first assignment he obtains a good discharge. If he has not paid the second assignee before receiving notice of the first assignment then, depending on the applicable law, he can either still pay the second assignee (the solution adopted by the UNIDROIT Principles, n 75 above, or invoke appropriate procedures such as interpleader or a payment into court. But the case where only one notice of assignment is given makes the point more sharply that the party from whom the debtor can get a good discharge by payment does not have to be the one with the strongest title to the debt.

[78] Catherine Walsh, 'Receivables Financing and the Conflict of Laws: The UNCITRAL Draft Convention on the Assignment of Receivables in International Trade' (2001–2002) 106 *Dickinson Law Review* 159, 174.

> as collateral for a secured obligation. This practical reality makes application of the law governing the assigned debt a commercially inefficient solution. The assignee would need to scrutinize each of the assigned contracts to determine the applicable law and would then have to conform to the priority rules of all relevant states. Priority would vary for different receivables depending on their governing law, increasing the costs of dispute resolution and insolvency administration. If the assignment included future receivables owing by as-yet-unidentified debtors, the assignee might not even be able to predict which laws might potentially apply.
>
> It is the practical demands of modern receivables financing which ultimately led the [UNCITRAL] Commission to endorse the law of the assignor's location as the most appropriate choice of law rule for priority. It is the only approach capable of supplying a single predictable governing law for the global assignment of multiple receivables owing by debtors in different states and for the assignment of future receivables, thereby vastly reducing the inquiry and monitoring burden on the assignee.
>
> The superiority of the assignor location rule has been recognized by analysts who have examined the issue with the practical realities of modern global assignment practices in mind.

To illustrate the point, let us suppose that an assignor based in London wishes to assign to an assignee also based in London, under an agreement expressed to be governed by English law, the assignor's rights under four sale contracts, one of which is governed by French law, one by German law, one by Spanish law and the fourth by Italian law. Does it really make sense to have a rule that requires the validity of the assignment as between assignor and assignee to be separately tested against French law for the first assignment, German law for the second, Spanish law for the third and Italian law for the fourth? By contrast, the case for adopting the law of the assignor's habitual residence has been convincingly demonstrated not only by Professor Walsh but by other scholars.[79]

Supposed Artificiality of the Distinction

These considerations make it difficult to understand the desire to remove what the Report refers to as 'the current artificial distinction between property aspects, as between assignor and assignee and against third parties'.[80] There would be force in this observation in the case of the assignment of a single debt, which could sensibly be treated in the same way as the sale of goods, where the *lex situs* is applied both to the transfer of ownership as between seller and buyer and to the effects of the sale vis-à-vis third parties. But in the case of assignments of multiple debts, the distinction between the assignor-assignee relationship and third party relationships, far from being artificial, responds to commercial realities. What the parties want is one law to govern the effects of the assignment as between themselves. They do not want to find such effects dependent on a possible diverse range of laws governing different claims each of which can be determined only by examining the terms of each assigned contract.

[79] See p 375 below.

[80] BIICL Final Report, n 33 above, 402, 409.

Law of the Assignor's Habitual Residence

If there is to be one rule it is surely clear that it cannot be the law applicable to the assigned claim. The factoring and invoice discounting industry would not be willing to accept it because of the substantial additional burdens imposed, while, on the other hand, the Report argues that there could be difficulty in defining factoring and invoice discounting for the purpose of a carve-out. That should not be beyond the wit of man. But the simpler solution is to say that all third party proprietary effects are governed by the law of the assignor's habitual residence. The securitisers say that this would impose an additional burden on them. But that is surely to view the matter from the wrong end of the telescope. We are only talking about third party effects. It must be much easier and cheaper for securitisers to examine a single law, the law of the assignor's habitual residence, than it is to look at the variety of legal systems covering the securitised claims. Moreover, securitisers already have to look at the law of the assignor's place of business to see whether assignments of receivables are required to be registered and, if so, to search the register,[81] and, more generally, will conduct a due diligence exercise on the assignor as originator. Factors and invoice discounters, for their part, would face major additional burdens, and, indeed, have to change their systems, if they had to examine every assigned contract and then research each applicable law to determine the third party effects of the assignment.

As noted above, the habitual residence rule is that adopted by the 2001 UN Convention on the Assignment of Receivables in International Trade,[82] and its several advantages were trenchantly described by a Dutch scholar and practitioner in the following terms:

> There are good reasons for adopting this conflicts rule. First of all, the place of business or residence of the assignor is the connecting factor that places the issues in their natural environment. That is where his wealth is showing, where he participates in trade and commerce, where third parties act on the appearance of solvency, where he is declared insolvent or bankrupt …
>
> Secondly, the place of business of the assignee is an easily ascertainable connecting factor. It is stable and foreseeable for all parties involved …
>
> Thirdly, the proposed conflicts rule does not incur the practical difficulties that would result from conflicting rules that apply the law governing the debt, or the law of the domicile of the debtor, it is practical both for global assignments of many debts in one transaction and for the assignment of future debts. It provides certainty from the start about the law that will govern the transaction.[83]

To this one might add that in those jurisdictions which require registration of assignments, it is against the assignor that registration will be effected and searches made.

[81] A number of legal systems require registration not only of security assignments but also of outright assignments,

[82] See Art 22. See to similar effect, see the *UNCITRAL Legislative Guide on Secured Transactions*, n 11 above, recommendation 208.

[83] Teun HD Struycken, 'The Proprietary Aspects of International Assignment of Debts and the Rome Convention, Article 12' (1998) *Lloyd's Maritime and Commercial Law Quarterly* 345, 357.

Change of Habitual Residence and Competing Connecting Factors: The 'Super Conflict' Rule

The Report also addressed the question of competing connecting factors. If, for example, the connecting factor were to be the assignor's habitual residence, what should be the position if there were successive assignments in favour of different assignees and the assignor's habitual residence changed between the two assignments?

The Report raises the possibility of a 'super conflict' rule by which the first assignee, by following a particular procedure such as the giving of written notice to the debtor, could fix the applicable law once and for all by reference to the circumstances prevailing at the time of the first assignment.[84] But there are serious problems with this suggestion. For one thing, it totally overlooks the fact, of which the Study Group cannot have been unaware, that the vast proportion of receivables financing, including securitisation, takes the form of non-notification finance. There are several reasons for this, succinctly set out by Professor Philip Wood in his analysis of securitisation:

> Notice will not normally be given to the debtors because of the inconvenience and expense, because it is preferable for the originator to continue collection (the originator has the data and the system), because the debtors might be confused by notice of an assignment and because the originator wishes to maintain its relationship with its customers.[85]

To this one might add that it is not only the debtors who would be confused. What could the assignee be expected to make of a payment from a debtor for whom the assignee maintains no accounts and whose payment relates to a transaction in respect of which the data are held by the assignor, not by the assignee? And what of the assignor, whose accounts will show that the debtor appears to be in default? So the last thing any of the parties would want is for the obligor to be given notice of assignment purely to fix the applicable law.

Secondly, the proposed rule would run counter to the well-established 'last event' rule in the conflict of laws by which it is the law of the last dealing or event which determines whether the purchaser or assignee has acquired an overriding title or whether the *nemo dat* rule applies, so that the title of the purchaser or assignee depends on that of his own seller or assignor. So, if the connecting factor is the assignor's habitual residence, which is in Ruritania, and this changes to Urbania between the first and the second assignment, the court should apply Urbanian law in the first instance. Only if this does not give the second assignee an overriding title will it be necessary for the court to resort to Ruritanian law to determine the title of the first assignee.[86] There seems no good reason to depart from a rule that respects

[84] BIICL Final Report, n 33 above, 401.

[85] Philip Wood, *Project Finance, Securitisations, Subordinated Debts* (London, Sweet & Maxwell, 2007) para 6-045.

[86] The Report refers at different points to the last event rule but starts with the law governing the first assignment and then applies the law governing the second assignment to determine if the first assignee's title is overridden. This produces the same result but is less economical than beginning with the law of the second assignment, which may make it unnecessary to refer to the law governing the first assignment. Hartley, 'Choice of Law regarding the Voluntary Assignment of Contractual Obligations under the

laws found in every jurisdiction by which, in given circumstances, a non-owner can pass a good title. Nor is it easy to see why such laws should be displaced by a law determined under a prior transaction to which one of the parties to the later transaction was not a party and of which it may have had no knowledge.

Thirdly, why should the position of a later assignee be fixed with a law applicable to a prior assignment of which it may have no knowledge by reason of a notice which will be equally invisible?

Finally, if prior to the giving of the notice by the first assignee the second assignee has already acquired priority under the last event rule or whatever other rule is applicable, why should that priority be retrospectively disturbed?

The BIICL was clearly not unaware of problems such as these and wisely omitted reference to the 'super conflict' rule in its final recommendations.

CONCLUSION

Neither the BIICL nor the Expert Group can be blamed for the inconclusive results of the study. These reflect a problem common in attempts at harmonisation, namely, that of securing consensus on a result when there is a sharp difference of opinion. Evidently the only way forward was the compromise solution recommended in the Report, a recognition that the best is often the enemy of the good. It is, however, to be hoped that in due course the European Commission will resuscitate its original proposal that third party effects of an assignment should be governed by the law of the assignor's habitual residence, however defined. Such rules would allow for third party effects to be governed by a single law without the need for a carve-out in favour of any particular industry sector. As the Report states, there is no single ideal solution. But we need to move on. To leave things in limbo to be dealt with by national conflict of laws rules is not a commercially sensible option.

Rome I Regulation', n 25 above, suggested that the problem of changing habitual residences made it difficult to decide which assignment should have priority and that this was best left to the law of the assigned obligation. However, in an exchange of views Prof Hartley readily accepted that the solution I have proposed in the text is the correct one.

20

Compulsory Central Clearing of OTC Derivatives

The Changing Face of the Provision of Collateral

LOUISE GULLIFER*

INTRODUCTION

I FIRST MET Hugh Beale when he kindly took account of what I had to say about floating charges in the light of the Law Commission's project on security interests. I ended up as a consultant to the project, and we have worked together since on a number of projects relating to secured transactions, including two editions of a book, and have taught together for a number of years in Oxford. During that time we have debated numerous issues relating to this area of law, but one of the most complicated and intractable has been the law relating to financial collateral. As part of the Law Commission project on security interests, Hugh attempted to rationalise the law relating to security interests in financial collateral in a way that was consistent with the Financial Collateral Directive,[1] and which also included priority rules modelled on articles 8 and 9 of the Uniform Commercial Code.[2] Although the Law Commission's recommendations were not enacted, there was support for many, though not all, of the proposals in relation to financial collateral.[3] While writing the first edition of *The Law of Personal Property Security*,[4] it fell to Hugh to disentangle the law on the scope of the Financial Collateral Arrangements

* This essay has benefitted from discussions with a number of practitioners. I would particularly like to thank Matthew Dening of Sidley Austin and Edward Murray of Allen and Overy.

[1] Council Directive 2002/47/EC of 6 June 2002 on financial collateral arrangements [2002] OJ L168.

[2] Law Commission, *Company Security Interests: A Consultative Report* (Law Com No 176, 2004) ch 4; Law Commission, *Company Security Interests* (Law Com No 296, 2005) ch 5.

[3] City of London Law Society Financial Law Committee, *The Registration of Companies' Security Interests (Company Charges): Comments of the Financial Law Committee of the City of London Law Society on the DTI's Consultation Document July 2005* (City of London Law Society, 2005) paras 47 and 105; Dermot Turing, 'New Growth in the Financial Collateral Garden' (2005) 1 *Journal of International Banking and Financial Law* 4.

[4] A book Hugh and I co-authored with Professors Michael Bridge and Eva Lomnicka; the first edition was published in 2007.

(No 2) Regulations 2003[5] (FCARs) in the course of a chapter on 'Perfection of Security Interests over Financial Collateral'. In the second edition[6] we decided that financial collateral merited a free-standing chapter, and Hugh and I spent many long hours debating the current state of the law in the light of the *Gray* case,[7] the new non-exhaustive definition of 'possession'[8] and the extension of 'financial collateral' to include credit claims.[9]

The subject has not become less intractable. Despite the decision of Briggs J in *Re Lehman Brothers International (Europe) (In Administration)*,[10] the scope of the FCARs still remains unclear.[11] However, the landscape of financial collateral is changing. New regulations brought in as a result of the global financial crisis mean that more reliance than ever is being placed on collateral, not just as mitigation of credit risk in bilateral financing transactions, but as one of the main techniques supporting the architecture of the regulated capital markets. This is particularly true in the derivatives market, where, for transactions which meet a specified degree of standardisation, compulsory clearing through central counterparties is being introduced pursuant to the decision taken at the G20 summit in Pittsburgh in September 2009.[12]

The EU Regulation introducing compulsory central clearing in Europe (EMIR),[13] takes an ambivalent attitude towards collateral. On one hand, it makes the provision of collateral to central counterparties (CCPs) compulsory,[14] in order to protect CCPs from credit risk if their counterparties default. On the other hand, it mandates particular collateral holding models, in order to protect counterparties from the risk of CCP insolvency, and to protect clients from the risk of their clearing broker's

[5] Financial Collateral Arrangements (No 2) Regulations 2003, SI 2003/3226.

[6] Published in 2012.

[7] *Gray v G-T-P Group Ltd; Re F2G Realisations Ltd (in liquidation)* [2010] EWHC 1772 (Ch).

[8] Introduced into the FCARs by Financial Markets and Insolvency (Settlement Finality and Financial Collateral Arrangements) (Amendment) Regulations 2010, SI 2010/2993, reg 4(2)(c).

[9] Introduced by Council Directive 2009/44/EC of 6 May 2009 amending Directive 98/26/EC on settlement finality in payment and securities settlement systems and Directive 2002/47/EC on financial collateral arrangements as regards linked systems and credit claims [2009] OJ L146 and Financial Markets and Insolvency (Settlement Finality and Financial Collateral Arrangements) (Amendment) Regulations 2010, SI 2010/2993.

[10] *Re Lehman Brothers International (Europe) (In Administration)* [2012] EWHC 2997 (Ch).

[11] Simon Goldsworthy, 'Taking Possession and Control to Excess: Issues with Financial Collateral Arrangements Under English Law' (2013) *Journal of International Banking and Finance Law* 71; Louise Gullifer, 'Piecemeal Reform: Is It the Answer?' in Frederique Dahan (ed), *Secured Lending in Commercial Transactions* (Cheltenham, Edward Elgar Publishing, 2014). See also Financial Markets Law Committee, *Analysis of Uncertainty regarding the Meaning of 'Possession or … Control' and 'Excess Financial Collateral' under the Financial Collateral Arrangements (No 2) Regulations 2003*, FMLC Paper: Issue 1 (2012).

[12] This was confirmed by the decision taken by the G20 leaders at the summit in Toronto in June 2010.

[13] The relevant legislation is the European Market Infrastructure Regulation (EMIR) (Council Regulation (EU) 648/2012 of 4 July 2012 on OTC derivatives, central counterparties and trade repositories [2012] OJ L201/1) and the delegated regulations passed to supplement EMIR (for a full list see European Securities and Markets Authority (ESMA), *Questions and Answers on the Implementation of EMIR* (ESMA/2013/324, 2013), available at www.esma.europa.eu/system/files/2014-164_qa_vi_on_emir_implementation_-_11_february_14.pdf.

[14] Whereas when transactions are bilateral, the provision of collateral is currently a matter of agreement between the parties and, particularly for 'buy-side' parties, will depend on assessment of their credit risk by the counterparty.

insolvency.[15] Both these requirements result in vastly increased demand for quality collateral.[16] For many market participants this is only achievable at considerable cost. There is every incentive for the market to develop ways of reducing the amount of collateral that is required to be posted, and to enable the available collateral to 'go further'. The chief technique used is netting of transactions: the more netting there is, the less exposure and therefore the less collateral is required. One of the benefits of central clearing is reduction of exposure through multilateral netting. However, netting at lower levels brings its own costs and difficulties. The market challenge has been to produce a range of collateral holding models so that participants can choose the particular balance of risks and costs which suits them.

The purpose of this essay is to examine the new structure in relation to central clearing,[17] as well as some of the market solutions, to analyse the legal position of each under English law[18] and the resulting mix of risks and protections offered by each technique.

PURPOSE OF FINANCIAL COLLATERAL

The core use of collateral on the financial markets[19] is the same as in more straightforward secured transactions: protection against credit risk. However, because of the need to preserve the integrity and liquidity of the markets, collateral is usually used to meet outstanding obligations on default, whether or not the debtor is insolvent. The collateral taker thus has little or no risk of lack of liquidity caused by time delays in enforcement,[20] which reduces the likelihood of a domino effect. This is achieved by several techniques, such as close-out netting[21] and appropriation.[22] The types of assets used as collateral on the financial markets reflect this purpose; they are typically either cash or liquid securities: such collateral is referred to here as 'financial collateral'.[23]

Thus, the provision of financial collateral serves two desirable purposes: protection against credit risk for individual parties and against systemic risk for the markets. By

[15] For an explanation of the interrelation between clients, clearing brokers and CCPs, see p 387 below.

[16] There have been some eye-watering estimates of the amount of extra collateral required, in the hundreds of billions of dollars, see Che Sidanius and Filip Zikes, *OTC Derivatives Reform and Collateral Demand Report,* Financial Stability Report 18 (Bank of England, 2012); Daniel Heller and Nicholas Vause, *Collateral Requirements for Central Clearing of OTC Derivatives*, Bank of International Settlement, Working Paper No 373 (2012).

[17] The new rules on the provision of collateral for uncleared OTC derivatives are not considered here: that will have to wait for another paper.

[18] It is, of course, quite likely that another law will apply to at least some of the links in the relevant chain, or to the insolvency of one or more of the parties involved.

[19] For further discussion, see Louise Gullifer, 'What Should We Do about Financial Collateral?' (2012) 65 *Current Legal Problems* 377.

[20] This is bolstered by statutory carve-outs from restrictions on enforcement contained in the insolvency regimes, see FCARs, Pt 3.

[21] See definition in FCARs, reg 3, and discussion in Louise Gullifer (ed), *Goode: Legal Problems of Credit and Security,* 5th edn (London, Sweet & Maxwell, 2013) para 7.21.

[22] See FCARs, regs 17 and 18 and Gullifer, *Goode: Legal Problems of Credit and Security*, n 21 above, para 6.50.

[23] See FCARs, reg 3 which defines financial collateral as cash, securities and credit claims, which are loan receivables owed to banks and other financial institutions.

reducing risk it reduces the cost of transactions, and increases their frequency, thus aiding liquidity, as well as reducing 'domino' risk in interconnected markets. As with all good things, there are downsides which need to be balanced against this universal good. These mainly affect the collateral provider (CP).[24]

First, the method by which collateral is provided may give rise to the risk that the collateral taker (CT) may become insolvent and unable to return the collateral. One such method is title transfer: CT becomes the full owner of the collateral, owing merely a personal obligation to return equivalent collateral.[25] CP retains no proprietary interest in the collateral. Without more, CP is exposed to the insolvency risk of CT in relation to the whole of the collateral provided, but the operation of close-out netting means that the only risk is in fact in relation to any surplus value in the collateral after the secured obligation has been met.[26]

The other method is by grant of a security interest to CT. Here CP remains the owner of the collateral, and CT's interest is limited to the amount of the secured obligation. Thus, in theory, any surplus value on enforcement is held on trust by CT for CP.[27] Three techniques used in practice, though, reduce this protection. The first is the use of appropriation: the effect of this is that CT only owes a personal obligation to CP in relation to surplus value.[28] The second is that CTs often have the right to re-use or rehypothecate the collateral.[29] Depending on the nature of the use, CP will lose all or substantially all its proprietary interest in the collateral and will have (at best) a proprietary interest in a claim of CT against a third party and (at worst) merely a personal obligation owed by CT to return the collateral. The third is that it is common for the collateral to be held by CT in an account in its name. If provided under a security arrangement, any surplus collateral will, of course, be held on trust for CP, but this is only satisfactory to the extent that the collateral can be traced into that account. If the collateral is mixed with collateral provided by other CPs or, even worse, with CT's own assets, it may be hard to trace the particular collateral provided by CP, so that if CT becomes insolvent, it will only have an unsecured claim.

These risks to the CP will increase the cost of collateral provision, either because (costly) steps are taken to avoid them, or because the risk of loss has to be factored into the cost. There are other possible costs. If certain types of collateral are required, there is the potential cost of collateral transformation: the CP may have to turn the securities it holds into 'better' securities or cash by means of repos or other devices.[30] As the CP will want to use all its available collateral to best effect, the

[24] In relation to derivatives, both parties are likely to be collateral providers, see p 383 below.

[25] This is unlike a mortgage, where, although ownership passes, this is subject to the mortgagor's equity of redemption, a proprietary interest.

[26] It should be noted that netting will normally apply not just to an individual transaction but to all transactions between the parties, depending on the nature of the agreement used.

[27] *Charles v Jones* (1887) 35 Ch D 544, 549.

[28] FCARs, reg 18.

[29] This is so that the collateral can be used for other purposes while it is held by the CT, which may reduce the costs of the provision of collateral.

[30] This is a service which is increasingly being offered by banks and custodians, see, eg Bank of New York Mellon, 'Collateral Services' (2013), available at www.bnymellon.com/collateralservices/index.html. For a discussion of the risks of collateral transformation, see Richard Ellis, Collateral Transformation: Liquidity and Market Risk Issues (Sapient Global Markets, 2012), available

market is developing 'collateral optimisation' services (at a price).[31] CPs also may suffer the opportunity cost of not being able to take advantage of market movements in relation to securities it holds, since they are not in a position to trade them.

PLACE OF COLLATERAL IN DERIVATIVES TRADING

Derivatives[32] are financial products 'the value of which is derived from another financial product',[33] which can be used for hedging risks arising from other transactions, or for speculation. Unlike, say, a loan or a sale transaction, it is not necessarily obvious from the outset which party will be paying which: this will depend upon the financial product from which the derivative transaction is derived. In a simple interest rate swap where one party agrees to pay a fixed rate and the other a floating rate, the amounts payable will be netted off, and who pays the balance will depend on which rate is higher during the relevant period. So if liability is to be collateralised, the amount of collateral, and the identity of CP, will change from time to time, depending on the market and who is 'in the money'.[34] In the absence of regulation or of a central counterparty imposing collateral requirements, it is a matter for the parties whether they require collateral at all, or whether one party requires collateral from its less credit-worthy counterparty while refusing to provide it itself. Since many derivative transactions are entered into between a dealer on one side and a customer (the 'buy-side') on the other, it has in the past been customary for only the buy-side firm to post collateral, or, at least, for the dealer not to have to post initial margin.[35]

These features have led the market to divide up collateral requirements into two types. The marked to market exposure, which changes daily or even more frequently, is covered by variation margin (VM), which can be called for, or returned, on a very frequent basis. Any other risks, such as losses during delays in calculating and calling for variation margin (including intraday losses), losses from a failure of the counterparty to provide variation margin, losses after default and before closing out is finalised, and losses too small to trigger a call for variation margin,

at www.sapient.com/assets/ImageDownloader/1415/Collateral_Transformation.pdf. It has been pointed out that as collateral transformation may well involve third parties who are banks or other financial institutions, the phenomenon is likely to increase interconnectedness which contributes to systemic risk; see David Murphy, *OTC Derivatives: Bilateral Trading and Central Clearing* (London, Palgrave Macmillan, 2013) 162.

[31] See, eg JP Morgan, 'Collateral Optimisation' (2013), available at www.jpmorgan.com/cm/BlobServer/is_collateral_optimization_overview.pdf?blobkey=id&blobwhere=1320609134755&blobheader=application/pdf&blobheadername1=Cache-Control&blobheadervalue1=private&blobcol=urldata&blobtable=MungoBlobs.

[32] It should be pointed out that there are other means of controlling risk arising from derivative transactions apart from the posting of collateral, such as netting (see above) and requirements for participants to hold capital (under Basel III).

[33] Alastair Hudson, *The Law on Financial Derivatives*, 5th edn (London, Sweet & Maxwell, 2012) para 1-06. Examples are interest rate swaps and credit default swaps, see the definition in EMIR, art 2(5), referring to Council Directive 2004/39/EC of 21 April 2004 on markets in financial instruments, Annex I, s C(4)–(10) [2004] OJ L145 (MiFID).

[34] Collateral is usually required on the basis of the net position between the parties taking into account all the transactions between them.

[35] Initial margin is discussed at p 384 below.

are covered by initial margin (IM).[36] This amount is posted at the commencement of the transaction, though more could be called later. It is the IM that is dispensed with if a party is seen as highly creditworthy; further adjustment can also come from an agreement that only IM calculated at a higher amount than an agreed threshold will be called. It will be seen that, provided that VM is calculated accurately, CP is not exposed to the insolvency risk of CT in respect to it, since if there is a default the loss will be netted off against the obligation to return the margin which should leave little or no surplus, unless there are significant intraday market movements. However, IM is far less accurately calculated: there is quite likely to be a surplus since the whole point is for it to provide a collateral buffer.[37] Therefore, unless steps are taken to avoid it, CP is exposed to the insolvency risk of CT.

CENTRAL CLEARING OF DERIVATIVES

Even before the financial crisis, many derivative transactions were cleared through central counterparties,[38] even financial derivatives.[39] However, credit default swaps (CDS) were not. It was perceived by governments and regulators that the interconnectedness of the CDS market was one of the main factors why Bear Sterns and AIG had to be bailed out during the financial crisis.[40] Moreover, the opacity of the over-the-counter[41] (OTC) CDS market meant that unravelling the CDS transactions entered into by Lehman was a lengthy and difficult process, leading to great market uncertainty, while the transactions Lehman entered into on the cleared futures market, either as principal or as a clearing member for clients, were resolved quickly, easily and without market disruption.[42] This led to a transnational resolve to introduce compulsory central clearing for as many derivative transactions as possible.[43] This has been introduced in the United States in the Dodd-Frank legislation,[44] and in Europe through EMIR.

An OTC derivative transaction is entered into by two parties, either two dealers or a dealer and a buy-side firm, who are in contractual privity with each other.

[36] This is also called an 'independent amount'. See ISDA, MFA and SIFMA, *Independent Amounts*, IA White Paper (2010).

[37] There are other reasons for overcollateralisation, such as the liquidity of the positions, which affect the length of time closing out would take, and the desire to speed up the acceptance of trades for clearing, see Murphy, *OTC Derivatives: Bilateral Trading and Central Clearing*, n 30 above, 173, 192.

[38] The first futures exchanges and clearing houses started in the nineteenth and early twentieth centuries (see Craig Pirrong, 'The Clearinghouse Cure' (2008–2009) 31 4 *Regulation* (Winter) 44, 45). See also Guido Ferrarini and Paolo Saguato, 'Reforming Securities and Derivatives Trading in the EU: From EMIR to MIFIR' (2013) 13 *Journal of Corporate Law Studies* 319, 327.

[39] Richard Squire, 'Clearing Houses and Liquidity Partitioning', (2014) 99 *Cornell Law Review* 857, available at http://papers.ssrn.com/sol3/papers.cfm?abstract_id=2185064.

[40] ibid 873–76.

[41] That is, not centrally cleared.

[42] Anupam Chander and Randall Costa, 'Clearing Credit Default Swaps: A Case Study in Global Legal Convergence' (2010) 10 *Chicago Journal of International Law* 639, 655–57.

[43] For a detailed history of this decision see Chander and Costa, n 42 above. For a description of the history of the European regulation, including EMIR, see Ferrarini and Saguato, 'Reforming Securities and Derivatives Trading in the EU: From EMIR to MIFIR', n 38 above, 328–30.

[44] Dodd-Frank Wall Street Reform and Consumer Protection Act, Pub L No 111-203, 124 Stat 1376 (2010).

In theory, in a cleared transaction, the clearing house is interposed between the two parties, so that each contracts with the clearing house (CCP) through novation. However, only members of a clearing house (known as clearing members or CMs) can contract with a CCP, and so non-members must contract with a CM, who will itself contract with the CCP. In Europe this is done on a principal to principal basis.[45] If a party to a transaction defaults, the party affected is now the CCP and not the trade counterparty: its counterparty is now the clearing house. Therefore, the domino effect created by interconnectedness of the market participants is negated. However, the CCP needs to protect itself against default risk,[46] which it does by requiring transactions with it to be fully collateralised. The imposition of compulsory clearing therefore has the effect, thought by regulators to be desirable, of compelling the full collateralisation of derivative transactions.[47] This has the effect that parties who would not previously have been required to post initial margin will have to do so, causing a greatly increased need for collateral.[48]

There are further advantages to central clearing. One is that transactions between members can be subject to multilateral netting, which reduces exposure, although this benefit is reduced the more clearing houses there are.[49] Another is that transactions are standardised, which enables more and better information to be available, both for regulatory purposes and for when a party defaults. Increased transparency also means that margin can be calculated more accurately.[50] Moreover, steps can be taken to protect both the CCP and the clients from the insolvency of a CM. The CCP protects itself by requiring all members to contribute to a 'default fund', so that losses are 'mutualised', that is, borne by all the members rather than individual CMs.[51] Protection of clients is achieved by arrangements to 'port' (that is, transfer) their (collateralised) positions with one (insolvent) CM to another solvent CM, provided the latter agrees. Thus, market disruption should be minimised.

It has been vigorously pointed out that the upshot of all these arrangements is to shift losses arising from default from CMs and clients to the other creditors of the insolvent CM, who would otherwise benefit from those positions open at the time of default which are profitable.[52] Moreover, it is said, requiring central clearing,

[45] An agency basis is usually used in the United States.

[46] It is protected against market risk since for every contract with a CM it has an equal and opposite one with another CM.

[47] Squire, 'Clearing Houses and Liquidity Partitioning', n 39 above.

[48] Manmahan Singh, *New Regulations and Collateral Requirements: Implications for the OTC Derivatives Market*, SWIFT Institute Working Paper No 2012-004 (2013). It should be pointed out that under the EMIR regime, discussed below, not all counterparties are required to use central clearing and therefore not required to post initial margin, see n 58 below. Non-financial companies who do not qualify for clearing also do not fall under the margin requirements for OTC derivatives.

[49] One way of overcoming this is to allow netting between clearing houses, under a system of interoperability, see Carl Baker, 'CCP Margining of OTC Derivatives: Towards the Missing Link' (2013) 28 *Journal of International Banking Law and Regulation* 201. For a view that interoperability is unlikely to occur to any significant extent, see Singh, *New Regulations and Collateral Requirements*, n 48 above.

[50] Chander and Costa, 'Clearing Credit Default Swaps', n 42 above, 675–76. See also Murphy, *OTC Derivatives: Bilateral Trading and Central Clearing*, n 30 above, 148, although he also points out that transparency as such comes from trade repositories and not central clearing (at 175 n 333).

[51] ibid.

[52] Pirrong, 'The Clearinghouse Cure', n 38 above, 44; Mark Roe, 'Clearinghouse Overconfidence' (2013) 101 *California Law Review* 1641. For an argument that clearing does create value rather than just shift losses, see Squire, 'Clearing Houses and Liquidity Partitioning', n 39 above.

though making the position of the CMs safer, will push risk into other areas less able to cope with it,[53] and, further, clearing is not the answer to a systemic collapse such as occurred in 2008–2009.[54] It is not intended to engage with these debates here. The purpose of this chapter is narrower: to consider the provision of collateral in the system of central clearing now introduced in Europe.

EMIR CENTRAL CLEARING REGIME

The types of derivatives which are to be the subject of compulsory clearing[55] will be defined by ESMA (the European Securities and Markets Authority) in regulatory technical standards.[56] No standards have yet been published. Compulsory clearing will apply to all derivatives of those types entered into by two financial counterparties,[57] but only applies to derivatives contracts entered into by non-financial counterparties over a certain threshold.[58] It would obviously be disastrous to the system if a CCP were to fail. This risk is mitigated in several ways. Primarily, to be an authorised CCP, an entity must be approved by the relevant authority in the relevant Member State[59] according to certain criteria designed to make sure that the CCP is sufficiently capitalised[60] and meets certain organisational and prudential standards.[61] The full collateralisation of transactions is mandated by strict rules concerning the provision of margin to the CCP:[62] this will operate as a 'primary line of defence' for the CCP.[63] The CCP must also maintain a default fund, which is funded by contributions from the clearing members (CMs), to cover any losses not met by the provision of margin.[64] Losses potentially caused to the CCP if a CM fails are to be met, first, by the margin posted by that CM; then by the default fund

[53] The liquidity risk arising from increased margin requirements is forcefully described in Murphy, *OTC Derivatives: Bilateral Trading and Central Clearing*, n 30 above.

[54] Roe, 'Clearinghouse Overconfidence', n 52 above.

[55] Some of the new regime has already been brought into force, but the first clearing obligations are expected to be in force by late 2014.

[56] EMIR, art 5. The standards will have to be approved by the Commission. They will take into account the degree of standardisation of the relevant class of derivatives, the size of the market and the availability of reliable pricing information (art 5(4)).

[57] EMIR, art 4(1). 'Financial Counterparty' is defined in art 2(8), and refers to regulated financial institutions. Non-financial counterparties are EU undertakings that are not financial counterparties (art 2(9)). Certain transactions involving non-EU parties are also included (art 4(1)).

[58] The thresholds are high, starting at EUR1 billion of notional amount for credit derivatives, and do not include derivatives used for hedging commercial or treasury risk. However, an account must be taken of the derivatives activity of all non-financial entities within a non-financial counterparty's worldwide group. There are also other exceptions, such as derivatives entered into between group companies, EMIR, art 4(2).

[59] EMIR, art 14.

[60] EMIR, recital 48, art 16.

[61] EMIR, recital 49, Title IV. The detailed requirements are set out in Commission Delegated Regulation (EC) 152/2013 of 19 December 2012 supplementing Council Regulation (EU) 648/2012 with regard to regulatory technical standards on capital requirements for central counterparties [2012] OJ L52/37 and Commission Delegated Regulation (EC) 153/2013 of 19 December 2012 supplementing Council Regulation (EU) 648/2012 with regard to regulatory technical standards on requirements for central counterparties [2012] OJ L52/41.

[62] EMIR, arts 41, 45 (which specify the type of collateral which is acceptable).

[63] EMIR, recital 70.

[64] EMIR, art 42.

contributions of that CM; then its own dedicated resources; and only after those are all exhausted, the default fund contributions of other CMs.[65] It cannot use margin posted by other (non-defaulting) CMs to cover losses caused by the default of one CM.[66]

Individual clients are protected against the insolvency of any individual CM by the porting provisions,[67] which also have the effect of maintaining stability in the market. If a CM defaults, the CCP is obliged to transfer the positions held by clients with the defaulting CM to another CM, provided that that CM has already agreed.[68] If transfer is not possible, the CCP must liquidate (close out) the CM's position and return collateral to the clients. The extent to which porting and return of collateral will be possible will depend upon which collateral holding model is adopted, and it is to discussion of these models which I now turn.

PROVISION OF COLLATERAL IN THE CENTRAL CLEARING REGIME[69]

Provision of Margin between CM and CCP

In a cleared transaction the CCP stands between the two parties. However, if the parties are not clearing members, but their clients, the structure is as shown in Figure 20.1, with all relationships being principal to principal.[70]

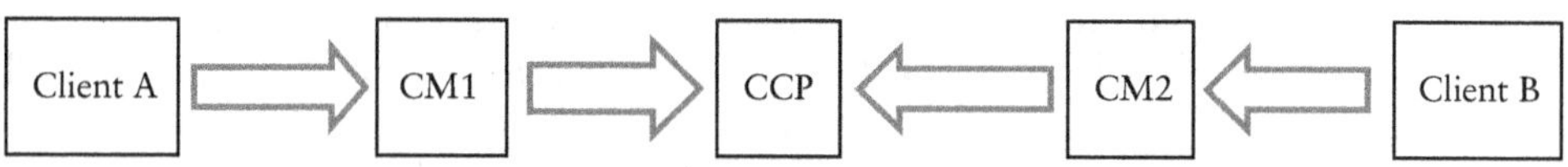

Figure 20.1: Simplified model of clearing structure.

The contract between client A and CM1 will mirror that between CM1 and CCP in commercial terms, and the contracts between CM1 and CCP, and CM2 and CCP will be equal and opposite in commercial terms. EMIR obliges the CCP to call for margin from each CM to cover potential exposures.[71] The collateral posted must

[65] EMIR, art 45. This is called the 'default waterfall'.
[66] EMIR, art 45(4).
[67] EMIR, art 48.
[68] It is difficult to see why a CM would agree to be a back-up unless the transferring client was already its client: this may lead to clients doing business with more than one CM, which, while it may aid portability, is not good for netting, see Murphy, *OTC Derivatives: Bilateral Trading and Central Clearing*, n 30 above, 160.
[69] ISDA and the FOA (Futures and Options Association) has produced a model disclosure document in accordance with EMIR, art 39(7) for CMs to give to their clients setting out the various collateral models and the risks and benefits of each, available at www2.isda.org/emir/ ('ISDA/FOA Disclosure Document'). See also the ISDA/FOA Client Cleared OTC Derivatives Addendum ('ISDA/FOA Addendum'), available at http://www.isda.org/publications/isda-clearedswap.aspx. Much of the analysis in this section is informed by these documents.
[70] It is entirely likely that there may be no CM2 and no client B, since the transaction may be between client A and CM1's house account. However, for the purposes of exposition it will be assumed that the situation is as in the diagram.
[71] EMIR, art 41.

be liquid and of high quality,[72] and, if not cash, must include a level of 'haircut' sufficient to cover such fluctuations in quality as might occur between a valuation and the liquidation of the collateral.[73] The CM must therefore call for collateral from the client not only to protect it against counterparty credit risk (which it might or might not have done under the previous system) but also to enable it to meet its obligations to the CCP. If the collateral provided by the client is not of the necessary type, it will need to be transformed by CM1 into that type, by some form of collateral transformation.[74]

The CCP will call for both IM and VM from CM1. VM is calculated according to the amount of exposure a party has on a transaction when that transaction is valued against the market ('marked to market'). Thus, in relation to a particular transaction, if CM1 is 'out of the money', so that VM is payable by it to the CCP, CM2 will be 'in the money', so that a similar amount of VM is payable to it by the CCP.[75] To the extent that a CCP calls for VM from those CMs who are, on a net basis, 'out of the money' on any one day, it will, in theory, have to pay out an equivalent amount to its CMs who are 'in the money'.[76] As the CCP needs to be able to use VM for this purpose, it invariably requires it to be in cash,[77] and on a title transfer basis. Thus, ownership of the cash passes to the CCP, and it can pass it to CM2 or use it for other purposes, without any express right of re-use. If the exposure of CM1 eventuates, its liability will be set off against the CCP's obligation to return the cash: this protects the CCP, who is also protected against its liability to CM2 (who is 'in the money'), as this liability is set off against CM2's obligation to return the VM. These rights of set-off, which are both contractually provided for[78] and which fall

[72] Such as cash, or government bonds, see EMIR, art 46 and Commission Delegated Regulation 153/2013, n 61 above, arts 38 and 39.

[73] EMIR, art 46. A 'haircut' is a percentage of market value added to the amount of (non-cash) collateral required over and above the calculated amount of exposure, to cover the risk that, were the collateral to be turned into cash, it would realise less than its quoted market value. See Richard Comotto, *Shadow Banking and Minimum Haircuts on Collateral* (EU Committee on Economic and Monetary Affairs, 2013) 14, available at www.europarl.europa.eu/RegData/etudes/note/join/2013/507462/IPOL-ECON_NT(2013)507462_EN.pdf.

[74] See p 382 above.

[75] This analysis also applies to whole positions, in which exposures on individual transactions are netted off against each other.

[76] Although this is the theory, it does not necessarily work like this in practice, since margin that is called on an 'intraday' basis is not usually required, under the clearing house agreements, to be passed on to 'in the money' CM. This mismatch is made even worse by the fact that it is possible for client 2 to choose to clear its transactions through a different CCP from client 1, so without netting between CCPs the amount of VM required to each CCP increases. See letter from ISDA to BIS and IOSCO, 2 February 2012, available at www2.isda.org/functional-areas/risk-management/page/7. Mismatches may also occur because of different types of netting applied to different CMs and clients, depending on the segregation approach adopted for each.

[77] This is market standard for CCPs, see, eg, Eurex, 'Margining Process' (2014), available at www.eurexclearing.com/clearing-en/risk-management/margining-process/148612. See also ISDA, *Margin Survey 2013*, 27–28, and the 2013 version of the ISDA Credit Support Annex (English law) para 10 definition of 'VM eligible credit support' (both available at www.isda.org/publications/pubguide.aspx). Although EMIR does not require a CCP to require cash for VM, it does require collateral to be 'highly liquid' (art 46).

[78] This is achieved by a combination of para 6 of the ISDA Credit Support Annex and the provisions for close-out netting in para 6 of the ISDA Master Agreement.

within insolvency set-off since they are mutual debts,[79] are required for protection of all parties as under a title transfer collateral arrangement the only right the CP has is a personal one to return of 'equivalent collateral' (here, a payment in cash).[80]

The categories of assets which can be used for IM are wider, although limited by EMIR.[81] It is increasingly likely that the market will require initial margin to be provided by the grant of a security interest over the collateral, rather than by title transfer.[82] This is because initial margin is being held against the overall risk of default rather than against any specific exposure, so the value of the collateral could well exceed any liability, giving rise to a surplus payable to the CM.[83] If the collateral were provided on a title transfer basis, the CM would be taking the insolvency risk of the CCP in relation to that surplus: a security interest is therefore preferable.[84]

Provision of Collateral from Client to CM

As mentioned earlier, the client will provide collateral to the CM, who will, effectively, pass it on to the CCP in order to meet its own margin obligations. The client is then exposed to the insolvency risk of both the CM and the CCP in relation to obligations to return the collateral. The risks are more complicated than those discussed above in relation to a two party transaction,[85] since there is no contractual privity between the client and the CCP. Thus, if the CM fails having passed on collateral to the CCP, the client might only have an unsecured claim against the CM and no claim at all against the CCP (for collateral provided on a title transfer basis) or (in relation to the surplus under a security arrangement) a proprietary claim against the CCP only for assets which could be traced. One way of mitigating these risks is for the client's positions and collateral to be transferred ('ported') to another CM if the original CM defaults: the client's transactions would then just carry on operating as before. Another way is for the client to have a direct claim against the CCP for close-out of all positions (including netting) and direct return of any surplus collateral, bypassing the (insolvent) CM.

EMIR provides for both these solutions.[86] It also stipulates methods of holding collateral which CCPs must offer,[87] which offer differing levels of protection to clients, both in terms of making porting easier, and in terms of preserving proprietary

[79] This is on the basis that UK insolvency law applies, see p 381 above.

[80] See definition of 'title transfer collateral arrangement' in FCARs, reg 3.

[81] Government bonds (or similar), other securities which meet certain conditions of quality and liquidity, bank guarantees issued to guarantee a non-financial CM and gold (Commission Delegated Regulation, n 61 above, reg 39 and Annexes 1 and 2).

[82] This is different from the standard ISDA Credit Support Annex terms under English law, where all margin was provided on a title transfer basis. In order to create a security interest, the ISDA credit support deed would have to be used.

[83] For other reasons for overcollateralisation, see n 30 above.

[84] The same argument applies in relation to provision of IM by the client to the CM, see below.

[85] See p 387–88 above.

[86] EMIR, art 48.

[87] EMIR, art 39.

rights to improve the client's chances of obtaining return of its collateral.[88] The CM must explain the choices to the client[89] and must offer them on 'reasonably commercial terms' (as must the CCP to CMs). The different ways in which collateral can be posted, and the market response to the requirements of EMIR will now be analysed, in the light of English law. Various legal issues arise. First, there is the question of the precise legal analysis (who owns what and who owes what to whom). Although this will, to some extent, depend on the exact wording of the agreements between the parties, some general points can be made. Second, there is the question of whether the arrangements benefit from disapplication of statutory provisions relating to insolvency under Part VII of the Companies Act 1989, or the more comprehensive disapplication of statutory provisions under the FCARs.[90] Third, there is the question of the application of the client money rules under the Financial Conduct Authority (FCA)'s Client Assets Sourcebook (CASS).

Individual and Omnibus Accounts

It should first be noted that a CCP is obliged to keep separate accounts of positions and assets for each CM in its own records.[91] Within each account, it must segregate the CM's own 'house' account, an 'omnibus' account for all the clients of the CM who have opted for this model[92] and individual accounts for any clients of the CM who have opted for this model.[93] Each CM must also keep its own records showing its own positions and assets as separate from those of its clients.[94] As will be seen, a client who opts for an individual account will have the benefit of increased safety, both in terms of likelihood of 'porting' of its positions to another CM, and also in terms of recovery of surplus collateral. However, the cost of such an account will be considerably more than of an omnibus account. The market has developed a number of variations on both themes so that clients can choose between expensive, but safer, options or cheaper, but riskier, options.

[88] For diagrams of how this might be achieved, see LCH Clearnet, *Account Structures under EMIR* (2014) 5, available at www.lchclearnet.com/Images/account%20structures%20brochure_21%202%2014_v1_tcm6-63942.pdf and Eurex, 'Client Asset Protection' (2014), available at www.eurexclearing.com/clearing-en/risk-management/client-asset-protection/143894/.

[89] EMIR, art 39(5) and (7). The ISDA/FOA Disclosure Document, n 69 above, is a model for CMs to use for this purpose.

[90] In relation to all financial collateral arrangements, this includes disapplication of various insolvency rules, and protection of close-out netting agreements (Pt 3). In relation to security financial collateral arrangements, this includes disapplication of registration requirements (Pt 2) and protection of agreements for right of use and appropriation (Pt 4).

[91] EMIR, art 39(1). There is, however, no need under EMIR for the CCP to keep separate accounts in respect of each CM at the bank or CSD at which it holds the collateral, see p 394 below.

[92] EMIR, art 39(2). It will be seen that CCPs tend to offer several types of omnibus accounts, but they are only obliged to offer one type under EMIR.

[93] EMIR, art 39(3).

[94] ibid art 39(4).

Individual Client Accounts

Under the requirements of EMIR for individual segregation, the CCP is required to keep in its own books a record of margin posted in relation to that individual client (client A account), and also of the transactions entered into by that client (client A positions).[95] Collateral recorded in client A account can only be used in relation to exposure on client A positions. If client A's transactions are 'ported' to another CM ('CM2'), client A account and client A positions would remain in the CCP's books, but would now relate to CM2.[96] Porting may, of course, mean that contracts beneficial to the (insolvent) CM1 are transferred to CM2, thus removing this benefit from that available to the insolvent CM1's creditors, which would not be possible under normal insolvency law. However, the porting mechanism is protected from the operation of such law by amendments to Part VII of the Companies Act 1989.[97] Porting is relatively straightforward under this holding model, since both the positions and assets of client A are identified in the records of the CCP. It is also made easier by the fact that CM1 is obliged to post any 'excess margin' to the CCP.[98] This is collateral it holds for client A relating to transactions cleared through a particular CCP which is in excess of the amount called by that CCP from CM1. This collateral can also be ported to the new CM, who will then be (at least) fully collateralised in relation to client A.

If client A's transactions are not ported, the CCP must close them out, and any sums owed by CM1 to the CCP in respect of client A positions will be set off against the CCP's obligation to return collateral of the amount in client A account.[99] One major advantage of individual segregation is that positions are segregated as well as assets posted as margin, so that client A's transactions cleared through the CCP will be only netted off against each other and not against transactions entered into by other clients of CM1.[100] Ordinary insolvency set-off, which would otherwise apply to all debits and credits between CM1 and CCP, is disapplied by section 182A of the Companies Act 1989.

It is less clear that this section disapplies insolvency set-off in relation to transactions between client A and CM1 (including non-cleared transactions and transactions cleared with another CCP): the wording of the section does not appear to apply to such contracts.[101] If CM1 entered liquidation before porting, insolvency set-off would apply automatically, and client A's positions would not remain intact to be ported. Although the contracts between client A and CM1 will probably exclude set-off between these contracts and transactions which are centrally cleared, it is trite law that parties cannot contract out of insolvency set-off.[102] If the A/CM1

[95] ibid art 39(3). The actual nature of these accounts is examined below.

[96] ibid art 48(6).

[97] Companies Act 1989, Pt VII, particularly s 159(1) (as amended by Financial Services and Markets Act 2000 (Over the Counter Derivatives, Central Counterparties and Trade Repositories) (No 2) Regulations 2013, SI 2013/1908, reg 2(5)(a)), and ss 163–65.

[98] EMIR, art 39(6)

[99] Securities may have to be valued or liquidated, see below.

[100] In contrast to some omnibus accounts, see below.

[101] See ISDA/FOA Disclosure Document, n 69 above.

[102] *National Westminster Bank Ltd v Halesowen Presswork and Assemblies Ltd* [1972] AC 785.

contracts provided for close-out netting in relation to each type of contract (cleared with first CCP, cleared with second CCP, non-cleared), but excluded set-off between different types of contracts, it is possible that such provisions in those contracts could be characterised as 'close-out netting provisions' within regulation 3 of the FCARs (if the arrangement for the provision of collateral were a financial collateral arrangement within the FCARs), in which case regulation 12 of the FCARs provides that a close-out netting provision should take effect according to its terms notwithstanding that CP or CT is in insolvency proceedings. There are two problems with this argument. First, it would require the provision of collateral from client A to CM1 in relation to transactions cleared with CCP1 to be characterised as a separate financial collateral arrangement, so that regulation 3, which appears to envisage only a close-out netting provision covering all the obligations under a single financial collateral arrangement, would apply. Second, the express disapplication of the insolvency set-off provisions in regulation 12[103] only applies to a limited part of the relevant rules.[104] It has been argued that the rest of the insolvency set-off rules do then apply, so that where insolvency set-off operates before the operation of the close-out netting provisions, those provisions operate subject to insolvency set-off having already taken place.[105]

If, after close-out by the CCP, the amount in client A account exceeds the exposure on the positions, the CCP must pay that amount directly to the client,[106] thus bypassing the (insolvent) CM1. This, of course, has the effect that client A receives this surplus in full rather than having to prove in the insolvency of CM1: the relevant insolvency rules are, again, disapplied.[107]

Omnibus Client Accounts

The other sort of mandated segregation is an omnibus account,[108] whereby positions and assets of all clients of a single CM are segregated on the books of a CCP from the house account of that CM and all positions and assets relating to other CMs. The market is already developing variations on this theme: the two most common are where the required margin is calculated on a net basis across all the client positions of a single CM ('net omnibus') and where it is calculated per client position (as with an individual segregated account) but then held in an omnibus account ('gross

[103] FCARs, reg 12(4).

[104] ibid reg 12(4) refers to Insolvency Rules 1986, rules 2.85(4)(a), (c) and 4.90(3)(b), but it is reasonably clear that this should now read rules 2.85(2)(a), (d) and 4.90(2)(c) (Look Chan Ho, 'The Financial Collateral Directive's Practice in England' (2011) 26 *Journal of International Banking Law and Regulation* 151, 167). These rules prevent debts arising in administration being mutual debits or credits.

[105] Robin Parsons and Matthew Dening, 'Financial Collateral: An Opportunity Missed' (2011) 5 *Law and Financial Markets Review* 164, 172.

[106] EMIR, art 48(7).

[107] The payment would be a qualifying property transfer under Companies Act 1989, ss 159(1)(h) and 155A(4) (as amended by Financial Services and Markets Act 2000 (Over the Counter Derivatives, Central Counterparties and Trade Repositories) (No 2) Regulations 2013, SI 2013/1908, reg 2(3)(a). There is some concern as to whether a payment falls within this protection if the cash is returned by the CCP to the CM who then returns it to the client (this is envisaged under art 48(7) where the identity of the client is not known to the CCP, see Financial Markets Law Committee, *Response to FCA's Consultation Paper CP 12/22* (FMLC, 2013).

[108] EMIR, art 39(2)

omnibus').[109] These forms of accounts are obviously more risky for clients than individual segregation, but are cheaper, with a net omnibus account being the cheapest, but the most risky.

Under a net omnibus account porting is difficult as neither client positions nor assets are identified, so it is unlikely that they could be transferred to another CM. Where margin is provided on a gross basis, the positions will be identifiable and so porting is easier. Under a net omnibus account, if only some client positions are available for porting (for example, because only those clients have made prior arrangements with another CM) there may not be sufficient assets in the account to cover these positions, since the margin was provided on a net basis across all client accounts.[110] There is also a danger that there may not be sufficient assets to return to everyone if the positions are closed out, since the assets provided to the omnibus account can be used to cover losses on other clients' positions. Where margin is provided on a gross basis, there are likely to be sufficient assets to cover all positions, even though assets can be used in relation to any client's losses, since there will be more in the pool. Some clearing houses are offering a 'gross omnibus with excess' option, where excess margin is also posted to the CCP and held in the omnibus account.[111] This, of course, makes it even more likely that there will be sufficient assets to enable porting.

Variation and Initial Margin

Variation Margin: Cash (Transfer of Title)

CM1's call for VM from a client in relation to the latter's exposure will be calculated taking all transactions with the client into account. However, it only needs to post VM to a CCP in relation to transactions which are cleared with that CCP. As the arrangement is by title transfer, full ownership of the cash will pass from client A to CM1 and from CM1 to the CCP. Since it owns the cash, the CCP is free to use it to provide variation margin to counterparty CMs. Cash not used in this way will be held in a bank account in the name of the CCP: the CCP is limited as to the banks in which they can hold cash.[112] Here it will be assumed that it is held at a central bank. The CCP owes a personal obligation to pay the amount of the VM to CM1, and CM1 owes a similar obligation to client A; both are subject to the netting of liabilities if there is default.

Provision of VM in this way is likely to qualify as a title transfer collateral arrangement within the terms of the FCARs, as title to the cash is transferred for the purpose of securing or covering the transferor's obligations and the transferee is

[109] The latter is not mandated by EMIR but has developed as a market alternative, particularly since a similar type of account is available in the United States under the Dodd-Frank legislation, called the 'Legally Segregated Operationally Commingled' account (LSOC).

[110] In practice, unless all clients agree to the same back-up CM, porting is very unlikely to occur anyway, since it will be impossible to disentangle the positions relating to the porting and non-porting clients.

[111] See Eurex, 'Client Asset Protection' (2014), available at www.eurexclearing.com/blob/clearing-en/51496-51498/700058/2/data/cap_overview_october_2013.pdf.

[112] EMIR, art 47(4) and Commission Delegated Regulation 153/2013, n 61 above, reg 45.

obliged to return the cash on discharge of those obligations.[113] Thus, it will benefit both from the disapplication of insolvency rules in Companies Act 1989, Part VII, and also from the slightly wider disapplication in the FCARs.[114] Further, provided that the VM is provided on a title transfer basis between both the client and CM1, and CM1 and the CCP, it will not be treated as client money under CASS.[115]

Individual Client Account When a CCP receives cash on a title transfer basis for a client who has opted for an individually segregated account, it must record it in a separate account in its books: 'client A cash account'. However, the cash itself will either be passed to other CMs as margin, or will be paid by the CCP into an account at a central bank. This account need not be a separate account identified as relating to client A, or even CM1: all the CCP must do is keep separate accounts at the central bank in relation to its own cash and in relation to the cash which has been provided by CMs as margin.[116] Thus, what the CCP owns is a debt owed to it by the central bank in relation to all the cash in the relevant account. 'Client A cash account' is merely part of a debt owed by the CCP to CM1.

CM1 must also post to the CCP 'excess margin' provided by the client to it in relation to the trades cleared by the CCP. [117] The terms on which such margin is posted are not entirely clear, though it is clear that the CCP is obliged to record it in its books separately from margin posted for any other client. Since client A has provided cash to CM1 on a title transfer basis, it would seem appropriate for the posting to the CCP to be on the same basis. As it will be segregated, and either ported[118] or returned to the client on the default of the CM, in the way described above, there is very little difference between it being provided to the CCP on a title transfer basis or another basis, unless the CCP becomes insolvent.

By providing margin on a title transfer basis, CM1 is at risk of the insolvency of the CCP to the extent that the margin provided exceeds the liability against which it will be set off. This seems to be a risk which a CM is expected to bear. In theory, unless CM1 is also insolvent, client A would have personal rights against it in relation to all the VM provided, whether margin required by the CCP or excess margin. It does, though, seem to be common for a CM to limit its liability in this respect to

[113] FCARs, reg 3.

[114] There is no need for registration provisions to be disapplied, as no security interest is created and therefore no registration is required.

[115] CASS 7.2.3.R and 7.2.4. This is confirmed by the Financial Services Authority in their policy statement 'Client Asset Regime: Changes Following EMIR' (PS12/23, 2012) 13. See also Financial Markets Law Committee, *Response to the Consultation of the Financial Conduct Authority Entitled: 'Review of the Client Assets Regime for Investment Business'*, Consultation Paper CP 13/5 (Issue 147: Client Monies, January 2014) para 3.3. Where the collateral is provided on a title transfer basis, the CASS Rules do not appear to offer the collateral taker a choice whether it treats the cash as client money or not, despite an indication to the contrary in the ISDA/FOA Disclosure Document, n 69 above, 9. If the client wishes for the cash it provides to be treated as client money, it would have to be provided on a different basis, such as a mortgage, see p 398 below.

[116] EMIR, art 47(5) and ESMA, n 13 above, CCP Question 8(e).

[117] EMIR, reg 39(6).

[118] If it is ported, this has the same deleterious effect on CM1's other creditors as mentioned above, but this is also protected by Pt VII of the Companies Act 1989 (as a qualifying collateral arrangement under s 155A(2)(b).

the amount of margin returned to it by the CCP,[119] which passes the risk of CCP insolvency onto the client. No doubt, if a client required further protection in this regard, it would be at a considerable cost. However, EMIR does provide for other safeguards against CCP insolvency, as mentioned earlier.[120]

Omnibus Account Although the amount of VM required will vary depending on whether the account is a net or gross omnibus account, in either case the CCP will record in its own books different accounts for different CMs, but will not record separate accounts for different clients of each CM.[121] The position on CM1 default is similar to that discussed in relation to an individually segregated account, except that porting may be more difficult for the reasons mentioned above.[122] If, on close-out, there is a balance due, the CCP may well not know to which clients it relates, in which case it cannot pay it directly to clients, and will pay it to the (insolvent) CM1.[123] This payment will form part of the insolvent CM1's estate, and client A will have an unsecured claim against CM1 for any amount due to it, subject, of course, to any rights of set-off. Although EMIR, article 48(7) provides that the money is paid to the CM 'for the account of its clients', this cannot have the effect of creating a proprietary interest in favour of client A when none existed before, given that the cash was provided by client A to CM1 on a title transfer basis.[124]

Initial Margin: Cash (Security Interest)

This section considers the position if IM is provided on a security interest basis[125] and in cash.[126] If, as is likely, the cash is initially paid into a bank account in CM1's name, provision by client A to CM1 would (under English law) be a legal mortgage. Legal title to the cash would be transferred to CM1, who would have legal title to the debt owed by the bank. It is important that CM1 has the ability to post the cash to the CCP as margin. In theory, if the cash is posted to the CCP also on a security interest basis, under English law this could be sub-mortgage; that is, a mortgage of CM1's interest under the mortgage granted to it by the client.[127] The advantage of such an arrangement is that there would be no need to provide for a right of use in the security agreement between client A and CM1, nor to rely on the FCARs for that right to be valid;[128] it would also mean that client A would have a proprietary right to any surplus vis-à-vis both CM1 and the CCP.

[119] See ISDA/FOA Disclosure Document, n 69 above.
[120] See p 386 above.
[121] The actual cash is, of course, passed on to other CMs or held in an account at a central bank, as discussed earlier.
[122] See p 393 above.
[123] EMIR, art 48(7).
[124] Nor can the client money rules apply if they did not before, see n 115 above.
[125] See p 382 above.
[126] Securities could also be posted (see p 389 above) but cash seems to be surprisingly common, see ISDA, *Margin Survey 2013*, n 77 above, tables 7.2. and 7.3.
[127] This would only be possible if the exposure secured by the sub-mortgage to the CCP was smaller or (perhaps) equal to that secured by the mortgage to CM1. See discussion in Hugh Beale, Michael Bridge, Louise Gullifer and Eva Lomnicka, *The Law of Security and Title-based Financing*, 2nd edn (Oxford University Press, 2012) para 6.51.
[128] FCARs, reg 16.

A different analysis appears to be envisaged by the industry, which is that CM1 will have a right of use,[129] and that, on the posting of the collateral to the CCP, ownership passes to CM1 who then grants a security interest to the CCP. Since the cash transferred to the CCP will be held in an account in its name at a central bank, the security interest will be a legal mortgage.[130] This analysis is also consistent with the wording of regulation 16 of the FCARs, which envisages the collateral taker dealing with the collateral 'as if it were the owner of it'.[131] As mentioned earlier, there appears to be no necessity for the CCP to place the cash relating to CM1 in a separate account at the central bank: it is enough that it has separate accounts for cash it holds for all CMs and its own cash.[132] Thus, in relation to the former account, the CCP is the legal owner of the debt due to it from the central bank subject to the jointly held equities of redemption of all its CMs.

The security interest granted by CM1 to the CCP is a market charge under section 173 of the Companies Act 1989. Thus, to aid the prompt operation of the default procedures, the normal restrictions on enforcement which apply on the appointment of an administrator are disapplied.[133] However, the Companies Act provisions do not disapply registration requirements;[134] these will only be disapplied if the security interest is a security financial collateral arrangement under the FCARs. Under the reformed system of registration of company charges,[135] all charges are registrable unless they fall within a specific exception (such as the FCARs): it is therefore important to know whether the security interest does qualify. To be a security financial collateral arrangement, the CCP must have 'possession or control' of the charged asset. As the central bank account is in the name of the CCP, it is likely to have 'possession' under the revised definition in the FCARs,[136] provided that

[129] ISDA/FOA Disclosure Document, n 69 above, 9. This would require an adaptation of the ISDA credit support deed, which expressly excludes any right of use.

[130] In theory, IM could be provided to the CCP by granting an equitable mortgage or charge over cash which remained in a bank account in the name of CM1. However, this would make enforcement and porting difficult if CM1 defaulted, and seems to have no advantages in terms of preserving assets for client A (unlike where securities are held at a third party custodian, see p 402 below), so this model is unlikely to be used.

[131] Whether the mortgage granted by client A to CM1 is a security financial collateral arrangement is discussed at p 397 below.

[132] See n 116 above.

[133] Companies Act 1989, s 175. Market charges also have priority over other interests, to the extent that this is necessary for default procedures to occur, ss 177–180.

[134] Nor are the priority rights of certain creditors on insolvency of the chargor if the charge is held to be floating disapplied. These include liquidator's or administrator's expenses (Insolvency Act 1986, s 176ZA and Insolvency Act 1986, Sch BI, para 99); preferential creditors (Insolvency Act 1986, s 175, applied to administration by Insolvency Act 1986, Sch BI, para 65(2)) and the prescribed part for unsecured creditors (Insolvency Act 1986, s 176A).

[135] Introduced by the Companies Act 2006 (Amendment of Pt 25) Regulations 2013, SI 2013/600.

[136] Introduced by Financial Markets and Insolvency (Settlement Finality and Financial Collateral Arrangements) (Amendment) Regulations 2010, SI 2010/2993, reg 4(2)(c). This provides that '"possession" of financial collateral in the form of cash or financial instruments includes the case where financial collateral has been credited to an account in the name of the collateral-taker or a person acting on his behalf (whether or not the collateral-taker, or person acting on his behalf, has credited the financial collateral to an account in the name of the collateral-provider on his, or that person's, books) provided that any rights the collateral-provider may have in relation to that financial collateral are limited to the right to substitute financial collateral of the same or greater value or to withdraw excess financial collateral'.

the collateral provider (here CM1) has no more rights than rights to substitute, or withdraw excess, collateral.[137]

Is the mortgage granted by client A to CM1 a security financial collateral arrangement under the FCARs, that is, does CM1 have 'possession or control' of the collateral? We are considering a situation where CM1 pays the cash into a bank account and almost immediately exercises the right of use and transfers some or all of it to the CCP. Where there is a right of use, arguably, the requirement of possession can only sensibly apply until that right is exercised, after which time the collateral will usually have been transferred out of any account into which the CT put it.[138] Thus, the relevant time to decide if the CT has possession of the collateral could be said to be the moment the collateral is posted to it. Further, where a right of use is exercised, the CP remains 'dispossessed' even if the CT loses possession: the requirements of 'possession or control' in the FCD and the FCARs are based on a policy decision to limit the scope of the disapplication to where there is dispossession of the CP.[139]

Alternatively, it could be said that CM1 has control of the collateral. It seems reasonably clear from the two decisions of the English courts on the matter,[140] that 'control' in the FCARs means negative control, that is, the lack of ability of CP to dispose of the collateral, rather than positive control, which is the ability of CT to dispose of the collateral.[141] If this focus on the rights (or lack of them) of the CP is correct, then, provided that CP's rights are limited to substitution and withdrawal of excess collateral,[142] the CM would have the necessary control, and it would not matter that it had passed the collateral to the CCP.

The rights of client A against CM1 will depend on the wording of the right of use. Without more,[143] the client may become an unsecured creditor of the CM in relation to the posted cash (although any liability of client A would be set off, so it would only be unsecured as to the surplus).[144] This would be consistent with the FCARs, which provide that, on exercise of the right of use, the collateral taker's obligation to replace equivalent collateral is a personal obligation.[145] Another model, though, would be for the security agreement to include a provision that the CM held its rights against the CCP in respect to the collateral (that is, its equity of redemption)

[137] The precise meaning of this restriction is not unproblematic, see material referred to at n 11 above and p 402–03 below.

[138] This interpretation is possible on the actual wording of the amended regulation, see n 136 above.

[139] FCD, recital 10. See also discussion in the *Lehman* case, n 10 above, paras 78–152 and Gullifer, n 11 above.

[140] *Gray*, n 7 above and *Lehman*, n 10 above. In both cases the focus of the court was on the rights of the CP and not those of the CT.

[141] This is also the view of Hugh Beale, originally expressed in Law Commission Consultative Report, n 2 above, paras 5.53–54 and then in Beale et al, *The Law of Security and Title-based Financing*, n 127 above, para 3.47.

[142] FCARs, reg 3. See n 137 above.

[143] This analysis is subject to the operation of the EMIR system on CM default and of the client money rules. Both these are discussed below.

[144] This is the position which appears to be envisaged in the ISDA/FOA Disclosure Document, n 69 above.

[145] FCARs, reg 16(2).

on trust for the client.[146] This would mean that the client would have a proprietary right to the surplus.

Individual Account Where client A opts for individual segregation, it has two possible methods of protection, even where it might otherwise have lost its proprietary right to the surplus as a result of the exercise of the right of use. First, the operation of the EMIR system under the individual segregation model means that the client is protected against the insolvency of CM1. If porting occurs, the client has the same rights against CM2 that it had against CM1: provided CM2 is solvent, it will be able to meet any personal obligation to return the surplus. If porting does not occur, the CCP is obliged to return any surplus directly to client A, thus bypassing the insolvent CM1.[147] Where the margin is cash and the amount is made clear by the credit entry in client A account, then it probably matters little whether the CCP's obligation to return the cash is personal or proprietary, as long as the CCP is solvent. If the CCP becomes insolvent, client A has personal rights against CM1.[148] If both the CCP and CM1 are insolvent, it may well matter whether client A has proprietary or personal rights to the surplus in the hands of the CCP, subject to the discussion which follows.

The cash provided to CM1 on a security interest basis will probably count as client money under the CASS rules.[149] In general, the CASS rules provide that a firm holding client money holds it under a statutory trust for the purposes of the client money rules.[150] CM1 is permitted to transfer such money to a CCP in the form of margin,[151] and this presumably includes granting a security interest over it.[152] The money does not cease to be client money when the security interest is granted,[153] which means that the rights that CM1 has against the CCP are themselves client money and are held under the statutory trust,[154] of which CM1 must give the CCP notice.[155] While the client money rules normally provide for all client money to form a single pool on the insolvency of a firm,[156] the rules have been modified to avoid money held by a CCP (including the CM's rights against the CCP) forming part of that pool,[157] so that the money held by the CCP can be ported or distributed as envisaged by the EMIR system. The money does not appear to be client money in the hands of the CCP, so the client is exposed to the insolvency risk of the CCP, as discussed above.

146 A clause to this effect was considered in the Australian case of *Lift Capital Partners Pty Ltd v Merrill Lynch International* (2009) 253 ALR 482, see esp para 91. The exercise of the right of use in that case was a securities lending agreement, not the grant of a security interest.

147 EMIR, art 47(6).

148 Though these may be limited as mentioned above (text to n 119).

149 CASS 7.2.5 and see FSA Policy Statement, n 115 above, 12.

150 CASS 7.7.2. The firm must deal with client money in specified ways, such as segregating it, keeping certain records in respect of it and so on, see CASS 7.3, 7.4 and 7.6.

151 CASS 7.5.2R.

152 In the FSA Policy Statement, n 115 above, it seems to be envisaged that the margin is provided to the CCP by way of title transfer, but the permission under the rules must surely include transfer by way of a legal mortgage.

153 CASS 7.2.15.

154 FSA Policy Statement, n 115 above, 12.

155 The reporting requirements under CASS 3.2.2 are also triggered.

156 CASS 7A.

157 CASS 7A.2.4.3(a).

Omnibus Account Porting is much less likely to occur if the cash is held under the omnibus account model.[158] If it does not, the CCP will close out all the positions and must, in theory, return excess collateral to the clients. However, especially if the margin is provided on a net basis, there is unlikely to be any excess cash. Further, if the clients are not identified the CCP may well not know to whom to return cash, and so will pay it to CM1, who also may not know to whom to return the cash. This may well not matter if the cash is to be treated as client money, which is likely. The client money rules have been modified to deal with this situation. If client A opts for a net omnibus account and CM1 calls for margin from each client on a gross basis,[159] CM1 will itself hold excess margin from each client. This will be client money, since it was provided under a mortgage. On a primary pooling event, it will therefore form part of the client money pool.[160] The FSA considered that any money received by the CM from the CCP in respect of money held in the net omnibus account should be treated in the same way, and therefore this will also form part of the client money pool.[161] The client money pool is distributed rateably among clients according to the CASS Rules.[162]

If, however, the money is held at the CCP on a gross omnibus basis, and surplus is returned to the CM, this is not to be pooled, and is to be returned to the clients, to the extent that their entitlement can be identified.[163] The FSA justified this treatment on the basis that the position of the client under the gross omnibus model is similar to that under the individual segregation model, and the inconsistency under the net omnibus model of some money relating to the CCP transactions being in the pool and some out of it (the reason for the rule in the last paragraph) does not apply here.[164] However, it is not entirely clear on what basis the money is to be returned to the clients. The analysis above[165] would seem to indicate that the money is held on trust for the clients, first because CM1's rights against the CCP are held under the statutory trust for the clients, and this money is the proceeds of those rights, and also because, as between the CM and the client, the money belongs to the client subject to a security interest in favour of the CM. Further (though this would not otherwise be definitive) Article 48(7) says the money is held 'for the account of clients'.[166]

Initial Margin: Securities (Security Interest)

The following assumes that securities are provided as collateral on a security interest basis. Much of the above analysis applies, although one obvious difference is that the CASS client money rules do not apply, although the CASS custody rules may

[158] See p 392–93 above.
[159] That is, netting off all of one client's transactions.
[160] CASS 7A.2.4.
[161] CASS 7A.2.4.(3)(b). See FSA Policy Statement, n 115 above, 22.
[162] CASS 7A.2.4.(2) and 7.7.2.
[163] CASS 7A.2.4.3(c) and 7A.2.4A.3.
[164] See FSA Policy Statement, n 115 above, 23.
[165] See p 398 above.
[166] If this is right, then claims CM1 has against client A cannot be set off against the obligation to return the cash: *Lehman Brothers International (Europe) (In Administration) v CRC Credit Fund Ltd* [2009] EWHC 3228 (Ch), para 331.

do,[167] as may the collateral rules.[168] Another is that the margin requirements in relation to securities (unlike cash) are calculated using a 'haircut'.[169] Securities can either be held directly[170] or indirectly in an account with an intermediary.[171] A CCP is likely to require the securities to be transferred into an account in its name, either with CREST,[172] or with an intermediary, to make both enforcement and porting easier. In the following discussion, the term 'CSD' will be used for both CREST and an intermediary. Securities held in the name of the CCP in a CREST account will be owned by it at law, and so its security interest will be a legal mortgage. If they are held by an intermediary in an account in the name of the CCP, it will have (under English law) a beneficial interest under a trust or sub-trust, so that its mortgage will be equitable.[173] Where the securities are held at a CSD in the name of the CCP, the analysis of whether the security interests granted by CM1 to the CCP and client A to CM1 fall within the FCARs is the same as above.[174]

It is also possible, in theory, for the securities to be held at a CSD in the name of CM1 and for a charge to be granted by CM1 to the CCP. In order for enforcement or porting to take place, the CCP would need positive control, that is, the CSD would have to agree to dispose of the securities according to the directions of the CCP.[175] Unless there was also negative control,[176] this would not fall within the FCARs. A variant on this model, which is being developed as a way of giving clients more protection, is discussed below.

If porting does not occur, the CCP has the right, on CM1's default, to liquidate both the clients' positions and their assets in order to manage its risks.[177] Thus, the actual securities held may be sold in order to generate cash to close out the clients' positions, or, if the agreement between the CCP and CM1 includes a right of appropriation and it is a security financial collateral arrangement, the securities may be appropriated. In these cases, the CCP is only obliged to return cash to the client: there is no obligation to return the actual securities posted.[178] This may be unfortunate for a client who has used as collateral its portfolio of securities, on which it

[167] CASS 6. This would be where the firm holds financial instruments belonging to a client in the course of its MiFID business (CASS 6.1.1.1B). The custody rules do not apply if securities are provided under a title transfer collateral arrangement (CASS 6.1.6).

[168] CASS 3.

[169] See n 73 above.

[170] In paper form (which is unlikely), in which case they will have to be held physically by the CCP or by a custodian or (if UK securities) in dematerialised form through the CREST system.

[171] In this case, the top of the intermediary chain will either be a CREST account or an account at a CSD holding an immobilised global note. There are limits as to the institutions which can be permitted to hold financial instruments posted to CCPs as margin, see EMIR, art 47(3) and Commission Delegated Regulation 153/2013, n 62 above, art 44.

[172] This would only be possible with UK dematerialised securities. For details of which securities can be held through the CREST system, see UK depositories as made by the Uncertificated Securities Regulations 2001, SI 2001/3755, as amended by the Uncertificated Securities (Amendment) (Eligible Debt Securities) Regulations 2003, SI 2003/1633.

[173] Both these situations differ from where cash is held in a bank in the name of the CCP: there the CCP has ownership of the debt owed to it by the bank and takes the credit risk of the bank.

[174] See p 397 above.

[175] In some jurisdictions, this is referred to as a 'control agreement', see UNIDROIT Convention on Substantive Rules for Intermediated Securities (2009), Arts 1(k) and 12(3)(c).

[176] See p 397 above.

[177] EMIR, art 48(6).

[178] This result seems to follow from the broad wording of EMIR, art 48(7).

was hoping to make capital gains, particularly given that the amount of securities posted will include a 'haircut'.[179]

Individual Account Since there is no requirement for the CCP to hold securities relating to each individual client, or even each CM, in a separate account at the level of the CSD,[180] securities of a particular type will be held in an omnibus account at CSD level, and the interest of all the CMs in those securities (pursuant to their equities of redemption) will be a joint interest.[181] Thus, the identification in the records of the CCP in respect of the individual client ('client A securities account') would relate to equivalent securities and not to the very securities posted.[182] The purpose of having an individually segregated account is so that the assets of client A cannot be used to meet losses on the account of client B. It might be thought that this purpose would not be achieved if there is a shortfall in securities at the level of the CCP's account at the CSD. However, the CCP would be obliged to make up any such shortfall because of its contractual obligation to return margin to CM1 or (on CM1's default) its obligations under EMIR to port or to return client A's assets.[183] Depending on its agreement with CM1, the CCP may have a limited right of use of the posted securities, but again the CCP would be obliged to return equivalent securities since this right of use would be that described in regulation 16 of the FCARs.[184] Thus, the client is protected against the insolvency of the CM, but less so against the insolvency of the CCP.

As might be expected, the market has been developing methods of holding securities as collateral which correspond to the appetite of clients for bearing, or avoiding, any sort of risk. The safest methods are, of course, the most expensive, but may be attractive where absolute safety of assets has tangible benefits, such as lowering capital requirements. Thus, the risk of shortfall in a CCP's account at CSD level can be obviated if the collateral is segregated at that level, either in an account in the name of the CCP but identified as for client A, or in an account in the name of client A.[185] In the latter case, the interest of the CCP would have to be by way of charge.

[179] See n 73 above.

[180] See n 116 above.

[181] This does not prevent there being an effective trust of the securities (or, here, of any surplus) see Gullifer, *Goode: Legal Problems of Credit and Security*, n 21 above, para 6-14; *In the Matter of Lehman Brothers International (Europe) (In Administration)* [2009] EWHC 2545 (Ch), para 56; *Lehman Brothers International (Europe) (In Administration)* [2010] EWCA Civ 917, para 171; *Re Lehman Brothers International (Europe) (In Administration)* [2010] EWHC 2914 (Ch), paras 232–39; *Mr Peter Eckerle, Mr Willem Bertheux, Mr Stephan Hallensleben v Wickeder Westfalenstahl GmbH, Dnick Holding plc* [2013] EWHC 68 (Ch), para 14(g).

[182] This appears to be the meaning of the answer given in ESMA, n 13, Question 8(d): 'Accordingly it is not sufficient that the account at the CCP identifies only the value due to the account of the client. It must identify the specific assets (eg the particular *or equivalent securities*) due to the account of the client' (emphasis added).

[183] Depending on the reason for the shortfall, the CSD might also be obliged to make it up.

[184] The right of use permitted by EMIR, art 39(8) only arises in relation to a security financial collateral arrangement under the FCD. Commission Delegated Regulation 153/2013, n 61 above, art 44(3) limits the right of reuse to where it is for 'making payments, managing the default of a clearing member or in the execution of an interoperable arrangement'.

[185] This model is offered by Eurex, 'Client Asset Protection' (2014), available at www.eurexclearing.com/clearing-en/risk-management/client-asset-protection/. It also offers a model where securities are held in an omnibus account, but each client is 'tagged' which appears to correspond to that described in the text. See also ISDA/FOA Disclosure Document, n 69 above, 23.

Further, client A may be able to avoid any risk of loss of collateral in transit between it and CM1 or CM1 and the CCP by providing collateral directly to the CCP under a quadparty collateral agreement.[186] This arrangement, which is developed from the widespread 'triparty collateral arrangement',[187] starts by the client moving securities into a 'longbox' at a custodian.[188] When margin is called for by CM1 (and therefore the CCP), the custodian decides which collateral is most appropriate,[189] and confirms to the CCP that it holds that collateral for it in an account in its name (though segregated for transactions of client A).

The structure of the security interests in such an arrangement would appear to be complex. The client's obligations in relation to the derivative transactions are to CM1 and not the CCP, whose contractual partner is CM1. However, if the idea is to bypass CM1 and provide security directly to the CCP (so as to avoid the insolvency risk of CM1), the client would be granting a security interest in its assets to someone to whom it did not owe an obligation. While such a security interest was said to be valid in a recent *Lehman* case,[190] this conclusion is not uncontroversial. However, for the client to undertake an obligation direct to the CCP would undermine the principal to principal model of central clearing that is used throughout the European market.

Further, it is likely that CM1 would want client A to grant it a security interest over the collateral as well, since it would otherwise be exposed to the risk of default and insolvency of the client.[191] There would presumably be contractual provisions as to the ranking of these interests. The interest of the CCP could be a mortgage, if the account were in its name:[192] it would then be likely to have 'possession' under the revised definition in the FCARs discussed above.[193] If the account were in the name of client A, the CCP's interest would be a charge, as would that of CM1. In this case, neither party can have possession, but could have negative control as discussed earlier, provided that client A's rights are limited to rights of substitution or withdrawal of excess collateral.[194]

The meaning of 'excess' collateral in the FCARs is not entirely clear. It could refer to collateral not required to cover actual exposures of the CT to the CP, or to collateral not required by the CT as a matter of agreement, that is, where the parties

[186] See David Field, 'Three Hearts Beating as One' (2013) 67 *Securities Lending Times* 18.

[187] See, eg SWIFT, 'Triparty Collateral Management Factsheet' (2011), available at www.swift.com/dsp/resources/documents/factsheet_triparty_collateral_management.pdf, and Euroclear, 'Triparty Collateral Management Services' (2012), available at www.euroclear.com/dam/PDFs/Collateral%20Management/MA1557-Triparty-collateral-management-services.pdf. Field, 'Three Hearts Beating as One', n 186 above; A Gordon-Orr, 'The Benefits and Pitfalls of Triparty Collateral Arrangements' (2013) 10 *Journal of International Banking and Finance Law* 627.

[188] Which custodians could be used will be limited, see n 171 above.

[189] This will enable effective 'collateral management'.

[190] *Lehman*, n 10 above, para 44.

[191] Field, 'Three Hearts Beating as One', n 186 above.

[192] This would be an equitable mortgage, since the legal title would be in the custodian: this analysis assumes that English law applies to the custody arrangement, which may be unlikely.

[193] See n 136 above. This is provided that client A has no more rights than rights to substitute, or withdraw excess, collateral.

[194] It is clear from Briggs J's decision in *Lehman*, n 10 above, that the requisite level of control is that the CP should have no more rights than these, see para 134.

agree to a threshold in respect of which margin will not be called. While the latter is the preferable view, it might be thought to be inconsistent with the decision in the *Lehman* case.[195] There, collateral was held to cover exposures to A, B and C, but a right to withdraw collateral over and above the exposure to just A was held to be more than a right to withdraw excess collateral and therefore fatal to A having 'possession or control'.[196] Fortunately, this uncertainty is unlikely to apply in the present context, since the CCP is obliged under EMIR to be fully collateralised (with no threshold) and since CM1's charge is over the same collateral as the CCP's, there seems to be no reason why it should not be on the same terms (that is, with no threshold).

Omnibus Account If the client opts for the omnibus account option, the CCP will clearly hold the securities in an unsegregated account (for all CMs) at CSD level, and its books will record the amount of securities held for each CM, but not for each client. Most of the analysis above also applies here, with one point of difference. If the CM held excess collateral for the client because margin was called on a gross basis and only posted to the CCP on a net basis, the client may be able to recover any surplus intact: this will, however, depend on the method used by the CM (or its insolvency officer) to enforce its security interest if necessary. Any surplus, in whatever form, will be held on trust for the client.[197]

CONCLUSION

The reliance on full collateralisation of centrally cleared derivative transactions in EMIR, while reducing counterparty risk and some systemic risk, has given rise to increased risk to market participants in relation to the insolvency of a collateral taker. These risks can be mitigated in a number of ways; this essay has examined those based on the way collateral is posted and held. The greater the safety for the collateral provider, the greater the cost, both in terms of intermediary fees and in terms of the amount of collateral that is required as margin. EMIR has provided two choices for collateral providers, each providing a different balance of cost and risk. The market is busy developing more nuanced ways of balancing risk and cost. Various clearing houses, clearing members and custodians are all offering slightly different models. This is good for competition, but increases complexity, particularly since many of these models will also be in different jurisdictions and governed by different laws. To add into the mix, the regulatory environment is particularly complex: EMIR is not an isolated piece of regulation, and has to be read in the light of others, such as the FCARs and the client money rules. In order to make an

[195] *Lehman*, n 10 above.
[196] ibid para 139.
[197] *Charles v Jones* (1887) 35 Ch D 544, 549.

informed choice, the actual ramifications of choosing a particular model need to be clear.[198]

The purpose of this essay is to analyse, in a generalised way, the risks and protection arising from the legal position of some of the more common models, on the basis that they are governed by English law. It remains to be seen how many of these models actually make it into common market practice, and whether they actually do the job of enabling market participants to achieve the balance of cost and risks that they actually want.

198 EMIR has gone some way to ameliorating this issue by requiring CMs to explain to clients the level of protection and costs of the choices offered (art 39(7)) and the ISDA/FOA Disclosure Document, n 69 above, which is a dynamic document amended regularly to take account of market practice and views, is very helpful in providing a basis for the provision of relevant information.

21

European Secured Transactions Law at a Crossroad

The Pitfalls of a 'Piecemeal Approach' to Harmonisation

ANNA VENEZIANO*

INTRODUCTION

PROFESSOR HUGH BEALE is one of the foremost experts in, amongst other topics, comparative and European secured transactions law (though with characteristic understatement, he would certainly object to this well-deserved praise). He was actively involved in national reform endeavours and in developing European principles and rules, with special consideration to the need to discuss transparently the fundamental policy choices involved in law-making. I feel justified therefore in presenting here, as a contribution to the essays in his honour, a plea towards a larger design and a more considered approach in European secured transactions law. It will start from a critical view of the specialised and fragmented approach that seems to characterise European legislation in this field. I will pose two questions: one dealing with what is currently happening and one asking what should be happening. For the first question I will focus on the Financial Collateral Directive and the regulation on retention of title in sales contracts. The answers to the second question are not, of course, meant to be conclusive but to contribute to the ongoing debate in this important sector of the law.

WHAT IS HAPPENING IN EU LEGISLATION IN THE FIELD OF SECURED TRANSACTIONS?

A short answer could be: apparently, very little and only in highly specialised fields (such as financial markets); in practice, more than one would think. Let me circumstantiate this assumption, by looking briefly at some of the existing (or attempted) EU legislation concerning certain aspects of secured transactions law.

* This essay benefited from discussions held at the Department of Private Law of the University of Oslo and at the Centre for the Study of European Contract Law at the University of Amsterdam. I would like to thank all participants and in particular Knut Bergo, Aukje van Hoek, Marco Loos and Rolef de Weijs for their comments. The views expressed, and all errors and omissions, are mine alone. Furthermore, they do not represent the views of UNIDROIT.

Financial Collateral Directive

Undoubtedly, the most relevant output of the European legislator in the field of secured transactions law is represented by the Financial Collateral Directive that was first approved in 2002 and subsequently modified in 2009.[1] The Directive was drafted to address specifically the need to ensure the stability of the financial system, the liquidity of the market as well as the reduction of its systemic risk, through the removal of legal obstacles to the cross-border use of risk mitigation techniques already widely used in practice.[2] Its aim was therefore to facilitate the use of collateral arrangements both in the form of traditional rights *in rem* (pledges) and of transfer of title within the financial market. In order to reach this result, a series of fundamental principles was thought to be necessary and was implemented, in particular relating to the disapplication of administrative burdens, formal acts and cumbersome procedures existing in the law of the Member States to create, validate, perfect, enforce or admit in evidence financial collateral arrangements or the provision of financial collateral, as well as the disapplication of those rules of national insolvency law that would limit the effective realisation of financial collateral or cast doubt on the validity of techniques such as close-out netting.[3]

The Directive's original scope of application was limited to financial collateral, defined as 'financial instruments' (investment securities such as shares and bonds and analogous instruments) and 'cash' (held in a bank or other account in connection with the operation of a financial collateral or close-netting arrangement), where at least one of the parties was a public authority, central bank or a financial institution (and the secured party had possession or 'control' over the collateral).[4] In the Evaluation Report issued in 2006 an extension of the scope of application of the Directive was recommended.[5] The European legislator amended the Directive taking such recommendations into account, in particular by expanding the notion of financial collateral to encompass not only financial instruments and cash but also 'credit claims', that is loans granted by banks to firms.[6] This latter type of

[1] Council Directive 2002/47/EC of 6 June 2002 on financial collateral arrangements [2002] OJ L168/43 (Financial Collateral Directive), as amended by Council Directive 2009/44/EC of 6 May 2009 amending the Settlement Finality Directive and the Financial Collateral Arrangements Directive [2009] OJ L146/37.

[2] European Commission, Proposal for the Financial Collateral Directive of 27 March 2001, COM(2001)168 final.

[3] See Financial Collateral Directive, esp recitals 5, 9 and 10.

[4] On the subjective and objective scope of application of the Directive as well as the meaning of 'possession' and 'control', see Hugh Beale, Michael Bridge, Louise Gullifer and Eva Lomnicka, *The Law of Security and Title Based Financing*, 2nd edn (Oxford University Press, 2012) 34.

[5] European Commission, *Evaluation Report on the Financial Collateral Arrangements Directive (2002/47/EC) of 20 December 2006*, COM(2006)833 final, 6. A decisive factor was also the decision of the European Central Bank to include credit claims in the list of eligible collateral for the Eurosystem in 2007.

[6] According to Financial Collateral Directive, art 2(1)(o), 'credit claims' are 'pecuniary claims arising out of an agreement whereby a credit institution, as defined in Art 4(1) of Banking Consolidation Directive 2006/48/EC of 14 June 2006 relating to the taking up and pursuit of the business of credit institutions [2006] OJ L 177, including the institutions listed in Art 2 of that Directive, grants credit in the form of a loan'.

financial collateral, however, was not subject to all the provisions of the Directive.[7] In addition, Member States were given the option to introduce further exceptions to the general regime and to continue to require formal acts for the effectiveness of collateral arrangements concerning credit claims in relation to (the debtor and) third parties.[8]

Despite certain shortcomings and lack of sufficient clarity in respect of a few provisions, the system introduced by the Directive is generally considered as a step forward by its addressees.[9] The critical remarks that I will make below do not purport to deny this, but rather stem from the different perspective of looking at the special discipline applicable in the field of financial markets from the angle of what would be a good regime for general secured transactions law, and questioning whether the direction in which European efforts at harmonisation seem to head is truly convincing.[10]

Attempts Towards Harmonised Rules on Retention of Title: Late Payment Directive, Insolvency Regulation, Proposal for a Common European Sales Law

Two references to retention of title clauses in sales contracts are contained in the *acquis communautaire* so far. First of all, the Late Payment Directive introduced a short (and rather obscure) provision requiring recognition of the retention of title in its simple form (that is, when the seller retains title only to the sold goods until full payment of their price) if minimal conditions are met (express stipulation before delivery).[11] In the interpretation of the European Court of Justice (CJEU), however, this provision does not prohibit Member States from keeping additional formal requirements for the proprietary effects of the retention of title clause as against third parties.[12]

Retention of title is further mentioned in article 7(1) of the Insolvency Regulation, according to which '[t]he opening of insolvency proceedings against the purchaser of an asset shall not affect the seller's rights based on a reservation of title where at the time of the opening of proceedings the asset is situated within the territory of a Member State other than the State of opening of proceedings'.[13] The exact import of this provision is unclear, since either a conflict of laws or a substantive-oriented

[7] In particular, Financial Collateral Directive, art 5 on the right of use of financial collateral under security financial collateral arrangements does not apply to credit claims.

[8] See ibid recital 23 and the modifications to art 3(1) introduced by Directive 2009/44/EC. See below.

[9] See COM(2006)833 final, 5.

[10] For a (critical) view of the Directive in this more general perspective, see Thomas Keijser, *Financial Collateral Arrangements* (Deventer, Kluwer, 2006) 339; Louise Gullifer, 'What Should We Do about Financial Collateral?' (2012) 65 *Current Legal Problems* 377.

[11] Former Council Directive 2000/35/EC of 29 June 2000 on combating late payment in commercial transactions, art 4 [2000] OJ L200/35, now substituted with no modifications by Council Directive 2011/7/EU of 16 February 2011 on combating late payment in commercial transactions, art 9 [2011] OJ L48/1.

[12] C-302/05 *European Commission v Italian Republic* [2006] OJ C326/16–17.

[13] Council Regulation (EC) 1346/2000 of 29 May 2000 on insolvency proceedings [2000] OJ L160/1.

interpretation is abstractly possible. Based on the purpose of the Insolvency Regulation, I am personally inclined to adhere to the former view.[14]

Finally, the recent Draft Report of the European Parliament on the Commission Proposal for a Regulation on a Common European Sales Law (CESL) favoured the introduction of a specific provision on retention of title in the proposed optional instrument.[15] The new text has a limited practical effect on the current discussion, being a mere clarification of the obligations of the parties and not addressing issues of third party proprietary effects of the clause.[16] The Report, however, in another amendment to the proposal concerning its recitals, envisaged that in reviewing the functioning of the CESL after five years of its operation, amongst other things, the need to include further rules relating to the matter of retention of title clauses should be taken into account.[17] This open-ended recommendation, although certainly not binding and not specific in its content, does not exclude future attempts at introducing a more encompassing regulation on the cross-border recognition of retention of title clauses within the proposed optional instrument.

On the whole, the impact of European legislation on retention of title devices so far has been negligible. As I will try to explain in the following paragraphs, this limited impact should not be seen as a failure but as a blessing, because it avoids the danger of developing ad hoc rules on the proprietary effects of retention of title clauses and leaves open the opportunity for a more considered approach to security devices in European law.

WHAT *SHOULD* HAPPEN IN EUROPEAN SECURED TRANSACTIONS LAW?

The temptation to make sweeping critical statements on the law as it is and on how it should be under a normative approach, and to expect a legislator to follow, it is a typical *faiblesse* of academic writing. It could come across as both over-ambitious and unrealistic, especially when that legislator has the difficult task of developing supranational rules. There is much wisdom in believing that it is better to reach a workable result, however imperfect, than to strive for a perfect solution that could still be controversial and not universally accepted.

In this perspective, and as mentioned above, the Financial Collateral Directive represented a remarkable achievement in many respects. It is difficult to deny that

[14] For a discussion of the import of art 7(1) of the Insolvency Regulation and reference to case-law, see Burkhard Hess, Paul Oberhammer and Thomas Pfeiffer (eds), *European Insolvency Law* (Oxford, Beck-Hart-Nomos, 2013) 202.

[15] CESL, art 91a, inserted by amendment 135, Committee on Legal Affairs, Co-rapporteurs Klaus-Heiner Lehne and Luigi Berlinguer, *Draft Report on the Proposal for a Regulation of the European Parliament and of the Council on a Common European Sales Law*, COM(2011)0635–C7-0329/2011–2011/0284 (COD) ('Draft Report'): 'If a retention of title clause has been agreed, the seller shall not be obliged to transfer ownership of the goods until the buyer has fulfilled the obligation to pay the price as agreed in that clause'.

[16] According to the explanatory comment to CESL, art 91a, '[s]imilarly to Article 9 of the Late Payments Directive, the proposed text is confined to the obligation side of a retention-of-title clause, while substantive property law remains outside of its scope'.

[17] Draft Report, n 15 above, amendment 21 to recital 35.

many of the principles on which the Directive is based are equally compelling if we look at them in the light of designing an efficient general legal regime for secured transactions. The 'functional' approach to transfer of title (as regards in particular admissibility, validity requirements and opposability against other creditors and in insolvency) when it fulfils in practice a security function, for example, is a convincing model also outside of the specific sector of financial markets. Another area of greater import than the limited scope of application of the Directive is represented by the enforcement of creditors' rights. Clear and simple rules that guarantee a swift recovery in case of default by the debtor are a key element in any modern regulation of secured transactions. The protection of debtors and of third parties is better served by introducing sufficient ex post safeguards during enforcement proceedings, such as the reasonability test used in the Directive, than by striking down parties' agreements as invalid, inter alia, through the traditional prohibition of *pactum commissorium*. In this latter respect, the role played by the Directive in influencing Member States' reforms of the law of general secured transactions, as happened in France and, more recently, in Belgium, is to be welcomed.[18]

Turning to the topic of retention of title clauses, again it is difficult to deny that were retention of title clauses created in the jurisdiction of one Member State accepted, and their proprietary effects fully recognised, in another jurisdiction, sellers would have a useful tool at their disposal to secure payment of the price in a cross-border situation, thereby facilitating the operation of the internal market, offering an incentive for sellers to conclude contracts with counterparts based in other Member States and permitting buyers to acquire goods on credit.[19] At least as between traders it would be an advantageous step forward. Moreover, the attempts, on the part of the European Parliament, to regulate at least the *inter partes* effects of retention of title in sales may be justified by the need to avoid a mistaken interpretation of the other provisions of the CESL on the seller's obligation to transfer property in the goods sold.[20]

Whilst this is true, I would like to make use of the privilege to take a 'bird's eye view' of what is happening in apparently unconnected sectors of the law and ask some questions, in particular as to whether the chosen path could lead, eventually, to undesirable results. Thus, I am firmly convinced that a fragmented, one could even say 'creeping' harmonisation of some parts only of secured transactions law does not represent a good approach. Such a statement may still seem to be premature given the relatively circumscribed area of the intervention of the European legislator; the steps taken until now, however, or those that are planned for the near future, appear to go in the direction of devising ad hoc rules instead of considering the whole picture.

[18] See for the abolition of the formal prohibition of the *pactum commissorium* in French law, Laurent Aynès and Pierre Crocq, *Droit civil: Les sûretés, la publicité foncière*, 4th edn (Paris, LJDJ, 2009) 13). On the recent Belgian reform, introduced with Loi du 11 juillet 2013, Eric Dirix, *La réforme des sûretés réelles mobilières* (Deventer, Kluwer, 2013).

[19] See generally Michael Veder, *Cross-Border Insolvency Proceedings and Insolvency Rights* (Deventer, Kluwer, 2004) 57.

[20] I owe this insight to comments received from Marco Loos.

I should note that what I will submit here is influenced by a strong bias on my part, that is the belief that the problem of cross-border recognition of commercial proprietary security in Europe would be better, and more practically, addressed by devising an efficient, balanced and possibly complete regulation for an autonomous *European* security right that parties could choose if they wished to do so (without necessarily modifying the current domestic legal systems except for the need to ensure full implementation of the proprietary effects of the European regime).[21] The development of an optional European instrument is in fact one of the possible purposes of the soft-law regulation provided in Book IX of the Draft Common Frame of Reference (DCFR) on 'Proprietary Security over Movables',[22] that was drafted by a team lead by Ulrich Drobnig within the DCFR project and to which Hugh Beale contributed both as national adviser and as member of the Compilation and Redaction Team of the Network of Excellence that prepared the entire DCFR.[23]

In order to justify such a plea in favour of a more considered approach in the area of secured transactions, I would like to briefly focus on two issues, namely, the preferential treatment of the creditor's rights in the insolvency of the debtor and the question of the publicity of security devices.

Preferential Treatment of Creditor's Rights

One of the most important aims of the harmonised rules on financial collateral is to apply a preferential treatment to creditors' rights in the insolvency of the debtor. The encumbered assets are insulated from the ordinary discipline of collective procedures against the collateral giver and the creditor prevails over conflicting holders of rights on the same assets. Not only is the creditor entitled to enforce as against the insolvency administrator whatever type of domestic procedure is opened (including 'rescue' proceedings) but the creditor is also exempted from the application of the various national provisions on the ineffectiveness of preferential claims (deriving from agreements concluded in the period immediately before the opening of an insolvency procedure).

Undoubtedly, this dramatically improves the position of the holder of financial collateral covered by the Directive, which was the aim of the Directive in the first place, but it does so at a cost, ie by worsening the chances of all other competing creditors. In this wider perspective, the disapplication of the general rules should be justified by comparing the policy reasons underlying the preferential treatment with

[21] For the difference between an optional instrument in the field of contract law (which would leave domestic law unaffected) and in the area of property law (where at the very least the relationship between domestic and European interests should be regulated) see Hugh Beale, 'The Future of Secured Credit in Europe: Concluding Remarks' in Horst Eidenmüller and Eva-Maria Kieninger (eds), *The Future of Secured Credit in Europe* (*European Company and Financial Law Review*, Spec Vol 2, 2008) 376, 380.

[22] Christian von Bar and Eric Clive (eds), *Principles, Definitions and Model Rules of European Private Law: Draft Common Frame of Reference, Full Edition* (Munich, Sellier, 2009) vol 6, 5389; Ulrich Drobnig, 'The Rules on Proprietary Security in Book IX DCFR' in Elena Lauroba Lacasa and Jaume Tarabal Bosch (eds), *Garantías reales en escenarios de crisis: presente y prospective* (Madrid, Pons, 2012) 15.

[23] On the origin, structure and purpose of the DCFR, I would like to refer here, generally, to Hugh Beale, 'The Nature and Purposes of the Common Frame of Reference' (2008) XIV *Juridica International* 10.

those of the insolvency regulations that would otherwise curb secured creditors' rights in specific circumstances.[24] My contention is not that those exceptions are per se unfounded. The wholesale financial market has technical and economic specificities that may well warrant a differentiated legal regime. Avoidance of systemic risks and 'domino' effects created by the insolvency of one actor represent strong arguments in this direction. The more we cover areas of the law that are distant from the original circumscribed scope of application of the Directive, however, either subjectively or objectively, the less easy it is to agree on an unqualified acceptance of such exceptions.[25]

In this light, looking at the amendments to the original Directive introduced in 2009, it is not surprising to see that whilst coverage of the harmonised rules was extended to credit claims, the drafters themselves, and some national legislators implementing the Directive, showed reluctance in introducing a completely new regime for security rights on these assets. As mentioned above, Member States are allowed to keep in place the formal requirements, however antiquated, of their general obligation and property laws as to the effectiveness of creditor's rights towards third parties and in insolvency. Italy, for example, followed this latter route, by retaining the publicity requirements of the Civil Code on third party enforceability of assignments of claims.[26]

If we move towards a general secured transactions regime, any preferential treatment of a secured creditor should be considered in the context of the rights of other interest holders on the same assets, as well as other claimants against the debtor's estate (including unsecured creditors, be they voluntary or involuntary). Whilst this ample coverage may be an unrealistic aim in the case of formal harmonised rules, at a minimum a debate should be initiated concerning this larger picture.

In doing so, we should keep in mind that there are other contractual devices that, despite a different formal allocation of title on the assets as between the two parties, fulfil in practice the function of securing a creditor's claim with an *in rem* right opposable to third parties. This brings us to the question of how to approach the treatment of retention of title devices in sales contracts. Admittedly, the inclusion of retention of title devices in the general scheme of a secured transaction regime is far from uncontroversial, especially with reference to European jurisdictions, and it represents a difficult issue on which one should tread carefully.[27] I would like to put forward, however, some arguments in favour of such an inclusion, for the moment leaving aside the (even more controversial) issue of publicity.

[24] See Gullifer, 'What Should We Do about Financial Collateral?', n 10 above, 391, 396.

[25] Thus, I wholly agree with the conclusion drawn by Louise Gullifer, ibid 409, that 'disapplication [of insolvency and commercial law rules] can be justified either if the purpose of the rule does not apply to a certain type of collateral arrangement or if, in relation to a certain type of arrangement, there is a cost of applying the rule that outweighs the value of the rule'.

[26] Legislative Decree No 48 of 24 March 2011 introduced a new para in art 3 of Legislative Decree No 170 of 21 May 2004 which implemented the Financial Collateral Directive in Italy, according to which enforceability as against third parties for collateral arrangements on credit claims is still subject to the publicity requirements of the Italian Civil Code (notification to or acceptance by the account debtor).

[27] For a thoughtful discussion of this issue, see, among others, Eva-Maria Kieninger, 'Evaluation: A Common Core? Convergences, Subsisting Differences and Possible Ways for Harmonisation' in Eva-Maria Kieninger, *Security Rights in Movable Property in European Private Law* (Cambridge University Press, 2009) 647.

Cross-border recognition of the seller's right to enforce its title retention upon the buyer's default amounts, in practice, to conceding a preferential position to the creditor of the sale price of goods. There may be excellent reasons to do so, but such reasons should be embraced in a transparent way, taking into account the economic purpose of the device rather than, exclusively, its formal legal structure. The seller's claims should be openly weighed against the interests of other competitors over the value of the assets, and, possibly, all devices fulfilling an analogous economic purpose should be subject to the same treatment, at least regarding priority rules, again notwithstanding their formal legal structure. This is why I do not favour the proposal to introduce harmonised rules *on the proprietary effects as against third parties* of retention of title clauses within an instrument dealing principally with sales contracts and parties' rights and obligations stemming from them, such as the CESL. This approach is dangerous, because it can lead to fragmentary rules that may be reasonable in the specific context but could end up being less so if considered in a wider perspective.

There is another element to be considered in relation to the issue of the treatment of retention of title devices in a possible future European regime: the prevailing trend in uniform law on secured transactions. In fact, existing worldwide international instruments have clearly opted for an inclusive approach. Thus, a treaty that is now in force in 54 states in the world, ie the Cape Town Convention on International Interests on Mobile Equipment together with its Aircraft Protocol,[28] applies to 'international interests' on the specific mobile collateral covered by the Convention system.[29] The international interest encompasses not only traditional (limited) rights *in rem* (an agreement granting, or transferring, a property right to secure a loan), but also devices based on retention of title, such as a conditional sale and a lease. The three categories are subjected to the 'same basic framework':[30] in particular, the creation, registration and priorities rules apply generally. The characterisation of an agreement as security, conditional sale or lease (characterisation that depends on the applicable domestic law), however, plays a role inasmuch as it affects the rules on enforcement.[31] Likewise, the UNCITRAL *Legislative Guide*

[28] Cape Town Convention on International Interests in Mobile Equipment (2001), text available at www.unidroit.org/instruments/security-interests/cape-town-convention and Protocol on Matters Specific to Aircraft Equipment ('Aircraft Protocol'), text available at www.unidroit.org/instruments/security-interests/aircraft-protocol; Roy Goode, *Convention on International Interests in Mobile Equipment and Protocol thereto on Matters Specific to Aircraft Equipment, Official Commentary,* 3rd edn (Rome, UNIDROIT, 2013). The Convention and the Protocol were jointly approved by the International Institute for the Unification of Private Law (UNIDROIT) and ICAO, on the basis of a Preliminary Draft developed by the former.

[29] In addition to the Aircraft Protocol, two other Protocols have been adopted, though they have not yet entered into force: the 2007 Luxembourg Protocol on Matters Specific to Railway Rolling Stock ('Rail Protocol') and 2012 Protocol on Matters Specific to Space Assets ('Space Protocol').

[30] Michel Deschamps, 'The Perfection and Priority Rules of the Cape Town Convention and the Aircraft Protocol: A Comparative Law Analysis' (2013) 2 *Cape Town Convention Journal* 51, 53.

[31] If the creditor is a chargee, it will be satisfied out of the value of the collateral up to the secured sum, with an obligation to account for the remaining proceeds, and the exercise of its remedies will be subject to notice requirements and some other restrictions depending on the contracting state's declarations in this respect. The conditional seller and the lessor, being the 'owners' of the equipment, are allowed to simply terminate the agreement and take possession. See generally Goode, *Official Commentary*, n 28 above, 45.

on Secured Transactions,[32] a soft law instrument that contains a discussion of the main policy issues relating to the topic together with recommendations for national legislators, showed a marked preference for a 'unitary approach' to acquisition financing devices (defined so as to encompass both traditional security devices enabling a person to acquire assets and title retention arrangements with the same purpose).[33]

Taking into account this trend is important at least in two respects. First of all, whilst the specificities of European financing markets should be considered and any uncritical importation of models, however accepted worldwide, should be avoided, there is little advantage, in my view, in adopting a system that is wholly unconnected with the most recent developments in the wider context of international trade. Secondly, the example of the cited uniform law instruments shows that including retention of title devices in the general scheme of secured transactions does not imply their recharacterisation as security rights for all purposes, nor does it mean that the legal regime should be the same on all accounts.

This explains why an analogous approach was followed in the already cited Book IX of the DCFR.[34] Book IX covers both contractual 'security rights' and 'ownership retained under retention of ownership devices'.[35] The applicable regime is for the most part the same, but not identical for the two types of devices; more importantly, however, the differentiated treatment that is exceptionally applied to retention of title devices is extended to all contractual agreements that fulfil the same economic purpose, ie financing the acquisition of assets by the debtor.[36]

It is interesting to note that including retention of title clauses within the area of secured transactions does not represent a totally innovative approach even in current European legal systems. Admittedly, the prevailing view is to treat retention of title devices as something inherently different from traditional limited security rights and to subject them to a completely separate legal regime.[37] There are, however, a few relevant instances of adoption of a more functional categorisation, followed by the application of analogous rules to both security rights and retention of title to specific purposes. (Just to offer a few well-known examples: the traditional treatment, in German case-law and now insolvency legislation, of the seller's claims in

[32] UNCITRAL, *Legislative Guide on Secured Transactions*, available at www.uncitral.org/pdf/english/texts/security-lg/e/09-82670_Ebook-Guide_09-04-10English.pdf.

[33] This issue was widely debated during the preparatory works, so that alternative solutions applying a non-uniform approach to acquisition finance devices were also suggested. See UNCITRAL, *Legislative Guide on Secured Transactions*, n 32 above, ch IX, 319, esp 334; Spiros Bazinas, 'The UNCITRAL Draft Legislative Guide on Secured Transactions' (2005) *Uniform Law Review* 141.

[34] See n 22 above.

[35] DCFR, art IX.-101. Retention of ownership devices are further defined as 'seller's retention under a contract of sale', 'supplier's retention under a hire-purchase agreement', 'ownership of the lessor under a financial leasing', 'supplier's ownership under a consignment with intention of effect to create a security': DCFR, art IX.-1:103.

[36] The only exceptional rules that are specific to retention of title devices concern enforcement of creditor's rights. For a critical appraisal, see generally Anna Veneziano, 'The DCFR Book on Secured Transactions: Some Policy Choices made by the Working Group' in Sjep van Erp, Arthur Salomons and Bram Akkermans (eds), *The Future of European Property Law* (Munich, Sellier, 2012) 123, 133. On the requirement of public registration of retention of title devices, see p 415 below.

[37] For all Kieninger, 'Evaluation: A Common Core?', n 27 above; Ulrich Drobnig, 'Security Rights in Movables' in Arthur Hartkamp et al (eds), *Towards a European Civil Code*, 4th edn (Deventer, Kluwer, 2010) ch 43.

the buyer's insolvency when the seller had secured its claim to the price by extending the retention of title on the original goods to the future receivables derived from the sale of such goods or to the future products derived from the transformation of the original assets;[38] in English law, the inclusion of reservation of title by an unpaid seller and chattel leasing along with security rights for the purpose of applying the rules on moratorium when an administration procedure is opened against the debtor;[39] in the recent French reform of secured transactions law, the inclusion of retention of title clauses in sales within the new Book IV of the Code civil on security rights and the application of the principle according to which the buyer has the right to receive any difference between the value of the assets and the outstanding debt).[40] It is far from being a coherent landscape, and neither the rules themselves nor their formal justification are the same in each legal system; nonetheless, they represent instances of recognition of the practical function of retention of title, at least in sales contracts.

Publicity of Security Devices

A second point that is causing me some concern, and that I would like to briefly address here, is the issue of the publicity of security devices. The Financial Collateral Directive, in devising a set of rules that facilitate the conclusion and the enforcement of collateral arrangements, opted for a strict limitation of all formalities that was intended to serve as requirements for the *inter partes* validity of the agreements or as requirements for their opposability to third parties. Member States cannot impose any formalities or administrative procedures in relation to, inter alia, perfection and enforceability of financial collateral arrangements or the provision of financial collateral under such arrangements; registration requirements are expressly mentioned as being part of the excluded cumbersome formalities.[41]

Again, this option may be justified in view of the nature of the collateral as well as the specificities of the financial market. Possession or 'control' are the alternative methods through which the balance between market efficiency and the safety of the parties to the arrangement and third parties is achieved. It is, however, questionable whether such a 'silent' system would be the best choice in the wider context of a more general regime of secured transactions law in Europe. Book IX of the DCFR, for example, clearly indicates that for non-possessory security devices, publicity in the form of a filing in a unified electronic European registry should be required to ensure third party effects of the agreement. Thus, the filing system provided by Book IX DCFR applies to all kinds of collateral, including intangibles such as receivables.

[38] 'Absonderungsrecht' under Insolvenzordnung (InsO), s 52. The simple retention of title, on the other hand, still enjoys the full 'Aussonderungsrecht' as per InsO, s 47. On the long-standing development of these rules in case-law, see generally (in English) Rolf Serick, *Securities in Movables in German Law: An Outline* (Tony Weir (trans), Dewenter, Kluwer, 1990).

[39] See generally Beale et al, *The Law of Security and Title Based Financing*, n 4 above, 641.

[40] Code civil, art 2371(3).

[41] Financial Collateral Directive, recital 10 and art 3.

The main justification lies in providing an efficient and simple system for solving priority issues among holders of rights on the same (future) assets.

DCFR, Book IX, as already mentioned, also covers retention of title devices. In principle, the filing requirement equally applies to the latter. In order to take the specific function of such agreements into account, however, as mentioned earlier, a series of exceptions were carved out of the general rule. In particular, retention of title agreements enjoy what is called a 'super-priority' as against ordinary security rights even with prior filing (if they are duly registered and if notification duties are fulfilled).[42] The point that I would like to stress again is that this differentiated treatment was extended to all devices that specifically finance the acquisition of assets by the debtor, whatever their formal structure, since it is based on economic reasons.

I tend to believe that requiring filing of retention of title devices, with all, or some, adjustments or exceptions could represent a good solution, in particular in the perspective of an autonomous European security right such as the one envisaged by Book IX of the DCFR. There may well be reasonable arguments against the introduction of such a generalised filing requirement for retention of title devices in the context of European secured transactions law, or different views on whether there should be exceptions and how best to regulate them. My submission here is that the discussion on such policy choices should not be avoided, or hidden behind the development of ad hoc rules, but should be openly acknowledged.

CONCLUDING REMARKS

In this chapter I have tried to look at recent developments in EU legislation regarding specific sectors within the law of secured transactions from a more general perspective.

My main (and admittedly limited) aim was to point out that in an area of great economic significance such as secured transactions, more thought should be given to the underlying policy decisions concerning it, especially when envisaging uniform or harmonised rules for cross-border transactions. In particular, a more open and general discussion on the reasons for granting preferential treatment to certain creditors, as well as on the reasons for applying a differentiated legal regime to devices that fulfil the same practical function would be, in my opinion, highly desirable. It may well be that such preferences or differentiated rules turn out to be justified, or acceptable in the light of prevailing policy reasons, but this should represent the conclusion and not the starting point of a supranational legislative activity. I like to think that Hugh Beale, as an academic, a former member of the English Law Commission, an influential participant in the development of European law and, above all, an optimist, would agree with me in this regard.

42 DCFR, art IX.-4:102. The super-priority is justified under economic and fairness considerations, ie to allow the debtor to acquire new assets injecting 'new money' in its activity: see Book IX, 5554.

22

How Secure is Security?

SARAH WORTHINGTON

INTRODUCTION

PROFESSOR HUGH BEALE'S intellectual legacy ranges over so much of national and European private law. Taking one small aspect of that work, this chapter examines the various common law and statutory rules which inhibit the intended operation of legal security, in particular security by way of charge. The topic is selected by way of tribute to Hugh Beale's influential scholarship in this area. He was Law Commissioner for England and Wales from 2000–2007, during which time he delivered the substantial project on the Registration of Security Interests over Property Other than Land.[1] Perhaps predictably, but nevertheless regrettably, the legal and business community baulked at the initial proposal for comprehensive personal property security legislation.[2] Worse still, and despite the Law Commission's substantial scaling back in its Final Report,[3] the only proposals so far adopted are relatively minor practical changes to the registration of company securities.[4]

Whether the United Kingdom stands firm against the tide of change that has already swept through much of the common law world delivering personal property security Acts,[5] or whether it eventually succumbs to what (from here) seems inevitable, it remains true that we need to understand our own rules well. Typically such exercises ask what is essential for valid security, and what rights then follow.

[1] See the three substantial outputs: a Consultation Paper, *Registration of Security Interests: Company Charges and Property Other Than Land* (Law Com CP No 164, 2002), a more detailed Consultative Report, *Company Security Interests* (Law Com CP No 176, 2004), and a Final Report, *Company Security Interests* (Law Com No 296, 2005) ('Final Report No 296'). These are all available at www.lawcommission.justice.gov.uk/areas/company-security-interests.htm. See also Hugh Beale, Michael Bridge, Louise Gullifer and Eva Lomnicka, *The Law of Security and Title-Based Financing*, 2nd edn (Oxford University Press, 2012).

[2] For detail, see Beale et al, *The Law of Security and Title-Based Financing*, n 1 above, ch 23. See also Roy Goode, 'The Exodus of the Floating Charge' in David Feldman and Frank Meisel (eds), *Corporate and Commercial Law: Modern Developments* (London, Lloyd's of London, 1996) ch 10, 202–3, who has long argued for a comprehensive statutory regime. For the contrary arguments, see Richard Calnan, *Proprietary Rights and Insolvency* (Oxford University Press, 2010) ch 1 generally.

[3] Final Report No 296, n 1 above, paras 21–24.

[4] Companies Act 2006, s 859Aff, discussed in Michael Bridge, Louise Gullifer, Gerard McMeel and Sarah Worthington, *The Law of Personal Property* (London, Sweet & Maxwell, 2013) paras 14-089–14-104.

[5] Starting with US Uniform Commercial Code, art 9 but now adopted in modified form in Canada, New Zealand and Australia, and contemplated for other common law jurisdictions.

But sometimes it is just as helpful to consider what *inhibits* the creation of effective security. That is the endeavour here.

The emphasis is on common law impediments, although the relevant statutory inhibitions are also outlined. In particular, modern case law suggests we still live with uncertainties in defining which assets can be made the subject of security; resolving characterisation problems; answering priorities problems; and addressing a good number of enforcement problems, especially those involving the anti-deprivation principle and relief from forfeiture. These issues all impinge on the value of the parties' intended security. Hence the title of this essay—How secure is security?

Given the limits of space, the focus here is exclusively on corporate debtors, and on legal securities by way of charge. The question in issue is whether the third party creditor has a valid security interest which can be enforced against the insolvent company. To put this in context, however, something should be said about the much broader range of security interests considered in Professor Beale's significantly larger Law Commission endeavour.

BASIC BUILDING BLOCKS IN SECURED FINANCING

The Law Commission's project on secured financing examined both legal security and functional security,[6] whether provided by companies or by individuals, so long as the protection was delivered by proprietary means, not personal means (eg excluding personal guarantees). This broad functional approach is the one adopted by personal property security legislation elsewhere.

By contrast, legal security is a much narrower concept. It is limited to instances where a debtor grants some sort of proprietary interest in the *debtor's* property to the creditor in order to support performance of the underlying obligation. Such legal security can be used to support performance of any type of obligation, but its most common use is in debt transactions and, for simplicity, that terminology is used here. As soon as the debt is discharged, so too is the security interest. But if the debt is not paid, then the creditor can have recourse to the secured property in whatever manner is anticipated in the security agreement.[7] Typically,[8] the security allows the creditor to sell the secured asset, and apply the proceeds of sale to discharge the unperformed obligation. The security interest is thus the creditor's 'hostage' against the debtor's failure to perform the secured obligation.[9]

English law recognises only four forms of security: pledges, possessory liens, mortgages and charges.[10] The first two are necessarily common law possessory

[6] See, eg retention of title agreements, finance leases, hire purchase arrangements, etc.

[7] *Bristol Airport v Powdrill* [1990] Ch 744, 760 (Browne-Wilkinson V-C): 'Security is created where a person ("the creditor") to whom an obligation is owed by another ("the debtor") by statute or contract, in addition to the personal promise of the debtor to discharge the obligation, obtains rights exercisable against some property in which the debtor has an interest in order to enforce the discharge of the debtor's obligation to the creditor'. See also *Re Bond Worth* [1980] Ch 228, 248 (Slade J).

[8] But, eg possessory liens do not include a right of sale, unless specifically agreed between the parties.

[9] Hugh Collins, *Regulating Contracts* (Oxford University Press, 1999) 102.

[10] *Re Cosslett (Contractors) Ltd* [1998] Ch 495 (CA) at 508 (Millett LJ).

security interests.[11] By contrast, mortgages may be legal or equitable interests; charges are equitable only (unless created under a statute); and both may be granted over tangible or intangible assets.[12]

All consensual security interests must be created by properly authorised parties; secure identified obligations;[13] attach to specific assets (so as to render the security binding between debtor and creditor);[14] and be perfected as required by law, typically by possession or registration (so as to render the security binding between the insolvent debtor and third parties in favour of the creditor).[15]

In practice, charges are the most important of the four categories of English securities. They are distinguishable from the other three categories in that they alone involve the creation of a new type of proprietary right in the creditor. This proprietary right recognises that the secured property is made liable for the payment of a debt, even though the debtor (the chargor) retains both ownership and (typically) possession and the creditor (the chargee) obtains neither. Ninety years ago, in *National Provincial and Union Bank of England v Charnley*,[16] Atkin LJ defined a charge as follows:

> I think there can be no doubt that where in a transaction for value both parties evince an intention that property, existing or future, shall be made available as security for the payment of a debt, and that the creditor shall have a present right to have it made available, there is a charge, even though the present legal right which is contemplated can only be enforced at some future date, and though the creditor gets no legal right of property, either absolute or special, or any legal right to possession, but only gets a right to have the security made available by an order of the Court. If those conditions exist I think there is a charge. If, on the other hand, the parties do not intend that there should be a present right to have the security made available, but only that there should be a right in the future by agreement, such as a licence, to seize the goods, there will be no charge.

To avoid the need for the court order mentioned by Atkin LJ, modern security agreements typically provide that on the debtor's default the creditor may assume possession of the secured asset, sell it, recoup the outstanding debt from the proceeds of sale, and return any excess to the debtor.

Charges may be fixed or floating and, crucially, the Insolvency Act 1986 makes floating charges far less attractive than fixed charges. The critical distinction turns on the rights of the debtor to deal with the charged assets for its own benefit during

[11] So only available over tangible assets which can be possessed. Note that an equitable lien is a completely different interest, being a charge which arises by operation of law rather than by agreement between the parties.

[12] For details, see, eg Bridge et al, *The Law of Personal Property*, n 4 above, esp ch 7; Beale et al, *The Law of Security and Title-Based Financing*, n 1 above, esp ch 6; Duncan Sheehan, *The Principles of Personal Property Law* (Oxford, Hart Publishing, 2011) esp ch 14.

[13] There is no security until the obligation exists: *Rogers v Challis* (1859) 27 Beav 175; 54 ER 68.

[14] The assets have to be ascertainable at the time of enforcement, if not before.

[15] Most perfection requirements, such as registration, are concerned with the validity of the security as against the liquidator or administrator of the debtor's assets. Prior to insolvency, these statutory requirements do not touch the debtor-creditor arrangements, and then any conflict between competing third party claims against the debtor's assets is resolved by normal priority rules.

[16] *National Provincial and Union Bank of England v Charnley* [1924] 1 KB 431 (CA) at 449–50.

the term of the charge.[17] As is usual, the court's categorisation is based on the substance of the arrangement between the parties, not the label the parties themselves attach to their dealing.

These charges and the various rules which limit their effectiveness form the subject of the rest of this chapter.

STATUTORY RULES WHICH LIMIT SECURITY INTERESTS

Security is valuable in supporting increased trade, but, more negatively, if the debtor fails, then security forces the unsecured creditors to shoulder more of the loss on the debtor's insolvency. Several statutory rules aim to limit this imbalance, requiring public notice to third parties that the debtor's property is encumbered; preventing the unacceptable garnering of priority on the doorstep of insolvency; and compelling certain security holders (notably only floating chargees) to shoulder some of the losses which would otherwise be suffered exclusively by the unsecured creditors.[18]

In the first category, intended security interests may be defeated if they do not comply with perfection requirements, typically possession[19] or control[20] or statutory registration requirements.[21] Subject to very limited exceptions,[22] all consensual corporate securities (ie excluding interests arising by operation of law) need to be registered. If particulars are not registered within 21 days of the creation of the charge or such longer period as allowed by the court (Companies Act (CA) 2006, section 859F), then the security is void against the liquidator, administrator and any creditor of the company (CA 2006, section 859H(3)), although the personal obligation remains effective, and indeed the money secured becomes immediately payable (CA 2006, section 859H(4)).

In the second category, even if the security is properly perfected, it may, if it is a floating charge, be rendered ineffective if it is found to have been granted on

[17] *Re Spectrum Plus Ltd* [2005] UKHL 41; [2005] 2 AC 680 (HL). See, eg *Gray v G-T-P Group Ltd* [2010] EWHC 1772 (Ch) (a floating charge, not a trust).

[18] For an outline, see Bridge et al, *The Law of Personal Property*, n 4 above, para 38-014. For more detail, see the standard corporate law and corporate finance texts: Paul L Davies and Sarah Worthington, *Gower and Davies: Principles of Modern Company Law*, 9th edn (London, Sweet & Maxwell, 2012) ch 32; Eilis Ferran and Look Chan Ho, *Principles of Corporate Finance Law*, 2nd edn (Oxford University Press, 2014) ch 12; Louise Gullifer and Jennifer Payne, *Corporate Finance Law: Principles and Policy* (Oxford, Hart Publishing, 2011) ch 6; Roy Goode, *Principles of Corporate Insolvency Law*, 4th edn (London, Sweet & Maxwell, 2011); Vanessa Finch, *Corporate Insolvency Law: Perspectives and Principles*, 2nd edn (Cambridge University Press, 2009).

[19] For common law possessory securities.

[20] For financial collateral arrangements: Financial Collateral Arrangements (No 2) Regulations 2003, SI 2003/3226, r 4. See Louise Gullifer, *Goode on Legal Problems of Credit and Security*, 5th edn (London, Sweet & Maxwell, 2013) paras 6.24–6.26, 6-32–6-52; Beale et al, *The Law of Security and Title-Based Financing*, n 1 above, ch 3; Gullifer and Payne, *Corporate Finance Law*, n 18 above, 262–67. See also *Gray v G-P-T Group Ltd*, n 17 above, para 48 (Vos J); Martin Hughes, 'The Financial Collateral Regulations' (2006) 21 *Journal of International Banking and Financial Law* 64; Look Chan Ho, 'The Financial Collateral Directive's Practice in England' (2011) 26 *Journal of International Banking Law and Regulation* 151.

[21] Companies Act 2006, s 859A. See also Bridge et al, *The Law of Personal Property*, n 4 above, para 14-085.

[22] Including the financial collateral rules noted at n 20 above.

the doorstep on insolvency and without new consideration.[23] This restriction is in addition to the more general provisions in the Insolvency Act 1986 which permit a liquidator or administrator to unwind certain preferences, undervalue transactions, transactions defrauding creditors and extortionate credit transactions.[24]

Finally, in the third category, there are provisions directed exclusively at floating charges, requiring the recoveries of the floating chargee to be subordinated to the costs and expenses of administration and liquidation;[25] allowing an administrator to dispose of assets subject to a floating charge without first obtaining court approval;[26] allowing preferential creditors to rank ahead of the floating charge holder in their call on assets subject to the floating charge;[27] and providing that a statutory proportion of floating charge realisations may have to be set aside for the unsecured creditors.[28] Because of these rules, parties prefer fixed charges, and resist judicial recharacterisation of their arrangements as floating.

STATUTORY RULES WHICH IMPOSE LIABILITIES ON THE SECURITY HOLDER

The above rules all have direct effect. Statutory rules may also impact indirectly on the net value of a secured creditor's recoveries. Security agreements over shares may give the secured creditor some form of voting control over those shares. This 'control' can, in some circumstances, make the controller liable. Typical risks, even if their incidence is rare, include pensions financial support directions, environmental and competition law obligations, shadow director possibilities,[29] and so forth.[30] Similar consequences could follow where control is demonstrated on other grounds. This argument is clearly exceptional, but may merit thought in drafting the security agreement.

ASSETS OVER WHICH SECURITY CAN BE TAKEN: CHARGE BACKS AND NON-ASSIGNABLE PROPERTY

Since a floating charge can be taken over all of a company's 'assets and undertaking', it is easy to imagine that there are no limits to the assets over which such security might be given: the 'assets' do not even have to have proprietary characteristics—a charge over all a company's 'assets and undertaking' effectively charges the benefits

[23] Insolvency Act (IA) 1986, s 245: a floating charge created for no new value in the period immediately leading up to insolvency may be set aside. No equivalent exists for fixed charges, which can only be set aside if they involve a preference (IA 1986, s 239).

[24] IA 1986, ss 238–42, 244–45.

[25] IA 1986, Sch B1, paras 70, 99, and IA 1986, s 176ZA.

[26] IA 1986, Sch B1, paras 70–71.

[27] IA 1986, ss 40, 175(2)(b), Sch B1, para 65(2) and Sch 6, paras 8–12.

[28] IA 1986, s 176A.

[29] Although this may seem unlikely after *Triodos Bank NV v Dobbs* [2004] EWHC 845 (Ch) at 210–15 (Lewison J), contrast the approach in *Vivendi SA v Richards* [2013] EWHC 3006 (Ch).

[30] See Dominic Griffiths and John Clarke, 'Not so clever? The potential dangers of taking security over shares' (2012) *Journal of International Banking and Financial Law* 351.

of the company's personal rights as well as the company's tangible and intangible property.

But a floating charge can only be given over the same *types* of assets as a fixed charge. The test of whether security by way of a charge is possible comes from considering what rights a charge delivers to the chargee, and whether, in practical terms, it is possible for the chargee to enforce the security which the chargor has purported to grant.

Charge Backs

The first and well-documented debate over this issue concerned the conceptual possibility of a 'charge back'. The possibility arises with banks attempting to enlarge the security they take from their borrowing customers. If customers have substantial deposits with the bank, can the bank take a charge over its own indebtedness to the customer to secure its loan to the customer (ie may the bank take a 'charge back')? The issue has now been resolved in favour of this form of security, but only after some debate.[31]

One school of thought was that charge backs were conceptually impossible.[32] The arguments were that the chargor could not assign to the bank the debt it was owed by the bank, since this would operate as a release of the debt, which would destroy the subject matter of the charge; that the debt could not be appropriated to the payment of the amount secured, since enforcement would involve the bank suing itself; that, as between debtor and creditor, a debt is a matter of obligation and not ownership and so cannot be the subject of a proprietary interest; and, finally, that a purported charge back was, in effect, simply a contractual set-off, and to the extent that it secured an indebtedness from a third party it would undermine the restrictions on insolvency set-off.

The contrary view was that this form of security was not only conceptually possible, but was commercially desirable and already well used in practice.[33] Lord Hoffmann, in dicta in *Re BCCI (No 8)*,[34] pointed out, rightly, that a charge does not involve a transfer of title, so a charge back would not effect a release of the debt (indeed, the debt may be for an amount greater than the sum secured), and was therefore distinguishable from set-off; that it would be enforced by book entry;

[31] Whether a 'mortgage-back' is possible is considered in Bridge et al, *The Law of Personal Property*, n 4 above, para 7-087.

[32] Roy Goode, *Legal Problems of Credit and Security*, 1st edn (London, Sweet & Maxwell, 1982) 86–87 and 2nd edn (London, Sweet & Maxwell, 1988) 124–29; and Roy Goode, *Commercial Law*, 2nd edn (London, Penguin, 1995); Bridge et al, *The Law of Personal Property*, n 4 above, 128, 660; *Re Charge Card Services Ltd* [1987] 1 Ch 150, esp 175–76 (Millett J); *Broad v Commissioner of Stamp Duties (NSW)* [1980] 2 NSWLR 40 (Lee J); Nick Segal, 'Conceptual Impossibility in the Court of Appeal' [1996] 8 *Journal of International Business and Law* 307; David Pollard, 'Credit Balances as Security' (1988) *Journal of Business Law* 127; Richard Calnan, 'Fashioning the law to suit the practicalities of life' (1998) 114 *Law Quarterly Review* 174, 176.

[33] Beale et al, *The Law of Security and Title-Based Financing*, n 1 above, para 6.23, noting that several jurisdictions confirmed the possibility by legislation. See also Fidelis Oditah, *Legal Aspects of Receivables Financing* (London, Sweet & Maxwell, 1991) para 5.10.

[34] *Re BCCI (No 8)* [1997] UKHL 44; [1998] AC 214, esp at 227.

and would be proprietary, binding both the liquidator and any assignees (subject to the rules of priority).[35]

Charges Over Non-assignable Rights

A similar question might be asked about taking security over non-assignable property.[36] A great deal has been written on purported assignments or trusts of non-assignable rights, but not on taking security over them. Is it possible to grant a charge over a non-assignable right?[37] The question is important, since contractual rights are increasingly being made non-assignable, yet charges over receivables or over all the chargor's assets and undertaking are very common. If the contractual agreement between an obligor and the obligee is agreed to be non-assignable, can the obligee/debtor nevertheless grant a charge to a third party creditor over the obligee's non-assignable right?[38] The non-assignable right may be a debt owed by the obligor, or a right due to the obligee under a construction contract or an insurance contract. Even though non-assignable, the right is nevertheless likely to deliver value to the obligee, eventually, and thus appears to provide potentially valuable security to a creditor.

Creating a charge over a non-assignable right looks unproblematic in doctrinal terms, despite the lack of authority.[39] Creation of a charge does not require assignment by the obligee of the charged property, and the obligor is not inherently

[35] For the detail of the arguments on both sides, see Beale et al, *The Law of Security and Title-Based Financing*, n 1 above, paras 6.25–6.29, 6.65.

[36] Non-assignment clauses can be worded, and construed, in different ways, but the restriction is unlikely to be held invalid on the grounds of public policy: *Linden Gardens Trust Ltd v Lenesta Sludge Disposals Ltd* [1994] 1 AC 85 (HL) at 106–7. See also the text below. But see Roy Goode, 'Inalienable Rights?' (1979) 42 *Modern Law Review* 553, 556, suggesting if such clauses operate to affect rights between the assignor and assignee, then they should be seen as repugnant to the assignor's rights of ownership. See also Darling J in *Shaw & Co v Moss Empires (Ltd)* (1908) 25 TLR 190, 191, suggesting that a non-assignment clause (as between assignor and assignee) 'could no more operate to invalidate the assignment than it could to interfere with the laws of gravitation'. But this misses the point that the assignor's 'rights of ownership' are those defined in the contract creating the intangible asset (the chose in action), except where the limiting clause can be struck down on public policy or other grounds, and the purported assignment in defiance of the prohibition is not invalidated as a contract: damages for breach may be claimed—whether the contract has proprietary effect is another matter. Put another way, not every purported assignment, even if agreed for consideration, is necessarily effective to deliver property rights to the intended assignee.

[37] Gullifer, *Goode on Legal Problems of Credit and Security*, n 20 above, para1-59 suggests it is not possible to grant security over non-assignable rights. The assertion is worded generally, but is doubted unless restricted to the forms of security requiring assignment of the property to the secured creditor. Also doubting that such charges are possible, see Peter Turner, 'Charges of Unassignable Rights' (2004) 20 *Journal of Contract Law* 97.

[38] There are thus three parties in what follows. The obligor and obligee have a contract, the terms of which specify that it is non-assignable, ie the obligee is prohibited from assigning the benefits of the contract to third parties. The same obligee, now as debtor, owes money under a separate debt contract to a creditor, and purports to grant security to the creditor, including security over the non-assignable contract right. If the debt contract is secured by way of charge, the debtor is the chargor, and the creditor the chargee. The secured assets include the non-assignable contract.

[39] But, to the contrary, see Turner, 'Charges of Unassignable Rights', n 37 above.

adversely affected.[40] But when it comes to enforcing the security, the typical and indeed assumed means of enforcement is for the creditor/chargee to take control of the secured asset, sell it (which clearly requires assignment) and use the proceeds to satisfy the unmet secured obligation. How is that possible with non-assignable assets? Put like that, enforcement might be problematic. And without enforcement mechanisms, it seems senseless to insist that the chargee has a charge. But further reflection suggests that enforcement *is* possible, although only via limited means.

First, if the time for performance by the obligor has arrived, then the non-assignment clause is unlikely to create problems. This is so because charging agreements typically provide that enforcement of the security will be carried out by a receiver appointed by the chargee, but acting as agent of the obligee/chargor. Recovery made by such a receiver, as agent for the obligee/chargor, directly against the obligor, can thus be pursued without the need for assignment.

By contrast, if the due date for performance by the obligor is too far into the future, then the usual strategy would be to sell the secured asset to third parties and use the sale proceeds to meet the outstanding secured debt. Can this be done? Here, the fact that the receiver acts as agent for the chargor does not meet the problem. Perhaps a third party could be persuaded to purchase these non-assignable rights in any event. But from all that has been written about what a purported assignment of a non-assignable asset might deliver to an assignee, they would be quite unwise to do so.[41]

This is because any purported assignment will not entitle the assignee to pursue the assigned claims directly against the obligor, since that would defeat the non-assignment clause:[42] in particular, the assignee certainly cannot obtain legal title to the assigned contract claim,[43] and it seems unlikely that the assignor/chargee would

[40] It follows that a non-assignment clause should not be construed as barring security agreements, unless clearly worded to have such effect. In *Re Turner Corporation Ltd (In Liquidation)* (1995) 17 ACSR 761, para 22 (Sackville J), where the Federal Court of Australia took the view that a clause prohibiting assignment also prohibited a charge, counsel had conceded the point (para 20), and the Court gave no reasons. See also *Foamcrete (UK) Ltd v Thrust Engineering Ltd* [2000] EWCA Civ 351. And, equally, the security agreement in question should be examined to assess whether it is in fact an assignment by way of mortgage: many cases treat the two as equivalent with no material consequences, whereas in this context the formal difference between the two structures matters.

[41] See Bridge et al, *The Law of Personal Property*, n 4 above, ch 29, paras 14-052–14-055 and 15-065–15-071; Marcus Smith and Nico Leslie, *The Law of Assignment*, 2nd edn (Oxford University Press, 2013) ch 29; Gullifer and Payne, *Corporate Finance Law*, n 18 above, para 8.2.2. See also Goode, 'Inalienable Rights?', n 36 above; Bob Allcock, 'Restrictions on the Assignment of Contractual Rights' (1983) 42 *Cambridge Law Journal* 328; Andrew Tettenborn, 'Trusts and Unassignable Agreements Again' [1999] *Lloyd's Maritime and Commercial Law Quarterly* 353; Andrew Tettenborn, 'Trust of Unassignable Agreements' [1998] *Lloyd's Maritime and Commercial Law Quarterly* 498; Gerard McCormack, 'Debts and Non-Assignment Clauses' [2000] *Journal of Business Law* 422; Andrew McKnight, 'Contractual Restrictions on a Creditor's Right to Alienate Debts: Part 2' (2003) 18 *Journal of International Business Law* 43; Greg Tolhurst, 'The Efficacy of Contractual Provisions Prohibiting Assignment' (2004) 26 *Sydney Law Review* 161; Alexander Trukhtanov, 'Trust of a Non-Assignable Contractual Benefit: *Barbados Trust Company v Bank of Zambia*' (2007) 70 *Modern Law Review* 848; Orkun Akseli, 'Contractual prohibitions on assignment of receivables: an English and UN perspective' [2009] *Journal of Business Law* 650.

[42] The *Vandepitte* procedure notwithstanding: see the arguments in Smith and Leslie, *The Law of Assignment*, n 41 above, ch 29.

[43] *Linden Gardens Trust Ltd v Lenesta Sludge Disposals Ltd*, n 36 above; *Helstan Securities Ltd v Hertfordshire County Council* [1978] 3 All ER 262 (QBD).

be deemed to hold the assigned (but non-assignable) right on constructive trust for the assignee.[44] This is because the contract of assignment can hardly be regarded as specifically enforceable in these circumstances, so that equity will 'treat as done that which ought to be done', deeming the assignor to hold the right on constructive trust for the assignee, 'since equity will not enforce the performance of an obligation which constitutes a breach of a prior contract with a third party [here, the obligor]'.[45] This is a perfectly general rule: equity will not 'treat as [already] done that which ought to be done', nor insist on specific performance of contracts where the underlying obligations are conditional and the conditions have not yet been met.[46]

The textbooks then typically consider whether, alternatively, it is possible for the obligee in these circumstances to declare a *trust* of its non-assignable contractual rights for the benefit of the third party. The cases suggest this is possible,[47] although the reasoning is doubted.[48] In any event, it will be a rare chargee (or, more accurately, its receiver acting as agent for the obligee/chargor) who will be minded to deal with secured assets by opting to become a trustee of them, even in exchange for immediate cash.

Timing chronologies in creating the non-assignable obligation and the security interest do not affect this reasoning. In particular, it does not matter whether the debtor's charge agreement pre-dates or post-dates the debtor's/obligee's contract containing a non-assignment clause. What matters is whether the charge agreement is worded to capture, or 'attach' to, the asset in question. If the security agreement is worded to capture all the debtor's current and future receivables, or the debtor's more broadly defined contract claims, then the contract containing the non-assignment clause will fall within the security net even though it was not in existence at the time the security arrangement was agreed. But the secured creditor then takes these secured assets with all their inherent limitations, including their non-assignment

[44] See following notes.

[45] *Ex p Floods of Queensferry* [1998] 1 WLR 1496 (CA) at 1501 (Millett LJ). Also see Smith and Leslie, *The Law of Assignment*, n 41 above, para 25.24; Andrew McKnight, 'Contractual Restrictions on a Creditor's Right to Alienate Debts: Part 2' (2003) 18 *Journal of International Banking Law and Regulation* 43, 46.

[46] See, most dramatically, *Brown v Heffer* (1967) 116 CLR 344 (AustHCt); and *Sainsbury plc v O'Connor* [1991] 1 WLR 963 (CA). This is the general rule unless the condition is inserted for the benefit of the assignee *and* (it is suggested) has been waived by him: *Wood Preservation Ltd v Prior* [1969] 1 WLR 1007 (CA) (where the possibility of waiver was considered sufficient, given the court's interpretation of the tax legislation). Generally, see Sarah Worthington, *Proprietary Interests in Commercial Transactions* (Oxford University Press, 1996) 197–215; Smith and Leslie, *The Law of Assignment*, n 41 above, paras 25.23–25.25. By contrast, see *Linden Gardens Trust Ltd v Lenesta Sludge Disposals Ltd*, n 36; Allcock, 'Restrictions on the Assignment of Contractual Rights', n 41 above, 335–36, both suggesting the rights may be held on trust for the third party assignee.

[47] *Don King Productions Inc v Warren* [2000] Ch 291, esp 630–4 (Lightman J); *Barbados Trust Company Ltd v Bank of Zambia* [2007] EWCA Civ 148 (CA).

[48] Smith and Leslie, *The Law of Assignment*, n 41 above, para 25.2 generally and para 25.32(4) specifically; Bridge et al, *The Law of Personal Property*, n 4 above, para 15-066. See also Gullifer, *Goode on Legal Problems of Credit and Security*, n 20 above, paras 3-40–3-42. Also against a trust, see McKnight, 'Contractual Restrictions on a Creditor's Right to Alienate Debts: Part 2', n 45 above; Gerard McMeel, 'The Modern Law of Assignment: Public Policy and Contractual Restrictions on Transferability' (2004) *Lloyd's Maritime and Commercial Law Quarterly* 483; Turner, 'Charges of Unassignable Rights', n 37 above.

clauses. This is not controversial: the debtor/chargor cannot grant security over rights it does not have.[49]

That is not quite the end of the story, however. All this suggests that the chargee *cannot* readily enforce its security in the orthodox manner, by sale of the secured assets and recoupment of the outstanding debt from their proceeds. But, despite this, it remains true that the debtor/chargor has agreed to hold these non-assignable assets as security for the debt owed to the chargee. As between the chargor (or the chargor's liquidator) and chargee, can the chargor or its liquidator simply take the benefit of these assets on its own account? Arguably not. In the context of assignments, it is commonly said that even if the assignment of the non-assignable contract right gives the assignee no proprietary interests in any asset, the obligee/assignor will hold the *fruits* of the non-assignable contract on constructive trust for the assignee.[50] This may be too broad. What little authority there is suggests this is certainly true where the relationship between the assignor and assignee is fiduciary.[51] This seems correct. Equally, it is suggested, the same result would obtain where the relationship is one of chargor and chargee, ie where the transaction has been by way of grant of security rather than assignment, since such transactions are inevitably specifically enforceable[52] and give rise to consequential rights in the chargee and strict limitations on the chargor's ability to deal with, or treat as its own, any fruits of unauthorised dealings with the charged property (being dealings against the chargee's interests).[53]

If this is right, then the plight of a chargee with security over a non-assignable contract right is certainly not that of an unsecured creditor, even though realisation of the benefits of the security may require a little more thought about the consequences of the agreed limitations to the obligee/chargor's property. In particular, on the analysis above, recovery may be delayed until the chargor receives the fruits of the non-assignable right.

Perhaps because of these complications, the Law Commission has suggested that non-assignment clauses in receivables should be deemed to have no effect as against

[49] This notwithstanding the court's contrary conclusions in *Foamcrete (UK) Ltd v Thrust Engineering Ltd* [2002] BCC 221. Of the same view, see Gullifer, *Goode on Legal Problems of Credit and Security*, n 20 above, para 3-45; McKnight, 'Contractual Restrictions on a Creditor's Right to Alienate Debts: Part 2', n 45 above, 47.

[50] See, eg Goode, 'Inalienable Rights?', n 36 above, 556; Roy Goode, 'Contractual Prohibitions against Assignment' [2009] *Lloyd's Maritime and Commercial Law Quarterly* 300; John Armour and Jennifer Payne (eds), *Rationality in Company Law* (Oxford, Hart Publishing, 2009) 362; Smith and Leslie, *The Law of Assignment,* n 41 above, para 25-32; Gullifer, *Goode on Legal Problems of Credit and Security*, n 20 above, para 3-34; Bridge et al, *The Law of Personal Property*, n 4 above, para 29-033, although compelling judicial authority is scant.

[51] *Re Turcan* (1888) 40 ChD 5 (CA) (settlement on trust); *Don King Productions*, n 47 above (partners and declaration of trust); *Barbados Trust*, n 47 above (declaration of trust). The issue was left open in *Linden Gardens Trust Ltd v Lenesta Sludge Disposals Ltd*, n 36 above, 107–9.

[52] See Worthington, *Proprietary Interests in Commercial Transactions*, n 46 above, 198–201.

[53] And dealing with a secured asset on the chargor's own account, for the chargor's benefit, *will* be unauthorised. Of course, if the agreed security is merely a floating charge, not a fixed charge, then the chargor is entitled to deal with the charge assets (and their proceeds, unless separately charged) as his own until the charge crystallises, and the fruits are then not captured in the manner indicated here.

third party assignees (ie not just against chargees).[54] With respect, this seems to be allowing the security tail to wag the property dog. It is true that this change would mean that financing for debtors would be easier. But surely the basic principle is that a debtor may only deal with the assets it *has*. Here its asset is flawed, being subject to a non-assignment clause. It is hardly the job of the legislature to override the parties' agreed limitations on the obligee/debtor's property, whatever the benefits to the debtor, especially when the obligor's own rights may not be met by a simple claim against the obligee for damages for breach of contract. If a parallel is needed, in creating a better market for shares, non-assignment or restrictive assignment clauses in shares are not overridden; rather, *if* the parties want to trade on a stock exchange, then their shares must be freely transferable. This seems the right way around.

By way of completing the picture, note that it is perfectly possible for the parties to grant security over (or assign, or declare a trust of) the *proceeds* or *fruits* of these non-assignable contract rights, rather than the rights themselves.[55] The non-assignment clause is unlikely to be interpreted as preventing such dealings.[56] An agreement for security over the fruits will attach in equity to the fruits immediately they are received,[57] although until then the purported assignee has no proprietary interest in anything,[58] and the debtor/obligee will not owe the creditor any fiduciary duties in dealing with the precursor non-assignable rights themselves.[59]

CHARACTERISATION RULES WHICH LIMIT SECURITY INTERESTS

For reasons noted earlier, secured creditors prefer fixed charges to floating charges, since the former are not devalued by various third party claims with statutory priority.[60] Characterisation is therefore crucial. It is a matter of law, with the courts looking at the rights agreed by the parties, not the label applied by the parties

[54] Final Report No 296, n 1 above, 4.35–4.40, and 6.73. Also see Gullifer and Payne, *Corporate Finance Law*, n 18 above, 388 n 169, for a list of the countries which have adopted this approach to varying degrees. The argument in favour is that small business debtors (ie chargors/assignors) have no bargaining power to contract out of the standard non-assignment terms imposed by their large customers, and small businesses then find it difficult to obtain finance from receivables financiers. However, in response it might be suggested that the large customers will simply adjust their terms, re-pricing their risk, and small businesses may not see much benefit.

[55] Smith and Leslie, *The Law of Assignment*, n 41 above, paras 25.32(5)–25.36.

[56] To do so would be repugnant to the obligee's rights of ownership, and any attempt ought therefore to be struck down: Gullifer, *Goode on Legal Problems of Credit and Security*, n 20 above, 556.

[57] *Tailby v Official Receiver* (1888) 13 App Cas 523, binding the property as soon as it comes into existence, although, for the purpose of priorities, the agreement is treated as having been effective from the date of the earlier agreement to assign: *Re Lind; Industrials Finance Syndicate Ltd v Lind* [1915] 2 Ch 345. See generally Worthington, *Proprietary Interests in Commercial Transactions*, n 46 above, 198–201.

[58] See *Bawejem Ltd v MC Fabrications Ltd* [1999] 1 All ER (Comm) 377 (CA), 382 (Robert Walker LJ); *Masri v Consolidated Contractors International Co* [2008] 1 All ER (Comm) 305 (QBD) at 123–26; *Norman v FCT* (1963) 109 CLR 9 (Aust HCt); *Shepherd v FCT* (1965) 113 CLR 385 (Aust HCt). Also see Bridge et al, *The Law of Personal Property*, n 4 above, paras 29-14–29-17.

[59] Smith and Leslie, *The Law of Assignment*, n 41 above, para 25.32(6).

[60] See p 421 above.

themselves.[61] The House of Lords' clarified the distinction between fixed and floating charges almost a decade ago in *Re Spectrum Plus Ltd (In Liqudation)*:[62] a charge is fixed if the chargor is required to preserve the charged assets or their permitted substitutes for the benefit of the chargee; otherwise the charge is floating. In particular, it is floating if the chargor is free to remove the charged assets and their substitutes from the scope of the security and use them for its own benefit in the course of its business during the time before the charge crystallises or the chargee intervenes to enforce the security.

Although the test is easily stated, it continues to generate discord. Recent concerns raised by the Financial Law Committee of the City of London Law Society are illustrative.[63] The Committee acknowledges the test is easily stated, and easily applied in clear cases, but suggests that most cases are not clear, and require unacceptably fact-specific determinations without clear guidance from the courts. The Committee gave four examples of this lack of clarity: (i) where, in a property financing transaction, the borrower is able to collect rents until enforcement of the security; or (ii) where, in an asset finance transaction (for instance, in relation to a ship or an aircraft), the borrower is able to collect charter hire or lease rental before enforcement; or (iii) where, with a share charge, the borrower is able to receive dividends or to vote the shares before enforcement; or (iv) where, with security over assets in custody, the borrower can direct the management of the fund, within limits, before enforcement.[64]

These examples are not described in detail in the Committee's paper, but the test provided by the House of Lords in *Re Spectrum Plus Ltd (In Liquidation)*[65] seems to provide clear answers to all four cases.[66] First, *Spectrum* does not insist that an asset and its proceeds are a single unit, nor that the right to use proceeds is equivalent to the right to deal with the asset, nor, marginally more subtly, that a charge over an asset must be a floating charge if the chargor is entitled to use at will any proceeds that are generated by the asset. These are not the crucial distinctions identified in *Spectrum*. *Spectrum* was a case about debts, whereas the above examples ask how the *Spectrum* test will be used to characterise charges over other revenue-generating assets.

Some of these cases are easy. A charge over freehold, including freehold generating a rental income as in the first example, will be a fixed charge notwithstanding that the rental income is at the disposal of the chargor, not the chargee. This is because

[61] See, eg Beale et al, *The Law of Security and Title-Based Financing*, n 1 above, generally; Bridge et al, *The Law of Personal Property*, n 4 above, chs 7 and 14; Davies and Worthington, *Gower and Davies: Principles of Modern Company Law*, n 18 above, ch 32. Also see Joshua Getzler and Jennifer Payne (eds), *Company Charges: Spectrum and Beyond* (Oxford University Press, 2006).

[62] *Re Spectrum Plus Ltd (In Liquidation)* [2005] UKHL 41; [2005] 2 AC 680 (HL); also see *Re Brumark Investments Ltd* [2001] UKPC 28; [2001] 2 AC 710 (PC).

[63] Financial Law Committee of the City of London Law Society, *Secured Transactions Reform: Discussion Paper 2 Fixed and Floating Charges on Insolvency* (London, February 2014) esp paras 15–20.

[64] ibid para 19.

[65] *Re Spectrum Plus Ltd (In Liquidation)*, n 62 above.

[66] For more detail, see Sarah Worthington, 'Floating Charges: The Use and Abuse of Doctrinal Analysis' in Joshua Getzler and Jennifer Payne (eds), *Company Charges: Spectrum and Beyond* (Oxford University Press, 2006) ch 3; and also Sarah Worthington, 'An "Unsatisfactory Area of the Law": Fixed and Floating Charges Yet Again' (2004) 1 *International Corporate Rescue* 175.

the charged asset, the land, remains fully preserved for the benefit of the chargee notwithstanding the chargor's use of the rental income. The same is true of a charge over a ship or an aircraft, or, more prosaically, over a fleet of vehicles run by a car-hire company, or over equipment (computers, televisions, furniture, etc) hired out to customers. It is irrelevant that the equipment is subject to wear and tear, and at risk of destruction from such use. Here, the charged assets remain preserved for the benefit of the chargee even though the chargor is entitled to the benefit of the proceeds. It is only if the charged asset itself (the land or equipment) is at the free disposal of the chargor that the charge is floating.[67]

The same approach is appropriate if the charge is over shares, even if the chargor is entitled to use the dividends at will[68] or vote the shares.[69] In all of these cases, the charged assets are themselves preserved intact for the benefit of the chargee, so the charge is fixed. The context of the final example is less clear, but if the 'directions' do not concern delivering distributions from the charged fund to the chargor, then this too is a fixed charge.

But this approach is not appropriate if the charges are not over the underlying assets, but are instead over the rental or lease agreements which might be entered into in relation to those assets. In these cases, the correct analogy *is* with debts. If the chargor is entitled to the benefit of the revenue generated by the lease, then the secured asset *is* being removed from the ambit of the charge for the benefit of the chargor, not the chargee.

In the case of debts, the removal is commonly effected in one fell swoop when the debt is collected and the proceeds become available for the benefit of the chargor. But it cannot really matter that the removal is instead effected in tranches, via periodic payments, so that at the end of a defined period (even a long period) and after a series of payments, the secured asset is wholly converted to cash proceeds, which proceeds have been used for the benefit of the chargor, not the chargee. The analogy between charges over debts repayable by instalment and charges over lease agreements is obvious.[70] Similarly, a charge over contractual performance rights will be floating if the chargor, not the chargee, is entitled to the benefits of performance; and a charge over an insurance contract will be floating if the chargor, not the chargee, is entitled to use the insurance proceeds for its own benefit.

In reaching this conclusion it is irrelevant that there are still assets subject to the security, and that those assets remain of sufficiently high value to fully protect the secured obligation notwithstanding the benefits delivered to the chargor. A security is not fixed or floating depending upon whether it continues to provide adequate cover to support the underlying obligation; the sole test is whether the nominated

[67] *Re Cosslett (Contractors) Ltd*, n 10 above.

[68] *Arthur D Little (In Administration) v Ableco Finance LLC* [2002] EWHC 701 (Ch).

[69] Although the chargee may bargain for additional protection in this regard, and there is in any event likely to be some limitation on the exercise of the rights so as to preserve the underlying secured asset.

[70] This suggests that the controversial decisions in *Re Atlantic Computer Systems Plc* [1992] Ch 505 (CA) and *Re Atlantic Medical Ltd* [1993] BCLC 485 cannot be supported. In both cases, the assignments of chattel sub-leases and rental payments were held to be fixed charges even though the assignor was free to use the proceeds of the rental streams in its business. This outcome appears inconsistent with the *Spectrum* and *Brumark* decisions, and the arrangements might be better characterised as floating charges in both cases.

assets are wholly reserved, and preserved, for the benefit of the chargee. If they are not, the charge is floating.[71] This is the tough fixed/not-fixed boundary issue demanded by the test in *Spectrum*.

Perhaps underlying the questions raised by the Financial Law Committee of the City of London Law Society is the notion that it *ought* to be possible to deliver fixed charge security over long-term leasing agreements even though the chargor takes the benefit of the ongoing rental stream. This pragmatic approach would give the chargee the benefit of a fixed charge over the asset, and the chargor the benefit of the ongoing rental stream in circumstances where the value of the asset is such that it can fully protect both interests. But this wishful thinking is inconsistent with the definition of fixed and floating charges accepted in both *Spectrum* and *Brumark*.[72]

What must be remembered is that this dividing line, rendered crucial by the Insolvency Act 1986, exists not because it tracks some difficult doctrinal distinction between fixed and floating charges, nor any analytical difficulty in the delivery of a floating security to the chargee, but because it tracks a divide settled on by the legislature to define a class of secured creditors where their security will be used to advance the interests of *both* the secured and the unsecured creditors.[73] It may be simpler to change this statutory rule, rather than try to finesse a statutory line between fixed and floating charges when both are underpinned by the same doctrinal analysis of equitable security interests.

PRIORITIES

The perfection requirement of registration does not of itself confer priority or give any protection to a charge holder, although of course, as noted previously, non-registration has almost fatal consequences for the security. Instead, priority is determined by the normal rules, with timing issues determined by the date of creation of the interest,[74] not the date of registration, provided the registrable interests are indeed properly registered. Given that parties generally have 21 days to register security agreements, this gives rise to the 'the 21-day invisibility problem' which would have been eliminated if the Law Commission's proposals for 'notice filing' and associated priority rules had been introduced.

The doctrine of constructive notice has not been abolished in regard to particulars of charges held by the registrar, and so everyone dealing with a company is deemed to have notice of the particulars which are required by statute to be registered.[75] These are defined in Companies Act 2006, section 859D, and include the date of

[71] In reaching these conclusions, the 'tree/fruit' analysis so commonly relied upon may be confusing rather than helpful. See Worthington, *Proprietary Interests in Commercial Transactions*, n 46 above, 77–78, and my erroneous discussion of the *Atlantic Medical* and *Atlantic Computer* cases, subsequently recanted in various published works.

[72] *Re Spectrum Plus Ltd (In Liquidation)*, n 62 above; *Re Brumark Investments Ltd*, n 62 above.

[73] See p 421 above.

[74] *George Barker Ltd v Eynon* [1974] 1 WLR 462 (CA) (contractual lien); *Champagne Perrier-Jouet SA v HH Finch Ltd* [1982] 1 WLR 1359 (company's lien on its shares).

[75] The final version of the amended Companies Act 2006 omits specific reference to constructive notice. An earlier draft included a proposed section 859R, which made explicit provision: see www.bis.gov.uk/assets/biscore/business-law/docs/e/12-1028-explanatory-notes-draft-regulations-part-25-companies.pdf.

creation of the charge, the nature of the charge (fixed or floating), the amount secured, short particulars of the property charged, and the persons entitled to the charge, and, by way of change from the earlier rules, whether the charge includes a 'negative pledge' clause (ie a provision by which the company undertakes not to create other charges ranking in priority to or *pari passu* with the charge[76]).[77]

So the question then becomes, how do the priority rules typically affect the chargee's security?[78]

Certain rules are notable, but not controversial. Charges which appear to sweep up all the company's assets cannot, by that mere assertion, also capture recoveries gleaned from third parties which only the company's liquidator, not the company, can claim. This includes all the statutory claw-back claims noted earlier.[79] These recoveries are therefore distributable only to the unsecured creditors, not attached by charges granted to secured creditors.[80]

More specifically, a floating charge generally authorises the company to deal with the charged assets in the ordinary course of business, at least until the company defaults in its obligations. It follows that, in the absence of specific provisions to the contrary in the charge document itself, the company may not only use, sell and buy such property during the currency of a floating charge, but may also create subsequent mortgages and fixed charges (and sometimes even floating charges[81]) ranking in priority to the floating charge itself.[82] It also follows that, because a floating charge does not operate as an assignment to the debenture holder of the company's book debts and other choses in action, then, until the charge has crystallised, the company's unsecured creditors may continue to set off debts due by the company against sums which they owe to it.[83]

Finally, there is nothing to prevent the secured creditors reaching their own agreements on priority as between themselves (ie subordination agreements), and they may do this without the consent of the debtor company.[84]

None of this is especially troubling. But one case in particular merits special mention as it departs from the generally understood rules. In *Macmillan Inc v Bishopsgate Investment Trust Plc (No 3)*,[85] shares held on trust were used, without authority, to provide security by way of equitable mortgage to secure funding for the Maxwell Group. At the time the security was agreed, the lender had no knowledge

[76] CA 2006, s 859D(2)(c).

[77] This eliminates the constructive notice problem illustrated in *Siebe Gorman & Co Ltd v Barclays Bank Ltd* [1979] 2 Lloyd's Rep 142 (Ch).

[78] See, eg Bridge et al, *The Law of Personal Property*, n 4 above, ch 36 generally, and esp paras 36-021–36-028; Smith and Leslie, *The Law of Assignment*, n 41 above, ch 27.

[79] See p 421 above.

[80] *Re Oasis Merchandising Services Ltd* [1998] Ch 170 (CA); *Re MC Bacon Ltd* [1991] Ch 127.

[81] See, eg *Re Automatic Bottle Makers Ltd* [1926] Ch 412 (CA), where the first charge expressly empowered the company to do so. Where no such power is reserved, commentators generally agree that the first charge, being first in time, should have priority.

[82] See, eg *Re Castell and Brown Ltd* [1898] 1 Ch 315 (subsequent fixed charge). But the company cannot grant a subsequent *floating* charge over the same assets and having priority over the earlier floating charge: *Re Benjamin Cope & Sons Ltd* [1914] 1 Ch 800; the equities being equal, the first in time prevails.

[83] *Biggerstaff v Rowatt's Wharf Ltd* [1896] 2 Ch 93 (CA).

[84] *Cheah Theam Swee v Equiticorp Finance Group Ltd* [1992] 1 AC 472 (PC).

[85] *Macmillan Inc v Bishopsgate Investment Trust Plc (No 3)* [1995] 1 WLR 978 (Ch).

of the beneficiaries' prior equity, although the information became known later on. But the creation of the equitable mortgage (rather than a charge) had been by way of delivery of the share certificates and transfer forms to the lender, so the lender could get in the legal title without recourse to the mortgagor. Millett J, as he then was, held that the lender was free to do so, and would then hold legal title free of the earlier equitable interest. He explained the outcome as follows:[86]

> A transferor who delivers to a transferee a share certificate together with an executed transfer may still retain the legal estate for the time being, but he has done everything in his power to vest it in the transferee, while the transferee for his part has it within his own power to vest the legal estate in himself without further recourse to the transferor. As between the transferee who has given value on the one hand and the transferor and those claiming under him on the other, this rather than the time when the transferee actually obtains the legal title is to my mind the appropriate time for the question of notice to be tested ... As the facts of the present case show, modern commercial lending often involves frequent substitution of security, and this makes registration inconvenient and commercially unattractive ... To expose [the lender] to the ... risk of being bound by an adverse claim of which he had no notice when he advanced his money, and from which he would have been free if he had obtained registration, is in my judgment commercially unacceptable. It is welcome to find that it is also legally unsound.

This conclusion provides a salutary reminder of the occasional surprises in priorities disputes. All priorities disputes raise the possibility that competing interests may make substantial inroads into the value of a lender's security. But in large measure these surprises are what the company charges registration system is designed to prevent, although that must now be read with the Financial Collateral Arrangements (No 2) Regulations 2003, SI 2003/3226, as amended at various times, and all the exemptions from registration which that permits.

ANTI-DEPRIVATION PRINCIPLE

The next inroad into security agreements is provided by the common law. Counter-intuitive though it may seem, finance deals are sometimes deliberately structured so as to defeat consensual security interests on the happening of specified events. Where the event is the security holder's *own* insolvency, then the knock-on effect of the loss of security may be a diminished pool of assets available for distribution on the security holder's liquidation. The statutory claw-back rules considered earlier do not touch this sort of arrangement, and modern cases have therefore asked whether there is a common law rule which protects the security holder's creditors against this. The answer is 'yes', there is a rule, although the protection afforded is flimsy.

These odd security-defeating terms may be inserted into complex financial deals in order to obtain triple-A ratings for a lender's investment securities. This was so in *Belmont Park Investments Pty Ltd v BNY Corporate Trustee Services Ltd*.[87]

[86] ibid 1003–4.

[87] *Belmont Park Investments Pty Ltd v BNY Corporate Trustee Services Ltd* [2011] UKSC 38; [2012] 1 AC 383 (SC), para 111. Discussed in Roy Goode, 'Flip clauses: the end of the affair?' (2012) 128 *Law Quarterly Review* 171; Sarah Worthington, 'Good Faith, Flawed Assets and the Emasculation of the UK Anti-Deprivation Rule' (2012) 75 *Modern Law Review* 112.

There, the Supreme Court was asked to strike down a priority flip clause which switched the secured priority over collateral away from a Lehman Brothers credit default swaps counterparty (LBSF) and in favour of third party noteholders (including Belmont Park Investments Pty Ltd) in defined circumstances, to the potential detriment of the now insolvent Lehman Brothers counterparty, or, more particularly, Lehman's unsecured creditors.[88] The Supreme Court declined to strike down the clause, holding, as had all the courts below, that the priority flip clause did not offend the common law 'anti-deprivation rule'.

This rule is part of an overarching common law principle which insists that 'there cannot be a valid contract that a man's property shall remain his until his bankruptcy, and on the happening of that event shall go over to someone else, and be taken away from his creditors'.[89] As now conceived, this principle has two distinct limbs, directed at maintaining, respectively, the proper distribution and the maximum size of the pool of debtor assets available to be distributed on insolvency.[90]

The first limb is the *pari passu* rule (or the contracting out rule). This ensures that the insolvency 'pool' is distributed according to the Insolvency Act 1986 rules, not according to some private arrangement between the parties. For example, in *British Eagle v Air France*,[91] a contractual netting-out agreement between international airline companies was held inoperable against British Eagle on its insolvency because its effect was to vary the collection and distribution of assets which would otherwise apply. According to the Supreme Court in *Belmont*, this is a rule of strict application:[92] it is irrelevant that the parties acted in good faith, with no intention to avoid the insolvency legislation; all that matters is the effect of clause. A clause will be struck down if, on insolvency, it provides for a distribution of assets which is different from the distribution mandated by statute.

The second limb, the anti-deprivation rule (or, more informatively, the insolvency-triggered deprivation rule) ensures that the 'pool' itself is not depleted on the event of insolvency by a clause seeking to achieve just that outcome by a specific insolvency-trigger.[93] This was the issue in *Belmont Park Investments Pty Ltd v BNY Corporate Trustee Services Ltd*,[94] with parallel proceedings in the United States.[95] Given the statements of the anti-deprivation principle in the old cases, it is perhaps easy to see why LBSF's administrator thought it might have a good case in relation to the insolvency-triggered flip clause.

The majority of the Supreme Court held that although the policy behind the anti-deprivation rule is clear, ie that parties cannot, on bankruptcy, deprive the

[88] The court also addressed the treatment of 'unwind costs' between these parties, but the focus here is on the fate of the flipped security interest.

[89] *Ex p Jay* (1880) 14 Ch D 19, 26 (Cotton LJ).

[90] *Lomas v JFB Firth Rixson Inc* [2012] EWCA Civ 419, paras 96–98. It is sometimes said that, on given facts, it can be difficult to distinguish between the two rules.

[91] *British Eagle v Air France* [1975] 1 WLR 758 (HL).

[92] *Belmont Park Investments Pty Ltd v BNY Corporate Trustee Services Ltd*, n 87 above, para 13.

[93] Deprivations caused by any other event are not touched by this rule.

[94] *Belmont Park Investments Pty Ltd v BNY Corporate Trustee Services Ltd*, n 87 above.

[95] *Lehman Brothers Special Financing Inc v BNY Corporate Trustee Services Ltd* Case no 09-01242 (Bankr SDNY, 25 January 2010), reaching the conclusion that the flip clause offended the statutory *ipso facto* rule and, more questionably, that it did so whether the flip was triggered by LBIE's own insolvency or that of its parent company.

bankrupt of property which would otherwise be available for creditors, that policy can be given a common-sense application so that bona fide commercial transactions which do not have as their predominant or main purposes the insolvency-triggered deprivation of the debtor's property do not fall foul of the anti-deprivation rule. Here, the parties had no such intention, and had genuine commercial reasons for inserting the flip clause in their agreement. Accordingly, the clause did not offend the anti-deprivation principle, and thus it took its intended effect on LBSF's insolvency. The contrast between the applicability of the first and second limbs of the anti-deprivation principle could not be more stark: the first limb is judged by the unacceptable effect of the clause; the second by the unacceptable intention of the parties.

In taking this approach, the majority was clearly alive to the damage they thought could be done to substantial and complex financial markets if legitimate expectations as to the validity of standard form contracts (as these were), freely agreed by the parties, were frustrated by the court's over-zealous application of a rule they said was designed to deal only with deliberate evasion of the bankruptcy legislation. But, as Lord Mance noted in his separate judgment, the principle of party autonomy cannot automatically override third party insolvency rights.[96] If parties need a safe harbour allowing for these sorts of terms, then the argument that this is more appropriately achieved by statute, as in the United States, seems unassailable.[97]

Instead, the Supreme Court's focus on the parties' intentions allowed it to sidestep the only really difficult doctrinal issue of whether such a flip clause does indeed deliver a deprivation, or whether it simply describes a perfectly legitimate 'flawed asset'. The 'flawed asset' argument suggests that the insolvency-triggered flip clause describes a limitation which is integral to the definition of the asset owned by the creditor, so that—when insolvency intervenes—the creditor's assets are not 'lost': the creditor has exactly the asset it had before, although the event renders that asset less valuable to the insolvent than it might otherwise have been.

This 'flawed asset' argument relies on the central truth in insolvency law that creditors must take their insolvent debtor as they find him, flawed assets included.[98] Of course, this follows only if the flaw itself is one which the law permits the parties to include in their agreement, and, with respect and despite *Belmont*, it seems impossible to uphold the anti-deprivation principle and yet permit such insolvency-triggered flaws. The flawed asset argument is in any event conceded to be impossible outside the context of choses in action.[99]

For completeness, note that these rules do not outlaw subordination arrangements. In *Belmont*, the question was not whether the issuer (a special purpose vehicle)

[96] *Belmont Park Investments Pty Ltd v BNY Corporate Trustee Services Ltd*, n 87 above, para 159. Although he reached the same conclusion as the majority by finding that the clause did not effect a 'deprivation' of assets.

[97] In the United States, there is a safe harbour for derivative contracts which in effect removes the *ipso facto* rule for swap agreements. Perhaps oddly, this safe harbour was held not to extend to terms governing priority over the collateral. This separation of proprietary security from the underlying obligation does not seem entirely convincing, but that is a matter of statutory interpretation, where one might expect the approach to safe harbours to favour limiting their scope.

[98] Calnan, *Rights and Insolvency*, n 2 above, para 1.20, taking a liberal view of flawed assets.

[99] See, eg *British Eagle*, n 91 above, 780 (Lord Cross), and Sarah Worthington, 'Insolvency Deprivation, Public Policy and Priority Flip Clauses' (2010) 7 *International Corporate Rescue* 28.

could offer security over its assets in a way that, *on its insolvency*, prioritised one secured creditor (LBSF, the first chargee) in some circumstances, and a second chargee (Perpetual Trustee) in other circumstances. If the secured creditors agree, this flipping of agreed subordination is possible. The issuer's unsecured creditors are completely unaffected by the arrangement, and so have nothing to complain about. But this was not the question in *Belmont*. There the question was, did the priority flip effect a deprivation of LBSF's assets when triggered by LBSF's insolvency?

RELIEF FROM FORFEITURE

Finally, there is the possibility (perhaps a slim one) that enforcement of the chargee's security may be upset by an order for relief from forfeiture protecting the chargor from actual or threatened forfeiture of its assets to a chargee who has enforceable security over them. Such an order will permit the chargor to retain or redeem the charged assets, but only on terms, as described below. The jurisdiction is limited, both practically and legally.[100]

Practically, the conditions for relief will at a minimum require the chargor to meet any outstanding obligations due to the chargee, including the costs of delay and probably certain other sums covering incidental losses. If the chargee has these funds to hand, then the security is perhaps unlikely to have been enforced in the first place.

Legally, the jurisdiction is seen as motivated by the same concerns as underpin the equity of redemption; ie equity's distaste for property-owners losing their property for failing to pay money strictly on time.[101] But running against that is the competing argument that properly agreed contract terms should be enforced.[102] The jurisdiction is therefore most often illustrated where the forfeiture provision is added by way of security, and the primary object of the bargain can be delivered, by appropriate payment, when the matter comes before the court.[103] But the jurisdiction is not so wide as to routinely permit late payment of outstanding sums, plus any incidental losses, despite delay and notwithstanding the parties' agreement:[104]

> The word 'appropriate' [in considering the appropriate circumstances in which to exercise the jurisdiction] involves consideration of the conduct of the applicant for relief, in particular whether his default was wilful, of the gravity of the breaches, and of the disparity

[100] See Bridge et al, *The Law of Personal Property*, n 4 above, paras 15-130–15-135. See also Mark Pawlowski, 'The Scope of Equity's Jurisdiction to Relieve against Forfeiture of Interests in Property Other than Land' [1994] *Journal of Business Law* 372; Lionel Smith, 'Relief Against Forfeiture: A Restatement' [2001] *Cambridge Law Journal* 178; Michael Bryan, 'Equitable Relief from Forfeiture: Performance or Restitution?' in Charles EF Rickett (ed), *Justifying Private Law Remedies* (Oxford, Hart Publishing, 2008) 363; Sarah Worthington, 'What is Left of Equity's Relief against Forfeiture?' in Elise Bant and Matthew Harding (eds), *Exploring Private Law* (Cambridge University Press, 2010) ch 11.

[101] *Cukurova Finance International Ltd v Alfa Telecom Turkey Ltd* [2013] UKPC 20 (PC) at para 86 (Lord Neuberger).

[102] *Shiloh Spinners v Harding* [1973] AC 691 (HL) at 722–23 (Lord Wilberforce).

[103] ibid.

[104] ibid 722–23, cited in *Cukurova Finance International Ltd v Alfa Telecom Turkey Ltd*, n 101 above, paras 88–89.

between the value of the property of which forfeiture is claimed as compared with the damage caused by the breach.

This last consideration would seem to explain why the jurisdiction is commonly illustrated by older cases of foreclosure of mortgages of land, or forfeiture of leases, where the potential loss to the defaulting mortgagor or lessee far outweighs the damage caused to the mortgagee or lessor by the breach of covenant. By contrast, there seems little need to afford protection when the security is by way of charge, since enforcement by sale and appropriation of the outstanding sums does not deliver a windfall to the chargee. Indeed, until last year there appear to be no illustrations of relief from forfeiture for securities by way of charge.

But last year a rather unusual case came before the Privy Council. In *Cukurova Finance International Ltd v Alfa Telecom Turkey Ltd*,[105] Alfa Telecom Turkey Ltd (ATT) lent US$1.352 billion to Cukurova Finance International Ltd (CFI). The interest rates were high,[106] and the loan was secured on shares in the Cukurova group. These shares gave control of Turkcell, Turkey's largest mobile telephone company. The chargor executed blank transfers of the shares and handed them over to ATT. The Financial Collateral Arrangements (No 2) Regulations 2003, SI 2003/3226 entitled ATT to appropriate the shares in the event of a default. This ATT did in 2007.[107] In fact, this had been its goal all along: it was more interested in securing control of Turkcell than in recovery of its loan.

Notwithstanding this appropriation, about six weeks later CFI tendered the total sums due (including sums for default interest for late payment). ATT refused to accept the tender, on the basis it had already legitimately appropriated the shares. Despite this, CFI held the funds in an escrow account for three years. The parties litigated until 2013.

The material issue for present purposes is whether ATT was entitled to enforce its security, or whether CFI was entitled to relief from forfeiture. The Privy Council held that this was a classic case for the exercise of the jurisdiction to grant relief,[108] and nothing in the Financial Collateral Arrangements (No 2) Regulations 2003 altered that.[109] If disparity between the value of the property forfeited as compared with the damage caused by the breach were needed, then that was found in the failure of the parties in agreeing their valuation formula (as required under the financial collateral regulations) to recognise the financial value of the control premium in ATT's acquisition of the shares.[110] But it is hard to resist the conclusion that the Board was heavily influenced by the fact that, all along, ATT's goal was to acquire control, not secure its loan, and had acted accordingly in enforcing its security, even if those actions were not legally 'improper'.[111]

[105] *Cukurova Finance International Ltd v Alfa Telecom Turkey Ltd*, n 101 above.

[106] Interest was payable at an annual rate of 8 per cent over LIBOR, with provision for a default rate of 11.5 per cent over LIBOR.

[107] Although in the ensuing litigation ATT was enjoined from registering the transfer.

[108] *Cukurova Finance International Ltd v Alfa Telecom Turkey Ltd*, n 101 above, paras 80–97. See also *Shiloh Spinners Ltd v Harding*, n 102 above; *BICC Plc v Burndy Corp* [1985] Ch 232.

[109] ibid paras 98–115.

[110] ibid para 125(a).

[111] ibid para 125(d) and generally.

The need for commercial certainty was recognised by the Board,[112] but the outcome is unlikely to make parties feel secure, especially in the cases where white knights fund ailing companies on a 'loan-to-own' basis.

In other contexts, the more important outcome of this litigation is its findings concerning the terms on which relief from forfeiture will be granted.[113] Typically relief from forfeiture is granted in short order, and the party in default pays up on its outstanding obligations, at the penalty rate of interest for delay if that has been imposed, plus additional sums for other losses and expenses incurred by the chargee. If that rule were applied here, CFI would be liable for six years of interest payments at the penalty rate notwithstanding its early tender of what the parties assumed to be the full amount outstanding, and which it had held, at its own expense, in escrow for three years.

In the end, the Board agreed unanimously that, from the time of CFI's initial tender of the outstanding sum plus penalty interest, interest should not run at all for the time the funds were in escrow, and should then only run at the standard contractual rate of 8 per cent over LIBOR, and not the penalty rate of 11.5 per cent over LIBOR. However, the members disagreed vehemently as to the principles by which they arrived at that conclusion. The majority regarded the courts' discretion as much wider than the minority did,[114] while agreeing that in general the overriding factor guiding the court in settling terms would be the underlying contractual agreement between the parties.[115] With respect, it seems very hard to argue with the logic of the minority that when a mortgagor is permitted by the court to invoke its right to redeem, the court is simply extending the time within which the money due under the mortgage must be paid,[116] and the terms on which relief is granted must follow inexorably from that.[117]

CONCLUSION

Exposing the scope and scale of these modern dilemmas suggests that, even if elegant, English security law is not so clear and certain as its adherents often suggest. The law reports are testament to that. Whether or not we eventually adopt Professor Beale's Law Commission proposals for personal property security legislation, these uncertainties will need resolution. And, however elegant the current English rules on security, they will not be taken up elsewhere if they cannot be laid out clearly and coherently for comparative assessment. Since commercial activity is increasingly international, we will then be left, literally and metaphorically, as an island nation.

[112] ibid para 126; see also *Cukurova Finance International Ltd v Alfa Telecom Turkey Ltd*, n 101 above, paras 43–44 (Lord Mance) and para 122 (Lord Neuberger).

[113] *Cukurova Finance International Ltd v Alfa Telecom Turkey Ltd*, n 101 above.

[114] For the majority, Lords Mance (delivering the judgment), Kerr and Clarke; and for the minority, Lords Neuberger and Sumption delivering separate judgments but agreeing with each other.

[115] *Cukurova Finance International Ltd v Alfa Telecom Turkey Ltd*, n 101 above, para 13.

[116] ibid paras 79 and 110–11 (Lord Neuberger), and paras 178–80 (Lord Sumption).

[117] But see Peter Turner, '"Mending Men's Bargains" in Equity: Mortgage Redemption and Relief against Forfeiture' (2014) 130 *Law Quarterly Review* 188, suggesting neither the majority nor the minority got this right.

Trends in Transnational and European Commercial Law

23

The Numerus Clausus *of Property Rights: A European Principle?*

CHRISTIAN VON BAR*

INTRODUCTION

THE FOLLOWING LINES, dedicated to Hugh Beale with my heartfelt congratulations on his retirement and in thankful memory of our common years as members of the Commission on European Contract Law and the Study Group on a European Civil Code, discuss the question whether the principle of a *numerus clausus* of property rights is a common principle of European private law. It deserves our attention because this principle has never been accepted without reservations throughout the European Union and has recently become subject to substantial debate. Some regard the *numerus clausus* principle as fundamental and universal,[1] others as a main cause of a (perceived or actual) scientific backwardness of property law and the lack of theoretical interest it purportedly attracts.[2]

PREDETERMINED TYPE, PREDETERMINED CONTENT, *NUMERUS CLAUSUS*

Property rights having third party effect or an 'effect *in rem*' require counterweights in the rules on the protection of legitimate third party expectations. Many identify as such a counterweight the theory that property rights may only arise and exist in those forms provided for and pre-defined in their outlines by the law. That is the core idea behind what one habitually refers to by the short-hand of *numerus clausus* (closed catalogue) principle on the continent. Often this principle is further differentiated into the principles of predetermined type and of predetermined content. The principle of predetermined type means that one may only use those types of property rights provided for by the law, while the principle of predetermined content means that one may only fill them with a content accepted by the law.

* Translation by *Christoph Karl Sliwka*.

1 S van Erp, in S van Erp and B Akkermans (eds), *Cases, Materials and Text on Property Law*, Ius Commune Casebooks for the Common Law of Europe (Oxford, Hart Publishing, 2012) 38.

2 JAC Vieira, *Direitos reais* (Coimbra, Coimbra Editora, 2008) 210 (whose analysis so far remained without practical effect; few legal systems adhere as strictly to the principle of *numerus clausus* as the Portuguese one).

A legal rule illustrating the principle of predetermined type is, for example, found in Spanish Civil Code, article 525 under which property rights of use and habitation (Spanish Civil Code, article 524) may not be let or transferred to another person under any type of title. The principle of predetermined type is weakened where, for example, security rights may be transformed into rights of use through mere party agreement. Greek Civil Code, article 1221 decrees that it could 'be agreed that the pledgee retains the profits from use of the pledged goods'. By consequence, the right of pledge, intended as a security right, assumes traits of a right of use under such an agreement; the law thus accepts the creation of hybrid forms in spite of the 'generally' inherent principle of predetermined type. The differentiation between the principles of predetermined type and of predetermined content is, as a matter of fact, impossible to maintain in a precise manner. A legal system, for example, which denies parties the ability to create a pledge without transfer of possession to the pledgee (predetermined type) necessarily also prevents them from agreeing on a waiver of the transfer of possession (predetermined content). At the very least such an agreement would remain without effect against third parties (*numerus clausus*).

HEARTLANDS OF *NUMERUS CLAUSUS*

The numerical majority of European legal systems treats the principle of *numerus clausus* as a mere expression of the perfectly obvious. It is quite true that overall there are few legal provisions explicitly establishing the principle as such. Portuguese Civil Code, article 1306(1) is a rare example. 'Not permitted', the article says, 'is the creation of restrictions of the right of ownership or subdivided forms of this right, unless in those cases provided for by the law'. Article 1306(1) is supplemented by Portuguese Civil Code, article 406(2) under which a contract has 'against third parties ... effects only in those instances and rules expressly provided for by the law'. The effect of this provision is not only to hinder the creation of a trust with proprietary effect under Portuguese law.[3] Portuguese courts went beyond that in refusing, based on Portuguese Civil Code, article 1306(1), to treat an agreement on the retention of title as an agreement creating a proprietary right of use or security for the benefit of the vendor. Accordingly, a retention of title was found to be different in nature from a property right.[4] Relying on the principle of *numerus clausus*, the Supreme Court further denied any proprietary effect to the conditions of sale of a municipality. The municipality had sold pieces of land it owned to different buyers through public auction. The buyers had promised to the municipality

[3] MJRC Vaz Tomé and D Leite de Campos, *Propriedade fiduciária (trust)—estudo para a sua consagração no direito português* (Coimbra, Almedina, 1999) 277–90, esp 287–89, however, proclaim Portuguese law's *propriedade fiduciária* and with it the trust itself an atypical property right (a *direito real atípico*). According to them, legal theory should be able to enforce such a *direito real atípico* against the prevalence of the *numerus clausus* principle since the latter is said to be of no pratical value and a piece from the museum of conceptual jurisprudence. At the very least, these authors submit, it should be possible to enlarge the number of exisiting property rights; still more preferable would it be in their view to allow for their creation through party autonomy.

[4] STJ 2 November 2004, CJ(ST) XII (2004–3) 102, 103; STJ 9 October 2008, Processo 07A3965, available at www.dgsi.pt.

to limit building activity on the land acquired to a certain measure, but not all buyers adhered to that promise. A lawsuit brought by those buyers faithful to the contract, and fearful of a loss in value of their own land, against their neighbours falling victim to a building frenzy failed. The court refused to assume the creation of an easement for the benefit of the claimants and went on to explain that no other property right could have been created in light of the rule in Portuguese Civil Code, article 1306(1).[5]

An even more direct reference to the principle of predetermined type in property rights is found in Greek Civil Code, article 973: 'Rights granting an unmediated power over objects, with effect against everybody (property rights), are ownership, easement, pledge and mortgage'. Other property rights are unknown to the Greek Civil Code and citizens are not free to bring them into being either.[6] For example, the courts repeatedly concluded from the application of the *numerus clausus* principle that possession was no property right since it was not mentioned in Greek Civil Code, article 973.[7] From this it could further be concluded that a transfer of possession in immovable property required neither written form nor, and even less so, a notary deed.[8] Likewise, possession of a right of way (be it in good or bad faith) was not found to establish a proprietary right since possession of a right was again not mentioned in Greek Civil Code, article 973.[9]

The Italian legislator chose to limit his express recognition of the *numerus clausus* principle in Italian Civil Code, article 2741(2) to security rights (and not to extend it to rights of use), but courts[10] and scholars[11] agree that it amounts to a general principle of property law. Thus, it would be impossible to create, through autonomous party decision, property rights other than those provided for by the law. This view is derived from the consideration that the transferability of objects would be unduly hindered if private individuals assumed the power to break apart the right of ownership at their discretion with effect against all the world. The foregoing would, moreover, conflict with the general principle of relativity of contractual relationships (Italian Civil Code, article 1372).[12] For property rights in land, reference is further made to Italian Civil Code, article 2643 and the rules on the *trascrizione* (registration) in the land register. From this it is said one could conclude that property rights in land are limited to a conclusive catalogue which, in turn, is said to again

[5] STJ 29 June 1989, BMJ 388 (1989) 520.

[6] AS Georgiades, *Empragmato Dikaio I* (Athens, Sakkula, 1991) s 2, para 8; NT Triantos, *Astikos kodikas* (Athens, Nomike Bibliotheke, 2009) 1185; IS Spyridakis, *Empragmato Dikaio* (Athens, Ant N Sakkoulas, 1983) 19; DE Papasteriou, *Empragmato Dikaio I* (Athens/Thessaloniki, Sakkoulas, 2008) 29.

[7] See, eg Areopag 1593/1979, No B 28 (1979) 1120; Areopag 291/1989, EEN 34 (1990) 70 and Areopag 220/2000, EllDik 41 (2000) 762.

[8] Areopag 220/2000, n 7 above.

[9] Athens Court of Appeal 6099/2000, EllDik 46 (2005) 498; Patmos Local Court 4/1997, available at www.dsanet.gr.

[10] Established case-law, see, eg Cass 29 February 1960, no 392, Rep Giur it 1960, 2502; Cass 23 August 1978, no 3931, Mass Giust civ 1978, 1642 and Cass 26 February 2008, no 5034, NGCC 2008, I, 1272.

[11] See generally S Troiano, in S Grundmann and A Zaccaria (eds), *Einführung in das italienische Recht* (Frankfurt aM, Verlag Recht und Wirtschaft, 2007) 270–71.

[12] M Comporti, *Contributo allo studio del diritto reale* (Milan, Giuffrè, 1997) 287; A Natucci, *La tipicità dei diritti reali* (Padua, Cedam, 1982) vol 1, 160; F Gazzoni, *Manuale di diritto privato*, 13th edn (Naples, Edizioni scientifiche italiane, 2007) 212.

confirm the general principle.[13] Austrian ABGB, section 308 finally contains a kind of legal catalogue of property rights. According to it, 'property rights are the right of possession, of ownership, of pledge, of easement and of heredity'. This catalogue is, however, rather hapless. Today, one no longer counts personal rights to heredity at all[14] and possession only to a limited degree amongst property rights; by contrast, Austrian ABGB, section 308 (yet) fails to mention numerous property rights created (through special acts of law) over time.

While the principle of *numerus clausus* of property rights has not been cast into legal form in Germany, the Netherlands and (with the exception of Slovenian SPZ, article 2) all Member States of Middle Eastern Europe, it still amounts to binding law. Scholars and courts conclude on the principle from the overall system of the respective codifications and strictly adhere to it.[15] Time and again it is stressed that the principles of predetermined type and of predetermined content are essential for reasons of legal certainty and legal clarity. Legal relationships relating to objects necessarily need to be recognisable from an outside perspective; fuzzy criteria (such as the widespread limitation of rights through the principle of good faith in the law of obligations) should be reduced to a minimum when it comes to property law. For the Czech Republic, *Eliáš* goes so far as to proclaim the principle of *numerus clausus* a necessary consequence of the absolute nature of property rights.[16] This certainly overshoots the mark but it illustrates the importance ascribed to the principles of predetermined type and predetermined content for the wider understanding of property law in those parts of the world. In Poland the validity of the *numerus clausus* principle is apparently taken to be so self-explanatory that local study books limit themselves to noting that only law itself could define satisfactory rules on the third party effect of personal rights, while property rights are immune to attempted modifications without proper legal basis.[17] One additional and important reason for the general adherence to the principles of predetermined type and predetermined content is said to lie, as *Menyhárd* points out for Hungary, in continental law's abstract notion of ownership. According to him, whenever one resolves, for the benefit of unimpeded transferability of titles in land, to avoid a permanent separation between

[13] A Gambaro, *Il diritto di proprietà* (Milan, Giuffrè, 1995) 67.

[14] OGH 22 October 2003, SZ 2003/134.

[15] See, eg FHJ Mijnssen, AA van Velten and SE Bartels, in C Asser, *Carel Asser's handleiding tot de beoefening van het Nederlands burgerlijk recht. Zakenrecht. Eigendom en beperkte rechten*, 15th edn, no 2 (Deventer, Kluwer, 2008) 2; F Szilágyi, in W Faber and B Lurger, *National Reports on the Transfer of Movables in Europe*, vol 3, *Germany, Greece, Lithuania, Hungary* (Munich, Sellier, 2011) 458–59; E Gniewek, *Prawo rzeczowe*, 7th edn (Warsaw, Beck, 2008) 14, para 35 and 20–21, paras 49–50, as well as Polish SN 13 January 2011, III CSK 85/10, Lex-No 686143; A Menyhárd, *Dologi jog* (Budapest, Osiris, 2007) 18; BGH 13 September 2013, NZM 2013, 733, 734; A Stadler, 'Einleitung zum Sachenrecht' in HT Soergel (ed), *Bürgerliches Gesetzbuch*, 13th edn (Stuttgart, Kohlhammer, 2002) vol 14, para 41; HH Seiler, 'Buch 3: Sachenrecht: Einleitung zum Sachenrecht' in J Staudinger (ed), *J von Staudingers Kommentar zum Bürgerlichen Gesetzbuch mit Einführungsgesetz und Nebengesetzen*, 2007 update (Berlin, Sellier–de Gruyter, 2007) para 39; J Švestka and J Dvořák, *Občanské právo hmotné*, 5th edn (Prague, Wolters Kluwer, 2009) 273; P Venedikov, *Novo veshtno pravo* (Sofia, Izd-vo SIBI, 1995) 33, para 19.

[16] K Eliáš et al, *Občanský zákoník. Velký akademický komentář* (Prague, Linde, 2008) vol I, 511.

[17] J Ignatowicz and K Stefaniuk, *Prawo rzeczowe*, 2nd edn (Warsaw, LexisNexis, 2006) 35; E Gniewek, *Prawo rzeczowe*, 8th edn (Warsaw, Beck, 2010) 19–22, paras 49–53.

the right to transfer title in a piece of land and the right to use it, one is bound to adhere to the principle of *numerus clausus*.[18]

OWNERSHIP AS A SECURITY RIGHT: A CONTENTIOUS ISSUE

It is, nevertheless, not always true that commitment to the same principle results in identical conclusions. This is illustrated by the development of so called *security ownership* in movables. German courts early on recognised this instrument, arguing that from a property law perspective it is ownership, not a 'new' kind of pledge which would conflict with the principle that a pledge in movables requires a transfer of possession and thus with German law's principle of *numerus clausus*.[19] Similar views are expressed by the predominant opinion in Greece[20] and Hungary, respectively.[21] In France, however, courts treated the matter the other way round. According to them, security ownership had to be denied recognition because French law of movable property only knows a pledge by transfer of possession while security ownership is a mere attempt to circumvent this requirement.[22] For the same reasons, in Austria security ownership is only recognised where it is indeed accompanied by a (permanent) transfer of ownership to the secured party.[23] In addition, several other provisions on a pledge in movable property are applied to security ownership.[24]

FRANCE AND SPAIN: *NUMERUS APERTUS* INSTEAD OF *NUMERUS CLAUSUS*?

In France, our issue recently reacquired a surprising topicality. Only a limited number of French scholars still maintain the view that it is impossible to create new property rights with an *erga omnes* effect by autonomous party agreement.[25] These authors point to French Code Civil, article 543, under which 'one can have in goods ownership, a simple right of use or just easements'. This catalogue is regarded as conclusive. Especially the organisation of ownership in land is treated as *d'ordre public* because of its over-arching importance for third parties, for the limited number of possible ways to transfer ownership and for legal certainty.[26] Moreover,

[18] Menyhárd, *Dologi jog*, n 15 above, 142.

[19] See already the seminal decision RG 8 November 1904, RGZ 59, 146, 148.

[20] See, eg Areopag 1307/1994, No B 44 (1994) 419; Court of Appeal Thessaloniki 2642/1992, EllDik 35 (1992) 629 and Court of Appeal Athens 6395/1976, No B 25 (1976) 406.

[21] See, eg Menyhárd, *Dologi jog*, 2nd edn (Budapest, ELTE Eötvös Kiado, 2010) 396.

[22] Cass civ 8 July 1969, Rev crit dr int priv 1971, 75 (note Fouchard).

[23] Seminal OGH 22 June 1926, SZ 8/200; established case-law ever since.

[24] B Eccher, in H Koziol, P Bydlinski and R Bollenberger (eds), *Kurzkommentar zum ABGB*, 2nd edn (Vienna, Springer, 2007) s 358, para 4.

[25] See especially J Carbonnier, *Droit civil* (Paris, Quadrige, 2004) vol II, 1588, para 706; H and L Mazeaud and F Chabas, *Introduction à l'étude du droit*, Leçons de droit civil, 12th edn (Paris, Ed Montchrestien, 2000) 273, para 163; F Zenati-Castaing and T Revet, *Les biens*, 3rd edn (Paris, Presses Universitaires de France, 2008) 458, para 296 and 473, para 313.

[26] See especially F Terré and Y Lequette, *Grands arrêts de la jurisprudence civile*, 10th edn (Paris, Dalloz, 1994) 267; similar F Terré and P Simler, *Les biens*, 6th edn (Paris, Dalloz, 2002) 60, para 52.

several 'younger' laws (ie those published after the Code Civil) expressly stressed the proprietary character of the rights they created. This is, for example, true for the Law of 26 June 1902 about the hereditary building lease or *emphyteusis* (the *bail emphytéotique*), and for Code de la construction et de l'habitation, art 251-1 about the *bail à construction*. It is concluded that if one needed a new law in order to create a property right, parties in turn could not be free to create them in their own right.[27] However, not everyone accepts these arguments.[28] On the contrary, the point is made that even the hereditary building right is nowhere expressly qualified as a property right by law, despite the early, and today entirely undisputed, recognition as one by the courts.[29] Moreover, nothing is said to be found in the wording of French Code Civil, article 543 that would support the thesis that it established a closed catalogue. By contrast, it is said to follow from the principle of freedom of contract that parties are capable of creating any rights not expressly forbidden by the law, including rights transferring direct power over an object to their holder, even if the law has not expressly endorsed them in its list of property rights.[30]

It turned out decisive for legal practice that the Court of Cassation had already renounced a universal application of the *numerus clausus* principle in a decision dating back to 13 February 1834: 'Les articles 544, 546, 552 du Code civil sont déclaratifs du droit commun relativement à la nature et aux effets de la propriété, mais ne sont pas prohibitifs'.[31] Accordingly, neither articles 544, 546 and 552 of the Code Civil nor any other rule of law prohibit modifications to the right of ownership. It would hence be (and actually is) possible to create new property rights, especially rights of use, by way of contract or unilateral act. Nevertheless, judicial recognition of such property rights created by party agreement remains a rare phenomenon. In 1834, there was a case on a form of co-ownership in the fruits and yields of a riparian strip of land different from the model of the Civil Code; in 1873, on the recognition of a hereditary building right;[32] in 1984, on the right to mount placards on the wall of a house;[33] and in 1992, first on a sole and exclusive right to use part of a court co-owned by several owners of residential apartments,[34] and, some months later, a right of pasture, the 'right to the second grass' (*droit*

[27] Such is the view expressed by (in spite of their rather cirtical stance towards the *numerus clausus* principle) P Malaurie and L Aynès, *Les biens*, 3rd edn (Paris, Defrénois, 2007) 89, para 358.

[28] Among the publications arguing against the reign of the *numerus clausus* principle are, eg M Planiol, G Ripert and M Picard, *Les biens*, 2nd edn (Paris, Librairie générale de droit et de jurisprudence, 1952) 54, para 48 and C Larroumet, *Les biens. Droits réels principaux*, Droit civil, 5th edn (Paris, Economica, 2006) 33, para 51. See further to the discussion especially C Atias, *Les biens*, 10th edn (Paris, LexisNexis, 2009) 51, para 74 and P Jourdain, *Les biens* (Paris, Dalloz, 1995) 10, para 8.

[29] The *droit de superifice* is generally classified as a *variété de droit de propriété* since Cass 16 December 1873, DP 1874, I, 249. It does not expire through non-use, persists, unless the parties agree otherwise, forever, can be charged with a mortgage and even be acquired through adverse possession. The beneficiary of a *droit de superificie* disposes of all advantages of ownership: *usus*, *fructus* und *abusus* (Malaurie and Aynès, *Les biens*, n 27 above, 284, para 904; Jourdain, *Les biens*, n 28 above, 238, para 177).

[30] Malaurie and Aynès, *Les biens*, n 27 above, 90, para 358.

[31] Cass req 13 February 1834, S 1834, 1, 205; D 1834, 1, 218. Translation: 'Articles 544, 546, 552 of the Code Civil describe the common legal basis regarding the nature and the effects of ownership but have no prohibitive function.'

[32] Cass 16 December 1873, DP 1874, I, 249.

[33] Cass civ 18 January 1984, D 1985, 504 (note Zenati).

[34] Cass civ 4 March 1992, D 1992, 386 (note Atias) confirmed in Cass civ 24 October 2007, Bull civ 2007, III, no 183.

de seconde herbe).[35] In France, one can thus observe a softening of the principle of *numerus clausus*, but examples remain few in number and rather undramatic. The Court of Cassation ultimately only accepted modifications to property rights already known as such, but not the creation of entirely new property rights 'out of the blue'.[36]

In Spain, the *numerus clausus* principle is equally not beyond criticism. Leading representatives of legal scholarship even promote the opinion that instead of following it, Spanish law adheres to a *numerus apertus* ('open catalogue') principle.[37] To support this view, it has been argued (i) that the Civil Code lacks a legal basis for a *numerus clausus* principle, and (ii) that Ley Hipotecaria (LH), article 2, read in conjunction with Reglamento Hipotecario (RH), article 7, expressly provides for the possibility to enter into the land register not only the rights mentioned in the Civil Code but 'any other right' (*y otros cualesquirea reales*). Whether this and the development of the law as practised for the past roughly 100 years support the notion that Spain is a country following a *numerus apertus* principle, may be deemed an open question. Ultimately, in Spain everything again boils down to determining the limitations of party autonomy in relation to property rights provided for by the law as well as those not (yet) contained in any rule of law.[38] Regarding the first group, Díez-Picazo is of the opinion that Spanish law of property is sufficiently flexible to adapt its contents to meet the requirements of an individual case by way of a broad interpretation. By contrast, the legal framework does not provide for the creation of entirely new property rights. In his view, while the law authorises parties to modify existing property rights on the basis of the written model, party autonomy falls short of allowing for the creation of new, atypical property rights.[39]

An examination of registration practice confirms this. The most important exception from the rule that parties are not free to create entirely new property rights can probably be found in the introduction of the hereditary building right (which today has long since been subject to statutory regulation). A more recent example can be found in so-called time-sharing, which was already awarded the character of a property right when a clarification to that effect was not yet in place.[40] Otherwise, decisions mostly concerned rather moderate steps of development: the Dirección General de los Registros y del Notariado (DGRN, the decision-making body of the land registrars) has, for example, recognised the right to install placard boards on foreign ground as a property right in immovable property which is capable of registration.[41] It has furthermore accepted a number of extensions of the *derechos*

[35] Cass 25 March 1992, D 1993, 65 (note de la Marnierre).

[36] Larroumet, *Les biens*, n 28 above, 33, para 51.

[37] See in this sense, inter alia, M Albaladejo, *Derecho civil. Tomo III: Derecho de bienes*, 10th edn (Madrid, Edisofer, 2004) 30; C Lasarte Álvarez, *Principios de derecho civil. Tomo IV: Propiedad y derechos reales de goce*, 9th edn (Madrid, Marcial Pons, 2009) 14 and X O'Callaghan Muñoz, *Compendio de derecho civil. Tomo III: Derechos reales e hipotecario*, 5th edn (Madrid, Dijusa, 2007) 36.

[38] So correctly L Díez-Picazo, *Fundamentos del derecho civil patrimonial. Tomo III: Las relaciones jurídico-reales. El registro de la propiedad. La posesión*, 5th edn (Madrid, Ec Civitas, 2008) 141.

[39] Díez-Picazo, *Fundamentos*, n 38 above, 136–37.

[40] DGRN 4 March 1993, RAJ 1993 no 2471, 3176.

[41] DGRN 25 November 1992, RAJ 1992 no 9494, 12432.

de adquisición preferente (rights to preferred acquisition of an object).[42] Such *derechos de adquisición preferente* may assume the form of purely contractual rights, but the parties are free to endow them with the characteristics of a property right.[43] Parties have, in other words, the ability to ascribe the character of a property right to a *derecho de adquisición preferente*, but only where they expressly agree to do so; where no such agreement is concluded, such a right remains a purely contractual one.[44] The Tribunal Supremo agrees with this view.[45] Entered into the land register were mutual rights to preferred acquisition of a piece of land on the respectively other side of a common border, securing a countertrade.[46] It is furthermore possible to agree with an effect *in rem* on a right for the benefit of the acquirer of one of two neighbouring pieces of land allowing him to build an underground carpark stretching below the seller's remaining piece of land in the future.[47] Entered into the land register was finally an administrative decision by a public authority permitting a public limited company to charge a piece of land which held a palace with a mortgage. The administrative decision included the right for the company to maintain a hotel in the palace for 55 years.[48]

NUMERUS CLAUSUS PRINCIPLE IN ENGLISH AND IRISH PROPERTY LAW

The system of English and of Irish common law equally only allows for the translation of interests in objects into property rights where objective law provides a corresponding design. This is only warranted in a limited number of cases.[49] '[I]t must not therefore be supposed' according to the rule in *Keppel v Bailey*, 'that incidents of a novel kind can be devised and attached to property at the fancy or caprice of any owner'.[50] This principle, however, only applies without qualifications to common law, but not to equity. Equity is, according to a familiar saying, still in its 'fertile age'.[51] For rights in land, section 1(1) and (2) of the English Law of Property Act 1925 contains (from a continental European perspective) an express legal confirmation of the *numerus clausus* principle of common law, and section 1(3) of the same Act adds that

[42] It is important that such rights may be granted without an express legal basis (as eg in Spanish Civil Code, art 1507, for a right *in rem* to repurchase) through party agreement. This concerns, inter alia, the *derecho de tanteo* and the *derecho de opción de compra* (J Puig Brutau, *Fundamentos de Derecho Civil. Prenda, anticresis, hipoteca inmobiliaria y mobiliaria, reserva de dominio, venta fiduciaria, anotación preventiva, tanteo, retracto, opción censos*, 3rd edn (Barcelona, Bosch, 1983) 395). However, they have to fulfil the conditions of RH, art 14 in order to be recognised as a property right.

[43] The DGRN specified the further conditions for a right *in personam* to be 'promoted' to a property right within this group in Resolución 20 September 1966, RAJ 1966 no 4020.

[44] DGRN 6. March 2001, RAJ 2002 no 2172.

[45] TS 3 March 1995, RAJ 1995 no 1776, 2303.

[46] DGRN 20 September 1966, RAJ 1966 no 4020, 4020.

[47] DGRN 14 May 1984, RAJ 1984 no 2588, 1993.

[48] DGRN 16 July 2002, RAJ 2002 no 9317, 17179.

[49] TW Merrill and HE Smith, 'Optimal Standardization in the Law of Property: The Numerus Clausus Principle' (2000) 110 *Yale Law Journal* 1, 3.

[50] *Keppell v Bailey* (1834) 39 ER 1042, 1049.

[51] Further (also on the quite obscure origin of this image) PV Baker and PSJ Langan, *Snell's Equity*, 29th edn (London, Sweet & Maxwell, 1990) 11.

rights in land not mentioned in this list may only 'take effect as equitable interests' in land. *Keppell v Bailey* equally concerned rights in *land*. Today, however, one treats this principle as an expression of a general idea. It contains a kind of *numerus clausus* principle that includes property rights in movable property.[52] It is not established by law and, unlike in many continental legal systems, it does not amount to a strict principle of property law. This decision, nevertheless, reflects a general stance, it is an expression of a generally restrictive attitude towards the recognition of new property rights. Despite the fact that nothing in principle prevents courts, outside the ambit of land law, from recognising new common law rights in chattels, they generally deny them recognition. Apart from legal ownership, the common law only recognises few rights in chattels, such as the special property of a pledgor or other bailee, all of them linked to or derived from possession. By contrast, a mere lessee of a movable has, leaving aside cases of incitement to a breach of contract, no rights against the buyer of the property where the seller and lessor is still in possession of the object and refuses to cede possession to the lessee. The contract of lease alone transfers no property right to the lessee before transfer of possession. The lessee is restricted to mere rights *in personam* against the lessor.[53]

The principle that an owner is not free to create novel *property rights* at his discretion is in most instances neither particularly stressed in the relevant study books nor discussed under the topic of a '*numerus clausus*' principle.[54] The latter is rarely discussed even in individual scientific analyses;[55] neither case-law nor scholarly writing developed a proper term for the rule that property law only deals with a closed catalogue of property rights. In substance, however, common law courts treat property rights in much the same way as continental European legal practice; they equally assume that the types of property rights recognised today form a conclusive list, which only a legislative act could extend or abridge.[56] Outside the law of immovable property, it assumes the character of a rule of interpretation of the common law, which in turn has the effect of a rule of judicial self-restraint.[57] One should, however, not forget to add that (expressed in continental European terms) common law cushions its rather strict principle of predetermined type with a rather lenient principle of predetermined content. Case-law maintains a rather

[52] One is dealing with a 'closed, or very nearly closed' list of property rights in pure personalty: W Swadling, in P Birks (ed), *English Private Law* (Oxford University Press, 2000) vol I, para 4-186.

[53] Further R Goode, *Commercial Law*, 3rd edn (London, LexisNexis, 2004) 34–35.

[54] The key term of the '*numerus clausus*' of property rights is, eg, neither found in the table of contents nor in the glossary of the 1,600 page *oeuvre* by R Megarry and W Wade, *The Law of Real Property*, 7th edn (London, Sweet & Maxwell, 2008); nor in the (shorter only by a third) textbook by EH Burn and J Cartwright, in GC Cheshire and EH Burn (eds), *Modern Law of Real Property*, 17th edn (Oxford University Press, 2006). A notable exception is marked by A Clarke and P Kohler, *Property Law* (Cambridge University Press, 2005) 159–60 and ch 9.

[55] An exception is marked by the essay mentioned in Merrill and Smith, 'Optimal Standardization in the Law of Property', n 49 above, and a further by the work of B Rudden, *Economic Theory v. Property Law: The Numerus Clausus Problem*, Oxford Essays in Jurisprudence, Third Series (Oxford, Clarendon Press, 1987) 239 (critically commented on in turn by P Sparkes, 'Certainty of Property: Numerus Clausus or the Rule with No Name?' (2012) *European Review of Private Law* 769).

[56] Merrill and Smith, 'Optimal Standardization in the Law of Property', n 49 above, 10.

[57] Merrill and Smith, 'Optimal Standardization in the Law of Property', n 49 above, 10; Clarke and Kohler, *Property Law*, n 54 above, 9, point out that 'courts [are] extremely reluctant to recognise new types of property rights'.

broad margin of discretion for future development within the outer boundaries of the subjective property rights specified (or predetermined) by common law. This is, inter alia, confirmed by the law of easements. Readiness for innovation may indeed be more limited for so-called 'negative' easements (by which a certain conduct is prohibited for the owner of the servient estate) than it is for 'positive' or 'affirmative' easements (entitling the owner of the dominant estate to perform certain acts on the estate of the servient owner).[58] Nevertheless, one is ultimately willing to preserve the ability to adapt both groups to varying circumstances.[59]

It is, for example, generally impossible to secure a right to hike or ramble on foreign land (ie with a differing direction and for purposes of relaxation) with an effect *in rem* by way of an easement because it thus would amount to a *jus spatiandi*.[60] Nevertheless, exceptions have been made from this rule, for example, for the benefit of the respective owners of apartments in a block adjacent to a park and garden area.[61] In *Middleton v Clarence*, an Irish court even accepted the right to dispose of waste from a quarry on foreign land as possible content of an easement.[62] Another development in property law concerns the status of the tenant. Common law has always attributed to the lessee in possession (tenant) property rights. However, the courts only recently moved on to concede the same rights to a person that acquired possession without consideration.[63] By contrast, an (older) example for the maintenance of *numerus clausus* and the principle of predetermined type is *Hill v Tupper*, a case concerning a provider of leisure boats on a canal. The claimant was unable to show that he held an estate or interest. According to the court, 'none of the cases cited are at all analogous to this, and some authority must be produced before we can hold that such a right can be created. To admit the right would lead to the creation of an infinite variety of interests in land, and an indefinite increase of possible estates'.[64] At the same time the case, nonetheless, shows that at common law the question as to the nature of a right as a right *in rem* can be posed time and again, while in most continental European countries it can be settled by mere consultation of the relevant statutes. The issue arising in *Hill v Tupper* would not even have come up in these countries.

All common law property rights can also be created in equity, albeit that the reverse is not true. There is no closed catalogue of equitable property rights, neither regarding land nor regarding movables. By consequence, there are equitable property rights without equivalent in the realm of common law property rights. However, even in equity 'new' property rights will only be recognised where they show a sufficient similarity to those rights already recognised. While there is, hence, room for new developments, even at equity they only evolve in small steps. The most important innovation established through equity in the past 150 years is

58 JCW Wylie, *Irish Land Law*, 3rd edn (Dublin, Butterworth, 1997) 364.

59 'The category of servitudes and easements must alter and expand with the changes that take place in the circumstances of mankind' (*Dyce v Lady James Hay* (1852) 1 Macq 305, 312–13 per Lord St Leonards, here quoted after Wylie, *Irish Land Law*, n 58 above).

60 *Henry Ltd v McGlade* [1926] NI 144.

61 *Re Ellenborough Park* [1956] Ch 131.

62 *Middleton v Clarence* (1877) IR 11 CL 499.

63 *Skipton BS v Clayton* (1993) 66 P & CR 223, 230 (Sir Christopher Slade).

64 *Hill v Tupper* (1863) 2 H & C 122, 128; 159 ER 51, 53 (per Martin B).

probably the so-called restrictive covenant (or equitable negative servitude). Only in Ireland was the restrictive covenant (taking a reverse route of legal policy) 'elevated' from a mere equitable interest to a right at common law.[65]

PROTECTION OF THIRD PARTIES AND PROPERTY LAW: SWEDEN

In Sweden the basic understanding of property law shifted. What Swedish scholars perceived as a dramatic change has not least widened the group of objects of property law. It is part and consequence of the thesis that it would be wrong to ascribe special significance to the differentiation between the law of obligations and the law of property. It is said that all that ultimately mattered was to know if and how far a given position at law had effect against a certain third party. Where this is answered in the affirmative it is said to enjoy 'protection *in rem*' (or protection against third parties, *tredjemansskyddet*). At the same time, one is eager to stress that this does not mean the same as when, for example in Germany, the corresponding capacity is qualified as a personal property right. The law of property was initially a sharply delineated area of law. It only covered a few property rights, precisely and up-front defined by the law. These in turn would only relate to such objects that could, in their spatial dimensions, be precisely delineated against all other objects in which one may have property rights.[66] In the area of *lös egendom* ('movable property'), for example, one used to count among the property rights ownership, pledge, the right to retention and a few other rights derived from these three basic forms. Consequently, they also formed the sole object of the leading account of Swedish property law from the first half of the twentieth century.[67] New property rights could not be created through party autonomy; *sakrätt* was (and in principle still is today) cogent law. A strict differentiation between the law of obligations and the law of property, to be more precise: the differentiation between the law of obligations and the law of property described above, has been perceived as increasingly unsatisfactory by Scandinavian theory in the second half of the twentieth century. One turned to an analysis and development of the law of obligations and the law of property as parts of an interconnected system. According to legal scholarship, the necessary differentiations could not be achieved as long as a limited number of property rights (as it then was ownership (*äganderätt*), security rights (*säkerhetsrätter*) and, in relation to land, rights of use (*nyttjanderätter*)) demanded to qualify all other rights as part of the law of obligations. The result was a change of perspective. One began to attribute particular importance to the differentiation between interests only subject to agreement *inter partes* and those interests that had or should have

[65] Land and Conveyancing Law Reform Act 2009, s 49.

[66] H Hessler, *Allmän sakrätt. Om det förmögenhetsrättsliga tredjemansskyddets principer* (Stockholm, Norstedt, 1973) 4.

[67] See B Östen Undén, *Svensk sakrätt* (Lund, Gleerup, 1927) 1st edn published in 1927 (and 10th edn published in 1976). It treated, under the law of property in movables, ownership (*äganderätt*), pledge (*panträtt*) and a few other security rights (*säkerhetsrätter*), and under the law of immovable property apart from ownership, mostly the right of use (*nyttjanderätt*). It is today perceived as a classic of the older theory of property law (T Håstad, *Sakrätt.·Avseende lös egendom,* 6th edn (Stockholm, Norstedts Juridik AB, 2001) 18 and Hessler, *Allmän sakrätt*, n 66 above, 3).

effect against third parties. It is said that there are good grounds for the recognition of such rights, even if the interest in question could not be expressed in the terms of a traditional personal right of property. Though, for example, conventional Swedish law of property failed to recognise rights of use in movable property, a need is perceived to enable, at least in some areas, the enforcement of such rights created by contractual agreement against successors in possession where these act in bad faith. The required flexibility could not be found in either the law of contract or the traditional law of property; one would, therefore, have to free oneself from and look beyond these categorisations to determine the effects of a contractual agreement against third parties.[68] Whether one has, thus, really torn down the differentiation between the law of obligations and the law of property is an open question. It is probably equally adequate to express this development by saying that Sweden widened its range of property rights over time.

This was, however, only possible because Swedish law has never fixed the *numerus clausus* principle in legal terms; it is well possible that one has to go as far as to say that, from a formal perspective, it does not even apply in Sweden. At the very least, the reluctance of the Swedish legislator left sufficient room for the courts to free themselves from a narrowly limited number of precisely defined absolute property rights over corporeal objects and instead focus on the 'functional' question of the protection of a given position at law against third parties (*tredjemansskyddet*), that may be answered differently depending on the circumstances of the individual case.[69] Sweden and the other Scandinavian countries are, hence, inaccessible to a general classification as countries with or without a *numerus clausus* principle. The so-called 'Scandinavian functionalism' often aims to balance a far wider range of interests in solving conflicts that involve third parties. Rights and capacities outside the initially closed catalogue of personal property rights may, thus, assume 'protection *in rem*', or put differently: the boundaries against the initially narrowly delimited right of 'movable property' have been blurred.[70] In return, however, the idea of ownership lost much of its once supreme importance as a means of solving issues of property law. When modern law talks about a 'conflict of property rights' it typically refers to a social conflict where two parties both claim an object in possession of a third party for themselves while only one of these claims can be fulfilled. The function of property law here is said to be the establishment of an order of precedence. The expression 'law of property' (*sakrätt*) thus assumed an ambiguous character. In a narrow (static or substantial) sense, it includes the 'classical' rights in corporeal objects, in a wider (dynamic or functional) sense, all capacities with effect against third parties in any type of object capable of being subject to legal transactions, ie including but not limited to corporeal objects.

The recognition of 'protection *in rem*' is, beyond the rights of use mentioned above, for example, discussed regarding option rights, restrictions of use or a prohibition to cease possession. For none of these possible agreements between parties

[68] Hessler, *Allmän sakrätt*, n 66 above.

[69] Håstad, *Sakrätt*, n 67 above, 16; M Lilja, in W Faber and B Lurger (eds), *National Reports on the Transfer of Movables in Europe*, vol 5, *Sweden* (Munich, Sellier, 2011) 13–16.

[70] G Millqvist, *Sakrättens grunder. En lärobok i sakrättens grundläggande frågeställningar avseende lös egendom*, 5th edn (Stockholm, Norstedts Juridik, 2009) 13–14.

to a contract could it be once and for all said that they take the character of a property right or of an obligation; the result could rather vary depending on the circumstances of the case. For example, legal literature today recognises restrictions of use or a prohibition to cease possession, initially a specific phenomenon of family law and the law of heritage, as having effect against third parties where agreed in a contract of donation,[71] but not where they have been agreed in a contract of sale. A third party acquiring the object is not bound by the agreement between seller and initial acquirer.[72] Option rights equally do not enjoy protection *in rem* as a general rule. Exceptionally, however, they take precedence over the interests of a pledgee.[73] Similar observations can be made for rights of use. Again, they generally enjoy no protection *in rem*.[74] However, certain exceptions are recognised. The limited legal effect of rights of use in movables is explained with reference to the historical context of short-term toll manufacturing. It is further said that today's situation has entirely changed and that it would therefore be of utmost importance for the courts to reconsider and extend the measure of protection afforded to rights of use. Overall, this approach has not only shifted the meaning of the term 'property law' but necessarily also the meaning of ownership, which is by now increasingly characterised in an anaemic fashion, remindful of English law, as a mere bundle of rights.[75] Sandsted described it to the point: 'For a substantialist (ie a lawyer of continental European background) creditor protection can normally be derived from the concept of ownership, whereas the Nordic approach in particular treats the transfer situation as a legal fact–legal effect scenario, ie *without using the concept of ownership* [emphasis added]'.[76] By contrast, one remains faithful to the principle of *numerus clausus* in Sweden in so far as it is still accepted that only the legal order as such (and not the parties autonomously) has the power to decide whether or not a given position at law has effect against third parties.[77]

[71] Millqvist, *Sakrättens grunder*, n 70 above, 19. Some legal rules (eg Preskriptionslag (1981:130) s 2) still expressly differentiate between a property right (*sakrätt*) and mere obligations (*fordringsrätt*).

[72] HD 10 March 1998, NJA 1998, 135.

[73] Millqvist, *Sakrättens grunder*, n 70 above.

[74] HD 2 October 1975, NJA 1975, 528.

[75] Lilja, in Faber and Lurger, *National Reports*, vol 5, n 69 above, 16–20.

[76] J Sandstedt, *Förarbeten till en komparativ sakrättsdialog. Substantialismens blick på den nordiska funktionalismen med exemplifiering genom valda fragment* (Bergen, Universitas Bergensis, 2012) VI. A pointed example can be found in HD 16 February 1960, NJA 1960, 9. B had acquired a lorry from A and later bought tyres for this lorry from C. Both contracts were concluded under a reservation of ownership (generally called a 'right to reacquire possession' in the Swedish language so as to avoid the notion of ownership) for the benefit of the supplier. When B failed to pay, A took the lorry back; C demanded the tyres. The court did not ask whether or not the tyres formed a constituent part of the lorry and thus became the property of A; the term property was not even used. Instead, the court reviewed at length the individual circumstances of the case and the interests at stake in answering the question whether C's reservation of the right to reacquire possession had effect against A. The court denied this, with 3:2 votes by the judges. The result (no right to reacquire possession for C) could have been different had B still been in possession of the lorry and A not yet enforced his own right to reacquire possession. In this case, according to Håstad, *Sakrätt*, n 67 above, 188–89, the situation could have been understood as a mere two-party relationship, resulting in a right for C to demand 'his' tyres back from B.

[77] Hessler, *Allmän sakrätt*, n 66 above; Millqvist, *Sakrättens grunder*, n 70 above, 17–18.

CONCLUSION

So what is the outcome of our short stroll through a number of important legal systems of the European Union? It seems to me that, in the gist of the matter, it confirmed the reign of the *numerus clausus* principle but that one cannot ignore a certain softening of its margins. In general, it is probably permissible to say: the lower the number of property rights, the more pressing, on the one hand, the effects of the *numerus clausus* principle, and the higher, on the other hand, the pressure on the legislator, the courts and legal scholarship to provide remedies. Many of the exceptions from the 'principle' of a closed catalogue of personal property rights ultimately do not at all lead to a further drifting apart of European legal systems but rather a renewed coalescence. By contrast, commitment to the same 'principle' far from guarantees that it will produce the same results in national legal systems. A real creation of entirely new property rights through party autonomy is such a rare phenomenon that it does not fundamentally question the common point of origin. However, there are differing margins of tolerance towards the stretching of recognised rights, especially in the law on the use of land, and there are, in the law on the protection of rights in movables *in rem*, regional methodological differences. The question whether the principle of a closed catalogue of personal property rights is a 'European principle' must, in turn, ultimately face the objection whether it is a sensible one at all. Before the entire landscape of European property law has been mapped, neither an affirmation nor a denial of our initial question seems to lead to meaningful results.

24

New Principles in the Legal World: The Hague Principles on the Choice of Law in International Commercial Contracts

BÉNÉDICTE FAUVARQUE-COSSON

INTRODUCTION

ONE OF THE most remarkable recent phenomena in our legal environment is the emergence of a 'collective legislative doctrine' gathered in trans-border groups which are either European or international.[1] Some of these groups contribute to the elaboration of common sets of rules, often referred to as 'Principles'. In the field of contract law, the Principles of European Contract Law are the first and most well-known work carried out by European academics.[2] Hugh Beale's contribution to the elaboration and reputation of this work was remarkable.[3] Subsequently, Hugh Beale played a leading role both in the Study Group on a European Civil Code, which drafted the DCFR,[4] and in the group of experts designated

[1] R Zimmermann, 'Comparative Law and the Europeanization of Private Law' in Mathias Reimann and Reinhard Zimmermann (eds), *The Oxford Handbook of Comparative Law* (Oxford University Press, 2006) 539, 558. P Deumier, 'La doctrine collective législatrice: une nouvelle source de droit?' (2006) *RTDCiv* 63. For an illustration in private international law, see the work of the European Group for Private International Law, created in 1991 (www.gedip-egpil.eu/gedip_groupe.html).

[2] Ole Lando and Hugh Beale (eds), *Principles of European Contract Law, Parts I and II, combined and revised, prepared by the Commission on European Contract Law* (The Hague, Kluwer Law International, 2003), available at http://frontpage.cbs.dk/ law/commission on_european_contract_law.

[3] Hugh Beale joined the first Commission of European Contract Law in 1987 and took an active part in the work of the three successive commissions (often named after their founder and chairman, Ole Lando, and referred to as 'the Lando Commission'). Together with Ole Lando, Hugh Beale is the editor of the Principles (Parts I and II, combined and revised) and co-authored the Introduction which establishes the purposes for which the Principles are designed, notably to 'provide a foundation to contract law within the European Union, on the basis of which more specific harmonization measures can be elaborated'.

[4] C von Bar, E Clive and H Schulte-Nölke (eds), *Principles, Definitions and Model Rules of European Private Law: Draft Common Frame of Reference (DCFR), Outline Edition* (Munich, Sellier, 2009); and H Beale et al, *Principles, Definitions and Model Rules of European Private Law: Draft Common Frame of Reference (DCFR), Full Edition* (Munich, Sellier, 2009). On this group, see C von Bar, 'Le groupe d'études sur un Code civil européen', (2001) 53 *Revue internationale de droit comparé* 127. Hugh Beale co-authored the introduction to the DCFR and co-edited the work. Those who participated in this unique European enterprise will recall Hugh Beale's powerful contributions, at all sessions, always carefully prepared and constantly aimed at clarifying the debate and finding appropriate solutions, particularly when this appeared impossible due to strongly conflicting views, a frequent situation.

by the European Commission to prepare a 'Feasibility Study' to serve as a basis for an optional regulation in the field of European contract law, a project that was eventually mainly limited to sales law.[5] Over the last decade, the debate on European contract law has been so intense, the opposition so fierce, that Hugh Beale has been regularly invited to explain the reasons for and the methodology of the work accomplished. His voice is famous all over Europe.[6]

Little did Hugh Beale anticipate, when he joined the Anglo-French group on contract law in the mid-1980s, that his input would be so important for the destiny of European contract law.[7] Nor could he have foreseen, while he worked tirelessly to make the dreams of so many Europeans in the field of contract law come true, that his influence would reach beyond the law of contracts, beyond the confines of academia and beyond Europe. And he certainly could not have expected the Hague Conference on Private International Law to take the risk of shifting from the preparation of conventions to that of principles.[8]

The Hague Conference on Private International Law, the oldest of the Hague international legal institutions, developed its operations on the heritage of Tobias Asser, an eminent Dutch lawyer who received the Nobel Peace Prize in 1911 and prepared the ground for subsequent work on the unification of private international law.[9] The Conference operates as an intergovernmental institution whose primary tool is multilateral treaties. The number of states participating in the work of the Hague Conference has grown steadily (74 states and the European Union, that is 75 members from all continents), and with it the representation of different legal traditions, with the exception of particular legal systems, notably those based on Shar'iah law traditions, that still hesitate to join certain treaties. The principle of the universal application of conventions (they apply regardless of whether the applicable laws are those of a state party to the treaty or those of another state) has found wide acceptance and so have, in their respective fields of application, the notion of habitual residence as a connecting factor and the freedom of parties to select the

[5] Proposal for a Regulation of the European Parliament and of the Council on a Common European Sales Law, COM(2011)635 final.

[6] For those generations that are too young to have followed this most stimulating debate in the field of comparative contract law, Hugh Beale left a wealth of written contributions and took a leading part in the two editions of a unique casebook in Europe: H Beale, B Fauvarque-Cosson, J Rutgers, D Tallon and S Vogenauer, *Cases, Materials and Texts on Contract Law*, Ius Commune Casebooks on the Common Law of Europe, 2nd edn (Oxford, Hart Publishing, 2010). Chapter 1 of this edition contains important developments in European contract law. This book would never have been published without Hugh Beale's determination, knowledge and kind support of his co-authors.

[7] See H Beale's own testimony in H Beale, 'Partial and Temporary Impossibility in English and French Law' in *Mélanges en l'honneur de Denis Tallon* (Société de législation comparée éd, Paris, 1999) 19.

[8] O Lando, 'The Draft Hague Principles on the Choice of Law in International Contracts and Rome I' in *A Commitment to Private International Law: Essays in Honour of Hans van Loon* (Intersentia, Cambridge, 2013) 299. As explained by the author, 'this article is about the Principles and their relationship with the EC Regulation of 17 June 2008 on the law applicable to contractual obligations (Rome I) and the soft laws, notably the UNIDROIT Principles of International Commercial Contracts (PICC) published by UNIDROIT in Rome in 2011, the Principles of European Contract Law (PECL) prepared by the Commission on European Contract Law and published in 2000 and 2003–4 and the Draft Common Frame of Reference of 2005 (DCFR) prepared by the Study Group on a European Civil Code'.

[9] Hans van Loon, 'The Hague Conference on Private International Law: Asser's Vision and an Evolving Mission' (2012) 30/3 *Netherlands International Privaatrecht* 358.

applicable law or to choose the court before which disputes will be heard. However, the problem with conventions is that the number of ratifications is often limited.

The adoption of the Convention of 30 June 2005 on Choice of Court Agreements was a significant step in the work of the Hague Conference to promote party autonomy in international contracts on an international scale. However, this Convention only deals with the parties' freedom to choose a jurisdiction. It does not settle the issue of the choice of the applicable law in international contracts, which has formed the subject of research by the Permanent Bureau since 2006.[10]

The gradual unification of private international law is typical of the work of the Conference. Since its creation in 1893, the Hague Conference on Private International Law has developed international conventions that respond to global needs in various areas: international legal cooperation and litigation, international commercial and finance law, etc. The new choice of law instrument in the field of international commercial contracts[11] does not deviate from this piecemeal ('*petits pas*') approach: it only covers the parties' choice of law, and not the law applicable when the parties have not made a choice of law.[12] Also, it only applies to international commercial contracts, not to consumer and employment contracts.[13]

In 2006, the Special Commission on General Affairs and Policy of the Hague Conference invited the Permanent Bureau to prepare a Feasibility Study for an instrument relating to choice of law in international contracts. Two comparative law studies were drafted: one relating to the existing rules generally applied in court proceedings, and the other focusing on the situation in the area of international arbitration. These studies revealed that the promotion of party autonomy in the area of international contracts on a worldwide scale would respond to a genuine need in international trade. A Working Group on the Choice of Law in International Contracts was duly established, with experts in the fields of private international law, international commercial law and international arbitration law participating.[14]

[10] *Feasibility Study on the Choice of Law in International Contracts, Report on Work Carried Out and Suggested Work Programme for the Development of a Future Instrument*, Prel Doc No 7 (March 2009) para 20; M Pertegas, 'Les travaux de la Conférence de La Haye sur un instrument non contraignant favorisant l'autonomie des parties' in S Corneloup and N Joubert (eds), *Le Règlement communautaire 'Rome I' et le choix de loi dans les contrats internationaux* (Paris, LexisNexis Litec, 2011) 19–33; Permanent Bureau of Hague Conference on Private International Law, 'Choice of Law in International Commercial Contracts: Hague Principles?' (2010) 15 *Uniform Law Review* 883; M Pertegás, 'Hague Principles on Choice of Law in International Contracts' in P Lindskoug et al (ed), *Essays in Honour of Michael Bogdan* (Lund, Juristförlaget, 2013) 461.

[11] For a comprehensive commentary, see S Symeonides 'The Hague Principles on Choice of Law for International Contracts: Some Preliminary Comments' (2013) 61 *American Journal of Comparative Law* 873.

[12] For a criticism of this exclusion, see Lando, 'The Draft Hague Principles on the Choice of Law in International Contracts and Rome I', n 8 above, 307: with his usual perspicacity, Ole Lando notes that in March 2009 the Permanent Bureau recommended that the future instrument should cover conflicts of law; besides, the Draft Commentary specifies (at 5): 'Eventually, the Principles may be transformed into a binding convention covering additional choice of law issues raised by international contracts'. Obviously, it would be more difficult to reach a consensus on an instrument intended to cover all choice of law issues in contract conflicts (*cf* Symeonides, 'The Hague Principles on Choice of Law for International Contracts', n 11 above, 877).

[13] Symeonides, 'The Hague Principles on Choice of Law for International Contracts', n 11 above, esp 876 on the scope of the Principles.

[14] The Working Group held meetings in The Hague from January 2010 to January 2014. It was chaired by Prof Daniel Girsberger from Switzerland. For further information, see all the Reports established by the Permanent Bureau, available on the website of the Hague Conference, together with other documents.

The Hague Principles on the Choice of Law in International Commercial Contracts ('Hague Principles') are the first legal instrument to address the choice of law in international commercial contracts at a global level.[15] They consist of 12 articles and a Commentary. They are intended to be used in both judicial and arbitral proceedings and affirm party autonomy. This may not seem innovative, since party autonomy is part and parcel of the law in many legal systems, in particular of the law of the 28 EU countries, of Russia and China and of most of the 50 states in the United States of America.[16] However, there are countries, notably in South America, that do not accept party autonomy or only do so to a limited extent. The studies conducted by the Permanent Bureau of the Hague Conference, the enquiries it made by means of questionnaires addressed to the Members of the Conference, the International Chamber of Commerce, arbitration centres and other international institutions led the Conference to conclude that legal predictability in contractual relations at the international level justified investing efforts in a global instrument that would respond to the expectations of international business operators.[17]

The adoption of 'Principles' by the Hague Conference on Private International Law is meaningful, both from a methodological and a substantive perspective. It encourages and institutionalises the use of Principles, which moreover promote a new dimension of party autonomy, based on the freedom to choose non-state rules.

CHOICE OF 'PRINCIPLES' BY THE HAGUE CONFERENCE ON PRIVATE INTERNATIONAL LAW

First Non-binding Legal Instrument Produced by the Hague Conference

Despite the fact that the notion of international unification by way of instruments less binding than international conventions was endorsed by the Member States of the Hague Conference as early as 1980,[18] the choice of law principles represent the first non-binding legal instrument produced by the Hague Conference. The

[15] For the text, the Draft Commentary, preparatory materials (notably those entitled Prel Doc) and a bibliography, see www.hcch.net.

[16] Lando, 'The Draft Hague Principles on the Choice of Law in International Contracts and Rome I', n 8 above, 299.

[17] Prel Doc No 7, n 10 above, para 9; Prel Doc No 6 (March 2010) para 4: 'In order to set out the parameters of the Instrument to be developed, the Permanent Bureau continued its evaluation of the current role of party autonomy in international commercial contracts. Special attention was devoted to the current practice as to the use of choice of law clauses and the extent to which they were respected. In that respect, the Permanent Bureau notes that differences in the recognition of party autonomy continue to be reported in doctrinal writings and case law in different parts of the world. The basic idea for the work of the Conference was therefore precisely the fact that promoting party autonomy worldwide would meet the needs of the actors in international trade'. The Inter-American Convention on the Law Applicable to International Contracts1994, which establishes the principle of party autonomy, has at present only been ratified by Mexico and Venezuela.

[18] Permanent Bureau of Hague Conference on Private International Law, 'Final Act of the Fourteenth Session (25 October 1980)' in *Actes et documents de la Quatorzième session*, vol I, *Miscellaneous Matters* (The Hague, 1982) I-63. See also Prel Doc No 7, n 10 above, para 20; Prel Doc No 5 (February 2008) para 10.

contemporary international and European contract law environment justifies that choice. The success of earlier initiatives in the area of contract law played its part in the Conference's decision, as did the fact that the term 'Principles' has gained world-wide recognition in describing such non-binding instruments.[19] The Introduction of the Draft Commentary phrases it thus:

> The Hague Principles add to the growing number of instruments that have achieved particular success in unifying rules relevant to international commerce. The hope is that the Hague Principles will do for choice of law what the United Nations Convention on Contracts for the International Sale of Goods ('CISG'), the UNIDROIT Principles of International Commercial Contracts ('UPICC'), the Principles on European Contract Law have done for the substantial law of contracts.[20]

When the Special Commission of Member States met, in November 2012, to discuss the draft Principles, a query was raised as to whether it would not be better to refer to the Principles as 'Model Rules'. Both the non-binding nature of the instrument and its primary aim of promoting party autonomy eventually tipped the scales in favour of the term 'Principles'.[21]

The Principles: A Mere Step Towards a Convention?

There are various reasons for an international organisation to draft Principles, composed of black letter rules together with comments, themselves enriched with illustrations. First, the comments make them more readily understandable and more likely to be uniformly interpreted. However, as already noted by Ole Lando, this pedagogical advantage is only one of the many reasons why this form of non-binding instrument is chosen and indeed is probably not even the most compelling one, since an international body can always publish an explanatory report or comments to its instruments.[22]

Probably the most important reason for drafting Principles rather than an international convention is the record of past experience and an awareness of the many hurdles that stand in the way of adoption of an international convention. In preparing its work, the Permanent Bureau referred not only to 'the positive experiences of

[19] For a criticism of the use of the word 'Principles', qualified as a 'convenient smokescreen', see Zimmermann, 'Comparative Law and the Europeanization of Private Law', n 1 above, 561.

[20] *Draft Commentary on the Draft Hague Principles on Choice of Law in International Contracts* (November 2013) 5, available at www.hcch.net/upload/wop/princ_com.pdf.

[21] The Special Commission meeting was attended by 119 experts from 42 Member States, as well as by representatives from the European Union. Seven observers from non-Member States, and 11 observers from prominent international organisations also participated: *Report of the November 2012 Special Commission Meeting on the Choice of Law in International Contracts* (February 2013) 4, available at www.hcch.net/upload/wop/contracts_rpt2012e.pdf. 'It was said that using the term "Principle" would reinforce their non-binding nature, allowing them to be more widely considered as a source of reference (where they could have broadest impact as a source of inspiration for law drafters and legislators). This was said to also allow the Principles to be applied flexibly, providing practical guidance for those involved in interpreting all kinds of rules of law: adjudicators (judges and arbitrators alike), legal practitioners and interested commercial parties.'

[22] See, eg Mario Giuliano and Paul Lagarde, 'Report on the Convention on the Law Applicable to Contractual Obligations' [1980] OJ C282/1.

other organizations such as UNIDROIT or UNCITRAL in the field of international commerce' and to the fact that 'the Principles, Model Laws and Good Practice Guides developed by these international organizations benefit from high credibility and usefulness ratings among the interested parties in the field',[23] but also to the experience of the Hague Conference in preparing international conventions:

> To begin with, it is today almost impossible to obtain a voluntary agreement on the part of States on the necessity of a binding instrument. Many States, already bound by a regional instrument, do not feel the need to invest their efforts in a project of international proportions. They also feel that some specific substantive law conventions are sufficient to regulate any problems that may arise.

The Permanent Bureau views the resort to a non-binding instrument as 'a preliminary stage which, in a more distant future, might facilitate the adoption of a veritable international convention'. Indeed, such an instrument would not only be drafted without the restrictions and compromises that are inherent in treaty negotiation, but it could also

> progressively evolve outside a conventional setting, thanks to the objectivity and scientific quality of the experts involved together with the solutions retained. Furthermore, the absence of any obligatory force of the future instrument would avoid all risk of conflict of norms. For example, there would be no direct interference with the Rome Convention or with the Rome I Regulation within the European Community, or with the Hague Conventions on the Law Applicable to Agency, to Contracts for International Sales, or to Securities held with an Intermediary. In fact, the vocation of the future instrument would be principally to become a constant source of inspiration for the progressive development of uniform rules in the field of the law applicable to international contracts.[24]

The Draft Commentary even anticipates the following: 'The Hague Principles' non-binding nature means that they can operate alongside, and hopefully influence the reform of, both national legislation and regional instruments on choice of law' (Preamble, paragraph 2). Such instruments include Regulation (EC) 593/2008 of the European Parliament and of the Council of 17 June 2008 on the law applicable to contractual obligations ('Rome I Regulation') and the Inter-American Convention of 17 March 1994 on the Law Applicable to International Contracts ('Mexico City Convention').[25]

The previous experience of both PECL and UPICC affords ample evidence that the Principles constitute a distinct new category of instrument, which in spite of—or perhaps more accurately thanks to—their lack of binding force has gained great persuasive value. Many are those, be they legislators or judges, who draw inspiration from these models, which are also the source of new regional initiatives towards the codification of contract law. The Principles thus promote convergences in the field of contract law.

[23] Prel Doc No 7, n 10 above, paras 20, 23; see also Prel Doc No 5 (February 2008) para 10.
[24] Prel Doc No 7, n 10 above, para 24.
[25] Draft Commentary, n 20 above, Introduction.

Principles are Becoming Quasi-Official Instruments

Over the years, the conditions for the development of Principles capable of playing such a role have been refined. The process has become public and the promoters of such instruments are anxious to show that the working groups are representative of the different legal traditions and professional interests involved. Little by little, in the field of contract law, the Principles have been 'institutionalised'. While they were initially drafted discreetly by working groups (as was the case for the PECL, prepared by the three Commissions chaired by Ole Lando), the infrastructure of international organisations, together with the use of the Internet, have permitted a major shift. This evolution is particularly noteworthy as regards the publication of the three successive editions of the UPICC (1994, 2004, 2010). Gradually, UNIDROIT has encouraged the attendance at its working sessions of numerous observers representing important international organisations, and all the preparatory work is accessible on the UNIDROIT website.[26]

The methodology used for the Hague Principles clearly illustrates this development. From the very beginning, the Permanent Bureau played a leading role: it addressed questionnaires to Member States and stakeholders, it drafted reports and feasibility studies and engaged in substantial comparative work before forming the Working Group in 2009,[27] with specialists in private international law and international arbitration law drawn from different legal systems from all over the world. During the drafting process, the Member States and the European Union were invited to a Special Commission meeting on choice of law in international contracts (November 2012). The Special Commission discussed the Draft Hague Principles proposed by the Working Group, unanimously approved a revised form of the Principles, and made a number of recommendations relating to the completion of the Principles (particularly as regards article 3, which will be discussed below) and the Commentary. In April 2013, the Council endorsed the 'Draft Hague Principles'. In January 2014, 'guided by the mandate given by the Council on General Affairs and Policy of the Conference ('Council') and the recommendations for the commentary outlined by the Special Commission, the participating experts continued and completed their discussions of the wording of the Commentary accompanying the Draft Hague Principles'. Some Member States, as well as the European Union, had provided comments on the Draft Commentary, which were taken into consideration on this occasion. The 'complete package' consisting of the revised version of the Principles and the Draft Commentary in English and French (the two official languages of the

[26] However, it is important to specify that neither this evolution, nor the fact that the Governing Council of UNIDROIT must approve the work, affected the independence of those who were members of the three successive Working Groups, all chaired by an academic, Michael Joachim Bonell.

[27] All the documents issued since 2006 are accessible on the Hague Conference website (www.hcch.net). Compare the start of work at UNIDROIT: after the UNIDROIT Governing Council decided to take up this subject, 'a small Steering Committee, composed of Professors René David, Clive M Schmitthoff and Tudor Popescu, representing the civil law, the common law and the socialist systems, was set up with the task of conducting preliminary inquiries into the feasibility of such a project' (Introduction to UNIDROIT Principles (1994) xxii).

Hague Conference) should be circulated to members for consideration prior to the Council meeting in April 2014.[28]

While the 'private' character of the Principles is being gradually erased, the unification and harmonisation of law is being 'privatised': indeed, even if that process is still subject to the effective guidance of some international institution, it is no longer exclusively geared to the development of instruments adopted between states in the shape of Conventions.

Towards New Forms of Competition Between Competing International Institutions

The development of soft law instruments generates new forms of competition between international institutions which are becoming the leading producers of 'official international soft law'. The capability of these instruments to develop a common model for legislators, judges and parties is becoming a crucial factor. While the issue of the number of ratifications by Member States is irrelevant (so long as these instruments are not turned into international conventions), each instrument, each provision draws its authority from its innate quality as well as from its ability to be understood and interpreted harmoniously. Hence the importance of the comments that accompany the rules. Hence also the attention paid by these instruments to organising the co-existence of hard law and soft law, through the elaboration of Preambles and black letter rules which define the extent of freedom enjoyed by the parties and give guidance on the articulation between internationally mandatory rules and other rules (see the Preambles, and PECL, article 1:103;[29] UNIDROIT Principles, article 1.4).

THE PRINCIPLES: AN INSTRUMENT FOR THE DEVELOPMENT OF PARTY AUTONOMY

By allowing the choice of non-state rules, the Hague Conference not only aims at promoting party autonomy worldwide; it also acknowledges its new dimensions, based on the development of the Principles in the field of contract law, and paves the way for potentially eligible instruments. In this respect, the model set forth in article 3 of the Hague Principles is not only very meaningful but also highly controversial.

Party Autonomy Promoted Worldwide

As regards the traditional aspects of party autonomy, the Hague Principles follow the European model: affirmation of autonomy; recognition of express and tacit choice;

[28] *Report of the Fifth Meeting of the Working Group on Choice of Law in International Contracts* (27–28 January 2014).

[29] PECL, art 1:103: 'Mandatory Law: (1) Where the law otherwise applicable so allows, the parties may choose to have their contract governed by the Principles, with the effect that national mandatory rules are not applicable. (2) Effect should nevertheless be given to those mandatory rules of national, supranational and international law which, according to the relevant rules of private international law, are applicable irrespective of the law governing the contract'.

no connection required between the law chosen and the case at hand (article 2(4), choice of a law with no connection to the parties or their transaction permitted, *dépeçage*; article 2(2) permits parties to choose laws or rules of law to apply to different parts of the contract); severability; exclusion of *renvoi*; overriding mandatory rules and public policy. There is, however, one remarkable and bold innovation: the Principles allow the parties to choose 'rules of law' within certain limits set out by article 3.

Choice of a Non-State Law Permitted

The recognition of the choice of a non-state law, in so far as the Preamble to the Principles contemplates that the Hague Principles may be applied by the courts, gives a new dimension to party autonomy.[30] The Working Group discussed this at length, first adopting a very liberal approach,[31] but subsequently redrafting article 3 in much stricter terms.[32]

Article 3 of the Draft Hague Principles on the Choice of Law in International Contracts, entitled 'Rules of Law', only allows a choice of non-state rules on specific conditions:

> Under these Principles, the law chosen by the parties may be rules of law that are generally accepted on an international, supranational or regional level as a neutral and balanced set of rules, unless the law of the forum provides otherwise.

This solution is clearly the result of a compromise.[33]

At the Special Intergovernmental Commission meeting in November 2012, objections were raised and arguments put forward, in particular by the representative of the European Union, in favour of removing this provision or at least limiting it substantially. A first concern was the potential use by the party with greater bargaining power of unfair unilateral terms. A second concern was that the courts' task of judging would be made more difficult and more unpredictable, given the variety of potential rules of law to be applied. It was also argued that the role of gap-filling rules should be filled by national laws, but this is another issue as in this specific situation, the rules of law are chosen by the parties.

Those who favoured the choice of non-state rules of law referred to the very purpose of the Principles: the promotion of party autonomy. They also recalled the existing limits to the application of unfair terms. They further added that the restrictive approach would conflict with the promotion of uniform and harmonised choice

[30] By contrast, such a choice should raise no difficulties in the field of international arbitration, where the arbitrator has no *lex fori* and where the rules of non-state law are allowed.

[31] For a strong and convincing justification of such an approach, which would permit the parties to choose the UPICC, see B Audit, 'Le choix des Principes d'Unidroit comme loi du contrat et le droit international privé' in *Liber amicorum Camille Jauffret-Spinosi* (Paris, Dalloz, 2013) 13, esp 17.

[32] For a detailed history of art 3, and a critical analysis of the result that was reached, see R Michaels, 'Non-State Law in the Hague Principles on Choice of Law in International Contracts' in K Purnhagen and P Rott (eds), *Varieties of European Economic Law and Regulation—Essays in Honour of Hans Micklitz* (Heidelberg, Springer, 2014).

[33] See *Report of the November 2012 Special Commission Meeting on the Choice of Law in International Contracts*, n 21 above; Symeonides, 'The Hague Principles on Choice of Law for International Contracts', n 11 above, esp 894.

of law principles and with contemporary arbitration and international practice, as embodied in various UNCITRAL, arbitration and international sales of goods texts, where the parties choose the 'rules of law' applicable to their contract.

Article 3, which was included as a separate provision in order to emphasise the novelty of the rule, allows the parties to choose rules of law that 'are generally accepted on an international, supranational or regional level as a neutral and balanced set of rules'.[34] Subsequently, only a small number of soft law instruments in the field of international trade law may be chosen by the parties as *lex contractus*. It was felt that it might be difficult to determine precisely what constitutes a 'neutral and balanced' set of rules and the Special Commission invited the Working Group to provide further guidance in the Commentary. The draft Commentary cites the 'classics': the UNIDROIT Principles, the United Nations Convention on Contracts for the International Sale of Goods, the Principles of European Contract Law, the Common European Sales Law (CESL). This is not an exhaustive list and there will be many potential candidates for inclusion given the evolving nature of international commercial law.

The Principles do not distinguish between arbitration and court proceedings but they recognise that a limitation on the freedom to choose rules of law is justified in judicial proceedings where the law of the forum restricts the parties' freedom to a choice of state law ('unless the law of the forum provides otherwise' is the last and perhaps most important provision of article 3).

CONCLUSION

The success of the Hague Principles will mainly depend on their capacity to become a model for national and regional legislators, who may choose the entire instrument,[35] or only those provisions that suit them, provided some coherence is maintained. To a lesser extent, it may also depend on the parties' willingness and judges' ability to refer to them, but this will take time, as evidenced by earlier models in the field of contract law, still unfamiliar to the contracting parties.[36]

Provided the Hague Principles become a universal model, the Hague Conference might eventually transform them into an international convention. This perspective was certainly one of the reasons for the strong input of the Hague Conference: from

[34] For a detailed critical assessment of art 3, see Michaels, n 32 above, who considers it 'a rather problematic provision in what should otherwise be a rather uncontroversial legal document', adding that 'The Hague Conference, by including Article 3 in the Hague Principles, takes a gamble. The hope is that the authority of the Hague Conference can finally bring about what earlier attempts failed at—to bring state courts to allow parties to choose non-state law'. However, Michaels considers that while allowing the choice of non-state law responds to a few existing needs, this provision 'is deeply problematic for the law and creates a great risk for the acceptance of the Hague Principles' (Part V, Evaluation).

[35] In May 2013, when the Principles were still being prepared, the Senate of Paraguay presented a 'Proyecto de Ley "Sobre el Derecho aplicable a los contratos internacionales"', which takes as a basis the Hague Draft Principles and reproduces them in their quasi-totality (www.hcch.net/upload/wop/contracts_legisl_py.pdf).

[36] In order to promote the parties' awareness and choice of the UNIDROIT Principles, UNIDROIT has published 'Model Clauses for Use by Parties of the UNIDROIT Principles of International Commercial Contracts' (2013).

the very beginning, the enterprise called for great international legitimacy. Information and transparency were of the essence and all the work in progress is accessible through the website of the institution. While this institutionalisation of the Principles gives them no additional binding force, it does elevate them in the informal hierarchy of soft law instruments.[37]

Not only do such instruments contribute to the renewal of international law, but they also profoundly change the nature of comparative law: nowadays, comparative studies no longer deal solely with foreign laws but must embrace and compare all these other models. Despite the complexity of the world and the internationalisation of business life, despite the division of the world into distinct legal families, a common language based on a common set of rules is taking shape. In the current global context, the sources of law are multiple. Soft law instruments compete with international conventions. International organisations themselves have come to realise that what matters is not the binding force of the model, but its persuasive authority: an instrument which is a constant source of inspiration for the development of uniform rules is of the greatest importance.

[37] While soft law 'hardens', it is striking to see that part of hard law is 'softening'. This is the case, in particular, of the Vienna Convention on International Contracts for the Sale of Goods (CISG) which has itself organised an opt-out mechanism, allowing the parties to exclude its application if they so wish (Art 6). Another example may be found in the Common European Sales Law (CESL): while the CESL is contained in an EU Regulation, it is meant to become an 'optional' EU Regulation which only applies if designated by the parties to a dispute or a contract.

25

Ex Officio *Application in Case of Unenforceable Contracts or Contract Clauses*

EU Law and National Laws Confronted

ARTHUR S HARTKAMP

INTRODUCTION

THIS ESSAY IS dedicated to Hugh Beale. He has greatly contributed to the success of such projects as the Principles of European Contract Law of the Lando Commission, the Principles of European Law of the Study Group on a European Civil Code and the *Ius Commune Casebook on Contract Law*, to mention only those projects in which the two of us have worked together. At a certain moment our ways have parted because we were engaged in national functions which took up most of our time. It is a great pleasure for me to be back on his track.

This chapter combines my two non-national interests in law, ie comparative private law and EU private law, in particular the case-law of the European Court of Justice (CJEU). The two have much to learn from each other, as I hope will be illustrated by this contribution dealing with the *ex officio* application of mandatory rules of law. It is restricted to two instances of (possible) *ex officio* application: starting with the power of a court to allow a claim on another ground (or to allow another claim) than the one brought forward by the claimant, it proceeds to its main subject, viz the power of the court to declare a contract or a contract term null (or unenforceable, void or non-binding) due to the violation of a mandatory rule of law. The essay pays attention to the case-law of the CJEU on Treaty on the Functioning of the European Union (TFEU), Article 101 and on EU Directives relating to consumer protection, in particular the Directive on unfair terms in consumer contracts, and to instances of *ex officio* application in a number of Member States, both within and without the realm of public policy.

There are some concluding remarks, but the main conclusion is not there, but right here: in present-day Europe, any attempt to create a convincing European contract law must incorporate both general principles underlying the national contract laws of the Member States and private law originated within the European Union, of which the case-law of the CJEU is a far from negligible component.

EX OFFICIO APPLICATION OF TFEU, ARTICLE 101: *VAN SCHIJNDEL* AND ITS AFTERMATH

In the Dutch case of *Van Schijndel*,[1] the question was raised whether the national courts are obliged to apply Article 81 of the EC Treaty (prohibition of cartels, currently TFEU, Article 101) of their own motion, that is to say even if the party with an interest in the application of that article does not rely on it. The CJEU ruled, with reference to *Rewe*,[2] that this question must be answered in the affirmative where, by virtue of domestic law, the courts must or may raise of their own motion points of law based on binding domestic rules which have not been raised by the parties; if that is the case, the courts must also of their own motion apply binding Community rules. This ruling is based on the principle of equivalence, but it goes further because under European law the courts are actually *obliged* to raise such points of law where under domestic law the courts merely 'may' (have power to) do so.

The CJEU went on to examine the second question referred by the Dutch Supreme Court, namely, whether such an obligation of *ex officio* or automatic application also exists 'where, in order to apply of its own motion the aforementioned Community rules, the court would have to abandon the passive role assigned to it by going beyond the ambit of the dispute defined by the parties themselves and/or by relying on facts and circumstances other than those on which the party to the proceedings with an interest in application of the provisions of the treaty bases his claim'. This question refers to the situation where the obligation of *ex officio* application does not exist under domestic law and therefore concerns the principle of effectiveness. The CJEU stated first and foremost that each case in which a national procedural provision renders application of Community law impossible or excessively difficult must be analysed

> by reference to the role of that provision in the procedure, its progress and its special features, viewed as a whole, before the various national instances. In the light of that analysis the basic principles of the domestic judicial system, such as protection of the rights of the defence, the principle of legal certainty and the proper conduct of procedure, must, where appropriate, be taken into consideration.

The CJEU attached great weight to the principle of domestic law that a court hearing civil proceedings must keep to the subject matter of the dispute and base its decision on the facts put before it. This limitation is justified by the principle that, in a civil suit, it is for the parties to take the initiative, the court being able to act of its own motion only in exceptional cases where the public interest requires its intervention. This principle reflects conceptions prevailing in most of the Member States as to the relations between the state and individuals; it safeguards the rights of the defence; and it ensures proper conduct of proceedings by, in particular, protecting them from the delays inherent in examination of new pleas. In those circumstances,

[1] Case C-430/93 *Van Schijndel and Van Veen v Stichting Pensioenfonds voor Fysiotherapeuten*, 14 December 1995 [1995] ECR I-04705. My remarks on the *Van Schijndel* case-law partly follow my *European Law and National Private Law: Effect of EU Law and Human Rights Law on Legal Relationships between Individuals* (Deventer, Kluwer, 2012) para 124.

[2] Case 120/78 *Rewe v Bundesmonopol* [1979] ECR 649.

so the CJEU continued in paragraph 22, the answer to the second question must be that Community law does not require national courts to raise of their own motion an issue concerning the breach of provisions of Community law where examination of that issue would oblige them to abandon the passive role assigned to them by going beyond the ambit of the dispute defined by the parties themselves and relying on facts and circumstances other than those on which the party with an interest in application of those provisions bases his claim. However, in paragraph 21 the CJEU recognised the possibility for the national court to act of its own motion in exceptional cases where the public interest requires its intervention.

Van Schijndel concerned a physiotherapist who challenged the obligation to participate in an occupational pension scheme pursuant to the Dutch Occupational Pension Scheme (Obligatory Participation) Act. He alleged that the pension fund made a requirement it was not allowed to make under the Act, and claimed that the relevant obligation be declared inapplicable to him. When this claim was held to be unfounded in primary proceedings and on appeal, he lodged an appeal in cassation and (for the first time) raised the plea that the Act was non-binding on account of incompatibility with EC Treaty, Article 81 (at that time still EC Treaty, Article 85, currently TFEU, Article 101) and alleged that the lower court should of its own motion have reviewed the Act for compatibility with this article. Article 101 is normally concerned with contracts being null and void because of infringement of paragraph (1), but Van Schijndel's allegation referred to the specific application of this article imposing a duty on Member States not to adopt or maintain in force any measure which could deprive the article of its effectiveness, which would be the case, in particular, if a Member State were to require or favour the adoption of agreements, decisions or concerted practices contrary to the article or to reinforce their effects.[3] Such measure would be non-applicable due to the violation of EU law and Van Schijndel relied precisely on that doctrine.

The Supreme Court referred the above questions to the CJEU for a preliminary ruling, after finding that Van Schijndel had raised new facts, which under Dutch law is not permitted in cassation proceedings,[4] and that he contended that the court would of its own motion have to assess his claim on a different basis than the one on which he had founded it, which is contrary to Dutch procedural law.[5] The CJEU replied (implicitly) that the Dutch court was not required to derogate from its national law of procedure to enable it to apply EC Treaty, Article 81 of its own motion, which would compel the court to go beyond the ambit of the dispute defined by the parties themselves.

In my opinion, the CJEU has, in subsequent judgments relating to contracts violating EC Treaty, Article 81, refined or even partly revoked the ruling that Article 81 must not be applied automatically beyond the ambit of the dispute defined by the parties themselves. In *Manfredi*,[6] the CJEU ruled by way of an obiter dictum (paragraph 31) that Article 81 is a matter of public policy which must be automatically applied by national

[3] See, eg Case 311/85 *Vlaamse reisbureaus v Sociale Dienst* [1987] ECR 3801.
[4] Dutch Code of Civil Procedure, art 410.
[5] ibid art 48 Rv old (currently arts 24 and 25).
[6] Joined Cases C-295/04–C-298/04 *Manfredi and others* [2006] ECR I-6619.

courts.[7] *Manfredi* was confirmed by *T-Mobile*,[8] which was about the term 'concerted practices' as used in TFEU, Article 101(1). The CJEU began its exposition of the term with an introductory consideration (paragraph 49), in which it stated as follows:

> It should be borne in mind at the outset that article 81 EC, first, produces direct effects in relations between individuals, creating rights for the persons concerned which the national courts must safeguard and, second, is a matter of public policy, essential for the accomplishment of the tasks entrusted to the Community, which must be automatically applied by national courts (see, to that effect, Case C-126/ 97 *Eco Swiss* [1999] ECR I-3055, paragraphs 36 and 39, and Joined Cases C-295/04 to C-298/04 *Manfredi and Others* [2006] ECR I-6619, paragraphs 31 and 39).

The discrepancy between *Van Schijndel* and *Manfredi* is understandable if one appreciates that the problem of *ex officio* application which was the subject of *Van Schijndel* potentially pertains to many different kinds of legal rules, two of which will be discussed here. The first situation relates to the (legal and factual) grounds on which a claim is based. On the one hand, as far as the legal ground is concerned, it is sufficient for the plaintiff to state what he claims from the defendant and on which factual grounds; in most legal systems it is not necessary to refer to the provisions of law on which the claim is based, because the court will independently assess whether the law justifies allowing the claim on the basis of the facts that have been alleged. On the other hand, the court must keep within the ambit of the dispute as defined by the parties. The court is bound by the facts and the *petitum* brought forward by the claimant; it examines and decides the case on that basis. Consequently, on the basis of the claim made and the factual basis alleged in support of the claim, the court decides on which legal ground it can be allowed; if the legal ground alleged by the plaintiff is incorrect or insufficient, but another legal ground is available that justifies allowing the claim, the court includes this ground and allows the claim on that basis.[9] But the court may not allow a claim other than the one made, nor allow the claim on another basis than the one alleged by the plaintiff.[10] It was this problem—the claim and its basis—that was at issue in *Van Schijndel*: the original claim was based on the assumption that a legal provision was *binding* but it was argued that it should not be applied to the specific case; in cassation proceedings it was argued that the district court should of its own motion have examined whether,

[7] Interestingly, even before the *Manfredi* judgment was pronounced, the Dutch Supreme Court ruled that courts deciding questions of fact (in the case under consideration the Appeal Court) must, in so far as necessary of their own motion, establish the invalidity of an agreement that is contrary to EC Treaty, art 81 if the allegations made by the parties do not imply the invocation of such invalidity with sufficient clarity (*Vreugdenhil v BVH*, HR 3 December 2004, NJ 2005, 118).

[8] Case C-8/08 *T-Mobile Netherlands v NMA* [2009] ECR I-4529.

[9] I leave aside procedural requirements based on due process, such as allowing the parties to express themselves on the legal grounds proposed by the court.

[10] These rules seem to prevail in many legal systems. See Simon Whittaker, 'Who Determines What Civil Courts Decide? Private Rights, Public Policy and EU Law' in Dorota Leczykiewicz and Stephen Weatherill (eds), *The Involvement of EU Law in Private Law Relationships* (Oxford University Press, 2013) 89, discussing German, French and English law; Jeroen Chorus, 'Le relevé d'office de moyens de droit et de fait: l'application de règles du droit européen par le juge national: étude de droit comparé et d'histoire du droit' in Letizia Vacca (ed), *Scienza giuridica, interpretazione e sviluppo del diritto Europeo* (Napoli, Jovene, 2013) 123, 149. However, according to Whittaker (at 96, 105) the first rule ('ius curia novit') does not apply in English law (but see also Chorus, 149). Both rules exist in Dutch law.

and have established that, the legal provision was (in effect) *non-binding* because it was incompatible with EC Treaty, Article 81. If the district court had done so, it would have examined and (might have) allowed Van Schijndel's claims on a different basis, which is prohibited by the law of civil procedure.

A different situation is that of the nullity of legal acts. If two parties have a dispute about the performance of a contract, for example, thus that the plaintiff claims specific performance and the defendant alleges that he has already made payment, the question arises whether the court may dismiss the claim on another ground than the one put forward by the defendant. This question certainly has a relationship with the one discussed above, because it might be argued (and often it is argued) that what has been said about the (legal and factual) ground on which a claim is based equally applies to the (legal and factual) ground on which a defence is based. However, this is not true in all respects. For instance, if on the basis of the alleged (and established) facts in the case just mentioned the court comes to the conclusion that the contract at its face is contrary to public policy, then the court must nullify the contract and dismiss the claim, notwithstanding the fact that in this situation the court decides beyond the ambit of the dispute as defined by the parties (this concept being used here in the usual sense of the dispute as defined by the claims and defences of the parties and the allegations of fact on which they are based). However, the fact that the court has the power (and the duty) to dismiss the claim on this ground, does not imply that he would have also the power to allow a claim on another ground than the one brought forward by the claimant. Under Dutch law, the *Van Schijndel* case would not be decided differently after *Manfredi*, which declared EC Treaty, Article 81 a matter of public policy to be automatically applied by national courts.[11] For that situation *Van Schijndel* is still good law; all the considerations relating to the second question in the preliminary reference (paragraphs 16–22) continue to apply, notwithstanding the fact that the article generally was declared a matter of public policy in *Manfredi* and *T-Mobile*.

Admittedly, the example of a contract violating public policy is not surprising since probably all legal systems would allow or even oblige a court to strike down such a contract on its own motion. However, it is a good starting point to argue that the case of enforceability of contracts essentially is not covered by *Van Schijndel*. The question put by the Dutch Supreme Court was too general and so was the answer given by the CJEU. The answer was correct for the case under consideration (the lee-way a national court has in modifying the legal basis of a claim or in awarding a claim different from the one put forward by the claimant) and it has remained correct after the CJEU labelled TFEU, Article 101 generally as a provision of public policy. But it is not correct for the review of contracts for illegality, which requires different standards for review based not only in procedural law but also in substantive private law. That second point has afterwards been decided by *Manfredi* and *T-Mobile*. The CJEU did so by upgrading Article 101 from a rule with a mere 'binding character' to a rule with a public policy character.

[11] In fact, the Dutch Supreme Court decided a case which was of the same nature as *Van Schijndel* in the same way; see *Cagemax v Staat*, HR 11 September 2009, NJ 2010, 369.

In my view, the outcome of the *Manfredi* and *T-Mobile* judgments is correct, but to achieve that outcome perhaps it was unnecessary to invest Article 101 with a public policy character. As will be explained below, in most European legal systems mandatory provisions leading to absolute nullity of illegal contracts other than provisions with a public policy character may be applied *ex officio*; and the CJEU has even gone a step further by creating a system of *ex officio* application for Directives protecting consumers which by their nature do not lead to absolute nullity.

I shall now first devote some remarks to the possible *ex officio* application of mandatory provisions in general, before proceeding to the firmer ground of the Directive on unfair terms in consumer contracts.

EX OFFICIO APPLICATION OF MANDATORY PROVISIONS OF NATIONAL CONTRACT LAW LEADING TO 'ABSOLUTE NULLITY'

In the present author's legal system there is a strong prevailing view to the effect that a duty of *ex officio* application only exists in the case of statutory provisions (or rules of unwritten law) which have a public policy character (French: *ordre public*). This view has been expressed, for example, in a judgment of the Supreme Court holding that article 6 of the Dutch Competitive Trading Act, which is the national equivalent of TFEU, Article 101, is a binding (mandatory) rule but does not have a public policy character and for that reason must (and may) not be applied by a court on its own motion.[12] This view does not have a firm statutory basis; it seems to be based on the general provision in the Code of Civil Procedure that a court must 'examine and decide a case on the basis of that on which the parties have based their claim, application or defence, unless otherwise provided by statute'.[13] The exception relating to public policy is not provided by statute, but nevertheless accepted. There are no other exceptions, at least not in the field of contract law. I have opposed this view because it is not difficult to imagine rules of mandatory law but not of a public policy character which should be applied by a court even if parties do not rely on them, for example, provisions that make the validity of a contract subject to compliance with a formal requirement.

I do not intend to argue this problem of Dutch law more in detail here,[14] but I would like to contrast it to the solutions adopted in some other European legal systems. I cannot contrast it with rules of EU law, because there is no case-law on this point.

[12] *Gemeente Heerlen v Whizz*, HR 16 January 2009, NJ 2009, 54. See in this sense HJ Snijders, 'New Developments in National Rules for ex Officio Raising of Points of Community Law by National Courts' in AS Hartkamp et al, *The Influence of EU Law on National Private Law*, 2nd edn (The Hague, Kluwer Law International, 2014) vol I, 95–117.

[13] Dutch Code of Civil Procedure, art 24.

[14] See Hartkamp, *European Law and National Private Law*, n 1 above, para 128; AS Hartkamp, *Ambtshalve aanvulling van rechtsgronden naar Europees recht en naar Nederlands recht* (Deventer, Kluwer, 2007); AS Hartkamp, 'De verplichting tot ambtshalve toepassing van Europees recht door de Nederlandse rechter. Vervolg' in PJM Von Schmidt auf Altenstadt, FE Vermeulen and BTM van der Wiel (eds), *Middelen voor Meijer: Liber amicorum RS Meijer* (Den Haag, Boom Juridische Uitgevers, 2013) 133–49.

I shall indicate the type of nullity relevant for this section with the term 'absolute nullity', meaning a legal rule leading to nullity (or unenforceability) of a contract which can be relied on by any person but which is not a rule characterised in the relevant legal system as a rule concerning public policy (*ordre public, öffentliche Ordnung, ordine pubblico, openbare orde)*. Public policy in this sense means someting along the lines that the rule is fundamental for a society because it helps in shaping the foundations of the legal, economic and moral order on which the society is based. Some legal systems make a distinction between public policy and 'good morals' (*bonnes moeurs, gute Sitten, goede zeden, buon costume*), to which no attention is paid here since the legal consequences for illegal contracts are the same.[15] I have tried to investigate which legal systems allow or prescribe the court to apply such rules automatically (*ex officio*, *ex proprio motu,* of its own motion), that is, even when it is not relied on by the claimant or the defendant.

In German law an absolute nullity (BGB, § 134) must be applied automatically by the courts.[16] This rule is supplemented by an aspect which is unknown to the other legal systems mentioned here,[17] which is called the '*Schlüssigkeitsprinzip*'.[18] A German court must, in examining a claim or a defence, investigate of its own motion whether the facts brought forward by a party justify the award of the claim or defence in the light of the applicable legal provisions. This is not only true if one party fails to appear in court, but also if both parties take part in the proceedings. The '*Schlüssigkeitsprinzip*' is also at the basis of the '*Hinweispflicht*', laid down in § 139 Zivilprozessordnung (ZPO), meaning that the court must see to it that the parties express themselves timely and exhaustively about all facts relevant to the decision of the dispute. The '*Hinweis*' must take place before the claim may be rejected '*wegen fehlender Schlüssigkeit*' (due to lack of compelling argument).[19] The '*Hinweispflicht*' does not comprise suggestions for supplementing the claim or the defence, but that does not mean that it is restricted to the ambit of the dispute as defined by the parties. It comprises all relevant aspects of the case, both of procedural and of substantive law.[20] Evidently, this includes matters, both procedural and substantive, which the court must take into consideration *ex proprio motu.*[21]

[15] In Germany, § 138 BGB only refers to '*gute Sitten*', which is supposed to include '*öffentliche Ordnung*' (deleted from the first draft of the article). See Flume, *Allgemeiner Teil des Bürgerlichen Rechts II*: *Das Rechtsgeschäft* (Berlin, Springer-Verlag, 1992) 368; Larenz/Wolf, *Allgemeiner Teil* (Munich, Beck, 2004) § 41, para 9.

[16] Larenz/Wolf, *Allgemeiner Teil,* n 15 above, § 27, para 65; § 44, para 5; *MünchKomm* (2012) ad § 125 BGB, para 42 (Einsele); *MünchKomm* (2012) ad § 134, para 103 (Armbrüster); Palandt/Ellenberger (2013), vor § 104, para 27.

[17] But according to my information the same applies in Polish law.

[18] '*Schlüssig*' means something like cogent, compelling, logical, sound (reasoning).

[19] Stein/Jonas (Leipold) 2005, § 139, para 52.

[20] Procedural aspects are covered by § 139(3), substantive law by paras (1) and (2) See *MünchKommZPO,* § 139, para 53 (Wagner); Stein/Jonas, § 139, para 92.

[21] In exercising its discretion as concerns substantive law the court is bound to the facts brought forward by the parties ('*Parteivortrag*' or '*von den Parteien unterbreitete Rechtsstoff*'), but not by the facts which they have put at the basis of the claim or defence. The restriction of the '*Parteivortrag*' does not apply to procedural aspects of the dispute. See Wagner, n 20 above; Stein/Jonas, § 139, para 52. Wagner makes clear that all this relates not only to '*Sittenwidrigkeit*' but implies also eg provisions that make the validity of a contract subject to compliance with a formal requirement.

I remark in passing that the '*Schlüssigkeitsprinzip*' also applies in case of review of unreasonable clauses in general conditions (which are, of course, not covered by the concept of absolute nullity as set out above). The court examines *ex officio* whether a clause relied on by a party is unreasonable in the sense of statutory requirements; if it finds that it is, the claim or defence will be rejected. It is probably for this reason that the CJEU case-law on the *ex officio* application of the Directive on unfair terms in consumer contracts has met much less resistance in Germany (and related legal systems) than initially in the Netherlands. I shall come back to this case-law in the next section.

Also in French law an absolute nullity must be applied automatically by the courts. For the correct understanding of French law two peculiar aspects of that legal system must be kept in mind.

In the first place, French law distinguishes between several kinds of '*ordre public*', one distinction being the one between '*l'ordre public de direction*' and '*l'ordre public de protection*'.[22] Rules belonging to *l'ordre public de direction* must be applied *ex officio* by the courts.[23] Less clear is the situation where *l'ordre public de protection* is concerned. Apparently, rules belonging to this public order in principle may not be applied *ex officio*, but there are important exceptions, such as consumer law.[24]

In the second place, the concept of *ordre public* as used in Civil Code, article 6[25] is a very broad one and includes, differently from, for example in the Netherlands, all cases of absolute nullity in the sense mentioned above. For this reason, the question discussed in Dutch law whether also cases of absolute nullity which are not related to public policy must be applied *ex officio*, in French law is moot. I note in passing that Dutch law also included the provisions of article 6 of the French Civil Code, but in the new Civil Code of 1992 this provision was deleted, because it was felt to be not only unnecessary in the light of Dutch Civil Code, article 3:40(1) (which declares legal acts contrary to public order and good morals null and void), but also unclear since not all mandatory law has a public policy character.

Interestingly, the Civil Code of Québec of 1994, which is to a large extent based on the French legal tradition, contains a provision which elucidates this matter in the following way: 'La nullité absolue d'un contrat peut être invoquée par toute personne qui y a un intérêt né et actuel; le tribunal la soulève d'office' (The absolute nullity of a contract may be invoked by any person having a present and actual interest in doing so; it is invoked by the court of its own motion) (article 1418).

Belgian law is based on the same principles as French law; it has the same Civil Code, article 6 which must be construed in the same broad way.[26] So here, too, the

[22] This distinction was explained by the French Government in the *Rampion* case (Case C-429/05 *Rampion v Franfinance* [2007] ECR I-8017, para 58).

[23] J Ghestin, *La formation du contrat* (Paris, LGDJ, 1993) para 113; F Terré, Ph Simler and Y Lequette, *Les obligations* (Paris, Dalloz, 2009) para 391; Ph Malaurie, L Aynes and Ph Stoffel-Munck, *Les Obligations* (Paris, Dalloz, 2005) para 699.

[24] Code de la Consommation, art-141 (in force since 2008) reads: 'Le juge peut soulever d'office toutes les dispositions du présent code dans les litiges nés de son application' ('The court may invoke the provisions of this Code of its own motion in proceedings to which it is applicable').

[25] Code Civil, art 6 reads: 'On ne peut pas déroger, par des conventions particulières, aux lois qui intéressent l'ordre public et les bonnes moeurs' ('Statutes relating to public policy and morals may not be derogated from by private agreements').

[26] Walter van Gerven, *Algemeen Deel* (Antwerp, Standaard, 1973) 345.

courts are under the obligation to apply automatically an absolute nullity.[27] This was confirmed in a recent judgment of the Belgian Supreme Court, which dealt with a case where a contract was at variance with a statute of a rather technical nature.[28] An interesting aspect of this case is the following. In Belgian law, as in French law, a nullity, even an absolute one, must at the request of the interested party be pronounced by the court (so that the absolute nullity is brought about by an 'annulment'). In the case at hand, the lower court had pronounced the nullity, although 'annulment' was not part of the claim. For this reason, the Supreme Court quashed the judgment of the lower court. It held that whereas a court may find *ex officio* that a contract is null and void (meaning in effect: is affected by a ground for nullity) and reject a claim for performance based on that contract, it is not allowed to pronounce the nullity ('annul' the contract), because by so doing it would award a claim which has not been raised (decision *ultra petita*). This was particularly clear in the present case, because the parties, at the request of the court (compare the German '*Hinweis*', discussed above) had declared that they did not seek the nullity of the contract. This agreement did not preclude the court from finding that the contract was affected by a ground for nullity, but the court could go no further than that and was not allowed to formally pronounce the nullity and annul the contract. The decision is interesting, because it reminds of the distinction discussed above in the framework of the *Van Schijndel* judgment: awarding a claim other than one instituted by a party must be distinguished from a judgment relating to the nullity or unenforceablity of a contract per se. The fact that an *ex officio* decision in the first sense is not allowed does not preclude an *ex offico* decision in the second sense.

For Italian law the position is clearly expressed in Codice Civile, article 1421, providing: 'Salvo diverse disposizioni di legge, la nullità può essere fatta valere da chiunque vi ha interesse e può essere rilevata d'ufficio dal giudice' (Unless statutory provisions state differently, the nullity may be invoked by any interested person and may be invoked by the court ex officio). The references in article 1418 make clear that nullity includes violation of mandatory rules (*norme imperative*) other than rules relating to public policy (article 1343) as well as violation of formal requirements (article 1325).[29] This means that the situation is, in principle, identical to French and Belgian law, but unlike those legal systems public policy is clearly distinguished from (other) mandatory norms, and moreover the possibility (not an obligation) of the courts to act *ex officio* is part of the statutory provision (as in the Québec Code). The *ex officio* intervention of the Italian courts in the majority of cases was limited to the rejection of the claim for performance (compare the Belgian judgment discussed above), but recently the Supreme Court has extended the reach

[27] Walter Van Gerven (mmv Sofie Covemaeker), *Verbintenissenrecht* (Leuven, Acco, 2006) 147; T Tanghe, *Tijdschrift voor Privaatrecht* (2012) 705 ev, 738.

[28] Hof van Cassatie, 28 September 2012, AR 120048N, annotated by Tanghe in (2013) 5 *Revue Générale de Droit Civil Belge* 234. See for another recent example of *ex officio* application of absolute nullity in Belgian law Case C-202/11 *Anton Las v PSA Antwerp NV*, 16 April 2013 (nyr).

[29] See R Sacco and G de Nova, *Il Contratto* (Turin, UTET, 1993) 579: normally a defect as to form is to be applied *ex officio*.

of article 1421 to a case where the declaraton of nullity 'exceeded' the claim which was directed at setting aside the contract on account of breach.[30]

For a contintal lawyer it is always difficult to form an opinion of English law, and this is of course also true in a thorny matter like this one, where even the scanty and incomplete support of continental Code provisions like those cited above is lacking. With this *caveat* it seems to me that the concept of public policy is used both in a broad sense and in a more narrow sense. In the broad sense it serves as criterion for the (un)enforceability of contracts in general.[31] In the narrow sense it closely resembles the continental concept of assumptions and rules which are fundamental for a society.[32]

Another relevant concept in this connection is that of illegality, which in English law is a broad concept encompassing all cases of legal wrongs, both conduct that is contrary to a statute and conduct that is contrary to unwritten rules of common law.[33] This means that the concept of illegality includes but is not restricted to public policy in the narrow sense.

The criterion for a nullity or unenforceability to be pronounced *ex officio* seems to be whether a contract is 'on its face illegal'. Whittaker writes: 'So, where a contract is on its face illegal the court will not enforce it, whether the illegality is pleaded or not: here, therefore, the court can and ought to raise and to determine the issue of illegality of its own motion'.[34] He speaks of a significant exception in a legal system which acknowledges a strong adversarial character of legal proceedings.

In conclusion, it seems to me that the expression 'on its face illegal' does not coincide with public policy in the narrow sense. English law allows an *ex officio* intervention in illegal contracts at large, provided that the illegality is clear. Consequently, English law concurs with the continental systems discussed above, with the exception of the Dutch one.

[30] Antonino Barletta, *Extra e ultra petizione. Studio sui limiti del dovere decisorio del giudice civile* (Milan, Giuffrè, 2012) 162, 168.

[31] See, eg *Chitty on Contracts* (2012) para 16-001: 'The enforcement of contractual claims is in certain circumstances against public policy'. See for Scots law WW McBryde, *The Law of Contract in Scotland* (Edinburgh, Thomson/W Green, 2007) para 19-16.

[32] Cheshire, *Fifoot and Furmston's Law of Contract* (2007) 471.

[33] See Law Commission, *Illegal Transactions: The Effect of Illegality on Contracts and Trusts*, Consultation Paper No 154 (1999) 2: 'an illegal transaction is any transaction which involves … the commission of a legal wrong … or conduct which is otherwise contrary to public policy'. See also *Treitel on the The Law of Contract* (London, Thomson/Sweet & Maxwell, 2007) para 11-003 and for Scots law, McBryde, *The Law of Contract in Scotland*, n 31 above, para 19-14.

[34] Whittaker, 'Who Determines What Civil Courts Decide?', n 10 above, 96. In the same sense *Chitty on Contracts* (2012) para 16-208, stressing that a court will not enforce a contract which is *ex facie* illegal, that is when the court is satisfied that all the relevant facts are before it and it can clearly see from them that the contract had an illegal object. See also *Principles of European Contract Law, Part III* (Deventer, Kluwer, 2003) 220: 'Courts will take notice of illegality on their own motion and dismiss actions accordingly'. At this place there is also a reference to HL McQueen and JM Thomson, *Contract Law in Scotland* (Edinburgh, Butterworth, 2000) para 4.67, which although the *ex officio* aspect is not mentioned there seems pertinent to me since MacQueen was the reporter for this chapter in the *PECL*.

EX OFFICIO APPLICATION BASED ON CONSUMER LAW DIRECTIVES: *OCÉANO* AND ITS AFTERMATH

The above observations concerned the possible automatic application of TFEU, Article 101 and of rules leading to 'absolute nullity', meaning a legal rule leading to nullity (or unenforceability) of a contract which can be relied on by any person, but which is not a rule characterised in the relevant legal system as a rule concerning public policy in the narrow sense of the word. We now turn our attention to cases where under European law the power or obligation of the courts to review legal acts of their own motion may also arise from a Directive, in particular Directive 93/13/EEC on unfair terms in consumer contracts. I briefly mention the most important cases.[35]

The matter arose in the well known *Océano* judgment of the CJEU,[36] following a reference by a Spanish court asking whether it may determine of its own motion whether a term of a contract (*in casu* a jurisdiction clause) is unfair when making its preliminary assessment as to whether a claim should be allowed to proceed before the ordinary courts. The CJEU answered in the affirmative, following the arguments put forward by the Advocate General and by the French Government that:

> [I]t is hardly conceivable that, in a system requiring the implementation of specific group actions of a preventive nature intended to put a stop to unfair terms detrimental to consumers' interests, a court hearing a dispute on a specific contract containing an unfair term should not be able to set aside application of the relevant term solely because the consumer has not raised the fact that it is unfair. On the contrary, the court's power to determine of its own motion whether a term is unfair must be regarded as constituting a proper means both of achieving the result sought by Article 6 of the Directive, namely, preventing an individual consumer from being bound by an unfair term, and of contributing to achieving the aim of Article 7, since if the court undertakes such an examination, that may act as a deterrent and contribute to preventing unfair terms in contracts concluded between consumers and sellers or suppliers. (paragraph 28)

In *Mostaza Claro*,[37] the CJEU took the matter further and elaborated its reasoning. The case was about a mobile telephone contract concluded between Ms Mostaza Claro and Centro Movíl Milenium SL. The contract contained an arbitration clause to the effect that any dispute relating to the contract would be settled by arbitration. Since Mostaza Claro had not complied with the minimum subscription period, Centro Movíl initiated arbitration proceedings. Centro Movíl granted Mostaza Claro a period of 10 days in which to refuse arbitration proceedings, informing her of the fact that, in the event of refusal, she could still bring legal proceedings. Mostaza Claro presented arguments on the merits of the dispute, but did not repudiate the arbitration proceedings nor claim that the arbitration agreement was void.

After the arbitrator had found against her, Mostaza Claro contested the award before the court, submitting that the arbitration agreement she had concluded was

[35] See for a recent survey V Trstenjak, 'Procedural Aspects of European Consumer Protection Law and the Case Law of the CJEU' (2013) *ERPL* 451.

[36] Case C-240-244/98 *Océano Gruppo Editorial v Murciano Quintero* [2000] ECR I-4941.

[37] Case C-168/05 *Elisa Mostaza Claro v Centro Movíl Milenium SL* [2006] ECR I-10421.

null and void since the arbitration clause was an unfair term within the meaning of Directive 93/13/EEC. The Spanish court decided that there was no doubt that the arbitration agreement included an unfair contractual term and was therefore null and void under Spanish law. Since Mostaza Claro had not pleaded that the agreement was invalid in the context of the arbitration proceedings, and in order to interpret the national law in accordance with the Directive, the court referred the question to the CJEU for a preliminary ruling whether Article 6 of the Directive must be interpreted thus that the court, finding that the arbitration agreement is void, must annul the award even if the voidness issue was raised for the first time in the annulment proceedings and not in the arbitration proceedings.

The CJEU answered this question in the affirmative, adding (on its own initiative) that the courts are even *obliged* to do so of their own motion. Citing earlier judgments (*Océano, Cofidis*),[38] in which it had spoken of the *competence* of automatic application, the CJEU considered that the system of protection introduced by the Directive is based on the idea that the consumer is in a weak position vis-à-vis the seller, as regards both his bargaining power and his level of knowledge, which leads to the consumer agreeing to terms drawn up in advance by the seller without being able to influence their content. This imbalance between the consumer and the seller can only be corrected by positive action unconnected with the actual parties to the contract. On this basis, the CJEU ruled that the power of the national court to determine of its own motion whether a term is unfair constitutes a means of achieving the results sought by the Directive, namely, on the one hand, by preventing an individual consumer from being bound by an unfair term, and on the other hand, by increasing the preventive 'deterrent' effect which contributes to preventing unfair terms from being included in contracts concluded between consumers and sellers. In paragraph 38, the court held:

> The nature and importance of the public interest underlying the protection which the Directive confers on consumers justify, moreover, the national court being required to assess of its own motion whether a contractual term is unfair, compensating in this way for the imbalance which exists between the consumer and the seller or supplier.

The *Pannon* judgment[39] confirmed this ruling: the national courts must examine of their own motion whether a contractual term is unfair where they have available to them the legal and factual elements necessary for that task. The CJEU added that after examining of its own motion whether the term is unfair, the court is not obliged to disapply the term in question if the consumer, after having been informed by that court, does not intend to assert its unfair or non-binding status, and therefore opposes non-application of the term (paragraphs 33 and 35).[40]

It is not yet entirely clear what is the scope of the obligation imposed by the CJEU case-law on the national courts. From *Pannon* it might be concluded that the obligation exists only on the basis of the legal and factual data known to the court from the file; and that it is arguable that the court is obliged to give either party or both parties the opportunity to provide further information, if the summons or the

[38] *Océano*, n 36 above; Case C-473/00 *Cofidis v Fredout* [2002] ECR I-10875.

[39] Case C-243/08 *Pannon GSM Zrt. v Erzsébet Sustikné Győrfi* [2009] ECR I-4713.

[40] Frequently repeated, eg in Case C-488/11 *Asbeek Brusse v Jahani BV*, 30 May 2013 (nyr).

documents submitted should give the court reason to suspect that terms which are relevant to the subject matter of the dispute are unfair. However, the judgment in *Pénzügyi Lizing*[41] extends the obligation to investigating facts, holding

> that the national court must investigate of its own motion whether a term conferring exclusive territorial jurisdiction in a contract concluded between a seller or supplier and a consumer, which is the subject of a dispute before it, falls within the scope of the Directive and, if it does, assess of its own motion whether such a term is unfair.

As in *Océano*, the case dealt with a jurisdiction clause and it has been held (as it was after *Océano*) that the ruling only relates to that clause. However, later judgments have shown this not to be the case.[42] In general, developments since *Océano* have shown that it is usually not realistic to give a restrictive interpretation to the judgments of the CJEU in this matter.

For the purposes of this chapter, from this case-law the following inferences may be drawn. The obligation to apply *ex officio* the Unfair Terms Directive[43] is not based on public policy (in the narrow sense), but on the public interest which the Directive is intended to serve. It is not a coincidence, I think, that the CJEU in its judgments does not justify the duty of *ex officio* application by referring to public policy, but to the 'public interest' underlying the protection which the Directive confers on consumers, since these two concepts are not identical.[44] In all language versions the concept of public interest is used (*intérêt public, öffentliches interesse, interesse pubblico, openbaar belang*) as opposed to public order (*ordre public, öffentliche Ordnung, ordine pubblico, openbare orde*); the latter terminology is consistently used in a different context, both in the Treaties[45] and in the case-law on TFEU, Article 101.[46] In my view the difference is entirely logical, since a nullity based on public policy is absolute and can be relied on by any interested person, even by the co-contractant and even against the will of the consumer, which is not appropriate here.[47] The Unfair Terms Directive provides that the terms are 'not binding on the consumer' ('ne lient pas les consommateurs, für den Verbraucher unverbindlich sind, non vincolano il consumatore, de consument niet binden'). So we have here the concept of 'relative' nullity or '*annullabilité*', which explains why, according to *Pannon*, in spite of a court's power to intervene *ex officio*, in the end it is the consumer who decides whether he prefers the nullity of the term or its

41 Case C-137/08 *Pénzügyi Lizing v Ferenc Schneider* [2010] ECR I-847.

42 See, eg; Case C-618/10 *Banco Espagnol de Credito (Banesto) v Calderon*, 14 June 2012 (nyr) para 44; Case C-472/11 *Banif Plus Bank v Csaba Csipai*, 21 February 2013 (nyr) para 24.

43 Of course, in horizontal relationships it is not the Directive which is applied *ex officio*, but the implementing legislation. The Directive requires the Member States to create this power for their courts.

44 The distinction seems to be overlooked by Whittaker, 'Who Determines What Civil Courts Decide?', n 10 above, 121, 123. It is vigorously denied by Snijders, 'New Developments in National Rules', n 12 above. In this connection it is interesting to note that in *Asbeek Brusse*, n 40 above, the referring court (the Amsterdam Court of Appeal) asked specifically (perhaps in the light of the discussion on that matter in the Netherlands) whether the Dutch implementing legislation must be considered to have a public policy character. The CJEU did not answer that question and relied on its previous case-law.

45 In particular in several free movement provisions (TFEU, arts 36, 45(3), 52 and 65(1)(b)). The expression 'public interest' is not found in the TFEU.

46 *Manfredi*, n 6 above, para 31; *T-Mobile*, n 8 above, para 49.

47 Even in French law, which brings the concept of protection under '*ordre public*', it refers to a separate kind of '*ordre public*' which does not entail absolute nullity; see above.

continuing existence. The CJEU's case-law has not replaced the concept of relative nullity by absolute nullity, which would run counter to the need of consumer protection, but has added to the concept of 'relative' nullity an additional protection by extending the power of the courts.[48]

It is true that in some CJEU judgments on the Unfair Terms Directive, mention is made of public order, but then we are faced with a different context. I take *Asturcom* as an example.[49] At issue was the enforcement of an arbitral award, given on the basis of an arbitration clause included in general conditions applying to a contract made between an undertaking and a consumer. That was the same situation as in *Mostaza Claro*, discussed above. There, the consumer herself had submitted the arbitral award to the civil court to be declared void; so the arbitral award had not yet become final. But in *Asturcom*, the consumer had been entirely passive, and continued so even when the undertaking, after the arbitral award had become final, applied to the court for leave to enforce the award (*exequatur*). The CJEU held, in the light of previous judgments on *res judicata*, that in this situation the public interest does not require the court to assess the clause of its own motion and therefore does not require it to annul the award of its own motion either. But the same public interest does require that Article 6 of the Directive is regarded as a provision of equal standing with a national rule of public policy, so that if national law confers power on the court to assess of its own motion whether an arbitration clause is in conflict with (domestic) public policy, even after the award has become final, it must also assess of its own motion whether the clause is unfair in the light of Article 6 (paragraphs 52 and 53). The fact that the CJEU applied the principle of equivalence indicates that the 'public interest' just mentioned does not entail that Article 6 is itself a rule of public policy but that in the situation at hand it must be treated in the same way as a national rule of public policy. There are other cases, too, where the Court mentions public order in the framework of the principle of equivalence,[50] but in this framework the relevant point of contact may also be a different national concept, such as 'basic morality' or 'prohibited by the law'.[51]

The conclusion is that the obligation of *ex officio* application, based on the public interest which the Directive is intended to serve, is formulated by the CJEU for the normal proceedings in first instance. In other types of procedures the obligation is not simply based on this ground, but either on the principle of equivalence which may find its point of reference in the obligation of *ex officio* application of

[48] Very clear in this sense a recent judgment of the Dutch Supreme Court: *Heesakkers v Voets*, HR 13 September 2013, ECLI:NL:HR:2013:691, RvdW 2013/1060. The Court ruled that Dutch law allows an interpretation of the relevant Code provisions in accordance with the requirements imposed by the Directive. This, too, was a hotly debated issue in legal doctrine. In my view the parliamentary history of the new Civil Code, entered into force in 1992, but written long before the Directive came into being, already made it clear that this interpretation is possible, irrespective of the later developments in EU law. See Hartkamp, *European Law and National Private Law*, n 1 above, para 188.

[49] Case C-40/08 *Asturcom Telecomunicaciones, SL v Cristina Rodríguez Nogueira* [2009] ECR I-9579, para 53.

[50] See *Asbeek Brusse*, n 40 above.

[51] Case C-76/10 *Pohotovost' v Iveta Kor ovská* [2010] ECR I-1157, para 52: 'a payment laid down by an arbitration award where that payment is prohibited by law or where it contravenes basic morality'.

a national rule of public policy or a comparable standard of review,[52] or, if such a point of reference is missing, on the principle of effectiveness.[53]

The obligation of *ex officio* application is not restricted to the Unfair Terms Directive. It was also pronounced with regard to three other Directives. The first time that the CJEU ruled to this effect was in *Rampion*,[54] regarding national provisions enacted in the process of transposing Directive 87/102/EEC on credit agreements for consumers.[55] If under national legislation the termination or annulment of a credit agreement results by operation of law in the nullity or termination of a purchase agreement, the courts must be able to apply the nullity or termination of their own motion. The court speaks, in the same vein as *Océano*,[56] of 'allowing national courts to apply of their own motion' that provision (paragraph 69), whereas in *Mostaza Claro*[57] (and later judgments on the Unfair Terms Directive) it is stated that the national court is 'required' to assess of its own motion whether a contractual term is unfair. The reason may be (apart from the way the reference was worded) that in this case the issue was not a national provision closely following a Directive provision (Article 6 of the Unfair Terms Directive), but national provisions which elaborated the protection provided by the Directive in sanctions not imposed by it.

The next case concerned national provisions enacted in the process of transposing Directive 85/577/EEC on contracts negotiated away from business premises. The Spanish Door-to-Door Sales Act provided that in the absence of a written instrument referring to the right of withdrawal, the contract may be annulled by the court. In *Martín Martín*,[58] the CJEU ruled that the national court can declare such annulment on its own motion. The Court stated that the obligation to give notice of the right of cancellation laid down in the Directive plays a central role in the overall scheme of that Directive, as an essential guarantee for the effective exercise of that right and, therefore, for the effectiveness of consumer protection sought by the Community legislature. Therefore it comes under the public interest justifying (within the meaning of the *Van Schijndel* case-law) a positive intervention by the national court in order to compensate for the imbalance between the consumer and the trader in the context of contracts concluded away from business premises.

In this case, too, the judgment grants the power of *ex officio* application instead of imposing an obligation. The reasons may be the same as just mentioned in connection with *Rampion*; moreover, the Court points out, first, that the possibility

[52] See *Pohotovost'*, n 51 above (proceedings to obtain an *exequatur* of an arbitration award that has become final), and *Asbeek Brusse*, n 40 above (proceedings in appeal).

[53] See Case C-618/10 *Banco Espagnol de Credito (Banesto) v Calderon*, 14 June 2012 (nyr). This case was about proceedings to obtain a payment order for a claim arising out of a contract containing an onerous term on interest for late payment; in the absence of an objection by the consumer the applicable Spanish legislation did not allow the court to assess *ex offico* the term. The same situation arose in another case, Case C-415/11 *Mohamed Aziz v Caixa*, 14 March 2013 (nyr): a loan agreement, containing an onerous term on annual default interest, secured by a mortgage, led to a claim which the bank sought to enforce in proceedings which did not allow the court to assess the term or grant interim relief. In both cases the CJEU held that the legislation, which apparently did not allow relief on any ground (including public policy), did not comply with the principle of effectiveness.

[54] Case C-429/05 *Rampion v Franfinance* [2007] ECR I-8017.

[55] Also *Pohotovost'*, n 51 above, is concerned with this Directive (para 77).

[56] See *Océano*, n 36 above, para 29.

[57] See *Mostaza Claro*, n 37 above, para 38.

[58] Case C-227/08 *Martín Martín v EDP Editores* [2009] ECR I-11939.

is not ruled out that other measures might ensure the same level of protection, and, secondly, referring to *Pannon*,[59] that the national court may also have to take account, in certain circumstances, of the consumer's wish not to have the contract at issue cancelled.

Finally, the matter of *ex officio* arose within the framework of Directive 99/44/EC on sale of consumer goods. It was not concerned with contract terms which were void or not binding, but with the consumer's right to reduction of the price under Article 3(5) of the Directive. The consumer had brought proceedings for the rescission of the contract because of lack of conformity, which was denied by the national court because the lack of conformity was minor. Due to procedural restrictions in the national law it was no longer possible for the consumer to claim reduction of the price. The CJEU[60] held that this state of affairs was precluded by the Directive if the national legislation did not allow the court hearing the dispute to grant of its own motion an appropriate reduction in the price. The decision is interesting because it is the first time that the CJEU has imposed the duty of *ex officio* application in order to allow a claim which has not been brought by the claimant—the subject of the case leading to the *Van Schijndel* case-law.

In view of the case-law on Directives discussed here it seems probable to me that the duty or the power of *ex officio* application will be accepted by the CJEU in all matters related to the Directives on consumer law.

CONCLUDING OBSERVATIONS

When taking stock of the case-law of the CJEU on *ex officio* application it must be pointed out in the first place that it is dangerous to draw from a specific judgment of the Court far-reaching conclusions for other cases, even if it contains legal considerations of a general character, such as *Van Schijndel*. Cases where *ex officio* application is or may be appropriate differ widely. In this essay I have restricted myself to two instances of (possible) *ex officio* application: the power to allow a claim on another ground (or to allow another claim) than the one brought forward by the claimant; and the power of the court to declare a contract or a contract term null or unenforceable due to the violation of a mandatory rule of law. There are many others, both of a procedural and of a substantive nature, some of which we know from CJEU cases, eg *Eco Swiss*[61] and *Van der Weerd*.[62] It is submitted that all instances have to be analysed taking into account their specific aspects and nature. Sometimes inspiration for the handling of an instance may be drawn from other instances, sometimes not. References in a judgment to another judgment (eg in *Manfredi* to *Eco Swiss* or in *Martín Martín* to *Van Schijndel*), and *a fortiori* the lack

[59] See *Pannon*, n 39 above.

[60] Case C-32/12 *Soledad Duarte Hueros v Autociba SA en Automóviles Citroën Espana SA*, 3 October 2013 (nyr).

[61] Case C-126/97 *Eco Swiss China Time Ltd v Benetton International NV* [1999] ECR I-3055.

[62] Case C-222/05 *Van der Weerd and others v Minister van landbouw* [2007] ECR I-4233. In European procedural law it is a doctrine of its own; see, eg Case C-89/08P *E uropean Commission v Ireland* [2009] ECR I-11245 and Case C-272/12P *European Commission v Ireland*, 10 December 2013 (nyr).

of such references, should be considered with caution; in my view, they are often not sufficient as a basis for a general argumentation.

Restricting myself to the two instances dealt with in this chapter, we have seen that *Van Schijndel* is still a convincing judgment for the case which led to that judgment. In fact, I have only found one case in which the CJEU accepted the power to award a claim which was not brought by the claimant, ie *Soledad Duarte*, discussed above. I have not found such cases in national legal systems, but I must admit that my main focus was the second instance, the nullity of contracts. In that context we have seen that many legal systems allow for an *ex officio* intervention of the courts not only where rules of public policy in the narrow sense are violated, but also where contracts are at variance with rules of a mandatory character not relating to public policy. The CJEU has not elaborated as yet this second category, but it has recognised its existence in *Asbeek Brusse* (paragraph 51):

> For the same reasons as those set out in paragraphs 43 and 44 of the present judgment, it follows that, where the national court has the power, under internal procedural rules, to annul of its own motion a term which is contrary to public policy *or to a mandatory statutory provision the scope of which warrants such a sanction*, which, according to the information provided in the order for reference, is true in the Netherlands judicial system with regard to a court ruling in appeal proceedings, it must also annul of its own motion a contractual term which it has found to be unfair in the light of the criteria laid down by the directive. (emphasis added)

Moreover, the CJEU has allowed or even prescribed *ex officio* application in the framework of Directives aiming at the protection of consumers, in particular the Unfair Terms Directive, but also several other Directives and the national implementing measures providing for a sanction of nullity or unenforceability not set out in the Directives. Here, the obligation of *ex officio* application is not based on public policy, but on the public interest underlying the Directive. Founding the unenforceability on public policy would not be appriopriate since the nature of these regulations requires a nullity of a more limited scope which is at the disposal of the protected person.

The fact that the obligations of *ex officio* application of TFEU, Article 101 and of the Directives are based on a different legal ground does not mean that the solutions reached may not interact. For example, the (limited) duty to investigate facts which was accepted in *Pénzügyi Lizing* (see above) could play a useful role in the context of TFEU, Article 101 as well. In fact, without an active attitude of the court, the obligation of *ex officio* application of that provision will prove to be of a very limited importance, given the complicated factual nature of many competition cases.

On the basis of these considerations it is submitted that the power or the obligation to automatically apply European law can be based on the following six grounds.

(1) The first ground is any express provision of law requiring the courts to automatically apply a rule of EU law. Such a provision could occur in one of the Treaties, a Directive or a Regulation. As far as I know, no such provision exists.

(2) The second ground is an interpretation given by the CJEU to a rule of (written or unwritten) EU law to the effect that the rule must be automatically applied. This is the ground that is the basis of the obligation of automatic application within the scope of Directives such as the Unfair Terms Directive 93/13/EEC. It could

also be used for rules of the type discussed above, ie mandatory provisions the scope of which warrant this sanction (see *Asbeek Brusse*, cited above).

(3) The third ground is a provision or judicial interpretation from which it can be deduced that a rule of EU law is a rule of public policy. It may be assumed that in this case the rule must be applied automatically. As far as I know this has never been decided in a general sense, but the connection follows from several of the judgments mentioned, in particular *Manfredi* and *T-Mobile.*

(4) and (5) The fourth and fifth grounds are the well-known principles of (4) effectiveness and (5) equivalence. Where a right safeguarded by EU law is to be enforced before the national courts and by applying national law, the rules of the national legal system must be compatible with these two principles, entailing the requirement that they may not make it virtually impossible or extremely difficult to exercise the right conferred by EU law (principle of effectiveness) and that they may not make the conditions for enforcing the right less favourable than those relating to similar rights of a domestic nature (principle of equivalence).

(6) The principle of equivalence is further tightened by what is known as the 'may is must' rule: if the national courts *may* apply a rule of national law of their own motion, they *must* of their own motion apply the corresponding rule of EU law. This principle was formulated in *Van Schijndel, Asturcom* and *Asbeek Brusse*.

The present situation is that EU law, as interpreted by the CJEU, in the area of contract law requires *ex officio* application of TFEU, Article 101 and of the consumer law Directives. It is hard to predict whether other rules of EU law will so qualify in the future. TFEU, Article 102 is a safe guess. Further, one might think of Directives of a protective nature other than those relating to consumer law, eg relating to the protection of employees or commercial agents.[63] Regulations, too, may contain prohibitions leading to nullity of contracts or contract clauses the scope of which warrant the sanction of *ex officio* application.[64] An interesting field of potential *ex officio* application has been opened up by the case-law in which Treaty provisions have been accorded direct horizontal effect, in particular most free movement provisions and prohibitions of discrimination; the latter have also been recognised as general principles of EU law and since 2009 they are enshrined in the Charter of Fundamental Rights. This subject cannot be pursued here,[65] but it is submitted that such provisions are not less 'essential for the accomplishment of the tasks entrusted to the Community' than TFEU, Article 101, as pronounced in *Manfredi* (see above). Even if they are not recognised by the CJEU as rules and principles of public policy, a duty of *ex officio* application may be based on other grounds mentioned above.

[63] In labour law there is an older judgment of the CJEU declaring the protection of Directive 77/187/EEC on employees' rights in case of transfer of undertakings to be a matter of public policy, so that it is not possible to derogate from the rules of the Directive: Case 324/86 *Foreningen af Arbejdsledere i Danmark v Daddy's Dance Hall A/S* [1988] ECR 739. It is easily imaginable that this protection must be applied *ex officio* by national courts.

[64] Eg prohibitions on dangerous goods or substances being marketed or exported. See Hartkamp, *European Law and National Private Law*, n 1 above, para 196. Whittaker, 'Who Determines What Civil Courts Decide?', n 10 above, 126 mentions the provisions in the Rome I Regulation and Rome II Regulation aiming at the protection of consumers and employees.

[65] See Hartkamp, *European Law and National Private Law*, n 1 above, paras 53, 105.

Index

www.ingramcontent.com/pod-product-compliance
Lightning Source LLC
LaVergne TN
LVHW052211200926
848481LV00001B/78